# DEEP ECOLOGY FOR THE TWENTY-FIRST CENTURY

# DEEP ECOLOGY
## *for the*
# TWENTY-FIRST CENTURY

*Edited by George Sessions*

SHAMBHALA

*Boston & London*

*1995*

Shambhala Publications, Inc.
Horticultural Hall
300 Massachusetts Avenue
Boston, Massachusetts 02115

9  8  7  6  5  4  3  2  1

FIRST EDITION
Printed in the United States of America on acid-free paper ♾
Distributed in the United States by Random House, Inc.,
and in Canada by Random House of Canada Ltd

Library of Congress Cataloging-in-Publication Data

Deep ecology for the twenty-first century/edited by George Sessions.
   —1st ed.
      p.  cm.
   ISBN 1-57062-049-0 (alk. paper)
    1. Deep ecology.  I. Sessions, George, 1938–  .  II. Title: Deep
ecology for the 21st century.
GE195.D44  1994                                    94-13967
363.7—dc20                                         CIP

# CONTENTS

# PREFACE

THE LONG-RANGE DEEP ECOLOGY movement emerged more or less spontaneously and informally as a philosophical and scientific social/political movement during the so-called Ecological Revolution of the 1960s. Its main concern has been to bring about a major paradigm shift—a shift in perception, values, and lifestyles—as a basis for redirecting the ecologically destructive path of modern industrial growth societies. Since the 1960s, the long-range Deep Ecology movement has been characterized philosophically by a move from anthropocentrism to ecocentrism, and by environmental activism.

## THE ECOCENTRIC ROOTS OF DEEP ECOLOGY AND THE ECOLOGICAL REVOLUTION OF THE 1960s

The philosophical roots of the Deep Ecology movement are found in the ecocentrism and social criticism of Henry David Thoreau, John Muir, D. H. Lawrence, Robinson Jeffers, and Aldous Huxley.[1] Influential ecological/social criticism has been also derived from the writings of George Orwell and Theodore Roszak, and from the critiques of the problems created by the rise of civilizations written by the maverick historian Lewis Mumford.[2] Further inspiration for contemporary ecological consciousness and the Deep Ecology movement can be traced to the ecocentric religions and ways of life of primal peoples around the world, and to Taoism, Saint Francis of Assisi, the Romantic Nature-oriented countercultural movement of the nineteenth century with its roots in Spinoza, and the Zen Buddhism of Alan Watts and Gary Snyder (which influenced many professional ecologists as well as the countercultural movement of the 1960s).[3]

The birth of the Deep Ecology movement paralleled the rise to public prominence of the science of ecology and the "ecological perspective" as popularized by Aldo Leopold, Rachel Carson, and other ecologists. The main inspiration for the movement during the 1960s came from Leopold's ecocentric "land ethic" and from Rachel Carson, Dave Brower, Paul Ehrlich, and other biologists, field ecologists, and conservation organization leaders concerned with the rapidly widening ecological crisis. These biologists and environmental activists were convinced that the dominant anthropocentric orientation of Western civilization was seriously misguided as well as inadequate to deal with the crisis.

The Ecological Revolution of the 1960s is usually dated from the publication of Rachel Carson's *Silent Spring* in 1962. Carson's indictment of the indiscriminate use of pesticides raised overall questions about the serious threats posed by the fruits of modern technology to human health. But since she was a marine biologist and a lover of birds, the ocean, and other wild places—and inspired by the science of ecology and Albert Schweitzer's Reverence for Life principle—her concerns went deeper to encompass a respect and concern for the biological integrity of the Earth and all its species. As a result, in *Silent Spring,* Carson questioned the direction and goals of Western society, including the human competence and "right" to dominate and manage the Earth. More generally, she posed a philosophical challenge to the *anthropocentrism* of Western culture. She claimed that "the 'control of nature' is a phrase conceived in arrogance, born of the Neanderthal age of biology and philosophy, when it was supposed that nature exists for the convenience of man."[4]

The whole question of the environmental crisis as fundamentally a crisis of the West's anthropocentric philosophical and religious orientations and values was raised even more forcefully by the U.C.L.A. historian Lynn White, Jr., in 1966.[5] White argued that Christianity had desacralized Nature, encouraged its exploitation, and promoted an anthropocentric worldview in which humans are superior to, and in charge of, the rest of Nature. He claimed that "since the roots [of the ecological crisis] are so largely religious, the remedy must also be essentially religious, whether we call it that or not. We must rethink and refeel our nature and destiny." According to White:

> Especially in its Western form, Christianity is the most anthropocentric religion that the world has seen. . . . Christianity, in absolute contrast to ancient paganism and Asia's religions . . . not only established a dualism of man and nature but also insisted that it is God's will that man exploit nature for his proper ends.

Modern science and technology, White claimed, are "permeated with Christian arrogance toward nature." He further argued that Marxism and other so-called "post-Christian" ideologies in the West are Judeo-Christian heresies that promote the same exploitive attitudes toward Nature. In an effort to reform Christianity ecologically, White proposed a return to the views of Saint Francis, who preached "the equality of all creatures."

As executive director of the Sierra Club during the 1960s, David Brower was the best-known conservation activist of this period. He was responsible for radicalizing the Club ecologically and turning it into the most influential environmental organization in the world. Historian Stephen Fox has referred to Brower as "Muir reincarnate." And like Muir, Brower was an ecocentrist, claiming in 1967 that "I believe in wilderness for itself alone. I believe in the rights of creatures other than man."[6]

In summarizing the 1960s Ecological Revolution, the Norwegian philosopher Arne Naess points out that

> classical nature conservation did not include fighting the power-centers which were pushing mindless "development." The environmental fight, from 1963 to 68, in California (and the U.S. generally) inspired the rest of the world. The 1972 United Nations Environmental Conference in Stockholm was the first acknowledgement by the establishment of social and political environmental conflicts.[7]

## THE RISE OF ANTHROPOCENTRIC SURVIVAL ENVIRONMENTALISM

Another version of environmentalism arose in the 1960s in reaction to the increasing industrial/chemical pollution of the environment after World War II. Many of the leaders of this aspect of environmentalism, such as the biologist Barry Commoner and Ralph Nader, did not have a background either in ecology or in the Thoreau/Muir/Leopold conservation tradition. Partly as a result, this newer strain of "human survival environmentalism" was anthropocentric, urban pollution–oriented, and narrowly focused on the issue of human survival. Commoner was once quoted as saying that "I happen to think that humans are more important than whooping cranes."[8] Commoner soon took the position, against Paul Ehrlich and most other ecologists, that there was no human overpopulation problem in the world. While urban pollution problems have become an increasingly central and crucial part of the environmental crisis since the 1960s, the major flaw in "human survival environmentalism" has been the failure to take a wider "ecological perspective" that involves a concern for the ecological integrity of the Earth and the well-being of other species, along with humans.[9] And sometimes the *quality* of life (for both humans and nonhumans) is more important than mere *survival*.

The philosophical split between the ecocentrists and the anthropocentric "survival environmentalists" in the 1960s had as its historical precedent the dispute between John Muir's ecocentrism and Gifford Pinchot's anthropocentric Resource Conservation and Development position at the beginning of the twentieth century. As the first head of the U.S. Forest Service, Pinchot claimed that there were just "people and resources." Even wilderness and other species had no value for their own sake; they were just human "resources" to be either exploited through resource extraction or enjoyed for their recreational or esthetic values, or to be saved for the enjoyment of future generations of *humans*.[10]

## ARNE NAESS AND THE "SHALLOW/DEEP ECOLOGY" DISTINCTION

Professional philosophers began to explore the immense philosophical implications raised by the environmental crisis in the late 1960s. For example, Arne Naess first began lecturing and writing on "Philosophy and Ecology" at the University of Oslo in 1968 and later at the University of Hong Kong in 1972. As long-time chairman of the philosophy department at the University of Oslo, and as a result of the influence of his books on semantics and the history of philosophy in the Norwegian school system, Naess's name has been nearly synonomous with philosophy in Norway for over fifty years.

At a Third World Futures conference held in Bucharest in 1972, Naess pointed out that two environmental movements had arisen during the 1960s: a "shallow" anthropocentric technocratic environmental movement concerned primarily with pollution, resource depletion, and "the health and affluence of people in the developed countries," and an ecocentric "Deep, Long-Range Ecology movement" (see the 1973 Naess paper in Part Two). Since first coining the term in 1972, Naess has continued to develop and refine the Deep Ecology position to the present day.

The Pulitzer Prize–winning poet and essayist Gary Snyder also worked out a unique Deep Ecological position beginning in the 1960s. Together with fellow Californians Peter Berg and the ecologist Raymond Dasmann, Snyder has developed the foundations for ecocentric bioregionalism.[11] Snyder has had an immense impact for over twenty-five years on the rise of the Deep Ecology movement. He and Naess are its two most influential international exponents.

Naess's "shallow/Deep Ecology" distinction was largely unknown outside Scandinavia until the 1980s, when it began to receive widespread attention among philosophers and environmentalists.[12] Worldwide awareness of the Deep Ecology movement resulted, in large part, from the publication of *Deep Ecology* by Bill Devall and George Sessions in 1985, and as a result of the publicity arising from the ecological activist group Earth First! throughout the 1980s.[13]

## DEEP ECOLOGY AND ITS CRITICS

Since the 1980s Deep Ecology has been discussed in many articles and books. While a great deal of this discussion has been positive, some has involved criticism of various aspects of Deep Ecology which is often based on misinterpretation and misunderstanding.

For example, Earth First! promoted an ecocentric orientation anad claimed to be an activist component of the Deep Ecology movement. While the Earth First! movement played a crucial role in reviving a sagging reform environmental movement during the anti-ecological Reagan era, some Earth First! activists unfortunately made apparently misanthropic remarks which are antithetical to Deep Ecology philosophy. The Deep Ecology critic Murray Bookchin, among others, seized upon these remarks in an attempt to discredit the Deep Ecology movement while, at the same time, promoting his own Social Ecology position.[14]

More recently, Vice President Al Gore, Jr. (in his best-selling book, *Earth in the Balance*), also referred to Earth First! activists' remarks in an attempt to portray the Deep Ecology movement as inherently misanthropic. Mr. Gore also made the very strange and unsubstantiated claim that Arne Naess's ecophilosophy portrays humans as being "an alien presence on the earth" and as having no free will. Deep Ecology has been misrepresented and used as a foil by Mr. Gore to promote his own human-dominant Christian stewardship position.[15]

The philosophy of the Deep Ecology movement is characterized essentially by ecocentrism, as outlined in the 1984 Deep Ecology platform. For critics such as Bookchin and Gore to substantiate their claims that the Deep Ecology position is inherently misanthropic, they would have to show that *ecocentrism* is essentially misanthropic. To my knowledge, no such serious argumentation has occurred and the case has not been made. On the other hand, powerful arguments have been made by ecophilosophers to the effect that anthropocentric positions in general, including those of Bookchin and Gore, are an unjustifiable form of "species chauvinism" and are thus ultimately indefensible.[16]

Certain Ecofeminists have criticized Deep Ecology for still different reasons.[17] (For critical discussions of Ecofeminism, Bookchin's Social Ecology, and Christian stewardship positions, see Part Four.) These kinds of misrepresentations of the Deep Ecology movement have resulted in considerable misunderstanding and confusion concerning what Deep Ecology actually is and what it stands for.

## PREVIOUS PRESENTATIONS OF THE DEEP ECOLOGY POSITION

The initial introduction of Deep Ecology concepts has been another source of confusion and misunderstanding. For example, *Deep Ecology* (1985) by Devall and Sessions helped popularize the concepts of the movement to a wide audience, but it had serious flaws, both substantive and stylistic, from its inception and it is now theoretically out of date in many respects.[18]

Arne Naess's *Ecology, Community, and Lifestyle* originally appeared in Norwegian in 1973 as *Økologi, samfunn, og livsstil* (it was the first ecophilosophy book written by a professional philosopher in any language) and it went through five Norwegian editions and a Swedish edition during the 1970s. Finally revised and translated into English in 1989 with help from David Rothenberg, *Ecology, Community, and Lifestyle* is Naess's main treatise on Deep Ecology (and on his own philosophical position, called Ecosophy T). While it is an authoritative contemporary statement of the Deep Ecology position, general readers may find certain parts of the book technical and difficult to understand.[19]

As with any philosophical/social position, Deep Ecology has evolved to some extent over the years, and some of this evolution has been the result of rethinking the position in light of sincere criticism and changing circumstances. One of the main purposes of this collection of papers is to attempt to clear up the misinterpretations and misunderstandings that have grown up recently around the Deep Ecology position, to respond to contemporary critics, and to lay out a contemporary version of the Deep Ecology position in a clear, easily accessible, but sophisticated manner. Correspondingly, many of the most up-to-date papers and interpretations of the position by leading theorists, activists, and historians of the movement have been assembled here.

## PARADOXES AND INCONSISTENCIES IN PRESENT ENVIRONMENTAL POLICY

Considerable theoretical refinement of ecophilosophical positions and conservation strategies has occurred throughout the 1980s and '90s.[20] At the same time, overall environmental destruction has increased dramatically. In the 1980s major global environmental problems appeared, such as ozone layer depletion and the greenhouse effect.

There has also been a tremendous accelerating loss of wild ecosystems, species, and species habitats worldwide. The Harvard conservation biologist E. O. Wilson claims that human-caused species extinction has accelerated from approximately 1,000 species per year in the 1970s to more than 10,000 species per year at present.[21] According to most biologists, this situation will continue to worsen dramatically in the coming decades unless there is a miraculous turnaround in the way modern societies behave on the planet.

As I write this, the world environmental situation consists of a welter of cruel paradoxes and inconsistencies. For instance, many of the world's "charis-

matic megafauna" are headed toward *imminent* extinction. The world-renowned wildlife biologist George Schaller has recently documented the
Chinese fiasco over protecting the giant pandas.[22] The San Diego Zoo and
other American zoos want pandas for display to enhance their images; China
has taken inadequate measures to protect panda habitat; and poachers are
getting $10,000 for panda pelts on the Asian black market.

The wild tiger situation in Asia in many ways parallels that of the panda,
and provides a typical and poignant example of the kinds of problems faced
by large mammals throughout the world. A recent issue of *Time* magazine
has a picture of a tiger on the cover with the caption "doomed."[23] According
to *Time*, 95 percent of the wild tiger population has been destroyed in the
twentieth century (the 95 percent figure now shows up repeatedly in terms of
the destruction of the wild world!). The Caspian tiger went extinct in the
1970s, and there are reportedly only 50 of the South China tigers left. Especially hard-hit has been Southeast Asia, where 90 to 95 percent of the rainfor-
ests (tiger habitat) have been clear-cut since World War II. The Bali tiger went
extinct in the 1940s, the Javan tiger in the 1980s, and there are only approximately 650 Sumatran tigers left. Incidentally, the Javan rhino is also on the
verge of extinction.

After massive deforestation throughout most of Asia (especially Southeast
Asia), the latest and final round of extinctions is occurring primarily as a result
of rapid human population growth impinging on the tiger preserves, and from
poaching for the exotic medicinal black trade market in China, Taiwan, and
Korea. Some Asians believe that concoctions made up of ground-up tiger
bones and rhino horns will restore potency in old men and cure other assorted
ailments. This has led conservationists to cut the horns off rhinos in Africa in
a desperate effort to save them from poachers.

According to *Time,* the Siberian (Amur) tiger has 800 miles of unbroken
pine forest habitat still remaining. But after the breakdown of the Soviet
Union, unchecked poaching for Asian bone markets has reduced Siberian
tiger numbers in a few short years to fewer than 200. There are at present no
wardens to help protect these tigers. What *Time* fails to point out is that Russia
is now in the process of awarding contracts to Japanese corporations to begin
clear-cutting these Siberian forests.

Most of the remaining tiger populations live in India. In 1972, the prime
minister of India, Indira Gandhi, launched Project Tiger, which established
India's ambitious network of tiger reserves. But, according to *Time,* these reserves are now suffering from the pressures of rapid human population
growth in and around the reserves, and are now being heavily poached to
supply Asian markets. Captive breeding of endangered species, such as the
tiger, and trying to reintroduce them to the wild at a later date, is rejected by

Schaller and other leading conservationists as "inefficient and unrealistic." If there are to be wild tigers, they must be protected in their wild habitat now!

In what amounts to a strange paradox, the Indian social ecologist Rama-chandra Guha recently complained (from a rather narrow anthropocentric "social justice" perspective) that India's tiger reserves are an example of "elite ecological imperialism," which has resulted in "a direct transfer of resources from the poor to the rich."[24]

There are also major problems on the North American continent (and throughout the world) with bears being poached for their gallbladders, which are then smuggled to Asia to supply the exotic "medicinal" market. The story in the United States is that there are insufficient funds to hire game wardens to enforce existing laws and prevent the decimation of North American wild-life as a result of increased poaching.

Also in the news is a $35-million project by researchers at San Diego's Scripps Institute to send sound waves through thousands of miles of deep ocean to study global warming; an interesting environmental paradox that involves endangering marine mammals in order to study another environmen-tal problem. The U.S. Navy has just proposed an explosives experiment in a marine mammal sanctuary off the coast of California. The Navy (along with the other branches of the military) has not been known for its environmental sensitivity—or concern for marine mammals: it trains dolphins for underwater suicide missions and, during World War II, used whales for submarine bomb-ing practice.[25] After conservationists have gone to extreme lengths over the years to protect marine mammals, instead of demanding a halt to this seem-ingly inane and largely unnecessary "experiment," they have meekly suggested that the Navy move its experiment further out to sea, where there will pre-sumably be "less" damage to these mammals.

Environmentalists in Holland and Germany are now trying to stop NATO low-level bomber-training flights over traditional Innu Indian lands in Labra-dor. According to Jerry Mander:

> More than 10,000 times each year, airplanes scream overhead at 700 miles per hour, just 50 feet above the trees, causing animals to scatter in shock and panic [and waterfowl to leave their habitat, and mink and foxes to eat their young], and utterly disrupting the millennia-old Innu hunting-and-gathering practices, not to mention the peace and quiet of their still-beautiful world.[26]

Another recent news article points out that environmentalists are opposing U.S. Air Force plans to take over a 13,000-acre area in southwestern Idaho for a bombing range that was previously slated for federal wilderness and wildlife protection. As the "cold war" winds down and the military withdraws from Europe, military leaders want to expand their training areas for supersonic jets and tanks in the United States. According to the news story, environmental battles similar to the one in Idaho are now being waged between the military establishment and environmentalists over wilderness and wildlife habitat in California, Arizona, Nevada, Colorado, New Mexico, Utah, and Alaska.

The cost of cleaning up radioactive and toxic wastes carelessly disposed of at military bases and weapons plants has been estimated at $400 billion. Superfund toxic cleanups are so costly that political leaders are now saying that we cannot afford to clean them up totally. Overall, military activities alone are estimated to cause between 10 and 30 percent of the total environmental degradation of the Earth.[27]

In other news, 95 percent of the ancient forests have been logged (mostly clear-cut) in the United States, but a judge has just given the go-ahead to log another 2,000 acres of ancient forest (and spotted owl habitat) in the Pacific Northwest and California: a move "eagerly sought by the Clinton administration and accepted by many environmentalists." At the same time, the Sierra Club is involved in an internal battle over whether to adopt a policy banning any further cutting of old-growth forests in the National Forests.

Most of the timber corporations have been guilty of poor and nonsustainable forestry practices for a long time. Now most of the remaining trees being cut (or pulp produced) are sent to Japan, long-time lumbering families and communities up and down the West Coast are put out of work, and the corporations then shut down the mills and look for profits elsewhere.

In conjunction with the attempt to protect what remains of the old growth forests, commercial ocean fishing is also being shut down along both the West and East coasts of the United States, and in many places throughout the world. Huge drift nets, radar, spotter planes, large processing ships—all the latest technology of modern fishing—coupled with increased demand for seafood and simple greed have depleted fish stocks in a great many areas. Paul Ehrlich and other ecologists predicted in the 1970s that this would happen, but regulatory agencies have been reluctant to face reality and angry fishermen, and to take the necessary steps to protect fish stocks until it is now all but too late in many cases.

Another news clipping reports that large sums of money are to be spent by the Interior Department in Clinton's administration to conduct a National Biological Survey to provide a huge computer data base and computer models of the remaining wild areas and wildlife in the United States. This is projected to take over twenty years to complete. This survey appears to have some merit but it also runs the same kind of risk as the Forest Service's essentially failed attempt to make responsible logging decisions based upon computer models of the forests.[28] As the semanticist Alfred Korzybski once remarked, "The map is not the territory."

The survey will have the advantage of providing long-term job security for the biologists who inventory what's left of the flora and fauna, but it also involves trapping, radio-collaring, and otherwise disturbing and "managing" the wildlife. More significantly, during the twenty years it will take to complete the survey, many of these wild areas (and plants and animals) will be destroyed through continued human encroachment and commercial "development." On the other hand, the world-renowned Stanford ecologist Paul Ehrlich claimed, in 1985, that "in a country like the United States, there is not the slightest excuse for developing one more square inch of undisturbed land."[29] This highlights the paradoxes and inconsistencies in trying to protect the remaining wildlife and habitat versus laying out huge sums of money, and wasting precious time, in "studying" the problem (a typical governmental bureaucratic alternative to making the necessary hard choices and taking appropriate action).

The Clinton administration has just announced its opposition to a bill (endorsed by the Sierra Club) that would protect 21 million acres of wilderness in Oregon, Washington, Idaho, Montana, and Wyoming. A Clinton administration Forest Service representative remarked, "We do not share the view that there is a crisis of the magnitude this bill would seem to presume." In terms of priorities and funding, given the severity of the contemporary wildlife and biodiversity crisis, the remaining wildlands and wildlife in this country (and the rest of the world) need to be protected *now!*

On a slightly different—but obviously related—tack, President Clinton and most other world leaders are now vigorously promoting the "new world order" of interlocking global economic markets and free trade (GATT and NAFTA, to which many environmentalists, including the Sierra Club, are opposed) to increase economic growth and consumption throughout the world. At the same time, in a glaring inconsistency, Vice President Gore refers to the United States as a "dysfunctional civilization" as a result of its addiction to consumption.[30] Clinton's economic "new world order" approach is consistent with the anthropocentric/economic emphasis of the 1987 United Nations "environmental" Brundtland Report (and the approach of the world leaders at the 1992 global Rio environmental summit), which promotes the concept of "sustainable development" as *the* environmental panacea. On the other hand, many environmentalists (both shallow and deep) consider the concept of "sustainable development" to be an oxymoron. Further, the "sustainable development" approach of the United Nations Brundtland report is inconsistent with the 1982 United Nations World Charter for Nature, which asserts that "Nature shall be respected and its essential processes shall not be disrupted." Ultimately, the majority of Americans (and citizens of other industrialized countries) refuse to face the fundamental inconsistency in their desire for *both* adequate environmental protection of the biosphere and continued economic growth and development.

Noel Brown, the director of the United Nations Environmental Program, said in 1989 that an Ecological Council (comparable to the Security Council) could soon be a reality.[31] This United Nations Council presumably could determine ecological disaster areas around the world, such as the periodic slaughter of African wildlife by poachers and military troups, or the Siberian tiger situation, and send "peacekeeping" troups, if necessary, to protect the wildlife and habitat temporarily until more permanent arrangements could be made. A perfect example of this is Rwanda, where a civil war has recently broken out. In addition to the horrible carnage taking place among the Rwandan people, the caretakers have abandoned the mountain gorilla preserve founded by Dian Fossey, which contains 300 of the last 600 mountain gorillas remaining in the world. The caretakers fear that the gorillas will be killed by poachers and soldiers.

But the Ecological Council is still not a reality. After adopting the ecocentric World Charter for Nature in 1982, why hasn't the United Nations developed a consistent environmental philosophical approach to the ecological crisis, implemented a realistic and aggressive environmental protection program, and integrated its environmental and population programs in a unified Biosphere protection approach?

The list of cruel and thoughtless environmental paradoxes and inconsistencies goes on and on. The world's "charismatic megafauna" on the verge of extinction—pandas, tigers, rhinos, bears, elephants poached for their ivory, gorillas subject to being wiped out by civil war; the world's wilderness areas and wildlife preserves too small and disconnected to prevent extinction; amphibians, birds, and ten thousand "lesser" species a year, all disappearing as a result of accelerating human overpopulation, ozone layer depletion, unending "development" and luxury consumption, inadequate, and (in some cases) insincere wildlife protection strategies, and lack of funds to adequately protect the few remaining wild ecosystems and to prevent poaching. Worldwide destruction of the last of the ancient forests. Marine mammals endangered by inane and expensive experiments. Why are there large sums of money for these kinds of experiments and projects, and why do we consider even tolerating such experiments, when the funds to take the necessary steps to protect wildlife and habitat are totally inadequate? And this is only a sampling of the contempory environmental inconsistencies and disordered priorities in the modern world.

# THE CONTEMPORARY ECOLOGICAL "STATE OF THE WORLD"

Government leaders and economic elites in Industrial Growth Societies continue to push for endless economic growth and development. Consumerism in the industrial world is now both a way of life and an addiction. New Age visions promote megatechnology solutions to economic and environmental ills, and propose massive high-tech global management and development schemes for the biosphere. Third World countries are now entering global markets and trying to become First World countries by destroying their ecosystems and wild species as they emulate the industrial and consumer patterns of the ecologically destructive unsustainable First World.

The leading ecotheologian Thomas Berry recently claimed that modern people "just don't get it. They don't comprehend how deeply rooted it is, the crisis that confronts us! . . . the order and magnitude of the present catastrophic situation is . . . so enormous, so widespread, and we don't know what we are doing." Berry further claims that

> reconciliation between [the developers and the ecologists] is especially difficult because the commercial-industrial powers have so overwhelmed the natural world in these past two centuries that there is, to the ecologist, no question of further adaptation of natural systems to the human. The oppression of the natural world by the plundering of the industrial powers has so endangered the basic functioning of natural forces that we are already on the verge of total dysfunctioning of the planet. We cannot mediate the situation as though there were presently some minimal balance already existing that could be slightly modified so that a general balance could come into being. The violence already done to the earth is on a scale beyond all understanding. . . . The change required by the ecologist is a drastic reduction in the plundering processes of the commercial industrial economy. . . . Never before has the human community been confronted with a situation that required such a sudden and total change in life style under the threat of a comprehensive degradation of the planet.[32]

Berry is surely correct to point out that the "opposition between the industrial entrepreneur and the ecologist has been both the central human issue and the central earth issue of this late 20th century."[33]

The 1992 Worldwatch Institute report contained a lead paper by Sandra Postel entitled "Denial in the Decisive Decade."[34] Documenting the continuing exponential deterioration of the world environment—the greenhouse effect, ozone layer depletion, desertification, exponential human population growth, air and water pollution, the pollution of the world's oceans, loss of topsoil, the continuing loss of ancient forests throughout the world, and the rate of species extinction (which she estimates at 140 per day), Postel claimed that the 1990s is the "decisive decade" to begin to turn things around. And we are halfway through that decade already! What we are getting instead is what Thomas Berry calls "microphase solutions to macrophase problems" or, in most cases, no realistic solutions at all. Most people, Postel claimed, are in a *psychological state of denial* concerning the seriousness and magnitude of the global ecological threat. One measure of the degree of this denial is how the industrial media have been able to convince so many people that if they just *recycle* they are "doing their part" for the environment, while they continue with their high-consumption lifestyles and all the other environmentally destructive practices that take place in industrial growth societies.[35]

The distinguished ecologists Anne and Paul Ehrlich have also recently discussed the dimensions of the current environmental crisis and proposed realistic solutions to our environmental problems. They claim that "the ravaging of biodiversity . . . is the most serious single environmental peril facing civilization." They further point out that the overall solution to the environmental crisis is to *"reduce the scale of the human enterprise."*[36]

The major reform environmental organizations have in some cases performed brilliantly, and in other cases they have compromised miserably, in their piecemeal political/economic/legal/technological approaches to protecting the environment. By failing to take an ecocentric integrated long-range perspective, by failing to be guided by realistic visions of ecological sustainable societies, and by failing to adequately address the root causes of the ecocrisis, they have managed only to delay some of the worst of the environmental degradation. Overall their strategies and efforts are failing to stem the tide of global environmental destruction.

The crucial paradigm shift the Deep Ecology movement envisions as necessary to protect the planet from ecological destruction involves the move from an anthropocentric to a spiritual/ecocentric value orientation. The wild ecosystems and species on the earth have intrinsic value and the right to exist and flourish, and are also necessary for the ecological health of the planet *and* the ultimate well-being of humans. Humanity must drastically scale down its industrial activities on Earth, change its consumption lifestyles, stabilize and then reduce the size of the human population by humane means, and protect and restore wild ecosystems and the remaining wildlife on the planet. This is a program that will last far into the twenty-first century. The crucial question is how much irreversible global ecological destruction humanity will continue to cause before existing trends can be significantly reversed.

# THE PLAN OF THE BOOK

In Part One of this anthology, various theorists discuss their views of the nature of Deep Ecology and the issues the movement addresses. Finally, it is claimed by Arne Naess that the Deep Ecology movement should be thought of as being characterized by the deep questioning process, the Deep Ecology platform, by the need for humans to identify with the nonhuman, and by nonviolent environmental activism, which stems from having a "total view." Andrew McLaughlin explains how the Deep Ecology platform functions as the heart of the movement.

Part Two discusses the history of the development of the Deep Ecology movement. The movement is a direct outgrowth of the ecocentric theorizing of Thoreau and Muir, the rise of the science of ecology, and Rachel Carson and the Ecological Revolution of the 1960s.

Part Three consists of papers by Arne Naess (most of them updated and/or previously unpublished) that discuss the finer points of Deep Ecology and Naess's own ecological philosophy (Ecosophy T). Naess also replies to various criticisms and misunderstandings of the Deep Ecology position.

Part Four addresses the issue of the relation of the Deep Ecology movement to Social Ecology, Ecofeminism, the New Age, and the Greens. This includes discussions by Naess of what he calls "the three great movements" and involves the issues of the relation of Deep Ecology to gender issues, and to issues of social justice. Critiques are also made of New Age anthropocentric megatechnological Disneyland utopian scenarios for the future.

Part Five involves discussions of wilderness and the wild, and explores what Thoreau meant by "In wildness is the preservation of the world." Reasons for protecting wilderness and wildness (both human and nonhuman) are examined. Some papers reply to critics of wilderness protection. Others discuss the new field of conservation biology and the most recent conservation strategies designed to protect wildlife and biodiversity by increasing the size of wildlife preserves together with interconnecting corridors.

Part Six centers on discussions of the politics of ecological sustainability. There are critiques of the concept of "sustainable development" as promoted at the 1992 Rio environmental conference. Sustainable development is thought by some to be essentially an attempt on the part of governmental leaders and economic/corporate elites in First World countries to coopt the main concerns of the environmental movement while they continue with their destructive path of economic growth and development at the expense of the Third and Fourth worlds, biodiversity protection, and genuine global ecological sustainability. Other papers discuss bioregional proposals and the possibilities of what the future holds if we do, or do not, adopt a Deep Ecological/ecocentric approach to the twenty-first century.

# ACKNOWLEDGMENTS

The sheer volume of high-quality writing in the general area of Deep Ecology by many authors is now immense. To begin to do justice to this literature would have required a collection of readings at least twice the length of this volume. In order to cover adequately what I consider to be the most important issues and topics in the area of Deep Ecology, to make this collection accessible to the general reader, and to make the book manageable in size, I was faced with the difficult and unpleasant task of deleting key papers (including a last-minute cut of approximately one hundred pages) by close friends and long-time academic associates. I hope that they can forgive me.

This project initially began years ago as a collection of Arne Naess's writings on Deep Ecology and only later was reconceived of as a more general collection for a general readership. Since I think that Naess, of all the theorists, has thought most deeply and carefully over a long period of time about the philosophical and technical aspects of Deep Ecology, I have decided to rely heavily throughout this collection on his exposition of the Deep Ecology position. I deeply regret that so many important papers (some of them my favorites) by leading Deep Ecological theorists and activists such as Bill Devall, Alan Drengson, Robyn Eckersley, Neil Everndon, Stephen Fox, Harold Glasser, Patsy Hallen, Sigmond Kvaloy, John Livingston, Joanna Macy, Stephanie Mills, Max Oelschlaeger, Theodore Roszak, Jeremy Rifkin, Kirkpatrick Sale, John Seed, Charlene Spretnak, and Michael Zimmerman could not be included. Readers are encouraged to seek out these and other writings in the bibliographies.

I want to thank Anne and Dave Brower, Michael and Valerie Cohen, Alan Drengson, Dave Foreman, Patsy Hallen, Dolores LaChapelle, Andrew McLaughlin, Max Oelschlaeger, Paul Shepard, Doug Tompkins, and Michael Zimmerman for their collegiality, friendship, and inspiration over the years. I have especially valued the hospitality and warm friendship of Gary Snyder and Carole Koda, and our many discussions about "the wild." Snyder has been one of the *major* influences in my thinking, and on my life, since the late 1960s. I have also greatly benefited from the discussions at the Deep Ecology seminars with Dolores and Max held in Silverton and Aspen, Colorado. I want to thank Doug and all his staff for the hospitality, insightful discussions about Third World problems, and the opportunity for uninterrupted work on the book at his ranch and alerce forest protection project in Chile in the fall of 1993.

Along with Gary Snyder, Arne Naess has also been a major influence on my life and thinking since the mid-1970s. I have worked closely with Arne for many years, and more intensely with Arne and Harold Glasser of the Department of Applied Sciences, University of California, Davis, during the last four years. I thoroughly enjoyed the hospitality of Arne and Kit Fai in Oslo and at Tvergastein, and the interaction with members of the philosophy department and the Center for Development and the Environment at the University of Oslo during the fall of 1992. Of special significance to me was the high-spirited discussions of the finer points of Deep Ecology with Arne and Harold in the Sonoran desert in the spring of 1993 and at various get-togethers with Michael Soulé at the University of California, Santa Cruz. Harold is a brilliant young ecophilosopher and friend who knows as much about Arne's technical philosophy as anyone, other than Arne. Harold has provided me with a number of crucial insights into Arne's technical philosophy that Arne was too polite to point out to me. I would also like to thank Ruth and Jim, Richard, David, and Aimeé for their special kinds of support over the years. And I want to thank my father, Al Sessions, for introducing me to the wildness of the Sierra at an early age.

I would also like to thank Doug, Jerry, Quincey, Dolly, and the Foundation for Deep Ecology for very generous financial and other kinds of support for this project. Thanks to Jerry Mander for his extraordinary book *In the Absence of the Sacred,* which tied many loose ends together for me. Thanks also to Danny Moses at Earth Island Institute Books for astute advice and support, and to Sierra College for the sabbaticals during the fall semesters of 1992–93, which helped make this book possible.

Finally, I would like to thank Peter Turner for excellent friendly editorial advice and support, and to Jonathan Green and everyone else at Shambhala for expediting the publication of this book.

# NOTES

1. For discussions of the roots of the Deep Ecology movement, see George Sessions, "Shallow and Deep Ecology: A Review of the Philosophical Literature," in J. Donald Hughes and Robert Schultz (eds.), *Ecological Consciousness: Essays from the Earthday X Colloquium* (Washington, D.C.: University Press of America, 1981), pp. 391–462; George Sessions, "The Deep Ecology Movement: A Review," *Environmental Review* 11, 2 (1987): 105–25; Roderick Nash, *The Rights of Nature: A History of Environmental Ethics* (Madison: University of Wisconsin Press, 1989); Max Oelschlaeger, *The Idea of Wilderness: From Prehistory to the Age of Ecology* (New Haven: Yale University Press, 1991). See also Part Two of this anthology.

2. For a discussion of Mumford's contribution to ecological awareness, see Anne Chisholm, *Philosophers of the Earth: Conversations with Ecologists* (New York: Dutton, 1972); see also F. F. Darling and J. Milton (eds.), *Future Environments of North America* (Garden City, N.Y.: Natural History Press, 1966); Lewis Mumford, *The Myth of the Machine* (New York: Harcourt, Brace & World, 1967); Lewis Mum-

ford, *The Pentagon of Power* (New York: Harcourt Brace Jovanovich, 1970); Theodore Roszak, *Person/Planet: The Creative Disintegration of Industrial Society* (Garden City, N.Y.: Doubleday, 1978), which the author dedicated to Lewis Mumford.

3. Two best-selling books that brilliantly summarize much of the social/ecological criticism of the 1960s are Charles Reich's *The Greening of America* (New York: Random House, 1970) and Theodore Roszak's *Where the Wasteland Ends: Politics and Transcendence in Postindustrial Society* (Garden City, N.Y.: Doubleday, 1972); see also Raymond F. Dasmann, "Conservation, Counterculture, and Separate Realities," *Environmental Conservation* 1 (1974): 133–37; Roderick Nash, *Wilderness and the American Mind,* 3rd ed. (New Haven: Yale University Press, 1982) pp. 237–62.

4. Rachael Carson, *Silent Spring* (Boston: Houghton Mifflin, 1962), p. 297; see also Paul Brooks, *The House of Life: Rachel Carson at Work* (Boston: Houghton Mifflin, 1972).

5. Lynn White's paper ("The Historical Roots of Our Ecologic Crisis") was read at a meeting of the prestigeous American Association for the Advancement of Science in December 1966 and published in *Science* 155 (1967): 1203–7; reprinted in Donald VanDeVeer and Christine Pierce (eds.), *Environmental Ethics and Policy Book* (Belmont, Calif.: Wadsworth, 1994), pp. 45–51. For discussions of the impact of White's thesis, see Stephen Fox, *John Muir and His Legacy: The American Conservation Movement* (Boston: Little, Brown, 1981), pp. 358–74; Roderick Nash, *The Rights of Nature,* pp. 87–120.

6. For a discussion of Brower as "Muir reincarnate," see Stephen Fox, *John Muir and His Legacy,* pp. 250–90; see also Michael Cohen, *The History of the Sierra Club: 1892–1970* (San Francisco: Sierra Club Books, 1988), pp. 187–322; for Brower's comments, see John McPhee, *Encounters with the Archdruid* (New York: Farrar, Straus & Giroux, 1971), pp. 74, 84–85, 226.

7. Personal correspondence, March 1992.

8. The Commoner quote appears in Fox, *John Muir and His Legacy,* p. 306. Fox's book contains the best short account of the ecological/environmental developments of the 1960s, including the disputes between the ecocentrists and the anthropocentrists (chap. 9). Fox also points out (p. 292) that the Social Ecologist Murray Bookchin, who, like Commoner, has a Marxist background and approach to environmental issues, wrote a book in 1962 (under the pseudonym Lewis Herber) entitled *Our Synthetic Environment,* which was also concerned primarily with urban pollution problems. But the book was immediately overshadowed by the publication of Carson's *Silent Spring.* Also like Commoner, Bookchin was to argue, against the ecologists, that there was no human overpopulation problem. One can seemingly hold this view only if one believes that humans have the whole Earth at their disposal, but this seems to imply a total lack of concern for wild species and their need for adequate habitat.

For another excellent short history of the development of environmentalism beginning with the 1960s, see Kirkpatrick Sale, *The Green Revolution: The American Environmental Movement 1962–1992* (New York: Hill and Wang, 1993).

9. For a more complete discussion of these issues, see George Sessions, "Ecocentrism and the Anthropocentric Detour," in Part Two of this anthology.

10. For a discussion of the split between Muir and Pinchot, see Fox, *John Muir and His Legacy*, pp. 110–30.

11. See, for example, Gary Snyder, "Re-inhabitation," in Gary Snyder, *The Old Ways* (San Francisco: City Lights Books, 1977), pp. 57–66; Peter Berg and Raymond Dasmann, "Reinhabiting California," in Peter Berg (ed.), *Reinhabiting a Separate Country* (San Francisco: Planet Drum Foundation, 1978); for historical discussions of the bioregional/reinhabitory movement, see Kirkpatrick Sale, *Dwellers in the Land: The Bioregional Vision* (San Francisco: Sierra Club Books, 1985); Dave Foreman, "Who Speaks for Wolf?" in Dave Foreman, *Confessions of an Ecowarrior* (New York: Harmony Books, 1991), pp. 37–50.

12. For a detailed discussion of the development of the Deep Ecology movement, see Warwick Fox, *Toward a Transpersonal Ecology* (Boston: Shambhala Publications, 1990).

13. Bill Devall and George Sessions, *Deep Ecology: Living as if Nature Mattered* (Salt Lake City: Gibbs Smith, 1985).

14. Dave Foreman's remarks about "not giving aid to Ethiopians and allowing them to starve" appeared in an interview with Bill Devall, "A Spanner in the Woods," in the Australian periodical *Simply Living* 2, 12 (1987). Murray Bookchin's 23-page diatribe against Deep Ecology ("Social Ecology versus 'Deep Ecology': A Challenge for the Ecology Movement") was delivered before a large audience at the first U.S. Green meeting in Amherst, Massachusetts, in July 1987. This talk was later revised and published as "Social Ecology versus Deep Ecology" in the *Socialist Review* 88, 3 (1988): 11–29, and has been reprinted in VanDeVeer and Pierce, *Environmental Ethics and Policy Book*, pp. 228–38. For a critique of Bookchin's Green meeting attack on Deep Ecology, see Kirkpatrick Sale, "Deep Ecology and Its Critics," *The Nation* 22 (May 14, 1988): 670–75.

　　Bookchin and Foreman later met at a forum in an attempt to resolve their differences. This dialogue was published in Steve Chase (ed.), *Defending the Earth: A Dialogue between Murray Bookchin and Dave Foreman* (Boston: South End Press, 1991). Foreman essentially apologized for his remarks, but Bookchin did not modify his anthropocentrism.

15. Al Gore, Jr., *Earth in the Balance: Ecology and the Human Spirit* (Boston: Houghton Mifflin, 1992), pp. 216–18. When questioned during an interview, Gore as much as admitted that he had made a "straw man" out of the Deep Ecology position. See Jordan Fisher-Smith, "Environmentalism of the Spirit: An Interview with Senator Al Gore," *Orion* 11, 3 (Summer 1992): 75–79.

16. See, for example, Richard and Val Routley, "Against the Inevitability of Human Chauvinism," in K. Goodpasture and K. Sayre (eds.), *Moral Philosophy for the Twenty-first Century* (South Bend, Ind.: University of Notre Dame Press, 1979);

Paul Taylor, *Respect for Nature: A Theory of Environmental Ethics* (Princeton: Princeton University Press, 1986), pp. 129–56; Warwick Fox, *Toward a Transpersonal Ecology,* pp. 13–22; Andrew McLaughlin, *Regarding Nature: Industrialism and Deep Ecology* (New York: State University of New York Press, 1993), chap. 8.

The ecologist David Ehrenfeld's *The Arrogance of Humanism* (Oxford: Oxford University Press, 1978) is a defense of ecocentrism and an extended critique of the philosophy of humanism understood as an anthropocentric position. Ehrenfeld devotes a chapter to the issue of misanthropy. See also David Ehrenfeld, *Beginning Again: People and Nature in the New Millenium* (Oxford: Oxford University Press, 1993).

17. The Australian sociologist Ariel Salleh's "Deeper than Deep Ecology: The Ecofeminist Connection," *Environmental Ethics* 6, 4 (1984): 339–45, was the first academic Ecofeminist critique of Deep Ecology.

18. The Devall/Sessions book was hastily written in Utah over a two-week period at the insistence of the publisher, based upon a previously contracted book of academic papers. The haste was thought necessary in order to compete with another book of the same title—Michael Tobias (ed.), *Deep Ecology* (San Diego, Calif.: Avant Books, 1985)—which, as it turned out, had little to do with Deep Ecology. For a critical discussion of the development of the Devall/Sessions and Tobias books, see Dolores LaChapelle, *Sacred Land Sacred Sex: Rapture of the Deep* (Durango, Colo.: Kivaki Press, 1988), pp. 12–15.

19. Arne Naess, *Ecology, Community and Lifestyle: Outline of an Ecosophy* (Cambridge: Cambridge University Press, 1989). While David Rothenberg is listed as the editor and translator of the book, Naess has subsequently claimed that he made almost all of the revisions: hence the book should be considered "pure Naess."

20. Much of the academic debate over the various ecophilosophical positions (Deep Ecology, Environmental Ethics, Ecofeminism, Social Ecology, and Animal Rights) has taken place over the last fifteen years in the pages of *Environmental Ethics* journal, founded in 1979 under the able editorship of Eugene Hargrove, who is chairman of the philosophy department at North Texas State University.

21. E. O. Wilson, *The Diversity of Life* (Cambridge, Mass.: Harvard University Press, 1992), p. 351.

22. George Schaller, *The Last Panda* (Chicago: University of Chicago Press, 1993).

23. *Time* 143 (March 28, 1994): 44–51.

24. Ramachandra Guha, "Radical American Environmentalism and Wilderness Preservation: A Third World Critique," *Environmental Ethics* 11, 1 (1989): 71–83; reprinted in VanDeVeer and Pierce, *Environmental Ethics and Policy Book,* pp. 548–56. Guha made this remark as part of an overall critique of what he understood to be the Deep Ecology position. For Arne Naess's reply to Guha's critique, see Part Five of this anthology.

25. See Farley Mowat, *Sea of Slaughter* (Boston: Atlantic Monthly Press, 1984).

26. Jerry Mander, *In the Absence of the Sacred: The Failure of Technology and the Survival of the Indian Nations* (San Francisco: Sierra Club Books, 1991), p. 389.

27. Sale, *The Green Revolution,* p. 75.

28. For a discussion of the failure of the Forest Service's computer modeling program, see Mander, *In The Absence of the Sacred,* p. 58.

29. Paul Ehrlich, "Comments," *Defenders of Wildlife,* Nov./Dec. 1985.

30. Al Gore, Jr., *Earth in the Balance,* pp. 216–37.

31. W. R. Prescott, "The Rights of Earth: An Interview with Noel Brown," *In Context* 22 (Summer 1989): 29–34.

32. Marjorie Hope and James Young, "A Prophetic Voice: Thomas Berry," *The Trumpeter: Canadian Journal of Ecosophy* 11, 1 (1994): 2–9; Thomas Berry, "The New Political Alignment," unpublished manuscript, 1993.

33. This quote is from the Thomas Berry essay "The Viable Human" in Part One.

34. Sandra Postel, "Denial in the Decisive Decade," in Lester R. Brown (ed.), *State of the World: A Worldwatch Institute Report on Progress toward a Sustainable Society* (New York: W. W. Norton, 1992), pp. 3–8.

35. Anne and Paul Ehrlich, in the introduction to *Healing the Planet: Strategies for Resolving the Environmental Crisis* (Reading, Mass.: Addison-Wesley, 1991), point out how the industrial media hype surrounding, for example, Earth Day 20 (1990) essentially coopts realistic environmental action by encouraging people to follow trendy, superficial, socially approved "ecological" changes in lifestyle which feed into the Industrial Growth Society, such as merely recycling or buying "green" products, thereby deflecting attention away from the real causes of the ecological crisis.

36. Ehrlich and Ehrlich, *Healing the Planet,* pp. 35–37; other books which comprehensively discuss the environmental crisis and propose realistic solutions are G. Tyler Miller, *Living in the Environment,* 8th ed. (Belmont, Calif.: Wadsworth, 1994), and Paul Harrison's, *The Third Revolution: Environment, Population and a Sustainable World* (London: I. B. Tauris, 1992).

PART ONE | # WHAT IS DEEP ECOLOGY?

# INTRODUCTION

THIS FIRST SELECTION OF essays attempts to provide a general overview of many of the issues that concern Deep Ecology theorists and activists. One should be able to read through these essays and get an overall sense of the flavor and concerns of the Deep Ecology movement. The last two essays, by Arne Naess and Andrew McLaughlin, discuss the Deep Ecology platform as the common ground for Deep Ecology as a philosophical and social activist movement. While many of the issues raised in these essays, and elsewhere throughout the book, are more or less implied by the Deep Ecology platform, others are more speculative and belong to the personal ecosophies and total views of individual Deep Ecology supporters.

In "The Viable Human," the leading Catholic ecotheologian, Thomas Berry, provides an overview of the contemporary environmental situation. In Berry's view, a major religious/philosophical paradigm shift in society is required—from an anthropocentric to a biocentric [or ecocentric] sense of reality and value—to deal effectively with the environmental crisis. Berry's ecocentrism is expressed in the claim that "the community of all living species is the greater reality and the greater value."

The global industrial establishments, Berry claims, are primarily responsible for the magnitude and severity of the contemporary environmental crisis in that they have shaped the contemporary social paradigm of reality and value. Industrial entrepreneurs have promoted an economic/technological/consumerist "wonderworld," whereas in actuality they are creating a "wasteworld" for both humans and the rest of Nature. Reducing the planet to a resource base for consumer use, he maintains, "is already a spiritual and psychic degradation." Echoing Orwell's analysis of "Newspeak," Berry claims that contemporary language has been degraded to support the industrial/consumerist vision, and that this degradation helps support "the most extravagant modes of commercial advertising to create the illusory world in which the human community is now living." Industrial control of the media, he claims "is among the most devastating forces threatening the viability of the human." Further, education has been warped from its original purposes to the point where it now prepares young people primarily for jobs in the destructive industrial society.

Educational and religious professionals, Berry claims, are failing to adequately address the environmental crisis and to provide effective guidance for
humanity. Berry sees the conflict between the industrialist and the ecologist as
"both the central human issue and the central earth issue of this late twentieth
century."

Berry offers important suggestions to help move us in the direction of a
spiritual/ecological paradigm, but his analysis fails to mention the crucial role
of human overpopulation in the environmental crisis. Elsewhere he has agreed
that population stabilization and eventual reduction are ecologically necessary.

The physicist Fritjof Capra essentially agrees with Berry when he claims
that a major scientific/spiritual/social paradigm shift to a Deep Ecology worldview is necessary to deal adequately with the contemporary environmental/
social crisis. Capra focuses specifically on the problems that have resulted from
the rise of the Cartesian mechanistic paradigm in the seventeenth century. He
stresses the more scientific and economic aspects of the shift: from a mechanistic anthropocentric worldview to an organic, ecologically interrelated, holistic
systems view. Capra also thinks that the move to the new paradigm is more
or less historically inevitable.

The 1982 interview with Arne Naess—"Simple in Means, Rich in Ends"—
provides a short, clear introduction to the main ideas of Deep Ecology, although in this interview he had not yet separated his own personal Ecosophy
T views from the more philosophically neutral views of the Deep Ecology
platform. Naess claims that the essence of Deep Ecology is to ask deeper questions. This leads to questioning the values of our society, and to the development of a total view. He discusses the importance of the norms of ecological
equality and Self-realization.

Naess further argues that science and technology alone cannot solve our
environmental problems. And since logic can't prove one's starting point, people must go beyond narrow rationality and reliance on "authorities" and learn
to cultivate and trust their basic intuitions as a basis for environmental action
and meaningful personal values. And echoing Thoreau's injunction that we
simplify our lives, Naess claims that the cultivation of an ecological self involves a materially simple lifestyle, and values that maximize the quality and
richness of our experience.

Another major area of concern for Deep Ecology theorists is now being
referred to as "ecopsychology." Concern with the psychological/spiritual dimensions of humanity's relationship to wild Nature can be traced back to
Thoreau and Muir, and ultimately to the primal peoples of the world. The
papers by Glendinning, Snyder, and LaChapelle all discuss various aspects of
this old/new interest in "ecopsychology." Arne Naess's concept of human self-
realization (the "ecological self") directly addresses the key issues of ecopsy-

chology, and human psychological maturity (see his "Self-realization" in Part Three), and Warwick Fox has developed an important ecopsychology he calls "transpersonal ecology." In addition, Theodore Roszak, in his book *The Voice of the Earth* (1992), has helped define the new field of ecopsychology and has been influential in interesting professional psychologists in ecopsychology. Roszak claims that "the core of the mind is the ecological unconscious. For ecopsychology, repression of the ecological unconscious is the deepest root of collusive madness in industrial society."

The psychologist Chellis Glendinning provides a very insightful thumbnail ecopsychoanalysis of industrial society. She claims that people in modern technological/industrial societies are suffering from the "Original Trauma" of separation from Nature. This separation has led to a failure of modern industrial humans to satisfy our most basic needs. The result is widespread psychopathological and addictive behavior. We are "awash in a sea of addictions," she claims, including consumerism and what she calls "Techno-Addiction." By contrast, Glendinning refers to Paul Shepard's discussions (in *Nature and Madness,* 1982) of primal peoples and their normal cultural ways of satisfying primary needs. A psychological recovery for technological society will require a renewed sense of connectedness to Nature.

This recent interest in ecopsychology, and a concern for a renewed sense of connectedness to Nature, has begun to refocus attention on Thoreau's enigmatic statement that "in wildness is the preservation of the world" (see the Turner paper in Part Five for further exploration of Thoreau's statement). Best-selling books such as Clarissa Pinkola Estés's *Women Who Run with the Wolves* (1992) claim that there is a wild creature inside of each of us that we must cultivate to avoid becoming domesticated. Recent popular films such as *Never Cry Wolf* and *Dances with Wolves* also explore the wild/domestic theme. This new interest in human wildness, however, runs the risk of becoming the latest fad, and of being deflected into some superficial New Age version of urban "spiritual" self-absorption.

On the other hand, Paul Shepard, Gary Snyder, and Dolores LaChapelle have provided sophisticated discussions of human wildness in their writings for many years. Developing themes raised by Rousseau, Thoreau, Muir, Huxley, Orwell, and, more recently, Jerry Mander (see, for example, "Killing Wilderness" by Wayland Drew in Part Two), Shepard and Snyder claim that humans have a genetic need for the wild as a result of our evolutionary development as hunters and gatherers under Pleistocene conditions. Shepard has developed the ecopsychological theory that intimate identification with wild Nature is part of our natural human developmental (ontogenetic) processes. The destruction of the Earth's wildness, together with the attempt at total domestication of humans by the urban/industrial/technological project of modernity, is destroying our essential humanness. To be fully human we must protect and nurture our wildness, which involves bioregional living, intimate contact with wild animals and plants in wild ecosystems, animistic perception, and primal nature rituals. Gary Snyder's *The Practice of the Wild* (1990) provides a keenly perceptive entry back into the wild world. Viewed from this perspective, the "wild/domestic" issue is a key philosophical concern raised by the ecological crisis.

In "Gary Snyder and the Practice of the Wild," Jack Turner provides an overview of Snyder's life and writings, and discusses selections from *The Practice of the Wild* and Snyder's bioregional way of life on the North San Juan ridge of Northern California.

In "Cultured or Crabbed" Snyder points out that, for Thoreau and Muir, there are two kinds of knowing: cultured and wild. Unlike primal peoples, contemporary people are cultivated stock, but we can return to the wild. The Deep Ecology movement holds that "the health of natural systems should be our first concern" while trying to create a "culture of wilderness" from within civilization. The environmental concerns of some people and societies are focused on human welfare, but, as Snyder points out, "there can be no health for humans and cities that bypasses the rest of nature." He makes the crucial point that we must distinguish between "nature" and the "wild."

Dolores LaChapelle explores the role that ritual plays among traditional peoples. Ritual is essential, she claims, in that it connects us to each other and to the nonhuman world with "the whole of our being."

Dave Foreman discusses the significance of Deep Ecology and ecocentrism from the perspective of an involved activist. During the 1970s the major reform conservation/environmental organizations were still trying to save wilderness and wild places in a piecemeal manner based upon anthropocentric rationales such as aesthetics and recreation. The need to protect entire ecosystems and to maintain ecosystem integrity was ignored, and unecological compromises were the norm in conservationist strategy. The rise of environmental ethics, Deep Ecology, the new field of conservation biology, and radical local environmental groups in the 1980s has changed the whole tenor of conservation efforts. Earth First! and the New Conservation movement, Foreman claims, have been instrumental in bringing about an ecocentric philosophical revolution in the environmental community in which wilderness areas are now understood to be key elements in the new ecological vision of interconnected nature preserves. It should also be mentioned that Earth First! was largely instrumental in making the protection of old growth forests a major environmental issue.

Naess's "The Deep Ecology Movement," written in 1986, is the best short contemporary statement of the Deep Ecology position. Naess provides illuminating contrasts between shallow and deep ecological positions on issues such as pollution, resources, human overpopulation, cultural diversity and appropriate technology, land and sea ethics, and education and the scientific enterprise.

Naess also introduces the Apron Diagram and the Eight Point Deep Ecology platform, which was developed in 1984. Widely differing cultural and philosophical/religious diversity of views necessarily and positively exists at Level I of the diagram. This diversity can nevertheless converge, at Level II, to support the Deep Ecology platform, which is basically an ecocentric/ecological approach to the Earth and its environmental problems. Level III of the diagram consists of hypotheses and factual statements about the state of the world, such as statements about ozone layer depletion, the rates of species extinction, and so forth. At Level IV of the diagram, specific environmental actions and social structures will also exhibit a certain amount of cultural diversity, while nevertheless remaining consistent with, and following logically from, the platform. (For a more detailed discussion of the Deep Ecology platform and the Apron Diagram, see the introduction and relevant papers by Naess in Part Three.) Naess also describes his own personal philosophical total view (which he calls Ecosophy T). Ecosophy T is developed from his single Level I norm "Self-realization."

In addition to the Deep Ecology platform, Naess points out that the Deep Ecology movement is characterized by the deep questioning process, and by environmental activism which is spiritual. Spiritual activism means, for Naess, acting from the basis of a fundamental philosophic/religious ecosophy (or "total view") and acting nonviolently.

In the last essay, Andrew McLaughlin reinforces Naess's view of the Deep Ecology platform as providing the main common ground for Deep Ecology as a social/political movement. McLaughlin points out that critics have missed the unique "logic" of the Deep Ecology position. In order to criticize the Deep Ecology movement in a relevant manner, criticism must be directed at some aspect of the Deep Ecology platform. Criticism is often made of some aspect of a Deep Ecology supporter's personal ecosophy (such as Naess's Ecosophy T, or statements made by environmental activists). But such criticism is "beside the point" in that it is not criticism of the position of the Deep Ecology movement.

McLaughlin explains in detail the significance of each of the platform's Eight points. The platform nevertheless provides for cultural and philosophic/religious diversity in terms of its ultimate Level I ecosophical justifications. Ultimately, the Deep Ecology movement is concerned to bring about the "profound social change" that is necessary to resolve the environmental crisis.

# 1 | THE VIABLE HUMAN
## *Thomas Berry*

To be viable, the human community must move from its present anthro-pocentric norm to a geocentric norm of reality and value. Within the solar system, the earth is the immediate context of human existence. And we recognize the sun as the primary source of earth's energies. Beyond the sun, however, is our own galaxy, and beyond that is the universal galactic system that emerged some fifteen billion years ago through some ineffable mystery.

To establish this comprehensive context is important; it is the only satisfactory referent in our quest for a viable presence of the human within the larger dynamics of the universe. We suppose that the universe itself is *the* enduring reality and *the* enduring value even while it finds expression in a continuing sequence of transformations. In creating the planet Earth, its living forms, and its human intelligence, the universe has found, so far as we know, the most elaborate manifestation of its deepest mystery. Here, in its human form, the universe is able to reflect on and celebrate itself in a unique mode of conscious self-awareness.

Our earliest human documents reveal a special sensitivity in human intellectual, emotional, and aesthetic responses to the natural world. These responses reveal cosmic and biologic realms of thought as well as anthropocentric life attitudes. These realms were all centered in each other, the later dependent on the earlier for survival, the earlier dependent on the later for their manifestation.

Instinctively, humans have always perceived themselves as a mode of being *of* the universe as well as distinctive beings *in* the universe. This was the beginning. The emergence of the human was a transformative moment for the earth as well as for the human. As with every species, the human being needed to establish its niche, a sustainable position in the larger community of

Originally published in *ReVision* 9, no. 2 (Winter-Spring 1987). Reprinted with permission of the Helen Dwight Reid Education Foundation. Published by Heldref Publications, 1319 Eighteenth St., N.W., Washington, D.C. 20036-1802.

life, to fulfill its need for food, shelter, and clothing, for security, for family and community. The need for community was special because of the unique human capacity for thought and speech, aesthetic appreciation, emotional sensitivities, and moral judgment. The fulfilling of these needs resulted in a cultural shaping that established the specific identifying qualities of the human being.

Whatever the cultural elaboration of the human, its basic physical as well as psychic nourishment and support came from the surrounding natural environment. In its beginnings, human society was integrated with the larger life society and the larger earth community composed of all the geological as well as biological and human elements. Just how long this primordial harmony endured we do not know beyond the last hundred thousand years of the Paleolithic period. Some ten thousand years ago, the Neolithic and then the Classical civilizations came into being. It must suffice to say that with the classical and generally literate civilizations of the past five thousand years, the great cultural worlds of the human developed, along with vast and powerful social establishments whereby humans became oppressive and even destructive of other life forms. Alienation from the natural world increased, and new ideals of human well-being neglected the needs of other living species. Because of this human dysfunctional relation with the earth, some of these earlier human cultures became nonsustainable. We can observe this especially in the classical Mediterranean civilizations of Greece and Rome. Even so, the human species as a whole was not seriously endangered; these experiences were regional and limited in their consequences. In recent times, however, this has changed.

A deep cultural pathology has developed in Western society and has now spread throughout the planet. A savage plundering of the entire earth is taking place through industrial exploitation. Thousands of poisons unknown in former times are saturating the air, the water, and the soil. The habitat of a vast number of living species is being irreversibly damaged. In this universal disturbance of the biosphere by human agents, the human being now finds that the harm done to the natural world is returning to threaten the human species itself.

The question of the viability of the human species is intimately connected with the question of the viability of the earth. These questions ultimately arise because at the present time the human community has such an exaggerated, even pathological, fixation on its own comfort and convenience that it is willing to exhaust any and all of the earth's resources to satisfy its own cravings. The sense of reality and of value is strictly directed toward the indulgences of a consumer economy. This nonsustainable situation can be clearly seen in the damage done to major elements necessary for the continued well-being of the planet. When the soil, the air, and the water have been extensively poisoned, human needs cannot be fulfilled. Strangely, this situation is the consequence of a human-centered norm of reality and value.

Once we grant that a change from an anthropocentric to a biocentric sense of reality and value is needed, we must ask how this can be achieved and how it would work. We must begin by accepting the fact that the life community, the community of all living species, is the greater reality and the greater value, and that the primary concern of the human must be the preservation and enhancement of this larger community. The human does have its own distinctive reality and its own distinctive value, but this distinctiveness must be articulated within the more comprehensive context. The human ultimately must discover the larger dimensions of its own being within this community context. That the value of the human being is enhanced by diminishing the value of the larger community is an illusion, the great illusion of the present industrial age, which seeks to advance the human by plundering the planet's geological structure and all its biological species.

This plundering is being perpetrated mainly by the great industrial establishments that have dominated the entire planetary process for the past one hundred years, during the period when modern science and technology took control not only of our natural resources but also of human affairs. If the viability of the human species is now in question, it is a direct consequence of these massive ventures, which have gained extensive control not only of our economies but also of our whole cultural development, whether it be economics, politics, law, education, medicine, or moral values. Even our language is heavily nuanced in favor of the consumer values fostered by our commercial industrial establishment.

Opposed to the industrial establishment is the ecological movement which seeks to create a more viable context for the human within the framework of the larger community. There must, however, be a clear understanding that this question of viability is not an issue that can be resolved in any permanent manner. It will be a continuing issue for the indefinite future.

The planet that ruled itself directly for the past millennia is now determining its future through human decision. Such has been the responsibility assumed by humans when we ventured into the study of the empirical sciences and their associated technologies. In this process, whatever the benefits, we endangered ourselves and every living organism on this planet.

If we look back over the total course of planetary development, we find that there was a consistent fluorescence of the life process in the larger arc of its development over some billions of years. There were innumerable catastrophic events in both the geological and biological realms, but none of these had the distinguishing characteristics or could cause such foreboding as Earth experiences at present.

The total extinction of life is not imminent, though the elaborate forms of life expression in the earth's ecosystems may be shattered in an irreversible manner. What is absolutely threatened is the degradation of the planet's more brilliant and satisfying forms of life expression. This degradation involves extensive distortion and a pervasive weakening of the life system, its comprehensive integrity as well as its particular manifestations.

While there are pathologies that wipe out whole populations of life forms and must be considered pernicious to the life process on an extensive scale, the human species has, for some thousands of years, shown itself to be a pernicious presence in the world of the living on a unique and universal scale. Nowhere has this been more evident than in the Western phase of development of the human species. There is scarcely any geological or biological reality or function that has not experienced the deleterious influence of the human. The survival of hundreds of thousands of species is presently threatened. But since the human survives only within this larger complex of ecosystems, any damage done to other species, or to the other ecosystems, or to the planet itself, eventually affects the human not only in terms of physical well-being but also in every other phase of human intellectual understanding, aesthetic expression, and spiritual development.

Because such deterioration results from a rejection of the inherent limitation of earthly existence and from an effort to alter the natural functioning of the planet in favor of a humanly constructed wonderworld for its human occupants, the human resistance to this destructive process has turned its efforts toward an emphasis on living creatively within the functioning of the natural world. The earth as a bio-spiritual planet must become, for the human, the basic reference in identifying what is real and what is worthwhile.

Thus we have the ecologist standing against industrial enterprise in defense of a viable mode of human functioning within the context of a viable planetary process. This opposition between the industrial entrepreneur and the ecologist has been both the central human issue and the central earth issue of this late 20th century. My position is that the efforts of the entrepreneur to create a wonderworld are, in fact, creating a wasteworld, a nonviable environment for the human species. The ecologist is offering a way of moving toward a new expression of the true wonderworld of nature as the context for a viable human situation. The current difficulty is that the industrial enterprise has such extensive control over the planet that we must certainly be anxious about the future.

But we are tempted to diminish our assessment of the danger lest we be overwhelmed with the difficulty, for indeed, we are caught in a profound cultural pathology. We might even say that, at present, our dominant institutions, professions, programs, and activities are counterproductive in their consequences, addictive to a consumer society; and we are paralyzed by our inability to respond effectively. Such a description is well merited if we consider the extent to which we have poisoned our environment, the air we breathe, the water we drink, and the soil that grows our food.

Having identified the magnitude of the difficulty before us, we need to establish a more specific analysis of the problems themselves. Then we need to provide specific programs leading toward a viable human situation on a viable planet.

The industrial entrepreneur is in possession of the natural resources of the planet, either directly, by corporate control, or indirectly, through governments subservient to the industrial enterprise. This possession is, of course, within limits. Fragmentary regions of the planet have been set aside as areas to be preserved in their natural state or to be exploited at a later time. These regions survive at the tolerance of the industrial establishment. Some controls now exist through governmental and private protection. These must be expanded.

Ecologists recognize that reducing the planet to a resource base for consumer use in an industrial society is already a spiritual and psychic degradation. Our main experience of the divine, the world of the sacred, has been diminished as money and utility values have taken precedence over spiritual, aesthetic, emotional, and religious values in our attitude toward the natural world. Any recovery of the natural world will require not only extensive financial funding but a conversion experience deep in the psychic structure of the human. Our present dilemma is the consequence of a disturbed psychic situation, a mental imbalance, an emotional insensitivity, none of which can be remedied by any quickly contrived adjustment. Nature has been severely, and in many cases irreversibly, damaged. Healing can occur and new life can sometimes be evoked, but only with the same intensity of concern and sustained vigor of action as that which brought about the damage in the first place. Yet, without this healing, the viability of the human is severely limited.

The basic orientation of the common law tradition is toward personal rights and toward the natural world as existing for human use. There is no provision for recognition of nonhuman beings as subjects having legal rights. To the ecologists, the entire question of possession and use of the earth, either by individuals or by establishments, needs to be profoundly reconsidered. The naive assumption that the natural world exists solely to be possessed and used by humans for their unlimited advantage cannot be accepted. The earth belongs to itself and to all the component members of the community. The entire earth is a gorgeous celebration of existence in all its forms. Each living thing participates in the celebration as the proper fulfillment of its powers of expression. The reduction of the earth to an object simply for human possession and use is unthinkable in most traditional cultures. To Peter Drucker, the entrepreneur creates resources and values. Before it is possessed and used, "every plant is a weed and every mineral is just another rock" (*Innovation and Entrepreneurship,* 1985, p. 30). To the industrial entrepreneur, human possession and use is what activates the true value of any natural object.

The Western legal tradition, with its insistence on personal rights and the freedom of the human to occupy and use the land and all its component forms, is the greatest support for the entrepreneur. There is no question of other natural beings having rights over the human. Human use is not limited by any legally recognized rights of other natural beings but only by human determination of the limits that humans are willing to accept.

To achieve a viable human-earth community, a new legal system must take as its primary task to articulate the conditions for the integral functioning of the earth process, with special reference to a mutually enhancing human-earth relationship. Within this context, each component of the earth would be a separate community and together they would constitute the integral expression of the great community of the planet Earth.

In this context, each individual being is also supported by every other being in the earth community. In turn, each contributes to the well-being of every other. Justice would consist in carrying out this sequence of creative relationships. Within the human community there would, of course, be a need for articulating patterns of social relationships, in which individual and group rights would be recognized and defended and the basic elements of personal security and personal property would be protected. The entire complex of political and social institutions would be needed. Economic organizations would also be needed. But these would be so integral with the larger earth economy that they would enhance rather than obstruct each other.

Another significant aspect of contemporary life, wherein the industrial entrepreneur has a dominant position, is language. Since we are enclosed in an industrial culture, the words we use have their significance and validation defined within this industrial framework. A central value word used by our society is "progress." This word has great significance for increasing our scientific understanding of the universe, our personal and social development, our better health and longer life. Through modern technology, we can manufacture great quantities of products with greater facility. Human technology also enables us to travel faster and with greater ease. So on and on, endlessly, we see our increasing human advantage over the natural world.

But then we see that human progress has been carried out by desolating the natural world. This degradation of the earth is the very condition of the "progress" presently being made by humans. It is a kind of sacrificial offering. Within the human community, however, there is little awareness of the misunderstanding of this word. The feeling that even the most trivial modes of human progress are preferable to the survival of the most sublime and even the most sacred aspects of the natural world is so pervasive that the ecologist is at a loss as to how to proceed. The language in which our values are expressed has been co-opted by the industrial establishments and is used with the most extravagant modes of commercial advertising to create the illusory world in which the human community is now living.

One of the most essential roles of the ecologist is to create the language in which a true sense of reality, of value, and of progress can be communicated to our society. This need for rectification of language was recognized very early by the Chinese as a first task for any acceptable guidance of the society. Just now, a rectification is needed for the term "progress." As presently used, this word might be understood more properly to mean "retardation" or "destruction." The meaning of the term "profit" also needs to be rectified. Profit according to what norms and for whom? The profit of the corporation is the deficit of the earth. The profit of the industrial enterprise can also be considered the deficit of the quality of life, even for human society.

Gender has wide implications for our conception of the universe, the earth, and the life process, as well as for the relation of human individuals toward each other and for identifying social roles. The industrial establishment is the extreme expression of a non-viable patriarchal tradition. Only with enormous psychic and social effort and revolutionary processes has this control been mitigated with regard to the rights of serfs, slaves, women and children, ethnic groups, and the impoverished classes of our society. The rights of the natural world of living beings other than humans is still at the mercy of the modern industrial corporation as the ultimate expression of patriarchal dominance over the entire planetary process. The four basic patriarchal oppressions are rulers over people, men over women, possessors over nonpossessors, and humans over nature.

For the ecologist, the great model of all existence is the natural ecosystem, which is self-ruled as a community wherein each component has its unique and comprehensive influence. The ecologist, with a greater understanding of the human as a nurturing presence within the larger community of the geological and biological modes of earth, is closer to the feminine than to the masculine modality of being and of activity.

The purpose of education, as presently envisaged, is to enable humans to be "productive" within the context of the industrial society. A person needs to become literate in order to fulfill some function within the system, whether in the acquisition or processing of raw materials, manufacturing, distributing the product in a commercially profitable manner, managing the process or the finances, or finally, spending the net earnings in acquisition and enjoyment of possessions. A total life process is envisaged within this industrial process.

All professional careers now tend toward the industrial-commercial model, especially medicine, law, and the engineering sciences.

In a new context, the primary educator as well as the primary lawgiver and the primary healer would be the natural world itself. The integral earth community would be a self-educating community within the context of a self-educating universe. Education at the human level would be the conscious sensitizing of the human to those profound communications made by the universe about us, by the sun and moon and stars, the clouds and rain, the contours of the earth and all its living forms. All the music and poetry of the universe would flow into the student, the revelatory presence of the divine, as well as insight into the architectural structures of the continents and the engineering skills whereby the great hydrological cycle functions in moderating the temperature of the earth, in providing habitat for aquatic life, in nourishing the multitudes of living creatures. The earth would also be our primary teacher of sciences, especially the biological sciences, and of industry and economics. It would teach us a system in which we would create a minimum of entropy, a system in which there is no unusable or unfruitful junk. Only in such an integral system is the future viability of the human assured.

Much more could be said about the function of the natural world as educator, but this may be sufficient to suggest the context for an education that would be available to everyone from the beginning to the end of life, when the earth that brought us into being draws us back into itself to experience the deepest of all mysteries.

In this ecological context, we see that the problems of human illness are not only increasing but also are being considerably altered in their very nature by the industrial context of life. In prior centuries, human illness was experienced within the well-being of the natural world with its abundance of air and water and foods grown in a fertile soil. Even city dwellers in their deteriorated natural surroundings could depend on the purifying processes of the natural elements. The polluting materials themselves were subject to natural composition and reabsorption into the ever-renewing cycles of the life process.

But this is no longer true. The purifying processes have been overwhelmed by the volume, the composition, and the universal extent of the toxic or non-biodegradable materials. Beyond all this, the biorhythms of the natural world are suppressed by the imposition of mechanistic patterns on natural processes.

The profession of medicine must now consider its role, not only within the context of human society, but in the context of the earth process. A healing of the earth is now a prerequisite for the healing of the human. Adjustment of the human to the conditions and restraints of the natural world constitutes the primary medical prescription for human well-being. Nothing else will suffice.

Behind the long disruption of the earth process is the refusal of our Western industrial society to accept any restraints upon its quest for release—not simply from the normal ills to which we are subject but release from the human condition itself. There exists in our tradition a hidden rage against those inner as well as outer forces that create a challenge or impose a limitation on our activities.

Some ancient force in the Western psyche seems to perceive limitation as the demonic obstacle to be eliminated rather than as a discipline to evoke creativity. Acceptance of the shadow aspect of the natural world is a primary condition for creative intimacy with the natural world. Without this opaque or even threatening aspect of the universe we would lose our greatest source of creative energy. This opposing element is as necessary for us as is the weight of the atmosphere that surrounds us. This containing element, even the gravitation that binds us to the earth, should be experienced as liberating and energizing rather than confining.

Strangely enough, it is our efforts to establish a thoroughly sanitized world that have led to our toxic world. Our quest for wonderworld is making wasteworld. Our quest for energy is creating entropy on a scale never before witnessed in the historical process. We have invented a counterproductive society that is now caught in the loop that feeds back into itself in what can presently be considered a runaway situation. This includes all our present human activities, although it is most evident in the industrial-commercial aspects of contemporary life.

The communications media are particularly responsible for placing the entire life process of the human in an uncontrolled situation. Producer and consumer feed each other in an ever-accelerating process until we experience an enormous glut of basic products. But we see unmatched deprivation for the growing numbers of people living in the shantytowns of the world.

There are no prominent newspapers, magazines, and periodicals that have consistently designated space for commentary on the ecological situation. There are sections for politics, economics, sports, arts, science, education, food, entertainment, and a number of other areas of life, including religion; but only on rare occasions are there references to what is happening to the planet. Of course, these periodicals are supported by the great industrial establishment, and the ecological situation is considered threatening or limiting to the industrial enterprise. In reality, industrial control of the media is among the most devastating forces threatening the viability of the human.

Efforts are made to mitigate the evils consequent to this industrial-commercial process by modifying the manner in which these establishments function, reducing the amount of toxic waste produced as well as developing more efficient modes of storing or detoxifying waste. Yet all of this is trivial in relation to the magnitude of the problem. So, too, are the regulatory efforts of the government; these are microphase solutions for macrophase problems.

We also witness the pathos of present efforts to preserve habitats for wildlife in some areas while elsewhere the tropical rain forests of the earth are being destroyed. Other efforts to alter present destructive activities are made by confrontational groups such as Greenpeace, Earth First!, and People for the Ethical Treatment of Animals. These are daring ventures that dramatize the stark reality of the situation. That such tactics (to save the whales at sea, the wilderness life on the land, and the millions of animals being tortured in laboratories under the guise of scientific research) are needed to force humans to examine and question our behavior is itself evidence of how deep a change is needed in human consciousness.

Beyond the mitigating efforts and confrontational tactics is the clarification of more creative modes of functioning in all our institutions and professions, especially through movements associated with reinhabiting the various bioregions of the world such as the Regeneration Project of the Rodale Institute, the Land Institute in Salina, Kansas, and the two North American Bioregional Congresses. These new and mutually enhancing patterns of human-earth relationships are being developed on a functional as well as a critical-intellectual basis. Among these organizations, the Green movement may be one of the most creative and effective in its overall impact as the years pass. This movement is finding expression in politics, in economics, in education, in healing, and in spiritual reorientation. These recent movements, oriented toward a more benign human relationship with the environment, indicate a pervasive change in consciousness that is presently our best hope for developing a sustainable future.

We might also now recover our sense of the maternal aspect of the universe in the symbol of the Great Mother, especially the Earth as the maternal principle out of which we are born. Once this symbol is recovered, the dominion of the patriarchal system that has brought such aggressive attitudes into our activities will be eliminated. If this is achieved, our relationship with the natural world should undergo its most radical readjustment since the origins of our civilization in classical antiquity.

We might also recover our archetypal sense of the cosmic tree and the tree of life. The tree symbol gives expression to the organic unity of the universe but especially of the earth in its integral reality. Obviously, any damage done to the tree will be experienced through the entire organism. This could be one of our most effective ways of creating not simply conscious decisions against industrial devastation of the earth but a deep instinctive repulsion to any such activity. This instinct should be as immediate as the instinct for survival itself.

In the United States, the educational and religious professionals should be especially sensitive in discerning what is happening to the planet. These professions present themselves as guides for the establishment of our values and interpretors of the significance of our lives. The study of education and religion should awaken an awareness of the world in which we live, how it functions, how the human fits into the larger community of life, and the role that the human fulfills in the great story of the universe, the historical sequence of developments that have shaped our physical and cultural landscape. Along with an awareness of the past and present, education and religion should guide the future.

The pathos of these times, however, is precisely the impasse we witness in our educational and religious programs. Both are living in a past fundamentalist tradition or venturing into New Age programs that are often trivial in their consequences, unable to support or to guide the transformation that is needed in its proper order of magnitude. We must recognize that the only effective program available is the program offered by the earth itself as our primary guide toward a viable human mode of being.

Both education and religion need to ground themselves within the story of the universe as we now understand this story through empirical knowledge. Within this functional cosmology we can overcome our alienation and begin the renewal of life on a sustainable basis. This story is a numinous revelatory story that could evoke the vision and the energy required to bring not only ourselves but the entire planet into a new order of magnificence.

Meanwhile, in the obscure regions of the human unconsciousness, where the primordial archetypal symbols function as ultimate controlling factors in human thought, emotion, and in practical decision making, a profound reorientation toward this integral human-earth relationship is gradually taking place. This archetypal journey must be experienced as the journey of each individual, since the entire universe has been involved in shaping our psyche as well as our physical being from that first awesome moment when the universe began. In the creation of a viable human, the universe reflects on and celebrates itself in conscious self-awareness, and finds a unique fulfillment.

# 2 | DEEP ECOLOGY
## A NEW PARADIGM
### *Fritjof Capra*

IT IS BECOMING INCREASINGLY apparent that the major problems of our time cannot be understood in isolation. The threat of nuclear war, the devastation of our natural environment, the persistence of poverty along with progress even in the richest countries—these are not isolated problems. They are different facets of one single crisis, which is essentially a crisis of perception.

The crisis derives from the fact that most of us and especially our large social institutions subscribe to the concepts and values of an outdated worldview, which is inadequate for dealing with the problems of our overpopulated, globally interconnected world. At the same time, researchers at the leading edge of science, various social movements, and numerous alternative networks are developing a new vision of reality that will form the basis of our future technologies, economic systems, and social institutions.

## CRISIS AND TRANSFORMATION

My theme, then, is the current fundamental change of worldview in science and society, a change of paradigms that amounts to a profound cultural transformation.

The paradigm that is now receding has dominated our culture for several hundred years, during which it has shaped our modern Western society and has significantly influenced the rest of the world. This paradigm consists of a number of ideas and values, among them the view of the universe as a mechanical system composed of elementary building blocks, the view of the human body as a machine, the view of life in society as a competitive struggle

---

A longer version of this essay originally appeared in *Earth Island Journal* 2, 4 (1987). Reprinted with permission.

for existence, the belief in unlimited material progress to be achieved through economic and technological growth, and last but not least, the belief that a society in which the female is everywhere subsumed under the male is one that follows a basic law of nature. In recent decades, all of these assumptions have been found to be severely limited and in need of radical revision.


## DEEP ECOLOGY

The newly emerging paradigm can be described in various ways. It may be called a holistic worldview, emphasizing the whole rather than the parts. It may also be called an ecological worldview, using the term "ecological" in the sense of deep ecology. The distinction between "shallow" and "deep" ecology was made in the early seventies by the philosopher Arne Naess and has now been widely accepted as a very useful terminology to refer to the major division within comtemporary environmental thought.

Shallow ecology is anthropocentric. It views humans as above or outside of nature, as the source of all value, and ascribes only instrumental, or use value to nature. Deep ecology does not separate humans from the natural environment, nor does it separate anything else from it. It does not see the world as a collection of isolated objects but rather as a network of phenomena that are fundamentally interconnected and interdependent. Deep ecology recognizes the intrinsic values of all living beings and views humans as just one particular strand in the web of life.

The new ecological paradigm implies a corresponding ecologically oriented ethics. The ethical framework associated with the old paradigm is no longer adequate to deal with some of the major ethical problems of today, most of which involve threats to non-human forms of life. With nuclear weapons that threaten to wipe out all life on the planet, toxic substances that contaminate the environment on a large scale, new and unknown micro-organisms awaiting release into the environment without knowledge of the consequences, animals tortured in the name of consumer safety—with all these activities occurring, it seems most important to introduce ecologically oriented ethical standards into modern science and technology.

The reason why most of old-paradigm ethics cannot deal with these problems is that, like shallow ecology, it is anthropocentric. Thus the most important task for a new school of ethics will be to develop a non-anthropocentric theory of value, a theory that would confer inherent value on non-human forms of life.

Ultimately, the recognition of value inherent in all living nature stems from the deep ecological awareness that nature and the self are one. This, however, is also the very core of spiritual awareness. Indeed, when the concept of the human spirit is understood as the mode of consciousness in which the individual feels connected to the cosmos as a whole, it becomes clear that ecological awareness is spiritual in its deepest essence and that the new ecological ethics is grounded in spirituality.

In view of the ultimate identity of deep ecological and spiritual awareness, it is not surprising that the emerging new vision of reality is consistent with the "perennial philosophy" of spiritual traditions, for example, with that of Eastern spiritual traditions, the spirituality of Christian mystics, or the philosophy and cosmology underlying the Native American traditions.

In our contemporary culture, the spiritual essence of the deep ecological vision seems to find an ideal expression in the feminist spirituality advocated within the women's movement. Feminist spirituality is grounded in the experience of the oneness of all living forms and of their cyclical rhythms of birth and death. It is thus profoundly ecological and is close to Native American spirituality, Taoism, and other life-affirming, Earth-oriented spiritual traditions.

To discuss further aspects and consequences of the current shift of paradigms, I shall first outline the old paradigm and its influence on science and society, and shall then describe some implications of the new ecological vision of reality.

## THE MECHANISTIC WORLDVIEW

The mechanistic worldview was developed in the seventeenth century by Galileo, Descartes, Bacon, Newton, and several others. Descartes based his view of nature on the fundamental division into two separate, independent realms: mind and matter. The material universe, including the human organism, was a machine that could in principle be understood completely by analyzing it in terms of its smallest parts.

Descartes' central metaphor was the clockwork, which had reached a high degree of perfection at that time and was seen as the ultimate machine. Thus Descartes wrote about the human body: "I consider the human body as a machine. My thought compares a sick man and an ill-made clock with my idea of a healthy man and a well-made clock."

The enthusiasm of Descartes and his contemporaries for the metaphor of the body as a clock has an interesting parallel in the enthusiasm of many people today for the metaphor of the human brain as a computer.

Like the Cartesian metaphor of the body as clockwork, the metaphor of the brain as a computer has been very useful, but both are now outdated. Our body often carries out machine-like functions, but it is not a machine; it is a living organism. Our brain may seem to carry out computer-like functions, but it is not a computer; the brain, too, is a living organism. This difference is crucial, but it is often forgotten by computer scientists and even more by lay people. And since computer science uses expressions like "intelligence," "memory," or "language" to describe computers, we tend to think that these refer to the well-known human phenomena. This grave misunderstanding is the main reason why modern computer technology has perpetuated and even reinforced the Cartesian image of human beings as machines.

As humans, we face problems that even the most sophisticated machines will never be able to handle, and our ways of thinking and communicating are totally different from those of a computer. Therefore, we have to draw a clear distinction between human intelligence and machine intelligence. Human intelligence, human judgments, human memory, and human decisions are never completely rational, but are always colored by emotions. We can never separate human rationality from emotion, nor from intuition. Moreover, our thinking is always accompanied by bodily sensations and processes. Even if we often tend to suppress these, we always think *also* with our body. But computers do not have such a body, and truly human problems will therefore always be foreign to their intelligence.

These considerations imply that certain tasks should never be left to computers: all those tasks that require genuine human qualities like wisdom, compassion, respect, understanding, or love. Decisions and communications that require those human qualities—such as those of a judge or a general—will dehumanize our lives if they are made by computers. In particular, the use of computers in military technology should not be increased but, on the contrary, should be radically reduced. It is tragic that our government and the business community have removed themselves very far from such considerations.

## DOMINATION AND CONTROL

The mechanistic, fragmented approach is one basic characteristic of the old worldview. Another is the obsession with domination and control. In our society, political and economic power is exerted by a hierarchically structured corporate elite. Our science and technology are based on the belief that an *understanding* of nature implies *domination* of nature by man. I use the word "man" here on purpose, because I am talking about a very important connection between the mechanistic worldview in the science and patriarchal value system, the male tendency of wanting to control everything.

In the history of Western science and philosophy, this connection occurred in the seventeenth century. Before the scientific revolution of Galileo, Descartes, Bacon, and Newton, the goals of science were wisdom, understanding of the natural order, and living in harmony with that order. Since the seventeenth century, the goal of science has been knowledge that can be used to control, manipulate, and exploit nature. Today both science and technology are used predominantly for purposes that are dangerous, harmful, and profoundly anti-ecological.

## THE IMPASSE OF ECONOMICS

For a further example of the limitations of Cartesian thought, I would now like to turn to economics. Most economists fail to recognize that the economy is merely one aspect of a whole ecological and social fabric. They tend to dissociate the economy from this fabric, in which it is embedded, and to describe it in terms of simplistic and highly unrealistic models. . . .

The narrow, reductionist framework of conventional economics has resulted in an orientation of economic policies that is fundamentally erroneous. The essence of these policies is the pursuit of economic growth, understood as the increase of the gross national product, i.e. as purely quantitative in terms of maximization of production. The assumption is that all growth is good and that more growth is always better. It makes you wonder whether these economists have ever heard of cancer.

## THE NEW PARADIGM

With these examples, to which many more could be added, I have tried to illustrate the limitations of the mechanistic and patriarchal ways of thinking in today's science and society. The shift to the paradigm of deep ecology is now crucial for our well-being—even for our survival!—and such a shift is indeed occurring. Researchers at the frontiers of science, various social movements, and numerous alternative networks are now developing a new vision of reality that will be the basis of our future technologies, economic systems, and social institutions.

In science, the theory of living systems, which originated in cybernetics in the 1940s but emerged fully only during the last ten years or so, provides the most appropriate scientific formulation of the ecological paradigm.

All natural systems are wholes whose specific structures arise from the interactions and interdependence of their parts. Systemic properties are destroyed when a system is dissected, either physically or theoretically, into isolated elements. Although we can discern individual parts in any system, the nature of the whole is always different from the mere sum of its parts.

The systemic, or deep ecological, way of thinking has many important implications not only for science and philosophy, but also for our society and our daily lives. It will influence our attitudes toward illness and health, our relationship with the natural environment, and many of our social and political structures. . . .

## NEW VALUES

. . . The shift to a new worldview and a new mode of thinking goes hand in hand with a profound change in values. What is so fascinating about these changes, to me, is a striking connection between the change of thinking and the change of values. Both can be seen as a shift from self-assertion to integration. As far as thinking is concerned, we can observe a shift from the rational to the intuitive, from analysis to synthesis, from reductionism to holism, from linear to nonlinear thinking. I want to emphasize that the aim is not to replace one mode by the other, but rather to shift from the overemphasis on one mode to a greater balance between the two.

As far as values are concerned, we observe a corresponding shift from expansion to conservation, from quantity to quality, from competition to cooperation, from domination and control to nonviolence.

## THE RISING CULTURE

The new values, together with new attitudes and lifestyles, are now being promoted by a large number of movements: the ecology movement, the peace movement, the feminist movement, the holistic-health and human-potential movements, various spiritual movements, numerous citizens' movements and initiatives, Third World and ethnic liberation movements, and many other grassroots movements. Since the early eighties, several of these movements have begun to coalesce, recognizing that they represent merely different facets of the same new vision of reality, and have started to form a powerful force of social transformation. The political success of the European Green movement is the most impressive example of that process of coalescence.

I have called the newly emerging social force the "rising culture," borrowing this image from Arnold Toynbee's description of the patterns of rise and fall in the process of cultural evolution. In the current cultural transformation, the declining culture—represented by the established political parties, the large corporations, the large academic institutions, etc.—is still dominating the scene. It refuses to change, clinging ever more rigidly to its outdated ideas. However, being based on a framework of concepts and values that is no longer viable, today's dominant culture will inevitably decline and will eventually disintegrate. The cultural forces representing the new paradigm, on the other hand, will continue to rise and, eventually, will assume the leading role.

This process of transformation is now clearly visible in our society and can also be experienced by each one of us as an inner transformation. One question arises: Will there be enough time? Will the turning point be reached soon enough to save the world? As my reply, I would like to quote the late E. F. Schumacher, author of *Small Is Beautiful* and prophet of the ecology movement:

> Can we rely on it that a "turning around" will be accomplished by enough people quickly enough to save the modern world? This question is often asked, but no matter what the answer, it will mislead. The answer "Yes" would lead to complacency, the answer "No" to despair. It is desirable to leave these perplexities behind us and get down to work.

# 3 | SIMPLE IN MEANS, RICH IN ENDS
## AN INTERVIEW WITH ARNE NAESS

*Stephan Bodian*

STEPHAN BODIAN: Arne, how did you become involved in deep ecology?

ARNE NAESS: When I was four or five years old, I had the opportunity to explore the shoreline of fjords in Norway, and I was intrigued by the fantastic variety of life forms, especially the tiny fishes and crabs and shrimps which would gather around me in a very friendly way. I lived with these other beings throughout the summer. When I was nine or ten, I learned to enjoy the high mountains where my mother had a cottage. Because I had no father, the mountain somehow became my father, as a friendly, immensely powerful being, perfect and extremely tranquil. Later, pressures from school, from society, from the man-made world, made me happy to be where nothing pressured me into behaving or evaluating in any particular way. For example, clouds talk to us, but they don't pressure us into believing anything. Even a work of art somehow intends something, informs us about something. But nature is overwhelmingly rich and good and does not impose anything upon us. We are completely free, our imagination is free. Of course, if we are careless, an avalanche might bury us or we might drown, but in nature, there are always warnings. I never have had the feeling that nature is something to be dominated or conquered; it is something with which we coexist.

Modern astronomy, which I have followed since the 1930s, indicates that the universe is growing, and I feel that I am growing with the universe; I

This interview was originally published in 1982 by *The Ten Directions*, Los Angeles Zen Center. Reprinted with permission.

identify with the universe—the greater the universe, the greater I am. Some people feel threatened when they realize that the cosmos is so immense and we are so small. But we can be just as big as the cosmos, in a sense. We ourselves, as human beings, are capable of *identifying* with the whole of existence.

These feelings then led me into ecology when there was an international movement developing. I did not do it for fun. I think social movements are actually boring. I would rather be in nature, but I think we must all contribute to saving a little of what is left of this planet—this is the last century in which we will have the chance. That is why I am in Los Angeles today and not in the mountains or the desert.

S.B.: From the beginning, then, your interest as a philosopher involved nature in some way.

NAESS: Because people found my interests so strange, I had somehow to label and rationalize them. This prompted me to ask deeper questions about the meaning of life. In this way, philosophy was my focus very early. A philosopher, in contrast to a professor of philosophy, is one whose philosophy is expressed in his or her life. I have tried to be both in the last ten years.

S.B.: You coined the term *deep ecology*. What do you mean by deep ecology exactly, and how is it different from shallow ecology?

NAESS: The essence of deep ecology—as compared with the science of ecology, and with what I call the shallow ecological movement—is to ask deeper questions. The adjective "deep" stresses that we ask why and how, where others do not. For instance, ecology as a science does not ask what kind of a society would be the best for maintaining a particular ecosystem—that is considered a question for value theory, for politics, for ethics. As long as ecologists keep narrowly to their science, they do not ask such questions. What we need today is a tremendous expansion of ecological thinking in what I call ecosophy. *Sophy* comes from the Greek term *sophia,* "wisdom," which relates to ethics, norms, rules, and practice. Ecosophy, or deep ecology, then, involves a shift from science to wisdom.

For example, we need to ask questions like, Why do we think that economic growth and high levels of consumption are so important? The conventional answer would be to point to the economic consequences of not having economic growth. But in deep ecology, we ask whether the present society fulfills basic human needs like love and security and access to nature, and, in so doing, we question our society's underlying assumptions. We ask which society, which education, which form of religion, is beneficial to all life on the planet as a whole, and then we ask further what we need to do in order to make the necessary changes. We are not limited to a scientific approach; we have an obligation to verbalize a total view.

Of course, total views may differ. Buddhism, for example, provides a fitting background or context for deep ecology, certain Christian groups have formed platforms of action in favor of deep ecology, and I myself have worked out my own philosophy, which I call ecosophy T. In general, however, people do not question deeply enough to explicate or make clear a total view. If they did, most would agree with saving the planet from the destruction that's in progress. The differing ecosophies can provide a motivating force for all the activities and movements aimed at saving the planet from human domination and exploitation.

S.B.: It seems that, if we ask deeply enough, our questions will require us to make a radical shift in the way we see the world, what some people have called a paradigm shift.

NAESS: Yes. I think it's a shift from being dominated by means, instruments, gadgets, all the many things we think will give us pleasure or make us happy or perfect. The shift comes about when we seriously ask ourselves, "In what situations do I experience the maximum satisfaction of my whole being?" and find that we need practically nothing of what we are supposed to need for a rich and fulfilling life. And if we make that shift toward a life simple in means but rich in goals, we are not threatened by plans for saving the planet elaborated by environmentalists. For instance, we can see that, instead of an energy crisis, we have a crisis of consumption—we have more than enough energy. There is no reason to continue increasing our consumption of energy or of any of the other material aspects of life. In countries like the United States, the crisis is rather one of lifestyle, of our traditions of thoughtlessness and confusion, of our inability to question deeply what is and is not worthwhile in life. Within fifty years, either we will need a dictatorship to save what is left of the diversity of life forms, or we will have a shift of values, a shift of our total view such that no dictatorship will be needed. It is thoroughly natural to stop dominating, exploiting, and destroying the planet. A "smooth" way, involving harmonious living with nature, or a "rough" way, involving a dictatorship and coercion—those are the options.

S.B.: What then would you consider the fundamental characteristics or attributes of deep ecology, and how do they differ from those of shallow ecology?

NAESS: One of the basic norms of deep ecology is that every life form has in principle a right to live and blossom. As the world is made, of course, we have to kill in order to eat, but there is a basic intuition in deep ecology that we have no right to destroy other living beings without sufficient reason. Another norm is that, with maturity, human beings will experience joy when other life forms experience joy, and sorrow when other life forms experience sorrow. Not only do we feel sad when our brother or a dog or a cat feels sad, but we will grieve when living beings, including landscapes, are destroyed. In our civilization, we have vast means of destruction at our disposal but extremely little maturity in our feelings. Only a very narrow range of feelings have interested most human beings until now.

For deep ecology, there is a core democracy in the biosphere. The shallow ecology movement tends to talk only about resources for humans, whereas in deep ecology we talk about resources for each species. Shallow ecology is concerned about overpopulation in developing countries but not about overpopulation in industrial countries—countries which may destroy one hundred times per capita than a country like Bangladesh. In deep ecology, we have the goal not only of stabilizing the human population but also of reducing it to a sustainable minimum by humane means which do not require a revolution or a dictatorship. I should think that we would not need more than one billion people in order to have the variety. of human cultures we had one hundred years ago. We need the conservation of human cultures, just as we need the conservation of animal species. We need diversity of both human and non-human life!

S.B.: So diversity is of great value at the human level as well as at the level of plants and animals.

NAESS: Yes. Personally, I think that, to maximize self-realization—and I don't mean self as ego but self in a broader sense—we need maximum diversity and maximum symbiosis. Diversity, then, is a fundamental norm and a common delight. As supporters of the deep ecology movement, we take a natural delight in diversity, as long as it does not include crude intrusive forms, such as Nazi culture, that are destructive to others.

A long-range view is characteristic of deep ecology—we feel responsible for future generations, not just the first, but the second, third, and fourth generation as well. Our perspective in time and space is very long. By contrast, the shallow ecological movement tends to repair only some of the worst consequences of our lifestyle and social structure—it does not address itself to fundamental questions.

S.B.: What do you mean when you say that maximum self-realization and maximum diversity are closely related?

NAESS: Self-realization is the realization of the potentialities of life. Organisms that differ from each other in three ways give us less diversity than organisms that differ from each other in one hundred ways. Therefore, the self-realization we experience when we identify with the universe is heightened by an increase in the number of ways in which individuals, societies, and even species and life forms realize themselves. The greater the diversity then, the greater the Self-realization. This seeming duality between individuals and the totality is encompassed by what I call the Self, and what the Chinese call the Tao. Most people in deep ecology have had the feeling—usually, but not always, in nature—that they are connected with something greater than their ego, greater than their name, their family, their special attributes as an individual—a feeling that is often called oceanic because many have had this feeling on the ocean. Without that identification, one is not so easily drawn to become involved in deep ecology.

Many people have had this feeling when they see a death struggle—for instance when they see tiny animals like flies or mosquitoes fighting for their lives. When they see animals suffering, they may identify with a life form they usually don't identify with. Such situations offer us an opportunity to develop a more mature point of view. Insofar as this conversion, these deep feelings, are religious, then deep ecology has a religious component. People who have done the most to make societies aware of the destructive way in which we live in relation to nature have had such religious feelings. Rachel Carson, for example, said that we *cannot* do what we have been doing, that we have no religious or ethical justification for behaving as we have toward nature. Her argument was not calculated or "reasonable" in the usual sense of saying that if we continue poisoning nature, we will be less healthy, or will have fewer resources, and so on. She said that we cannot permit ourselves to behave in that way. Some will say that nature is not man's property, it's the property of God; others will say it in other ways. Deep ecology may be said to have a religious component, fundamental intuitions that everyone must cultivate if he or she is to have a life based on values and not function like a computer. Shallow ecology, if taken to its logical extreme, is like a computerized cost-benefit analysis designed to benefit only humans.

S.B.: You mention a long time frame. On the other hand, of course, the situation is critical right now—species are becoming extinct at a very rapid rate, ecosystems are being destroyed. How do you balance the need for a long time frame with the very urgent need for immediate action?

NAESS: It is very natural to combine the two, because the long perspective in time and space motivates one to act in a profound and consistent way. That is to say, being concerned with the whole, with the religious and philosophical background, one learns, for example, that there are practically no more rain forests on far away Sumatra, and only six percent left on Sri Lanka, and one is motivated immediately by some deep evaluation that says, "This cannot go on, this must be changed." So the long time frame—absolutely necessary in questions of population reduction, for instance—is necessary both because of certain facts and because of the motivation we derive from eternal concerns like Self-realization, identification with the universe, and other religious notions that involve millennia or even eternity, rather than five or ten years.

s.b.: Deep ecology, then, is a fundamental view of the world that at the same time calls for immediate action. In addition to contrasting it with shallow ecology, can you suggest ways in which the two might work together? Can deep ecology inform movements which may be anthropocentric and may not articulate a fundamental world view yet are also large and effective?

NAESS: I think that the deep ecology movement must cooperate with various movements, including what we call narrow or shallow environmental organizations. The Sierra Club, for example, cannot have deep ecological principles in its statutes but must include people who are very anthropocentric and think only about the maximum benefit for human beings within a ten or twenty year time frame. We need to work with movements whose members do not know anything about deep ecology and may not have contact with wilderness or personal relationships with animals other than cats and dogs. And of course we can cooperate with movements that deal with related issues, such as the antinuclear movement and certain Christian movements for the dignity of life, at the same time trying to expand and deepen their views in a new direction.

However, we must also have programs that may not be meaningful to those who are not supporters of deep ecology—the reduction of human population, for instance. We must be flexible but never forget fundamental principles, because, like Buddhism and certain other philosophies in the Western and Eastern traditions, deep ecology involves basic views of man and the world.

s.b.: Some people, particularly in this country, have great faith that, once we've perfected our computer technology and can process all the available information, we'll be able to make informed decisions. You, on the other hand, have spoken about the importance of admitting that we don't know, admitting our ignorance in the face of the complexity of nature, and at the same time be willing to trust our intuition and stand up and say, "I know in my heart that this is what we need to do."

NAESS: I think that, one hundred and fifty years ago, in government decision making in America and in Europe, more information was available in proportion to the amount needed than is available today. Today, we are using thousands of new chemicals, and we don't know their combined long-range effects. We interfere a million times more deeply in nature than we did one hundred years ago, and our ignorance is increasing in proportion to the information that is required.

S.B.: In other words, many more questions are being raised, but fewer answers are being provided.

NAESS: Exactly. One indication is that, if you take the number of scientific articles published each year with neat, authoritative conclusions and divide it by the number of questions posed to scientists by responsible people concerned with the consequences of our interventions in nature, you will find that the quotient approaches zero. That is, the number of questions is becoming indefinitely large very quickly, whereas the number of answers is increasing very slowly indeed. And, in any case, within a hundred years, we'll run out of paper to print the billion articles that supply the relevant answers needed each year.

S.B.: So you don't think that, if we just perfect our science and technology, our answers will somehow catch up with the number of questions being raised?

NAESS: On the contrary, technology is more helpless than ever before because the technology being produced doesn't fulfill basic human needs, such as meaningful work in a meaningful environment. Technical progress is sham progress because the term *technical progress* is a cultural, not a technical term. Our culture is the only one in the history of mankind in which the culture has adjusted itself to the technology, rather than vice versa. In traditional Chinese culture, the bureaucracy opposed the use of inventions that were not in harmony with the general cultural aims of the nation. A vast number of technical inventions were not used by the populace because it was simply not permitted. Whereas here we have the motto, "You can't stop progress," you can't interfere with technology, and so we allow technology to dictate cultural forms.

S.B.: In connection with that, it has been pointed out that the hazardous nature of the materials used to generate nuclear power will have unforeseen political consequences.

NAESS: Yes. Security, for instance, is a major problem. And even more importantly, such technology presupposes a tremendous, centralized society, whereas, in more ecologically defensible societies, energy creation and energy sources would be decentralized and widely distributed, with small groups in local communities in control of their own resources. As it is now, we have increasing centralization, which fosters diminished self-determination for individuals and local cultures, and diminished freedom of action. The more centralized our energy sources, the more dependent we are on centralized institutions hundreds of miles away.

There's no reason to believe there won't be another war. On the contrary, the statistics give us every reason to believe we will continue to have wars in the future. During World War II, people were highly self-sufficient—they could raise pigs, they could burn wood—whereas, in a war today some nations could be conquered almost immediately because all resources are centralized. We don't know how to grow food, we don't have anything to burn. In the year 2000, we will be so dependent that, if an aggressor were to take over the energy sources and the political institutions, ninety-nine percent of the population would have to surrender, whereas in the last war we were able to continue our culture. Deep ecology is concerned with these long-range problems, particularly with the question of war and peace, because, of all man-made ecological catastrophes, nuclear war would be the most devastating.

S.B.: This brings us back to the question of information versus intuition. Your feeling is that we can't expect to have an ideal amount of information but must somehow act on what we already know.

NAESS: Yes. It's easier for people in deep ecology than for others because we have certain fundamental values, a fundamental view of what's meaningful in life, what's worth maintaining, which makes it completely clear that we in the rich countries are opposed to further development for the sake of increased domination and an increased standard of living. The material standard of living should be reduced and the quality of life, in the sense of basic satisfaction in the depths of one's heart or soul, should be maintained or increased. This view is intuitive, as are all important views, in the sense that it can't be proven. As Aristotle said, it shows a lack of education to try to prove everything, because you have to have a starting point. You can't prove the methodology of science, you can't prove logic, because logic presupposes fundamental premises.

All the sciences are fragmentary and incomplete in relation to basic rules and norms, so it's very shallow to think that science can solve our problems. Without basic norms, there is no science. Of course, we need science—in fact, a thousand times more than we have—if we are to answer scientifically the questions politicians ask about the consequences of our actions. As it is now, we have to say, for the most part, that we don't know although we can make informed guesses. And since politicians give priority to increased growth and consumption, their reply is, "If you can't tell us authoritatively what the bad consequences will be from this project, then we'll go ahead with it." For example, they may give researchers so many dollars to discover the effects of oil spills on plankton. And after a year, we may have to say as scientists that we don't really know, we are just beginning to understand. But common sense and intuition tell us that, if we continue to dump more oil into the sea, we will cause the destruction of life forms on a vast scale.

S.B.: Nowadays, people have been trained to defer taking a stand on an issue until all the facts are in. As an example, some experts say that nuclear reactors are unsafe, others say that they are safe, and people are bewildered.

NAESS: I tell people that if they make clear their fundamental assumptions about what is needed for a life simple in means and rich in ends, they will necessarily come to the conclusion that it is not a lack of energy consumption that makes them unhappy. They can then oppose nuclear power without having read thick books and without knowing the myriad facts that are used in newspapers and periodicals. And they must also find others who feel the same way and form circles of friends who give one another confidence and support in living in a way that the majority finds ridiculous, naive, stupid, and unnecessarily simplistic. But in order to do that, one must already have enough self-confidence to follow one's intuitions—a quality very much lacking in broad sections of the populace. Many people follow the trends and advertisements and tend to become philosophical and ethical cripples.

S.B.: What do you consider the priorities for action in the deep ecology movement over the next twenty-five years?

NAESS: Each of us has to act on a different part of a very broad frontier. One of the most important activities for the next five to ten years will be to disseminate the knowledge we have—regarding the destruction of the tropical rain forests, for example, or the climatic changes and other global factors that are now getting out of hand. Communication is crucial, and all of us can do something. In deep ecology, another major question is how to get along with the various religious populations—Christians, Buddhists, and others—in which a minority, especially the young, is completely aware of the destruction of the planet and believes that it must not be permitted. We must cooperate with these religious movements because, as I've mentioned, the motivation for strong action must come from deep sources in philosophy and ethics.

In the matter of political action, I am very much inspired by the Gandhian approach of maximizing the communication on a friendly footing—that is, even if people don't want to talk with you at a certain moment, try to be personally helpful and to make personal contact. Another way to make contact is to canvass from house to house. I think the personal approach has not been sufficiently explored, especially with labor organizations. Many actions in Norway have been unsuccessful because the intellectuals and the middle class have not communicated with the working classes. Laborers are concerned about unemployment and think ecology is a kind of fad among the upper classes, whereas, in an ecological crisis, laborers and others with limited economic means will actually be the hardest hit. The credibility and effectiveness of the ecological movement will remain low as long as we don't make contact with working people. We must learn to talk with them in language they are familiar with. Canvassing should not mean that we talk only with people who think like us.

S.B.: The head of the machinists' union at an aerospace company involved in a great deal of defense contracting recently made a similar point. He stressed that, if the disarmament movement wanted to join with workers in the arms industry, it would have to emphasize the conversion of weapons manufacturing to peace-time industry. Otherwise, it would be threatening their livelihood and would never win their support.

NAESS: That relates also to what we are doing now in Norway. In trying to compete with Japan, Singapore, and various other countries, we have had to build large, centralized, automated factories. Instead, what we need to do is to reduce our imports and therefore our exports, convert our big factories into small-scale, labor-intensive industry that makes products we need, and continue to sustain our culture as it has been, rather than try to compete on the world market. Then we will have very little unemployment, and work will be much more meaningful. If we come to the workers with this kind of program, they will be more receptive than if we come from our middle- or upper-class residences and talk to them in our own language about our rather abstract concerns.

S.B.: How important do you feel it is for individuals to practice deep ecology in their own lives? And I was wondering how you practice it in yours?

NAESS: I think that, in the long run, in order to participate joyfully and wholeheartedly in the deep ecology movement, you have to take your own life very seriously. People who successfully maintain a low material standard of living and successfully cultivate a deep, intense sense of life are much better able to consistently maintain a deep ecological view and to act on behalf of it. As I sit down and breathe deeply and just feel where I am, I can ask myself where and when I really enjoy my life and what would be the minimum means necessary to maintain these enjoyable feelings and situations. For example, I myself have been too eager to go climbing in the Himalayas, whereas the peculiar satisfaction I have as a mountaineer could be had in Norway. If you concentrate on what gives you satisfaction, you will find that it can be obtained much more easily and simply than we are educated to believe in our society, where the bigger, the more elaborate, and the more expensive are considered better.

S.B.: I like what you said recently about spending an hour or two just looking at a little patch of ground.

NAESS: Yes. Look at this (holding up a tiny flower). If you took the forms and the symmetries and made them into a painting, you might win first prize in any competition.

S.B.: I have relatives in England who take endless delight in climbing the same mountains in Wales and the same hills near their home.

NAESS: That's right. A hill is never the same in a repetitious way! The development of sensitivity toward the good things of which there are enough is the true goal of education. Not that we need to limit our goals. I'm not for the simple life, except in the sense of a life simple in means but rich in goals and values. I have tremendous ambition. Only the best is good enough for me. I like richness, and I feel richer than the richest person when I'm in my cottage in the country with water I've carried from a certain well and with wood I've gathered. When you take a helicopter to the summit of a mountain, the view looks like a postcard, and, if there's a restaurant on top, you might complain that the food is not properly made. But if you struggle up from the bottom, you have this deep feeling of satisfaction, and even the sandwiches mixed with ski wax and sand taste fantastic.

# 4 | RECOVERY FROM WESTERN CIVILIZATION

## Chellis Glendinning

IN WESTERN CULTURE, WE live with chronic anxiety, anger, and a sense that something essential is missing from our lives, that we exist without a soul. What could be wrong with us?

I believe Western culture is suffering from "Original Trauma," caused by the systemic removal of our lives from nature, from natural cycles, from the life force itself. This removal began slowly with the introduction of agriculture (about three hundred generations ago) and has grown to crisis proportions in technological society (which began only about five generations ago). With it comes the traumatic loss of a sense of belonging on the Earth.

Some of the symptoms of psychological distress displayed by our culture and government are the recognized symptoms of post-traumatic stress disorder: hyperreactions; inappropriate outbursts of anger; psychic numbing; constriction of the emotions; and loss of a sense of control over our destiny.

Behaviors like these are surely troublesome, but we have to come to accept them as normal. We have become accustomed to people acting out their feelings about childhood neglect and abuse both in their personal lives and in public life. But what if such behavior is not normal at all? What if it is a desperate expression of coping by people who find themselves in an extreme situation?

If so, what is that extreme situation? It's our homelessness. It's our alienation from the only home we will ever have, from the Earth.

In his brilliant book, *Nature and Madness* (Sierra Club Books, 1982), the ecologist Paul Shepard talks about the psychology of hunter/gatherer culture and compares it to agricultural psychology. In hunter/gatherer society, survival is dependent on particular psychological qualities: openness, attunement, spon-

This essay originally appeared in the *Elmwood Quarterly* 8, 1 (1992). Reprinted with permission.

taneity, solidarity with other people, wonderment and appreciation. Survival is dependent on the sense of communication with other people, made possible by a secure and supple sense of boundaries. It is also dependent on the ability to heal, which in hunter/gatherer cultures often involves a natural psychotherapeutic process including ceremony, communion with the natural world, herbs, and nonordinary states of consciousness. As Shepard points out:

> The logic of man's domination of nature, the zealous control of things organic, the fear of the body's natural processes and their analogies in nature, the haunting sense of fall from affinity with nature, are the relentless expressions of subterranean disaster whose roots lie deep in our culture and deep in our personal psyches.
>
> It was not always so. While foible and weakness may always have been human, those shadows of fear were not. Our minds, like our bodies, are programmed by the circumstances of a vanished world, a world in which we create a culture in the freedom of small group self-determination, an environment infinitely rich in totemic nature, abundant in material resources, in lives socially participatory and richly ceremonial.
>
> The erosion of those things is history. In our modern struggle to cope with epidemics of dementia, posthistorical societies reveal all the desperate, autistic rationalizations, projections, obsessions and other symptoms of the clinical diagnosis of schizophrenia and paranoia. The rage to conquer nature is a kind of madness.
>
> Madness always signifies flaws of childhood. What civilization does to nature it does by corrupting its children, ravaging their ontogeny. Fear of the natural world is the fear of separation prolonged past its time.
>
> Natural childbirth is a first step toward a recovery of harmony with the world. But what is a natural infancy, or childhood, or adolescence? Only as we recover them does the life of the planet and its endangered species have a chance.

In another marvelous book, *The Continuum Concept* (Addison-Wesley, 1975), anthropology writer Jean Liedloff compares the child rearing practices of hunter/gatherers to our child rearing—and again, we are amazed at the contrast. In hunter/gatherer cultures there were no distinctions between work and play, no separate rooms, no disconnection of experience. Infants were with adults *all the time,* constantly being touched and held. They slept with people, they were always in someone's arms. A sense of connectedness and security that we can only imagine was built into their lives from the beginning.

These books helped me to see that the very issues that we in the technological West are struggling with—personal boundaries, community, a sense of belonging, how to heal personal wounds and address archetypal issues—the issues that we just can't make sense of, that we have to go through incredibly painful processes of unraveling in order to heal, these are the very qualities that were the daily reality in the lives of hunter/gatherers.

One result of the introduction of agriculture was the loss of these qualities. And what follows losses like these? Often, it's the addictive process: a reaction to a loss of satisfaction of our primary needs. This process is a rather ingenious attempt by the organism to satisfy primary needs with secondary sources. But of course, secondary sources will never work because they don't really satisfy and we become obsessed with them.

So here we are in this technological culture and we are absolutely awash in a sea of addictions: romantic love, sex, shopping, drugs, alcohol, self-destruction, fast cars, abuse of other people, and on and on. We know that people who have severe addiction problems are often people who were neglected or abused by people who were neglected or abused, and the problem spirals back further and further to previous generations but there's little talk about how it all got started.

I look at these addictions as symptoms crying out for us to look deeper. I believe that the central addiction of Western society is what I call *Techno-Addiction*—an addiction both to a mechanistic way of seeing the world and to specific machines such as computers, television sets and missiles. Uprooted from our home in nature, uprooted from natural cycles, separated from other creatures, we feel lost and terrified. This is something that happened over a long period of time. Slowly, as our physical reality became less wild and more technological, we needed to create a new psychic context for ourselves. But since we did this out of terror, we ended up dreaming a dream of a world that fit our desperate needs; we ended up dreaming a dream of a world in which we humans had complete control. We created techno-utopia.

I have been talking the language of trauma and addiction. Now I want to talk about recovery. I think the ultimate goal of recovery is to refind our place in nature.

The first step is to break through denial about this predicament. The second step is to feel, to come alive, to come out from under the deadening of the machines and the mechanistic worldview. In this step, the first layer of feelings that most people go through is frustration—very deep, painful, and real—about their current lives. Subsequently, people encounter the neglect, regimentations, and assaults that many of us experienced growing up in a society that was trying to make us all into machines. But this is the point in therapy where most people stop.

The next layer of feelings is crucial. It is our feelings about the loss of our relationship to the natural world—both as we remove ourselves from it into cities and as we witness the natural world being destroyed. How many people have ever both deeply and consciously felt this loss?

When we begin to heal the wounding, what arises is the sense of connectedness. What happens is the return of the things that we've lost: a more solid
sense of ourselves, a sense of connectedness to our deeper selves, to other
people, to the world, to the animals, and a deeper communication with soul,
body, and Earth. When we have these feelings, the imagination comes in touch
with our deeper selves, and we reconnect to our long-lost souls. We come back
to Earth.

As we in Western technological culture go through this process, we need to
integrate into our lives a new philosophy that reflects the wisdom of what we
are learning in our recovery and the wisdom of the kind of cultures that all
humans once enjoyed—earth-based, ecological, and indigenous.

# 5 | GARY SNYDER AND THE PRACTICE OF THE WILD

## Jack Turner

FOR THE PAST FORTY years, Gary Snyder has pursued a radical vision which integrates Zen Buddhism, American Indian practices, ecological thinking and wilderness values. The vision has informed his poetry, shaped the cause of Deep Ecology, and produced a distinctive answer to the eternal question of what it is to live a human life.

He was born in 1930 and raised near Puget Sound in Washington. His early interest in nature led him to climb Mount St. Helens when he was fifteen years old. At seventeen he had reached the summit of many of the northwest's major snow peaks. He joined the Mazamas Climbing Club and the Wilderness Society, beginning an association with mountaineering and wilderness that continues to the present.

Snyder graduated from Reed College in 1951 with a major in literature and anthropology. After briefly studying linguistics at Indiana University he completed three years of graduate work in Asian languages at the University of California at Berkeley. He also worked on the docks in San Francisco, read Buddhist philosophy, wrote poetry, and became a founding father of the Beat Generation.

After Snyder and Jack Kerouac climbed Matterhorn Peak in the northern Sierra Nevada, Kerouac used Snyder as the model for Japhy Ryder, the itinerant mountain-climbing poet of *Dharma Bums* (1958), a man who took his Zen practice beyond the confines of formal study. "The secret of this kind of climbing," said Japhy in a tone that might be reminiscent of Snyder's, "is like Zen. Don't think. Just dance along. It's the easiest thing in the world, actually easier than walking on flat ground." For contemporary American life in the

Originally published in the *Patagonia* catalogue, Fall-Winter 1991. Reprinted with permission.

1950s, Snyder, as vagabond-mountaineer-Zen scholar-poet, was scouting new ground for his generation and those that have followed.

In 1956 Snyder left for Japan. For twelve years he studied Rinzai Zen Buddhism, worked as a researcher and translator of Zen texts, and traveled throughout Asia, including a six-month sojourn through India where he had a memorable meeting with the Dalai Lama in 1962. He also worked for nine months in the engine room of a tanker visiting ports in the Pacific and the Persian Gulf (he still has Seaman's Papers). In 1969 Snyder returned to the United States and settled on a mountain farmstead on San Juan Ridge in the foothills of the northern Sierra Nevada, where he continues to live as a poet, teacher, and spokesman for wilderness.

Gary Snyder has published fourteen books of poetry and prose. *Turtle Island* received the Pulitzer Prize for Poetry in 1975. Since 1985 he has spent half of each year at the University of California, Davis, where he teaches Ethno-Poetics, Creative Writing, and the Literature of Wilderness. At present, Snyder is finishing *Mountains and Rivers Without End,* his poem cycle evoking the whole planet as watershed and habitat.

The following profile is drawn from his writings, recent conversations and excerpts from *The Practice of the Wild,* his new book of essays published by North Point Press, 1990.

In 1832, after excursions among the Plains Indians prior to the genocide that destroyed their culture, the artist George Catlin called for the preservation and protection of wilderness and gave us the idea of "a nation's Park, containing man and beast." Numerous public lands now preserve wilderness, plants, and animals, but the unity of place, man, and beast that was, for the Indian, a life of wholeness and integrity—the life that Catlin saw and cherished—is gone. We have succeeded in preserving wilderness only by isolating it from a central position in our lives, creating a dichotomy between wilderness and our increasingly urban culture that benefits neither ourselves nor the Earth. We no longer inhabit the wilderness; we have diminished it to remote "islands" used mainly for recreation and summer vacations.

This dichotomy is as abnormal as it is pervasive. As Snyder says, "There has been no wilderness without some kind of human presence for several hundred thousand years." Our common task is to again create this synthesis. "We need a civilization that can live fully and creatively together with wildness. We must start growing it right here, in the New World."

We have forgotten that, when our bison were the Earth's largest herd of mammals, when flocks of pigeons blackened our skies, and salmon choked our streams, when grizzlies fed on the carcasses of whales along the beaches of California—at this time "North America was all populated."

This home territory was entirely mapped by song and story, myth and lore, filled with critical information about distance, water, animals, plants, weather, shelter—a string of ecological and economical connections between human being and place, an interdependence that resulted from necessity, the "life and death lessons of subsistence economies."

In contrast, the citizens of an urban civilization are often not aware of its interdependence with place. Our songs and stories and myths do not arise so much from necessity, nor do they provide information critical to survival. They primarily serve as entertainment. Urban inhabitants, freed from producing their own food, clothing, warmth, and shelter, ignorant of where their water comes from and where their garbage goes, released from educating their children and deprived of community, are blinded to biological continuities and dependencies. At the same time, wild nature—forest fires, earthquakes, drought, disease—is seen as a malevolent intrusion on the human world. Our reaction is to seek more control, our way of measuring progress, regardless of the pernicious effect on the planet or even our own destruction. This has become our story, our song, and we are beginning to realize that not only do we not like the ending, we are accelerating toward that ending:

> By the sixteenth century the lands of the Occident, the countries of Asia, and all the civilizations and cities from the Indian subcontinent to the coast of North Africa were becoming ecologically impoverished. . . . People who grew up in towns or cities, or on large estates, had less chance to learn how wild systems worked. Then major blocks of citified mythology (Medieval Christianity and then the "Rise of Science") denied first the soul, then consciousness, and finally even sentience to the natural world. Huge numbers of Europeans, in the climate of a nature-denying mechanistic ideology, were losing the opportunity for direct experience of nature.

But for those who still had a direct experience of nature, claims Snyder, "the world is as sharp as the edge of a knife":

> The wilderness pilgrim's step-by-step breath-by-breath walk up a trail, into those snowfields, carrying all on back, is so ancient a set of gestures as to bring a profound sense of body-mind joy. The same happens to those who sail in the ocean, kayak fjords or rivers, tend a garden, peel garlic, even sit on a meditation cushion. The point is to make contact with the real world, real self. Sacred refers to that which helps us (not only human beings) out of our little selves into the whole mountains-and-rivers mandala universe. Inspiration, exaltation, and insight do not end when one steps outside the doors of a church. The wilderness as temple is only a beginning.

With such raw contact we learn what primary cultures learned, that nature can be a ferocious teacher of the way things are—a profoundly wild, organic world of system and raw process, a maze of networks, webs, fields, and communities, all interdependent, interrelating, and mirroring each other. Thoreau says, "In wildness is the preservation of the world." Snyder responds, "Wildness is not just the 'preservation' of the world, it is the world. . . . Nature is ultimately in no way endangered; wilderness is. The wild is indestructible, but we might not see the wild."

In our emphasis on species loss and habitat destruction we forget our own peril. "Human beings themselves are at risk—not just on some survival-of-civilization level, but more basically on the level of heart and soul. We are ignorant of our own nature and confused about what it means to be a human being."

This confusion stems from judging ourselves independent from and superior to other forms of life rather than accepting equal membership in the seemingly chaotic and totally interdependent world of wildness. To remove an animal or plant or hunter-gatherer from its place automatically compromises its inherent qualities and integrity and leads to the infinite sadness of zoos, aquariums, and reservations.

How do we remedy this situation? "To resolve the dichotomy of the civilized and the wild, we must first resolve to be whole." And if we are going to make this resolution we must first figure out what we might mean by "wild." The practice of the wild refines our thinking about the wild, extending it beyond the realm of vacation spots, beyond the facts and equations of scientific explanation, to a place familiar to any child who persists in asking "Why?" Children know that natural metaphors of plants and animals penetrate to the wild place, that fairy tales are true, that they are little animals. That is why they so vigorously oppose the forces of domesticity and civilized education. They know quite well that they would be better off in forests, the mountains, the deserts, and the seas. "Thoreau wrote of 'this vast savage howling mother of ours, Nature, lying all around, with such beauty, and such affection for her children, as the leopard; and yet we are so early weaned from her breast to society.' " This is cause of great sorrow, and points to the source of our society's grave ills:

> The world is our consciousness, and it surrounds us. There are more things in mind, in the imagination, than "you" can keep track of—thoughts, memories, images, angers, delights, rise unbidden. The depths of mind, the unconscious, are our inner wilderness areas, and that is where the bobcat is right now. I do not mean personal bobcats in personal psyches, but the bobcat that roams from dream to dream. The conscious agenda-planning ego occupies a very tiny territory, a little cubicle somewhere near the gate, keeping track of some of what goes in and out (and sometimes making expansionistic plots), and the rest takes care of itself. The body is, so to speak, in the mind. They are both wild.

To fully accept our wildness we must embody it, we must take up residence in a biological order; to become whole we must live as part of a larger system of plant and animal communities governed by reciprocity. The acid test is this: to see yourself as food. "To acknowledge that each of us at the table will eventually be part of the meal is not just being 'realistic.' It is allowing the sacred to enter and accepting the sacramental aspect of our shaky temporary personal being."

To take up residence in a biological order is to inhabit a place, to belong to a particular network of wild systems, a distinctive web of flora and fauna, landforms, elevation and other natural criteria, what we are learning to call a bioregion, a mixture of home, commons, and wilderness all necessary for the health of the region. "Bioregional awareness teaches us in specific ways. It is not enough just to 'love nature' or want to 'be in harmony with Gaia.' Our relation to the natural world takes place in a place, and it must be grounded in information and experience."

When your lunch depends upon a mutual effort between you and huckleberry bushes, you oppose their destruction. When the health of your children (and grandchildren) is dependent, in space and time, upon the health of a commons, communities extend the little "self" of self-interest into the future and challenge modern economies that reduce both commons and community to raw material for short-term profit. Bioregional cultures resist exploitation. Their cohesion of place and life engages the heart, and an engaged heart grounds political action—the effectiveness of grassroots politics. Grassroots politics is local, the politics of "locale." To take up residence in a wild system is a political act.

When you are informed by your place, you become the voice of its spirit. Snyder quotes a Crow elder: "You know, I think if people stay somewhere long enough—even white people—the spirits will begin to speak to them. It's the power of the spirits coming from the land. The spirits and the old powers aren't lost, they just need people to be around long enough and the spirits will begin to influence them."

Gary Snyder has lived this vision. He and his friends reinhabited San Juan Ridge in the northern Sierra Nevada. They have practiced a quasi-subsistence economy, and they have established one of America's first lay Zen centers. They interact with their land, and they are devoted to grassroots politics. Over the years they have established numerous organizations—the San Juan Ridge Tax Payers Association, the Ridge Study Group—then recently they created the Yuba Watershed Institute, a bioregional organization devoted to the total Yuba River community—human, biological, and topographic. It presents public field days and talks on such subjects as "The Ecosystem of the Rotting

Tree," "Insects of the Forest," and "Forest Fires and Ecological Changes on San Juan Ridge." In conjunction with another local group, the Timber Framers Guild, the Institute is working with the BLM to set aside a forest area for cooperative timber management that will preserve old-growth forest. They are working in support of the South Yuba Citizens League to establish wild and scenic river status for all forks of the Yuba.

This is the real work of the real world. As Snyder reflects, "We are defending our own space, and we are trying to protect the commons. More than the logic of self-interest inspires this: a true and selfless love of the land is the source of the undaunted spirit of my neighbors."

# 6 | CULTURED OR CRABBED

## Gary Snyder

WE STILL ONLY KNOW what we know: "The flavors of the peach and the apricot are not lost from generation to generation. Neither are they transmitted by book-learning" (Ezra Pound). The rest is hearsay. There is strength, freedom, sustainability, and pride in being a practiced dweller in your own surroundings, knowing what you know. There are two kinds of knowing.

One is that which grounds and places you in your actual condition. You know north from south, pine from fir, in which direction the new moon might be found, where the water comes from, where the garbage goes, how to shake hands, how to sharpen a knife, how the interest rates work. This sort of knowledge itself can enhance public life and save endangered species. We learn it by revivifying culture, which is like reinhabitation: moving back into a terrain that has been abused and half-forgotten—and then replanting trees, dechannelizing streambeds, breaking up asphalt. What—some would say—if there's no "culture" left? There always is—just as much as there's always (no matter where) place and language. One's culture is in the family and the community, and it lights up when you start to do some real work together, or play, tell stories, act up—or when someone gets sick, or dies, or is born—or at a gathering like Thanksgiving. A culture is a network of neighborhoods or communities that is rooted and tended. It has limits, it is ordinary. "She's very cultured" shouldn't mean elite, but more like "well-fertilized."

(The term *culture* goes back to Latin meanings, via *colere,* such as "worship, attend to, cultivate, respect, till, take care of." The root *kwel* basically means to revolve around a center—cognate with *wheel* and Greek *telos,* "completion of a cycle," hence *teleology.* In Sanskrit this is *chakra,* "spinning wheel"—or "great wheel of the universe." The modern Hindu word is *charkha,* "spinning wheel"—with which Gandhi meditated the freedom of India while in prison.)

Originally published in Gary Snyder, *The Practice of the Wild* (San Francisco: North Point Press, 1990). Copyright © 1990 by Gary Snyder. Reprinted with permission of North Point Press, a division of Farrar, Straus & Giroux, Inc.

The other kind of knowledge comes from straying outside. Thoreau writes of the crab apple, "*Our* wild apple is wild only like myself, perchance, who belong not to the aboriginal race here, but have strayed into the woods from cultivated stock." John Muir carries these thoughts along. In *Wild Wool* he quotes a farmer friend who tells him, "Culture is an orchard apple; Nature is a crab." (To go back to the wild is to become sour, astringent, crabbed. Unfertilized, unpruned, tough, resilient, and every spring *shockingly* beautiful in bloom.) Virtually all contemporary people are cultivated stock, but we can stray back into the woods.

One departs the home to embark on a quest into an archetypal wilderness that is dangerous, threatening, and full of beasts and hostile aliens. This sort of encounter with the other—both the inner and the outer—requires giving up comfort and safety, accepting cold and hunger, and being willing to eat anything. You may never see home again. Loneliness is your bread. Your bones may turn up someday in some riverbank mud. It grants freedom, expansion, and release. Untied. Unstuck. Crazy for a while. It breaks taboo, it verges on transgression, it teaches humility. Going out—fasting—singing alone—talking across the species boundaries—praying—giving thanks—coming back.

On the mythical plane this is the source of the worldwide hero narratives. On the spiritual plane it requires embracing the other as oneself and stepping across the line—not "becoming one" or mixing things up but holding the sameness and difference delicately in mind. It can mean seeing the houses, roads, and people of your old place as for the first time. It can mean every word heard to its deepest echo. It can mean mysterious tears of gratitude. Our "soul" is our dream of the other.

There is a movement toward creating a "culture of the wilderness" from within contemporary civilization. The Deep Ecology philosophers and the struggles and arguments which have taken place between them and the Green movement, the Social Ecologists, and the Ecofeminists are all part of the emerging realization that this could be tried. Deep Ecology thinkers insist that the natural world has value in its own right, that the health of natural systems should be our first concern, and that this best serves the interests of humans as well. They are well aware that primary people everywhere are our teachers in these values (Sessions and Devall, *Deep Ecology,* 1985). The emergence of Earth First! brings a new level of urgency, boldness, and humor into environmentalism. Direct-action techniques that go back to the civil rights and labor movement days are employed in ecological issues. With Earth First!, the Great Basin finally steps onto the stage of world politics. The established environmental organizations are forced by these mavericks to become more activist. At the same time there is a rapidly growing grassroots movement in Asia,

Borneo, Brazil, Siberia. It is a cause for hope that so many people world-wide—from Czech intellectuals to rainforest-dwelling mothers in Sarawak—are awakening to their power.

The original American environmental tradition came out of the politics of public lands and wildlife (geese, fish, ducks—hence the Audubon Society, the Izaak Walton League, and Ducks Unlimited). For decades a narrow but essential agenda of wilderness preservation took up everyone's volunteer time. With the 1970s, "conservation" became "environmentalism" as concerns extended out of the wilderness areas to broader matters of forest management, agriculture, water and air pollution, nuclear power, and all the other issues we know so well.

Environmental concerns and politics have spread worldwide. In some countries the focus is almost entirely on human health and welfare issues. It is proper that the range of the movement should run from wildlife to urban health. But there can be no health for humans and cities that bypasses the rest of nature. A properly radical environmentalist position is in no way anti-human. We grasp the pain of the human condition in its full complexity, and add the awareness of how desperately endangered certain key species and habitats have become. We get a lot of information—paradoxically—from deep inside civilization, from the biological and social sciences. The critical argument now within environmental circles is between those who operate from a human-centered resource management mentality and those whose values reflect an awareness of the integrity of the whole of nature. The latter position, that of Deep Ecology, is politically livelier, more courageous, more convivial, riskier, and more scientific.

It comes again to an understanding of the subtle but critical difference of meaning between the terms *nature* and *wild*. Nature is the subject, they say, of science. Nature can be deeply probed, as in microbiology. The wild is not to be made subject or object in this manner; to be approached it must be admitted from within, as a quality intrinsic to who we are. Nature is ultimately in no way endangered; wilderness is. The wild is indestructible, but we might not *see* the wild.

A culture of wilderness starts somewhere in this terrain. Civilization is part of nature—our egos play in the fields of the unconscious—history takes place in the Holocene—human culture is rooted in the primitive and the paleolithic—our body is a vertebrate mammal being—and our souls are out in the wilderness.

# 7 | THE NEW CONSERVATION MOVEMENT

## Dave Foreman

## CONSERVATIONISTS SUPPORT MULTIPLE USE

IN THE 1970S, CONSERVATIONISTS were tub-thumpers for the concept of multiple use. No group would have considered opposing timber cutting, livestock grazing, mining, oil extraction, motorized recreational development, off-road vehicle (ORV) use, and other extractive uses as legitimate activities on the public lands. We fought pitched battles against logging, mining, and massive ski areas in certain places; we sometimes called for cutbacks in permitted livestock numbers; we urged restrictions on ORVs; but we rolled our beads and mumbled along to the multiple-use catechism that in concept all such activities were legitimate uses for the National Forests, BLM lands, and sometimes even for National Parks and Wildlife Refuges.

## CONSERVATIONISTS USE ANTHROPOCENTRIC ARGUMENTS FOR WILDERNESS

In the '70s, Wilderness Areas, National Parks, National Wildlife Refuges, and other protected areas were still viewed primarily as recreational and scenic resources—not as ecological reserves.

Wilderness Areas on the National Forests were established in the 1920s and 1930s to keep alive pioneer skills as old-time foresters reacted to the smoky spread of Ford's machine. Until the 1980s, conservationists argued most frequently from a recreational (including aesthetic) standpoint for the preserva-

A longer version of this essay was originally published in *Wild Earth* 1, 2 (1991). Reprinted with permission.

tion of Wilderness. Areas proposed for Wilderness status were those with a vigorous constituency of hikers, packers, climbers, fishers, hunters, and such. In most cases, it was the high country with glacial tarns, mountain meadows, and imposing peaks above timberline that drew the support of recreationists. To gain protection for a popular alpine core, conservation groups willingly whittled off from their proposals the surrounding lower elevation lands desired by timbermen—even though these forested areas were far more valuable ecologically than the highlands. I remember a founder of the New Mexico Wilderness Study Committee urging me to pare back my proposed Wilderness acreage on the Gila National Forest in southwestern New Mexico because his small high country wildernesses in the north were more attractive for recreation. He feared that if much of the drier, hotter, less classic landscape of the Gila was designated as Wilderness, correspondingly fewer of the Colorado-like roadless areas in northern New Mexico would be protected. The same old hiker refused to support Wilderness designation for what he considered unattractive lands at Bosque del Apache National Wildlife Refuge. There is even a tantalizing rumor of a California Sierra Club honcho meeting in the '70s where a decision was made to surrender the old-growth forests and concentrate on getting wilderness protection for the recreationally prime high country.

Such conservationists were making a strategic decision. They believed only a limited amount of land would receive Wilderness Area designation; they wanted it to be the areas in which they most enjoyed hiking, camping, fishing, climbing, and hunting.

The arguments for National Parks followed a similar theme. From the beginning with Yellowstone in 1872, it was not wilderness being preserved but the spectacles and curiosities of nature—the wonders of the world like the Grand Canyon, Yosemite Valley, Carlsbad Caverns, and Crater Lake. Alfred Runte, the preeminent scholar of the National Parks, calls this argument "monumentalism."

National Wildlife Refuges were in most cases established to provide breeding grounds and other habitat for huntable waterfowl or big game; seldom were refuges set up for critters like Whooping Cranes. Even rare species rescued from the brink of extinction, like the Desert Bighorn, paid their way in recreational terms—in the case of the Desert Bighorn by providing limited hunting opportunities on Cabeza Prieta and San Andres Game Ranges. Game species were further protected for hunters by predator extermination campaigns in National Parks and Wilderness Areas during the first third of this century. Even after scientists recognized the necessary ecological role of predators, conservationists did not dare advocate restoration of Gray Wolf, Grizzly Bear, or Cougar to areas where they had been exterminated.

For all of the protected areas, another anthropocentric rationale was what Runte calls the "worthless lands" argument. We could afford to set aside these areas and restrict full-blown multiple-use exploitation because they didn't have much in the way of resources. This approach, of course, reinforced the willingness of conservationists to exclude rich forestlands, grazing areas, and mineralized zones from their proposals.

Additionally, 1970s conservationists saw Wilderness Areas, National Parks, and Wildlife Refuges as islands—discrete, separate *units*. They were living museums, outdoor art galleries, backwoods gymnasiums, open-air zoos. Protective classification was not seen as a zoning process, but as the identification of delineated tracts to be honored as the "crown jewels" of American nature. Lines were drawn around these areas and they were viewed as standing apart from the land around them. Ecological concepts of habitat fragmentation were generally ignored (or unknown) by federal agencies and conservationists alike.

By 1980, these philosophical and organizational foundations were experiencing cracks. The zany excesses of Jim Watt helped the 1980s to become a transition period for conservation, but four other factors were actually more important in cracking the old foundations.

## ACADEMIC PHILOSOPHY

During the 1970s, philosophy professors in Europe, North America, and Australia began to look at environmental ethics as a worthy focus for discussion and explication. Sociologists, historians, anthropologists, and other liberal arts academics also began to study attitudes toward nature. By 1980, enough interest had coalesced for an academic journal called *Environmental Ethics* to appear. Also, several university faculty members, particularly Bill Devall and George Sessions, were popularizing in the United States the Deep Ecology views of Norwegian philosopher Arne Naess. An international network of specialists in environmental ethics developed, leading to one of the more vigorous debates in modern philosophy.

At first, little of this big blow in the ivory towers drew the notice of working conservationists, but by the end of the '80s, few conservation group staff members or volunteer activists were unaware of the Deep Ecology–Shallow Environmentalism distinction or of the general discussion about ethics and ecology. At the heart of this discussion was the question of whether other species possessed intrinsic value or had value solely because of their use to humans. Ginger Rogers to this Fred Astaire was the question of what, if any, ethical obligations humans had to nature or other species. Interestingly, advocates for intrinsic value and ethical obligations to ecosystems looked back to Aldo Leopold, the originator of the Wilderness Area concept on the National Forests, for inspiration. (One could argue that the evolution of the conservation movement's arguments from the '70s to the '90s recapitulated the personal evolution of Aldo Leopold.)

## CONSERVATION BIOLOGY

Despite the example of early-day wildlife scientists like Aldo Leopold and Olaus Murie, few biologists or other natural scientists were willing to enter the political fray in the 1970s. I remember trying to recruit zoologists, botanists, ecologists, and other scientists at New Mexico colleges to speak out in support of Wilderness Area designation. A handful did, but most excused themselves.

In the 1980s, however, two groups of working biologists appeared who were willing to provide conservationists with information, speak out in public, and even put their reputations on the line over preservation issues. One group consisted of agency scientists: ecologists, botanists, zoologists, soils scientists, and other researchers who worked for the Forest Service, National Park Service, Fish and Wildlife Service, and Bureau of Land Management. These research scientists studied old-growth forest ecosystems, investigated the needs of Endangered and sensitive species, and calculated the impact of resource extraction on a variety of ecosystems. In the 1970s Howard Wilshire, a geologist with the U.S. Geological Survey, had nearly gotten fired for publicizing his research revealing the unexpected damage done by ORVs. As could be expected, timbermen in the Pacific Northwest called for muzzling certain government old-growth researchers in the '80s as the researchers' findings began to draw attention. Their new data exploded old myths about biological deserts in old-growth and underlined the need to stop the fragmentation of habitats. Their research swayed some agency managers to tread a little easier, but, more importantly, conservation groups began to back up their preservation arguments with facts from the government's own researchers. (Closely allied to this factor of more outspoken scientists in government agencies was the emergence of other employees in the Forest Service and other agencies who, influenced by the scientists and by the conservation movement, began to take a less submissive role within the agencies and to agitate for internal reform. This led to the formation of the Association of Forest Service Employees for Environmental Ethics.)

The other group of ecologists joining the movement were university researchers largely working in tropical rain forests and other exotic locations who suddenly became aware that the natural diversity they were studying was fast disappearing. As their data accumulated, a growing number of them could not deny the inescapable conclusion: due to the activities of industrial human beings, the Earth was in the throes of an extinction crisis greater than any revealed in the geological record. Nowhere in the dusty bins of universities and museums or in the great fossil sites of the world was there evidence for a rate of extinction as high as that occurring in the late twentieth century.

These facts were so shocking—like the sudden buzz of a rattlesnake in tall grass—that a covey of biologists flushed into action and formed a new branch of biology. This "crisis discipline" (a term coined by one of its founders, Michael Soulé) was named Conservation Biology. The new field had dozens of books and a quarterly journal by the end of the 1980s. The warnings of conservation biologists were being heard through the national media. Even some politicians began to listen. By the decade's end, *biodiversity* had become a common term and a major issue. Conservation groups like The Wilderness Society hired staff ecologists. The Nature Conservancy redoubled its efforts to purchase ecologically sensitive tracts of land and began to talk about linkages and corridors. Tropical rain forests attracted much of the attention but temperate habitats in the United States gained considerable notice as well. One example of activist scientists was a group of botanists at the University of Wisconsin who proposed that large blocks of the National Forest acreage in Wisconsin be devoted to the restoration of old-growth conditions. . . .

## EARTH FIRST!

In *Confessions of an Eco-Warrior,* I discuss the whelping of Earth First! out of the mainstream movement, what the accomplishments of that remarkable phenomenon were during the '80s, and why I felt it had largely achieved its practical goals by the late '80s. Here, I want to emphasize something that rarely percolates to the surface in all of the volumes of media hype about Earth First!: The antiestablishment stance of Earth First! was a deliberate, strategic decision designed to effect certain defined goals. We founders of Earth First! did not believe that EF! was a replacement for the rest of the wilderness movement. In many respects, it was a kamikaze operation.

In the last chapter of *Confessions,* I sum up the accomplishments of Earth First!:

> Earth First! has led the effort to reframe the question of wilderness preservation from an aesthetic and utilitarian one to an ecological one, from a focus on scenery and recreation to a focus on biological diversity.
>
> Similarly, we have gone beyond the limited agenda of mainstream conservation groups to protect *a portion* of the remaining wilderness by calling for the reintroduction of extirpated species and the restoration of vast wilderness tracts. We have brought the discussion of biocentric philosophy—Deep Ecol-

ogy—out of dusty academic journals. We have effectively introduced nonviolent civil disobedience into the repertoire of wildland preservation activism. We have also helped to jolt the conservation movement out of its middle-age lethargy and re-inspire it with passion, joy, and humor. In doing all of this, Earth First! has restructured the conservation spectrum and redefined the parameters of debate on ecological matters.

It was necessary for a group to consciously step outside of the system, to eschew the temptations of political access, to deliberately try to stir the stew: to bring biocentric arguments for wilderness to the fore; to emphasize biological diversity values over recreational and utilitarian values; to help prepare the soil out of which could sprout a necessary spectrum of groups within the wilderness movement; and to make possible the serious discussion of previously taboo subjects such as predator reintroduction, wilderness restoration, and outlawing of timber cutting and livestock grazing on the public lands. Earth First! could not itself gain the visionary wilderness it proposed or shut down logging on the National Forests. But, intertwined like an orgy of serpents with environmental philosophers, conservation biologists, and independent grassroots groups, the Earth First! movement played a key role in creating the necessary conditions for the emergence of a New Conservation Movement for the '90s—which can accomplish much of what was first proposed by Earth First!.

A different situation exists today in the wilderness preservation movement than ever before. There is an obvious spectrum of groups with differing positions on a variety of issues, and there is no centralized general staff able to dictate national strategy. Things are in a happy boil, and a new vision is challenging old ways of thinking and doing. The cutting edge of wilderness preservation has passed from well-established, wealthy national groups with large memberships and guaranteed political access, to struggling, hungry grassroots organizations with their feet and hearts planted firmly in the wildwood. . . .

## WILDERNESS CONCEPT

The New Conservation Movement has largely turned its back on the old concept of Wilderness as primarily a recreational resource. Their arguments are solidly based in conservation biology, and recognize biological diversity as the fundamental value. Articulated and further developed by the visionaries, such ideas and reasoning are trickling down into the national mainstream. No longer are Wilderness Areas and National Parks viewed as islands of solitude for harried urbanites, but as core preserves in an unfinished North American *system* of ecological preserves linked together to provide necessary habitat for viable populations of sensitive and wide-ranging wilderness-dependent species, like Spotted Owl, Gray Wolf, Florida Panther, Ocelot, Grizzly, and many less "charismatic" species.

# 8 | RITUAL—THE PATTERN THAT CONNECTS
## *Dolores LaChapelle*

THE NORWEGIAN PHILOSOPHER Arne Naess says that "what we need today is a tremendous expansion of ecological thinking." Paradoxically we must write or talk about this alternative way of thinking while using the very same language system which is at the root of the problem. The nature of language is such that a particular language forces those who use it to think in the categories of that language. It is precisely the dualistic mode of thinking inherent in the European language system which has been one of the factors leading to the current devastation of the environment as well as modern stress-related physical and mental ills. Our language system acknowledges only the type of phenomena which support *this* particular system. Other phenomena are dismissed as either impossible or scientifically unproved.[1] To write about such holistic subjects as Deep Ecology it frequently is necessary to invent awkward new words or resort to using a mechanism such as Heidegger uses when he writes of man as a "being-in-the-world."

Ritual, however, allows us to bypass the limitations imposed by the structure of our language.

Most native societies around the world had three common characteristics: they had an intimate, conscious relationship with their place; they were stable "sustainable" cultures, often lasting for thousands of years; and they had a rich ceremonial and ritual life. They saw these as intimately connected. Out of the hundreds of examples of this, consider the following:

1. The Tukano Indians of the Northwest Amazon River basin, guided by their shamans, make use of various myths and rituals that prevent over-hunting and over-fishing. They view their universe as a circuit of energy in which the entire cosmos participates. This basic circuit of energy consists of "a limited

Previously published in *Deep Ecology: Living as if Nature Mattered,* by Bill Devall and George Sessions (Salt Lake City: Gibbs Smith, 1985).

quantity of procreative energy that flows continually between man and animals, between society and nature." Reichel-Dolmatoff, the Columbian anthropologist, notes that the Tukano have very little interest in exploiting natural resources more effectively but are greatly interested in "accumulating more factual knowledge about biological reality and, above all, about knowing what the physical world requires from men."[2]

2. The !Kung people of the Kalahari Desert have been living in exactly the same place for eleven thousand years! They have very few material belongings but their ritual life is one of the most sophisticated of any group.[3]

3. Roy Rappaport has shown that the rituals of the Tsembaga of New Guinea allocate scarce protein for the humans who need it without causing irreversible damage to the land.[4]

4. The longest-inhabited place in the United States is the Hopi village of Oraibi. At certain times of the year they may spend up to half their time in ritual activity.[5]

5. Upon the death of their old cacique, Santa Ana Pueblo in New Mexico recently elected a young man to take over as the new cacique. For the rest of his life he will do nothing else whatsoever but take care of the ritual life of the pueblo. All his personal needs will be taken care of by the tribe. But he cannot travel any further than sixty miles or one hour distance—his presence is that important to the ongoing life of the Pueblo. They know that it is ritual which embodies the people.[6]

Our Western European industrial culture provides a striking contrast to all these examples. We have idolized ideologies, "rationality," and a limited kind of practicality, and have regarded the conscious rituals of these other cultures as frivolous curiosities, at best. The results are all too evident. We've been here only a few hundred years and we have already done irreparable damage to vast areas of the country now called the United States. As Gregory Bateson once pointed out, "mere purposive rationality is necessarily pathogenic and destructive of life."[7]

We have tried to relate to the world around us through only the left side of our brain, and we are clearly failing. It we are to reestablish a viable relationship, we will need to rediscover the wisdom of these other cultures who knew that their relationship to the natural world required the whole of their being. What we call their "ritual and ceremony" was a sophisticated social and spiritual technology, refined through many thousands of years of experience, that maintained this relationship.

Gary Snyder writes of "animals speaking through the people and making their point." He further says that "when, in the dances of the Pueblo Indians and other peoples, certain individuals became seized, as it were, by the spirit of the deer, and danced as a deer would dance, or danced the dance of the corn maidens, or impersonated the squash blossoms, they were no longer speaking for humanity, they were taking it on themselves to interpret through their humanity, what these other life forms were."[8]

The human race has forgotten so much in the last two hundred years that we hardly know where to begin. But it helps to begin remembering. In the first place, *all* traditional cultures, even our own Western European cultural ancestors, had seasonal festivals and rituals.

The true origin of most of our modern major holidays dates back to these seasonal festivals. There are four major festivals: winter and summer solstice (when the sun reverses its travels) and spring and autumn equinox (when night and day are equal). But in between each of these major holidays are the "cross quarter days." For example, spring equinox comes around March 21 or 22 but spring is only barely beginning at that time in Europe. True spring (reliably warm spring) doesn't come until later. This is the cross quarter day (May 1) that Europe celebrated with maypoles, flower-gathering, and fertility rites. May became the month of Mary after the Christian church took over; May crownings and processions were devoted to Mary instead of the old "earth goddesses."

Summer solstice comes on June 21. The next cross quarter day is Lammas Day in early August. This is the only festival that our country does not celebrate in any way. The Church put the Feast of the Assumption on this day to honor Mary. Fall equinox comes on September 21—the cross quarter day is Hallowe'en, the ancient Samhain of the Celts. Then comes winter solstice—the sun's turnaround point from darkness to light. The cross quarter day between the solstice and spring equinox is in early February—now celebrated in the Church as Candlemas.[9]

The traditional purpose of seasonal festivals is periodically to revive the *topocosm*. Gaster coined this word from the Greek—*topo* for place and *cosmos* for world order. *Topocosm* thus means "the world order of a particular place." The topocosm is the entire complex of any given locality conceived as a living organism—not just the human community but the total community—the plants, animals, and soils of the place. The topocosm is not only the actual and present living community but also that continuous entity of which the present community is but the current manifestation.[10]

Seasonal festivals make use of myth, art, dance, and games. All of these aspects of ritual serve to connect—to keep open the essential connections within ourselves. Festivals connect the conscious with the unconscious, the right and left hemispheres of the brain, the cortex with the older three brains (this includes the Oriental *tan tien*—four fingers below the navel), as well as connecting the human with the nonhuman: the earth, the sky, the plants and animals.[11]

The next step after seasonal rituals is to acknowledge the non-human coin-habitants of your place. You can begin by looking into the records of the tribes of Indians who lived there and see what their totem was. Look into the accounts of the early explorers and very early settlers. Barry Lopez said that the Eskimos told him that their totem animal was always one who could teach them something they needed to learn.[12]

For example, Salmon is the totem animal for the North Pacific Rim. "Only Salmon, as a species, informs us humans, as a species, of the vastness and unity of the North Pacific Ocean and its rim. . . . Totemism is a method of perceiving power, goodness and mutuality in locale through the recognition of and respect for the vitality, spirit, and interdependence of other species," as Freeman House explains. For at least twenty thousand years, the Yurok, Chinook, Salish, Kwakiutl, Haida, and Aleut on this side of the rim, and, on the other rim of the Pacific, the Ainu (the primal people of Japan) ordered their daily lives according to the timing of the Salmon population.[13]

Several years ago I did some in-depth study of Celtic myth and discovered that Salmon was the totem animal for the Celts, too. According to their myth, there was a sacred well situated under the sea where the sacred Salmon acquired their supernatural wisdom. The famous Celtic hero, Finn, traditionally obtained his wisdom when he sucked on the thumb he had just burnt when picking up the Salmon he cooked.[14] It is not surprising that Salmon links all these areas. The North Pacific Rim and the British Isles are maritime climates in the northern half of the earth. Here is the perfect way to ritualize the link between planetary villagers around the earth—through their totem animal.

How can we learn from Salmon? One specific way is to reclaim our waterways so that Salmon can again flourish. And by so doing, we will also have reclaimed the soil, the plants, and the other species of the ecosystem—restored them to aboriginal health. And by doing this, we would be restoring full health to our children as well.

Freeman House feels that the people who live in or near the spawning grounds of Salmon should form associations—not law enforcement agencies such as the State Fish and Game Department—but educational groups and providers of ritual and ceremony that would celebrate the interdependence of species. Freeman was a Salmon fisherman on Guemes Island in Washington. Now he lives in Northern California where he is restocking Salmon rivers.

What relevance do these kinds of rituals have for people living in cities? All of us need seasonal and nature rituals wherever we live, but let me give you a specifically urban example.

Siena, Italy, with a population of about fifty-nine thousand people, has the lowest crime rate of any Western city of comparable size. Delinquency, drug addiction, and violence are virtually unknown. Class is not pitted against class nor young against old.

Why? Because it is a tribal, ritualized city organized around the *contrada* (clans)—with names such as Chiocciola (the Snail), Tartule (the Turtle) and the like—and the Palio (the annual horse race). The *contrada* function as independent city states. Each has its own flag, its own territorial boundaries, its own discrete identity, church songs, patron saint and rituals. Particular topographical features of each *contrada*'s area are ritualized and mythologized. The ritualized city customs extend clear back to the worship of Diana, the Roman goddess of the moon. Her attributes were taken over by the worship of Mary when Christianity came in.

Many famous writers, including Henry James, Ezra Pound, and Aldous Huxley, sensed the energy of the city and its events and tried to write about it. But none of them even faintly grasped the yearlong ritualized life behind it. About one week before the day of the Palio race, workers from the city of Siena begin to bring yellow earth (*la terra* from the fields outside Siena) and spread it over the great central square (the Campo) thus linking the city with its origins in the earth of its *place*. In fact, anytime during the course of the year when someone needs to be cheered up, the sad person is told not to worry because soon there will be "la terra in piazza" (soon there will be earth in the square).

The horse race serves two main purposes. In the intense rivalry surrounding the race, each *contrada* "rekindles its own sense of identity." The Palio also provide the Sienese with an outlet for their aggressions and, as such, is a ritual war. The horse race grew out of games which were actually mimic battles and were used to mark the ends of religious festivals.

The *Palio* is truly a religious event. On this one day of the year the *contrada*'s horse is brought into the church of its patron saint. In the act of blessing the horse, the *contrada* is itself blessed. This horse race is the community's greatest rite. "In the Palio, all the flames of Hell are transformed into the lights of Paradise," according to a local priest, Don Vittorio.[15]

If we want to build a sustainable culture, it is not enough merely to "go back to the land." That's exactly where our pioneering ancestors lived; as the famous Western painter Charles Russell said, "A pioneer is a man who comes to virgin country, traps off all the fur, kills off the wild meat, plows the roots up. . . . A pioneer destroys things and calls it civilization."

If we are truly to reconnect with the land, we need to change our perceptions and approach more than our location. As long as we limit ourselves to narrow rationality and its limited sense of "practicality," we will be disconnected from the Deep Ecology of our place. As Heidegger explains: "Dwelling is not primarily inhabiting but taking care of and creating that space within which something comes into its own and flourishes."[16] It takes both time and ritual for real dwelling. Similarly, as Roy Rappaport observes, "Knowledge will never replace respect in man's dealings with ecological systems, for the ecological systems in which man participates are likely to be so complex that he may never have sufficient comprehension of their content and structure to permit him to predict the outcome of many of his own acts."[17] Ritual is the focused way in which we both experience and express that respect.

Ritual is essential because it is truly the pattern that connects. It provides communication at all levels—among all the systems within the individual human organism; between people within groups; between one group and another in a city; and throughout all these levels between the human and the nonhuman in the natural environment. Ritual provides us with a tool for learning to think logically, analogically, and ecologically as we move toward a sustainable culture. Most important of all, perhaps, is that during rituals we have the experience, unique in our culture, of neither *opposing* nature or *trying* to be in communion with nature; but of *finding* ourselves within nature, and that is the key to sustainable culture.

# NOTES

1. Barrington Nevitt, *ABC of Prophecy: Understanding the Environment* (Toronto: Canadian Futures, 1980), 13.

2. G. Reichel-Dolmatoff, "Cosmology as Ecological Analysis: A View from the Rain Forest," in *Man: Journal of the Royal Anthropological Institute* 2, no. 3 (September 1978).

3. Richard B. Lee, "What Hunters Do for a Living, or, How to Make out on Scarce Resources," in *Man the Hunter,* edited by Richard B. Lee and Irven DeVore (Chicago: Aldine Publishing Co., 1968), 30–43.

4. Roy Rappaport, *Pigs for the Ancestors* (New Haven: Yale University Press, 1968).

5. John J. Collins, *Primitive Religion* (New York: Rowman and Littlefield, 1978).

6. Elizabeth Cogburn, from a personal communication.

7. Gregory Bateson, *Steps to an Ecology of Mind* (New York: Ballantine Books, 1972), 146.

8. Gary Snyder, *Turtle Island* (New York: New Directions Books, 1974), 109.

9. Dolores LaChapelle, *Sacred Land Sacred Sex, Rapture of the Deep: Concerning Deep Ecology and Celebrating Life* (Durango, Colo.: Kivaki Press, 1992), 231–238.

10. Gaster, Theodore H., *Thespis: Ritual, Myth, and Drama in the Ancient Near East.* New York: W. W. Norton, 1961.

11. Eugene G. d'Aquili and Charles D. Laughlin, Jr., "The Neurobiology of Myth and Ritual," in *The Spectrum of Ritual: A Biogenetic Structural Analysis,* edited by

Eugene G. d'Aquili, Charles D. Laughlin, Jr., and John McManus (New York: Columbia University Press, 1979), 152–182.

12. Barry Lopez, from a personal communication.

13. Freeman House, "Totem Salmon," in *North Pacific Rim Alive* (San Francisco: Planet Drum, 1979).

14. Tom Jay, "The Salmon of the Heart," in *Working the Woods, Working the Sea,* edited by Finn Wilcox and Jeremiah Gorsline (Port Townsend, Wash.: 1986), 100–124.

15. A Dundes and A. Falassi, *La Terra in Piazza: An Interpretation of the Palio of Siena* (Berkeley, Calif.: University of California Press, 1975).

16. Martin Heidegger, *The Piety of Thinking,* translated by James G. Hart and John Maraldo (Bloomington: Indian University Press, 1976), 131.

17. Roy Rappaport, *Ecology, Meaning, and Religion* (Berkeley, Calif.: North Atlantic Books, 1979), 100.

# 9 | THE DEEP ECOLOGICAL MOVEMENT
## SOME PHILOSOPHICAL ASPECTS

*Arne Naess*

## 1. DEEP ECOLOGY ON THE DEFENSIVE

INCREASING PRESSURES FOR CONTINUED growth and development have placed the vast majority of environmental professionals on the defensive. By way of illustration:

The field ecologist Ivar Mysterud, who both professionally and vigorously advocated deep ecological principles in the late 1960s, encountered considerable resistance. Colleagues at his university said he should keep to his science and not meddle in philosophical and political matters. He should resist the temptation to become a prominent "popularizer" through mass media exposure. Nevertheless, he persisted and influenced thousands of people (including myself).

Mysterud became a well-known professional "expert" at assessing the damage done when bears killed or maimed sheep and other domestic animals in Norway. According to the law, their owners are paid damages. And licensed hunters receive permission to shoot bears if their misdeeds become considerable.[1] Continued growth and development required that the sheep industry consolidate, and sheepowners became fewer, richer, and tended to live in cities. As a result of wage increases, they could not afford to hire shepherds to watch the flocks, so the sheep were left on their own even more than before. Continued growth also required moving sheep to what was traditionally considered

This essay originally appeared in *Philosophical Inquiry* 8, nos. 1–2 (1986). Reprinted with permission.

"bear territory." In spite of this invasion, bear populations grew and troubles multiplied.

How did Mysterud react to these new problems? Did he set limits to the amount of human/sheep encroachment on bear territory? Did he attempt a direct application of his deep ecological perspective to these issues? Quite the contrary. He adopted what appeared to be a shallow wildlife management perspective, and defended the sheepowners: more money to compensate for losses, quicker compensation, and the immediate hiring of hunters who killed mostly "juvenile delinquent" bears accused of killing many sheep.

Protectors of big carnivores noted with concern the change of Mysterud's public "image"; had he really abandoned his former value priorities? Privately he insisted that he hadn't. But in public he tended to remain silent.

The reason for M.'s unexpected actions was not difficult to find: the force of economic growth was so strong that the laws protecting bears would be changed in a highly unfavorable direction if the sheepowners were not soon pacified by accepting some of their not unreasonable demands. After all, it did cost a lot of money to hire and equip people to locate a flock of sheep which had been harassed by a bear and, further, to prove the bear's guilt. And the bureaucratic procedures involved were time-consuming. M. had not changed his basic value priorities at all. Rather, he had adopted a purely defensive compromise. He stopped promoting his deep ecology philosophy publicly in order to retain credibility and standing among opponents of his principles and to retain his friendships with sheepowners.

And what is true of Mysterud is also true of thousands of other professional ecologists and environmentalists. These people often hold responsible positions in society where they might strengthen responsible environmental policy, but, given the exponential forces of growth, their publications, if any, are limited to narrowly professional and specialized concerns. Their writings are surely competent, but lack a deeper and more comprehensive perspective (although I admit that there are some brilliant exceptions to this).

If professional ecologists persist in voicing their value priorities, their jobs are often in danger, or they tend to lose influence and status among those who are in charge of overall policies.[2] Privately, they admit the necessity for deep and far-ranging changes, but they no longer speak out in public. As a result, people deeply concerned about ecology and the environment feel abandoned and even betrayed by the "experts" who work within the "establishment."

In ecological debates, many participants know a lot about particular conservation policies in particular places, and many others have strong views concerning fundamental philosophical questions of environmental ethics, but only a few have both qualities. When these people are silent, the loss is formidable.

For example, the complicated question concerning how industrial societies can increase energy production with the least undesirable consequences is largely a waste of time if this increase is pointless in relation to ultimate human ends. Thousands of experts hired by the government and other big institutions devote their time to this complicated problem, yet it is difficult for the public to find out or realize that many of these same experts consider the problem to be pointless and irrelevant. What these experts consider relevant are the problems of how to stabilize and eventually decrease consumption without losing genuine quality of life for humans. But they continue to work on the irrelevant problems assigned to them while, at the same time, failing to speak out, because the ultimate power is not in their hands.

## 2. A CALL TO SPEAK OUT

What I am arguing for is this: even those who completely subsume ecological policies under the narrow ends of human health and well-being cannot attain their modest aims, at least not fully, without being joined by the supporters of deep ecology. They need what these people have to contribute, and this will work in their favor more often than it will work against them. Those in charge of environmental policies, even if they are resource-oriented (and growth tolerating?) decision makers, will increasingly welcome, if only for tactical and not fundamental reasons, what deep ecology supporters have to say. Even though the more radical ethic may seem nonsensical or untenable to them, they know that its advocates are, in practice, doing conservation work that sooner or later must be done. They concur with the practice even though they operate from diverging theories. The time is ripe for professional ecologists to break their silence and express their deepest concerns more freely. A bolder advocacy of deep ecological concerns by those working within the shallow, resource-oriented environmental sphere is the best strategy for regaining some of the strength of this movement among the general public, thereby contributing, however modestly, to a turning of the tide.

What do I mean by saying that even the more modest aims of shallow environmentalism have a need for deep ecology? We can see this by considering the World Conservation Strategy—prepared by the International Union for the Conservation of Nature and Natural Resources (IUCN) in cooperation with the United Nations Environmental Programme (UNEP) and the World Wildlife Fund (WWF). The argument in this important document is thoroughly anthropocentric in the sense that all its recommendations are justified exclusively in terms of their effects upon human health and basic well-being.[3]

A more ecocentric environmental ethic is also recommended apparently for tactical reasons: "A new ethic, embracing plants and animals as well as people, is required for human societies to live in harmony with the natural world on which they depend for survival and well-being." But such an ethic would surely be more effective if it were acted upon by people who believe in its validity, rather than merely its usefulness. This, I think, will come to be understood more and more by those in charge of educational policies. Quite simply, it is indecent for a teacher to proclaim an ethic for tactical reasons only.

Furthermore, this point applies to all aspects of a world conservation strategy. Conservation strategies are more eagerly implemented by people who love what they are conserving, and who are convinced that what they love is intrinsically lovable. Such lovers will not want to hide their attitudes and values, rather they will increasingly give voice to them in public. They possess a genuine ethics of conservation, not merely a tactically useful instrument for human survival.

In short, environmental education campaigns can fortunately combine human-centered arguments with a practical environmental ethic based on either a deeper and more fundamental philosophic or religious perspective, and on a set of norms resting on intrinsic values. But the inherent strength of this overall position will be lost if those who work professionally on environmental problems do not freely give testimony to fundamental norms.

The above is hortatory in the positive etymological sense of that word. I seek "to urge, incite, instigate, encourage, cheer" (Latin: *hortari*). This may seem unacademic but I consider it justifiable because of an intimate relationship between hortatory sentences and basic philosophical views which I formulate in section 8. To trace what follows from fundamental norms and hypotheses is eminently philosophical.

## 3. WHAT IS DEEP ECOLOGY?

The phrase "deep ecology movement" has been used up to this point without trying to define it. One should not expect too much from definitions of movements; think, for example, of terms like "conservatism," "liberalism," or the "feminist movement." And there is no reason why supporters of movements should adhere exactly to the same definition, or to any definition, for that matter. It is the same with characterizations, criteria, or a set of proposed necessary conditions for application of the term or phrase. In what follows, a platform or key terms and phrases, agreed upon by George Sessions and myself, are tentatively proposed as basic to deep ecology.[4] More accurately, the sentences have a double function. They are meant to express important points which the great majority of supporters accept, implicitly or explicitly, at a high level of generality. Furthermore, they express a proposal to the effect that those

who solidly reject one or more of these points should not be viewed as supporters of deep ecology. This might result because they are supporters of a shallow
(or reform) environmental movement or rather they may simply dislike one
or more of the eight points for semantical or other reasons. But they may well
accept a different set of points which, to me, has roughly the same meaning,
in which case I shall call them supporters of the deep ecology movement, but
add that they *think* they disagree (maybe Henryk Skolimowski is an example
of the latter). The eight points are:

1. The well-being and flourishing of human and non-human life on Earth
   have value in themselves (synonyms: intrinsic value, inherent worth).
   These values are independent of the usefulness of the non-human world
   for human purposes.
2. Richness and diversity of life forms contribute to the realization of these
   values and are also values in themselves.
3. Humans have no right to reduce this richness and diversity except to
   satisfy vital needs.
4. The flourishing of human life and cultures is compatible with a substantially smaller human population. The flourishing of non-human life *requires* a smaller human population.
5. Present human interference with the non-human world is excessive, and
   the situation is rapidly worsening.
6. Policies must therefore be changed. These policies affect basic economic,
   technological, and ideological structures. The resulting state of affairs
   will be deeply different from the present.
7. The ideological change will be mainly that of appreciating life quality
   (dwelling in situations of inherent value) rather than adhering to an increasingly higher standard of living. There will be a profound awareness
   of the difference between bigness and greatness.
8. Those who subscribe to the foregoing points have an obligation directly
   or indirectly to try to implement the necessary changes.

## COMMENTS ON THE EIGHT POINTS OF THE PLATFORM

RE (1): This formulation refers to the biosphere, or more professionally, to the
ecosphere as a whole (this is also referred to as "ecocentrism"). This includes
individuals, species, populations, habitat, as well as human and non-human
cultures. Given our current knowledge of all-pervasive intimate relationships,
this implies a fundamental concern and respect.

The term "life" is used here in a more comprehensive non-technical way
also to refer to what biologists classify as "non-living": rivers (watersheds),
landscapes, ecosystems. For supporters of deep ecology, slogans such as "let the
river live" illustrate this broader usage so common in many cultures.

Inherent value, as used in (1), is common in deep ecology literature (e.g., "The presence of inherent value in a natural object is independent of any awareness, interest, or appreciation of it by any conscious being").[5]

RE (2): The so-called simple, lower, or primitive species of plants and animals contribute essentially to the richness and diversity of life. They have value in themselves and are not merely steps toward the so-called higher or rational life forms. The second principle presupposes that life itself, as a process over evolutionary time, implies an increase of diversity and richness.

Complexity, as referred to here, is different from complication. For example, urban life may be more complicated than life in a natural setting without being more complex in the sense of multifaceted quality.

RE (3): The term "vital need" is deliberately left vague to allow for considerable latitude in judgment. Differences in climate and related factors, together with differences in the structures of societies as they now exist, need to be taken into consideration.

RE (4): People in the materially richest countries cannot be expected to reduce their excessive interference with the non-human world overnight. The stabilization and reduction of the human population will take time. Hundreds of years! Interim strategies need to be developed. But in no way does this excuse the present complacency. The extreme seriousness of our current situation must first be realized. And the longer we wait to make the necessary changes, the more drastic will be the measures needed. Until deep changes are made, substantial decreases in richness and diversity are liable to occur: the rate of extinction of species will be ten to one hundred or more times greater than in any other short period of earth history.

RE (5): This formulation is mild. For a realistic assessment, see the annual reports of the Worldwatch Institute in Washington, D.C.

The slogan of "non-interference" does not imply that humans should not modify some ecosystems, as do other species. Humans have modified the earth over their entire history and will probably continue to do so. At issue is the *nature and extent* of such interference. The per capita destruction of wild (ancient) forests and other wild ecosystems has been excessive in rich countries; it is essential that the poor do not imitate the rich in this regard.

The fight to preserve and extend areas of wilderness and near-wilderness ("free Nature") should continue. The rationale for such preservation should focus mainly on the ecological functions of these areas (one such function: large wilderness areas are required in the biosphere for the continued evolutionary speciation of plants and animals). Most of the present designated wilderness areas and game reserves are not large enough to allow for such speciation.

RE (6): Economic growth as it is conceived of and implemented today by the industrial states is incompatible with points (1) through (5). There is only a faint resemblance between ideal sustainable forms of economic growth and the present policies of industrial societies.

Present ideology tends to value things because they are scarce and because they have a commodity value. There is prestige in vast consumption and waste (to mention only several relevant factors).

Whereas "self-determination," "local community," and "think globally, act locally," will remain key terms in the ecology of human societies, nevertheless the implementation of deep changes requires increasingly global action: Action across borders.

Governments in Third World countries are mostly uninterested in Deep Ecological issues. When institutions in the industrial societies try to promote ecological measures through Third World governments, practically nothing is accomplished (e.g., with problems of desertification). Given this situation, support for global action through non-governmental international organizations becomes increasingly important. Many of these organizations are able to act globally "from grassroots to grassroots" thus avoiding negative governmental interference.

Cultural diversity today requires advanced technology, that is, techniques that advance the basic goals of each culture. So-called soft, intermediate, and alternative technologies are steps in this direction.

RE (7): Some economists criticize the term "quality of life" because it is supposedly vague. But, on closer inspection, what they consider to be vague is actually the nonquantifiable nature of the term. One cannot quantify adequately what is important for the quality of life as discussed here, and there is no need to do so.

RE (8): There is ample room for different opinions about priorities: what should be done first; what next? What is the most urgent? What is clearly necessary to be done, as opposed to what is highly desirable but not absolutely pressing? The frontier of the environmental crisis is long and varied, and there is a place for everyone.

The above formulations of the eight points may be useful to many supporters of the deep ecology movement. But some will certainly feel that they are imperfect, even misleading. If they need to formulate in a few words what is basic to deep ecology, then they will propose an alternative set of sentences. I shall of course be glad to refer to them as alternatives. There ought to be a measure of diversity in what is considered basic and common.

Why should we call the movement "the deep ecological movement"?[6] There are at least six other designations which cover most of the same issues: "Ecological Resistance," used by John Rodman in important discussions; "The New Natural Philosophy" coined by Joseph Meeker; "Eco-philosophy," used by Sigmund Kvaloy and others to emphasize (1) a highly critical assessment of the industrial growth societies from a general ecological point of view, and (2) the ecology of the human species; "Green Philosophy and Politics" (while the term "green" is often used in Europe, in the United States "green" has a misleading association with the rather "blue" Green agricultural revolution); "Sustainable Earth Ethics," as used by G. Tyler Miller; and "Ecosophy" (eco-wisdom), which is my own favorite term. Others could be mentioned as well.

And so, why use the adjective "deep"? This question will be easier to answer after the contrast is made between shallow and deep ecological concerns. "Deep ecology" is not a philosophy in any proper academic sense, nor is it institutionalized as a religion or an ideology. Rather, what happens is that various persons come together in campaigns and direct actions. They form a circle of friends supporting the same kind of lifestyle which others may think to be "simple," but which they themselves see as rich and many-sided. They agree on a vast array of political issues, although they may otherwise support different political parties. As in all social movements, slogans and rhetoric are indispensable for in-group coherence. They react together against the same threats in a predominantly nonviolent way. Perhaps the most influential participants are artists and writers who do not articulate their insights in terms of professional philosophy, expressing themselves rather in art or poetry. For these reasons, I use the term "movement" rather than "philosophy." But it is essential that fundamental attitudes and beliefs are involved as part of the motivation for action.

## 4. DEEP VERSUS SHALLOW ECOLOGY

A number of key terms and slogans from the environmental debate will clarify the contrast between the shallow and the deep ecology movements.[7]

### A. POLLUTION

Shallow Approach: Technology seeks to purify the air and water and to spread pollution more evenly. Laws limit permissible pollution. Polluting industries are preferably exported to developing countries.

Deep Approach: Pollution is evaluated from a biospheric point of view, not focusing exclusively on its effects on human health, but rather on life as a whole, including the life conditions of every species and system. The shallow reaction to acid rain, for example, is to tend to avoid action by demanding more research, and the attempt to find species of trees which will tolerate high acidity, etc. The deep approach concentrates on what is going on in the total ecosystem and calls for a high priority fight against the economic conditions and the technology responsible for producing the acid rain. The long-range concerns are one hundred years, at least.

The priority is to fight the deep causes of pollution, not merely the superficial, short-range effects. The Third and Fourth World countries cannot afford to pay the total costs of the war against pollution in their regions; consequently they require the assistance of the First and Second World countries. Exporting pollution is not only a crime against humanity, it is a crime against life in general.

## B. Resources

Shallow Approach: The emphasis is upon resources for humans, especially for the present generation in affluent societies. In this view, the resources of the earth belong to those who have the technology to exploit them. There is confidence that resources will not be depleted because, as they get rarer, a high market price will conserve them, and substitutes will be found through technological progress. Further, plants, animals, and natural objects are valuable only as resources for humans. If no human use is known, or seems likely ever to be found, it does not matter if they are destroyed.

Deep Approach: The concern here is with resources and habitats for all life-forms for their own sake. No natural object is conceived of solely as a resource. This leads, then, to a critical evaluation of human modes of production and consumption. The question arises: to what extent does an increase in production and consumption foster ultimate human values? To what extent does it satisfy vital needs, locally or globally? How can economic, legal, and educational institutions be changed to counteract destructive increases? How can resource use serve the quality of life rather than the economic standard of living as generally promoted by consumerism? From a deep perspective, there is an emphasis upon an ecosystem approach rather than the consideration merely of isolated life-forms or local situations. There is a long-range maximal perspective of time and place.

## C. Population

Shallow Approach: The threat of (human) "overpopulation" is seen mainly as a problem for developing countries. One condones or even applauds population increases in one's own country for short-sighted economic, military, or other reasons; an increase in the number of humans is considered as valuable in itself or as economically profitable. The issue of an "optimum population" for humans is discussed without reference to the question of an "optimum population" for other life-forms. The destruction of wild habitats caused by increasing human population is accepted as in inevitable evil, and drastic decreases of wildlife forms tend to be accepted insofar as species are not driven to extinction. Further, the social relations of animals are ignored. A long-term substantial reduction of the global human population is not seen to be a desirable goal. In addition, the right is claimed to defend one's borders against "illegal aliens," regardless of what the population pressures are elsewhere.

Deep Approach: It is recognized that excessive pressures on planetary life stem from the human population explosion. The pressure stemming from the industrial societies is a major factor, and population reduction must have the highest priority in those societies.

## D. Cultural Diversity and Appropriate Technology

Shallow Approach: Industrialization of the Western industrial type is held to be the goal of developing countries. The universal adoption of Western technology is held to be compatible with cultural diversity, together with the conservation of the positive elements (from a Western perspective) of present non-industrial societies. There is a low estimate of deep cultural differences in non-industrial societies which deviate significantly from contemporary Western standards.

Deep Approach: Protection of non-industrial cultures from invasion by industrial societies. The goals of the former should not be seen as promoting lifestyles similar to those in the rich countries. Deep cultural diversity is an analogue on the human level to the biological richness and diversity of life-forms. A high priority should be given to cultural anthropology in general education programs in industrial societies.

There should be limits on the impact of Western technology upon present existing non-industrial countries and the Fourth World should be defended against foreign domination. Political and economic policies should favor sub-cultures within industrial societies. Local, soft technologies should allow for a basic cultural assessment of any technical innovations, together with freely expressed criticism of so-called advanced technology when this has the potential to be culturally destructive.

## E. Land and Sea Ethics

Shallow Approach: Landscapes, ecosystems, rivers, and other whole entities of nature are conceptually cut into fragments, thus disregarding larger units and comprehensive gestalts. These fragments are regarded as the properties and resources of individuals, organizations or states. Conservation is argued in terms of "multiple use" and "cost/benefit analysis." The social costs and long-term global ecological costs of resource extraction and use are usually not considered. Wildlife management is conceived of as conserving nature for "future generations of humans." Soil erosion or the deterioration of ground water quality, for example, is noted as a human loss, but a strong belief in future technological progress makes deep changes seem unnecessary.

Deep Approach: The earth does not belong to humans. For example, the Norwegian landscapes, rivers, flora and fauna, and the neighboring sea are not the property of Norwegians. Similarly, the oil under the North Sea or anywhere else does not belong to any state or to humanity. And the "free nature" surrounding a local community does not belong to the local community.

Humans only inhabit the lands, using resources to satisfy vital needs. And if their non-vital needs come in conflict with the vital needs of nonhumans, then humans should defer to the latter. The ecological destruction now going on will not be cured by a technological fix. Current arrogant notions in industrial (and other) societies must be resisted.

## F. EDUCATION AND THE SCIENTIFIC ENTERPRISE

Shallow Approach: The degradation of the environment and resource depletion requires the training of more and more "experts" who can provide advice concerning how to continue combining economic growth with maintaining a healthy environment. We are likely to need an increasingly more dominating and manipulative technology to "manage the planet" when global economic growth makes further environmental degradation inevitable. The scientific enterprise must continue giving priority to the "hard sciences" (physics and chemistry). High educational standards with intense competition in the relevant "tough" areas of learning will be required.

Deep Approach: If sane ecological policies are adopted, then education should concentrate on an increased sensitivity to non-consumptive goods, and on such consumables where there is enough for all. Education should therefore counteract the excessive emphasis upon things with a price tag. There should be a shift in concentration from the "hard" to the "soft" sciences which stress the importance of the local and global cultures. The educational objective of the World Conservation Strategy ("building support for conservation") should be given a high priority, but within the deeper framework of respect for the biosphere.

In the future, there will be no shallow environmental movement if deep policies are increasingly adopted by governments, and thus no need for a special deep ecological social movement.

## 5. BUT WHY A "DEEP" ECOLOGY?

The decisive difference between a shallow and a deep ecology, in practice, concerns the willingness to question, and an appreciation of the importance of questioning, every economic and political policy in public. This questioning is both "deep" and public. It asks "why" insistently and consistently, taking nothing for granted!

Deep ecology can readily admit to the practical effectiveness of homocentric arguments:

> It is essential for conservation to be seen as central to human interests and aspirations. At the same time, people—from heads of state to the members of rural communities—will most readily be brought to demand conservation if they themselves recognize the contribution of conservation to the achievement of their needs as perceived by them, and the solution of their problems, as perceived by them.[8]

There are several dangers in arguing solely from the point of view of narrow human interests. Some policies based upon successful homocentric arguments turn out to violate or unduly compromise the objectives of deeper argumentation. Further, homocentric arguments tend to weaken the motivation to fight for necessary social change, together with the willingness to serve a great cause. In addition, the complicated arguments in human-centered conservation documents such as the World Conservation Strategy go beyond the time and ability of many people to assimilate and understand. They also tend to provoke interminable technical disagreements among experts. Special interest groups with narrow short-term exploitive objectives, which run counter to saner ecological policies, often exploit these disagreements and thereby stall the debate and steps toward effective action.

When arguing from deep ecological premises, most of the complicated proposed technological fixes need not be discussed at all. The relative merits of alternative technological proposals are pointless if our vital needs have already been met. A focus on vital issues activates mental energy and strengthens motivation. On the other hand, the shallow environmental approach, by focusing almost exclusively on the technical aspects of environmental problems, tends to make the public more passive and disinterested in the more crucial non-technical, lifestyle-related, environmental issues.

Writers within the deep ecology movement try to articulate the fundamental presuppositions underlying the dominant economic approach in terms of value priorities, philosophy, and religion. In the shallow movement, questioning and argumentation comes to a halt long before this. The deep ecology movement

is therefore "the ecology movement which questions deeper." A realization of
the deep changes which are required, as outlined in the deep ecology eight
point platform (discussed in #3 above) makes us realize the necessity of "questioning everything."

The terms "egalitarianism," "homocentrism," "anthropocentrism," and
"human chauvinism" are often used to characterize points of view on the
shallow-deep spectrum. But these terms usually function as slogans which are
often open to misinterpretation. They can properly imply that man is in some
respects only a "plain citizen" (Aldo Leopold) of the planet on a par with all
other species, but they are sometimes interpreted as denying that humans have
any "extraordinary" traits, or that, in situations involving vital interests, humans have no overriding obligations towards their own kind. But this would
be a mistake: they have!

In any social movement, rhetoric has an essential function in keeping members fighting together under the same banner. Rhetorical formulations also
serve to provoke interest among outsiders. Of the many excellent slogans, one
might mention "nature knows best," "small is beautiful," and "all things hang
together." But sometimes one may safely say that nature does not always know
best, that small is sometimes dreadful, and that fortunately things hang together sometimes only loosely, or not at all.

Only a minority of deep ecology supporters are academic philosophers, such
as myself. And while deep ecology cannot be a finished philosophical system,
this does not mean that its philosophers should not try to be as clear as possible.
So a discussion of deep ecology as a derivational system may be of value to
clarify the many important premise/conclusion relations.


# 6. DEEP ECOLOGY ILLUSTRATED AS A
# DERIVATIONAL SYSTEM

Underlying the eight tenets or principles presented in section 3, there are even
more basic positions and norms which reside in philosophical systems and in
various world religions. Schematically we may represent the total views logically implied in the deep ecology movement by streams of derivations from
the most fundamental norms and descriptive assumptions (level 1) to the particular decisions in actual life situations (level 4).

The pyramidal model has some features in common with hypothetico-
deductive systems. The main difference, however, is that some sentences at
the top (= deepest) level are normative, and preferably are expressed by imperatives. This makes it possible to arrive at imperatives at the lowest derivational level: the crucial level in terms of decisions. Thus, there are "oughts" in

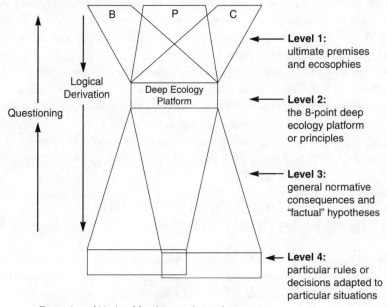

Logical
Derivation

Questioning

**B**  **P**  **C**

Deep Ecology
Platform

**Level 1:**
ultimate premises
and ecosophies

**Level 2:**
the 8-point deep
ecology platform
or principles

**Level 3:**
general normative
consequences and
"factual" hypotheses

**Level 4:**
particular rules or
decisions adapted to
particular situations

Examples of kinds of fundamental premises:
B = Buddhist
C = Christian
P = Philosophical (e.g., Spinozist or Whiteheadian)

our premises as well as in our conclusions. We never move from an "is" to an "ought," or vice versa. From a logical standpoint, this is decisive!

The above premise/conclusion structure (or diagram) of a total view must not be taken too seriously. It is not meant in any restrictive way to characterize creative thinking within the deep ecology movement. Creative thinking moves freely in any direction. But many of us with a professional background in science and analytical philosophy find such a diagram helpful.

As we dig deeper into the premises of our thinking, we eventually stop. Those premises we stop at are our ultimates. When we philosophize, we all stop at different places. But we all use premises which, for us, are ultimate. They belong to level 1 in the diagram. Some will use a sentence like "Every life form has intrinsic value" as an ultimate premise, and therefore place it at level 1. Others try, as I do, to conceive of it as a conclusion based on a set of premises. For these people, this sentence does not belong to level 1. There will be different ecosophies corresponding to such differences.

Obviously, point 6 of the 8 point deep ecology tenets (see section 3) cannot belong to level 1 of the diagram. The statement "there must be new policies affecting basic economic structures" needs to be justified. If no logical justification is forthcoming, why not just assert instead that ecologically destructive "business as usual" economic policies should continue? In the diagram I have had ecosophies as ultimate premises in mind at level 1. None of the 8 points of the deep ecology principles belong at the ultimate level; they are derived as conclusions from premises at level 1.

Different supporters of the deep ecology movement may have different ultimates (level 1), but will nevertheless agree about level 2 (the 8 points). Level 4 will comprise concrete decisions in concrete situations which appear as conclusions from deliberations involving premises at levels 1 to 3. An important point: supporters of the deep ecology movement act from deep premises. They are motivated, in part, from a philosophical or religious position.

## 7. MULTIPLE ROOTS OF THE DEEP ECOLOGY PLATFORM

The deep ecology movement seriously questions the presuppositions of shallow argumentation. Even what counts as a rational decision is challenged, because what is "rational" is always defined in relation to specific aims and goals. If a decision is rational in relation to the lower level aims and goals of our pyramid, but not in relation to the highest level, then this decision should not be judged to be rational. This is an important point! If an environmentally oriented policy decision is not linked to intrinsic values or ultimates, then its rationality has yet to be determined. The deep ecology movement connects rationality with a set of philosophical or religious foundations. But one cannot expect the ultimate premises to constitute rational conclusions. There are no "deeper" premises available.

Deep ecological questioning thus reveals the fundamental normative orientations of differing positions. Shallow argumentation stops before reaching fundamentals, or it jumps from the ultimate to the particular; that is, from level 1 to level 4.

But it is not only normative claims that are at issue. Most (perhaps all) norms presuppose ideas about how the world functions. Typically the vast majority of assertions needed in normative systems are descriptive (or factual). This holds at all the levels.

As mentioned before, it does not follow that supporters of deep ecology must have identical beliefs about ultimate issues. They do have common attitudes about intrinsic values in nature, but these can, in turn (at a still deeper level), be derived from different, mutually incompatible sets of ultimate beliefs.

Thus, while a specific decision may be judged as rational from within the derivational system (if there is such) of shallow ecology, it might be judged as irrational from within the derivational system of deep ecology. Again, it should be emphasized that what is rational from within the deep ecology derivational pyramid does not require unanimity in ontology and fundamental ethics. Deep ecology as a conviction, with its subsequently derived practical recommendations, can follow from a number of more comprehensive world views, from differing ecosophies.

Those engaged in the deep ecology movement have so far revealed their philosophical or religious homes to be mainly in Christianity, Buddhism, Taoism, Baha'i, or in various philosophies. The top level of the derivational pyramid can, in such cases, be made up of normative and descriptive principles which belong to these religions and philosophies.

Since the late '70s, numerous Christians in Europe and America, including some theologians, have actively taken part in the deep ecology movement. Their interpretations of the Bible, and their theological positions in general, have been reformed from what was, until recently, a crude dominating anthropocentric emphasis.

There is an intimate relationship between some forms of Buddhism and the deep ecology movement. The history of Buddhist thought and practice, especially the principles of non-violence, non-injury, and reverence for life, sometimes makes it easier for Buddhists to understand and appreciate deep ecology than it is for Christians, despite a (sometimes overlooked) blessedness which Jesus recommended in peace-making. I mention Taoism chiefly because there is some basis for calling John Muir a Taoist, for instance, and Baha'i because of Lawrence Arturo.

Ecosophies are not religions in the classical sense. They are better characterized as *general* philosophies, in the sense of total views, inspired in part by the science of ecology. At level 1, a traditional religion may enter the derivational pyramid through a set of normative and descriptive assumptions which would be characteristic of contemporary interpretations (hermeneutical efforts) of that religion.

Supporters of the deep ecology movement act in contemporary conflicts on the basis of their fundamental beliefs and attitudes. This gives them a particular strength and a joyful expectation or hope for a greener future. But, naturally, few of them are actively engaged in a systematic verbal articulation of where they stand.

# 8. ECOSOPHY T AS AN EXAMPLE OF A DEEP ECOLOGICAL DERIVATIONAL SYSTEM

I call the ecosophy I feel at home with "Ecosophy T." My main purpose in announcing that I feel at home with Ecosophy T is didactic and dialectic. I hope to get others to announce their philosophy. If they say they have none, I maintain that they have, but perhaps don't know their own views, or are too modest or inhibited to proclaim what they believe. Following Socrates, I want to provoke questioning until others know where they stand on basic matters of life and death. This is done using ecological issues, and also by using Ecosophy T as a foil. But Socrates pretended in debate that he knew nothing. My posture seems to be the opposite. I may seem to know everything and to derive it magically from a small set of hypotheses about the world. But both interpretations are misleading! Socrates did not consistently claim to know nothing, nor do I in my Ecosophy T pretend to have comprehensive knowledge. Socrates claimed to know, for instance, about the fallibility of human claims to have knowledge.

Ecosophy T has only one ultimate norm: "Self-realization!" I do not use this expression in any narrow, individualistic sense. I want to give it an expanded meaning based on the distinction between a large comprehensive Self and narrow egoistic self as conceived of in certain Eastern traditions of *atman*.[9] This large comprehensive Self (with a capital "S") embraces all the life forms on the planet (and elsewhere?) together with their individual selves (jivas). If I were to express this ultimate norm in a few words, I would say: "Maximize (long-range, universal) Self-realization!" Another more colloquial way to express this ultimate norm would be to say "Live and let live!" (referring to all of the life forms and natural processes on the planet). If I had to give up the term fearing its inevitable misunderstanding, I would use the term "universal symbiosis." "Maximize Self-realization!" could, of course, be misinterpreted in the direction of colossal ego trips. But "Maximize symbiosis!" could be misinterpreted in the opposite direction of eliminating individuality in favor of collectivity.

Viewed systematically, not individually, maximum Self-realization implies maximizing the manifestations of all life. So next I derive the second term, "Maximize (long-range, universal) diversity!" A corollary is that the higher the levels of Self-realization attained by any person, the more any further increase depends upon the Self-realization of others. Increased self-identity involves increased identification with others. "Altruism" is a natural consequence of this identification.

This leads to a hypothesis concerning an inescapable increase of identification with other beings when one's own self-realization increases. As a result, we increasingly see ourselves in other beings, and others see themselves in us. In this way, the self is extended and deepened as a natural process of the realization of its potentialities in others.

By universalizing the above, we can derive the norm, "Self-realization for

## Ecosophy T

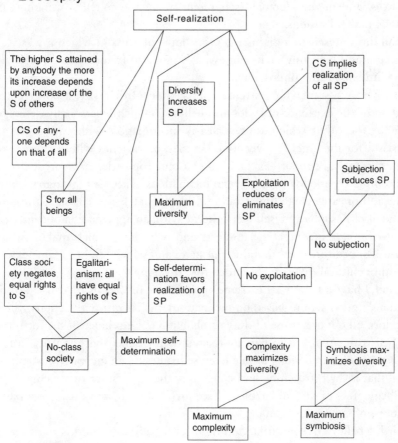

S = Self-realization
C = Complete
P = Potential
SP = Self-realization potentials

every being!" From the norm, "Maximize diversity!" and a hypothesis that maximum diversity implies a maximum of symbiosis, we can derive the norm "Maximize symbiosis!" Further, we work for life conditions such that there is a minimum of coercion in the lives of others. And so on![10] The eight points of the deep ecology platform are derived in a fairly simple way.

A philosophy as a world view inevitably has implications for practical situations. Like other ecosophies, Ecosophy T therefore moves on, without apologies, to the concrete questions of lifestyles. These will obviously show great variation because of differences in hypotheses about the world in which each of us lives, and in the "factual" statements about the concrete situations in which we make decisions.

I shall limit myself to a discussion of a couple of areas in which my "style" of thinking and behaving seem somewhat strange to friends and others who know a little about my philosophy.

First, I have a somewhat extreme appreciation of diversity; a positive appreciation of the existence of styles and behavior which I personally detest or find nonsensical (but which are not clearly incompatible with symbiosis); an enthusiasm for the "mere" diversity of species, or varieties within a genus of plants or animals; I support, as the head of a philosophy department, doctrinal theses completely at odds with my own inclinations, with the requirement only that the authors are able to understand fairly adequately some basic features of the kind of philosophy I myself feel at home with; an appreciation of combinations of *seemingly* incompatible interests and behaviors, which makes for an increase of subcultures within industrial states and which might to some extent help future cultural diversity. So much for "diversity!"

Second, I have a somewhat extreme appreciation of what Kant calls "beautiful actions" (good actions based on inclination), in contrast with actions which are performed out of a sense of duty or obligation. The choice of the formulation "Self-realization!" is in part motivated by the belief that maturity in humans can be measured along a scale from selfishness to an increased realization of Self, that is, by broadening and deepening the self, rather than being measured by degrees of dutiful altruism. I see joyful sharing and caring as a natural process of growth in humans.

Third, I believe that multifaceted high-level Self-realization is more easily reached through a lifestyle which is "simple in means but rich in ends" rather than through the material standard of living of the average citizens of industrial states.

The simple formulations of the deep ecology platform and Ecosophy T are not meant primarily to be used among philosophers, but also in dialogues with the "experts." When I wrote to the "experts" and environmental professionals personally, asking whether they accept the eight points of the platform, many answered positively in relation to most or all of the points. And this includes top people in the ministries of oil and energy! Nearly all were willing to let their written answers be widely published. It is an open question, however, as to what extent they will try to influence their colleagues who use only shallow argumentation. But the main conclusion to be drawn is moderately encouraging: there are views of the human/nature relationship, widely accepted among established experts responsible for environmental decisions, which require a pervasive, substantial change of present policies in favor of our "living" planet, and these views are held not only on the basis of shortsighted human interests.

# NOTES

1. For more about interspecific community relationships, see Arne Naess, "Self-realization in Mixed Communities of Humans, Bears, Sheep, and Wolves," *Inquiry* 22 (1979): 321–41; Naess and Ivar Mysterud, "Philosophy of Wolf Policies I: General Principles and Preliminary Exploration of Selected Norms," *Conservation Biology* 1, 1 (1987): 22–34.

2. These problems are discussed further in Naess's keynote address to the second international Conference on Conservation Biology held at the University of Michigan in May 1985; published as "Intrinsic Value: Will the Defenders of Nature Please Rise?" *Conservation Biology* (1986): 504–15.

3. IUCN, *World Conservation Strategy: Living Resource Conservation for Sustainable Development* (Gland, Switzerland, 1980) section 13 ("Building Support for Conservation").

4. The deep ecology principles (or platform) were agreed upon during a camping trip in Death Valley, California (April, 1984) and first published in George Sessions (ed.), *Ecophilosophy VI* newsletter (May, 1984). They have subsequently appeared in a number of publications.

5. Tom Regan, "The Nature and Possibility of an Environmental Ethics," *Environmental Ethics* 3 (1981): 19–34, citation on p. 30.

6. I proposed the name "Deep, Long-Range Ecology Movement" in a lecture at the Third World Future Research conference in Bucharest in September 1972. A summary of that lecture ("The Shallow and the Deep, Long-Range Ecology Movement") was published in *Inquiry* 16 (1973): 95–100. Within the deep ecology movement it is fairly common to use the term "deep ecologist," whereas "shallow ecologist," I am glad to say, is rather uncommon. Both terms may be considered arrogant and slightly misleading. I prefer to use the awkward, but more egalitarian expression "supporter of the deep (or shallow) ecology movement," avoiding personification. Also, it is common to call deep ecology consistently anti-anthropocentric. This has led to misconceptions: see my "A Defense of the Deep Ecology Movement," *Environmental Ethics* 5 (1983).

7. The "shallow/deep" dichotomy is rough. Richard Sylvan has proposed a much more subtle classification; see his "A Critique of Deep Ecology," *Discussion Papers in Environmental Philosophy,* RSSS, Australian National University, No. 12 (1985).

8. *World Conservation Strategy,* section 13 (concluding paragraph).

9. The term *atman* is not taken in its absolutistic senses (not as a permanent indestructible "soul"). This makes it consistent with those Buddhist denials (the *avatman doctrine*) that the *atman* is to be taken in absolutist senses. Within the Christian tradition some thelogians distinguish "ego" and "true self" in ways simi-

lar to these distinctions in Eastern religions. See the ecophilosophical interpretation of the gospel of Luke in Stephen Verney's *Onto the New Age* (Glasgow: Collins, 1976) pp. 33–41.

10. Many authors take some steps toward derivational structures, offering mild systematizations. The chapter "Environmental Ethics and Hope" (in G. Tyler Miller, *Living in the Environment,* 3rd ed. [Belmont: Wadsworth, 1983]) is a valuable start, but the derivational relations are unclear. The logic and semantics of simple models of normative systems are briefly discussed in my "Notes on the Methodology of Normative Systems," *Methodology and Science* 10 (1977): 64–79. For a defense of the thesis that as soon as people assert anything at all, they assume a total view, implicitly involving an ontology, methodology, epistemology, and ethics, see my "Reflections about Total Views," *Philosophy and Phenomenological Research* 25 (1964–65): 16–29. The best and wittiest warning against taking systematizations too seriously is to be found in Søren Kierkegaard, *Concluding Unscientific Postscript.*

For criticism and defense of my fundamental norm ("Self-realization"), together with my answer, see *In Sceptical Wonder: Essays in Honor of Arne Naess* (Oslo: University Press, 1982). My main exposition of Ecosophy T was originally offered in the Norwegian work, *Økologi, samfunn og livsstil* (Oslo: University Press, 5th ed., 1976). Even there, the exposition is sketchy. (Editor's note: Naess's Norwegian book has been revised and reissued as Arne Naess (translated and edited by David Rothenberg), *Ecology, Community and Lifestyle* [Cambridge: Cambridge University Press, 1989].)

# 10 | THE HEART OF DEEP ECOLOGY

## Andrew McLaughlin

IN THE LAST FEW hundred years, industrial society has encircled the earth and, in requiring massive disruptions of ecological processes for its ordinary functioning, threatens all forms of life on this planet. Both capitalist and social- ist variants of expansionary industrialism routinely require the destruction of species and ecosystems. Industrialism now threatens to disrupt atmospheric conditions fundamental to the whole biosphere. If ecological problems have roots in industrialism, then a perspective which takes industrialism itself as part of the problem is needed.[1]

The transformation of industrialism will, I believe, involve a multifaceted struggle over several generations. The changes required are of the magnitude of the agricultural and industrial revolutions.

Deep Ecology is one perspective which beckons us in the right direction. In just two decades, Deep Ecology as a theory—as distinct from Deep Ecology as a social movement—has become a benchmark in defining varieties of envi- ronmental philosophies.[2] In the course of its relatively short history, there has been considerable controversy surrounding Deep Ecology, but most of it has been misdirected. One reason for this has been the failure of critics to notice that the "logic" of Deep Ecology differs fundamentally in form from many other philosophical positions.

The heart of Deep Ecology is its platform, which consists of a number of inter-related factual and normative claims about humans and their relations with the rest of nature. The platform was intended as a description of a Deep Ecology social movement and as a basis for a larger unity among all those who accept the importance of nonanthropocentrism and understand that this en- tails *radical* social change.

The platform, articulated by Arne Naess and George Sessions while they

---

This essay (1993) is previously unpublished. Published with permission.

were camping in Death Valley in 1984, is a nontechnical statement of principles around which, it is hoped, people with differing *ultimate* understandings of themselves, society, and nonhuman nature, could unite. Thus, from the start, the platform was meant to be a terrain of commonality which allowed, recognized, and even encouraged differences in more logically ultimate philosophies.

## THE DEEP ECOLOGY PLATFORM

The platform itself consists of eight points.

1. *The well-being and flourishing of human and nonhuman Life on Earth have value in themselves (synonyms: intrinsic value, inherent value). These values are independent of the usefulness of the nonhuman world for human purposes.*

Essentially, this is a rejection of anthropocentrism. It is an assertion that human *and* nonhuman life should flourish. "Life," in this context, is understood broadly to include, for example, rivers, landscapes, and ecosystems. Accepting the idea that humans are not the *only* valuable part of nature is the watershed perception from which Deep Ecology flows.

This plank should not be taken as implying a commitment to any philosophically precise theory about intrinsic or inherent value. When Deep Ecologists use the language of moral discourse they are not usually trying to construct a formal ethical theory. If one wishes to speak outside the academy, one must use language which communicates in popular contexts. That language right now uses concepts of intrinsic or inherent value and rights. To take Devall and Sessions literally, when they ascribe an "equal right" to all things and claim they are "equal in intrinsic worth," is interpreting them out of context.[3] In the passage in which those phrases appear, they are writing with the intent of having practical effect within the environmental movement. They are not writing with philosophical precision, and for them to do so would counter their main purpose.[4]

Perhaps the search for some sort of value *in* nonhuman nature, be it inherent, intrinsic, or some other sort of nonanthropocentric value seems necessary because we cannot now fully imagine an adequate environmental ethic. Often an ethic is supposed to constrain people from doing what they otherwise would do. As both Warwick Fox and Val Plumwood point out, many ethical theorists implicitly assume that we would care about nonhuman nature "for itself" *only* if it has intrinsic value.[5] This assumption motivates the search for the elusive intrinsic value, but it may be overly constraining in the search for an environmental ethic. Simply put, we *can* care for the rest of nature for reasons which have nothing to do with whether or not it has intrinsic, inherent, or whatever sort of value. Such a caring can spring, for example, from a felt sense of relatedness to the rest of nature or a love of existence.

2. *Richness and diversity of life forms contribute to the realization of these values and are also values in themselves.*

This, along with the first point, is intended to counter the often-held image of evolution as resulting in "higher" forms of life. It involves a re-visioning of life and evolution, changing from understanding evolution as "progress" from "lower" to "higher" forms to understanding evolution as a magnificent expression of a multitude of forms of life. Cherishing diversity appreciates differences and rejects any single standard of excellence.

Valuing diversity means freeing large areas of the earth from domination by industrial economy and culture. Expand wilderness! But in interpreting this injunction, it should be remembered that "wilderness" is an outsider's construct. Most of what appears to industrial peoples as wilderness has been steadily occupied or traversed by indigenous peoples for eons. Thus, preserving such areas from industrial regimes is not only protecting wilderness, but is, in some cases, also preserving indigenous peoples. The struggle for wilderness is both for biological and human diversity.

3. *Humans have no right to reduce this richness and diversity except to satisfy vital needs.*

The key point in this claim is the implied distinction between "vital" and other needs. This distinction is denied by the consumerism inherent in industrialism. To lose sight of it is to become trapped within an endlessly repeating cycle of deprivation and temporary satiation. Making the distinction opens to the possibility of more enduring forms of happiness and joy. Of course, the distinction cannot be drawn precisely, since what is a vital need in one context may be a trivial want in another. There is a real difference between an Eskimo's wearing the skin of a seal and one worn for social status in an affluent society.

4. *The flourishing of human life and cultures is compatible with a substantial decrease in human population. The flourishing of nonhuman life requires such a decrease.*

Once recognition is given to other forms of life, then it is clear that we humans are too many already. We have already jostled many species out of existence and the near future promises an expansion of such extinctions. Recent projections by the United Nations indicate that current trends in population growth will involve converting about 80 percent of current nature reserves to human use.[6] This would drastically accelerate the already alarming trends towards the extinction of myriad species of life.[7]

The continuing increase in human numbers also condemns many humans to a life of suffering. Parents within industrial societies easily recognize that many children means fewer life prospects for each and limit themselves to fewer children, hoping to give them each a better life. We should collectively recognize that an increase in human numbers is not in the best interest of humans, much less the rest of life.

It is to the credit of the Deep Ecology movement that it clearly gives priority to human population as a problem and calls for a gradual decrease.[8] This does not imply misanthropy or cruelty to presently existing humans. In fact, it implies the reverse for there is considerable evidence indicating that the best way of moderating and then reversing the growth of human population is to find ways of providing a decent life for all.[9]

There is, of course, much more that might be said about the problem of overpopulation and the ways the human population might decline. In this regard, alliances between Deep Ecologists and Ecofeminists may be very helpful. The problem of coerced motherhood exists in all societies to some degree, but it is most acute in poorer countries where population growth is most rapid. Current evidence indicates that there has been a global increase in coerced pregnancy and motherhood and this trend must be reversed for there to be much hope in slowing population growth.[10] The worldwide struggle for the rights of women to choose the number of children they will bear will help in at least slowing the growth of human populations. Such a right includes the right to choose sexual partners and manage fertility in safe ways, which includes the right to access to safe abortions. Ecofeminists have much to contribute both theoretically and practically to success in this struggle.

5. *Present human interference with the nonhuman world is excessive, and the situation is rapidly worsening.*

This directs attention to current trends and claims that current levels of "interference" with the rest of nature is excessive. There are at least two sorts of such interference which need to be addressed. One sort is the destruction of existing areas of wilderness, such as old growth forests. This is irreparable within any moderate time scale and is wrong. In fact, the guiding principle should probably be the continuation of biological history, creating large enough wilderness areas to allow for the continued speciation of plants and animals. This does not involve dispossessing indigenous peoples who have found ways of living within those ecosystems without destroying them.

Another sort of interference is based on particular forms of technology. Many technologies disrupt natural cycles far more than is necessary. For example, agricultural practices involving large scale monocropping create expanding needs for fertilizer and pesticides. Multicropping, integrated pest management, and a variety of organic farming techniques interfere less with natural cycles and can enhance the fertility of soils.

6. *Policies must therefore be changed. These policies affect basic economic, technological, and ideological structures. The resulting state of affairs will be deeply different from the present.*

The scope of the changes needed is great. However, significant work is being done in trying to create adequate models for change. Although the concept remains obscure and controversial, "sustainability" is becoming a slogan in thinking about how economies should be restructured, even among those who remain within an anthropocentric perspective. We need to be clear about precisely "what" is to be sustained. For Deep Ecology, at least, we need to sustain the very conditions for the diversity of the myriad forms of life, including the cultural diversity of human life.

7. *The ideological change is mainly that of appreciating life quality (dwelling in situations of inherent value) rather than adhering to an increasingly higher standard of living. There will be a profound awareness of the difference between big and great.*

This point is especially important for industrial peoples enmeshed within an ultimately unsatisfying consumerism.[11] With a focus on quality, people can see that existing patterns of labor and consumption are not satisfying, but rather involve chronic dissatisfaction. Moving towards an appreciation of the *quality* of life, instead of quantities of things, leads to an *increase* in happiness, not a decrease. This is fundamental, since people are more apt to change when they experience change as improvement, rather than a grudging submission to necessity. As long as environmentalism seems to require only denial and sacrifice, its political effectiveness will be lessened. Deep Ecology seeks a more satisfactory way of living, an increase in vitality and joy.

8. *Those who subscribe to the foregoing points have an obligation directly or indirectly to try to implement the necessary changes.*

Although this is clear in claiming that we must begin to act now, it is vague in not indicating *particular* priorities. At this point in history, priorities cannot be made more specific. No one now knows *exactly* what positive changes are necessary. The problems with economic growth and the emptiness of consumerism are clear enough, but they do not show just what needs to be done now. People who accept the Deep Ecology platform may disagree about what is most urgent now, and there are many ways to attempt the needed changes. In the light of the value of diversity, such differences should be respected and not become occasions for sectarian squabble.

## THE LOGIC OF DEEP ECOLOGY

The eight-point platform is not "ultimate" or "basic" in a logical sense. That is, it is not put forward as requiring or allowing no further justification.

Rather, it is basic in being the most general view that supporters of Deep Ecology hold in common. There is no expectation nor need for wide agreement on logially more ultimate premises which might be used to render a deductive justification of the platform. In fact, disagreement on such ultimate premises is to be expected.

From a *historical* perspective, the platform as articulated by Naess and Sessions is unique to Deep Ecology. However, were it to become grounds for widespread unity within a movement directed toward transforming industrial society and creating a nonanthropocentric society, it might no longer be called a specifically "Deep Ecology" position. The platform is part of a program for what Robyn Eckersley calls an "ecocentric" Green political movement, a movement which will encompass many who might not identify themselves as "Deep Ecologists."[12] Thus, while it is now a specifically "Deep Ecology" platform, should it achieve its intended end, it might no longer be identified *as* a "Deep Ecology" platform. If it is successful in its intent, it might dissolve as a distinct position.

If one seeks a *justification* for the Deep Ecology platform, then discussion might proceed to more ultimate premises characteristically espoused by some deep ecologists. But other justifications might depend on "ultimate premises" of some other ecocentric perspective, such as ecofeminism or some variant of social ecology. The central point is that there is not only one possible justification for the platform.

The *platform* is the heart of Deep Ecology, and it is this platform, not the various justifications of it, which should be the focus of argument about the value of Deep Ecology.[13]

The development of a radical ecology movement must start its collective discussion somewhere, and the Deep Ecology platform is a good beginning. People may come to adopt this platform from quite diverse directions and for differing reasons. Those who start from social concerns and come to believe that an ecological perspective must be taken very seriously may come to the Deep Ecology position through an understanding of the ecological inadequacy of more traditional social ideologies. On the other hand, those who start with a concern about nonhuman nature are likely to arrive at the Deep Ecology platform more directly by reflecting on what follows from a rejection of anthropocentrism and a recognition of the worth of the flourishing of *all* of nature.

Although some Deep Ecologists have emphasized the process of expanding one's sense of self towards a larger identification with all of nature to arrive at a denial of anthropocentrism, this is surely not the only path. The Ecofeminist Marti Kheel argues persuasively that the differences in the ways men and women now typically form their identities makes *any* gender neutral concept of the self suspect. This means that different genders now may find different paths toward the Deep Ecology platform. Ecofeminism, in speaking to this historically conditioned difference between men and women, offers other routes to a justification of the platform. But, as Kheel argues, this unique strength of Ecofeminism does not entail any fundamental opposition between Ecofeminism and Deep Ecology.[14]

Even the *kinds* of reasons which might persuade a person to adopt a version of the platform may range from rational to nonrational to irrational. For example, acceptance might be based on philosophical reflection, religious conviction, personal experience, intuitions, mystical experience, aesthetic perception, or some other basis. *Allowing for a variety of paths to the same position is precisely the intent of the Deep Ecology platform.* It is not intended to be, nor is it, a systematic philosophical position; it proposes a common ground for defining an ecocentric movement for radical social change. Even the particular formulation of the platform is not final or the only acceptable expression.[15] The point of these principles is to define the Deep Ecology movement, create clarity within the movement, and make clear where real disagreement might exist.[16]

When the structure of Deep Ecology is understood this way, much of the controversy surrounding Deep Ecology can be seen as irrelevant. While argument directed against one, some, or all of the eight points is of great importance, criticism directed to one of the underlying philosophical positions used to justify the Deep Ecology platform is far less relevant. Clearly, one could reject a particular philosophical or religious justification of the platform, yet still believe that the platform is correct at this point in history. I think it has been a failure to appreciate this aspect of the structure of the Deep Ecology position which has led to much heated but fruitless controversy. Focusing on the platform may help us find the basis for unity among those who may disagree on more philosophically ultimate issues.

This approach to Deep Ecology does not make clear what is philosophically distinctive in the writings of deep ecologists. Although this question may be of great interest to theorists of Deep Ecology, it may be of less importance to movement activists. The platform is a proposal for us now, in this particular historical context. When that context changes, the platform may change. Perhaps Deep Ecology would even disappear as a distinctive position.

Without understanding the platform as the heart of Deep Ecology, attempts to justify the platform tend to create needless schisms. For example, the most exhaustive attempt to define what is distinctive about Deep Ecology is Warwick Fox's *Toward a Transpersonal Ecology.* He focuses on the nature of the self and explains Deep Ecology as involving an identification of self with all that is. But his specification of Deep Ecology, *unless* it is understood as one among many alternative justifications for the platform, creates unneeded friction. It leaves out others who accept the platform, but do not agree with Fox's notion of identification. Richard Sylvan and Jim Cheney, for example, both accept the platform, but are critics of Fox's Transpersonal Ecology.[17] Which is more important—finding differences or realizing unity?

If Deep Ecology is understood primarily as the attempt to spark profound social change, then the question of who is and who isn't a Deep Ecologist can be settled by referring to the platform. But disputes over possible justifications are of pressing importance only if they lead to differences over the platform.

The platform, then, is a proposal for a set of general agreements among radical ecocentrists, a common ground for those who value *all* nature. Deep ecologists have done a valuable service in bringing such a platform to the fore. Our urgent task is social change.

# NOTES

1. I have argued at length that industrialism *is* the core problem which we must confront. See Andrew McLaughlin, *Regarding Nature: Industrialism and Deep Ecology* (Albany: SUNY Press, 1993).

2. See Warwick Fox, *Toward a Transpersonal Ecology: Developing New Foundations for Environmentalism* (Boston: Shambhala Publications, 1990), 44–45 and the works referenced there. Deep Ecology as a social *movement* has origins which predate Naess's formulation of deep ecology as a *theory*.

3. Bill Devall and George Sessions, *Deep Ecology: Living as if Nature Mattered* (Salt Lake City: Gibbs Smith, 1985), 67.

4. See Warwick Fox's "Approaching Deep Ecology: A Response to Richard Sylvan's Critique of Deep Ecology," *Environmental Studies Occasional Paper 20* (Hobart: University of Tasmania, 1986), 37ff, and Fox's *Toward a Transpersonal Ecology* for extended discussions as to why it is an error to interpret Deep Ecology as an alternative axiology. For further discussion, see note 25 of chap. 9 in *Regarding Nature*.

5. Fox, "Approaching Deep Ecology," p. 79. Val Plumwood, "Nature, Self, and Gender: Feminism, Environmental Philosophy, and the Critique of Rationalism," *Hypatia* 6 (1991): 10. See also Anthony Weston, "Beyond Intrinsic Value: Pragmatism in Environmental Ethics," *Environmental Ethics* 7, no. 4 (Winter, 1985): 321–339.

6. Nafis Sadik, *The State of World Population: 1992* (New York: United Nations Population Fund, 1992), ii.

7. See Edward O. Wilson, *The Diversity of Life* (Cambridge: Harvard University Press, 1992), for a sobering discussion of this problem.

8. "Population reduction towards decent levels might incidentally require a thousand years." Arne Naess, *Ecology, Community and Lifestyle: Outline of an Ecosophy,*

translated by David Rothenberg (New York: Cambridge University Press, 1989), 127.

9. See Sadik, *The State of World Population: 1992.*

10. See Jodi L. Jacobson, "Coerced Motherhood Increasing," in Lester R. Brown et al., *Vital Signs: 1992* (New York: Norton & Co., 1992), 114–115.

11. See chap. 4 of my *Regarding Nature* for a fuller discussion of consumerism.

12. See Robyn Eckersley, *Environmentalism and Political Theory: Toward an Ecocentric Approach* (Albany: SUNY Press, 1992), especially chap. 3.

13. The centrality of the platform has been claimed by a number of Deep Ecology writers. See, for example, Arne Naess, "The Deep Ecological Movement," *Philosophical Inquiry* 8, nos. 1–2 (1986); 23–26 [This article is reprinted in this anthology. See pp. 64–85.—Editor's note]; Arne Naess, *Ecology, Community, and Lifestyle,* 27–32; Bill Devall, *Simple in Means, Rich in Ends: Practicing Deep Ecology* (Salt Lake City: Gibbs Smith, 1988) 12–18.

14. Marti Kheel, "Ecofeminism and Deep Ecology: Reflections on Identity and Difference," *The Trumpeter* 8, no. 2 (Spring 1991).

15. Other sketches are possible, even encouraged. Naess regards his own formulation as tentative. (See Naess, *Ecology, Community, and Lifestyle,* 31). He expects that others who identify with the Deep Ecology movement "will work out their own alternative formulations" (*Ecology,* 28). Bill Devall, one founder of Deep Ecology, prefers the concept of "worth" to "value." (See Devall, *Simple in Means,* 14.)

16. Naess, *Ecology,* 32.

17. See Richard Sylvan, "A Critique of (Wild) Western Deep Ecology," unpublished manuscript, 2; Jim Cheney, "The Neo-Stoicism of Radical Environmentalism," *Environmental Ethics* 11, no. 4 (Winter 1989): 295.

PART TWO | HISTORICAL ROOTS
OF DEEP ECOLOGY

# INTRODUCTION

In GRADUATE SCHOOL DURING the 1960s, partly as a result of reading Thomas Kuhn's *The Structure of Scientific Revolutions* (1962), I came to see that the history and philosophy of science cannot fruitfully be separated. I think the same is true of environmental history and ecophilosophy.

In terms of environmental history, there are the various cultural histories of the human/nature relationship, the history of the rise of modern reform environmentalism, the history of the modern rediscovery and development of ecocentrism and the rise of the Deep Ecology movement, together with the academic discipline of environmental history. The official journal of environmental history is the *Environmental History Review* (formerly the *Environmental Review*).

Unfortunately, cultural and ethical relativism, and anthropocentrism, have been an integral part of the social sciences (including the academic disciplines of history, and environmental history) since their inception. Also endemic to the social sciences is a human/nature dualism exemplified in the "second nature" view, which holds that civilization has "transcended" or "evolved out of" Nature and is thus not subject to evolutionary/ecological laws. Modern versions of the "second nature" view, in effect, insulate social and physical scientists, and others who hold it, from the apocalyptic warnings of primarily the biological scientists who have been actively concerned with the rapidly deteriorating ecological state of the world since at least the 1950s. Mainstream economics is a blatant example of this in continuing to support and refine economic growth theories in total disregard of biological limitations. Ecologically concerned economists, such as Herman Daly, have put forth theories of "steady state" economics, but they are widely ignored by mainstream economists.

In 1960, the ecologist Marston Bates (in *The Forest and the Sea*) pointed out that humanities scholars (including mainstream philosophers) as well as social scientists hold the "second nature" view. Many academics in the social sciences and humanities continue to operate out of their specialized compartmentalized niches in "second nature," spinning out theories and interpretations that are dangerous to humanity and the Earth in being totally out of touch with biological realities—a situation that the ecologist David Ehrenfeld refers to as "the arrogance of humanism." The philosopher Roderick French pointed out ("Is Ecological Humanism a Contradiction in Terms?," 1980) that "it is very unsettling . . . to be forced to consider the idea that the formation of human consciousness through training in literature, philosophy, history, religion and related disciplines may in fact inculcate values and behaviors that jeopardize the continuation of life itself" (p. 61). The Canadian naturalist John Livingston claimed (*One Cosmic Instant,* 1973) that the liberally educated humanist is the "key to the entire supranatural pyramid, because he is ancient anthropocentricity in its most highly developed form" (pp. 216–17).

A major debate is finally shaping up, centering around the leading environmental historians William Cronen and Donald Worster, over the issues of relativism, the validity of "progress" and continued growth and development in the modern world, and the "second nature" view as held by many environmental historians. According to Chris Lewis (in "Telling Stories about the Future," 1993), and in his projected book, *Science and the End of the Modern World*), Cronen claims that the proper task of historians is to "tell stories" about how different people have lived in the environment. Cronen (*Nature's Metropolis,* p. xvii) is a believer in the theory of "second nature," which he defines as "the artificial nature that people erect atop first nature." Donald Worster, on the other hand, asks whether just "telling stories" merely perpetuates the "state of nihilism, relativism, and confusion that modernistic history, and modernistic everything else, have left us in." Worster also challenges Cronen's concept of the human creation of a "second nature."

The Social Ecologist Murray Bookchin and the biologist Barry Commoner are also believers in the "second nature" theory. Chris Lewis points out that, unlike Paul Ehrlich and most other ecologists, Commoner (in *Making Peace with the Planet,* 1990) claims that

> if humanity must give up progress, economic growth, and development—give up the modern world—to end its war against nature and make peace with the planet, it would be a tragic defeat. Commoner refuses to accept calls for controlling population growth, ending economic growth and development, and transforming the modern world. He argues that because humanity lives in two worlds, the natural world or the ecosphere and a social world of its own creation—the technosphere—the environmental crisis is not an ecological problem but a social and political problem. . . .

In his 1993 paper, Lewis points to the November 1992 "World Scientists' Warning to Humanity," signed by 1575 leading scientists from sixty-nine countries, which claims:

> Human beings and the natural world are on a collision course. . . . We the undersigned, senior members of the world's scientific community, hereby

warn all humanity of what lies ahead. A great change in our stewardship of the earth and life on it is required if vast human misery is to be avoided and our global home on this planet is not to be irretrievably mutilated.

"Can environmental history," Lewis asks, "refuse to recognize the power of the modern biological sciences to help us evaluate competing stories about the human impact on the natural world?"

Underlying a certain segment of the "shallow" anthropocentric technocratic environmental movement, and the visions of the technological utopians, is an implicit or explicit belief that modern civilized humans are *literally* separated from the rest of Nature in an artificial technological "second nature" of their own creation. As such, they believe that modern society is immune to environmental apocalypse.

Lewis also points out that the United Nations Brundtland report is based upon the modernist vision of solving our environmental problems through continued growth and development. He sees that the Deep Ecology movement takes seriously the apocalyptic warnings of the biological scientists, rejects the "second nature" view, and is committed to moving beyond modernism to an ecological worldview.

Given humanity's largely uncritical commitment to the ideology of modernism over the last several hundred years, it is understandable why environmental history, like environmentalism itself, has been slow to come of age. George Perkins Marsh wrote his book, *Man and Nature,* in 1864, warning of humanity's destruction of Nature, but few paid any attention. Most people were caught up in the frenzy of industrialization and progress. Chris Lewis documents the increasingly steady stream of warnings of environmental disaster coming from biological scientists since World War II.

The first environmental history, Samuel Hays's *Conservation and the Gospel of Efficiency,* was not written until 1959, and this occurred somewhat by accident (Hays was mainly interested in the Progressive movement). Hays portrayed environmental history through the prevailing lenses of modernism, scientific/technological know-how, and progress. Roderick's Nash's *Wilderness and the American Mind* (1967) cracked open the door of intellectual environmental history by discussing the positions of Thoreau, Muir, and Leopold. It took a young historian, but an environmental history outsider, Stephen Fox, to write the first solid intellectual history of the environmental movement. In *John Muir and His Legacy: The American Conservation Movement* (1981) Fox chronicled the ecocentric origins of the environmental movement in John Muir (Fox was the first to make use of the Muir papers which had finally been made available to scholars by the Muir family in the 1970s). More recently, Fox has surveyed the field of environmental history, claiming that "the Muir tradition best defines conservation," and ties the Muir tradition to contemporary "anti-modernist" (i.e., "postmodernist") ecological trends.

Michael P. Cohen's *The Pathless Way: John Muir and American Wilderness* (1984), also based on the Muir papers, is the most insightful treatment of Muir's ecocentrism. Thoreau's radical ecocentrism was finally given its due in Donald Worster's *Nature's Economy* (1977) and Nash's *The Rights of Nature: A History of Environmental Ethics* (1989). This was followed by the ecophilosopher Max Oelschlaeger's monumental *The Idea of Wilderness: From Prehistory to the Age of Ecology* (1991), which updates the ecocentric scholarship on Thoreau, Muir, and Leopold.

In "Environmental Consciousness in Modern Literature," written in 1980, Del Ivan Janik traces modern environmental consciousness to the Romantic movement and the emergence of the ecocentric/bioregional perspectives of D. H. Lawrence, Aldous Huxley, Robinson Jeffers, and Gary Snyder. Janik points out, however, that, in these writers, the philosophical idealism, anthropocentrism, and subjectivism of Romanticism "has largely disappeared" and been replaced with what he calls a "posthumanism." Lawrence, Huxley, Jeffers, and Snyder, he claims, are "major modern writers" whose significance will only increase as "man moves toward the climactic confrontation with environmental realities. . . ."

Huxley's ecological concerns are further discussed by Wayland Drew in his wonderfully perceptive "Killing Wilderness" (1972). The three major anti-technological utopian novelists of the twentieth century—Eugene Zamiatin, Aldous Huxley, and George Orwell—all drew invidious comparisons between the developing totalitarian technological society and wilderness. (Birch refers to this developing totalitarian society as the "imperium" in his paper in Part Five; see also the critiques of megatechnological visions by Sessions and Mander in Part Four.) Only in wilderness, as Zamiatin, Huxley, and Orwell point out, can humans escape the total tyranny of the technocratic state. These authors seem to echo Thoreau's point that freedom and wildness are intimately connected, and that the technological/totalitarian state leads inevitably to the total domestication of humans.

Anticipating the critiques of "shallow" reform environmentalism by Naess and others, Drew points out that this "industrial establishment" kind of environmentalism has been coopted by the technological rationale. And anticipating as well the criticisms raised by Turner and Birch (in Part Five), Drew claims that the technocratic bureaucracy "has adroitly undercut the question raised by wilderness, and has reduced all wilderness issues to the status of managerial techniques."

The political philosopher John Rodman wrote some of the most sophisticated ecophilosophical analyses of the 1970s. In his essay Rodman summarizes these analyses in the form of a historical development of contemporary ecological sensibility or consciousness in the twentieth century. His critiques of Pinchot's anthropocentric Resource Conservation and Development position, and the "Moral Extensionism" theorizing of the animal liberationists (Singer and Regan), Christopher Stone, and Whitehead (and many contemporary environmental ethics theorists) are devastating and to the point. Rodman's critique of Muir's "wilderness preservation" emphasizes the "religious/esthetic" aspect of Muir's position, but this overlooks Muir's basic ecocentrism (post-1980 Muir scholarship was not available to him). And, in contrast with the attempts by Holmes Rolston, Baird Callicott, and other leading environmental ethics theorists to treat Leopold's "land ethic" as an early attempt to formulate an academic ethical position, Rodman argues persuasively that Leopold, in *Sand County Almanac,* was actually trying to bring about an ecocentric "paradigm shift" or change in perception and consciousness.

The classic ecocentric / Deep Ecological essays of the 1960s and early '70s are Lynn White's "Historical Roots of Our Ecologic Crisis" (1967); Paul Shepard's "Ecology and Man" (1969); Gary Snyder's "Four Changes" (1969); and Arne Naess's "The Shallow and the Deep Long-Range Ecological Movements" (1972). The historian Lynn White's essay linked Christian anthropocentrism with the ecological crisis. Modern secular ideologies, such as Marxism, are essentially Judeo-Christian heresies, White claimed, and have not deviated from Christian ideas of progress, and "man's rightful mastery over nature." Modern science and technology, having developed within a Christian matrix, are also "permeated with Christian arrogance toward nature." As a Christian solution to the ecological crisis, White proposed a return to the views of Saint Francis, who believed in "the equality of all creatures."

Paul Shepard also inspired much subsequent ecocentric ecophilosophical thought with his complex essay "Ecology and Man." He draws upon Alan Watts's popularizations of Zen Buddhism to distinguish between two views of the self: as an "isolated thing" (or ego) and as a self (similar to Naess's "ecological self") that is deeply immersed in and interrelated with the natural environment. Shepard provides an early discussion of both Greek and Judeo-Christian anthropocentrism and its role in the ecological crisis; he also points to the misunderstandings and misuses that have been made of Darwinian theory. Shepard claims that there is "an ecological instinct [or intuition] which probes deeper and more comprehensively than science . . . ," an ecological wisdom which manifests itself in many traditional cultures.

Shepard implicitly challenges the anthropocentric dualistic "second nature" theory by pointing out that Western academics have erroneously claimed that "only men were found to be capable of escape from predictability, determinism, environmental control, instincts and other mechanisms which 'imprison' other life forms. Even biologists such as Julian Huxley announced that the purpose of the world was to produce man, whose social evolution excused him forever from biological evolution."

Shepard was the first to refer to ecology as the "subversive science," claiming that the ideological status of ecology is that of a resistance movement. After chastising control-obsessed engineers and "corporation people selling consumption itself," Shepard concludes that "affirmation of its own organic essence will be the ultimate test of the human mind."

In "Four Changes" (1969), Gary Snyder prefigured the direction of radical ecological thinking with his vision of a future spiritual/ecological society. His ecocentrism is expressed in the claims that "all living beings are my brothers and sisters," and that "the unknown evolutionary destinies of other life forms are to be respected." He calls for population stabilization and reduction and an end to unnecessary consumption. "The five-millennia-long urbanizing civilization tradition," he claims, "must be transformed into a new ecologically-sensitive harmony-oriented wild-minded scientific-spiritual culture." Future ecological societies will live harmoniously and dynamically in a "world environment which is "left 'natural.' "

In his 1972 "Shallow/Deep Ecology" paper Arne Naess first coined the terms "shallow environmentalism" and "Deep Ecology." He wrote this paper in the spirit of a sociological description of a movement that he saw as having developed since the 1960s, and based upon the experiences of "field ecologists" and others closely associated with wild Nature. (For more discussion of this paper, see the introduction to Part Three.) These experiences included an awareness of the internal interrelatedness of ecosystems, ecological egalitarianism, and an appreciation of ecological diversity, symbiosis, and complexity. Like Shepard, Naess places emphasis upon ecological wisdom ("ecosophy") rather than ecological science. Ecology as a science only *inspires* the Deep Ecology movement: "Insofar as ecology movements deserve our attention," Naess claimed, "they are ecophilosophical rather than ecological."

In "Ecocentrism and the Anthropocentric Detour," I summarize the historical development of human/Nature views in the West. Anthropologists and historians claim that most primal peoples throughout the world held ecocentric views. Beginning with Socrates, Greek philosophy became increasingly anthropocentric. Greek and Roman anthropocentrism later combined with, and reinforced, Judeo-Christian anthropocentrism during the Middle Ages and the Renaissance. Contrary to the main thrust of Western culture, Saint Francis and Spinoza held nonanthropocentric views. The influence of Spinoza's nonanthropocentric metaphysics is traced through the Nature-oriented views of the Romantics, George Santayana, Bertrand Russell, Albert Einstein, Robinson Jeffers, and Arne Naess.

There are discussions of the beginnings of environmentalism with John Stuart Mill and George Perkins Marsh in the nineteenth century, and the recent scholarship which has established the ecocentric orientations of Thoreau and Muir. Because the rise of the Ecological Revolution, beginning after World War II and blossoming in the 1960s, has never received an in-depth philosophically sophisticated analysis by historians, considerable space is devoted to this period in environmental history. The connections between the rise of the global environmental crisis and the issue of human overpopulation throughout this period is emphasized. Also connected to the overpopulation issue is the contrast between those who conceive of the environmental crisis as *essentially* an urban/industrial pollution problem and those who see the primary ecological issue to be that of the protection of wildness, biodiversity, and the ecological integrity of the Earth.

# 11 ENVIRONMENTAL CONSCIOUSNESS IN MODERN LITERATURE
## FOUR REPRESENTATIVE EXAMPLES

*Del Ivan Janik*

ALTHOUGH THE SEVERITY OF the problems that modern society faces as a result of man's treatment of his natural environment since the age of the Industrial Revolution has only entered the public consciousness within the last two decades, literary men have been aware of those problems from the beginning. In the course of the last two hundred years there has emerged a movement within British and American literature toward a new environmental consciousness, involving a revaluation of man's place in the natural world as well as of the importance of nonhuman nature in itself and in its impact on human life. An awareness and understanding of this movement can contribute to the formation of a broader view of the environmental and cultural choices that face us today than has yet been taken by those in power in government, industry, and the mass media.

This new environmental consciousness in literature has its roots in the Romantic movement in England and America. The attitudes toward nature that characterized the Romantic period seem to have had three major sources. First, there was among literary men in the late eighteenth and early nineteenth centuries a reaction against the effects of the industrial revolution and a turning toward untouched natural settings as potential refuges from the ugliness and sordidness of industrialism. Second, there was an attraction to primitivism

A longer version of this essay was originally published in *Ecological Consciousness*, edited by Robert C. Schultz and J. Donald Hughes (Washington D.C.: University Press of America, 1981). Reprinted with permission.

as an antidote to the excessive rationality of the Enlightenment, and to agrarianism as an alternative to the emerging urban-industrial pattern of life. Finally, much Romantic literature reflected developments in eighteenth-century natural philosophy which had begun to challenge the foundations of Judeo-Christian religion. In the light of the discoveries and theories of seventeenth- and eighteenth-century science, it was increasingly difficult for intellectuals to sustain a faith in traditional revealed religion, yet poets like Wordsworth and Coleridge were unwilling to accept a purely mechanistic philosophy. . . .

The legacy of Romanticism for the modern literature of environmental consciousness is complex. The Romantic view of primitive or preindustrial modes of living as an attractive alternative to the prevailing progress-oriented, mechanistic worldview is reflected in the works of twentieth-century writers like D. H. Lawrence, Aldous Huxley, Robinson Jeffers, and Gary Snyder, as are the concepts of nature as unity (the world as organism) and the impulse toward pantheism or "nature worship." But these writers differ from their Romantic ancestors in significant ways. The philosophical idealism of Wordsworth, Coleridge, Emerson, and Thoreau has largely disappeared. Even Huxley and Snyder, heirs to the Transcendentalist interest in Eastern mysticism, base their defenses of the natural environment at least partly on observation and objective scientific knowledge. The fundamental—if disguised—anthropocentric humanism of the Romantics has been replaced in Lawrence, Huxley, Jeffers, and Snyder by a broader, biocentric view in which external nature is valued for its own sake and man is seen as one coequal partner in the process of the whole; it is a philosophy that represents such a significant departure that it might rightly be given the name "posthumanism."

D. H. Lawrence was dissatisfied with the anthropocentric assumptions that have dominated Western culture. That dissatisfaction emerged gradually out of his questioning of Western society's reliance on rational intellect. Lawrence thought in dichotomies, and for him the central dichotomy was the split between body and mind. Early in his career (1913) he enlisted himself on the side of the body:

> My great religion is a belief in the blood, the flesh, as being wiser than the intellect. We can go wrong in our minds. But what our blood feels and believes and says, is always true. The intellect is only a bit and a bridle.[1]

Lawrence soon modified this primitivistic position: In *The Rainbow* (1915) and *Women in Love* (1920) he presents a balance between the passions and the intellect as being the clue to successful self-integration and creative human relationships. Still, his belief that mind and spirit had for centuries been given more than their due led him to emphasize the need to liberate man's powers of physical awareness.

Lawrence's quarrel with the modern industrial system was that it made the individual less than a human being, forcing him to subordinate individual spontaneity to the needs of a mechanical system. His criticism of the nature of modern relationships among men and women and between them and the natural environment was based on his sense of the fundamental importance of the individual being, which he expressed in his concept of "otherness." In "Manifesto," (1917) Lawrence describes his sudden intuitive awareness of his wife's absolute separation from him, even in moments of intense passion; she is a distinct being, equal to but utterly different from himself. The poem leads to a vision of a new world in which that radical separateness might be acknowledged.

> Every man himself, and therefore, a surpassing singleness of mankind.
> The blazing tiger will spring upon the deer, undimmed,
> the hen will nestle over her chickens,
> we shall love, we shall hate,
> but it will be like music, sheer utterance,
> issuing straight out of the unknown,
> the lightning and the rainbow appearing in us unbidden, unchecked,
> like ambassadors.[2]

In *Birds, Beasts and Flowers* (1923), Lawrence explicitly extends this perception of radical otherness to man's relation to the nonhuman. Perhaps the most striking of these poems is "Fish," in which the speaker attempts to imagine the life of a fish but ultimately recognizes that it is impossible. Catching a fish and holding it in his hand, he realizes in a moment of illumination,

> I am not the measure of creation.
> This is beyond me, this fish.
> His God stands outside my God.[3]

This sense of otherness, of the absolute, inviolable value of that which is not oneself, informs *The Rainbow, Women in Love,* and *Lady Chatterley's Lover.* The great evil is the imposition of one's ego, one's will, upon the other— human or nonhuman.

Lawrence's belief in otherness was balanced by an awareness of the interrelatedness of all life, and of all living things with their environments. Lawrence's point of view was not that of the ecologist, but the mystic. He was intrigued by American Indian animism, with its insistence upon the spiritual vitality of all matter. In American Indian religion Lawrence recognized a worldview that acknowledged the wonder of material existence.

> It was a vast old religion, greater than anything we know: more starkly and
> nakedly religious. . . . In the oldest religion, everything was alive, not super-

naturally but naturally alive. There were only deeper streams of life, vibrations of life more and more vast. . . . For the whole life-effort of man was to get his life into direct contact with the elemental life of the cosmos, mountain-life, cloud-life, thunder-life, air-life, earth-life, sun-life.[4]

From his understanding of American Indian cultures and his speculations about that of the ancient Etruscans, Lawrence evolved a vision of a society in which the modern centralized social and political structure based on money and technological progress might be replaced by a fabric of small, organic communities in which life, not power or wealth, would be of primary value. In *Lady Chatterly's Lover,* the hero, Oliver Mellors, puts forth such a program for the revitalization of England, and in his own commentary Lawrence explained that the great imperative, for him, was reestablishment of intimate relationship between man and the rest of life: "We *must* get back into relation, vivid and nourishing relation to the cosmos and the universe. . . . Vitally, the human race is dying. It is like a great uprooted tree, with its roots in the air. We must plant ourselves again in the universe."[5]

Lawrence rejected humanism, with its focus on man and its belief in unlimited progress. He saw man as part of an organic universe, living best by acknowledging its wonder and rejecting the temptation to force his will upon it. In this sense he stands at the beginning of the modern posthumanist tradition and of the literature of environmental consciousness.

Lawrence was the model for Mark Rampion, one of the few positive characters in Aldous Huxley's 1928 novel *Point Counter Point.* One of the things that Huxley most admired in Lawrence was his empathy with the nonhuman.

> He seemed to know, by personal experience, what it was like to be a tree or a daisy or a breaking wave or even the mysterious moon itself. He could get inside the skin of an animal and tell you in the most convincing detail how it felt and how, dimly, unhumanly, it thought.[6]

Huxley shared Lawrence's concern about modern man's estrangement from the natural world, although at first that concern was expressed mainly in satire. In *Brave New World* (1932), Huxley contrasted an antiseptic, mind-controlled world civilization of the distant future with the world of the primitive past—represented by the reservation that produced John Savage—in which men were in intimate contact with the forces of nature but lived in filth, ignorance, and fear. Huxley disapproved of the modern mechanical, consumption-oriented society, but saw no sensible alternative.

In the late thirties and early forties, after he had come under the influence of Gerald Heard and had moved to California, Huxley became committed to what he called, after Leibniz, the "Perennial Philosophy": a belief, derived from Hinduism but manifested also in Mahayana Buddhism and among the

Sufis, the Catholic mystics, and the early Quakers, that, in Hindu terminology, "the *atman,* or immanent eternal Self, is one with Brahman, the Absolute Principle of all existence; and the last end of every human being is to discover the fact for himself, to find out Who he really is."[7] In his 1946 "Foreword" to a new edition of *Brave New World* Huxley explained, "If I were now to rewrite the book, I would offer the Savage a third alternative. Between the utopian and the primitive horns of his dilemma would lie the possibility of sanity: in a community where "the prevailing philosophy of life would be a kind of Higher Utilitarianism, in which the Greatest Happiness principle would be secondary to the Final End principle": the primary question would always be how a thought or a contemplated action would affect the possibility of achievement of intuitive knowledge of the universal self.[8]

Huxley created such an imaginary community in *Island,* his last novel (1962). His Pala, a Southeast Asian country with Mahayana Buddhist traditions, escaped colonization and industrialization but benefitted from the arrival in the middle of the nineteenth century of Andrew McPhail, a Scottish physician who in cooperation with the Raja of the time molded a civilization in which Western science and Eastern mysticism blended to produce a peaceful, self-sustaining mode of existence. In Pala, Huxley's true utopia, the population had been stabilized by birth control so that the local economy was sufficient to the people's material needs. Technology was limited to essentials: the production of electricity for refrigeration and labor-intensive light industry that did not deplete the island's natural resources. Government was centralized, but the basic unit of organization, as in Mellor's revitalized England, was the village. Medicine was preventive, relying primarily on diet and autosuggestion. Education was based on ecological principles, with scientific training centered on "the modest ambition is to live as fully human beings in harmony with the rest of life on this island at this latitude on this planet."[9] Religion was eclectic, founded on respect for life and the preparation for intuitive experience of universal Oneness. Like other writers of utopias, Huxley used Pala to reveal the follies of his own civilization: abstract materialism, egoism, and lust for power, represented in the novel by the neighboring "third world" dictatorship of Rendang-Lobo and the Western oil companies that seek to exploit Pala's petroleum deposits. Huxley's ideas closely resemble those of the economist E. F. Schumacher, who saw a hope for an environmentally sane future in the reduction of wants to needs and the introduction of small-scale "appropriate technology."

A view of man's relation to nature much like Lawrence's and Huxley's was stated explicitly by Robinson Jeffers in the Preface to *The Double Axe* (1948):

> Its burden, as of some previous work of mine, is to present a certain philosophical attitude, which might be called Inhumanism, a shifting of emphasis

and significance from man to not-man; the rejection of human solipsism and recognition of the transhuman magnificence. It seems time that our race began to think as an adult does, rather than like an egocentric baby or an insane person. This manner of thought is neither misanthropic nor pessimist, though two or three people have said so and may again.[10]

Jeffers' "Inhumanism" is much like what I call "posthumanism"; it received its greatest statement in the poem "The Answer" (1937):

> Integrity is wholeness, the
> greatest beauty is
> Organic wholeness, the wholeness of life and
> things,
> the divine beauty of the universe. Love
> that, not man
> Apart from that . . .[11]

Jeffers saw human effort in a larger context, and insisted in poems like "To the Stone-Cutters" and "Shine, Perishing Republic" that in that context the historical acts of men and the rise and fall of civilizations are insignificant. But Jeffers' "Inhumanism," if it is not misanthropic or pessimistic, is, at least in some of its manifestations, irresponsible and shortsighted. For example, the protagonist of "The Inhumanist," part II of "The Double Axe," is a recluse who preserves one small tract of land while environmental degradation continues unabated elsewhere; in "Shine, Perishing Republic" we are told, "when the cities lie at the monster's feet there are left the mountains."[12] It is a comforting thought for lovers of mountains, but not for those who revere "organic wholeness." Unlike Huxley, who looked beyond industrial civilization to the possibility that human beings could live in harmony with their surroundings, Jeffers seemed to advocate resignation and withdrawal. Jeffers seldom went beyond criticism of humanist anthropocentrism to suggest how a posthumanist society might function, and in that sense, his contribution to posthumanist thought is seriously limited. Nevertheless, his remains an important voice against the thoughtless embrace of what technological civilization calls progress, and for a new appreciation of the nonhuman.

The posthumanist philosophy that developed out of Romanticism is best expressed, among contemporary writers, by Gary Snyder, who was born in 1930 in San Francisco and grew up in Washington and Oregon. His work as logger and Forest Service lookout, his studies in anthropology and Oriental languages, and his experiences as a Zen Buddhist monk combined to form a unique perspective in which the problems of and potentials for humanity as part of the living world hold the central place. The first poem in his first book of poems, *Riprap* (1959), exemplifies Snyder's love of wilderness, his sensitivity to natural detail, and the directness of his verse.

> Down valley a smoke haze
> Three days heat, after five days rain
> Pitch glows on the fir-cones
> Across rocks and meadows
> Swarms of new flies
>
> I cannot remember things I once read
> A few friends, but they are in cities.
> Drinking cold snow-water from a tin cup
> Looking down for miles
> Through high still air.[13]

The poem is extremely simple, making virtually no assertions, but calling attention to a natural scene apprehended in its completeness, somewhat in the manner of Thoreau—swarms of flies as well as picturesque "smoke haze."

Snyder's early poetry reveals his debt to the Chinese nature poetry he translated, and reflects the influence of William Carlos Williams. But he soon developed a distinctive poetic voice that reflected his sense that poetry must be rooted in local experience. From his college years on he has been a student of American Indian folklore, and the Indian respect for the nonhuman impressed him as strongly as it had Lawrence. Snyder believes that "primitive" cultures had a great deal to teach "civilized" man. In "Poetry and the Primitive" he wrote that primitive cultures have "knowledge of connection and responsibility that amounts to spiritual ascesis for the whole community. . . . Class-structured civilized society is a kind of mass ego. To transcend the ego is to go beyond society as well. 'Beyond' there lies, inwardly, the unconscious. Outwardly, the equivalent of the unconscious is the wilderness: both of these terms meet, one step even farther on, as one."[14]

Snyder's interest in primitive modes of life and apprehension is not an exercise in exoticism. He is convinced that the technological civilization of the present century is an aberration, and that the coming exhaustion of fossil-fuel supplies will inevitably bring about the return of man to his normal condition, in which his survival will depend on his ability to cooperate with rather than exploit his surroundings. Hence Snyder seeks "a new definition of humanism and a new definition of democracy that would include the nonhuman, that would have representation from those spheres."[15] Traditional Western humanism, according to Snyder, is unequal to the task: "If we are on the verge of postcivilization, then our next step must take account of the primitive worldview which has traditionally and intelligently tried to open and keep open lines of communication with the forces of nature."[16] If we do not, he points out, "they will revolt against us. They will submit nonnegotiable demands about our stay on the earth. We are beginning to get nonnegotiable demands right now from the air, the water, the soil."[17]

Like Lawrence and Huxley, Snyder has a program, one that sees beyond the imperative of Gross National Product to a manner of living in which mankind might stabilize the pressures it places on the environment. He calls it "reinhabitation": the reestablishment of personal ties to the local ecosystem one finds oneself in, the cessation of the imposition of homogeneous technological methodologies between the inhabitant and the land. Snyder's idea of reinhabitation is a restatement, in less expansive terms, of Lawrence's belief that "we must plant ourselves again in the universe" and of Huxley's ideal "to live as fully human beings in harmony with the rest of life on this island at this latitude on this planet." It is stated most succinctly in the closing lines of his poem "For the Children":

> Stay together
> learn the flowers
> go light[18]

"Stay together" as a cohesive community, in touch with each other and with local realities; "learn the flowers"—know the natural world, both scientifically and intuitively; "go light," living responsibly as a part of the natural world.

The movement toward an environmental consciousness in literature of which Lawrence, Huxley, Jeffers, and Snyder are some of the most prominent representatives is perhaps still a relatively small one: it has not yet been recognized in literary histories. Nevertheless, it exists, and exists not as an esoteric self-conscious clique that issues manifestos in little magazines, but in the works of major modern writers who are familiar to the educated public. It is a movement whose significance and influence is likely to increase as man moves toward the climactic confrontation with environmental realities that its members have foreseen.

# NOTES

1. *The Collected Letters of D. H. Lawrence,* ed. Harry T. Moore, 2 vols. (London: Heinemann, 1962), I, 180.

2. *The Complete Poems of D. H. Lawrence,* ed. Vivian de Sola Pinto and F. Warren Roberts, 2nd ed. (New York: Viking Compass, 1971), 268.

3. *Complete Poems,* 339.

4. D. H. Lawrence, "New Mexico," *Phoenix,* ed. Edward D. McDonald (London: Heinemann, 1936), 146–147.

5. D. H. Lawrence, "A Propos of *Lady Chatterley's Lover,*" *Phoenix II,* ed. Warren Roberts and Harry T. Moore (London: Heinemann, 1968), 510.

6. *The Collected Letters of D. H. Lawrence, II,* 1265.

7. Aldous Huxley, *The Perennial Philosophy* (New York: Harper, 1945), 2.

8. Aldous Huxley, *Brave New World* (1932, 1946; rpt. New York: Bantam Books, 1958), viii–ix.

9. Aldous Huxley, *Island* (1962; rpt. New York: Perennial, 1972), 216.

10. Robinson Jeffers, *The Double Axe* (1948; rpt. New York: Liveright, 1977), xxi.

11. Robinson Jeffers, *Selected Poetry* (New York: Random House, n.d.), 594.

12. Jeffers, *Selected Poetry,* 168.

13. Gary Snyder, *Riprap and Cold Mountain Poems* (San Francisco: Four Seasons Foundation, 1969), 1.

14. Gary Snyder, *Earth House Hold* (New York: New Directions, 1969), 121–122.

15. Gary Snyder, *Turtle Island* (New York: New Directions, 1974), 106.

16. Snyder, *Turtle Island,* 107.

17. Snyder, *Turtle Island,* 108.

18. Snyder, *Turtle Island,* 86.

# 12 | KILLING WILDERNESS
## Wayland Drew

Oh, how great and divinely limiting is the wisdom of walls. This Green Wall is, I think, the greatest invention ever conceived. Man ceased to be a wild animal the day he built the first wall; man ceased to be a wild man only on the day when the Green Wall was completed, when, by this wall we isolated our machine-like, perfect world from the irrational, ugly world of trees, birds, and beasts.

Written in 1920, Eugene Zamiatin's novel *We,* quoted above, has never been published in its author's homeland, for the Soviet authorities quite correctly saw it to be subversive and dangerous. It describes a perfect, man-made environment, a cool, regimented, self-regulating utopia where the citizens, or Numbers, are entirely happy. Passion, ecstasy, rage, agony, heroism, and honor, all the extremes by which humanity once acknowledged and enlarged its animal inheritance have been systematically reduced to a ubiquitous Good. For happiness, Zamiatin's citizens have cheerfully traded their freedom. They are secure in the knowledge that the State will meet their every need, because the State will eliminate needs it cannot fulfill.

*We* is the first of three great anti-utopian novels to appear in English in the last half century. Both Huxley's *Brave New World* and Orwell's *Nineteen Eighty-four* are indebted to it, although all three books share a libertarian tradition that reaches back beyond Rousseau and the Romantic poets, a tradition exulting man's natural heritage in the face of encroaching Mechanism. Specifically, what these novels say is that a technological society will be totalitarian regardless of what political structures permit its development, for the essence of technique is efficiency and the autonomous individual, apt to be skeptical, irrational, and recalcitrant, is inefficient. For the general good therefore, the dangerous elements of individuality must be suppressed, and man must be severed from all the spiritual, intellectual, and emotional influences which might promote dissent. Man's integrity must be broken. He must be

Originally published in the *Ontario Naturalist* (September 1972). Reprinted with permission.

fragmented and reshaped to participate contentedly in the smooth functioning of the technological State—a State that is fundamentally inimical to his instinct and insulting to his intellect. In other words, the nature of man must be changed.

The protagonists of all three novels undergo this change and although the techniques vary they are uniformly relentless. The issue is never in doubt. "Reason," says Zamiatin's hero as he awaits his lobotomy, "must prevail." Since these are visions of perfectly rational States, it is clear that for the novelist freedom consists largely in irrationality, in instinctual response, and in the right to reject oppressive but reasonable options. Some people in *We* have retained the right. They are those who live in the wilderness beyond the Green Wall. The inhabitants of the State who know of their existence fear them deeply, for they pose a radical, primitive, viable alternative to the ethos of uniformity. In fact, the wilderness itself offers such an alternative. Vast and turbulent, it constantly invades the sterile, constructed world with reminders of its presence . . . "from some unknown plains the wind brings to us the yellowed honeyed pollen of flowers. One's lips are dry from this sweet dust. (It) somewhat disturbs my logical thinking." In its mystery and diversity, in its exuberance, decay, and fecundity, the perfection of the wilderness contrasts with the sterile and static perfection of the State. The difference between them is that between existence and life, between predictability and chance, between posturing and action. Wilderness, Zamiatin says, will threaten the totalitarian state while they co-exist, for the separation of man from nature is imperfect so long as man might recognize that a separation has occurred.

Zamiatin knew a good deal about the conquest of nature, for he was a civilized man. But to a Russian writing fifty years ago, the utter technological crushing of the wild and the free was inconceivable. He therefore assumed that State control would advance mainly on one front towards the subjugation, fracturing, and reconditioning of the individual. Huxley made the same assumption, but it is interesting to note that in *Brave New World* wilderness has been drastically diminished, to the point where Green Walls are no longer necessary. At the same time human techniques have been refined to near-perfect efficiency. "A love of nature," says the Director of Hatchery and Conditioning, "keeps no factories busy. . . . We condition the masses to hate the country . . . but simultaneously we condition them to love all country sports. At the same time, we see to it that all country sports shall entail the use of elaborate apparatus. So that they consume manufactured articles as well as transport."

In George Orwell's dreadful vision, written sixteen years later, man has been unraveled from the fabric of nature. Parks remain, where citizens might take collective hikes under surveillance, and a few pockets of wild land still offer seclusion. In one of these forgotten corners, reminiscent of the Golden Country of his dreams, Winston Smith first makes illicit love to Julia. "It was," Orwell tells us, "a political act," because it was instinctual and therefore subversive. Elsewhere, only memories remain, and truncated passions, and hopeless atavisms, all of which can be easily excised or altered by human techniques. "If you want a picture of the future," says O'Brien, the Thought Policeman, "imagine a boot stamping on a human face—forever." In the context of *Nineteen Eighty-four,* he is absolutely right; there is no escape.

Monitory novels should be read in groups, one after the other, for then their various crosscurrents are less diverting and the reader is better able to sense the drift of his own society. Many such novels have appeared in recent years, but these three remain predominant (*Brave New World* and *Nineteen Eighty-four* together still head their publisher's list in Canadian sales.) Huxley's vision of the future, forty years old this year, is closest to the present truth, for we have in fact passed beyond the necessity for Zamiatin's Green Wall and we have not yet realized the Orwellian nightmare. We are at the stage where, to quote one of *Brave New World*'s Controllers, "People are happy. They get what they want and they never want what they can't get. . . . they're so conditioned that they practically can't help behaving as they ought to behave." As for wilderness, it is seen as an archaic, anarchistic welter. When its mystique has been evaporated, its measurable components such as water, oxygen, minerals, timber, space, lie open to the service of technocracy.

That technocracy operates, as Huxley predicted, with subtlety and refinement. Its workings have been carefully traced by Jacques Ellul[1] and Herbert Marcuse.[2] Its dynamic is directed toward no less an end than the sterilization of the natural world and the substitution of total predictability. When it is understood that we are in its grip, the remaining wilderness assumes an awesome importance, for it is the sole index by which we can measure the extent of our own subjugation to unnatural forces. When wilderness has been consumed, our understanding of what is natural can be changed as required, and no facet of the human psyche or biology will be left invulnerable to revision. Reason, and only Reason, will prevail.

The South African novelist Laurens van der Post recently posed the challenge succinctly: "It is not reason that needs to be abolished," he said, "but the tyranny of reason."[3] But for the contemporary, existential urban man constantly assaulted by novelities, diversions, and facile, conflicting opinions, such a statement is already meaningless. What is reason if not consensus? And how can any tyranny exist in such a proliferation of choices, such an unprecedented prosperity and scope for self-expression? Already for millions of such men the rationale of the technocracy has become absolute, and the highest use of intelligence consists in maintaining their position in it. To be sure, their lives are fraught with problems and dilemmas, but none of these is insoluble within the terms of the artificial environment, an environment sufficiently elastic to desublimate repressed instincts in harmless ways. Promiscuity, drugs and alcohol, gambling, movies and television, violence and combativeness in sports and games, all are thus enlisted in the State's service. They divert and purge simultaneously, as do the debates generated by their presence, thereby obscuring criticisms of technocracy itself. Meanwhile, the Reason of the technocracy grows stronger by self-confirmation, for it can easily be shown that technological problems demand technological solutions. Everywhere we are acceding to the technocratic dictum that what is not known by experts cannot be known.

Only in wilderness is it possible to escape this tyranny. In wilderness a man or woman has physically left behind the milieu of conditioning—the pervasive sociability, the endless "information" from mass media, and so on. To some extent, the wilderness traveler will be reminded of his animal nature, and share again the profound, irrational correctness of trees, lakes, birds, and beasts. For urban men this can be a subverting experience. Some must react violently in an attempt to debase or destroy the source of their disturbance, and to bring ancient terrors to heel. But even on the most superficial level wilderness strengthens independence, for the man who has been freed from regimentation and finds that he can go anywhere at any time has been reminded of a basic animal right. Should he succeed in formulating the idea of *right*, then in a small but significant way he will become a critic of technological confinement. There is a fundamental difference between this animal freedom and technocracy's most popular accomplishment: the ability to travel thousands of miles in a regulated atmosphere, never once feeling the rain or the sun, never once drinking pure water, hearing a natural sound, or breathing unreconditioned air. The wilderness traveler is apt to find himself in a radical position, for he has passed beyond the "reasonable" arguments about public versus private transportation, or jumbo jets versus the SST, or whether or not we are economically capable of mass-producing a safe automobile. He has bypassed the mass of alternatives posed by the assumptions of the technological society and glimpsed a possibility which his society will tell him is reactionary, archaic, and impossible, but which his body and his spirit tell him is absolutely correct. He has positioned himself to breach the Reason of his society, to jump the Green Wall and confirm that there is something better than being a drugged and gratified utopian.

> The man of flesh and bone can maintain physical and mental sanity only to the extent to which he can have direct contact with a certain kind of reality not very different from the conditions under which he evolved.[4]

As the anti-utopian novelists foresaw, a force bent on total control must first confuse the inherited biological indices which tell us what types of behavior and what forms of environment are consistent with the dignity and survival of the human animal. The conservationists who now oppose that force recognize that the proper exercise of reason includes the defence of the instinctual and irrational, both inside man and in what remains of the natural world. Such people see in the issue of wilderness preservation a chance to negate what subjugates and diminishes them as individuals. They are saying in effect that they prefer freedom to happiness, even now. Like the Savage in *Brave New World,* they reject surrogates, and defiantly claim the right to God, to poetry, to real danger, to freedom, to goodness, to sin.

> "In fact," said Mustapha Mond, "you're claiming the right to be unhappy. . . . Not to mention the right to grow old and ugly and impotent; the right to have syphilis and cancer; the right to live in constant apprehension of what may happen tomorrow; the right to catch typhoid; the right to be tortured by unspeakable pains of every kind."
>
> There was a long silence.
>
> "I claim them all," said the Savage at last.

But it is one thing to have attained such a perception and quite another to know how to act upon it. Flight is still possible for us, as it is for Huxley's citizens, but most have been conditioned away from the necessary decisiveness and courage. Besides, at the present rate of technological expansion, escape could only be relative and temporary.

Environmental defense within the society seems to offer the larger hope. Traditionally, conservation has selected goals not incompatible with the objectives of the society at large—a stretch of marshland, a grove, a sand-spit, a strategic watershed, a particular species of endangered bird—such concerns coincide with the fragmenting process of technology and do not seriously threaten its advance. In fact, the stronger conservation has become the more it has hastened refinement of human and management techniques relative to land use, and the recent enlargement of its vision to include the Earth itself tends merely to reinforce the apparent need for tighter, global, technocratic controls. The threat of breakdowns in ecological systems can only be countered "realistically" by urging either the totalitarian management or replacement of those systems. "Spaceship earth," a current catchphrase among environmentalists, indicates their co-optation by the technological rationale, for the spaceship is the absolute in technical perfection. In its operation there is no room for the irrational and nothing can be left to chance. The survival of those who inhabit it depends on their subservience to technical processes, and hence on their diminishment as humans.

What conservation activities have accomplished, however, is the stubborn keeping alive of a fundamental question: What is man's correct relationship to the rest of nature? The technologist has one answer, the advocate for wilderness senses another. For 99 percent of the two million years on earth, cultural man has lived as a nomadic hunter-gatherer. It is of that way of life, the most successful and enduring that man has ever achieved, that wilderness reminds us. We have learned that it was not necessarily as nasty, brutish, and short as we had supposed, and yet our interest in it invariably takes the form of nostalgia for something irretrievably lost. No one advocates a return to the "primitive." In terms of the prevailing Reason it is absurd—almost literally unthinkable—to consider it except as part of an anthropological exercise. To do so would seem to deny history. Any politician proposing a serious reevaluation of the primitive would be scorned as whimsical, and no scientist would suggest its postulation as a legitimate end of scientific endeavor. Almost all philosophical and cultural traditions stand against it. No physician could consider it for a moment, and the very demographic projections made possible by the increased control of death point to its eclipse both in nature and in human thought.

Civilization has triumphed. And yet, it has not. Ecologically our civilization is as mindless as a cancer, and we know that it will destroy itself by destroying its host. Ironically, any remnants of humanity to survive the apotheosis of civilization will be returned, genetically mutilated, to that state which we have thought contemptible. If man does not survive, "interplanetary archeologists of the future will classify our planet as one in which a very long and stable period of small-scale hunting and gathering was followed by an apparently instantaneous efflorescence of technology and society leading rapidly to extinction. 'Stratigraphically,' the origin of agriculture and thermonuclear destruction will appear as essentially simultaneous."[5]

Reason severed from instinct is a monster. It is an affirmation of intellect, therefore, and not an abrogation, to defend as a viable development from civilization a way of life in which both instincts and intelligence have flourished freely; and while wilderness is still able to suggest man's proper place and deportment, it is a narrow, hubristic, suicidal, and tyrannical Reason which will not listen.

As civilized people, wilderness preservationists have been understandably reluctant to admit this. Together with the benefits of the advanced technological society they share the fallacy of infinite expansion, or seem to do so. Radical decentralization is too anarchistic and too negative a proposal for them to make. Whenever possible they seek positive political solutions, thereby allowing themselves to enter a dialectical process by which rational "concepts" of wilderness are formulated and wilderness itself is circumscribed in thought. Should they recognize the thralldom of politics to technocracy, they will say ruefully that they are at least "buying time." But while they debate, wilderness shrinks; when they compromise, wilderness is fragmented. To endorse any projection of society's "future needs" is to endorse the growth dynamic in which technology is founded, unless the radical shift to a steady-state economy has already occurred. At the present rate of expansion, technological demands on the environment will have been multiplied by a factor of thirty-two by the year 2040 within the lifetime of children now living. It is an insane projection. Long before then we shall either have scuttled civilization, or we shall have made a reality of the Orwellian nightmare. Such words as "individual" and "wilderness" will long since have been torn from their semantic moorings.

Redefinitions are already underway. This century has seen the insinuation of the term "wilderness park" by the technocratic bureaucracy, and its ready acceptance by conservationists. In this maneuver, the State has adroitly undercut the question raised by wilderness, and has reduced all wilderness issues to the status of managerial techniques. Dangerous negative perceptions are thereby deflected into the positivistic enterprise. When the principle of management has been accepted by everyone, then the containment of wilderness will be virtually complete. There will be continuing discussions, of course, but they will be discussions among the wardens and the gardeners. No longer might the phrase "wilderness park" be seen as a contradiction in terms, for what lies within the boundaries of such parks will be wilderness by definition, and it will remain so no matter what further technological ravishment it undergoes. Wilderness hotels, wilderness railroads and airports, wilderness highways, wilderness theaters and shopping plazas—all could ultimately be made to make sense, because there will be no basis for comparison left. "Don't you see," asks one of Winston Smith's colleagues in *Nineteen Eighty-four,* "that the whole purpose of Newspeak is to narrow the range of thought?" Should the State reserve natural areas, it will be as psychic purging-grounds for those atavistic citizens who still require such treatment, but those reserves will be parks, not wilderness.

While we are able to do so, let us note the distinction. A park is a managerial unit definable in quantitative and pragmatic terms. Wilderness is unquantifiable. Its boundaries are vague or nonexistent, its contents unknown, its inhabitants elusive. The purpose of parks is use; the earmark of wilderness is mystery. Because they serve technology, parks tend toward the predictable and static, but wilderness is infinitely burgeoning and changing because it is the matrix of life itself. When we create parks we bow to increased bureaucracy and surveillance, but when we speak for wilderness we recognize our right to fewer strictures and greater freedom. Regulated and crowded, parks will eventually fragment us, as they fragment the wilderness which makes us whole.

Only when wilderness can be circumscribed in thought can it be contained, reduced, and transformed in practice. If the horizons of reason are so narrowed as to exclude radically simple alternatives, that containment can be completed. For the moment, wilderness poses its silent, subversive question. We can avoid the question. We can erase it. We can easily, most easily, lose it in a morass of technological reductions and substitutions. If we continue to act expediently, we shall at some point stand like the deracinated Winston Smith, listening to his sad song,

> Under the spreading chestnut tree
> I sold you and you sold me . . .

At that point our idea of wilderness will be no more than a dream of the Golden Country, a country lost forever.

## NOTES

1. Jacques Ellul, *The Technological Society* (New York: Vintage Books, 1967).
2. Herbert Marcuse, *One-Dimensional Man* (Boston: Beacon Press, 1966).
3. Laurens van der Post, "A Region of Shadow," *The Listener* (August 5, 1971).
4. René Dubos, *Reason Awake* (New York: Columbia University Press, 1970).
5. Richard B. Lee and Irven DeVore, *Man the Hunter* (Chicago: Aldine Publishing, 1968).

# 13 | FOUR FORMS OF ECOLOGICAL CONSCIOUSNESS RECONSIDERED

## John Rodman

MY PRIMARY PURPOSE HERE is to describe and evaluate as succinctly as possible four currents of thought discernible in the history of the contemporary environmental movement. My secondary purpose is to recommend the still-emergent fourth form (Ecological Sensibility) as the starting point for a general environmental ethic. Along the way, I hope to suggest something of the complexity and ambiguity of the various forms—qualities sometimes lost in the rush to condemn the "shallow" and extoll the "deep."[1]

## RESOURCE CONSERVATION

The basic thrust of the Resource Conservation standpoint, taken in its turn-of-the-century context and seen as its advocates saw it, was to restrain the reckless exploitation of forests, soils, etc., characteristic of the pioneer stage of modern social development by imposing ethical and legal requirements that "natural resources" be used "wisely," meaning (in Gifford Pinchot's words) that they should be used "for the greatest good of the greatest number" (of humans), as distinct from being used to profit a few, and that the good should be considered over "the long run," that is, in terms of a sustainable society. Now that the novelty of this standpoint has worn off and more radical views have arisen, it clear that the ethic of "wise use" remained within the worldview of anthropocentric utilitarianism, since it assumed (without arguing the point)

Originally published in *Ethics and the Environment,* edited by Thomas Attig and Donald Scherer (Englewood Cliffs, N.J.: Prentice-Hall, 1983). Reprinted with permission.

that nonhuman natural entities and systems had only instrumental value as (actual or potential) "resources" for human use, so that the only reasons for humans to restrain their treatment of nonhuman nature were prudential ones flowing from considerations of enlightened self-interest.

What is a self and what is an interest, however, are not exactly given once and for all. To Pinchot's identification of human interests with economic prosperity and national power others have subsequently added such things as aesthetic enjoyment, scientific knowledge, and (more recently) biological survival. To Pinchot's and Theodore Roosevelt's extension of the self in space and time to comprise a national society and to include the interests of overlapping generations (ourselves, "our children, and our children's children"), others have superadded the notion of the human species as a kind of planetary society and the notion of obligations to a remoter posterity to which we are linked by the half-life of radioactive nuclear waste. Clearly, it is possible to engage in a good deal of persuasion by using and extending key terms and commitments within the Resource Conservation standpoint, as, for example, when Aldo Leopold redefined wealth and poverty in aesthetic terms so that an economically poor landscape might be seen as rich in beauty and therefore worth preserving. In the case of aesthetic contemplation and certain kinds of disinterested scientific knowledge (e.g., that of the field naturalist), we approach the boundaries of the Resource Conservation position in the sense that these are undeniable human interests that are so distant from the original and core (economic) sense of "use" (which involved the damming, logging, bulldozing, and transformation of nature into manufactured products) that the non- (or at least significantly less-) exploitative, more respectful senses of "use" can provide bridges for crossing over into the notion that there is intrinsic value in (some) natural entities and systems, which, after all, are beautiful or interesting to us partly in virtue of qualities than inhere *in them*.

Insofar as the Resource Conservation standpoint is retained in its core assumptions, however, it is vulnerable on several related grounds. First, the reduction of intrinsic value to human beings and the satisfaction of their interests is arbitrary, since it is neither necessary (for there are other human cultures that have not so reduced value), nor justified (for nobody has yet successfully identified an observable, morally relevant quality that both includes all humans and excludes all nonhumans). Second, the commitment to maximizing value through maximizing human use leads logically and in practice to an unconstrained total-use approach, whose upshot is to leave nothing in its natural condition (for that would be a kind of "waste," and waste should be eliminated); all rivers should be dammed for irrigation and hydropower, and all native forests replaced with monocultural tree plantations managed for "harvest." Given the arbitrariness of the first principle, the second amounts to an unjustifiable species imperialism.

Granted all this, it would be unfortunate if the contemporary environmental movement turned out to be simply what Steward Udall once called it, "the third wave of conservation." Yet it is also important to recognize the (limited) validity of the Resource Conservation standpoint in terms of its historical thrust. It emerged, in large part, as an attempt to constrain the destructive environmental impact of individuals and corporations who exploited nature for profit without sufficient regard for the larger social good or for the welfare of future generations. That issue has not died or become unimportant because broader ones have arisen. Some acts are wrong on several grounds: this is what makes possible the formation of honest coalitions, which are indispensable to political efficacy. Put in the most general way, the original thrust of the Resource Conservation movement was to enlarge in space and time the class of beings whose good ought to be taken into account by decision-makers, and to draw from that some conclusions about appropriate limits on human conduct. That Pinchot and his followers were inhibited by an unquestioning, almost unconscious, fidelity to an anthropocentric reduction of intrinsic value is cause for regret and for criticism, but the direction of thrust warrants respect from even the most radical environmentalists. In retrospect, the Resource Conservation standpoint appears to have been an early ideological adaptation on the part of a society that was still in the pioneering or colonizing stage of succession but had begun to get glimpses of natural limits that would require different norms of conduct for the society to become sustainable at a steady-state level. How different those norms might have to be was not yet clear.

## WILDERNESS PRESERVATION

At approximately the same time (1890–1914) that the Conservation movement was defining itself against the forces of unbridled resource exploitation, the Wilderness Preservation tradition, represented in part by John Muir and the Sierra Club, was also emerging as a social force.[2] At first allied with Pinchot against the common enemy and under the common banner of "conservation," Muir parted ways with him over issues such as the leasing of lands in the federal forest reserves to commercial grazing corporations and over the proposal to dam Hetch Hetchy Valley to make a reservoir for the growing population of San Francisco. What seemed a wise use to Pinchot, weighing the number of city dwellers, seemed a "desecration" to Muir. In contrast to the essentially economic language of Resource Conservation, Preservationists tended to articulate their vision in predominately religious and aesthetic terms. . . . On the other hand, if Muir had been asked outright whether Yosemite had value in itself, or for its own sake, independent of there being any actual or potential people to experience it, he would have surely said that it did. . . .

## MORAL EXTENSIONISM

Moral extensionism (which I called "Nature Moralism" in earlier papers) is an appropriately awkward term invented to designate a wide range of positions whose common characteristic is that they contend that humans have duties not only concerning but also directly to (some) nonhuman natural entities, and these duties derive from rights possessed by the natural entities, and that these rights are grounded in the possession by the natural entities of an intrinsically valuable quality such as intelligence, sentience, or consciousness. Quite different versions of this position can be found in the writings of such people as John Lilly, Peter Singer, Christopher Stone, and certain philosophers in the tradition of Whitehead (notably, Charles Hartshorne and John Cobb). All these writers *appear* to break with the anthropocentric bias of Resource Conservation and to resolve the ambiguity of Preservationism by clearly attributing intrinsic value to (at least some) natural items in their own right. The ground for human self-restraint towards nonhuman nature thus becomes moral in a strict sense (respect for rights) rather than prudential or reverential. Yet more radical environmentalists (e.g., the Routleys, Rodman, Callicott, Sessions, and Devall) object that the break with anthropocentrism and the resolution of the ambiguity are incomplete, and that all the variants of this position are open to the criticism that they merely "extend" (rather than seriously question or radically change) conventional anthropocentric ethics, so that they are vulnerable to revised versions of the central objection to the Resource Conservation standpoint, namely, that they are chauvinistic, imperialistic, etc.

Consider, for a starter, John Lilly's view that we ought to protect dolphins because they are very intelligent. Or consider, further along the spectrum of variants on this position, Peter Singer's argument that all sentient beings (animals down through shrimps) have an equal right to have their interests taken into consideration by humans who are making decisions that might cause them pain (pain being bad, and acts that cause unnecessary pain being wrong). Then consider, at the far end of the spectrum, the claim of various writers that all natural entities, including plants and rocks, have certain rights (e.g., a right to live and flourish) because they all possess some trait such as consciousness (though some possess it more fully than others). In the first two cases, the scope of moral concern is extended to include, besides humans, certain classes of nonhumans that are like humans (with regard to the specified quality), while the vast bulk of nature is left in a condition of unredeemed thinghood. In Singer's version, anthropocentrism has widened out to a kind of zoocentric sentientism, and we are asked to assume that the sole value of rain forest plant communities consists in being a natural resource for birds, possums, veneer manufacturers, and other sentient beings. In the third case, we are asked to adopt the implausible assumption that rocks (for example) are conscious. In all three cases, we end up with an only slightly modified version of the conventional hierarchy of moral worth that locates humans at the top of the scale (of intelligence, consciousness, sentience), followed by "higher" animals, "lower" animals, plants, rocks, and so forth. "Subhumans" may now be accorded rights, but we should not be surprised if their interests are normally overridden by the weightier interests of humans, for the choice of the quality to define the extended base class of those entitled to moral consideration has weighted the scales in that way.

Moreover, extensionist positions tend (when consistent, at least) to perpetuate the atomistic metaphysics that is so deeply embedded in modern culture, locating intrinsic value only or primarily in individual persons, animals, plants, etc., rather than in communities or ecosystems, since individuals are our paradigmatic entities for thinking, being conscious, and feeling pain. Yet it seems bizarre to try to account wholly for the value of a forest or a swamp by itemizing and adding up the values of all the individual members. And it is not clear that rights and duties (of which our ideas are fundamentally individualistic) can be applied to ecosystem relationships without falling into absurdity. Pretty clearly, what has happened is that, after both the prudential and the reverential stages of ideological adaptation by Resource Conservation and Wilderness Preservation came to seem inadequate, a more radical claim that nature had value "in its own right" seemed in order. Many of the attempts to make that claim plausible have, however, tried to extend the sphere of intrinsic value and therefore of obligatory moral concern by assimilating (parts of) nature to inappropriate models, without rethinking very thoroughly either the assumptions of conventional ethics or the ways in which we perceive and interpret the natural world. It is probably a safe maxim that there will be no revolution in ethics without a revolution in perception.

## ECOLOGICAL SENSIBILITY

The last form that I shall discuss is still emergent, so that description is not easily separated from prescription. The term "sensibility" is chosen to suggest a complex pattern of perceptions, attitudes, and judgments which, if fully developed, would constitute a disposition to appropriate conduct that would make talk of rights and duties unnecessary under normal conditions. At this stage of development, however, we can analytically distinguish three major components of an Ecological Sensibility: a theory of value that recognizes intrinsic value in nature without (hopefully) engaging in mere extensionism (in the sense discussed above); a metaphysics that takes account of the reality and importance of relationships and systems as well as of individuals; and an ethics that includes such duties as noninterference with natural processes, resistance to human acts and policies that violate the noninterference principle, limited intervention to repair environmental damage in extreme circumstances, and a style of coinhabitation that involves the knowledgeable, respectful, and restrained use of nature. Since there is not space to discuss all these components here, and since I have sketched some of them elsewhere,[3] I shall focus here on two basic dimensions of the theory of value, drawing primarily upon the writings of Leopold,[4] the Routleys,[5] and Rodman.

The first dimension is simple but sweeping in its implications. It is based upon the obligation principle that one ought not to treat with disrespect or use as a mere means anything that has a *telos* or end of its own—anything that is autonomous in the basic sense of having a capacity for internal self-direction and self-regulation. This principle is widely accepted but has been mistakenly thought (by Kant and others) to apply only to persons. Unless one engages in a high redefinition of terms, however, it more properly applies to (at least) all living natural entities and natural systems. (I leave aside in this essay the difficult and important issue of physical systems.) The vision of a world composed of many things and many kinds of things, all having their own *tele*, goes back (except for the recognition of ecosystems) to Aristotle's metaphysics and philosophy of nature and does not therefore involve us in the kinds of problems that arise from extending the categories of modern Liberal ethics to a natural world made up of the dead "objects" of modern thought. (To mention Aristotle is not, of course, to embrace all of his opinions, especially the very anthropocentric *obiter dicta*—e.g., that plants exist for the sake of animals, animals for humans, etc.—that can be found in his *Ethics* and *Politics*.) This notion of natural entities and natural systems as having intrinsic value in the specific and basic form, of having *tele* of their own, having their own characteristic patterns of behavior, their own stages of development, their own business (so to speak), is the basic ground in which is rooted the attitude of respect, the obligation of noninterference, etc. In it is rooted also the indictment of the Resource Conservation standpoint as being, at bottom, an ideology of human chauvinism and human imperialism.

It may be objected that our paradigmatic notion of a being having a *telos* is an individual human being or person, so that viewing nature is terms of *tele* involves merely another extension of an all-too-human quality to (part of) nature, retaining the conventional atomistic metaphysics and reinstating the conventional moral pecking order. I do not think that this is the case. It seems to me an observable fact that thistles, oak trees, and wombats, as well as rain forests and chaparral communities, have their own characteristic structures and potentialities to unfold, and that it is as easy to see this in them as it is in humans, if we will but look. For those unaccustomed to looking, Aldo Leopold's *Sand County Almanac* provides, in effect, a guidebook. Before the reader is introduced to the "land ethic" chapter (which is too often read out of the context of the book as a whole), he or she is invited to accompany Leopold as he follows the tracks of the skunk in the January snow, wondering where the skunk is headed and why; speculating on the different meanings of a winter thaw for the mouse whose snow burrow has collapsed and for the owl who has just made dinner of the mouse; trying to understand the honking of the geese as they circle the pond; and wondering what the world must look like to a muskrat eye-deep in the swamp. By the time one reaches Leopold's discussion of the land ethic, one has grown accustomed to thinking of different animals—and (arguably), by extension, different natural entities in general—as subjects rather than objects, as beings that have their own purposes, their own perspectives on the world, and their own goods that are differentially affected by events. While we can never get inside a muskrat's head and know exactly what the world looks like from that angle, we can be pretty certain that the view is different from ours. What melts away as we become intrigued with this plurality of perspectives is the assumption that any one of them (for example, ours) is privileged. So we are receptive when the "land ethic" chapter suggests that other natural beings deserve respect and should be treated as if they had a "right" in the most basic sense of being entitled to continue existing in a natural state. To want from Leopold a full-scale theory of the rights of nature, however, would be to miss the point, since the idea of rights has only a limited application. Moreover, Leopold does not present logical arguments for the land ethic in general, because such arguments could not persuade anyone who still looked at nature as if it were comprised of objects or mere resources, and such arguments are unnecessary for those who have come to perceive nature as composed of subjects. When perception is sufficiently changed, respectful types of conduct seem "natural," and one does not have to belabor them in the language of rights and duties. Here, finally, we reach the point of "paradigm change."[6] What brings it about is not exhortation, threat, or logic, but a rebirth of the sense of wonder that in ancient times gave rise to philosophers but is now more often found among field naturalists.

In further response to the objection that viewing nature in terms of *tele* is simply another version of anthropocentric Moral Extensionism, consider that a forest may be in some ways more nearly paradigmatic than an individual human for illustrating what it means to have a *telos*. A tropical forest may take five hundred years to develop to maturity and may then maintain a dynamic, steady state indefinitely (for million of years, judging from fossils) if not seriously interfered with. It exhibits a power of self-regulation that may have been shared to some extent by millennia of hunter-gatherer societies but is not an outstanding characteristic of modern humans, taken either as individuals or as societies. While there may be therefore some differences in the degree to which certain aspects of what it means to have a *telos* are present in one organism or one system compared with another, the basic principle is that all items having a *telos* are entitled to respectful treatment. Comparisons are more fruitfully made in terms of the second dimension of the theory of value.

The second dimension incorporates a cluster of value-giving characteristics that apply both to natural entities and (even more) to natural systems: diversity, complexity, integrity, harmony, stability, scarcity, etc. While the *telos* principle serves primarily to provide a common basic reason for respectful treatment of natural entities and natural systems (ruling out certain types of exploitative acts on deontological grounds), and to provide a criterion for drawing morally relevant distinctions between natural trees and plastic trees, natural forests and timber plantations, etc., this cluster of value-giving qualities provides criteria for evaluating alternative courses of permissible action in terms of optimizing the production of good effects, the better action being the one that optimizes the qualities taken as an interdependent, mutually constraining cluster. Aldo Leopold seems to have had something like this model in mind when he stated the land ethic in these terms:

> A thing is right when it tends to preserve the integrity, stability, and beauty of the biotic community. It is wrong when it tends otherwise.

(We may wish to modify Leopold's statement, omitting reference to beauty, and adding additional criteria, especially diversity [which stands as a principle in its own right, not merely as a means to stability]; moreover, an action can be right or wrong in reference to individuals as well as communities—but Leopold was redressing an imbalance, calling our attention to the supra-individual level, and can be forgiven for overstating his case.) More controversially, the cluster of ecological values can also be used to appraise the relative value of different ecosystems when priorities must be set (given limits on time, energy, and political influence) by environmentalists working to protect nature against the bulldozer and the chainsaw. The criteria of diversity, complexity, etc., will sometimes suggest different priorities than would result from following the aesthetic of the sublime or a criterion such as sentience, while a fully pantheistic philosophy of preservation provides no criteria at all for discriminating cases.

Since the cluster of value-giving principles applies generally throughout the world to living natural entities and systems, it applies to human beings and human societies as well as to the realm of the nonhuman. To the extent that diversity on an individual human level is threatened by the pressures of conformity in mass society, and diversity of social ways of life is threatened by the pressures of global resource exploitation and an ideology of worldwide "development" in whose name indigenous peoples are being exterminated along with native forests, it would be shortsighted to think of "ecological issues" as unrelated to "social issues." From an ecological point of view, one of the most striking sociopolitical phenomena of the twentieth century—the rise of totalitarian dictatorships that forcibly try to eliminate the natural condition of human diversity in the name of some monocultural ideal (e.g., an Aryan Europe or a classless society)—is not so much a freakish aberration from modern history as it is an intensification of the general spirit of the age. Ecological Sensibility, then is "holistic" in a sense beyond that usually thought of: it grasps the underlying principles that manifest themselves in what are ordinarily perceived as separate "social" and "environmental" issues.[7] More than any alternative environmental ethic, it attains a degree of comprehension that frees environmentalists from the charge of ignoring "people problems" in their preoccupation with saving nature. Insofar as Ecological Sensibility transcends "ecology" in the strict sense, its very name is metaphorical, drawing on a part to suggest the whole. Starting with issues concerning human treatment of the natural environment, we arrive at principles that shed light on the total human condition.

## NOTES

1. An earlier version of the "four forms" analysis was developed in a series of papers written in 1977–78. These included: "The Liberation of Nature?" (*Inquiry*, 20, Spring 1977); "Four Forms of Ecological Consciousness, Part One: Resource Conservation" (paper presented at the annual meeting of the American Political Association, 1976); and the paper listed below in note 3. The present essay is based on a paper read to the Department of Philosophy, Research School of Social Sciences, Australian National University, where I was a Visiting Fellow in the summer of 1981. It attempts to restate the "four forms" analysis so as to clear up misunderstandings, deal with criticisms, and incorporate suggestions. It omits much of the historical material and many peripheral arguments in an effort to focus on the central issues.

2. The hedge ("in part") is meant to acknowledge that, although Muir did articulate

the standpoint that I describe, there were other elements in his writings as well. I am analyzing a particular point of view, not presenting an exhaustive analysis of John Muir.

3. See my "Ecological Resistance: John Stuart Mill and the Case of the Kentish Orchid," paper presented at the annual meeting of the American Political Science Association, 1977.

4. Aldo Leopold, *A Sand County Almanac* (New York: Oxford University Press, 1949).

5. Richard and Val Routley, "Human Chauvinism and Environmental Ethics," in *Environmental Philosophy,* Don Mannison, Michael McRobbie, and Richard Routley, eds. (Department of Philosophy, Research School of Social Sciences, Australian National University, 1980); and Val and Richard Routley, "Social Theories, Self-Management, and Environmental Problems," also in *Environmental Philosophy.*

6. Obviously, I believe that those who see Leopold's land ethic as a mere extension of conventional ethics are radically mistaken.

7. See also Rodman, "Paradigm Change in Political Science," *American Behavioral Scientist* 24, no. 1 (September–October 1980): 67–69.

# 14 ECOLOGY AND MAN— A VIEWPOINT

## Paul Shepard

ECOLOGY IS SOMETIMES CHARACTERIZED as the study of a natural "web of life." It would follow that man is somewhere in the web or that he in fact manipulates its strands, exemplifying what Thomas Huxley called "man's place in nature." But the image of a web is too meager and simple for the reality. A web is flat and finished and has the mortal frailty of the individual spider. Although elastic, it has insufficient depth. However solid to the touch of the spider, for us it fails to denote the *eikos*—the habitation—and to suggest the enduring integration of the primitive Greek domicile with its sacred hearth, bonding the earth to all aspects of society.

Ecology deals with organisms in an environment and with the processes that link organism and place. But ecology as such cannot be studied; only organisms, earth, air, and sea can be studied. It is not a discipline: there is no body of thought and technique which frames an ecology of man.[1] It must be therefore a scope or a way of seeing. Such a perspective on the human is very old and has been part of philosophy and art for thousands of years. It badly needs attention and revival.

Man is in the world and his ecology is the nature of that in-ness. He is in the world as in a room, and in transience as in the belly of a tiger or in love. What does he do there in nature? What does nature do there in him? What is the nature of the transaction? Biology tells us that the transaction is always circular, always a mutual feedback. Human ecology cannot be limited strictly to biological concepts, but it cannot ignore them. It cannot even transcend them. It emerges from biological reality and grows from the fact of interconnectedness as a general principle of life. It must take a long view of human life and nature as they form a mesh or pattern going beyond historical time

Originally published in *The Subversive Science,* edited by Paul Shepard and Daniel McKinley (Boston: Houghton-Mifflin, 1969). Reprinted with permission.

and beyond the conceptual bounds of other humane studies. As a natural history of what it means to be human, ecology might proceed the same way one would define a stomach, for example, by attention to its nervous and circulatory connections as well as its entrance, exit, and muscular walls.

Many educated people today believe that only what is unique to the individual is important or creative, and turn away from talk of populations and species as they would from talk of the masses. I once knew a director of a wealthy conservation foundation who had misgivings about the approach of ecology to urgent environmental problems in America because its concepts of communities and systems seemed to discount the individual. Communities suggested to him only followers, gray masses without the tradition of the individual. He looked instead—or in reaction—to the profit motive and capitalistic formulas, in terms of efficiency, investment, and production. It seemed to me that he had missed a singular opportunity. He had shied from the very aspect of the world now beginning to interest industry, business, and technology as the biological basis of their—and our—affluence, and which his foundation could have shown to be the ultimate basis of all economics.

Individual man has his particular integrity, to be sure. Oak trees, even mountains, have selves or integrities too (a poor word for my meaning, but it will have to do). To our knowledge, those other forms are not troubled by seeing themselves in more than one way, as man is. In one aspect the self is an arrangement of organs, feelings, and thoughts—a "me"—surrounded by a hard body boundary: skin, clothes, and insular habits. This idea needs no defense. It is conferred on us by the whole history of our civilization. Its virtue is verified by our affluence. The alternative is a self as a center of organization, constantly drawing on and influencing the surroundings, whose skin and behavior are soft zones contacting the world instead of excluding it. Both views are real and their reciprocity significant. We need them both to have a healthy social and human maturity.

The second view—that of relatedness of the self—has been given short shrift. Attitudes toward ourselves do not change easily. The conventional image of a man, like that of the heraldic lion, is iconographic; its outlines are stylized to fit the fixed curves of our vision. We are hidden from ourselves by habits of perception. Because we learn to talk at the same time that we learn to think, our language, for example, encourages us to see ourselves—or a plant or animal—as an isolated sack, a thing, a contained self. Ecological thinking, on the other hand, requires a kind of vision across boundaries. The epidermis of the skin is ecologically like a pond surface or a forest soil, not a shell so much as a delicate interpenetration. It reveals the self ennobled and extended rather than threatened as part of the landscape and the ecosystem, because the beauty and complexity of nature are continuous with ourselves.

And so ecology as applied to man faces the task of renewing a balanced view where now there is man-centeredness, even pathology of isolation and fear. It implies that we must find room in "our" world for all plants and animals, even for their otherness and their opposition. It further implies exploration and openness across an inner boundary—an ego boundary—an appreciative understanding of the animal in ourselves which our heritage of Platonism, Christian morbidity, duality, and mechanism have long held repellent and degrading. The older countercurrents—relics of pagan myth, the universal application of Christian compassion, philosophical naturalism, nature romanticism and pantheism—have been swept away, leaving only odd bits of wreckage. Now we find ourselves in a deteriorating environment which breeds aggressiveness and hostility toward ourselves and our world.

How simple our relationship to nature would be if we only had to choose between protecting our natural home and destroying it. Most of our efforts to provide for the natural in our philosophy have failed—run aground on their own determination to work out a peace at arm's length. Our harsh reaction against the peaceable kingdom of sentimental romanticism was evoked partly by the tone of its dulcet facade, but also by the disillusion to which it led. Natural dependence and contingency suggest togetherness and emotional surrender to mass behavior and other lowest common denominators. The environmentalists matching culture and geography provoke outrage for their oversimple theories of cause and effect, against the sciences which sponsor them and even against a natural world in which the theories may or may not be true. Our historical disappointment in the nature of nature has created a cold climate for ecologists who assert once again that we are limited and obligated. Somehow they must manage in spite of the chill to reach the centers of humanism and technology, to convey there a sense of our place in a universal vascular system without depriving us of our self-esteem and confidence.

Their message is not, after all, all bad news. Our natural affiliations define and illumine freedom instead of denying it. They demonstrate it better than any dialectic. Being more enduring than we individuals, ecological patterns—spatial distributions, symbioses, the streams of energy and matter and communication—create among individuals the tensions and polarities so different from dichotomy and separateness. The responses, or what theologians call "the sensibilities" of creatures (including ourselves) to such arrangements grow in part from a healthy union of the two kinds of self already mentioned, one emphasizing integrity, the other relatedness. But it goes beyond that to something better-known to twelfth-century Europeans or Paleolithic hunters than to ourselves. If nature is not a prison and earth a shoddy way station, we must find the faith and force to affirm its metabolism as our own—or rather, our own as part of it. To do so means nothing less than a shift in our whole frame of reference and our attitude toward life itself, a wider perception of the landscape as a creative, harmonious being where relationships of things are as real as the things. Without losing our sense of a great human destiny and without intellectual surrender, we must affirm that the world is a being, a part of our own bodies.[2]

Such a being may be called an ecosystem, or simply a forest or landscape. Its members are engaged in a kind of choreography of materials and energy and information, the creation of order and organization. (Analogy to corporate organization here is misleading, for the distinction between social [one species] and ecological [many species] is fundamental.) The pond is an example. Its ecology includes all events: the conversion of sunlight to food and the food chains within and around it, man drinking, bathing, fishing, plowing the slopes of the watershed, drawing a picture of it, and formulating theories about the world based on what he sees in the pond. He and all the other organisms at and in the pond act upon one another, engage the earth and atmosphere, and are linked to other ponds by a network of connections like the threads of protoplasm connecting cells in living tissues.

The elegance of such systems and delicacy of equilibrium are the outcome of a long evolution of interdependence. Even society, mind, and culture are a part of that evolution. There is an essential relationship between them and the natural habitat: that is, between the emergence of higher primates and flowering plants, pollinating insects, seeds, humus, and arboreal life. It is unlikely that a manlike creature could arise by any other means than a long arboreal sojourn following and followed by a time of terrestriality. The fruit's complex construction and the mammalian brain are twin offspring of the maturing earth, impossible, even meaningless, without the deepening soil and the mutual development of savannas and their faunas in the last geological epoch. Internal complexity, as in the mind of a primate, is an extension of natural complexity, measured by the variety of plants and animals and the variety of nerve cells—organic extensions of each other.

The exuberance of kinds as the setting in which a good mind could evolve (to deal with a complex world) was not only a past condition. Man did not arrive in the world as though disembarking from a train in the city. He continues to arrive, somewhat like the birth of art, a train (in Roger Fry's definition) passing through many stations, none of which is wholly left behind. This idea of natural complexity as a counterpart to human intricacy is central to an ecology of man. The creation of order, of which man is an example, is realized also in the number of species and habitats, an abundance of landscapes lush and poor. Even deserts and tundras increase the planetary opulence. Curiously, only man and possibly a few birds can appreciate this opulence, being the world's travelers. Reduction of this variegation would, by extension then, be an amputation of man. To convert all "wastes"—all deserts, estuaries, tundras, ice fields, marshes, steppes, and moors—into cultivated fields and cities would impoverish rather than enrich life aesthetically as well as ecologically. By aesthetically, I do not mean that weasel term connoting the pleasure of baubles. We have diverted ourselves with litterbug campaigns and greenbelts while the fabric of our very environment is unraveling. In the name of conservation, too, such things are done, so that conservation becomes ambiguous. Nature is a fundamental "resource" to be sustained for our well-being. But it loses in the translation into usable energy and commodities. Ecology may testify as often against our uses of the world, even against conservation techniques of control and management for sustained yield, as it does for them. Although ecology may be treated as a science, its greater and overriding wisdom is universal.

That wisdom can be approached mathematically, chemically, or it can be danced or told as a myth. It has been embodied in widely scattered, economically different cultures. It is manifest, for example, among pre-Classical Greeks, in Navajo religion and social orientation, in Romantic poetry of the eighteenth and nineteenth centuries, in Chinese landscape painting of the eleventh century, in current Whiteheadian philosophy, in Zen Buddhism, in the worldview of the cult of the Cretan Great Mother, in the ceremonials of Bushman hunters, and in the medieval Christian metaphysics of light. What is common among all of them is a deep sense of engagement with the landscape, with profound connections to surroundings and to natural processes central to all life.

It is difficult in our language even to describe that sense. English becomes imprecise or mystical—and therefore suspicious—as it struggles with "process" thought. Its noun and verb organization shapes a divided world of static doers separate from the doing. It belongs to an idiom of social hierarchy in which all nature is made to mimic man. The living world is perceived in that idiom as an upright ladder, a "great chain of being," an image which seems at first ecological but is basically rigid, linear, condescending, lacking humility and love of otherness.

We are all familiar from childhood with its classifications of everything on a scale from the lowest to the highest: inanimate matter/vegetative life/lower animals/higher animals/men/angels/gods. It ranks animals themselves in categories of increasing good: the vicious and lowly parasites, pathogens, and predators/the filthy decay and scavenging organisms/indifferent wild or merely useless forms/good tame creatures/and virtuous beasts domesticated for human service. It shadows the great man-centered political scheme upon the world, derived from the ordered ascendency from parishioners to clerics to bishops to cardinals to popes, or in a secular form from criminals to proletarians to aldermen to mayors to senators to presidents.

And so is nature pigeonholed. The sardonic phrase, "the place of nature in man's world," offers, tongue-in-cheek, a clever footing for confronting a world made in man's image and conforming to words. It satirizes the prevailing philosophy of antinature and human omniscience. It is possible because of an attitude which—like ecology—has ancient roots, but whose modern form was shaped when Aquinas reconciled Aristotelian homocentrism with Judeo-Christian dogma. In a later setting of machine technology, puritanical capitalism, and an urban ethos it carves its own version of reality into the landscape like a schoolboy initialing a tree. For such a philosophy, nothing in nature has inherent merit. As one professor recently put it, "The only reason anything is done on this earth is for people. Did the rivers, winds, animals, rocks, or dust ever consider my wishes or needs? Surely, we do all our acts in an earthly environment, but I have never had a tree, valley, mountain, or flower thank me for preserving it."[3] This view carries great force, epitomized in history by Bacon, Descartes, Hegel, Hobbes, and Marx.

Some other post-Renaissance thinkers are wrongly accused of undermining our assurance of natural order. The theories of the heliocentric solar system, of biological evolution, and of the unconscious mind are held to have deprived the universe of the beneficence and purpose to which man was a special heir and to have evoked feelings of separation, of antipathy toward a meaningless existence in a neutral cosmos. Modern despair, the arts of anxiety, the politics of pathological individualism and predatory socialism were not, however, the results of Copernicus, Darwin, and Freud. If man was not the center of the universe, was not created by a single stroke of Providence, and is not ruled solely by rational intelligence, it does not follow therefore that nature is defective where we thought it perfect. The astronomer, biologist, and psychiatrist each achieved for mankind corrections in sensibility. Each showed the interpenetration of human life and the universe to be richer and more mysterious than had been thought.

Darwin's theory of evolution has been crucial to ecology. Indeed, it might have helped rather than aggravated the growing sense of human alienation, had its interpreters emphasized predation and competition less (and, for this reason, one is tempted to add, had Thomas Huxley, Herbert Spencer, Samuel Butler, and G. B. Shaw had less to say about it). Its bases of universal kinship and common bonds of function, experience, and value among organisms were obscured by preexisting ideas of animal depravity. Evolutionary theory was exploited to justify the worst in men and was misused in defense of social and economic injustice. Nor was it better used by humanitarians. They opposed the degradation of men in the service of industrial progress, the slaughter of American Indians, and child labor, because each treated men "like animals." That is to say, man were not animals, and the temper of social reform was to find good only in attributes separating men from animals. Kindness both toward and among animals was still a rare idea in the nineteenth century, so that using men as animals could mean only cruelty.

Since Thomas Huxley's day, the nonanimal forces have developed a more subtle dictum to the effect that, "Man may be an animal, but he is more than an animal, too!" The *more* is really what is important. This appealing aphorism is a kind of anesthetic. The truth is that we are ignorant of what it is like or what it means to be any other kind of creature than we are. If we are unable to truly define the animal's experience of life or "being an animal," how can we isolate our animal part?

The rejection of animality is a rejection of nature as a whole. As a teacher, I see students develop in their humanities studies a proper distrust of science and technology. What concerns me is that the stigma spreads to the natural world itself. C. P. Snow's "Two Cultures," setting the sciences against the humanities, can be misunderstood as placing nature against art. The idea that the current destruction of people and environment is scientific and would be corrected by more communication with the arts neglects the hatred for this world carried by our whole culture. Yet science as it is now taught does not promote a respect for nature. Western civilization breeds no more ecology in Western science than in Western philosophy. Snow's two cultures cannot explain the antithesis that splits the world, nor is the division ideological, economic, or political in the strict sense. The antidote he proposes is roughly equivalent to a liberal education, the traditional prescription for making broad and well-rounded men. Unfortunately, there is little even in the liberal education of ecology-and-man. Nature is usually synonymous with either natural resources or scenery, the great stereotypes in the minds of middle-class, college-educated Americans.

One might suppose that the study of biology would mitigate the humanistic—largely literary—confusion between materialism and a concern for nature. But biology made the mistake at the end of the seventeenth century of adopting a modus operandi or lifestyle from physics, in which the question why was not to be asked, only the question how. Biology succumbed to its own image as an esoteric prologue to technics and encouraged the whole society to mistrust naturalists. When scholars realized what the sciences were about it is not surprising that they threw out the babies with the bathwater: the informational content and naturalistic lore with the rest of it. This is the setting in which academic and intellectual America undertook the single-minded pursuit of human uniqueness, and uncovered a great mass of pseudo-distinctions such as language, tradition, culture, love, consciousness, history, and awe of the supernatural. Only men were found to be capable of escape from predictability, determinism, environmental control, instincts, and other mechanisms which "imprison" other life. Even biologists, such as Julian Huxley, announced that the purpose of the world was to produce man, whose social evolution excused him forever from biological evolution. Such a view incorporated three important assumptions: that nature is a power structure shaped after human political hierarchies; that man has a monopoly of immortal souls; and omnipotence will come through technology. It seems to me that all of these foster a failure of responsible behavior in what Paul Sears calls "the living landscape" except within the limits of immediate self-interest.

What ecology must communicate to the humanities—indeed, as a humanity—is that such an image of the world and the society so conceived is incomplete. There is overwhelming evidence of likeness, from molecular to mental, between men and animals. But the dispersal of this information is not necessarily a solution. The Two Culture idea that the problem is an information bottleneck is only partly true; advances in biochemistry, genetics, ethology, paleoanthropology, comparative physiology, and psychobiology are not self-evidently unifying. They need a unifying principle not found in any of them, a wisdom in the sense that Walter B. Cannon used the word in his book *Wisdom of the Body*[4] about the community of self-regulating systems within the organism. If the ecological extension of that perspective is correct, societies and ecosystems as well as cells have a physiology, and insight into it is built into organisms, including man. What was intuitively apparent last year—whether aesthetically or romantically—is a find of this year's inductive analysis. It seems apparent to me that there is an ecological instinct which probes deeper and more comprehensively than science, and which anticipates every scientific confirmation of the natural history of man. . . .

The humaneness of ecology is that the dilemma of our emerging world ecological crisis (overpopulation, environmental pollution, etc.) is at least in part a matter of values and ideas. It does not divide men as much by their trades as by the complex of personality and experience shaping their feelings toward other people and the world at large. I have mentioned the disillusion generated by the collapse of unsound nature philosophies. The antinature position today is often associated with the focusing of general fears and hostilities on the natural world. It can be seen in the behavior of control-obsessed engineers, corporation people selling consumption itself, academic superhumanists and media professionals fixated on political and economic crisis, neurotics working out psychic problems in the realm of power over men or nature, artistic symbol-manipulators disgusted by anything organic. It includes many normal, earnest people who are unconsciously defending themselves or their families against a vaguely threatening universe. The dangerous eruption of humanity in a deteriorating environment does not show itself as such in the daily experience of most people, but is felt as general tension and anxiety. A kind of madness arises from the prevailing nature-conquering, nature-hating, and self- and world-denial. Although in many ways most Americans live comfortable, satiated lives, there is a nameless frustration born of an increasing nullity. The aseptic home and society are progressively cut off from direct, organic sources of health and increasingly isolated from the means of altering the course of events. Success, where its price is the misuse of landscapes, the deterioration of air and water, and the loss of wild things, becomes a pointless glut, experience one-sided, time on our hands an unlocalized ache.

The unrest can be exploited to perpetuate itself. One familiar prescription for our sick society and its loss of environmental equilibrium is an increase in the intangible Good Things: more Culture, more Security, and more Escape from pressures and tempo. The "search for identity" is not only a social but an ecological problem having to do with a sense of place and time in the context of all life. The pain of that search can be cleverly manipulated to keep the status quo by urging that what we need is only improved forms and more energetic expressions of what now occupy us: engrossment with ideological struggle and military power, with productivity and consumption as public and private goals, with commerce and urban growth, with amusements, with fixation on one's navel, with those tokens of escape or success already belabored by so many idealists and social critics so ineffectually.

To come back to those Good Things: the need for culture, security, and escape [is] just near enough to the truth to take us in. But the real cultural deficiency is the absence of a true *cultus* with its significant ceremony, relevant mythical cosmos, and artifacts. The real failure in security is the disappearance from our lives of the small human group as the functional unit of society and the web of other creatures, domestic and wild, which are part of our humanity. As for escape, the idea of simple remission and avoidance fails to provide for the value of solitude, to integrate leisure and natural encounter. Instead of these, what are foisted on the puzzled and troubled soul as Culture, Security, and Escape are more art museums, more psychiatry, and more automobiles.

The ideological status of ecology is that of a resistance movement. Its Rachel Carsons and Aldo Leopolds are subversive (as Sears recently called ecology itself).[5] They challenge the public or private right to pollute the environment, to systematically destroy predatory animals, to spread chemical pesticides indiscriminately, to meddle chemically with food and water and to appropriate without hindrance space and surface for technological and military ends; they oppose the uninhibited growth of human populations, some forms of "aid" to "underdeveloped" peoples, the needless addition of radioactivity to the landscape, the extinction of species of plants and animals, the domestication of all wild places, large-scale manipulation of the atmosphere or the sea, and most other purely engineering solutions to problems of and intrusions into the organic world.

If naturalists seem always to be against something, it is because they feel a responsibility to share their understanding, and their opposition constitutes a defense of the natural systems to which man is committed as an organic being. Sometimes naturalists propose projects too, but the project approach is itself partly the fault, the need for projects a consequence of linear, compartmental thinking, of machinelike units to be controlled and manipulated.

True ecological thinking need not be incompatible with our place and time. . . . We must use it to confront the great philosophical problems of man— transience, meaning, and limitation—without fear. Affirmation of its own organic essence will be the ultimate test of the human mind.

# NOTES

1. There is a branch of sociology called Human Ecology, but it is mostly about urban geography.
2. See Alan Watts, "The World Is Your Body," in *The Book on the Taboo Against Knowing Who You Are* (New York: Pantheon Books, 1966).
3. Clare A. Gunn in *Landscape Architecture,* July 1966, p. 260.
4. Walter B. Cannon, *Wisdom of the Body* (New York: W. W. Norton, 1932).
5. Paul B. Sears, "Ecology—A Subversive Subject," *BioScience,* 14, no. 7 (July 1964): 11.

# 15 | FOUR CHANGES

## *Gary Snyder*

FOUR CHANGES WAS WRITTEN in the summer of '69 in response to an evident need for a few practical and visionary suggestions. Michael McClure, Richard Brautigan, Steve Beckwitt, Keith Lampe, Cliff Humphreys, Alan Watts, Allen Hoffman, Stewart Brand, and Diane di Prima were among those who read it during its formative period and offered suggestions and criticisms. It was printed and distributed widely, free, through the help of Alan Watts and Robert Shapiro. Several other free editions circulated, including one beautifully printed version by Noel Young of Santa Barbara. Far from perfect and in some parts already outdated, it may still be useful. Sections in brackets are recent commentary.

Whatever happens, we must not go into a plutonium-based economy. If the concept of a steady-state economy can be grasped and started in practice by say, 1980, we may be able to dodge the blind leap into the liquid metal fast breeder reactor—and extensive strip-mining—a path once entered, hard to turn back.

My Teacher once said to me,

> —become one with the knot itself,
>  til it dissolves away.
> —sweep the garden.
> —any size.

## I. POPULATION

### THE CONDITION

Position: Man is but a part of the fabric of life—dependent on the whole fabric for his very existence. As the most highly developed tool-using animal, he

---

Originally published in Gary Snyder, *Turtle Island* (New York: New Directions, 1974). Reprinted with permission. "Postscript" © 1995 by Gary Snyder.

must recognize that the unknown evolutionary destinies of other life forms are to be respected, and act as gentle steward of the earth's community of being.

Situation: There are now too many human beings, and the problem is growing rapidly worse. It is potentially disastrous not only for the human race but for most other life forms.

Goal: The goal would be half of the present world population, or less.

## ACTION

Social/political: First, a massive effort to convince the governments and leaders of the world that the problem is severe. And that all talk about raising food-production—well intentioned as it is—simply puts off the only real solution: reduce population. Demand immediate participation by all countries in programs to legalize abortion, encourage vasectomy and sterilization (provided by free clinics)—free insertion of intrauterine loops—try to correct traditional cultural attitudes that tend to force women into child-bearing—remove income tax deductions for more than two children above a specified income level, and scale it so that lower income families are forced to be careful too—or pay families to limit their number. Take a vigorous stand against the policy of the right wing in the Catholic hierarchy and any other institutions that exercise an irresponsible social force in regard to this question; oppose and correct simple-minded boosterism that equates population growth with continuing prosperity. Work ceaselessly to have all political questions be seen in the light of this prime problem.

[The governments are the wrong agents to address. Their most likely use of a problem, or crisis, is to seize it as another excuse for extending their own powers. Abortion should be legal and voluntary, but questions about vasectomy side-effects still come up. Great care should be taken that no one is ever tricked or forced into sterilization. The whole population issue is fraught with contradictions: but the fact stands that by standards of planetary biological welfare there are already too many human beings. The long-range answer is steady low birth rate. Area by area of the globe, the criteria of "optimum population" should be based on the sense of total ecological health for the region, including flourishing wildlife populations.]

The community: Explore other social structures and marriage forms, such as group marriage and polyandrous marriage, which provide family life but many less children. Share the pleasures of raising children widely, so that all need not directly reproduce to enter into this basic human experience. We must hope that no woman would give birth to more than one [two?] child, during this period of crisis. Adopt children. Let reverence for life and reverence for the feminine mean also a reverence for other species, and future human lives, most of which are threatened.

Our own heads: "I am a child of all life, and all living beings are my brothers and sisters, my children and grandchildren. And there is a child within me waiting to be brought to birth, the baby of a new and wiser self." Love, Love-making, a man and woman together, seen as the vehicle of mutual realization, where the creation of new selves and a new world of being is as important as reproducing our kind.

## II. POLLUTION

### THE CONDITION

Position: Pollution is of two types. One sort results from an excess of some fairly ordinary substance—smoke, or solid waste—which cannot be absorbed or transmitted rapidly enough to offset its introduction into the environment, thus causing changes the great cycle is not prepared for. (All organisms have wastes and by-products, and these are indeed part of the total biosphere: energy is passed along the line and refracted in various ways, "the rainbow body." This is cycling, not pollution.) The other sort is powerful modern chemicals and poisons, products of recent technology, which the biosphere is totally unprepared for. Such is DDT and similar chlorinated hydrocarbons— nuclear testing fall-out and nuclear waste—poison gas, germ and virus storage and leakage by the military; and chemicals which are put into food, whose long-range effects on human beings have not been properly tested.

Situation: The human race in the last century has allowed its production and scattering of wastes, by-products, and various chemicals to become excessive. Pollution is directly harming life on the planet: which is to say, ruining the environment for humanity itself. We are fouling our air and water, and living in noise and filth that no "animal" would tolerate, while advertising and politicians try and tell us we've never had it so good. The dependence of the modern governments on this kind of untruth leads to shameful mind-pollution: mass media and much school education.

Goal: Clean air, clean clear-running rivers, the presence of Pelican and Osprey and Gray Whale in our lives; salmon and trout in our streams; unmuddied language and good dreams.

### ACTION

Social/political: Effective international legislation banning DDT and other poisons—with no fooling around. The collusion of certain scientists with the pesticide industry and agri-business in trying to block this legislation must

be brought out in the open. Strong penalties for water and air pollution by
industries—"Pollution is somebody's profit." Phase out the internal combus-
tion engine and fossil fuel use in general—more research into non-polluting
energy sources; solar energy; the tides. No more kidding the public about
nuclear waste disposal: it's impossible to do it safely, and nuclear-generated
electricity cannot be seriously planned for as it stands now. [Energy: we know
a lot more about this problem now. Non-polluting energy resources such as
solar or tides, would be clearly inadequate to supply the power needs of the
world techno-industrial cancer. Five hundred years of strip-mining is not acceptable. To go into the liquid metal fast breeder reactor on the gamble that
we'll come out with the fusion process perfected is not acceptable. Research
should continue on nuclear power, but divorced from any crash-program
mentality. This means, conserve energy. "Do more with less." "Convert Waste
into Treasure."] Stop all germ and chemical warfare research and experimen-
tation; work toward a hopefully safe disposal of the present staggering and
stupid stockpiles of H-bombs, cobalt gunk, germ and poison tanks and cans.
Laws and sanctions against wasteful use of paper etc. which adds to the solid
wastes of cities—develop methods of recycling solid urban wastes. Recycling
should be the basic principle behind all waste-disposal thinking. Thus, all
bottles should be reusable; old cans should make more cans; old newspapers
back into newsprint again. Stronger controls and research on chemicals in
foods. A shift toward a more varied and sensitive type of agriculture (more
small-scale and subsistence farming) would eliminate much of the call for
blanket use of pesticides.

The community: DDT and such: don't use them. Air pollution: use less
cars. Cars pollute the air, and one or two people riding lonely in a huge car is
an insult to intelligence and the Earth. Share rides, legalize hitch-hiking, and
build hitch-hiker waiting stations along the highways. Also—a step toward
the new world—walk more; look for the best routes through beautiful coun-
tryside for long-distance walking trips: San Francisco to Los Angeles down
the Coast Range, for example. Learn how to use your own manure as fertilizer
if you're in the country—as the Far East has done for centuries. There's a
way, and it's safe. Solid waste: boycott bulky wasteful Sunday papers which
use up trees. It's all just advertising anyway, which is artificially inducing more
energy consumption. Refuse paper bags at the store. Organize Park and Street
clean-up festivals. Don't work in any way for or with an industry which pol-
lutes, and don't be drafted into the military. Don't waste. (A monk and an old
master were once walking in the mountains. They noticed a little hut up-
stream. The monk said, "A wise hermit must live there"—the master said,
"That's no wise hermit, you see that lettuce leaf floating down the stream, he's
a Waster." Just then an old man came running down the hill with his beard

flying and caught the floating lettuce leaf.) Carry your own jug to the winery and have it filled from the barrel.

Our own heads: Part of the trouble with talking about something like DDT is that the use of it is not just a practical device, it's almost an establishment religion. There is something in Western culture that wants to totally wipe out creepy-crawlies, and feels repugnance for toadstools and snakes. This is fear of one's own deepest natural inner-self wilderness areas, and the answer is, relax. Relax around bugs, snakes, and your own hairy dreams. Again, we all should share our crops with a certain percentage of buglife as "paying our dues." Thoreau says: "How then can the harvest fail? Shall I not rejoice also at the abundance of the weeds whose seeds are the granary of the birds? It matters little comparatively whether the fields fill the farmer's barns. The true husbandman will cease from anxiety, as the squirrels manifest no concern whether the woods will bear chestnuts this year or not, and finish his labor with every day, relinquish all claim to the produce of his fields, and sacrificing in his mind not only his first but his last fruits also." In the realm of thought, inner experience, consciousness, as in the outward realm of interconnection, there is a difference between balanced cycle, and the excess which cannot be handled. When the balance is right, the mind recycles from highest illuminations to the muddy blinding anger or grabbiness which sometimes seizes us all; the alchemical "transmutation."

## III. CONSUMPTION

### THE CONDITION

Position: Everything that lives eats food, and is food in turn. This complicated animal, man, rests on a vast and delicate pyramid of energy-transformations. To grossly use more than you need, to destroy, is biologically unsound. Much of the production and consumption of modern societies is not necessary or conducive to spiritual and cultural growth, let alone survival; and is behind much greed and envy, age-old causes of social and international discord.

Situation: Man's careless use of "resources" and his total dependence on certain substances such as fossil fuels (which are being exhausted, slowly but certainly) are having harmful effects on all the other members of the life-network. The complexity of modern technology renders whole populations vulnerable to the deadly consequences of the loss of any one key resource. Instead of independence we have overdependence on life-giving substances such as water, which we squander. Many species of animals and birds have become extinct in the service of fashion fads—or fertilizer—or industrial oil—the soil is being used up; in fact mankind has become a locustlike blight on the planet that will leave a bare cupboard for its own children—all the while in a kind of Addict's Dream of affluence, comfort, eternal progress—using the great achievements of science to produce software and swill.

Goal: Balance, harmony, humility, growth which is a mutual growth with Redwood and Quail; to be a good member of the great community of living creatures. True affluence is not needing anything.

## Action

Social/political: It must be demonstrated ceaselessly that a continually "growing economy" is no longer healthy, but a Cancer. And that the criminal waste which is allowed in the name of competition—especially that ultimate in wasteful needless competition, hot wars and cold wars with "Communism" (or "Capitalism")—must be halted totally with ferocious energy and decision. Economics must be seen as a small sub-branch of Ecology, and production/distribution/consumption handled by companies or unions or co-operatives, with the same elegance and spareness one sees in nature. Soil banks; open spaces [logging to be truly based on sustained yield; the U.S. Forest Service is—sadly—now the lackey of business]. Protection for all scarce predators and varmints: "Support your right to arm bears." Damn the International Whaling Commission which is selling out the last of our precious, wise whales; absolutely no further development of roads and concessions in National Parks and Wilderness Areas; build auto campgrounds in the least desirable areas. Consumer boycotts in response to dishonest and unnecessary products. Radical Co-ops. Politically, blast both "Communist" and "Capitalist" myths of progress, and all crude notions of conquering or controlling nature.

The community: Sharing and creating. The inherent aptness of communal life—where large tools are owned jointly and used efficiently. The power of renunciation: If enough Americans refused to buy a new car for one given year, it would permanently alter the American economy. Recycling clothes and equipment. Support handicrafts, gardening, home skills, mid-wifery, herbs—all the things that can make us independent, beautiful and whole. Learn to break the habit of unnecessary possessions—a monkey on everybody's back—but avoid a self-abnegating anti-joyous self-righteousness. Simplicity is light, carefree, neat and loving—not a self-punishing ascetic trip. (The great Chinese poet Tu Fu said, "The ideas of a poet should be noble and simple.") Don't shoot a deer if you don't know how to use all the meat and preserve that which you can't eat, to tan the hide and use the leather—to use it all, with gratitude, right down to the sinew and hooves. Simplicity and mindfulness in diet is a starting point for many people.

Our own heads: It is hard to even begin to gauge how much a complication of possessions, the notions of "my and mine," stand between us and a true, clear, liberated way of seeing the world. To live lightly on the earth, to be aware and alive, to be free of egotism, to be in contact with plants and animals, starts with simple concrete acts. The inner principle is the insight that we are interdependent energy-fields of great potential wisdom and compassion— expressed in each person as a superb mind, a handsome and complex body, and the almost magical capacity of language. To these potentials and capacities, "owning things" can add nothing of authenticity. "Clad in the sky, with the earth for a pillow."

## IV. TRANSFORMATION

### THE CONDITION

Position: Everyone is the result of four forces: the conditions of this known-universe (matter/energy forms and ceaseless change); the biology of his species; his individual genetic heritage and the culture he's born into. Within this web of forces there are certain spaces and loops which allow to some persons the experience of inner freedom and illumination. The gradual exploration of some of these spaces is "evolution" and, for human cultures, what "history" could increasingly be. We have it within our deepest powers not only to change our "selves" but to change our culture. If man is to remain on earth he must transform the five-millennia-long urbanizing civilization tradition into a new ecologically-sensitive harmony-oriented wild-minded scientific-spiritual culture. "Wildness is the state of complete awareness. That's why we need it."

Situation: Civilization, which has made us so successful a species, has over-shot itself and now threatens us with its inertia. There also is some evidence that civilized life isn't good for the human gene pool. To achieve the Changes we must change the very foundations of our society and our minds.

Goal: Nothing short of total transformation will do much good. What we envision is a planet on which the human population lives harmoniously and dynamically by employing various sophisticated and unobtrusive technologies in a world environment which is "left natural." Specific points in this vision:

- A healthy and spare population of all races, much less in number than today.
- Cultural and individual pluralism, unified by a type of world tribal council. Division by natural and cultural boundaries rather than arbitrary political boundaries.
- A technology of communication, education, and quiet transportation, land-use being sensitive to the properties of each region. Allowing,

thus, the Bison to return to much of the high plains. Careful but intensive agriculture in the great alluvial valleys; deserts left wild for those who would live there by skill. Computer technicians who run the plant part of the year and walk along with the Elk in their migrations during the rest.

• A basic cultural outlook and social organization that inhibits power and property-seeking while encouraging exploration and challenge in things like music, meditation, mathematics, mountaineering, magic, and all other ways of authentic being-in-the-world. Women totally free and equal. A new kind of family—responsible, but more festive and relaxed—is implicit.

## ACTION

Social/political: It seems evident that there are throughout the world certain social and religious forces which have worked through history toward an ecologically and culturally enlightened state of affairs. Let these be encouraged: Gnostics, hip Marxists, Teilhard de Chardin Catholics, Druids, Taoists, Biologists, Witches, Yogins, Bhikkus, Quakers, Sufis, Tibetans, Zens, Shamans, Bushmen, American Indians, Polynesians, Anarchists, Alchemists . . . the list is long. Primitive cultures, communal and ashram movements, co-operative ventures.

Since it doesn't seem practical or even desirable to think that direct bloody force will achieve much, it would be best to consider this a continuing "revolution of consciousness" which will be won not by guns but by seizing the key images, myths, archetypes, eschatologies, and ecstasies so that life won't seem worth living unless one's on the transforming energy's side. We must take over "science and technology" and release its real possibilities and powers in the service of this planet—which, after all produced us and it.

[More concretely: no transformation without our feet on the ground. Stewardship means, for most of us, find your place on the planet, dig in, and take responsibility from there—the tiresome but tangible work of school boards, county supervisors, local foresters—local politics. Even while holding in mind the largest scale of potential change. Get a sense of workable territory, learn about it, and start acting point by point. On all levels from national to local the need to move toward steady state economy—equilibrium, dynamic balance, inner-growth stressed—must be taught. Maturity/diversity/climax/creativity.]

The community: New schools, new classes, walking in the woods and cleaning up the streets. Find psychological techniques for creating an awareness of "self" which includes the social and natural environment. "Consideration of what specific language forms—symbolic systems—and social institutions constitute obstacles to ecological awareness." Without falling into a facile interpretation of McLuhan, we can hope to use the media. Let no one be ignorant of the facts of biology and related disciplines; bring up our children as part of the wildlife. Some communities can establish themselves in backwater rural areas and flourish—others maintain themselves in urban centers, and the two types work together—a two-way flow of experience, people, money and home-grown vegetables. Ultimately cities may exist only as joyous tribal gatherings and fairs, to dissolve after a few weeks. Investigating new life-styles is our work, as is the exploration of Ways to explore our inner realms—with the known dangers of crashing that go with such. Master the archaic and the primitive as models as basic nature-related cultures—as well as the most imaginative extensions of science—and build a community where these two vectors cross.

Our own heads: Is where it starts. Knowing that we are the first human beings in history to have so much of man's culture and previous experience available to our study, and being free enough of the weight of traditional cultures to seek out a larger identity; the first members of a civilized society since the Neolithic to wish to look clearly into the eyes of the wild and see our self-hood, our family, there. We have these advantages to set off the obvious disadvantages of being as screwed up as we are—which gives us a fair chance to penetrate some of the riddles of ourselves and the universe, and to go beyond the idea of "man's survival" or "survival of the biosphere" and to draw our strength from the realization that at the heart of things is some kind of serene and ecstatic process which is beyond qualities and beyond birth-and-death. "No need to survive!" "In the fires that destroy the universe at the end of the kalpa, what survives?"—"The iron tree blooms in the void!"

Knowing that nothing need be done, is where we begin to move from.


# POSTSCRIPT

Twenty-five years later. The apprehension we felt in 1969 has not abated. It would be a fine thing to be able to say, "We were wrong. The natural world is no longer as threatened as we said then." One can take no pleasure, in this case, in having been right. Larger mammals face extinction and all manner of species are being brought near extinction. Natural habitat is fragmented and then destroyed. The world's forests are being cut at a merciless rate. Air, water and soil are all in worse shape. Population continues to climb. The few remaining traditional people with place-based sustainable economies are driven into urban slums or worse. The quality of life for everyone has gone down, what with resurgent nationalism, racism, violence both random and organized, and increasing social and economic inequality. There are whole nations for whom daily life is an ongoing disaster. I still stand by the basics of "Four Changes."

—*Gary Snyder*
*1995*

# 16 | THE SHALLOW AND THE DEEP, LONG-RANGE ECOLOGY MOVEMENTS
## A SUMMARY

## *Arne Naess*

THE EMERGENCE OF ECOLOGISTS from their former relative obscurity marks a turning point in our scientific communities. But their message is twisted and misused. A shallow, but presently rather powerful movement, and a deep, but less influential movement, compete for our attention. I shall make an effort to characterize the two.

I. *The Shallow Ecology movement:*

Fight against pollution and resource depletion. Central objective: the health and affluence of people in the developed countries.

II. *The Deep Ecology movement:*

1. Rejection of the man-in-environment image a favor of *the relational, total-field image.* Organisms as knots in the biospherical net or field of intrinsic relations. An intrinsic relation between two things A and B is such that the relation belongs to the definitions or basic constitutions of A and B, so that without the relation, A and B are no longer the same thing. The total-field model dissolves not only the man-in-environment concept, but every compact thing-in-milieu concept—except when talking at a superficial or preliminary level of communication.

2. *Biospherical egalitarianism*—in principle. The "in principle" clause is inserted because any realistic praxis necessitates some killing, exploitation, and suppression. The ecological field-worker acquires a deep-seated respect, or

---

Originally published in *Inquiry* (Oslo), 16 (1973). Reprinted with permission.

even veneration, for ways and forms of life. He reaches an understanding from within, a kind of understanding that others reserve for fellow men and for a narrow section of ways and forms of life. To the ecological field-worker, *the equal right to live and blossom* is an intuitively clear and obvious value axiom. Its restriction to humans is an anthropocentrism with detrimental effects upon the life quality of humans themselves. The quality depends in part upon the deep pleasure and satisfaction we receive from close partnership with other forms of life. The attempt to ignore our dependence and to establish a master-slave role has contributed to the alienation of man from himself.

Ecological egalitarianism implies the reinterpretation of the future-research variable, "level of crowding," so that *general* mammalian crowding and loss of life-equality is taken seriously, not only human crowding. (Research on the high requirements of free space of certain mammals has, incidentally, suggested that theorists of human urbanism have largely underestimated human life-space requirements. Behavioral crowding symptoms, such as neuroses, aggressiveness, loss of traditions, are largely the same among mammals.)

3. *Principles of diversity and of symbiosis.* Diversity enhances the potentialities of survival, the chances of new modes of life, the richness of forms. And the so-called struggle for life, and survival of the fittest, should be interpreted in the sense of the ability to coexist and cooperate in complex relationships, rather than the ability to kill, exploit, and suppress. "Live and let live" is a more powerful ecological principle than "Either you or me."

The latter tends to reduce the multiplicity of kinds of forms of life, and also to create destruction within the communities of the same species. Ecologically inspired attitudes therefore favor diversity of human ways of life, of cultures, of occupations, of economies. They support the fight against economic and cultural, as much as military, invasion and domination, and they are opposed to the annihilation of seals and whales as much as to that of human tribes and cultures.

4. *Anti-class posture.* Diversity of human ways of life is in part due to (intended or unintended) exploitation and suppression on the part of certain groups. The exploiter lives differently from the exploited, but both are adversely affected in their potentialities of self-realization. The principle of diversity does not cover differences due merely to certain attitudes or behaviors forcibly blocked or restrained. The principles of ecological egalitarianism and of symbiosis support the same anti-class posture. The ecological attitude favors the extension of all three principles to any group conflicts, including those of today between developing and developed nations. The three principles also favor extreme caution toward any over-all plans for the future, except those consistent with wide and widening classless diversity.

5. *Fight against pollution and resource depletion.* In this fight ecologists have

found powerful supporters, but sometimes to the detriment of their total stand. This happens when attention is focused on pollution and resource depletion rather than on the other points, or when projects are implemented which reduce pollution but increase evils of other kinds. Thus, if prices of life necessities increase because of the installation of anti-pollution devices, class differences increase too. An ethics of responsibility implies that ecologists do not serve the shallow, but the deep ecological movement. That is, not only point five, but all seven points must be considered together.

Ecologists are irreplaceable informants in any society, whatever their political color. If well organized, they have the power to reject jobs in which they submit themselves to institutions or to planners with limited ecological objectives. As it is now, ecologists sometimes serve masters who deliberately ignore the wider perspectives.

6. *Complexity, not complication.* The theory of ecosystems contains an important distinction between what is complicated without any Gestalt or unifying principles—we may think of finding our way through a chaotic city—and what is complex. A multiplicity of more or less lawful, interacting factors may operate together to form a unity, a system. We make a shoe or use a map or integrate a variety of activities into a workaday pattern. Organisms, ways of life, and interactions in the biosphere in general, exhibit complexity of such an astoundingly high level as to color the general outlook of ecologists. Such complexity makes thinking in terms of vast systems inevitable. It also makes for a keen, steady perception of the profound *human ignorance* of biospherical relationships and therefore of the effect of disturbances.

Applied to humans, the complexity-not-complication principle favors division of labor, not *fragmentation of labor.* It favors integrated actions in which the whole person is active, not mere reactions. It favors complex economies, an integrated variety of means of living. (Combinations of industrial and agricultural activity, of intellectual and manual work, of specialized and non-specialized occupations, of urban and non-urban activity, of work in city and recreation in nature with recreation in city and work in nature . . .)

It favors soft technique and "soft future-research," less prognosis, more clarification of possibilities. More sensitivity toward continuity and live traditions, and—more importantly, towards our state of ignorance.

The implementation of ecologically responsible policies requires in this century an exponential growth of technical skill and invention—but in new directions, directions which today are not consistently and liberally supported by the research policy organs of our nation-states.

7. *Local autonomy and decentralization.* The vulnerability of a form of life is roughly proportional to the weight of influences from afar, from outside the local region in which that form has obtained an ecological equilibrium. This

lends support to our efforts to strengthen local self-government and material and mental self-sufficiency. But these efforts presuppose an impetus towards decentralization. Pollution problems, including those of thermal pollution and recirculation of materials, also lead us in this direction, because increased local autonomy, if we are able to keep other factors constant, reduces energy consumption. (Compare an approximately self-sufficient locality with one requiring the importation of foodstuff, materials for house construction, fuel and skilled labor from other continents. The former may use only five percent of the energy used by the latter.) Local autonomy is strengthened by a reduction in the number of links in the hierarchical chains of decision. (For example a chain consisting of a local board, municipal council, highest sub-national decision-maker, a state-wide institution in a state federation, a federal national government institution, a coalition of nations, and of institutions, e.g., E. E. C. top levels, and a global institution, can be reduced to one made up of a local board, nation-wide institution, and global institution.) Even if a decision follows majority rule at each step, many local interests may be dropped along the line, if it is too long.

Summing up then, it should, first of all, be borne in mind that the norms and tendencies of the Deep Ecology movement are not derived from ecology by logic or induction. Ecological knowledge and the life-style of the ecological field-worker have *suggested, inspired, and fortified* the perspectives of the Deep Ecology movement. Many of the formulations in the above seven-point survey are rather vague generalizations, only tenable if made more precise in certain directions. But all over the world the inspiration from ecology has shown remarkable convergences. The survey does not pretend to be more than one of the possible condensed codifications of these convergences.

Secondly, it should be fully appreciated that the significant tenets of the Deep Ecology movement are clearly and forcefully *normative*. They express a value priority system only in part based on results (or lack of results, cf. point six) of scientific research. Today, ecologists try to influence policy-making bodies largely through threats, through predictions concerning pollutants and resource depletion, knowing that policy-makers accept at least certain minimum norms concerning health and just distribution. But it is clear that there is a vast number of people in all countries, and even a considerable number of people in power, who accept as valid the wider norms and values characteristic of the Deep Ecology movement. There are political potentials in this movement which should not be overlooked and which have little to do with pollution and resource depletion. In plotting possible futures, the norms should be freely used and elaborated.

Thirdly, insofar as ecology movements deserve our attention, they are *ecophilosophical* rather than ecological. Ecology is a *limited* science which makes use of scientific methods. Philosophy is the most general forum of debate on fundamentals, descriptive as well as prescriptive, and political philosophy is one of its subsections. By an *ecosophy* I mean a philosophy of ecological harmony or equilibrium. A philosophy is a kind of *sophia* wisdom, is openly normative, it contains *both* norms, rules, postulates, value priority announcements *and* hypotheses concerning the state of affairs in our universe. Wisdom is policy wisdom, prescription, not only scientific description and prediction.

The details of an ecosophy will show many variations due to significant differences concerning not only "facts" of pollution, resources, population, etc., but also value priorities. Today, however, the seven points listed provide one unified framework for ecosophical systems.

In general systems theory, systems are mostly conceived in terms of causally or functionally interacting or interrelated items. An ecosophy, however, is more like a system of the kind constructed by Aristotle or Spinoza. It is expressed verbally as a set of sentences with a variety of functions, descriptive and prescriptive. The basic relation is that between subsets of premises and subsets of conclusions, that is, the relation of derivability. The relevant notions of derivability may be classed according to rigor, with logical and mathematical deductions topping the list, but also according to how much is implicitly taken for granted. An exposition of an ecosophy must necessarily be only moderately precise considering the vast scope of relevant ecological and normative (social, political, ethical) material. At the moment, ecosophy might profitably use models of systems, rough approximations of global systematizations. It is the global character, not preciseness in detail, which distinguishes an ecosophy. It articulates and integrates the efforts of an ideal ecological team, a team comprising not only scientists from an extreme variety of disciplines, but also students of politics and active policy-makers.

Under the name of *ecologism,* various deviations from the deep movement have been championed—primarily with a one-sided stress on pollution and resource depletion, but also with a neglect of the great differences between under- and over-developed countries in favor of a vague global approach. The global approach is essential, but regional differences must largely determine policies in the coming years.

# 17 | ECOCENTRISM AND THE ANTHROPOCENTRIC DETOUR

## *George Sessions*

IT IS NOW BECOMING fashionable among environmental ethics theorists and historians to say that Lynn White's paper resulted in the "greening of religion," whereas the "ethical extensionist" theories of the animal liberation philosophers Peter Singer and Tom Regan essentially brought about the "greening of philosophy." For example, Roderick Nash has claimed that the impact of Singer's writings "on the greening of American philosophy can be compared to the effect of Lynn White's 1967 paper on environmental theology."[1]

Actually, Lynn White's critique of Christian anthropocentrism and the ecological crisis, together with Aldo Leopold's ecocentric perspective, were major influences on the rise of ecophilosophy, as well as ecotheology, in the late 1960s and early 1970s.[2] Invidious comparisons were also made during this period between Western anthropocentrism versus the nature-oriented worldviews of the American Indians and other primal peoples, and Eastern religions such as Taoism and Zen Buddhism. These were all major factors that influenced Australian philosopher John Passmore to write his influential ecophilosophy book *Man's Responsibility for Nature* (1974), although Passmore was determined to reject these views and promote an orthodox Western anthropocentric position. The ecocentrism of Leopold's land ethic figured prominently in fellow Australian Richard Routley's early ecophilosophy paper "Is There a Need for a New, an Environmental, Ethic?" (1973).

In the United States during the late 1960s and early '70s, theologian John

Originally published in *ReVision* 13, 3 (1991). Revised 1993. Reprinted with permission of the Helen Dwight Reid Educational Foundation. Published by Heldref Publications, 1319 18th Street, N.W., Washington, DC 20036-1802. Copyright 1991.

Cobb, Jr., and philosophers Charles Hartshorne and Peter Gunter promoted the process philosophy of Alfred North Whitehead as a metaphysical basis for an ecological worldview.[3] And Arne Naess began lecturing on "Philosophy and Ecology" at the University of Oslo in 1968. The ecophilosophy and ecosophy he developed during this period were based upon the metaphysical systems of Spinoza and Gandhi.[4]

Animal liberation theory was a relative latecomer on the ecophilosophical scene and entered the ecophilosophical debate quite tangentially. Peter Singer published a review of animal liberation writing in the *New York Review of Books* in 1973; his book *Animal Liberation* did not appear until 1975. The roots of animal liberation were in the liberal "cruelty to domestic animals" movement of the nineteenth century, in contrast with the ecophilosophical theorizing that arose out of the 1960s as a result of the influence of Thoreau, Muir, Jeffers, Leopold, Carson, Huxley, White, and Snyder. The main concerns of animal liberation were concentrated on the mistreatment of domestic animals and were, at best, peripherially related to the issues raised by ecology and the environmental crisis.

In 1977 John Rodman provided a devastating ecophilosophical critique of the "ethical extensionism" of the animal liberation movement.[5] During the late 1970s, however, ecophilosophical concerns began to narrow in scope in some philosophical circles, moving away from broader metaphysical/ethical and ecopsychological concerns, and from social critiques, to the somewhat specialized search for an "environmental ethic" exemplified, for example, in the writings of J. Baird Callicott and Holmes Rolston III (who were inspired primarily by Leopold's formulation of the "land ethic"). Callicott's subsequent, and usually insightful, critiques of animal liberation theorizing, unfortunately, pitted Leopold's holistic ecosystem ethic against the emphasis of animal rights theorizing on the "rights" of individual nonhuman beings. This led to charges by Tom Regan and others that ecosystem ethics, by apparently discounting the importance of the individual, is fascistic. Nash points to Callicott's claim that "the extent of misanthropy in modern environmentalism may be taken as a measure of the degree to which it is biocentric."[6]

There is no reason why a holistic ecosystem approach (such as Leopold's) necessarily precludes respect for individual beings (human or nonhuman), or leads to misanthropy, and there is no reason to believe that Leopold intended this. For example, Naess's Ecosophy T combines respect for all individuals with respect for ecosystems. Further, John Rodman, in promoting Leopold's ecosystem approach to ecological sensibility, did not denigrate the importance of individuals, nor did he promote misanthropy.[7] From its beginnings in the 1960s, the concerns of ecophilosophy were more metaphysical, holistic, ecocentric, and radical than "ethical extensionist" or "environmental ethics" theorizing.

In what follows, I offer a brief summary of the historical development of human/Nature views in Western culture, together with an account of the rise of environmentalism and ecophilosophy, depicted here as the various twists and turns of Western ecocentric versus anthropocentric worldviews.


## ECOCENTRISM AND PRIMAL CULTURES

Although this issue has been hotly debated in the literature over the last thirty years, it seems accurate to say, based on recent scholarship, that the cultures of most primal (hunting/gathering) societies throughout the world were permeated with Nature-oriented religions that expressed the ecocentric perspective. These cosmologies, involving a sacred sense of the Earth and all its inhabitants, helped order their lives and determine their values. For example, anthropologist Stan Steiner describes the traditional American Indian philosophy of the sacred "Circle of Life":

> In the Circle of Life, every being is no more, or less, than any other. We are all Sisters and Brothers. Life is shared with the bird, bear, insects, plants, mountains, clouds, stars, sun.[8]

Countless expressions of this kind can be cited from primal cultures all over the globe. Despite the present five to six billion people on Earth, some anthropologists argue that the majority of humans who have lived on Earth over the two to four million years of human history have been hunters and gatherers. If so, this means that ecocentrism has been the dominant human religious/philosophical perspective throughout time.

With the beginnings of agriculture, most ecocentric cultures (and religions) were gradually destroyed, or driven off into remote corners of the Earth by pastoral and, eventually, "civilized" cultures (Latin: *civitas,* cities). It appears that one of the functions of the Garden of Eden story was to provide a moral justification for this process. The environmental crisis, in Paul Shepard's view, has been ten thousand years in the making:

> As agriculture replaced hunting and gathering it was accompanied by radical changes in the way men saw and responded to their natural surroundings. . . . [Agriculturalists] all shared the aim of completely humanizing the earth's surface, replacing wild with domestic, and creating landscapes from habitat.[9]

Religious traditions became more anthropocentric as they changed to reflect changes in ways of life from hunting and gathering to pastoral to urban. For example, while Taoism and certain other Eastern religions retained elements of the ancient shamanistic Nature religions, the Western religious tradition radically distanced itself from wild Nature and, in the process, became increasingly anthropocentric. Henri Frankfort claims that Judaism sacrificed

> the greatest good ancient Near East religion could bestow—the harmonious integration of man's life with the life of nature—Man remained outside nature, exploiting it for a livelihood . . . using its imagery for the expression of his moods, but never sharing its mysterious life.[10]

This overall analysis is also supported by the anthropologist Loren Eiseley, who points out:

> Primitive man existed in close interdependence with his first world . . . he was still inside that world; he had not turned her into an instrument or a mere source of materials. Christian man in the West strove to escape this lingering illusion the primitives had projected upon nature. Intent upon the destiny of his own soul, and increasingly urban, man drew back from too great an intimacy with the natural. . . . If the new religion was to survive, Pan had to be driven from his hillside or rendered powerless by incorporating him into Christianity.[11]

Similar conclusions were arrived at by D. H. Lawrence in his 1924 essay "Pan in America," which provides extraordinary insight into the mystical relationship of the American Indians with the Earth and other creatures:

> Gradually men moved into cities. And they loved the display of people better than the display of a tree. They liked the glory they got out of overpowering one another in war. And, above all, they loved the vainglory of their own words, the pomp of argument and the vanity of ideas. . . . Til at last the old Pan died and was turned into the devil of the Christians.[12]

The intellectual Greek strand in Western culture also exhibits a similar development from early ecocentric animistic Nature religions, the Nature-oriented (but less animistic) cosmological speculations of the Pre-Socratics, to the anthropocentrism of the classical Athenian philosophers. Beginning with Socrates, philosophical speculation was characterized by "an undue emphasis upon man as compared with the universe," as Bertrand Russell and other historians of Western philosophy have observed.[13]

With the culmination of Athenian philosophy in Aristotle, an anthropocentric system of philosophy and science was set in place that was to play a major role in shaping Western thought until the seventeenth century. Aristotle rejected the Pre-Socratic ideas of an infinite universe, cosmological and biological evolution, and heliocentrism. He proposed instead an Earth-centered finite universe wherein humans, by virtue of their rationality, were differentiated from, and seen as superior to, animals and plants. Aristotle promoted the hierarchical concept of the "Great Chain of Being," in which Nature *made* plants for the use of animals, and animals were *made* for the sake of humans (*Politics* 1.88).

In the medieval Christian synthesis of Saint Thomas Aquinas, there were problems reconciling Aristotle's naturalism with Christian otherworldliness (including the idea of an immaterial soul), but Aristotle's anthropocentric cosmology was quite compatible with Judeo-Christian anthropocentrism. In the Christian version of the great chain of being, the hierarchical ladder led from a transcendent God, angels, men, women, and children, down to animals, plants, and the inanimate realm.[14] In summarizing the medieval culmination and synthesis of Greek and Christian thought, philosopher Kurt Baier remarked:

> The medieval Christian world picture assigned to man [humans] a highly significant, indeed the central part in the grand scheme of things. The universe was made for the express purpose of providing a stage on which to enact a drama starring Man in the title role.[15]

The West has had several decisive historical opportunities to leave the path of the ecologically destructive "anthropocentric detour" and return to ecocentrism, but has failed to do so. In the twelfth century, the Jewish philosopher Maimonides argued that the world was good before man was created. "It should not be believed," he declared, "that all beings exist for the sake of the existence of man. On the contrary, all the other beings, too, have been intended for their own sakes and not for the sake of something else." In his classic paper of the 1960s, Lynn White, Jr., pointed out that Saint Francis of Assisi, in the thirteenth century, tried to undermine the Christian anthropocentric worldview:

> Francis tried to depose man from his monarchy over creation and set up a democracy of all God's creatures. . . . The greatest spiritual revolutionary in Western history, Saint Francis, proposed what he thought was an alternative Christian view of nature and man's relation to it: he tried to substitute the idea of the equality of all creatures, including man, for the idea of man's limitless rule of creation. He failed. . . .[16]

## THE RISE OF THE ANTHROPOCENTRIC MODERN WORLD

As the West underwent the major intellectual and social paradigm shift from the medieval to the modern world in the seventeenth and eighteenth centuries, the anthropocentrism of the Greek and Judeo-Christian traditions continued to dominate the major theorists of this period. For example, the leading philosophical spokesmen for the Scientific Revolution (Francis Bacon, René Descartes, and Gottfried Leibniz) were all strongly influenced by Christian anthropocentric theology. Bacon claimed that modern science would allow humans to regain a command over Nature that had been lost with Adam's Fall in the Garden. Descartes, considered the "father" of modern Western philosophy, argued that the new science would make humans the "masters and possessors of nature." Also in keeping with his Christian background, Descartes's famous "mind-body dualism" resulted in the view that only humans had minds (or souls): all other creatures were merely bodies (machines). Animals had no sentience (mental life) and so, among other things, could feel no pain. In the middle of the nineteenth century, Darwin had to argue, against prevailing opinion, that at least the great apes experienced various feelings and emotions!

The Scientific Revolution also overturned the age-old organic view of the world as a living organism and replaced it with a mechanistic clockwork image of the world as a machine.[17]

The anthropocentrism of the medieval Christian worldview, perpetuated in the philosophical systems of Bacon, Descartes, and Leibniz, was to combine with, and be reinforced by, Renaissance anthropocentric humanism, which arose prior to the Scientific Revolution (from classical Greek and Roman sources). Renaissance humanism was exemplified in the fifteenth-century pronouncements of Pico della Mirandola, and in Erasmus and Montaigne, and was to continue with the Enlightenment philosophers, and on into the twentieth century with Karl Marx, John Dewey, and the humanistic existentialism of Jean-Paul Sartre. Like medieval Christianity, Renaissance humanism portrayed humans as the central fact in the universe while, in addition, supporting the exalted view that humans had unlimited powers, potential, and freedom (what ecophilosopher Pete Gunter refers to as "man-infinite").

Modern science, however, turned out to be a two-edged sword. As we have seen, seventeenth-century science, on the one hand, was conceived within an anthropocentric humanist/Christian matrix with the avowed purpose, according to Bacon and Descartes, of conquering and dominating Nature. This led Lynn White to claim that both modern science, together with the more recent scientifically based technology of the Industrial Revolution, "is permeated with Christian arrogance toward nature."

On the other hand, the development of modern theoretical science, over the last three hundred years, has resulted in the replacement of the Aristotelian anthropocentric cosmology with essentially the original nonanthropocentric cosmological worldview of the Pre-Socratics; first in astronomy with heliocentrism, the infinity of the universe, and cosmic evolution; then in biology with Darwinian evolution. Ecology, as the "subversive science," has, to an even greater extent than Darwinian biology, stepped across the anthropocentric threshold, so to speak, and pointed toward an ecocentric orientation to the world. Thus, as the modern West has tried to cling to its anthropocentric illusions, each major theoretical scientific development since the seventeenth century has served to "decentralize" humans from their preeminent place in the Aristotelian/Christian cosmology. Lynn White also recognized this aspect of the development of modern science when he pointed out:

> Despite Copernicus, all the cosmos rotates around our little globe. Despite Darwin, we are not, in our hearts, part of the natural process. We are superior to nature, contemptuous of it, willing to use it for our slightest whim.[18]

## SPINOZA'S PANTHEISTIC METAPHYSICS AND THE ROMANTIC MOVEMENT

In the seventeenth century, the Dutch philosopher Baruch Spinoza developed a nonanthropocentric philosophical system designed to head off the Cartesian/Baconian drive for power over Nature. It provided the second opportunity (after Saint Francis) for Western culture to abandon the anthropocentric detour. The British Spinoza scholar Stuart Hampshire points out that

> Spinoza, alone of the great figures of that age, seems somehow to have antici-pated modern conceptions of the scale of the universe, and of man's relatively infinitesimal place with the vast system; in Descartes and in Leibniz . . . one is still in various ways given the impression of a Universe in which human beings on this earth are the privileged center around whom everything is arranged, almost, as it were, for their benefit; whatever their professed doc-trine, almost everyone still implicitly thought in terms of a man-centered universe, although Pascal also . . . had this inhuman vision of human beings as not especially significant or distinguished parts of an infinite system, which seems in itself vastly more worthy of respect and attention than any of our transitory interests and adventures. To Spinoza it seemed that men can attain happiness and dignity only by identifying themselves, through their knowl-edge and understanding, with the whole order of nature.[19]

Drawing upon ancient Jewish pantheistic roots, Spinoza attempted to resa-cralize the world by identifying God with Nature; God/Nature was conceived of as each and every existing being, human and nonhuman. Unlike Descartes, mind (or the mental attribute), for Spinoza, is found throughout Nature.

Spinoza's system is not a static substance metaphysics like that of his con-temporaries. Paul Wienpahl has interpreted it as a process metaphysics: "You find that you can view your world as a kind of fluidity. The ocean is a suitable simile. There is Being and the modes of being, constantly rising up from it, and just as constantly subsiding into it. . . . Perceived clearly and distinctly, God is Being."[20]

The implications Spinoza drew from his system were, however, not explicitly ecological. He held typically seventeenth-century European views of wild nature, including a utilitarian view of animals. In the nineteenth century, Schopenhauer pointed to Spinoza's anomolous attitude toward animals: "Spinoza's contempt for animals, as mere things for our use, and declared by him to be without rights . . . and in conjunction with pantheism is at the same time absurd and abominable." Arne Naess claims that "Spinoza was personally what we today call a speciesist, but his system is not speciesist."[21]

Spinoza's pantheistic vision did not derail the dominant Western philosophic and religious anthropocentrism and the dream of the conquest of Nature in the seventeenth century, but it influenced many who questioned and resisted this trend. Some of the leading figures of the eighteenth-century European Romantic movement (Coleridge, Wordsworth, Shelley, and Goethe) were inspired by Spinoza's pantheism.[22] The Romantic movement arose as the main Western countercultural force speaking on behalf of Nature and the wild, and against the uncritical and unbridled enthusiasm of the Scientific and Industrial Revolutions. Rousseau shocked Europeans by claiming they had lost their spontaneity and freedom, together with the morality and virtues associated with "natural man" living in primal societies, by becoming overly civilized and refined.

## THE NINETEENTH- AND EARLY-TWENTIETH-CENTURY ORIGINS OF ENVIRONMENTALISM

At the beginning of the nineteenth century, Parson Thomas Malthus inadvertently triggered the environmental debate with his "gloomy" thesis that unchecked human population growth is exponential, thus inevitably outrunning food production and resulting in "general misery." Malthus's concerns were not ecological: he was apparently not concerned with, or aware of, the negative effects of the pressures of continued population growth on natural systems and other species (his theory involved a simple human population/food equation). But the larger ecological and environmental issues were soon to be explored by John Stuart Mill, George Perkins Marsh, and John Muir.

**John Stuart Mill.**   The British philosopher and genius John Stuart Mill was a sharply divided personality: the cold logical expositor and developer of Bentham's utilitarianism, but also a botanizer, mountain walker, and admirer of Wordsworth's nature poetry. Mill had read Malthus as a young man and became concerned with the rising rate of human population growth. And, like

Rousseau, he also began to wonder whether modern humans were becoming too civilized. In *Of the Principles of Political Economy* (book IV, 1848) he questioned the ends of industrial progress and looked with aversion on the effects of human overcrowding and on "a world in which solitude is extirpated":

> Solitude, in the sense of being alone often, is essential to any depth of meditation or of character; and solitude in the presence of natural beauty and grandeur, is the cradle of thoughts and aspirations. . . . Nor is there much satisfaction in contemplating the world with nothing left to the spontaneous activity of nature; with every rood of land brought into cultivation . . . every flowery waste or natural pasture plowed up, all quadrupeds or birds which are not domesticated for man's use exterminated as his rivals for food, every hedgerow or superfluous tree rooted out; and scarcely a place left where a wild shrub or flower could grow without being eradicated as a weed in the name of improved agriculture.

As a result, Mill called for a "stationary [steady] state" society to replace continued population and industrial growth.

John Rodman tells the story of how Mill intervened to protect the Kentish orchid from being obliterated by overzealous botanists. Rodman once considered Mill to be the prototype of contemporary ecological sensibility and resistance.[23]

It is understandable why Malthus and Mill were concerned about the growth of human population: population had increased very slowly for many tens of thousands of years. By the time of the Roman Empire, it was estimated to be 250 million. By the year 1650, world population had doubled to 500 million. By 1850, it had doubled again (in only two hundred years) to one billion people, with most of this growth in the West. From an ecological perspective, Mill was right in suggesting a cessation of population and industrial growth and further destruction of the wild at that point in history.

A decade after Mill's work, Darwin shocked the world with the publication of *The Origin of Species* (1859), which located humans ecologically in the natural web of life.[24]

**Henry David Thoreau.**  As the result of recent scholarship, Henry David Thoreau is now recognized as the great ecocentric philosopher of the nineteenth century. Thoreau arrived at an evolutionary (and ecocentric/ecological) perspective before Darwin's works appeared, and certainly by the time of publication of *Walden* in 1854.

Thoreau's countrymen did not know what to make of his critique of the rising American preoccupation with economics and materialism, and his equating of freedom with wildness. As a result, he was not widely read. Roderick Nash points out that the British animal liberationist Henry Salt helped create Thoreau's reputation by writing a biography of him in 1890.[25] But still Thoreau's ecocentrism was misunderstood, and he remained in the shadow of his anthropocentric Transcendentalist mentor, Emerson. The ecological aspects of Thoreau's writings were more fully appreciated by Joseph Wood Krutch in his 1948 biography of Thoreau.[26]

Only now is the full significance of his philosophical achievement being recognized. Thoreau's 1851 statement "In wildness is the preservation of the world" provides the basis for modern ecocentric environmentalism. Concerning the philosophy of the wild that Thoreau developed throughout the 1850s, Roderick Nash comments that "such ideas are totally remarkable for their total absence in previous American thought. . . . Thoreau was not only unprecedented in these ideas, he was virtually alone in holding them.[27]

**George Perkins Marsh.** If Thoreau is now recognized as the first modern ecocentric philosopher then, as Anne and Paul Ehrlich suggest, the American geographer George Perkins Marsh should be considered the first modern environmentalist.[28] According to Nash, Marsh's *Man and Nature* (1864) was "the first comprehensive description . . . of the destructive impact of human civilization on the environment." Marsh pointed to "the necessity of caution in all operations which, on a large scale, interfere with the spontaneous arrangements of the organic and inorganic world; to suggest the possibility and the importance of restoration of disturbed harmonies and the material improvement of waste and exhausted regions. . . ." Marsh was concerned that "the multiplying population and the impoverished resources of the globe" (the impact of humans upon other species, the forests, the soil, and climate) could lead to disaster. Marsh argued his case, however, exclusively on the basis of human welfare.[29]

**John Muir.** Like Thoreau, John Muir's ecocentric philosophy was not fully understood and appreciated until quite recently. In Muir's case, his family had denied scholars access to his personal papers and journals until the mid-1970s.[30]

Muir had a pivotal experience in 1864 (at age twenty-six) during a walk through a Canadian swamp. Here he discovered rare white orchids far from the eyes of humans. It dawned on him that things exist for themselves; the world was not made for man. His ecocentric philosophy developed more fully during his thousand-mile walk to the Gulf of Mexico in 1867, leading to the rejection of the anthropocentrism of his strict Calvinist upbringing ("Lord Man"). Stephen Fox claims that Muir arrived at an ecocentric position based upon his own experiences in wild Nature; his reading of Thoreau and Emerson came later. The ecocentric pantheism of Thoreau and Muir had made a sharp break from the subjectivism of both the Romantics and Emerson's Transcendentalism.

For the next ten years, Muir wandered through Yosemite and the High Sierra, climbing mountains, studying glaciers, and further deepening his ecological consciousness. The major generalizations of ecology were arrived at by Muir through direct intuitive experiential understanding of natural processes and, like Thoreau, by the use of participatory scientific method (e.g., lying down on the glacial polished granite in order to "think like a glacier").[31]

Through his highly acclaimed writings, Muir awakened the American public to the need for protection of the wild, and was chosen to be the first president of the Sierra Club in 1892, a position he held until his death in 1914. Stephen Fox sees Muir as the founder of the American conservation movement.

Since Thoreau and Muir, ecocentrism has had to be discovered and rediscovered time and time again. During the late nineteenth and twentieth centuries, calls for an ecocentric perspective were increasingly "in the air." Victor Hugo proposed that "in the relations of man with the animals, with the flowers, with the objects of creation, there is a great ethic, scarcely perceived as yet, which will at length break forth into the light. . . ." In 1890, Arthur Schopenhauer pointed to a "fundamental error of Christianity . . . the unnatural distinction Christianity makes between man and the animal world to which he really belongs. It sets up man as all-important, and looks upon animals as merely things."

**George Santayana.**   Harvard University philosopher George Santayana is one of the most striking instances of early twentieth-century ecocentrism. Santayana had grown increasingly disillusioned with his anthropocentric pragmatist and idealist colleagues, and with the direction of urbanization and the economic/technological domination-over-Nature path of nineteenth-century America. Upon his retirement in 1911, Santayana came to the University of California, Berkeley to deliver a parting shot at the prevailing anthropocentric American philosophy and religion. Santayana remarked:

> A Californian whom I had recently the pleasure of meeting observed that, if the philosophers had lived among your mountains their systems would have been different . . . from what those systems are which the European genteel tradition has handed down since Socrates; for these systems are egotistical; directly or indirectly they are anthropocentric, and inspired by the conceited notion that man, or human reason, is the center and pivot of the universe. That is what the mountains and the woods should make you at last ashamed to assert. . . . These primeval solitudes [should] . . . suspend your forced sense

of your own importance not merely as individuals, but even as men. They allow you, in one happy moment, at once to play and to worship, to take yourselves simply, humbly, for what you are, and to salute the wild, indifferent, non-censorious infinity of nature.

While Calvinism saw both humans and Nature as sinful and in need of redemption, Emerson's Transcendentalism saw Nature as "all beauty and commodity." Transcendentalism was, for Santayana, a "systematic subjectivism"—a "sham system of Nature." The pragmatism of James and Dewey, and Hegelian idealism, were also anthropocentric. Western religion and philosophy, according to Santayana, failed to provide any restraints on the developing urban-industrial society (the "American Will"). If anything, they provided a justification for the technological domination of Nature.

In Santayana's view, only one American writer, Walt Whitman, had escaped anthropocentrism and the American "genteel tradition" by extending the democratic principle "to the animals, to inanimate nature, to the cosmos as a whole. Whitman was a pantheist; but his pantheism, unlike that of Spinoza, was unintellectual, lazy, and self-indulgent." Santayana looked forward to a new "noble moral imagination": an ecocentric revolution in philosophy.[32]

It is ironic that John Muir was still alive in California at the time of Santayana's Berkeley lecture. Perhaps Santayana looked upon Thoreau and Muir, in line with prevailing opinion, as mere extensions of Emerson's Transcendentalism. But, as we have seen, Thoreau and Muir exemplified the ecocentric revolution Santayana called for.

The development of environmentalism and ecocentrism, from Mill, Marsh, and Thoreau to Muir and Santayana in the early twentieth century, can be viewed as a third opportunity to abandon the anthropocentric detour. The turning point for early-twentieth-century American ecocentrism occurred in the confrontation between Muir, Gifford Pinchot, and Theodore Roosevelt. In 1903, Muir camped out with Roosevelt in Yosemite for three days and tried to influence his philosophical outlook. But Roosevelt ultimately turned away from Muir's ecocentrism (Roosevelt failed to invite Muir to the White House Governors' Conference for Conservation in 1908) and adopted, instead, Pinchot's anthropocentric policies of scientific/technological Resource Conservation and Development. For Pinchot, there were just "people and resources." In 1913, the Pinchot-backed congressional act was signed, damming Muir's Hetch Hetchy Valley in Yosemite to provide water for the growing city of San Francisco, an event some say broke Muir's heart. He died the following year. A unique opportunity to set America on an ecocentric ecological path was lost.[33]

## ECOCENTRISM AFTER WORLD WAR II

While America and the rest of Western culture continued with the anthropocentric detour, now under Pinchot's Resource Conservation and Development policies, ecocentrism remained alive from the 1920s through the 1950s in the writings of D. H. Lawrence, Robinson Jeffers, Joseph Wood Krutch, and various professional ecologists, including Aldo Leopold.

In addition to the influence of Spinoza on Santayana, Spinoza's pantheism continued to play a role in ecocentric thinking in the twentieth century. Two of the leading intellects of the early twentieth century, Bertrand Russell and Albert Einstein, were deeply influenced by Spinoza. Einstein called himself a "disciple of Spinoza," expressed his admiration, as well, for Saint Francis, and held that "cosmic religious feeling" was the highest form of the religious life.

Recent scholarship has revealed that Russell's cosmology, ethics, and religious orientation were essentially Spinozistic. At the end of the Second World War, and before there was any public awareness of the mounting environmental crisis, Russell was a lone philosopher (with the possible exception of Heidegger) speaking out against anthropocentrism and the instrumental use of Nature. He argued that the philosophies of Marx and Dewey were anthropocentric: they placed humans in the center of things and were "inspired by scientific *technique*." These are "power philosophies, and tend to regard everything non-human as mere raw material." Prophetically, Russell warned that the desire of Dewey and Marx for social power over Nature "contributes to the increasing danger of vast social disaster."[34]

Einstein and Russell were drawn to Spinoza largely from the perspective of cosmology and astronomy. An ecological expression of Spinoza's pantheism had to await the California poet Robinson Jeffers and the Norwegian philosopher Arne Naess.

From his perch on the Hawk Tower on the Carmel coast beginning in the 1920s, Jeffers developed a pantheistic philosophy, expressed through his poetry, which he called "Inhumanism" as a counterpoint to Western anthropocentrism. One Jeffers scholar claimed that Jeffers was "Spinoza's twentieth-century evangelist." Jeffers's ecocentric philosophy and poetry has had a major influence on David Brower, Ansel Adams, and other prominent contemporary environmentalists.[35]

World population growth and wild habitat and species destruction continued unabated. Human population continued to increase exponentially; it doubled in eighty years (from 1850 to 1930) to 2 billion, and was on its way to another doubling (in forty-six years) to 4 billion humans in 1976. Shortly after World War II, attention again focused on the wider issues of overpopulation and environmental destruction. In 1948, Sir Julian Huxley, as director general of UNESCO, warned of the dangers of overpopulation. He grossly underestimated the rate of increase, speculating that we might reach 3 billion by the twenty-first century, but claimed that "population must be balanced against resources or civilization will perish."[36]

Two influential books also appeared in 1948 (Fairfield Osborn's *Our Plundered Planet,* and William Vogt's *Road to Survival*), which, in the spirit of Marsh, warned apocalyptically of a population/resources/environmental crisis. Vogt specifically focused on the issue of American overconsumption, claiming the United States was overpopulated with 147 million people, and called for a social and values revolution.[37]

Aldo Leopold's *Sand County Almanac* appeared posthumously in 1949, although its ecocentric message typically was not appreciated and accepted until years later. It culminated in a statement of his "land ethic": "A thing is right when it tends to preserve the integrity, stability, and beauty of the biotic community." Leopold's "land ethic" became the basis of the burgeoning new philosophical field of environmental ethics in the 1970s. Leopold argued for the "biotic right" of plants, animals, waters, and soils to continued existence in our life communities. He began to think ecocentrically in the 1920s as he made the transition from being trained as a Pinchot resource manager to a more Muir-like position. Anne and Paul Ehrlich claim that "the works of Leopold, Vogt and Osborn . . . greatly influenced our own thinking and that of many other ecologists of our generation."[38]

In *Brave New World Revisited* (1959) Aldous Huxley stressed the dangers of overpopulation, claiming that it was the main factor leading the world toward totalitarianism. About the same time, an ecological perspective became central to Huxley's thought. In 1963, Huxley argued that accelerating population growth "will nullify the best efforts of underdeveloped countries to better their lot and will keep two-thirds of the human race in a condition of misery. . . ." He claimed that "the basic problem confronting twentieth-century man is an ecological problem" and that we should shift our concerns to the "politics of ecology." In his 1967 "Historical Roots" paper, Lynn White mentions having influential ecological conversations with Huxley.[39]

## ECOCENTRISM AND THE ECOLOGICAL REVOLUTION OF THE 1960s

The Ecological Revolution of the 1960s was quite remarkable in that ecocentrism emerged for the first time as a major intellectual and social force in American life, and provided yet another opportunity to abandon the anthropocentric detour. Environmental historian Carroll Pursell has described this as a transition "from conservation to ecology": from Pinchot's Resource Conservation and Development position to Thoreau, Muir, Leopold, Rachel Carson, and David Brower as guiding beacons. Supreme Court Justice William O. Douglas provides an interesting example of this philosophic shift from Pinchot back to Muir.[40]

**David Brower and the Sierra Club.**   At the 1959 Sierra Club Wilderness conference, professional ecologists argued that the efforts of conservation organizations to protect wilderness would be futile unless they also focused on overpopulation. Finally, in 1965 the Sierra Club "adopted a policy statement indicting overpopulation for threatening wilderness and wildlife while damaging the general quality of life." As the Club's executive director David Brower said at the time, "you don't have a conservation policy unless you have a population policy."[41] The on-going Wilderness Conferences held from the 1950s through the '70s became the main public forum for ecologists to link traditional conservation interests with the new ecological perspective.

Dave Brower was an ecocentrist, claiming that "I believe in wilderness for itself alone. . . . I believe in the rights of creatures other than man." His highly acclaimed Sierra Club Exhibit Format books—for example, *This Is the American Earth* (1960), *In Wildness Is the Preservation of the World* (1962), *Not Man Apart* (1964), and *Gentle Wilderness* (1964)—brought to a wide audience the ecocentric philosophies of Thoreau, Jeffers, and Muir amid stunning photographs of wild Nature. Throughout the '60s, Brower moved the Sierra Club philosophically, and in terms of his aggressive campaign tactics, increasingly in an ecocentric direction (culminating in his daring 1967 proposal for an "Earth International Park"). John McPhee called Brower the "archdruid," while historian Stephen Fox refers to him as "Muir reincarnate." Brower was fired as executive director in 1969 for what Susan Zakin calls "his difficult management style and fiscal freehandedness." He had become too radical and was moving environmentalism too fast for more conservative Club leaders.[42]

In addition to Brower's Muir-like radical leadership of the Sierra Club and publication of the Exhibit Format books, five major literary events can be singled out that helped define the philosophical basis of the Ecological Revolution of the 1960s. These were the publication of Rachel Carson's *Silent Spring* (1962), Steward Udall's *The Quiet Crisis* (1963), Lynn White's "Historical Roots of Our Ecologic Crisis" (1967), Roderick Nash's *Wilderness and the American Mind* (1967), and Paul Ehrlich's *The Population Bomb* (1968).

**Rachel Carson's *Silent Spring.***   Carson's book rightfully marks the beginning of the modern environmental movement; it was on the *New York Times* bestseller list for thirty-one weeks and sold more than half a million copies. While she argued her case against pesticides largely in terms of human welfare, as a biologist her underlying concerns extended more deeply to the natural world. She dedicated *Silent Spring* to Albert Schweitzer and was heavily influenced by his "reverence for life" principle. In the closing pages of the book she posed a challenge to Western anthropocentrism: "The 'control of nature,' " she claimed, "is a phrase conceived in arrogance, born of the Neanderthal age of biology and philosophy, when it was supposed that nature exists for the convenience of man." She confided to her editor that while her intention in writing the book was to emphasize the menace to human health, nevertheless she was convinced that the dangers pesticides posed to "the basic ecology of all living things . . . outweighs by far . . . any other aspect of the problem." And so the beginnings of the modern environmental movement with Carson were characterized by a deep and abiding ecocentrism.[43]

**Stuart Udall's** *The Quiet Crisis.*  John F. Kennedy's secretary of the interior, Stewart Udall (with help from Wallace Stegner), published *The Quiet Crisis* in 1963. Conceived of as launching "the third wave of conservation," it too became a best-seller, although it tended to be overshadowed by the shock waves caused by Carson's *Silent Spring.* It outlined the "conservation" crisis; helped popularize the ideas of Marsh, Thoreau, and Muir; mentioned Leopold; and pointed to changing attitudes toward the nature religions and "land wisdom" of the American Indians. Udall called for "modern Muirs" to step forward and carry on the conservation fight. In 1965, *Time* magazine asserted, "The real father of conservation is considered to be John Muir."[44]

**Lynn White's** "Historical Roots".  Lynn White, Jr., brought the anthropocentrism issue to center stage with his "Historical Roots" paper linking Christian anthropocentrism with the ecological crisis. It first appeared in the prestigious journal *Science* in 1967 and was soon reprinted in the *Sierra Club Bulletin,* the *Whole Earth Catalogue, Horizon Magazine,* Garrett DeBell's *Environmental Handbook,* and even *The Boy Scout Handbook,* as well as many other ecological anthologies which appeared in the late 1960s and early '70s.

Although White's paper served as the focus of the ensuing anthropocentrism/ecocentrism debate, criticism of Christian anthropocentrism had been widespread throughout the ecological community for years, having also been made by Muir, Schopenhauer, Jeffers, Krutch, Huxley, and Ian McHarg, among others. For example, in 1960, the ecologist Marston Bates worried about the "dizzy rate of population growth and the exhaustion of resources," criticized Christian anthropocentrism, referred to Schweitzer's "reverence for life" principle, called for philosophers to develop an ecological philosophy and, anticipating White, proposed Saint Francis as the patron saint of ecologists.

Stephen Fox has observed that "when Lynn White wrote his article in 1966, he was merely summarizing ideas with a long history among conservationists. . . . White's contribution was to bring the viewpoint to a larger audience, with the authority and literary panache of a skilled historian."[45]

**Roderick Nash's *Wilderness and the American Mind*.** Stuart Udall mentioned the difficulty he had in writing *The Quiet Crisis:* he thought it scandalous that no academic history of American conservation had ever been written. In a roundabout way (by discussing the "idea" of wilderness), the young graduate student Roderick Nash's Ph.D. dissertation, published as *Wilderness and the American Mind* (1967), became the first intellectual history of conservation. Nash later claimed that the timing was right: it went through "seven quick reprintings and into a second, revised edition in 1973."[46] In 1981, the *Los Angeles Times* listed it "among the one hundred most influential books published in the United States in the last quarter century." Nash's book began with European attitudes toward Nature and wilderness; discussed the Romantic movement and the philosophies of Thoreau, Muir, and Leopold; and chronicled various environmental battles. Nash soon became the major academic proponent of Leopold's thought and land ethic.

**Paul Ehrlich's *The Population Bomb*.** David Brower encouraged Stanford biologist Paul Ehrlich to write this book, which made human overpopulation a central issue in the environmental debate of the late '60s. Stephen Fox noted that it "sold three million copies over the next decade. It was the best-selling conservation book ever." Influenced by William Vogt, Ehrlich outlined the overpopulation/environmental crisis, using arguments similar to those advanced earlier by the Huxleys. He referred approvingly to Lynn White's paper on anthropocentrism, and claimed that "we've got to change from a growth-oriented exploitive system to one focused on stability and conservation. Our entire system of orienting to nature must undergo a revolution."[47]

Ehrlich became, along with Barry Commoner, a major "media star" of the environmental movement, giving innumerable talks on overpopulation and environment at college campuses right up through Earth Day, and serving as a counterpoint to Commoner's more narrowly focused urban pollution approach.

While Ehrlich became a "lighting rod" for attacks from leftists, capitalists, conservative Christians, and others opposed to a policy of human population stabilization and reduction, he was (like Lynn White) merely forcefully and influentially promoting ideas which, as we have seen, were widely advocated in conservationist and ecologist circles since the late 1940s, and which extended back to Marsh and Mill.

Paul Ehrlich helped establish the organization Zero Population Growth and, together with his wife, Anne, a biologist, wrote some of the earliest environmental/ecological textbooks. In the late '70s, with his former student Michael Soulé, Ehrlich helped found the new field of conservation biology.[48] In 1986 he announced his support of the Deep Ecology movement, claiming that it may be "the main hope for changing humanity's present course. . . ."[49]

If noncoercive low birth-rate population programs (promoted by Ehrlich and other ecologists and environmentalists of the 1960s) could have been agreed upon by the world community, building upon the impetus of Earth Day I and vigorously instituted and sustained globally throughout the 1970s and '80s, it might have been possible to stabilize world population at 5 to 6 billion people. Now United Nations projections are for world population to reach 10 to 15 billion people before stabilizing. The human overpopulation situation, together with the corresponding loss of wild species and ecosystems, is perhaps the most tragic aspect of the contemporary ecological crisis.

Finally, over forty years after William Vogt and the Huxleys issued warnings on the human overpopulation/environmental crisis, and twenty-five years after Paul Ehrlich wrote *The Population Bomb,* the conservative world scientific establishment has officially acknowledged the crisis. In February 1992, the National Academy of Sciences and the Royal Society of London jointly announced that the worldwide population growth of nearly 100 million people annually was the "core reason" for the loss of forests, global warming, and the rate of species extinction. They claimed that "the future of the planet is in balance" and called for the rapid stabilization of world population.

Two other books of this period deserve mention. Edward Abbey's *Desert Solitaire* (1968) immediately became an underground environmental classic and inspired a new generation of activists. In this book, Abbey attacked anthropocentrism, overpopulation, industrial tourism, and the anti-ecological growth policies of the industrial state, while promoting wildness and the ecocentric point of view. His later novel, *The Monkey Wrench Gang* (1976), inspired Dave Foreman and other founders of the Earth First! organization. Earth First! reinvigorated a sagging and compromised environmental movement during the 1980s, dramatically bringing the issues of wild ecosystem protection, human overpopulation, and ecocentrism again to public consciousness.

The other book is the *Environmental Handbook* (1970), edited by Garrett DeBell. David Brower, who was president of the newly formed Friends of the Earth, managed to have the book published in one month to be ready for the first Earth Day on April 22, 1970. Max Oelschlaeger claims the book

"became a virtual bible for the environmental teach-ins and consciousness raising activities associated with Earth Day I, going through three printings between January and April, 1970. What startles the contemporary reader is that virtually all the problems that characterize our present ecocrisis are identified there. Paul Ehrlich writing on "Too Many People." David Brower on the wilderness and its preservation. Kenneth Boulding on the paradox of an economics . . . sure to undercut nature's economy. Lynn White on the culpability and responsibility of Judeo-Christianity. Gary Snyder . . . on the necessity of creating an old-new mythos that would lead us into a post-modern age. And the list goes on and on.[50]

Earth Day I was an awe-inspiring event. As Kirkpatrick Sale describes it:

. . . April 22 saw probably the largest of all the demonstrations of the 1960's. According to the organizers, 1,500 colleges and 10,000 schools took part, many campuses had street demonstrations and parades, and large rallies were held in New York, Washington, and San Francisco. *Time* estimated that some 20 million people were part of what [Gaylord] Nelson called "truly an astonishing grass-roots explosion."

For a new generation, or those too young to remember, it is difficult to imagine the excitement of these mass demonstrations in support of the Earth, expressing an idealistic hope for a new ecological beginning for humanity. As one of the organizers of the event, Denis Hayes, later commented, "We hoped it would lead to a new kind of ideology, a new value system based on ecology and a reverence for life."[51]

## ECOCENTRISM VERSUS ANTHROPOCENTRIC SURVIVAL ENVIRONMENTALISM

Not all those participating in Earth Day recognized the need for, or aspired to, a new ecocentric value system or felt a "reverence for life." The main new ingredient in 1960s environmentalism was the rise of an anthropocentric urban/industrial "pollution consciousness" narrowly emphasizing the issue of human survival. Stephen Fox claims that the "newer man-centered leaders" of this aspect of environmentalism (such as Barry Commoner, Ralph Nader, and the Environmental Defense Fund) saw industrial pollution as the essence of the environmental problem. Barry Commoner (who had a Marxist background and was not trained as an ecologist) graced the cover of *Time* as "the Paul Revere of ecology," became known as the "pollution man," and was soon embroiled in a debate with Paul Ehrlich over whether or not human overpopulation was a major factor in the environmental crisis.[52]

In summary of this period, Susan Zakin claims that "when the children of the sixties tentatively pulled the two strands of old-style wilderness conservation and populist pollution fighting together on April 22, 1970, they created what is now considered the contemporary environmental movement."[53]

But things were not quite this simple. As urban pollution/survival environmentalism increasingly dominated the public's attention, more long-range ecocentric concerns such as wild ecosystem and species protection suffered. David Brower and Michael McCloskey (the new executive director of the Sierra Club) worried that the new anthropocentric "survival environmentalism" would overwhelm the deeper message of ecology (protection of wilderness, wild species, and the biological integrity of the Earth). McCloskey wrote in the early '70s that the "new environmentalism" looked upon wilderness protection as "parochial and old fashioned."[54] These two major orientations in environmentalism have competed with each other for public attention to the present day, despite the frantic warnings throughout the 1980s of E. O. Wilson, Paul Ehrlich, and other conservation biologists regarding the crucial necessity of protecting biodiversity and species habitat.

Furthermore, "old-style wilderness conservation" had been undergoing a sea change since the 1950s with its new emphasis upon resource depletion, pollution, and overpopulation, as well as wilderness protection (the 1960 Sierra Club Exhibit Format book *This Is the American Earth,* recently reprinted, dramatically illustrates this wider approach to the environment). The rationale for protecting wilderness, as we have seen, had shifted from an emphasis upon aesthetics and recreation to ecosystem and wild species protection. The Sierra Club Wilderness Conferences had focused on overpopulation and the ecosystem protection functions of designated wilderness areas since 1959. This emphasis continued at the 1969 Sierra Club Wilderness Conference which, according to Michael Cohen,

> focused on the role of wildlife in wilderness, particularly in Alaska; the ecological integrity of parks and wilderness was uppermost in the minds of organizers and participants. A critique of policy in national parks in 1969 insisted that the ecological well-being of parks and perpetuation of their natural biological communities must come before recreational needs, and that the parks were not islands. . . . In his keynote address at the conference Paul Erhlich denounced "the continuing delusion . . . that environmental problems can be separated from the population explosion."[55]

Many of Brower's radical ecological ideas, spurred on by the new environmental awareness surrounding Earth Day I, continued to influence policy in the Sierra Club for several years after his firing. As one old guard Sierra Club director, Richard Leonard, said in retrospect, these ideas "were carried out simply because Brower was right. His ideas were sound ideologically." Michael McCloskey had 400,000 copies of *Ecotactics: The Sierra Club Handbook for*

*Environmental Activists* published for Earth Day. The young new president of the Sierra Club, Phil Berry, promoted the aggressive global ecological agenda begun by Brower as well as aspects of survival environmentalism. The Club's statement of purpose was changed to reflect a concern for "preserving and restoring the integrity of the World's natural ecosystems," although it unfortunately still referred to the Earth as "natural resources." But during the 1970s, the Sierra Club gradually pulled back from this more aggressive stance, became more anthropocentric, bureaucratic, and pragmatic in philosophy and tactics (as did the other mainstream reform environmental organizations), thus creating a vacuum later to be filled by Earth First! and other ecocentric radical environmental groups.[56]

## THE RISE OF THE LONG-RANGE DEEP ECOLOGY MOVEMENT

Arne Naess grew up in the wild mountain and coastal areas of Norway. Given his early fascination with Nature, a lawyer he met in the mountains told him he should read Spinoza, and, by the time Naess reached the age of seventeen, Spinoza had become his favorite philosopher. Two years later, while he was a young student in Paris, Gandhi became of one his heroes as well, as a result of Gandhi's 1931 "salt march." As a professor of philosophy, Naess formed academic Spinoza study groups at the University of Oslo in the 1960s, which produced important and original Spinoza scholarship. While in California in the mid-1960s, he became aware of the environmental activism resulting from Rachel Carson's efforts. Together with his student Sigmond Kvaloy, Naess took part in direct action environmental campaigns in Norway. Then, partly at the urging of his students, he began to develop the philosophies of Spinoza and Gandhi into a coherent ecophilosophy (or ecosophy) to serve as a basis for ecological understanding and action. Naess claims that for Spinoza

> all particular things are expressions of God; through all of them God acts. There is no hierarchy. There is no purpose, no final causes such that one can say that the "lower" exist for the sake of the "higher." There is an ontological democracy or equalitarianism which, incidentally, greatly offended his contemporaries, but of which ecology makes us more tolerant today . . . no great philosopher has so much to offer in the way of clarification and articulation of basic ecological attitudes as Baruch Spinoza.[57]

Also during the 1960s, the California poet and essayist Gary Snyder began weaving together an ecocentric/Deep Ecological philosophy and lifestyle based upon Zen Buddhism, the religions and ways of life of American Indians and other primal peoples, and the science of ecology.

Max Oelschlaeger has referred to Snyder as the "poet laureate of Deep Ecology." He claims that Snyder's latest book, *The Practice of the Wild* (1990) "is the most inspiring statement of an environmental ethic since Aldo Leopold's *Sand County Almanac*," and ranks these two books alongside Thoreau's *Walden*.[58]

Gary Snyder's writings were very popular and influential in the 1960s and '70s, but have become even more influential during the last four or five years, as reinhabitory and bioregional thinking has begun to enter mainstream thinking and policy making in the United States. Snyder is the leading spokesperson for the American bioregional movement.

# NOTES

1. Nash, *The Rights of Nature: A History of Environmental Ethics* (Madison: University of Wisconsin Press, 1989), p. 137. Nash's history is required reading for students of ecophilosophy, but his strenuous efforts to interpret the development of ecophilosophy in terms of "ethical extensionism," and as the inevitable American liberal "rounding out" of liberty and the doctrine of natural rights, has serious philosophical problems. For a critique of Nash's interpretation, see Tom Birch, "The Incarceration of Wildness: Wilderness Areas as Prisons," *Environmental Ethics* 12, (1990): 3–26. A recent textbook that also tends to take the "animal rights as the greening of philosophy" approach is Joseph R. DesJardins, *Environmental Ethics* (Belmont, Calif.: Wadsworth, 1993).

2. See also Roderick French, "Is Ecological Humanism a Contradiction in Terms?: The Philosophical Foundations of the Humanities Under Attack," in J. Donald Hughes and Robert C. Schultz (eds.), *Ecological Consciousness: Essays from the Earthday X Colloquium* (Washington, D.C.: University Press of America, 1981), pp. 43–66.

3. For discussions of these ecophilosophical developments in the United States, Norway, and Australia during the late 1960s and early 1970s, see George Sessions, "Shallow and Deep Ecology: A Review of the Philosophical Literature," in Robert Schultz and J. Donald Hughes (eds.), *Ecological Consciousness*, pp. 391–462; George Sessions, "The Deep Ecological Movement: A Review," *Environmental Review* 11 (1987): 105–25; Sessions, "Paul Shepard: Ecological Elder," in Max Oelschlaeger (ed.), *Nature's Odyssey: Essays on Paul Shepard* (Denton: University of North Texas Press, 1995); Richard Routley's 1973 paper has been reprinted in Michael Zimmerman, J. Baird Callicott, George Sessions et al. (eds.), *Environmental Philosophy: From Animal Rights to Radical Ecology* (Englewood Cliffs, N.J.: Prentice-Hall, 1993), pp. 12–21. The early developments in Australian ecophilosophy are discussed in the introduction to Don Mannison, Michael McRobbie, and Richard Routley (eds.), *Environmental Philosophy* (Canberra: Philosophy Department, RSSS, Australian National University, 1980).

4. Arne Naess, *Økologi, Samfunn og Livsstil* (Oslo: Universitetsforlaget, 1973), went through five editions in Norwegian by 1976, and a Swedish edition, and was very influential throughout Scandinavia. This book arose out of a third, expanded edition of a short work, *Ecology and Philosophy,* Naess had begun in the late '60s. The book was revised and first published in English as *Ecology, Community, and Lifestyle* (Cambridge: Cambridge University Press, 1989). Historically, Naess's book deserves credit for being the first book written and published by a professional philosopher in ecophilosophy (preceding Passmore's, but unfortunately Naess's book was not available in English).

5. John Rodman, "The Liberation of Nature?" *Inquiry* (Oslo) 20 (1977): 83–131. This is one of the classic ecophilosophic papers of the 1970s, but its length has unfortunately precluded its being reprinted in anthologies; for a discussion of Rodman's critique, see Nash, *The Rights of Nature,* pp. 152–53; see also Sessions, "Paul Shepard: Ecological Elder."

6. Nash, *The Rights of Nature,* pp. 153–54; see J. Baird Callicott, "Animal Liberation: A Triangular Affair," *Environmental Ethics* 2 (1980): 311–28; Callicott, "Review of Tom Regan, *The Case for Animal Rights,*" *Environmental Ethics* 7 (1985): 365–72.

7. See John Rodman, "Four Forms of Ecological Consciousness Reconsidered," in Donald Scherer and Thomas Attig (eds.), *Ethics and the Environment* (Englewood Cliffs, N.J.: Prentice-Hall, 1983), pp. 82–92.

8. Stan Steiner, *The Vanishing White Man* (New York: Harper and Row, 1976), p. 113; see also J. Baird Callicott, "Traditional American Indian and Western European Attitudes toward Nature," *Environmental Ethics* 4 (1982): 293–328; J. Donald Hughes, *American Indian Ecology* (El Paso: Texas Western Press, 1983); Max Oelschlaeger, *The Idea of Wilderness: From Prehistory to the Age of Ecology* (New Haven: Yale University Press, 1991), pp. 1–30; Jerry Mander, *In the Absence of the Sacred: The Failure of Technology and the Survival of the Indian Nations* (San Francisco: Sierra Club Books, 1991), parts 3 and 4; John Grim, "Native North American Worldviews and Ecology," in M. Tucker and J. Grim (eds.), *World Views and Ecology* (Lewisburg, Pa.: Bucknell Univ. Press, 1993), pp. 41–54.

9. Paul Shepard, *The Tender Carnivore and the Sacred Game* (New York: Scribner's, 1973) p. 237; see also Paul Shepard, "A Post-Historic Primitivism," in M. Oelschlaeger (ed.), *The Wilderness Condition* (San Francisco: Sierra Club Books, 1992), pp. 40–89; Calvin Martin, *In the Spirit of the Earth: Rethinking History and Time* (Baltimore: Johns Hopkins University Press, 1992); Max Oelschlager, *The Idea of Wilderness* (New Haven: Yale University Press, 1991), pp. 1–30.

10. Henri Frankfort, *Kingship and the Gods* (Chicago: University of Chicago Press, 1948), pp. 342–44.

11. Loren Eiseley, "The Last Magician," in Eiseley, *The Invisible Pyramid* (New York: Scribner's, 1970), pp. 137–56.

12. D. H. Lawrence, "Pan in America," in E. McDonald (ed.), *Phoenix* (New York: Macmillan, 1936); see also Dolores LaChapelle, "D. H. Lawrence and Deep Ecology," *The Trumpeter (Canadian Journal of Ecosophy)* 7, 1 (1990): 26–30; for another

powerful account of American Indian nature mysticism (in which the world was "a place bristling and crackling with spiritual power"), see Calvin Martin, "The American Indian as Miscast Ecologist," in Schultz and Hughes, *Ecological Consciousness,* pp. 137–48.

13. Bertrand Russell, *A History of Western Philosophy* (New York: Simon and Schuster, 1945), pp. 72–73.

14. For a critical discussion of the Christian anthropocentric patriarchal "great chain of being" from an ecofeminist perspective, see Elizabeth Gray, *Green Paradise Lost* (Wellesley, Mass.: Roundtable Press, 1982).

15. Kurt Baier, "The Meaning of Life: Christianity versus Science," in A. Bierman and J. Gould (eds.), *Philosophy for a New Generation,* 2nd ed. (New York: Macmillan, 1973).

16. The Maimonides quote appears in Passmore, *Man's Responsibility for Nature,* p. 12; Lynn White, Jr., "Historical Roots of Our Ecologic Crisis," *Science* 155 (1967): 1203–7, reprinted in Ian Barbour (ed.), *Western Man and Environmental Ethics* (Reading, Mass.: Addison-Wesley, 1973).

17. For ecological critiques of Bacon, Descartes, and Leibniz, see Clarence Glacken, "Man against Nature: An Outmoded Concept," in H. H. Helfrich, Jr. (ed.), *The Environmental Crisis* (New Haven: Yale University Press, 1970); Theodore Roszak, *Where the Wasteland Ends* (New York: Doubleday, 1972), pp. 142–77; Max Oelschlaeger, *The Idea of Wilderness,* pp. 68–96; for critiques of the seventeenth-century machine image of the Earth, see Theodore Roszak, *Where the Wasteland Ends,* pp. 142–219; Carolyn Merchant, *The Death of Nature* (New York: Harper and Row, 1980); Fritjof Capra, *The Turning Point* (New York: Simon and Schuster, 1982).

18. For ecological critiques of humanism, see Roderick French, "Is Ecological Humanism a Contradiction in Terms?: The Philosophical Foundations of the Humanities Under Attack," in Hughes and Schultz, *Ecological Consciousness,* pp. 43–66; David Ehrenfeld, *The Arrogance of Humanism* (Oxford: Oxford University Press, 1978); John Livingston, *One Cosmic Instant,* pp. 216–17; White, "Historical Roots of Our Ecologic Crisis."

19. Stuart Hampshire, *Spinoza* (London: Faber and Faber, 1951), pp. 160–61.

20. See Paul Wienpahl, *The Radical Spinoza* (New York: New York University Press, 1979); Paul Wienpahl, "Spinoza's Mysticism," in Wetlesen, *Spinoza's Philosophy of Man;* George Sessions, "Western Process Metaphysics: Heraclitus, Whitehead, and Spinoza," in Bill Devall and George Sessions, *Deep Ecology* (Utah: Peregrine Smith Books, 1985), pp. 236–42; the pre-evolutionary nature of Spinoza's metaphysics has been criticized by Max Oelschlaeger, *The Idea of Wilderness,* pp. 341–43.

21. Arne Naess, "Environmental Ethics and Spinoza's Ethics: Comments on Genevieve Lloyd's Article," *Inquiry* (Oslo) 23, 3 (1980): 323.

22. For a balanced discussion of the Romantic movement, see Theodore Roszak, *Where the Wasteland Ends,* pp. 277–345.

23. John Rodman, "Ecological Resistance: John Stuart Mill and the Case of the Kentish Orchid," unpublished manuscript read at a meeting of the American Political Science Association, 1977. Rodman later substituted Aldo Leopold for Mill as his exemplar of Ecological Sensibility and Resistance.

24. For an excellent discussion of the ecological significance of Darwin, see Donald Worster, *Nature's Economy: The Roots of Ecology* (San Francisco: Sierra Club Books, 1977).

25. Roderick Nash, *The Rights of Nature*, pp. 27–31; Worster, *Nature's Economy*. Worster's chapter on Thoreau in *Nature's Economy*, together with the chapter on Thoreau in Max Oelschlaeger, *The Idea of Wilderness*, pp. 133–71, are important ecocentric interpretations of Thoreau.

26. As a result of Thoreau's influence, Krutch underwent a dramatic conversion from a New York superhumanist literary professor, critic, and pessimist to being a pantheist and passionate advocate of wild Nature, eventually moving to the Arizona desert in 1952. On Krutch and Thoreau, see Nash, *Rights of Nature*, pp. 74–76; Worster, *Nature's Economy*, pp. 333–38; Stephen Fox, *John Muir and His Legacy*, pp. 229–33.

27. Nash, *The Rights of Nature*, pp. 36–38.

28. See Anne and Paul Ehrlich, *Earth* (New York: Franklin Watts, 1987), chap. 7 ("The Coming of the Green"), pp. 157–79, for comments on Marsh and a summary of the development of environmentalism.

29. For discussions of Marsh, see Nash, *The Rights of Nature*, p. 38; Oelschlaeger, *The Idea of Wilderness*, pp. 106–9.

30. The ecocentric interpretations of Muir which are based on his personal papers include Stephen Fox, *John Muir and His Legacy* (1981); Michael P. Cohen, *The Pathless Way: John Muir and American Wilderness* (Madison: University of Wisconsin Press, 1984); Frederick Turner, *Rediscovering America: John Muir in His Time and Ours* (San Francisco: Sierra Club Books, 1985). See also Nash, *The Rights of Nature*, pp. 38–41; Oelschlaeger, *The Idea of Wilderness*, chap. 6.

31. For Muir's participatory science, see Cohen, *The Pathless Way;* for Thoreau's participatory science, see Worster, *Nature's Economy*.

32. George Santayana, "The Genteel Tradition in American Philosophy," in Santayana, *Winds of Doctrine* (New York: Scribner's, 1926), pp. 186–215; Santayana, "Dewey's Naturalistic Metaphysics," *Journal of Philosophy*, December 1925; for a discussion of Santayana's address in an ecological context, see William Everson, *Archetype West* (Berkeley: Oyez Press, 1976), pp. 54–60.

33. For the split between Muir, Pinchot, and Roosevelt, see Roderick Nash, *Wilderness and the American Mind*, 3rd ed. (New Haven: Yale University Press, 1982), pp. 129–40; Fox, *John Muir and His Legacy*, pp. 109–30; Cohen, *The Pathless Way*, pp. 160–61, 292ff. For the Hetch Hetchy controversy, see Michael P. Cohen, *The History of the Sierra Club: 1892–1970* (San Francisco: Sierra Club Books, 1988), pp. 22–33. The Resource Conservation and Development period of American con-

servation history (1890 through the 1950s) has been discussed in various places; see, e.g., Fox, *John Muir and His Legacy,* pp. 103–217; Cohen, *The History of the Sierra Club: 1892–1970.*

34. Albert Einstein, *The World as I See It* (New York: Philosophical Library, 1949), pp. 1–5, 24–29; B. Hoffman and H. Dukas, *Albert Einstein: Creator and Rebel* (New York: New American Library, 1972), pp. 94–95; Arne Naess, "Einstein, Spinoza, and God," in Alwyn van der Merwe (ed.), *Old and New Questions in Physics, Cosmology, Philosophy and Theoretical Biology* (Holland: Plenum Publishing Corporation, 1983), pp. 683–87; Kenneth Blackwell, *The Spinozistic Ethics of Bertrand Russell* (London: Allen and Unwin, 1985); Russell, *A History of Western Philosophy,* pp.–494, 788–89, 827–28.

35. David Brower (ed.), *Not Man Apart: Lines from Robinson Jeffers* (San Francisco: Sierra Club Books, 1965); Ansel Adams, *Ansel Adams: An Autobiography* (Boston: Little, Brown, 1985), pp. 84–87; George Sessions, "Spinoza and Jeffers on Man in Nature," *Inquiry* (Oslo) 20 (1977): 481–528; for the "Jeffers as Spinoza's evangelist" quote, see Arthur Coffin, *Robinson Jeffers: Poet of Inhumanism* (Wisconsin: University of Wisconsin Press, 1971), p. 255.

36. Huxley's speech is discussed in Raymond F. Dasmann, *Planet in Peril* (New York: World Publishing, 1972), p. x; see also Sir Julian Huxley, "The Age of Overbreed," *Playboy Magazine* (1966) reprinted in *Project Survival,* Playboy editors (Chicago: Playboy Press, 1971), pp. 43–64.

37. Fox, *John Muir and His Legacy,* pp. 307–11. Chapter 9 in Fox's book ("The Last Endangered Species") is an excellent summary of the intellectual events leading from the Vogt book through Rachel Carson to Earth Day I, 1970. For the social/political side of this period in history, see Kirkpatrick Sale, *The Green Revolution: The American Environmental Movement 1962–1992* (New York: Hill and Wang, 1993), chaps. 1, 2.

38. Anne and Paul Ehrlich, *Earth,* pp. 167–68. For discussions of Aldo Leopold's "land ethic" and immense contribution to twentieth-century environmentalism and ecocentric thought, see Oelschlaeger, *The Idea of Wilderness,* chap. 7; Fox, *John Muir and His Legacy,* pp. 244–49; Nash, *The Rights of Nature,* pp. 63–74; J. Baird Callicott (ed.), *Companion to A Sand County Almanac* (Madison: University of Wisconsin Press, 1987).

39. Aldous Huxley, "The Politics of Ecology," *Center* magazine (Center for the Study of Democratic Institutions, Santa Barbara, Calif.), 1963.

40. Carroll Pursell (ed.), *From Conservation to Ecology* (New York: T. Y. Crowell, 1973). On Douglas, See Fox, *John Muir and His Legacy,* pp. 239–44; Nash, *The Rights of Nature,* pp. 130–31.

41. See Stephen Fox, *John Muir and His Legacy,* p. 311; Michael Cohen, *The History of the Sierra Cub,* pp. 232–33. For an ecologist's view of the overpopulation problem in the early '60s, see Raymond F. Dasmann, *The Last Horizon* (New York: Macmillan, 1963), pp. 210–27.

42. John McPhee, *Encounters with the Archdruid* (New York: Farrar, Straus and Gir-

oux, 1971), pp. 74, 84–85, 226; David Brower, "Toward an Earth International Park," *Sierra Club Bulletin* 52, 9 (1967): 20. For discussions of Brower and the Sierra Club, see Fox, *John Muir and His Legacy,* pp. 250–90, 316–22; Michael Cohen, *The History of the Sierra Club,* pp. 67–434; Susan Zakin, *Coyotes and Town Dogs* (New York: Viking, 1993), p. 81.

43. The Carson quote appears in Nash, *The Rights of Nature,* p. 80. For a discussion of Carson and the influence of Schweitzer, see Fox, *John Muir and His Legacy,* pp. 292–99, 367–86. For the influence of Carson on the Sierra Club, see Michael Cohen, *The History of the Sierra Club,* pp. 285–91; see also Paul Brooks, *The House of Life* (New York: Houghton Mifflin, 1972); Ralph Lutts, "Chemical Fallout: Rachel Carson's *Silent Spring,* Radioactive Fallout, and the Environmental Movement," *Environmental Review* 9 (1985): 210–25.

44. On Udall's book, see Fox, *John Muir and His Legacy,* pp. 289–90; Cohen, *The History of the Sierra Club,* pp. 271–72.

45. For a recent assessment of White's thesis, see Elspeth Whitney, "Lynn White, Ecotheology, and History," *Environmental Ethics* 15, 2 (1993): 151–69; Marston Bates, *The Forest and the Sea* (New York: Random House, 1960), relevant sections reprinted in an excellent ecophilosophical anthology: Lorne Forstner and John Todd (eds.), *The Everlasting Universe: Readings on the Ecological Revolution* (Lexington, Mass.: Heath and Co., 1971), pp. 46–56; Fox, *John Muir and His Legacy,* p. 363.

46. Stuart Udall, *The Quiet Crisis* (New York: Holt, Rinehart, and Winston, 1963), pp. 203–26; Nash, *Wilderness and the American Mind,* 3rd ed. (1982), p. ix. Max Oelschlaeger's *The Idea of Wilderness* can be seen, in part, as an updated and greatly expanded philosophical reinterpretation of Nash's intellectual history.

47. See Stephen Fox, *John Muir and His Legacy,* pp. 311–13, 355; Paul Ehrlich, *The Population Bomb* (New York: Ballantine, 1968) pp. 169–72.

48. Richard Primack, *Essentials of Conservation Biology* (New York: Sinauer and Sunderland, 1993), p. 18; see Paul and Anne Ehrlich, *Extinction: The Causes and Consequences of the Disappearance of Species* (New York: Random House, 1981).

49. Paul R. Ehrlich, *The Machinery of Nature* (New York: Simon and Schuster, 1986), pp. 17–18; see also Paul and Anne Ehrlich, *Healing the Planet: Strategies for Resolving the Environmental Crisis* (Reading, Mass.: Addison-Wesley, 1991), pp. 257–58.

50. Max Oelschlaeger, *After Earth Day* (Denton: University of North Texas Press, 1992), p. viii.

51. Sale, *The Green Revolution,* p. 24; the Hayes quote appears in Zakin, *Coyotes and Town Dogs,* p. 37.

52. Stephen Fox, *John Muir and His Legacy,* pp. 302–306, 312–13, 355.

53. Susan Zakin, *Coyotes and Town Dogs,* p. 36.

54. Michael McClosky, "Wilderness Movement at the Crossroads," *Pacific Historical Review* 51 (August 1972): 346–62; see Michael Cohen, *The History of the Sierra Club,* pp. 443, 449.

55. Cohen, *The History of the Sierra Club,* pp. 436–37.

56. Ibid., pp. 439–44; for critiques of the reform environmentalism of the 1970s and '80s, see Christopher Manes, *Green Rage: Radical Environmentalism and the Unmaking of Civilization* (Boston: Little, Brown, 1990), pp. 45–65; Kirkpatrick Sale, *The Green Revolution;* Susan Zakin, *Coyotes and Town Dogs.*

57. Arne Naess, *Freedom, Emotion, and Self-Subsistance: The Structure of a Central Part of Spinoza's Ethics* (Oslo: Universitetsforlaget, 1975), pp. 118–19; see also Arne Naess, "Spinoza and Ecology," *Philosophia* 7 (1977): 45–54; Naess, "Spinoza and Attitudes toward Nature," unpublished manuscript, 1990; the Spinoza scholars Stuart Hampshire and Errol Harris also claimed that Spinoza's thought provided a philosophical solution to the ecological crisis: see Stuart Hampshire, "Morality and Pessimism" *New York Review of Books* 19 (1973): 26–33; reprinted in Stuart Hampshire, *Public and Private Morality* (Cambridge: Cambridge University Press, 1978); Errol Harris, *Salvation from Despair: A Reappraisal of Spinoza's Philosophy* (The Hague: M. Nijhoff, 1973), p. 3.

58. Max Oelschlaeger, *The Idea of Wilderness,* p. 261; Max Oelschlaeger, "Review of Gary Snyder, *The Practice of the Wild,*" *Environmental Ethics* 14, 2 (1992): 185–90.

# PART THREE

# ARNE NAESS ON DEEP ECOLOGY AND ECOSOPHY

# INTRODUCTION

By way of a short biography: Arne Naess was born in 1912 and grew up in a wealthy family in Oslo and among the fjords and mountains of Norway. He studied economics for a while—as did his two older brothers, who became very successful in the shipping industry—went to school in Paris, and studied with the Vienna circle of philosophers in Austria. Naess was appointed professor of philosophy at the University of Oslo at the age of twenty-seven. The previous year, he had built his little cabin, Tvergastein, in an arctic environment high on the side of a mountain between Oslo and Bergen that he has identified with as his home—his "place"—ever since. Naess introduced technical rock climbing (with pitons, carabiners, and ropes) to Norway in the 1930s and is a well-known Himalayan climber. In 1977, Naess was awarded the Sonningen Prize (Europe's highest academic honor) for his contributions to European culture.

In his charming essay "Living in the World," Richard Langlais describes his visit to Tvergastein and discusses some of Naess's achievements. Naess has written approximately thirty books and literally hundreds of papers in specialized philosophical topics and in ecophilosophy, many of which are out of print or were never published. He has always been concerned more with thinking and writing, and sending out his papers to friends and associates for discussion purposes, than with being bothered with the details of publishing. An edition of his selected works is now in preparation.

Arne points out that his philosophical work can be divided roughly into four periods or phases. The first period (up through about 1940) concentrated on the philosophy of science. The second period (from about 1940 through 1953) consisted of work in empirical semantics. A short third period concentrated on antidogmatism and the revival of "the largely forgotten classic Greek Pyrrhonic scepticism." The fourth period began about 1968, partly at the urging of his students, when his interests shifted to ecological philosophy. This work, combined with work in philosophical anthropology, Gestalt perception and ontology, and his important original studies in Spinoza and Gandhi, have found a unique summation in his development of Deep Ecology and Ecosophy T (for Tvergastein).

In his discussion of Deep Ecology as a derivational system (see "The Deep Ecological Movement" in Part One), Naess suggests that "while deep ecology cannot be a finished philosophical system, this does not mean that its philosophers should not try to be as clear as possible." As a major theorist in empirical semantics, and with his background in symbolic logic, Naess certainly makes strenuous efforts to be clear in terms of exactitude of expression and clarification of premise/conclusion relations. For instance, with his favorite philosopher, Spinoza, he has rendered a "central part of Spinoza's *Ethics*" into symbolic logical relationships coupled with a close empirical comparison of Spinoza's key terms. But, unlike most other philosophers with this kind of training, Naess combines these techniques with tremendous empirical and *intuitive* understanding and relating to the world, including nonhuman creatures and wild Nature.

This kind of logical and semantical precision can be irritating to people who are not trained in, or used to, the application of philosophical analytic techniques. And since Arne continually refines and rethinks his positions, which often results in his papers being revised over and over, this can present problems for those trying to edit his writings.

Environmental activists sometimes express annoyance with the theorists of the Deep Ecology movement: efforts to clarify ecophilosophical thinking and concepts are often looked upon as superfluous and a waste of time. This kind of misunderstanding between "thinkers" and "doers" has been going on since at least the time of Socrates. Naess, however, believes that it is of utmost importance that we *think clearly and deeply* about ecological issues, as well as in other areas of life. He feels that it is important to be *both* a thinker and an activist (for Naess, following the philosophies of Spinoza and Gandhi, thinking and acting are intimately related). Humans must be understood as a whole organism, not in terms of a mind/body split. Accordingly Naess has engaged in nonviolent "direct action" ecological campaigns in Norway.

In Naess's papers included in this part (as well as in other papers throughout this book), one can judge for oneself whether careful philosophical and analytical thinking illuminates ecophilosophical and environmental issues and problems, actually strengthens and clarifies our basic ecological intuitions, and is therefore crucial for thoughtful and effective environmental activism.

Naess has actually developed at least three different characterizations of the Deep Ecology position since the late 1960s, and this has certainly added to the confusion and misunderstanding of the position. The three *main* characterizations are (1) Naess's early *description* of the beliefs, attitudes, and lifestyles of supporters of the Deep Ecology movement in his 1972 Bucharest paper; (2) the continuing development, since the late 1960s, of Naess's own personal "total view" and Ecosophy T; and (3) the development in 1984 of the Deep Ecology platform together with a supporting "Apron Diagram" with four levels. These levels illustrate the relation of differing ultimate religious and philosophical commitments and belief systems (Level I) to the platform of Deep Ecology (Level II), and further, how the first two levels, together with hypotheses and norms about states of affairs in the world (Level III), lead logically to concrete ecological decisions and actions (Level IV).

1. *The 1972 Bucharest paper* was largely a sociological *descriptive* account (tidied up a bit, and interpreted philosophically) of what Naess saw as an international philosophical/social movement that had arisen during the 1960s, based upon the experiences of field ecologists such as Rachel Carson and others who were closely associated with wild Nature. These experiences, he claimed, resulted in scientific conclusions and Deep Ecological intuitions that were amazingly similar all over the world (see the Naess 1973 "Shallow-Deep" paper in Part Two).

2. *Ecosophy T.* Ecosophy T is Naess's own personal "total view" (or Level I ecosophy). As a total view, Ecosophy T actually extends from Level I down through Level IV of the Apron Diagram (other ecosophies will similarly extend down through the various levels of the diagram). As Naess points out, in ecosophies (or total views) there is an emphasis upon the need for thinking in terms of norms. (For Naess's discussion of Ecosophy T, together with a diagram, see Naess, "The Deep Ecological Movement," in Part One; for a more recent discussion of Ecosophy T, see Naess, *Ecology, Community and Lifestyle.*)

Naess's Ecosophy T starts with one ultimate (fundamental) philosophical norm: "Self-Realization!" (at Level I of the Apron Diagram). From this norm he derives various subnorms, such as "Self-Realization for all beings!," "No exploitation," "No class society!," "Maximum complexity!," "Maximum diversity!," and "Maximum symbiosis!" (at Level IV). That is, he derives these *norms* "somewhat loosely" from "Self-Realization!" plus an important set of descriptive sentences. He insists that an articulated ecosophy needs a host of descriptions of "hypotheses" and norms (at Level III of the diagram) describing states of affairs in the world: e.g., the greenhouse effect, the rate of species extinction, the need to protect habitat, and so forth.

What Naess means, in part, by "Self-Realization" is the Universe (Nature, the Tao), and all the individuals (human and nonhuman) of which it is comprised, realizing itself. In a sense, all the Level IV subnorms logically unfold from (or are implicitly packed into) the ultimate "Self-Realization" norm, properly understood, at Level I. Following the insights of Gandhi and Spinoza, human individuals attain personal self-realization, and psychological/emotional maturity when they progress from an identification with narrow ego, through identification with other humans, to a more all-encompassing identification of their "self" with nonhuman individuals, species, ecosystems, and with the ecosphere itself. This process of "wide identification" Naess takes to be a process of the development of the "ecological self."

Considerable confusion has arisen when this psychological process or thesis of Self-Realization is taken to be an identifying characteristic of the Deep Ecology movement. The "wide identification" process is not only a part of Naess's Ecosophy T, it is also the basis of Warwick Fox's "transpersonal ecology" (that is, it is a Level I ecosophy and *not* a part of the Deep Ecology platform at Level II). Thus, the Self-Realization norm or thesis is not an identifying characteristic of the Deep Ecology movement!

(3) The *1984 Deep Ecology platform* is now taken by Naess and other Deep Ecology supporters (together with having a total view, and the deep questioning process) as characterizing Deep Ecology as an ecophilosophical and social/political movement. The need to establish a common platform came about, I think, as a result of the realization by Naess that some of the characteristics listed in the 1972 Bucharest paper were too specific in that they did not allow for full cultural diversity (such as the principles of local autonomy and decentralization). In addition, they included certain fundamental ecophilosophical beliefs (namely, the doctrine of "internal relations" in characterizing ecosystems, and the belief in biocentric egalitarianism) not necessarily held by all supporters of the Deep Ecology movement. Ecosophical beliefs and ultimate premises needed to be conceptually separated from more philosophically neutral general beliefs and attitudes shared by most, or all, supporters of the Deep Ecology movement (the Level II platform), thus allowing for, and promoting, a diversity of widely differing ecosophies (such as Spinozist, Christian, Muslim, and Buddhist). Further, an "anti-social-class posture" (mentioned in the Bucharest paper), while held by most Deep Ecology supporters, is not specifically an *ecological* issue (for a discussion of this, see the papers by Naess in Parts Five and Six) and so is not included in the Deep Ecology platform. The platform is essentially a statement of philosophical and normative ecocentrism together with a call for environmental activism.

The following papers by Naess are divided into different topic areas. The first two papers are concerned with common features of the Deep Ecology movement ("deepness of questioning" and the Deep Ecology platform); the next five papers discuss various aspects of Naess's Ecosophy T total view; the last paper is a discussion of Deep Ecology lifestyles.

In "Deepness of Questions and the Deep Ecology Movement," Naess discusses the importance of "deep questioning" and provides examples of "why-chains." He points to what he claims is the absence of deep questioning in the "shallow" environmental movement. The deepness of questioning is an essential part of the Deep Ecology movement, and provides the movement with its name. Naess further holds that deep questioning should lead to an awareness of the need for deep changes in society.

Naess has thought long and hard about the formulation of the Deep Ecology platform (or what he often prefers to call the "Eight Points"). In "The Deep Ecology 'Eight Points' Revisited" he discusses various formulations of the points and replies to critics. He considers Fritjof Capra's suggestion that the platform include the idea of ecological interdependence ("all things hang together"). He also replies to Baird Callicott's claims that the Deep Ecology position essentially involves "mysticism" and a rejection of ethics. Ultimately criticisms such as those raised by Callicott are beside the point: to criticize the Deep Ecology position (as McLaughlin points out in Part One), one must criticize the Eight Points of the platform, not the various Level I personal ecosophies thought to held by various theorists and activists.

Naess discusses the philosophical and everyday uses of the terms "intrinsic value," "inherent value," and "rights." There is a long discussion of the point concerned with population stabilization and reduction. There is also a discussion of politics, charges of ecological fascism, and the importance of cultural diversity even among societies that are ecologically sustainable; Naess claims that there can be no "ecological blueprint" for deep ecological societies (see also Naess's "Politics" in Part Six).

Elsewhere, Naess has emphasized that points 6 and 8 of the platform imply ecological activism, and that social/political activism is *absolutely crucial*. One of the unique characteristics of the Deep Ecology movement, he claims, is "activism on a 'spiritual' basis"—that is, acting from the basis of a fundamental philosophic/religious ecosophy (or total view) and acting nonviolently.

The paper "Equality, Sameness, and Rights" begins the discussion of various aspects of Naess's Level I ecosophy views. It should be noted that the Deep Ecology platform does not contain a statement of "ecological (or biocentric) egalitarianism": it merely states that human and nonhuman life have value in themselves, not *equal* value. Instead of debating whether humans and nonhumans have *equal* intrinsic or inherent value (whatever that might mean!), Naess claims instead that his personal intuition is that all individuals, of whatever species, have the *same* right to live, although "the vital interests of our nearest, nevertheless, have priority."

Some critics have suggested that if all beings have the same right to live, then we could never justify killing or eating anything, or otherwise using other beings for our purposes. But even highly developed traditional humanistic ethical theories, such as utilitarianism and "rights theory," in which all humans are to be treated "equally," can provide no "hard-and-fast" rules for adjudicating conflicts, even among humans. Humans, of course, have the right to exist and flourish, just as everything else does. The main adjudicating concepts for Deep Ecology are "vital" versus "nonvital" needs (which are incorporated into point 3 of the platform). The environmental ethics theorist Paul Taylor (*Respect for Nature,* 1986) also finds it necessary to distinguish between the "basic" and "nonbasic" needs of humans in order to resolve conflicts between humans and nonhumans. As a general principle for deciding conflicts of interest, Naess suggests (in "The Deep Ecological Movement" in Part One) that "humans only inhabit the lands, using resources to satisfy vital needs. And if their nonvital needs come in conflict with the vital needs of nonhumans, then humans should defer to the latter."

Naess's paper "Self-Realization: An Ecological Approach to Being in the World" explores the concept of the self, develops his "wide-identification" theses, and discusses his concept of individual human self-realization. This paper is his most extensive contribution to "ecopsychology," in which he coins the term "ecological self." (See also the papers on ecopsychology in Part One.)

Arguing that one's "self" cannot be identified with one's body, he claims that the ecological self is "that with which this person identifies." Those who identify only with their narrow ego "self," or only with other humans, underestimate their psychological and emotional potentialities. Increasing maturity in humans corresponds with increased identification with others, which extends out to encompass the nonhuman realm. Naess's concept of Self-Realization purports to be a factual psychological thesis about human development and maturity. While apparently not going so far as to posit a normal human genetic ontogeny (like Paul Shepard's thesis in *Nature and Madness*), which involves an identification with the wild, Naess is nevertheless claiming that identification with the wild is an essential aspect of healthy human maturity.

One's "self-interest" expands with increasingly wider identification of the self, which then obviates the need for traditionally moral acts thought to be "altrustic." For Naess, "moral acts" in Kant's sense (acting against one's inclination and perceived self-interest) are replaced, in Kant's terminology, with "beautiful acts." This process of widening identification also involves identification with "place" as a part of one's "self." And contrasting this sense of "self-realization" with standard Western psychological and moral assumptions that humans are always seeking to maximize their pleasure or happiness, Naess suggests that "seeking self-realization" may be a good answer to questions concerning the meaning of life.

In "Ecosophy and Gestalt Ontology" the ecological maxims (and metaphysical principles) "Everything is interrelated" and "Everything hangs together" (what Naess referred to in his 1972 Bucharest paper as "the relational total-field image" and the doctrine of "internal relations") are understood in his Ecosophy T total view in terms of gestalt ontology and experience. The immediate experience humans have of the world is in terms of manifolds of gestalts, as opposed to the "abstract structures" of reality we find, for instance, in musical notation and science, or of the world as we are culturally conditioned to perceive it in terms of individual entities "externally related" to one another. The latter he calls the "supermarket view." The world of concrete contents is the real world we humans live in, and it is not "subjective." It is crucial, Naess claims, for members of the Deep Ecology movement to articulate reality in terms of gestalt perception and ontology, for the competing claims of developers and environmentalists are often based on egoistic atomistic "marketplace" perception, as opposed to ecological gestalts. (For more extended discussions of Naess's account of gestalt perception and ontology, see *Ecology, Community and Lifestyle,* and "The World of Concrete Contents," mentioned in the bibliography.)

In "Metaphysics of the Treeline," Naess provides a charming and sensitive description and example of how ancient forests can be experienced in terms of nonsubjective higher-order gestalts. He points out that artificial "tree farms" result in a massive "disordering" of our spontaneous gestalts.

Arne Naess's 1973 paper "The Place of Joy in a World of Fact" provides a good overview and summary of many of the ingredients that have been integrated into his Ecosophy T total view, as well as the spirit of his outlook. He points out how overworked environmentalists often fail to experience joy as a result of their failure to be in the wild often. And lack of joy is also a result of psychological immaturity in humans. Naess holds that Spinoza's psychology and theory of the emotions (like his metaphysics and theory of knowledge) is one of the most sophisticated ever developed: a crucial guide for the development of human maturity. With Spinoza's psychology (which is similar in many respects to Zen Buddhism), the key is to avoid *passivity* and to cultivate *activeness.* Activeness necessarily involves joy. Naess explores Spinoza's various concepts of joy and sorrow and their relation to self-realization, to gestalt perception and ontology, and to having a total view. From this perspective, dividing the world into the realms of "fact" and "value" is a false dichotomy which reinforces the culturally conditioned relativism that holds that "facts" are objective and "values" are subjective. Joy, he claims, is to be found right in the center of reality.

Much of Naess's thinking about ecophilosophy, the Deep Ecology platform, and Ecosophy T has been inspired by Spinoza's *Ethics:* for example, the emphasis upon individuals; the substitution of ontology for moralizing; the intellectual/emotional/physical integration and unity of the person as opposed to mind/body dualism; the "All things hang together" thesis, which Naess understands in terms of gestalt ontology and experience; a nonhierarchical ontological ecological egalitarianism; human freedom as attainable through self-realization; intuitive understanding of individuals (the third and highest level of understanding for Spinoza) that goes beyond the conceptual rational understanding found in metaphysical systems and theoretical science; and much more. As Naess has pointed out, "no great philosopher has so much to offer in the way of clarification and articulation of basic ecological attitudes as Baruch Spinoza."

In "Deep Ecology and Lifestyle," Naess describes the characteristics of the "simple in means, rich in ends" lifestyles he finds among many supporters of the Deep Ecology movement.

# 18 | LIVING IN THE WORLD
## MOUNTAIN HUMILITY, GREAT HUMILITY

## *Richard Langlais*

*Haiku to Arne*
Coming to visit;
am used to travelling up
to see the mountains.

We ski with heavy packs ever upward; Eva and I have brought enough supplies to feed four people for a week. In his terse note Arne hadn't mentioned whether his companion would be with him or not during our stay, so we planned to be on the safe side with sufficient food. It turns out that he's actually been up there alone for two weeks. And where has he gone now, anyway? The snow-covered Norwegian tundra rises in undulations until its abrupt end in the black cliffs which form the entire horizon ahead of us. No sign of him.

We keep climbing slowly, trying to avoid sweating. We're chasing a seventy-seven-year-old man who has sprung off ahead of us, perhaps in impatience, but certainly in anticipation of preparing tea for us in advance of our eventual arrival at his hut. He's only carrying a day pack, mind you; still, he disappeared behind the rim of a foreshortened ravine some time ago and we haven't seen him since. Slow step after slow step, then another rest, and we see him. He's far enough away that he appears to be just another tiny speck among the many specks which are the tips of boulders poking up against the white slopes.

The minute black figure skiing steadily ever mountainwards had once written that "the smaller we come to feel ourselves compared to the mountain, the nearer we come to participating in its greatness." This is the same scholar and practitioner of Spinozan ethics and Gandhian nonviolence who has become

Originally published in the *Alpine Club of Canada Journal* (1991). Reprinted with permission.

known, through his development of ecosophy, or ecological philosophy, as an inspiration in the formation of the Deep Ecology, environmental, social movement, which is becoming increasingly influential thoughout the West. This is Arne Naess, whose environmentally-oriented civil disobedience has made him a household name in Norway and in most of Scandinavia. It is the same man who founded the journal *Inquiry* and who led successful expeditions to Tirich Mir in 1950 and 1964; the same person who at 27 became Norway's youngest Professor, and yet gave up the same Chair in Philosophy in 1970 to devote himself full-time to "the urgent environmental problems facing humankind," convinced that a philosopher can actively contribute to their solution.

All his life Norwegians have known him as a fervent spokesman for the benefits of the "friluftsliv" movement, the conviction that an outdoor life can provide an antidote to the stresses of urban conditions. (When it was announced that the Norwegian Trygve Haavelmo had won the 1989 Nobel Prize for Economics, a frustrated world press could only report that their efforts to interview him would have to await his return from a trip into the forests. Informed of the prize, and well aware of the publicity it would bring, Haavelmo's reaction was said to be that he had gone out "pa tur"—the Norwegian euphemism for heading for the hills for a little peace and quiet.) And now this man Arne was rushing ahead of us for his hut, his true home, where we would share tea. I contemplated my man, my mountain.

Arne's hut stands on the edge of a perhaps hundred-meter-wide bench just below the black cliffs whose tops are disappearing into the snow-heavy clouds. It's quickly becoming a winter-dark day, even though it's early June. Here below the cliffs called Hallingskarven up on the great treeless plateau of the Hardangervidda, dominated by its central icefield, the Hardangerjokulen, it is winter at least ten months of the year, with only the intense respite of an arcticlike summer intervening. The hut, which Arne had named Tvergastein, after the locals' name for the quartz crystals found near the small tarn below it, at just over 1500 meters above sea level, is Norway's highest privately owned dwelling.

As we trudge up the last steep pitch below the hut, we admire how its low form fits in here. Much of its wooden construction is weather-beaten gray; the eye shifts smoothly from the grain of the wood to the patterns of the lichens on the rocks. Stones spaced out on the roof to hold it down against the gales remind us of hardy mountain dwellings in other of the world's more isolated regions. With its view out over several thousand square kilometers of the Hardangervidda, it is a true aerie. "Simple in means, rich in ends," as Arne has so famously put it. This is the place after which he has named his own philosophy, Ecosophy T. The *T* is for Tvergastein.

He greets us warmly at the door, wearing his sagging old sweater and woolen trousers and seeming happy at our unrestrained enthusiasm for the place. He says that he had been sitting at the picture window watching us as we climbed up the last few hundred meters. So the tea is just ready. "Have a glass of 'T'!" We sit on the rustic, homemade chairs in the living room, thankfully sipping the hot brew and listening to Arne's stories of the place and his life here. The chairs are before the large window where we would come to sit for many hours during the next week, brooding over the rarely relenting snowstorms and, before going outside to take advantage of the clear spells, waxing ecstatic over the panorama suddenly ours. This room, literally a living room, would be the one where we would spend all of our waking, indoor hours.

It was part of the original, smaller hut—eight meters by five meters—that Arne built in 1938; he later enlarged it to its current size of 100 square meters. The windward side, facing the prevailing westerlies, consisted of a workshop-cum-storage-room; along the northern wall there was a tiny toilet closet, a kitchen, and the entry hall, which also served as a storage room and which housed part of Arne's library. None of these areas were occupied very often, and so formed a buffer for the more often lived-in south-facing rooms. These were a compact library, which had a small brazier in it, a sleeping room (mattresses on the floor), the living room, and—the core of them all—the winter, or storm, room. Each of the south-facing rooms, unlike the northern ones which had only very small peepholes, had a large, sun-transmitting window. It was surprising how, even in whiteouts, a noticeable amount of warming solar radiation could be felt coming through the panes.

Arne has kept a log of how many days he has spent up here through the decades. Over 3,650 days—a total of ten years now. At one point earlier on, he and his wife and two young children lived in the hut, mostly in the storm room, for four and a half months. It was an experiment in living in extreme conditions. The storm room is double-insulated and the only one heated most of the time. The whole family ate and slept, played and worked within its five-by-two-and-a-half-meter sides. These days Arne lives in there, except when he has visitors, most of the time. It's much more efficient for him to keep that room slightly heated and just leave the rest at the same temperature as outside. He's completely devoted to trying to live in a way which is as little consuming of energy as possible, so he has even rigged up a stand above the glass chimney of his coal oil lamp where he sets a small kettle that provides him with boiling water for tea. His small space heater is only lit for short periods throughout the day, then it roars. Arne's idea is to heat up the stove as much as he can, fast, then let it die out immediately, so as to avoid having the room's heat get sucked up the chimney. He calculates and cuts the bits of fuel so that they burn completely, perhaps within half an hour to an hour. The room is so well-insulated that the stove's heat remains for a surprisingly long time.

Where does his fuel come from? Well, it's old roofing material. The roof has blown off three times and each time it has provided him with fuel for several years. Each bit of tar paper, each shard of wood gets painstakingly ripped or sawed into tiny squares for consumption in the stove. We are able to vouch for this firsthand, as one of our chores was to finish off the preparation of the last remaining box of roofing which a storm had so thoughtfully transformed into fuel for him. Oh yes; all the used toilet paper gets burned also. It is deposited delicately in a pail beside the toilet bench, rather than down the hole.

The spartan tale continues. His supplies get hauled up in bulk every three years. In the old days it was with horses, these days by snowmobile. One time, he read in a newspaper that a cannery was selling off its remaining inventory of blood pudding. For some reason, Arne thought it would be a matter of twenty cans or so. As it turned out, he had become the proud owner of 185 cans of blood pudding. When some of the people in the valley got wind of this, the rumor spread around that Arne Naess thought another world war was coming soon. As it was, he ended up eating it several times a week for a few years.

There is really no end to the fastidiousness with which Arne pursues his ideas of living in a way which does not harm or insult the mountains which he knows are his true home. The mountains have given him so much and he is fully aware of his impact. The point of all his spartan habits is that he is choosing to have it this way. Of course he could live in a materially more consuming manner and he realizes that few others would want to live as he does; the important thing for him, however, is that he wants to live as faithfully as he can to his own idea of a mountain ethic. This ethic is not only in accordance with his philosophy, but has also done much to influence its formulation. "Voluntary simplicity" speaks for much of it, and so does the idea of intense identification with the mountains—indeed, with all of nature, of which humans are a part. Besides his professional systematization of this, he has a starker—as he says, cruder—way of stating it:

> Mountains are big. Very big. But they are also great. Very great. They have dignity and other aspects of greatness. They are solid, stable, unmoving. A Sanskrit word for them is *a-ga,* that which does not go. But curiously enough, there are lots of movements in them. Thus a ridge is sometimes ascending, there is a strong upward movement, perhaps broken with spires, towers, but resuming the upward trend, toward the sky or even toward heaven. The ridge or contour does not only have movement up and up, but may point upward, may invite elevation. When we are climbing a mountain, it may

witness our behavior with a somewhat remote or mild benevolence. The mountain never fights against us and it will hold back avalanches as long as it can, but sometimes human stupidity and hubris and a lack of intimate feeling for the environment result in human catastrophes.[1]

It is this kind of sensitivity which leads Arne to request that all guests—both his and the mountains'—attempt, "when they can," to step only on the rocks between the alpine plants, at least in the immediate area of the hut; it is here, after all, where his impact, and hence his debt, are most concentrated. This also explains why every few weeks, like a Chinese gardener, he takes the bucket out from under the toilet bench and meticulously ladles its contents (not waste!) out around the bases of the plants at the periphery of the hut's impact zone. The hut's concentrated effects are thus at least slightly diluted. After a few days at Tvergastein, experiencing the intensity of Arne's careful routines, the area around the hut begins to resemble a zone of love. The mountain environment certainly doesn't seem diminished by this presence.

The days pass and we fall into the ways of the place. Arne figures it usually takes him at least a couple weeks up here before he can feel completely at home; then his thinking and writing really sharpen. We relish every minute of it, go out for ski trips in the whiteouts, navigating from boulder to boulder, and let the tranquillity seep into us. After every couple of hours' work writing indoors, Arne goes out for a short ski, often including a bit of bouldering while he's out there. We might have just come in to the hut and begun cooking our meal when Arne rushes out of the storm room and announces he'll be back in a little while; he's just going out to one of his favorite cliffs to do a bit of climbing. Or carrying rocks, from as far away from the hut as he can, to heighten the sheltering wall he's built on the windward side of the hut. Mind and body, action and thought, mustn't let this body stiffen with age and rot.

What with the steady snowfall, there really isn't so much to do, but one afternoon Arne declares that we're going downhill skiing. We look out the window: whiteout. We muster some enthusiasm, get out our gear, and follow him out. We've got our touring stuff on and Arne is wearing an old pair of plastic alpine skiing boots. He says we're going to the "Frankrike" slope, the large permanent snow patch which, from the hut, looks like the map of France, on the boulder slope below the cliffs. We're finding out that Arne has names for just about everything in the area; so it is with the creation of a world.

We shoulder bundles of bamboo poles and head off for the slope. In the near whiteout, we realize that when the angle steepens we should begin packing, so we start side-stepping our way up an imagined slalom course. Packing and tramping, we eventually trace out seven or eight gates and stick in a pole at each one. It is only slightly surreal. But we have a blast out there in the middle of the fog below some cliffs somewhere on the vast Hardangervidda. We each manage a few runs, regrooming the course on our climbs back up, before Arne nonchalantly excuses himself and says that he has to go back in to the hut. He'd seemed pretty spry and nimble, performing old-fashioned, yet pictur-esquely elegant hop turns with his beat-up slalom gear, so we wonder what he's got in mind. Well, he explains, a couple years ago he'd broken his leg and he still had a steel pin in his ankle from it. Because of the pressure of the rigid ski boots, the head of the pin has pushed through the skin and is now bleeding slightly. "Oh," we say, rather nonplussed. He is adamant that he can manage it by himself and that we needn't come in. Since a break in the snowfall seems to be forming, it's easy to stay out for a few more runs.

After skiing and admiring the view for a while longer, we rejoin Arne in the hut. He's all right, so we sit around together over some bowls of soup. There's a story of his that I'd read where he recounts an experience he'd had as a boy in the Jotunheimen Mountains. Wandering around in the deep snow at dusk, he needed to find some shelter and came across an hospitable old man who was doing some caretaking at one of the alpine club's huts. They ate only porridge for the whole week that Arne stayed with him; the evenings were passed with the old man telling the occasional story of the mountain life, or playing out complex rhythms on his violin. Arne talks of the effect that that stay had on him, how it was the beginning of a deep appreciation for the layers of richness that actually underlie the superficial harshness and spartan quality of mountain living.

In his story, Arne says nothing more about the old man. I ask if he ever sought him out again. He replies with a chuckle, saying that goodness, no, he was too young at the time to know enough about the full effects that his stay with the old fellow would have on him. He was too foolish and impatient for new things to have the idea that it might be worthwhile to try to find him again.

But with the passage of a few years, the realization of what he'd gained from him matured, and he began more and more to seek out mountain people. He became convinced that they had an inner relation with the mountains in which they lived. This was a "certain greatness, cleanness, a concentration upon what is essential, a self-sufficiency; and consequently a disregard of lux-ury, of complicated means of all kinds . . . and the obvious fondness for all things above the timberline, living or 'dead,' certainly witnessed a rich, sensual attachment to life, a deep pleasure in what can be experienced with wide-open eyes and mind" (quoted from Naess, in Tobias).

He points to the rocky, barely two-meter-wide ledge before the drop-off outside the window. "There, for example, is my garden," he muses. "As you can see, only some tiny, tough alpine flowers, some lichens and rock; but for fifty years now, those few square meters, always visible—even in storms, for the wind keeps it swept—have been my forest, my garden, my landscape. They have been more than enough."

While we'd been out skiing and the clouds had parted, Eva and I had noticed that up on a ledge near the crest of the cliffs there was a small, oddly rectangular object. What was that, Arne? "That is Tvergastein's Nest. It's another tiny hut, three by three meters, which I built in the forties." Our jaws drop. "Now it's in bad shape, for the roof has blown off and I've no longer been able to dedicate the energy to keep it maintained. I carried most of the materials up myself, board by board, up the gullies along a protected route which I'd secured. There you really get the feeling of being on the very brink of the abyss. It's two hundred meters higher than here. I wanted to have that feeling of a raven perched on the cliff for long periods. The building materials that are stacked in the entrance hall are intended for it. Some local young people are going to repair it, so the Nest will still be used for at least a few more years."

After the day's exertions and several days of not bathing, Eva shyly asks Arne if she can heat up a basin of water. She explains that it would also stave off the chill which she is feeling. Arne's warm agreement is pleasantly surprising; during our first couple of days here, we hadn't pushed such requests too much. We simply got the feeling that our adaptability was being tested. Although Arne tried, naturally, to be the perfect host, I think the fact that we would be staying for more than just one or two nights was a bit more demanding for him. He and I had only had a few previous encounters, while this trip was Eva's first meeting with him. When alone, he lives so entirely according to his own all encompassing, uncompromising discipline, that the sudden prolonged presence of two relatively unknown visitors in his hermitage took at least some effort of acclimatization. Besides, bathing could be an authentic chore.

Water was usually hauled up from a hole in the ice of the tarn a couple hundred meters off, although during our stay we were collecting it from beneath The Pyramid, an enormous boulder so appealingly true to its name, which is much nearer the hut. Melting snow for water is entirely too wasteful; as Arne says, taking snow from minus one degrees Celsius to plus one uses up as many calories as heating it from plus one to the boiling point, to say nothing of having to haul the fuel up here in the first place. The huge Primus kerosene-burning stove is temperamental as well, even though it is much cherished for its decades of faithful service. Its brass tank still has its dent from a fall down the university stairs in 1939. It stands in the unheated living room, so that when it's lit the windows fog up; the test of efficient cooking is just how much steam forms on the single pane. I guess we've kept the windows pretty clear, and that, combined with a few other things, is giving us a good rating. When Eva starts heating up her bath water, Arne's a real sweetheart by insisting that she take double the amount in her basin. It doesn't take much convincing for me to get my share as well.

When our sponge bath is finished, we come back into the living room to find that Arne has retired for the evening. From his room we hear some quiet classical music, but since it's one of the old 78s that are stacked in the living room, the scratches are quite audible. Power is from batteries that are kept charged by a solar cell panel on the south wall; the head lamp which Arne uses for his reading is powered in the same way.

Tomorrow, we have to go back down, as our host has an appointment in Oslo, so it seems like an evening for everyone to indulge in a little bit of a foretaste of the softer side of city living. I am moved by the obvious age of the recorded music and by the thought of how many times it must have mellowed the loneliest evenings over the decades, its harmonies taking the edge off of worry about the Nazi Occupation and the rumors of the Gestapo coming to take him away for questioning the next day, its melodies easing the strain of the sick children, or wondering about the strength of the storm and the roof holding.

The next morning it is dead calm and the sky perfectly clear. The surface of yesterday's newly fallen wet snow has frozen concrete-hard in the cold night. We get ready for a fast ski down. With all of the garbage stowed in them, our packs feel almost as heavy as when we came up; Arne is taking advantage of our willingness and our young backs to have some of several years' accumulated junk taken down. Above the hut the black cliffs stand huge against the blue sky. Where is it? The Nest? Yes, there it is, one of its walls silhouetted sharply by the brilliant dawn.

Perhaps next time. . . . Gazing up at the fantastic cliffs I'm reminded again of what Arne had written once:

> As I see it, modesty is of little value if it is not a natural consequence of much deeper feelings, and even more important in our special context, a consequence of a way of understanding ourselves as part of nature in a wide sense of the term. This way is such that the smaller we come to feel ourselves compared to the mountain, the nearer we come to participating in its greatness. I do not know why this is so.[2]

We fly down the mountain. Looking back at Hallingskarven, I can just make out the minute box that is Tvergastein. To the right of it is the raw gash of a huge break in the seemingly unending cliffs. I want to check with Arne if that is the location of a route we had been talking about a few days ago.

Careless, I enquire if that was the "valley" that he had been describing to me. His reaction is pained and I wonder what was wrong in what I said.

"I don't think that that place would like to hear itself called a 'valley'," he reprimands me. "It is too wild and violent and rugged a place to be called that." He stares admiringly up at it, his head tilted back at an angle usually reserved for contemplating very large masterpieces.

"A gorge?" I try.

"No, think of how it would feel at being called that," he reiterates.

"What about a cirque, or a ravine; a box canyon?"

"Hmm, no, not yet," is all he can say.

"Well, a cwm, then," I venture, thinking of Everest.

"Yes, not bad perhaps, but maybe just a bit a too soft," he replies, muttering about Scotland.

Humbled at having not been as precise as I would have liked to have been, I quietly state, "Whatever it is, it is truly great."

Arne Naess turns and looks at me with a smile and then we all turn to ski back down. I am feeling pretty small.

## NOTES

1. Arne Naess, "Modesty and the Conquest of Mountains," in *The Mountain Spirit,* edited by Michael Charles Tobias and Harold Drasdo (Woodstock, N.Y.: Overlook Press, 1979).
2. Naess, "Modesty."

# 19 DEEPNESS OF QUESTIONS AND THE DEEP ECOLOGY MOVEMENT[1]

*Arne Naess*

## I. HISTORICAL PROLOGUE

WHATEVER THE WEAKNESSES WE all are aware of, the term *deep* is going to remain central in the terminological structure of the Deep Ecology movement. Is the Deep Ecology terminological structure complicated? It is nothing compared to what we have to get accustomed to if we participate in social and political debates. Here, I focus on only one approach in trying to make the term *deep* more precise in the relevant sense (thus, eliminating interpretations which lead away from what is intended). The approach taken here is concerned with "premise/conclusion chains."[2] This approach is concerned with the *deepness of premises* used in debates over efforts to overcome the ecological crisis.

There are other approaches; for instance, the "deepness and broadness of attitude" approach. For example, the owner of a rock garden may treasure every life form in the garden for its own sake, but this attitude is limited only to the garden. The attitude is not deep enough for this person to generalize it beyond the confines of the garden. Further, the shortcomings of society may be seen and felt by this person, and result in unrest and frustration, but the attitude is not intense enough to make the owner of the garden "problematize" all aspects of society. Whereas the premise/conclusion approach, if carried out systematically, requires some education (but not knowledge) in logic, the "deepness of attitude" approach leads to social psychology and social science

---

Originally written in the 1970's and revised in 1990, this essay is previously unpublished. Published with permission.

in general. But only a small group of a movement's theorists can afford to spend much time on systematization.

Conservatism may be said to be the social movement which tries to conserve what is best in what already exists. Such short expressions of what a social movement "is" may have some value in some contexts, but generally a social movement requires fairly complex characterizations. Attempts to shorten them into one sentence, which is then treated as a so-called definition or criterion, are rarely successful—or the sentence gets to be too long and complicated. Definition may have a place in dictionaries, but rarely elsewhere.

In my paper "The Deep Ecology Movement: Some Philosophical Aspects" (1986), the contrast between the Deep and the Shallow ecological movements is characterized by using about two hundred words. One difference is said to be decisive: it "concerns a willingness to question and to appreciate the importance of questioning every economic and political policy in public." The questioning is "deep" and "public." Because I used the word "questioning," not the Germanic "problematizing," the misinterpretation arose that I found intellectual playful questioning of the kind found in graduate philosophy seminars sufficient. On the other hand, problematizing is a profound "existential" undertaking.

But in comparing the two movements, the relatively deeper questioning in the sense of "problematizing" (*Problematizierung*) of the Deep Ecology movement is quite manifest. It is my *hypothesis* that any systematic contemporary philosophy will, if it takes a stand on the ecological crisis, support the Deep Ecology movement. Supporters of the Deep Ecology movement, therefore, have no systematic philosophy to oppose. The modern ecological predicament is the result of thoughtlessness, rather than thought. In one sense we may say: if there is deep questioning, then this is compatible with Ecosophy T, or some other ecosophy articulating the perspectives of the Deep Ecology movement. But "deepness" must include not only systematic philosophical deepness, but also the "deepness" of proposed social changes.

## 2. PERSISTENT "WHYS" AND "HOWS"

Let us inspect the chain of questions in the following dialogue:

1. A: Turn on the gas!
2. B: Why?
3. A: Because we are going to boil the potatoes.
4. B: Why?
5. A: Because we ought to have dinner soon.
6. B: Why?

7. A: Because we should keep fit.
8. B: Why?
9. A: Because we should do what makes us feel happy.
10. B: Why?
11. A: Because happiness is what we ultimately desire.
12. B: Why?
13. A: "Happiness" means satisfaction of all biological and social needs.
14. B: Why?

At step 13 the pure why-chain turns from normative to descriptive. This may lead us into discussing the etymology of the term "happiness" and other unphilosophical specialties. The "why" at 10 and at 12 are within the traditions of philosophy and more profound, I would say, than at 8 or even at 13. Furthermore I would say, perhaps arbitrarily, that the "why" at 8 is profounder, or leads (or may more easily lead) into deeper water than 6. It is convenient to use two words here ("deep" and "profound") letting "deeper" refer to the premise/conclusion relations, and letting "profound" refer to nearness to philosophical and religious matters. The latter term I leave unanalyzed.

At the start of introductory philosophy courses, my habit of persistently asking "why?", whatever the answers to my questions (for instance, "What time is it?") makes the students bemused, bewildered, frustrated, or angry in a remarkably fruitful way for the whole course. Within less than 10 minutes, they are ready for anything.

Among other things, they realize that deep questions seem to be only "millimeters" away from the trivial, conventional, or silly. Some get unhappily bewildered because they feel that I am making fun of them, or that their sanity is being tested.

The unhappily bewildered remind me of the research on "tolerance of ambiguity" in the 1930s and '40s motivated by the astonishing popularity of fascist and National Socialist ideas. One working hypothesis held that intolerance of the ambiguity of a situation correlated highly with indicators of acceptance of fascist ideas: that there should always be rules for correctness. The only test for saneness is correctness: to be *comme il faux*. Certain questions could (should) be asked, others could not. Idle wondering is dangerous, therefore "keep straight at any cost." The *Führer* establishes the rules, thereby avoiding *embarrassing* bewilderment.

Suppose the above dialogue, at an early stage, went descriptive and explanatory:

1. A: Turn on the gas!
2. B: Why?
3b. A: Because if you do not turn on the gas the water will not boil.

4b.  B: Why?

5b.  A: Because cold water needs heat from the gas in order to reach boiling temperature.

6b.  B: Why?

7b.  A: Boiling requires that water molecules attain higher velocities and these must be transferred from the hot flame of the gas.

8b.  B: Why?

9b.  A: Because, ultimately, quantum mechanical and thermodynamical laws prescribe certain conditions to be fulfilled.

10b.  B: Why?

11b.  A: We have no good reason to think that heating might be done otherwise than in conformity with physical and chemical laws or theories accepted today.

12b.  B: Why?

Again, we have landed in philosophy. Why-strings in science inevitably lead us beyond science. Sequences of "how?" show similar traits. Sooner or later we arrive in fields of inquiry typical of philosophy.

1c.  A: Turn on the gas!

2c.  B: How?

3c.  A: Put your fingers here and turn to the left.

4c.  B: How?

5c.  A: Activate certain muscles of your underarm . . . !

6c.  B: How?

7c.  A: By deciding to do so.

8c.  B: How?

9c.  A: Pull yourself together!

10c.  B: How?

11c.  A: Use your free will!

It seems that we can lead a dialogue out of philosophy even when continuing our why's and how's, but not without certain kinds of diversionary steps or side-tracking maneuvers:

12c.  B: How?

13c.  A: By a careful study of the philosophy of personal development.

It might be possible to keep the dialogue within the borders of techniques of study a couple of steps further. But roughly the conclusion holds: persistent questioning leads to deeper questions.

The importance of this conclusion is limited because whereas question number n may lead deeper, question $n+1$ may lead back to trivialities as exemplified by 12c. And which concepts of "depth" are intended? "Deep

mathematical theorems" are one thing; "deep grammatical structure" is something else. And, is philosophy invariably "deep"? Deep waters can be distinguished from murky ones, but how are deep questions and answers
distinguished from murky ones? Let us say the dialogue takes this turn:

x.          There is something rather than nothing.
x + 1.    Why?
x + 2.    . . .

The Heideggerian literature at step x + 2 will be characterized by some of
us as murky rather than deep, or at least both murky and deep.

In a critical situation, a complex proposal A (concerning how to act) may be
said to be based on a set of premises, some of them explicitly formulated in A,
the others playing the role of unarticulated "presuppositions" (Collingwood).
Suppose a proposal B is based upon the same set of premises except one, an
unarticulated presupposition P. B questions (problematizes) P, doesn't find it
tenable and rejects proposal A. In this critical situation, B may be said to
*question deeper* than A, and the deeper question may be said to be "Why P?"

The above is meant just to touch upon the difficult questions we face when
trying to formulate fairly simple (but useful) analyses (precizations) of "deep
questions," "deeper questioning" and similar expressions.

These questions do not, in my view, undermine the usefulness and appro-
priateness of the designation "Deep Ecology movement." But they do justify
the remarks made by Warwick Fox, David Rothenberg, and others, that what
Deep Ecology theorists write is often sketchy, tentative, and preliminary (using
my words, rather than theirs). Theoreticians for the peace movement, and
especially the Marxist-inspired social justice movements, have produced much
heavier stuff together with highly elaborated doctrines. Unfortunately, the
widening of the ecological crisis seems to give us more than enough time to
gain in profoundness.

Comparing argumentation patterns within the shallow and deep movements, I find that supporters of the Deep Ecological movement (as characterized in certain texts) ask deeper questions. But they are rarely
zetetics—questioning everything. On the contrary—like Rachel Carson, they
tend to have firm convictions at a deep level. This is also true of people in
the two other great movements—the peace movement and the social justice
movements.

Inspecting my examples of why- and how-strings some might wonder: are
they not also suited for introducing concepts of "p being sillier than q"? This
question reminds us of the concept of *relevance*. When questions of what to do
(or not to do) in a given situation are relevant, why- and how-strings sooner
or later get to be irrelevant. They get sillier from the point of view of action.

For example, if we start a string of questions and answers concerning why and how we eat, eating gets more and more relevant as the hours pass. Action (in this case, eating) cuts the Gordian knot, but leaves all questions open, and leaves all answers invoked to account for decision and action questionable.

For example, the main reaction of the U.S. Department of Agriculture and the chemical industry to the accusations of Rachel Carson in her *Silent Spring* was: "wildly exaggerated!" If this factual and normative premise is accepted, then a whole area of questions raised by her are clearly irrelevant, and some of them are even silly. From 1963 to 1989 there have been vast differences of opinion concerning the gravity of the ecological situation. One may roughly distinguish between an extreme optimism, a moderate optimism, a moderate pessimism, and a black pessimism (the "doomsday prophets"). The supporters of the Deep Ecology movement consider the ecological crisis to be grave, and this may be seen by some as pessimism. Tremendous efforts will be necessary and the transition to wide ecological sustainability will be painful for most people. The supporters of the shallow movement tend toward optimism. Some do not even acknowledge that there is anything like a crisis, but support vigorous action to investigate the ozone layer situation, to restore forests with genetically altered trees which grow faster and are more resistant to pollutants, and other kinds of repair jobs. Some of these efforts are admirable and indispensible today from the Deep Ecology standpoint.

The tendency to refrain from discussion of deep questions in the shallow movement has, as its main cause, its perceived irrelevance: why bother? They believe that responsible ecological policies will be implemented in due time because of the clearly manageable magnitude of the implied problems.

When the use of pesticides increased by a very large percentage each year, only a few people were alarmed. But they found that strong forces were allied against the use of restraint. Even when the short-range undesirable consequences of pesticide use became clear, nothing decisive was done to decrease their use.

Few people asked "why?" or "how?" with persistence. But those who did were deeply concerned with the ecological situation. The answers to these questions relate not only to chemistry and biology; they involved increasingly more and more of various aspects of human affairs—economic, technological, social, cultural—and ultimately, philosophical and religious aspects. That is, those who went deeper, *both* questioned deeper in the sense of deeper premises, and *suggested deeper changes socially (in a wide sense)*.

The percentage increase of the sheer volume of impact, and the increase of pernicious impact (of special chemicals, especially on vulnerable regional changes) could not, and cannot, be precisely measured. There is always room for differences in degrees of optimism and pessimism. The effects of DDT were uncertain; the causes and effects of acid rain are still uncertain; climatic changes (ice age or warming of the planet, or both, or none?) are uncertain. Some point out that population growth correlates with the growth of wealth if proper technology is available—look at the history of Holland! With high income and education, population stabilizes. The implication is that there is no cause for alarm.

With modern degrees of optimism the strings of "Why?" and "How?" need not be long. Science and technology seem to furnish answers; also they do not touch fundamental social aspects, nor fundamental attitudes and value priorities.

The difference between the Deep and the Shallow ecological movements may be looked upon from a special point of view: namely, what is questioned and how deep the questioning goes. But *defining* the movements in terms of deepness of questioning is misleading.

The English term *questioning* is not as forceful as the German and French equivalents: *problematizieren, Problematizierung, problematique,* etc. In European philosophy and politics during the late '60s these terms were important— the whole industrial society was questioned: *problematiziert.* The movement to protect nature was *politiziert* in the sense that it had to face the economic and political forces that mobilized against major protection efforts. Without political changes there would be no shift to ecologically sane policies. In the United States, terms like *vested interests* and *hidden persuaders* were used, but did not gain much influence in questions of environmentalism. The profound *Problematizierung* of the sociologist C. Wright Mills came too early.

Looking at the relevant literature and public debates, my conclusion is (and has long been) that what characterizes the deep movement (in relation to the shallow) is not so much the *answers* that are given to "deep questions" but rather *that* "deep questions" are raised and taken seriously. Argumentation patterns within the shallow movement rarely touch the deeper questions: we do not find the complete social/philosophical *Problematizierung.* But if supporters of the Shallow movement are invited to answer the deeper questions, it is my experience that the points of view of the Deep Ecology movement are often accepted. (A pilot study in which influential people were invited to answer these kinds of questions confirms my impressions. More studies of this kind would be highly desirable.)

From this I conclude that the view is untenable that one is confronted, in the ecological crisis, with politicians and other influential people who invariably hold a different philosophy of life and a different view about humanity's place in the cosmic scheme, and who deliberately work against the realization of a Green Society (which implies respect for the richness and diversity of Life on Earth). They often say, "Yes, sure. Every living being has intrinsic value.

But what is your politically realistic proposal for solving the unemployment problem? Some forests may have to go."

The last few years have seen a lively interest among religious leaders in denouncing the arrogance toward, and ruthless exploitation of, the planet. Christian leaders proclaim the intrinsic value of all beings because they are the creation of God, and speak about human sinful behavior towards God's creation.

There is a central point, however, which this "new green wave" (on the philosophical and religious level) has not taken sufficiently seriously: *the necessity of a substantial change in economic, social, and ideological structures.* If the first Five Points of the Deep Ecology Platform are accepted, such changes are seen as necessary by most supporters of the Deep Ecology movement (cf. especially Point 6).

Should we now say then that deeper questioning is no longer what fundamentally makes Deep Ecology argumentation patterns different from those of the Shallow movement? The term *fundamentally* is too strong. I think the term *most clearly* is better.

To illustrate this, a concept of pure "why" strings was introduced. It introduced a simple concept of "deeper question" which was adapted to one of the many usages of the term *deeper*.

But there is *another* usage relevant to the choice of the designation "Deep Ecology movement": that of *"deepness of change."* Whereas the shallow movement suggests increases in environmental budgets, forcing polluters to pay for the pollution caused, and many other changes in social policies, these proposed changes are not "deep." Green political party programs usually imply changes on the same deep level as those implied by the Deep Ecology movement.

As an example, let's consider the philosophical norm of universalizability as applied to ecological policies. Because all major ecological problems are global as well as local, one society degrading the Earth to a much greater extent per capita than other societies cannot be tolerated as long as the global volume of interference is clearly excessive. Norms of justice derivable from the eight points may convince people that ethically justifiable levels of interference in ecosystems require much deeper social changes than is now widely anticipated. Societies must adopt policies which can be universalized without reducing the richness and diversity of Life on Earth.

It is of considerable importance that the Deep Ecology movement has so far faced no serious philosophically-based criticism. Sooner or later that will occur, but of course it has to be legitimate criticism, not a caricature, of the movement.

Jeremy Bentham was both a philosopher and social reformer who was not afraid to derive very special particular norms from general principles; for instance, which color would be best for ballot boxes. For every British custom and legal procedure he asked "Why so?" If a procedure did not satisfy his pleasure-principle, it was to be abandoned. That is, he questioned (problematized) every procedure in the light of his total-view, his special form of utilitarianism. Even if his way of doing this (through his "special" why-strings) was fictitious to some degree (like the *q.e.d.'s* in Spinoza's "proofs"), his reform movement was highly successful.

The ecological crisis requires an analogous scrutiny "of everything" in the light of broad, global long-range ecological sustainability. Here, why- and how-strings must mercilessly confront procedures with basic principles on the philosophical and religious levels.

# NOTES

1. This is a revised and shortened version of an unpublished manuscript, "Deepness of Questions," written in the 1970s and distributed to only a few people because of its manifest weaknesses. I have revised it because some interest in it persists, and because of the prominent place it received in Warwick Fox's important book, *Toward a Transpersonal Ecology* (1990)—G.S.

2. The term *chain* is important. The structure of systematization may be schematized as follows: from premises A and B, conclusion C is drawn. From premises C and D, conclusion E is drawn. From premises E and F, conclusion G is drawn. Thus, a chain of premise/conclusion relations is asserted. The rules of inference which are applied are rough. Requirements of logical validity lead to vast unnecessary complications for people other than professional logicians.

# 20 | THE DEEP ECOLOGY "EIGHT POINTS" REVISITED

## Arne Naess

TEN YEARS AGO IT was fairly common to express astonishment that people with very different philosophical and religious backgrounds could be supporters of the Deep Ecology movement. What did they have in common? Or, how could they have anything in common? How would they define what Deep Ecology really is?

The first question seemed to me to be the most important. It was important to emphasize that supporters of the Deep Ecology movement need not have philosophical or religious premises of a basic kind in common. They should have, and use, such premises, but they would not all be of the same kind because of cultural differences. The deeper the differences the better because of the value of deep differences in cultural backgrounds.

At that time (in the early '80s) it was important to point to views held in common. There were at least two ways in which things were clearly held in common: personal sorrow or despair was felt when environmental battles ended in defeat, and there was a corresponding feeling of joy when there was at least partial victory. There was also a high degree of agreement about the need for, and acceptance of, "direct actions" of some sort, and (what to me was a great thing) a clear consciousness about the limitations of the means to be used: nonviolence. Typically, many supporters had been active in the peace movement before becoming environmental activists. Reference to nonviolence should perhaps be included in the Eight Points.

Less clearly, the supporters had some *fairly general and abstract* views in common, or nearly in common. What the critics and doubters needed was a not too complex and detailed survey of such views, which should be put forth

---

Written in 1993, this essay is previously unpublished. Published by permission.

tentatively. The formulation of the Eight Points was the result. That these short points were called "principles," or expressions of a "platform," was perhaps unfortunate. A longer name for the Eight Points is indispensible, for instance "A set of fairly general and abstract statements that seem to be accepted by nearly all supporters of the Deep Ecology movement."

The term *seem* is included because what is meant is not only acceptance of the Eight Points as an articulate answer to a question, but acceptance in a wider, somewhat vague sense, as in sentences like "Mr. A accepted Mr. B's leadership," or "In the ashram they accepted the situation that snakes and scorpions were permitted to stay in their sleeping quarters during the night." The chance might be that an ashram member, if asked, would object to allowing certain snakes to come into the room, but so far there have been no such members. It has been encouraging how people say, "Yes, of course I accept those Eight Points, but so far I have not had the words to express my attitudes." What the Eight Points have offered is mainly to put words to views people have "always" had but have not expressed, at least not in public.

The reception of the set of eight formulations by supporters has been encouraging: from this I conclude that there is a broad similarity of views on the fairly general and abstract level. A further conclusion: the usefulness of the Eight Points as a convenient reference point suggests that alternative analogous sets should be developed. It is unnatural that only one way of formulation could be convenient.

The Eight Points are of course not intended to function as a definition of the Deep Ecology movement: neither as a rule-given definition of the term, nor as a plain description of how the expression "Deep Ecology movement" is actually used, nor as an expression of the essence of the Deep Ecology movement. I do not know of any satisfactory definitions at the dictionary level. For instance, I do not think a dictionary entry like the following is very helpful: "Deep Ecology movement: A movement within environmentalism which is activist, ecocentric rather than anthropocentric, and based on nonviolent philosophical or religious views."

Looking back, I am glad to have the opportunity to make some comments about the Eight Point list, not all of which are critical:

1. It has been suggested that the Eight Points should include reference to the "all things hang together" theme. The best way of including this seems to me to be the formulation of Fritjof Capra. He suggests the following alternative formulation of point 2: "The fundamental interdependence, richness and diversity contribute to the flourishing of human and non-human life on Earth."

This alternative formulation is important to me mainly because the three factors mentioned are presented as instrumental, not as values in themselves.

Such a presentation does not, of course, rule out the inherent value of richness and diversity, but I have thought that inherent value must be declared explicitly in the formulation of that point. But why "must"? Conclusion: the suggestion by Capra adds to *the set of alternative formulations* of the Eight Points (I have myself not found it possible to stick to only one single way of formulating the points).

Of course, to "hang together" as a kind of interdependence may be taken by some as a kind of threat. One hears such warnings: "remember humans are *unfortunately* dependent upon the health of the ecosystems. *Therefore* respect nature or you invite disaster!"

In short, I have so far not found sufficient reason to include in the Eight Points a reference to the "all things hang together" theme. It should not be necessary to add that anything like "nature mysticism" (the ultimate unity of all living beings and similar Level I views) has no place among views which supporters may have *in common.* The views about, and feelings of, the intimacy and kind of "hanging together" may, of course, differ in terms of degree of tightness. The interdependence referred to in the alternative formulation is of the kind that supporters do, in fact, talk about.[1]

However, I find it regrettable that J. Baird Callicott, a supporter of the Deep Ecology movement as far as I can understand, believes that some kind of nature mysticism is *implied* in being a Deep Ecology supporter. Callicott writes that "indeed [ Deep Ecologists] argue that ecology teaches us that the whole of nature is the true Self."[2] This is a strange formulation. Supporters of the movement have total views inspired in part by reactions to the ecological crisis. Such total views I have called ecosophies—I call my own Ecosophy T. Fortunately other supporters have different ecosophies. (One thing we have in common is that the articulation of our views is, and must be, fragmentary.) In the premise/conclusion systematization of Ecosophy T, "Self-Realization!" is designated as the one ultimate premise. Some feel at home with this, others do not. The Eight Points could not possibly contain that norm.

I do not feel badly when Professor Callicott mistakenly seems, more or less, to identify my opinions with those of Mahatma Gandhi. He quotes from a section of my "Self-Realization" paper which I introduce by writing: "I do not *defend* all the views presented here: rather I primarily wish to inform you about them." Later in the section I write: "Gandhi says: 'I believe in *advaita* (non-duality). I believe in the essential unity of man and, for that matter, all that lives. Therefore I believe that if one man gains spirituality, the whole world gains with him and, if one man fails, the whole world fails to that extent.'" The quotation from Gandhi reminds me of his (and my) belief in the individual. It shook the world when, as the accused before the judge, Gandhi uttered, "The individual is the supreme concern."

Professor Callicott also writes that "scientific ecology will not support the claim that the self is in reality the Self, that the individual is identical with the world." I might join him in saying that support of that claim might mean the end of scientific ecology. At any rate, no one has, to my knowledge, found that the Eight Points imply a kind of nature mysticism, although many supporters show various degrees of affinity with it.

Points 3 and 8 are the ones that most clearly belong to a (normative) ethic covering actions related to the ecological crisis. An *announcement* of an obligation is made in point 8, and an ethical *prohibition* is made in point 3. Both belong as part of an ethic of vast scope covering our relations to non-human beings. The search for an environmental ethic is, as I see it, a laudable undertaking from the point of view of the Deep Ecology movement. Some supporters would disagree, I suppose, but I am not sure that I know of any. Professor Callicott writes: "Deep ecology . . . rejects ethics outright" (p. 325), but his four supporting quotations (three from texts by Warwick Fox and one from me) don't justify Callicott's claim. Like many others, I distinguish between an ethic as a normative system (in Professor Callicott's terminology "a conceptual system"—p. 338) and acts of *moralizing:* that is, where one individual or group admonishes others to follow certain moral precepts. "We certainly need to hear about our ethical shortcomings," I write in the article quoted by Callicott, but I have emphasized, and continue to emphasize, the rather limited motivational force of moralizing. The Kantian distinction between "beautiful acts" and "moral acts" is convenient here (see my "Beautiful Action: Its Function in the Ecological Crisis" in *Environmental Values* 2, 1 [1993]). Beautiful acts are compared with policies facilitating attitude changes in the direction of ecologically responsible behavior. And Warwick Fox certainly does not hold, as Callicott seems to suggest, that ethical norms which have the structure of points 3 and 8 involve "narrow, atomistic, or particle-like conceptions of self."

2. In recent years considerable efforts have been made to distinguish two concepts; one is expressed by the term "intrinsic value" and the other by the term "inherent value" or "inherent worth." What I intend to express by the use of the term "intrinsic value" in the Eight Points is perhaps better conveyed by the term "inherent value."

Some critics tell me that I must enter the professional philosophical debate about what exactly might be meant by terms like "intrinsic value," "inherent value," and "value in itself" (which I use in my book *Ecology, Community and Lifestyle*). But even in my comments on the Eight Points (which consists of about four hundred words), entering this discussion would be misplaced. The Eight Point formulations admit of various interpretations, but nevertheless interpretations with reasonably small differences. The level of vagueness and ambiguity must be within tolerable limits, but professionalism would under-mine the aim of the Eight Points.

3. I try in my ecosophy to be consistent in my view that individual beings, and only individual beings, can have inherent value, and not classes of individ-uals as such (the term *intellectualis amor* in Spinoza's *Ethics* I likewise take to be the loving understanding of individuals). Point 2 (which discusses diversity) makes this difficult if landscapes, or the whole Earth, are not taken to be individual beings, and not classes of individual beings. If taken otherwise, I would attribute value to some kind of mere multiplicity. I do not attach inher-ent value to species or families (as classes or sets of beings with more than one individual or element) but to diversity, itself. From the "diversity norm," plus various hypotheses, I derive norms of priorities: the defense, for instance, of threatened orders or families should have higher priority than that of species or subspecies, if there are no special reasons not to attach higher priorities to the latter (for example, to families of insects as compared to species of mammals).

In the brief comments on the third of the Eight Points, it is not made sufficiently clear that the use of the expression "no right to" is an everyday use of the term "right" as in: "You have no right to eat your little sister's food!" It is not meant to be identical in meaning with "You ought not to eat. . . ." It does not imply an affirmative answer to the question of the existence of the "rights of man" or the "rights of animals." Because of vast controversies in professional philosophy about the concept of "rights," it may be unwise to use the expression "no right to" in point 3. I am not convinced about that, and the use of it opens up the good question, "Why can't animals have rights?" If the answer is "Because they can have no obligations," this leads to the question "What about babies? The mentally ill?" Such discussions tend to lead people in the direction of softening their rigid views about humans being apart from non-human nature.

Concerning the term "vital needs," several comments are readily at hand. What you *need* in your life is a small fraction of what you are led to desire in the rich countries whereas, in regions of desperate poverty, the vital needs of the majority of people are not satisfied whether or not they reduce the richness and diversity of life forms.

4. In the 1984 formulation, population was discussed in point 5. The con-tent of points 4 and 5 suggest that, in terms of logical order, the population issue should be discussed in point 4, rather than 5.

5. Many supporters of the Deep Ecology movement believe that a reduction in human population would, of course, be a great gain both for humanity and for non-human life, but they don't see how it could happen within the scope of a decent ethics. Some are willing to see reduction occur within a couple of

centuries. What seems a little odd to me is that, at the same time, they can envision population stabilization (zero growth) occurring (without "nature taking over" in the sense of catastrophic wars or massive famines, or both). If transition to zero growth is thought to be practicable, why could there not also occur a population reduction of, say, one-quarter of a percent per year? Within several centuries that would make a lot of difference. A firm acceptance of the population reduction point does not oblige one to speculate concerning how great a reduction one has in mind. That is a different question.

I seriously think that the Eight Points (or corresponding sets of points provided by other supporters) should be acceptable without hesitation to nearly all supporters of the Deep Ecology movement. I have found, therefore, that point 4 *might* be "softened," perhaps in the direction of formulations like the following: "It would be better for humans to be fewer, and much better for non-humans."

If the "decrease" or "reduction" terminology is retained in point 4, then comments should include these two points: the process of a slow but adequate reduction naturally will take more than a couple of centuries. The situation in some rich countries, where zero growth has been reached (or nearly reached) makes it important for governments to declare that nothing will be done to *counteract* a process of reduction in the next century. Those economists (and others) will be consulted who can show how a satisfactory economic situation can be maintained during the difficult transition period.

In a process of slow decrease of the population, there will be a *slight* increase in the percentage of people over the age of retirement. This could be partly allievated by motivating a slight increase in the age of retirement. The amount of capital per person will increase slightly, as well as the availability of resources in general. The chances of significant unemployment will also be slightly reduced, and so on.

But an adequate discussion of the economics of population reduction cannot be the aim of these remarks. Both strategically and tactically, it is of central importance, in my view, that more people outside of the economically richest countries realize that population reduction is compatible with maintaining, or increasing, the overall quality of life. Point 7 is meant to be relevant here. One cannot expect people in the poorer countries to believe in this point if very few people in the richest countries do.

The argument is often heard in rich countries that many sons are necessary in poor countries to provide security for one's old age. Actually there is a substantial minority of people in the poor countries who do not think this way (if four sons need sixteen sons, who need sixty-four, what happens then?).

Clearly, many people do not consider it possible that adults can have a close warm relationship to small children they have not themselves produced. But, in many cultures, architecture and the use of space make it possible for small children to walk around without danger and to be taken care of by neighbors and friends. In such situations, young parents do not have to worry when they go to work, and the kids might have close relationships, and even stay overnight, with "uncles" and "aunts." Adults who wish to have small children around them, and like to spend a lot of time with them, are highly esteemed and form an indispensible part of the community. Under such conditions, one may have closer and *more durable* relations with small children than parents in rich countries who have produced as many as four or five children.

I have spent so much space talking about the population issue because I think that, in some countries, now is the time to reconsider the design of cities, and policies of spacing, so as to anticipate a slow decrease of population which may begin in the near future in some countries; say, within a couple of generations, or even sooner.

6. The Deep Ecology terminology was introduced, during the late 1960s, in a highly politicized environment. "Every question is a political question" was a slogan you might have heard repeated every other day in Europe during this period. The very able students of the neo-Marxist and Frankfurt School knew very well that slogans and repetitions are indispensible in a social movement. When the Green movement suddenly surfaced in European cities (in Norway with the astonishing basic slogan "Green Grass!") it was laudable, in my view, that activism and the necessity of social and political change was made a central point. Economics, technology, and politics must be a subject of teaching and disucssion in any "environmental" movement. The combination of points 6 and 8 is supposed to express the seriousness of this insight. But it does not, of course, mean that all supporters of Deep Ecology must specialize in party politics or related activities.

Supporters of the Deep Ecology movement naturally work within the horizon of the "alternative future" movements. More specifically, they work with the supporters of the Green movement (which may roughly be said to require of a society that it has largely solved the peace, social justice, and ecological sustainability problems). The intimate cooperation and mutual respect among people (whose *activism* is quite naturally focused on one, but not all, of these three areas of problems) is excellent, and does not exclude strong utterances in favor of their own specialties. Such utterances strengthen our motivation.

Because the main work of supporters of the Deep Ecology movement concerns only a part of what is required of a Green society, there can be no such thing as a "Deep Ecology society." The Deep Ecological requirement of "wide" ecological sustainability (protecting the full richness and diversity of Life on Earth), however, limits the kinds of Green societies that would be acceptable. Because the intrinsic value, respect, and support of deep cultural differences are viewed (in accordance with points 1 and 2) on a par with attitudes towards richness and diversity of non-human life forms, any social or political trends of the fascist or Nazi kind runs counter to the requirement of full ecological sustainability.

In Germany, some people become worried when they hear about Deep Ecology: "Sacredness of the soil? I remember Himmler, the terrible Himmler, talking and talking about that!" But acquaintance with the movement dispels the worries.

Critics have deplored the lack of an authoritative Deep Ecology blueprint for a society satisfying the requirements of the Eight Points—they are apparently looking for texts like Edward Goldsmith's *Blueprint for Survival,* but updated. More or less broad visions of future Green societies are expressed within the Green movement, of which the Deep Ecology movement is only a part. Visions are needed, but scarcely blueprints.

Personally, I envision deep cultural differences existing among Green societies in different parts of the world. Valuable suggestions have been made since the 1960s, but they do not so far show, in my opinion, how diversity of thinking, acting, and cultural priorities may be normal among future societies which satisfy the three requirements of peace, social justice, and ecological sustainability.

In any case, point 6 is not the place to go into specific requirements of social change. A vague, general suggestion along these lines is made in point 7. But I am not sure that it is a good idea to have even a point like that. It only vaguely suggests something about the general direction of the political changes needed. At any rate, it has been a great satisfaction to note that no supporters have indicated that I overrate the importance of political change as a necessary condition of surmounting the ecological crisis.

There are supporters who think that the formulation of the Eight Points has been overrated and that they do not deserve the position of importance they are sometimes accorded. And obviously, if the points are taken to express *the* philosophy characteristic of the Deep Ecology movement, or even *the* principles of Deep Ecology, it would be, in a sense, a grave misinterpretation of those approximately two hundred words used to express those points. Maybe it should be repeated more often they they *only* present an attempt to formulate what *might be* accepted by the great majority of the supporters of the movement at a fairly general and abstract level. Different sets of formulations are needed to express something similar, but in the language of supporters in the non-industrialized parts of the Earth. As formulated, the Eight Points are in a sense provincial—adapted primarily to discussions among formally well-educated people in rich countries.

When introducing the Eight Points in non-industrialized societies, I have of course used very different formulations; sometimes, for instance, not speaking about the Earth at all, and limiting the intended validity of point 7 to the rich countries. It is a curious phenomenon that some people in the West think that poor people don't fight for the preservation of non-human beings for their own sake. In 1973, the families of a poor village in Nepal voted 46 to 0 to send their headman with a petition to *protect* their sacred mountain Tseringma (Gauri Shankar) from tourism—forgoing the vast financial income they might gain. (Incidentally, the name Tseringma means "the mother of the good long life.") Without having seen such phenomena, I would not talk about the broad *international* Deep Ecology movement.

In conclusion, I would like to ask forebearance for talking so much about such a small set of formulations. But they have so far been helpful in fostering feelings of being closely together in an immense task of supreme value.

# NOTES

1. The 18 points of my 1973 paper "The Shallow and the Deep, Long-Range Ecology Movements" smacked too much of the special metaphysics of a younger Naess, as I soon found out. They were discarded in favor of the Eight Points, to the regret of some readers (for example, Richard Sylvan, among ecophilosophers). The 1973 paper, for example, claimed the ego to be like "knots in the biospherical net or field of intrinsic relations." I still may use the sentence "all living beings are ultimately one" which embarrassed Sir Alfred Ayer in our one-hour debate. (See *In Reflexive Waters,* edited by Fons Elders (Souvenir Books, 1974), 31.

2. J. Baird Callicott, "The Search for an Environmental Ethic," in *Matters of Life and Death,* edited by Tom Regan, 3rd ed. (New York: McGraw Hill, 1993), 330.

# 21 | EQUALITY, SAMENESS, AND RIGHTS

## *Arne Naess*

MY INTUITION IS THAT the right to live is one and the same for all individuals, whatever the species, but the vital interests of our nearest, nevertheless, have priority. There are rules which manifest two important factors which operate when interests conflict: vitalness and nearness. The greater vital interest has priority over the less vital. And the nearer has priority over the more remote—in space, time, culture, and species. Nearness derives its priority from our special responsibilities, obligations, and insights as humans among humans.

The terms used in these rules are of course vague and ambiguous. But even so, the rules point toward ways of thinking and acting which do not leave us helpless in the many inevitable conflicts between norms. The vast increase of negative consequences for life in general, brought about by industrialization and the population explosion, necessitates new guidelines.

For example, the use of threatened species for food or fur clothing may be more or less vital for certain poor families in non-industrial human communities. But for people who are not poor, such use is clearly ecologically irresponsible. Considering the fabulous possibilities open to the richest industrial nations, it is their responsibility to cooperate with poor communities in ways such that undue exploitation or threatened species, populations, anad ecosystems can be avoided.

It may be of vital interest to a family of poisonous snakes to remain in a place where they have lived for hundreds of generations but where small children now play, but it is also of vital interest to the children and their parents that there be no accidents. The priority rule of nearness (and a sense of responsibility) makes it justifiable for the parents to relocate the snakes. But

---

Written in 1993, this essay is previously unpublished. Published with permission.

the priority of the vital interests of the snakes is important in deciding where to establish the playgrounds in the first place.

A personal testimony: I have injured thousands of individuals of the tiny arctic plant, *Salix herbacea,* during a ten-year period of living in the high mountains of Norway, and I shall feel forced to continue stepping on them as long as I live there. But I have never felt the need to justify such behavior by thinking that they have less of a right to live and blossom (or that they have less intrinsic value as living beings) than other living beings, including myself. It is simply not possible to live and move around in certain mountain areas without stepping on myriads of these plants, and I maintain that it *is* justifiable to live in these mountain areas. When I behave as I do, I can (at the same time) admire these plants and acknowledge their "equal" right to live and blossom with my right to do so: not less and not more. It is therefore a better formulation to say that living beings have a right (or intrinsic or inherent value, or value in themselves) to live and blossom that is the *same* for all. If we speak of differences in rights or value we do not speak of the rights or value I have in mind. It is not meaningful to speak of *degrees* of intrinsic or inherent value when speaking of the right of individuals to live and blossom.

What I have done here is to try to verbalize an intuition. But any such verbalization may be misleading, and it has certainly often mislead others. There are other intuitions and thousands of slight differences in attitude which reflect different valuations of various sorts. For example, if there is a choice concerning whether to step on a *Salix herbacea,* rather than on the small, more overwhelmingly beautiful and rarer *Gentiana nivalis,* I unhesitatingly and deliberately step on the former.

The abstract and somewhat grandiose term "biospherical egalitarianism in principle" (and certain similar terms which I have sometimes used) perhaps do more harm than good. They may be taken by some to suggest a major *doctrine* of sorts, but that goes way beyond my intentions. As I see it, the importance of the intuition I speak of resides in its capacity to counteract, perhaps only momentarily, the self-congratulatory and lordly attitude towards those beings which may seem, to some people, to be less developed, less complex, less beautiful, or less miraculous.

When I characterize this as an intuition, I do not imply the absence or lack of a rational basis for it, but rather that there are other factors operating here. For example, the increase in demand for rigor in mathematical proofs eliminated certain intuitions. But intuitions still operate, for instance, when choosing axioms and other fundamentals.

There is a rich variety of acceptable motives for being more reluctant to injure or kill a living being of kind A rather than a being of kind B. The cultural setting is different for each being in each culture, and there are few general norms—only vague general guidelines. The more narrow and specific the questions posed, the less vagueness there will be. For example, I have proposed norms relating to communities of bears, wolves, sheep, and sheepowners in Norway.[1]

Another relevant factor is the *felt nearness* of different living beings. This factor largely determines our capacity to strongly identify with a certain kind of living being, and to suffer when they suffer. One cannot put forth ethical rules of conduct without taking our limited capacities, and such personal feelings, seriously. If it is *difficult to avoid* killing A, for example, because of its smallness, whereas killing B is easily avoided, then we tend to protect B rather than A. And there is an obvious diversity of obligations. We obviously have special obligations towards our own children: any animal may be killed in order to feed one's starving child. Obligations toward individuals that have been members of our communities for long periods of time are greater than toward accidental visitors. Furthermore, there is, of course, the relevance of suffering: is the suffering of A less than that of B? Does A have the capacity to suffer?

The rather simple thing I am trying to convey here is that an ethic that attempts to deal with the *differences* between nonhuman living beings is of a comparable level of complexity with an ethic which concerns itself with our behavior toward different people and groups with which we interact.

Related to the above, I prefer the term *living being* to the term *organism*. The intuitive concept of "life" (or "living being") sometimes includes a river, a landscape, a wilderness, a mountain, and an arctic "waste." The intuition has a little, but not much, to do with biology or neurophysiology. Intrinsic value, as posited by the intuition, is influenced, but not decisively, by "biological news": for instance, news about the whale's "nervous system complexity comparable to humans."

The kind of intuition I have been speaking about I take to be rather common among supporters of the Deep Ecology movement. It is not easy to verify this in detail, however, because of terminological and conceptual differences. The broad stream of nature poetry, over thousands of years, is perhaps the best source of confirmation of the widespread intuitive appreciation of the *same* right of all beings to live and blossom.

# NOTE

1. For more about the relevance of tradition and culture, see Arne Naess, "Self-Realization in Mixed Communities of Humans, Bears, Sheep, and Wolves," *Inquiry* 22 (1979): 231–41; Arne Naess and Ivar Mysterud, "Philosophy of Wolf Policies I: General Principles and Preliminary Exploration of Selected Norms," *Conservation Biology* 1, no. 1 (1987): 22–34.

# 22 | SELF-REALIZATION
## AN ECOLOGICAL APPROACH
## TO BEING IN THE WORLD

### *Arne Naess*

### I

HUMANITY HAS STRUGGLED, FOR about 2,500 years, with basic questions about who we are, where we are headed, and the nature of the reality in which we are included. This is a short period in the lifetime of a species, and an even shorter time in the history of the Earth, to which we belong as mobile beings. I am not capable of saying very new things in answer to these questions, but I can look at them from a *somewhat* different angle, using somewhat different conceptual tools and images.

What I am going to say, more or less in my own way and in that of my friends, can be condensed roughly into the following six points:

1. We underestimate ourself. And I emphasize "self." We tend to confuse our "self" with the narrow ego.

2. Human nature is such that, with sufficient comprehensive (all-sided) maturity, we cannot help but "identify" our self with all living beings; beautiful or ugly, big or small, sentient or not.

The adjective comprehensive ("all-sided") as in "comprehensive maturity" deserves a note: Descartes seemed to be rather immature in his relationship with animals; Schopenhauer was not very advanced in his relationship to his family (kicking his mother down a staircase?); Heidegger was amateurish—to say the least—in his political behavior. Weak identification with nonhumans

This essay was originally given as a lecture, March 12, 1986, at Murdock University, Western Australia, sponsored by the Keith Roby Memorial Trust. Reprinted with permission.

is compatible with maturity in some major sets of relationships, such as those towards one's family or friends. And so I use the qualification *comprehensive* to mean "being mature in *all* major relationships."

3. Traditionally, the *maturity of the self* has been considered to develop through three stages: from ego to social self (comprising the ego), and from social self to a metaphysical self (comprising the social self). But in this conception of the maturity of the self, Nature is largely left out. Our immediate environment, our home (where we belong as children), and the identification with nonhuman living beings, are largely ignored. Therefore, I tentatively introduce, perhaps for the very first time, the concept of *ecological self.* We may be said to be in, and of, Nature from the very beginning of our selves. Society and human relationships are important, but our self is much richer in its constitutive relationships. These relationships are not only those we have with other humans and the human community (I have elsewhere introduced the term *mixed community* to mean those communities where we consciously and deliberately live closely together with certain animals).

4. The meaning of life, and the joy we experience in living, is increased through increased self-realization; that is, through the fulfillment of potentials each of us has, but which are never exactly the same for any two living beings. Whatever the differences between beings, nevertheless, increased self-realization implies a broadening and deepening of the self.

5. Because of an inescapable process of identification with others, with increasing maturity, the self is widened and deepened. We "see ourselves in others." Our self-realization is hindered if the self-realization of others, with whom we identify, is hindered. Our love of ourself will fight this hindering process by assisting in the self-realization of others according to the formula "Live and let live!" Thus, everything that can be achieved by altruism—the *dutiful, moral* consideration for others—can be achieved, and much more, by the process of widening and deepening ourselves. Following Kant, we then act *beautifully,* but neither morally nor immorally.

6. One of the great challenges today is to save the planet from further ecological devastation which violates both the enlightened self-interest of humans and nonhumans, and decreases the potential of joyful existence for all.

## II

Now, proceeding to elaborate these points, I shall start with the peculiar and fascinating terms *ego* and *self.*

The simplest answer to who or what I am is to point to my body. But clearly I cannot identify my self, or even my ego, with my body. For example, compare:

| I know Mr. Smith. | | My body knows Mr. Smith. |
|---|---|---|
| I like poetry. | | My body likes poetry. |
| The only difference between us is that you are a Presbyterian and I am a Baptist. |  | The only difference between our bodies is that your body is Presbyterian whereas mine is Baptist. |

In the above sentences, we cannot substitute "my body" for "I." Nor can we substitute "my mind" or "my mind and my body" for "I." More adequately, we may substitute "I as a person" for "I," but this does not, of course, tell us what the ego or the self is.

Several thousand years of philosophical, psychological, and social-psychological thinking has not brought us any adequate conception of the "I," the "ego," or the "self." In modern psychotherapy these notions play an indispensible role, but, of course, the practical goal of therapy does not necessitate philosophical clarification of these terms. It is important to remind ourselves about the strange and marvelous phenomena with which we are dealing. Perhaps the extreme closeness and nearness of these objects of thought and reflection adds to our difficulties. I shall offer only one single sentence which resembles a definition of the "ecological self." The ecological self of a person is that with which this person identifies.

This key sentence (rather than a definition) about the self shifts the burden of clarification from the term "self" to that of "identification," or rather "process of identification."

## III

I shall continue to concentrate on the "ecology of the self," but will first say some things about identification.

What would be a paradigm situation involving identification? It would be a situation which elicits intense empathy. My standard example involves a nonhuman being I met forty years ago. I was looking through an old-fashioned microscope at the dramatic meeting of two drops of different chemicals. At that moment, a flea jumped from a lemming which was strolling along the table and landed in the middle of the acid chemicals. To save it was impossible. It took many minutes for the flea to die. Its movements were dreadfully expressive. Naturally, what I felt was a painful sense of compassion and empathy. But the empathy was *not* basic, rather it was a process of identification: that "I saw myself in the flea." If I had been *alienated* from the flea, not seeing intuitively anything even resembling myself, the death struggle would have left me feeling indifferent. So there must be identification in order for there to be compassion and, among humans, solidarity.

One of the authors contributing admirably to a clarification of the study of the self is Erich Fromm. He writes:

The doctrine that love for oneself is identical with "selfishness" and an alternative to love for others has pervaded theology, philosophy, and popular thought; the same doctrine has been rationalized in scientific language in Freud's theory of narcissism. Freud's concept presupposes a fixed amount of libido. In the infant, all of the libido has the child's own person as its objective, the stage of "primary narcissism," as Freud calls it. During the individual's development, the libido is shifted from one's own person toward other objects. If a person is blocked in his "object-relationships," the libido is withdrawn from the objects and returned to his or her own person; this is called "secondary narcissism." According to Freud, the more love I turn toward the outside world the less love is left for myself, and vice versa. He thus describes the phenomenon of love as an impoverishment of one's self-love because all libido is turned to an object outside oneself.[1]

What Fromm attributes here to Freud we can now attribute to the shrinkage of self-perception implied in the fascination for ego-trips. Fromm opposes such a shrinkage of self. The following quotation from Fromm concerns love of persons but, as "ecosophers," we find the notions of "care, respect, responsibility, knowledge" applicable to living beings in the wide sense.

Love of others and love of ourselves are not alternatives. On the contrary, an attitude of love toward themselves will be found in all those who are capable of loving others. Love, in principle, is indivisible as far as the connection between "objects" and one's own self is concerned. Genuine love is an expression of productiveness and implies care, respect, responsibility, and knowledge. It is not an "effect" in the sense of being effected by somebody, but an active striving for the growth and happiness of the loved person, rooted in one's own capacity to love.[2]

Fromm is very instructive about unselfishness—it is diametrically the opposite of selfishness, but still based upon alienation and a narrow perception of self. We might add that what he says also applies to persons experiencing a sacrifice of themselves:

The nature of unselfishness becomes particularly apparent in its effect on others and most frequently, in our culture, in the effect the "unselfish" mother has on her children. She believes that by her unselfishness her children will experience what it means to be loved and to learn, in turn, what it means to love. The effect of her unselfishness, however, does not at all correspond to her expectations. The children do not show the happiness of persons who are convinced that they are loved; they are anxious, tense, afraid of the mother's disapproval, and anxious to live up to her expectations. Usually, they are affected by their mother's hidden hostility against life, which they sense rather than recognize, and eventually become imbued with it themselves. . . .

If one has a chance to study the effect of a mother with genuine self-love, one can see that there is nothing more conducive to giving a child the experience what love, joy, and happiness are than being loved by a mother who loves herself.[3]

We need environmental ethics, but when people feel that they unselfishly give up, or even sacrifice, their self-interests to show love for nature, this is probably, in the long run, a treacherous basis for conservation. Through identification, they may come to see that their own interests are served by conservation, through genuine self-love, the love of a widened and deepened self.

At this point, the notion of a being's interests furnishes a bridge from self-love to self-realization. It should not surprise us that Fromm, influenced as he is by Spinoza and William James, makes use of that bridge. "What is considered to constitute self-interest?" Fromm asks. His answer:

There are two fundamentally different approaches to this problem. One is the objectivistic approach most clearly formulated by Spinoza. To him self-interest or the interest "to seek one's profit" is identical with virtue.

"The more," he says, "each person strives and is able to seek his profit, that is to say, to preserve his being, the more virtue does he possess; on the other hand, in so far as each person neglects his own profit he is impotent." According to this view, the interest of humans is to preserve their existence, which is the same as realizing their inherent potentialities. This concept of self-interest is objectivistic inasmuch as "interest" is not conceived in terms of the subjective feeling of what one's interest is but in terms of what the nature of a human is, "objectively."[4]

"Realizing inherent potentialities" is one of the good, less-than-ten-word, clarifications of "self-realization." The questions "What are the inherent potentialities of the beings of species X?" and "What are the inherent potentialities of this specimen X of the species Y?" obviously lead to reflections about, and studies of, X and Y.

As humans we cannot just follow the impulses of the moment when asking what our inherent potentialities are. It is something like this that Fromm means when he calls an approach "objectivistic" as opposed to an approach "in terms of subjective feeling." Because of the high estimation of feeling and a correspondingly low estimate of so-called objectivization (*Verdinglichung,* reification) within Deep Ecology, Fromm's terminology is not adequate today, but what he means to say is appropriate. And it is obviously relevant when we deal with species other than humans: animals and plants have interests in the sense of ways of realizing inherent potentialities which we can study only by interacting with them. We cannot rely on our momentary impulses, however important they are in general.

The expression "preserve his being," in the quotation from Spinoza, is better than "preserve his existence" since the latter is often associated with physical survival and a "struggle for survival." An even better translation, perhaps, is to "persevere in his being" *(perseverare in suo esse)*. This has to do with acting from one's own nature. Survival is only a necessary condition, not a sufficient condition of self-realization.

The concept of self-realization, as dependent upon insight into our own potentialities, makes it easy to see the possibilities of ignorance and misunderstanding in terms of what these potentialities are. The "ego-trip" interpretation of the potentialities of humans presupposes a major underestimation of the richness and broadness of our potentialities. As Fromm puts it, "man can deceive himself about his real self-interest if he is ignorant of his self and its real needs."[5]

The "everything hangs together" (or "everything is interrelated") maxim of ecology applies to the self and its relation to other living beings, ecosystems, the ecosphere, and to the Earth, itself, with its long history.

## IV

The existence and importance of the "ecological self" is easy to illustrate with some examples of what has happened in my own country, Norway.

Scattered human habitation along the arctic coast of Norway is uneconomical and unprofitable, from the point of view of the current economic policy of our welfare state. Welfare norms require that every family should be connected by telephone (in case of illness); this costs a considerable amount of money. The same holds for the mail and other services. Further, local fisheries are largely uneconomical perhaps because a foreign armada of big trawlers of immense capacity is fishing just outside the fjords. And so, the availability of jobs is crumbling.

Therefore, the government heavily subsidized the resettlement of people from the arctic wilderness, concentrating them in so-called centers of development (small areas with a town at the center). But the people, as persons, are clearly not the same when their bodies have been thus transported. The social, economic, *and natural setting* is now vastly different. The objects with which they work and live are completely different. There is a consequent loss of personal identity. They now ask "Who am I?" Their self-respect and self-esteem has been impaired. What is adequate in the so-called periphery of the country is different from what is important in the so-called centers.

If people are relocated, or rather, transplanted from a steep mountainous place to the plains below, they also realize (but too late) that their home-place was a part of themselves and that they *identified* with features of that place. The way of life in the tiny locality, with the intensity of social relations there, has formed their personhood. Again, "they are now not the same as they were."

Tragic cases of this can be seen in other parts of the Arctic. We all regret the fate of the Eskimos; their difficulty in finding a *new identity,* a new social self, and a new more comprehensive ecological self. In addition, the Lapps of arctic Norway have been hurt by interference with a river for the purpose of developing hydroelectricity. Accused of an illegal demonstration at the river, one Lapp said in court that the part of the river in question was "part of himself." This kind of spontaneous answer is not uncommon among people. They have not heard about the philosophy of the wider and deeper self, but they talk spontaneously as if they had.

## V

We may try to make the sentence "This place is part of myself" intellectually more understandable by reformulations—for example, "My relation to this place is part of myself"; "If this place is destroyed something in me is destroyed"; "My relation to this place is such that if the place is changed, I am changed". . . .

One drawback with these formulations is that they make it easy to continue thinking of two completely separable, real entities: a self and the place, joined by an *external* relation. The original sentence rather conveys the impression that there is an *internal* relation of sorts. I say "of sorts" because we must take into account that the relation may not be reciprocal. If I am changed, or even destroyed, the place would be destroyed, according to one usual interpretation of "internal relation." From the standpoint of phenomenology and the "concrete contents" view, the reciprocity holds, but that is a special interpretation. We may use an interpretation such that if we are changed, the river need not be changed.

The newborn, of course, lacks any conceptions, however rudimentary, corresponding to the tri-partition—subject, object, and medium. Probably the conception (not the concept) of one's own ego comes rather late, say after the first year. First there is a vague net of relations. This network of perceived and conceived relations is neutral, similar to what in British philosophy was called "neutral monism." In a sense, we are trying to work out this basic sort of crude monism anew, not by trying to become babies again, but by better understanding our ecological selves. This understanding has not had favorable conditions for development, since prior to the time the Renaissance glorified our ego by placing it in opposition to the rest of reality.

What is the practical importance of this conception of a wide and deep ecological self? When we attempt to defend Nature in our rich industrial societies, the argument of our opponents is often that we are doing it to secure beauty, recreation, and other non-vital interests for ourselves. Our position is strengthened if, after honest reflection, we find that the destruction of Nature (and our place) threatens us in our innermost self. If so, we are more convincingly defending our vital interests, not merely something "out there." We are engaged in self-defense. And to defend fundamental *human* rights is vital self-defense.

The best introduction to the psychology of the self is still to be found in William James' excellent and superbly readable book, *The Principles of Psychology* (1890). His 100-page chapter on the consciousness of self stresses the plurality of components of the wide and deep self as a complex entity. (Unfortunately, he prefers to talk about a plurality of selves. I think it may be better to talk about the plurality of the components of the wide self.)

If we say about somebody that he or she is not himself today, we may refer to a great many different *relations* to other people, to material things, and certainly, I maintain, to what we call his or her environment: the home, the garden, the neighborhood. . . .

When James says that these relata *belong* to the self, of course, it is not in the sense that the self has eaten the home, the environment, etc. Such an interpretation would mean that the self is still identified with the body. Nor does it mean that an *image* of the house *inside* the consciousness of the person belongs to the self. When somebody says about a part of a river-landscape that it is part of himself, we intuitively grasp roughly what he means. But it is difficult, of course, to elucidate this meaning in philosophical or psychological terminology.

A last example from William James: We understand what is meant when someone says "As a man I pity you, but as an official I must show you no mercy." Obviously the self of an official cannot empirically be defined except as relationships in a complex social setting. Thus, the self cannot possibly be inside the body, or inside a consciousness.

Enough! The main point is that we do not hesitate *today,* being inspired by ecology and a revived intimate relationship to Nature, to recognize and accept wholeheartedly our ecological self.

## VI

The next section is rather metaphysical. I do not *defend* all the views presented here; rather I primarily wish to inform you about them. As a student and admirer of Gandhi's non-violent direct actions in bloody conflicts since 1930,

I am inevitably influenced by his metaphysics which personally furnished him with tremendously powerful motivation and contributed to keeping him going until his death. His ultimate aim was not India's *political* liberation. He, of course, led a crusade against extreme poverty, caste suppression, and against terror in the name of religion. This crusade was necessary, but the liberation of the individual human being was his supreme aim. It is strange for many to hear what he himself said about his ultimate goal:

> What I want to achieve—what I have been striving and pining to achieve these thirty years—is self-realization, to see God face to face, to attain *Moksha* (Liberation). I live and move and have my being in pursuit of that goal. All that I do by way of speaking and writing, and all my ventures in the political field, are directed to this same end.[6]

This sounds individualistic to the Western mind—a common misunderstanding. If the self Gandhi is speaking about were the ego or "narrow" self (*jiva*) of egocentric interest ("ego-trips"), why then work for the poor? For him, it is the supreme or universal Self—the *atman*—that is to be realized. Paradoxically, it seems, he tries to reach Self-realization through "selfless action"; that is, through a diminishment of the dominance of the narrow self or ego. Through the wider Self every living being is intimately connected, and from this intimacy follows the capacity of *identification* and, as a natural consequence, the practice of non-violence. No moralizing is needed, just as we don't need morals to make us breathe. Rather, we need to cultivate our insight: "The rock bottom foundation of the technique for achieving the power of non-violence is belief in the essential oneness of all life."

Historically, we have seen that Nature conservation is non-violent at its very core. Gandhi says:

> I believe in *advaita* (non-duality). I believe in the essential unity of man and, for that matter, all that lives. Therefore I believe that if one man gains spirituality, the whole world gains with him and, if one man fails, the whole world fails to that extent.

Surprisingly enough, Gandhi was extreme in his personal concern for the self-realization of nonhuman living beings. When traveling, he brought a goat along to satisfy his need for milk. This was part of a non-violent demonstration against certain cruel Hindu ways of milking cows. Some European companions who lived with Gandhi in his ashrams were taken aback that he let snakes, scorpions, and spiders move unhindered into their bedrooms—as animals fulfilling their lives. He even prohibited people from keeping a stock of medicines against poisonous bites. He believed in the possibility of satisfactory coexistence and he was proved right. There were no accidents. Ashram people would naturally look into their shoes for scorpions before using them. Even when moving over the floor in darkness one could easily avoid trampling on one's fellow beings. Thus, Gandhi recognized a basic common right to live and blossom, to self-realization in a wide sense applicable to any being that can be said to have interests or needs. Gandhi made manifest the interal relation between self-realization, non-violence, and what has sometimes been called biospherical egalitarianism.

In the environment in which I grew up, I heard that what is important in life is to get *to be* someone—to outdo others in something, to be victorious in comparing one's abilities with others. The ability to cooperate, to work with people, to make them feel good, of course, "pays" in a fiercely individualistic society, and high positions may require that—but only to the extent to which they are ultimately subordinated to one's career, to the basic norms of the ego-trip, not to a self-realization worthy of the name. To identify self-realization with ego-trips manifests a vast underestimation of the human self.

According to the usual translation of Pali or Sanskrit, Buddha taught his disciples that the human mind should embrace all living things as a mother cares for her son, her only son. Some who would never feel it to be meaningful or possible that a human *self* could embrace all living things, might stick to the usual translation. We shall then ask only that your *mind* embrace all living beings, together with your good intentions to care, feel, and act with compassion.

If the Sanskrit word translated into English is *atman,* it is instructive to note that this term has the basic meaning of "self," rather than "mind" or "spirit" as one usually sees in the translations. The superiority of the translation using the word *self* stems from the consideration that *if* your self (in the wide sense) embraces another being, you need no moral exhortation to show care. Surely you care for yourself without feeling any moral pressure to do it—provided you have not succumbed to a neurosis of some kind, developed self-destructive tendencies, or hate yourself.

Incidentally, the Australian Deep Ecology supporter and ecofeminist Patsy Hallen uses a formula close to that of Buddha's: We are here to embrace rather than conquer the world. It is of interest to notice that the term *world* is being used here rather than *living beings.* I suspect that our thinking need not proceed from the notion of living being to that of the world, but we will conceive reality, or the world we live in, as alive in a wide, not easily defined, sense. There will then be no non-living beings to care for.

## VII

If "self-realization" (or "self-fulfillment") is habitually associated today with lifelong ego-trips, then isn't it stupid to use this term for self-realization in

Gandhi's widely different sense or (in a less religiously loaded context) as a term for widening and deepening the "self" so that it embraces all life forms? Perhaps it is. But I think the very popularity of the term makes people feel safe, and they listen for a moment. In that moment the notion of a greater "self" should be introduced, pointing out that if they equate self-realization with ego-trips, then they seriously *underestimate* themselves. "You are much greater, deeper, generous and capable of more dignity and joy than you think! A wealth of non-competitive joys is open to you!"

But I have another important reason for inviting people to think in terms of deepening and widening their selves, *starting* with the ego-trip as the crudest, but inescapable, zero point. It has to do with a notion usually placed as the opposite of the egoism of the ego-trip; namely the notion of *altruism*. The Latin term *ego* has, as its opposite, the term *alter*. Altruism implies that the *ego* sacrifices its interests in favor of the other, the *alter*. In the latter case, one is motivated primarily by duty: it is said that we *ought* to love others as strongly as we love ourselves.

Unfortunately, what humanity is capable of loving from mere duty or, more generally, from moral exhortation, is very limited. From the Renaissance to the Second World War about four hundred cruel wars were fought by Christian nations for the flimsiest of reasons. It seems to me that, in the future, more emphasis has to be given to the conditions under which we most naturally widen and deepen the "self." With a sufficiently wide and deep "self," *ego* and *alter* as opposites are, stage by stage, eliminated. The distinction between *ego* and *alter* is, in a way, transcended.

Early in life, the social "self" is sufficiently developed such that we do not prefer to eat a big cake all by ourselves. We share the cake with our friends and our nearest. We identify with these people sufficiently to see our joy in their joy, and our disappointments in theirs. Now is the time to *share* with all life on our maltreated Earth through a deepening identification with all life forms and the greater units: the ecosystems and Gaia, the fabulous old planet of ours.

## VIII

Moral acts are acts motivated by the intention to follow the moral laws at whatever cost; that is, to do our moral duty solely out of respect for that duty. Therefore, the supreme *test* of our success in performing a pure moral act is that we do it completely against our inclination: that we, so to speak, hate to do it but are compelled to do it by our respect for the moral law. Kant was deeply awed by two phenomena: "the heaven with its stars above me and the moral law within me."

If we do something, we should do it according to the moral law, but if we do something out of inclination and with pleasure—what then? Should we abstain from performing the act, or try to work up some displeasure? Not at all, according to Kant. If we do what the moral law says is right on the basis of positive inclination, then we perform a *beautiful* act. Now, my point is that, in environmental affairs, perhaps we should try primarily to influence people towards performing beautiful acts. We should work on their inclinations rather than their morality. Unhappily, the extensive moralizing within environmentalism has given the public the false impression that we primarily ask them to sacrifice, to show more responsibility, more concern, better morality. As I see it, we need to emphasize the immense variety of sources of joy which are available to people through an increased sensitivity towards the richness and diversity of life, and the landscapes of free nature. We can all contribute to this individually, but it is also a question of local and global politics. Part of the joy stems from the consciousness of our intimate relation to something bigger than our ego; something which has endured for millions of years, and is worth continued life for many more millions of years. The requisite care flows naturally if the "self" is widened and deepened so that protection of free nature is felt and conceived as protection of ourselves.

Academically speaking, what I am suggesting is the supremacy of environmental ontology and realism over environmental ethics as a means of invigorating the environmental movement in the years to come. If reality is as it is experienced by the ecological self, our behavior *naturally* and beautifully follows strict norms of environmental ethics. We certainly need to hear about our ethical shortcomings from time to time, but we change more easily through encouragement and through a deepened perception of reality and our own self. That is, a deepened realism. How can that be brought about? The question needs to be treated in another paper! It is more a question of community therapy than community science: a question of healing our relations to the widest community—that of all living beings.

## IX

The subtitle of this paper is "An Ecological Approach to Being in the World." I now want to speak a little about "Nature," with all the qualities we spontaneously experience as being identical with the reality we live in. This means a movement from being in the world to being in Nature. Then, at last, I shall inquire into the goal or purpose of being in the world.

Is joy *in* the subject? I would say No. It is just as much, or as little, *in* the object. The joy of a joyful tree is primarily "in" the tree we should say—if pressed to choose between the two possibilities. But we should not be pressed:

there is a third position. The joy is a feature of the *indivisible,* concrete unit of subject, object and medium. In a sense, self-realization involves experiences of the infinitely rich joyful aspect of reality. It is misleading, according to my intuitions, to locate joys inside my consciousness. What is joyful is something that is not "subjective"; it is an attribute of a reality wider than a conscious ego. This is philosophically how I contribute to the explanation of the internal relations between joy, happiness, and human self-realization. But this conceptual exercise is of interest mainly to an academic philosopher. What I am driving at is probably something that may be suggested with less conceptual gymnastics: namely that it unwarranted to believe that how we feel nature to be is not how nature really is. Rather, it is that reality is so rich that we cannot see everything at once; we see separate parts (or aspects) in separate moods. The joyful tree I see in the morning light is not the sorrowful one I see that night, even if they are the "same" tree in terms of their abstract (physical) structure.

## X

It is very human to ask for the ultimate goal or purpose for being in the world. This may be a misleading way of putting the question. It may seem to suggest that the goal or purpose must somehow be outside of, or beyond, the world. Perhaps this can be avoided by living "in the world." It is characteristic of our time that we subjectivize and individualize the question asked of each one of us: What do *you* consider to be the ultimate goal or purpose for *your* life? Or, we leave out the question of priorities, and simply ask for goals and purposes.

The main title of this paper is motivated partly by the conviction that *self-realization* is an adequate key-term expression one would use to answer the question of the ultimate goal in life. Of course, it is only a key-term. An answer by a philosopher could scarcely be shorter than the little book, *Ethic,* by Spinoza.

In order to understand the function of the term *self-realization* in this capacity, it is useful to compare it with two other terms—*pleasure* and *happiness.* The first suggests hedonism; the second, eudaemonism, in professional philosophical (but just as vague and ambiguous) jargon. Both terms connote states of feeling (in a broad sense of the term). Experiencing pleasure or being happy is to *feel* well. One may, of course, find that the term *happiness* connotes something different from this, but the way I use *happiness,* one standard set of replies to the question "How do you feel?" would be "I feel happy" or "I feel unhappy." The following set of answers to the question would be rather awkward: "I feel self-realized" or "I do not feel self-realized."

The most important feature of self-realization, as compared with pleasure and happiness, is its dependence upon a certain view of human capacities (or better—potentialities). Again, this implies a particular view of human nature. In practice this does not imply a general doctrine of human nature. That is the work of philosophical fields of research.

An individual whose attitudes reveal that he or she takes self-realization to be the ultimate or fundamental goal in life has to have a view of his or her nature and potentialities. And the more one's nature and potentialities are realized, the more self-realization there is. The question "How do you feel?" may honestly be answered in the positive or negative, whatever the level of self-realization. If one has attained a certain level of self-realization, the question may be answered in the negative, in principle. But at this point, following Spinoza, I take the valid way of answering the question "How do you feel?" to be positive, because the realization of the fulfillment (using somewhat less philosophical jargon) of one's potentialities is *internally* related to happiness. But it is not related in such a way that by *deliberately seeking* happiness, one thereby realizes one's self. John Stuart Mill makes this point clearly in his philosophy: you should not deliberately go seeking for happiness ("Happiness, to be got, must be forgot"). That is a bad way to proceed even if, with Mill, you take happiness to be the ultimate goal in life. I think that it is much better to deliberately seek self-realization; to develop your capacities (using a rather dangerous word because it is easily interpreted in the direction of interpersonal, rather than intrapersonal, competition). But even the striving implied in the term *competition* may mislead. Dwelling in situations of intrinsic value, spontaneous non-directed awareness, relaxing from striving, are all conducive to self-realization as I understand it. But, of course, there are infinite variations among humans depending upon cultural, social, and individual differences. This makes the key term *self-realization* abstract in its generality. But nothing more can be expected when the question is posed as it is: "What might deserve the name of ultimate or fundamental goal in life?" We may reject the meaningfulness of such a question (I don't) but for those of us for whom it has meaning, an answer using few words is bound to be abstract and general.

Going back to the three key terms—*pleasure, happiness* and *self-realization*—the third has the merit of being clearly and forcefully applicable to any being with a specific range of potentialities. I limit this range to living beings, using "living" in a rather broad sense. I do not feel that the terms *pleasure* and *happiness* are so easily generalized. Having already introduced the rather general concept of "ecological self," the concept of self-realization naturally follows.

Let us consider the preying mantis, a formidable group of voracious insects. They have a nature which is fascinating to many people. Mating is part of their self-realization, but some males are eaten while performing the act of copulation. While being devoured, is he happy, is he experiencing pleasure? We don't know. But, well done if he does! Actually he feeds his partner so that she has strong offspring. But it does not make sense to me to attribute happiness to these males. Self-realization? yes; happiness? no. I maintain that there is an internal relation between self-realization and happiness among people, and among some animal groups. As a professional philosopher, I am tempted to add a point where I have been inspired by Zen Buddhism and Spinoza: I agree that happiness is a feeling, but the act of realizing a potential is always an interaction involving, as one single concrete unit (one gestalt, as I would say), three abstract aspects: subject, object, and medium. And what I have said about joyfulness in nature holds as well of happiness in nature; they should not be conceived as merely subjective feelings.

The richness of reality is becoming even richer through our specific human endowments; we are the first kind of living beings we know of which have the potentialities of living in community with all other living beings. It is our hope that all these potentialities will be realized—if not in the immediate future, then at least in the somewhat near future.

## NOTES

1. Erich Fromm, "Selfishness, Self-Love, and Self-interest," in *Self-Explorations in Personal Growth,* edited by Clark E. Mustakas, 58.

2. Ibid., p. 59.

3. Ibid., p. 62.

4. Ibid., p. 63.

5. Ibid.

6. This and the following quotations from Gandhi are taken from Arne Naess, *Gandhi and Group Conflict* (Oslo: 1974), 35, where the metaphysics of Self-realization is treated more thoroughly. For further detailed discussions of identification, see Naess, "Identification as a Source of Deep Ecological Attitudes," reprinted in *Radical Environmentalism,* edited by Peter List (Belmont, Calif.: Wadsworth, 1993), 24–38; Naess, "Man Apart and Deep Ecology: A Reply to Reed," *Environmental Ethics* 12, no. 2 (1990): 185–192.

# 23 | ECOSOPHY AND GESTALT ONTOLOGY

## *Arne Naess*

## EVERYTHING HANGS TOGETHER— EVERYTHING IS INTERRELATED

IT IS A MAXIM OF ecology that "everything hangs together." For example, certain kinds of segmented worms start to "swarm" fifty-four minutes after sunset: masses of them at the same time! What triggers this joint activity three days after a full moon in late October? A biological clock. How do biological clocks work? Of course, we know next to nothing about how and why. But, clearly, "things hang together" and form complexes of vast dimensions.

One dominant response to this is one of regret: because "things hang together" so intimately, human actions have innumerable unintended consequences, and many of them turn out to be detrimental to us, at least in the long run. Would a simpler world, less intimately interrelated, suit us better? A world of easily separated things? Some feel this would be a better world for humans.

For the ecosopher, this vast complex of interrelationships which makes up the world is a characteristic of our existence which we joyfully acknowledge, contemplate, and study. Because of our severely limited knowledge, the complexity of the world can get us into difficult situations, sometimes even causing death, but the "hanging together of everything" is nevertheless experienced and conceived of as a positive value. We participate in the world and try to be careful.

## INTERNAL AND EXTERNAL RELATIONS

There is a philosphical distinction that is highly relevant here: the distinction between an *external* relation and an *internal* relation. If I refer to "my body,"

This essay was originally published in *The Trumpeter* 6, 4 (1989). Reprinted with permission.

and "my telephone number," the relation between me and my telephone number is an *external* relation. That is, my telephone number can be changed without it affecting me *essentially*. But my relation to my body is of a very different character, at least in my view. I am *essentially* not the same self or person if I have a different body (or if my body gets a new self!). The relation between me and my body is an *internal* one.

Some people (for instance, Martin Luther) seem to have a different conception of this. He conceived himself to be somehow imprisoned in his body, and hoped to escape from it at death. Luther seemed to conceive of his self and his body as being externally related. Furthermore, the general tendency in the natural sciences is to conceive of things as being externally related.

## SPONTANEOUS HUMAN EXPERIENCE

In what follows I shall try to explain a way to conceptualize what I understand to be spontaneous human experience of reality. How are things (in the widest sense) related to each other in spontaneous experience? I will argue that they are internally related. (My answer is part of a total view I call "Ecosophy T".)

But first, the term "spontaneous" needs a couple of comments. If I say "The water looks yellow" or "The water seems yellow" I tend to imply that perhaps it is not really yellow. These statements, however, are based on a spontaneous experience I have had which is partly expressible by "yellow water" or "yellow water!" The use of the words "looks" and "seems" tends to reveal a moment of reflection, doubt, or inquiry. The latter is a criterion of non-spontaneousness. Instead of using the word "spontaneous" one could say "immediate" but the latter term is heavily burdened with philosophical theories.

## THE MEANING OF GESTALT

*Gestalt* is the central term of the ontology to be explained. It is generally associated with the maxim "the whole is greater than the sum of its parts." A common demonstration of this point consists of putting three dots on the blackboard. If the dots are not placed too erratically, a triangle is spontaneously experienced ("seen"), although a triangle obviously consists of more than just three dots. We experience spontaneously a gestalt, but we can *analyze* its structure.

An elementary example of a kind of gestalt, in the ontological sense, is that of a well-known melody. The phrase "kind of" is important because melodies, in general, can scarcely form a gestalt, only individual *occurrences* of a definite melody. Only *individual occurrences* are parts of reality: only they are genuine

contents of reality. If a person hears part of a well-known melody, the spontaneous experience that person has is colored by their attitudes towards the
melody as a whole as well as by many circumstances, past and present. These
all go to make up that particular occurrence of the melody. The spontaneous
experience had by this person constitutes a closed unity, or gestalt.

Prior to the advent of gestalt theory, the dominant term used to try to
describe these kinds of experiences was *association:* this meant that a part of
the well-known melody is "associated" with the rest of the parts and with past
experiences (for instance, a pleasant or unpleasant outing or concert). A cloud
of associations surrounded the perception (hearing) of the part *itself.* This conceptual framework implied a series of experiences: the part of the melody *and*
the associations. The gestalt framework, on the other hand, recognizes *one
single experience,* which can be reflected upon and analyzed. The part *itself* is
just an abstraction, defined by its structures.

## CONCRETE CONTENTS AND ABSTRACT STRUCTURES

An important distinction needs to be made between concrete contents and
abstract structures. The spontaneous experiences we have are the concrete
contents, whereas the interrelations between these experiences are the abstract
structures. When we reflect upon and analyze the gestalt experience, we are
clarifying the abstract relations between spontaneous experiences.

When we listen to a melody, or to a more complex musical unity (for instance, Beethoven's Fifth Symphony) there is a succession of spontaneous experiences. They all have, as one aspect, a certain color or atmosphere which is
specific to the symphony as a whole. Instead of just saying the whole is more
than the sum of the parts, other maxims are relevant: "The part is more than
a part." That is, if the melody is well-known, the part is "part-of-the-melody";
that is, the character of the whole melody colors the experience of the part, or
largely determines the spontaneous experience of the part. Put more bluntly,
"there is no spontaneous experience of the part merely as a part." It is internally related to the melody as a whole. But neither is there spontaneous experience of the whole. We may therefore also say "There is neither an experience
of a part, nor of a whole as separable entities." But there are important abstractions which are communicated interpersonally by refering (pointing to) musical notes, discs, video, etc. The "whole" Fifth Symphony may be printed on
100 pages: the first page is one percent of the "whole." This latter way of
using the terms *whole* and *part* refers to abstract structure, interpersonally
understandable.

What I am proposing, then, is to say that there is a gestalt, or rather sets of gestalts, made up of series of spontaneous experiences which are had by different people and related to Beethoven's Fifth Symphony; and defined interpersonally through published musical notes. What I further suggest is that the content of reality, insofar as it is at all experienceable by humans, is a manifold of gestalts. In order to stress the "content/structure" distinction, I contrast the "concrete contents" of reality with the totally "abstract structures" of reality.

The examples used in the foregoing smack, perhaps, of epistemological and ontological idealism, subjectivism, or even solipsism. But this is due to the mistaken assumption that ideas, subjects, and egos are not subject to gestalt scrunity. Subjects are not conceived of as "things in themselves" (Kant's *Ding an sich*). Let me use an example that might seem less elusive.

Hallingskarvet is a mountain in Norway, a small part of which can be seen from the train running between Oslo and Bergen. It is about twenty-five miles long and, here and there, fairly broad. Many people know Hallingskarvet well, and it plays a role in their life. A vast set of spontaneous experiences may appropriately be called "experiences of Hallingskarvet." Structurally and abstractly the mountain is defined through the use of maps. When people agree that they have been to places on Hallingskarvet, they refer to maps. They map the structure of reality. For instance, when skiing on Hallingskarvet in fog and wind, the spontaneous experience is not only of what little you can see, it is also an experience of Hallingskarvet. One is particularly eager to assess where one is at the moment, and where the nearest precipice is located. In short, one is intensely aware of the mountain and its "dangers"; for example, the possibility of not finding a proper way down and skiing over the many near-vertical cliffs. The spontaneous experiences will be colored by a manifold of aspects of the mountain and will have a pronounced gestalt character.

There is a fundamental relation of *comprehensiveness* between gestalts. For example, the character of the slow second movement of the Fifth Symphony is dependent upon the different characteristics of the first and third movements. The spontaneous experience of the second movement is intimately colored by the whole symphony, for those people who know the whole symphony. The gestalt of the second movement is less comprehensive than the gestalt of the whole symphony. The same holds for each movement. One might say, in a way, that the gestalt of the symphony is more "comprehensive" than that of his small pieces for the piano. But this would be misleading. It is better to talk about *subordinate* and *superordinate* gestalts. The movements of the symphony as gestalts are subordinate to the gestalt of the whole. But as spontaneous experiences of reality, this gestalt is again subordinate to more comprehensive ones, similar to the experience of a concrete occasion of listening or performing as a member of the orchestra.

The gestalt ontology is a conceptual framework adapted to humans and other conscious living beings. The world we live in spontaneously cannot be degraded by being characterized as being merely subjective. It is the real world we experience. Nothing is more real. Without going into philosophical niceties, I conclude that our life experience is not of "things in themselves" (Kant's *Ding an sich*), but this experience is not merely "subjective" either: not "things for me" (*Ding an mich*). Life experience is the experience of gestalts, and a conceptual framework is adapted to the spontaneous experience of the content of reality.

## GESTALT EXPERIENCE AND ECOSOPHY

What has all this to do with ecosophy? The relation is somewhat indirect. What may be called the dominant way of conceiving reality is roughly that of a vast supermarket stocked with individual things that are extrinsically related to each other: like primitive atomistic conceptions. These relations are no longer conceived to be Newtonian and mechanistic, but are still largely seen as extrinsic relations between things in themselves. Many supporters of the Deep Ecology movement, however, are inspired by ways of experiencing reality which clash with this dominant way of conceiving reality.

For example, a proposal is made to build a road through a large forest. Preservationists reject the proposal. But the proponents say, in all honesty, that the area spoiled by the road itself will be less than a tiny *fraction* of the forest. But they are neglecting the gestalt character of the forest. A quantitative abstract structure is taken to be identical with the contents.

The preservationists answer that the heart of the forest, or the forest as a whole, would be destroyed. (If you are deep in the forest and encounter a road, the forest as spontaneously experienced is no longer the same. The greatness and majesty, the dignity and purity, etc., is lost). But the proponents answer by saying that is only a "subjective" aspect. The forest is "objectively" a multiplicity of trees, etc., and a road would be only a tiny intrusion. (Even more "objectively," according to microbiology and biochemistry, the whole area is nothing but a great complex of externally related molecules without color, and anything we fancy, as subjects, is not out there in the "external world.") The preservationist will admit that there are trees in the forest. They are subordinate gestalts, as are many other features of the forest. But the forest as a whole is an extremely valuable superordinate gestalt and clearly vulnerable to "development," whatever the fraction of the area that is destroyed. An atomistic view of reality is arrived at by systematically "delearning" the gestalt view which dominates the child's experience.

Clearly, the economics of industrial societies are such that most conse-quences of gestalt ontology are viewed as undesirable. The atomistic view helps to value the forest in terms of market prices, of extrinsic parts, and tourism. "A tree is a tree. How many do you have to see?"

This "delearning" process (of not taking spontaneous experience of superor-dinate gestalts seriously) makes life progressively less rich, narrowing it down to a mass of externally connected details. The more people are adapted to the supermarket concept, the more dangerous is the appeal to the correctness of majority opinion. It seems that the ecosystem concept (and its corresponding gestalt experiences, popularized from the start of the Deep Ecology move-ment) is still not influential, and still has not been internalized, by policy mak-ers. Thus, the Barents Sea, one of the richest ecosystems in the world, has been treated in a narrow fashion as mainly a resource of marketable fish. If one species is nearly extinct, we then concentrate on the others, one at a time. The result has been one of the greatest marine environmental disasters of the century.

There are many causes of such a mistaken policy, but one cause seems to be the lack of clear and forceful thinking in terms of wholes, rather than frag-ments. The supporters of the Deep Ecology movement will profit from the further development, and forceful articulation, of gestalt perception and, more importantly, gestalt ontology. It must be defended against allegations of "sub-jectivism." The dominant "objectivism" leads, if used consistently and linked to natural science, to the confusion of the contents of reality with the useful but immensely abstract structures invented by mathematical physics.

Simple holism—the insistence that wholes be taken seriously—is not enough as a competing point of view. The argumentation must refer to experi-ence, and spontaneous experience in particular. And it must acknowledge hi-erarchies of wholes and their non-external, non-extensional, internal relations. The term *gestalt* may not be used, or used only sparingly, if more traditional terms can be found. But that is quite difficult.

# 24 | METAPHYSICS OF THE TREELINE

## Arne Naess

IN MANY PARTS OF the world, but perhaps most clearly in the far North, the treeline is full of symbolic value: enigmatic, mystical, threatening, liberating and alluring—and repulsive and ominous. No single person or animal has the capacity to experience all these tertiary qualities of the treeline. The same holds true for the drama of crossing the treeline, either from above or from below.

The term *treeline* is misleading. There is actually no line but rather a narrow or wide border area. If the terrain is nearly horizontal, the area is wide—perhaps miles wide. If the terrain is steep, the line is narrow but never sharp. Thus it is a shock to first see an artificial forest, actually a "tree farm," covering the slope high on the side of a valley and then suddenly coming to a halt.

Suddenly, there is not a single tree! From full-grown trees to nothing: an abnormality, an experience of something utterly valuable having been destroyed, the landscape desecrated, a personal loss even if one has never been near the place.

Here I shall relate the immensely rich reality that a certain group of people has experienced, a group that includes millions of people. I shall start with the simple, obvious experiences.

Moving up toward the treeline, there are signs of new challenges being met by the trees. In the strong winds and thinning soil, trees become smaller and take on gnarled and fantastic shapes. Some have fallen over. They tend to clump together, as we would do. Sometime there are only clusters of trees at particular spots, or single trees that are altogether isolated. They may be courageous, haughty, even triumphant, but also miserable.

But these characteristics of trees are subordinate gestalts, lesser forms of what is real. The higher-order gestalts predominate. One gestalt is that of

---

Originally published in *Appalachia* 188 (1989). Reprinted with permission.

upward movement, as far as possible, overcoming obstacles, trying to "clothe the mountain."

Some trees succeed in clothing the mountain. Compared with lowland trees, they resemble tiny bushes. They may be only a few feet tall, while their lowland kin soar fifty to one hundred feet or more. Yet call them stunted and they ask: "What am I lacking?" These trees have produced cones. They've realized all their possibilities, they've fulfilled essential functions. Mere size has nothing to do with the quality of life.

Others merely survive, stunted and deformed. No cones, no expression of fulfillment, half-dead from exposure to winter after winter, and summers that alternate from drenching rain to dry.

Each tree has a different life experience from birth. And still others thrive in small ways by managing merely to survive. The rough terrain and numerous variations in conditions have obvious consequences—no tree is identical to any other. Each tree is a mighty presentation of the drama of life. To some you feel near, others you feel further from.

A few people have the background to enlarge the high-order gestalts in the time dimension. These people will see the waves of cold and warm climates after the last ice age. They see waves of trees further clothing the mountain, or in retreat, leaving broken trunks clinging high on the open slopes. The treeline is seen as constantly moving up or down, never resting.

People living near thick spruce forests may see the forest density as a protective wall. Others feel that these trees block the view, or even one's existence, hindering free expression of life and thought. If the trees are old with drooping branches, they may communicate resignation, sorrow, melancholy. Swayed by the wind, large trees move in slow rhythms, and the music can have the heartbreaking feel of a funeral march. Or they may express slowly something like, "doomed, doomed, doomed. . . ." Through the dimness of night, the wall of trees may invite merciful death. The existence of the treeline somewhere high—reachable, but far away—then inevitably becomes a promise of freedom, a proof of limits to any sorrow, any prison, any doubt or guilt. As one approaches treeline, walls disappear. Trees shrink, gaps enlarge, light shines between them and between their branches. It has been my privilege to see all this.

When rich high-order gestalts contrast high/low, dark/light, they are apt to acquire metaphysical dimensions. Movement from low and dark toward high and light treeline strengthens this contrast. Lightness is further strengthened by the ease of movement at treeline. Being at treeline becomes an experience of reaching supreme freedom. For some, a change from a tragic to a more cheerful outlook on life occurs.

Those who live in the forest, or feel at home there, may have experiences that vary even more. The upper limit of the forest marks the end of security, the end of the world we master, the beginning of the harsh world of wind-driven snow, dangerous precipices, useless expanse.

Above treeline it is cold and hostile, below is warm and friendly. Even in these negative experiences there is a contrast of metaphysical dimensions. The positive and negative gestalts attest to the supreme gestalt of Janus-faced existence, comprising good and bad on an equal footing, or emphasizing one aspect more than another.

How is this metaphysical aspect to be understood? What insight can it offer? It is a meta-metaphysical question that can't be entirely answered here or anywhere. But certain essentials can be gleaned from three approaches.

1. *The Homocentrist.* The power of human imagination is overwhelming. There's no limit to what human genius is able to *project into* nature. The richness of treeline symbols attests to this. Flights of imagination soar from the plane of brute facts: the leaves are green, stems grow upward, . . . the rest is a wonderful projection of the human mind.

2. *The Idealist Philosopher.* Strictly speaking, the leaves are not green. Their atoms are colorless, not even grey, and the stem's electromagnetic waves or particles do not grow upward. There is a realm beyond the material world. The new physics confirms it—a spirit world beyond space and time, a spiritual realm. The human mind is in direct touch with this realm and "spiritualizes" nature.

3. *The Ecosopher.* The richness and fecundity of reality! How overwhelming! The treeline's abstract geographical structure points to a seemingly infinite variety of *concrete* contents! More is open to the human ecological self than can be experienced by any other living being.

The metaphysics of the treeline is a serious affair for the ecosopher. It lets us understand the spontaneous immediate experience of the treeline as an experience of reality, beyond the divisions between subject/object, and spiritual/material.

One of today's most chilling realizations is that present "reforestation" projects do not really restore a *forest*. Artificial tree plantations lack the immense biological richness and diversity of ancient forests, together with their metaphysical intensity and richness. With so many people now reacting negatively to sham reforestation, the time is ripe for a change in policy.

# 25 | THE PLACE OF JOY IN A WORLD OF FACT

## Arne Naess

THE SOLUTION OF ENVIRONMENTAL problems is presupposed in all uto-pias. For example, every family is to enjoy free nature under Marxian commu-nism. "In a communist society," Marx says in a famous passage, "nobody has one exclusive sphere of activity but each can be accomplished in any branch he wishes. Society regulates the general production and thus makes it possible for me to do one thing today and another tomorrow: to hunt in the morning, fish in the afternoon, tend cattle in the evening, engage in literary criticism after dinner, just as I have in mind, without ever becoming a hunter, fisher-man, shepherd, or critic." . . .

The complete individual is not a specialist; he is a generalist and an amateur. This does not mean that he has no special interests, that he never works hard, that he does not partake in the life of the community. But he does so from personal inclination, with joy, and within the framework of his value pri-orities.

. . . In the future ideal society, whether outlined by Marx, or by more bourgeois prophets, there will be people who might use most of their energy doing highly specialized, difficult things, but as amateurs—that is, from incli-nation and from a mature philosophy of life. There will be no fragmentary men. And certainly no fragmentary ecologists. . . .

We all, I suppose, admire the pioneers who, through endless meetings held in contaminated city air, succeeded in establishing wilderness areas in the United States. But their constant work in offices and corridors has largely ruined their capacity to enjoy these areas. They have lost the capacity to show, *in action,* what they care for; otherwise they would spend much more time (and even live) in the wilderness. Many people verbally admire wilderness

Originally published in *The North American Review* 258, no. 2 (1973). Reprinted with per-mission.

areas, but they have not stepped down from their exalted positions, as chairman of this or that, to enjoy these areas at least part of the year.

What I say here about advocates of wilderness seems unhappily to be valid for advocates of a better environment in general. Ordinary people show a good deal of skepticism toward verbally expressed values which are not expressed in the life style of the propagandist. The environmentalist sometimes succumbs to a joyless life that belies his concern for a better environment. This cult of dissatisfaction is apt to add to the already fairly advanced joylessness we find among socially responsible, successful people, and to undermine one of the chief presuppositions of the ecological movement: that joy is related to the environment, and to nature.

In short, the best way to promote a good cause is to provide a good example. . . . One ought not be afraid that the example will go unnoticed. For example, Albert Schweitzer hid himself in Africa, but his public relations prospered and so did the sale of his books.

So much for utopias. My next concern is with how to get nearer to our utopias. I shall take up only one aspect: the relation between personal lifestyle and teaching.

## THE LIFESTYLE OF ENVIRONMENTALISTS

Joy is contagious. But if we only talk about the joys of a good environment, it is of little avail.

I know that many *have* turned their backs on more lucrative careers and on a life of security cultivating well-established sciences. But this is not enough. Life should manifest the peaks of our value priorities. Working for a better environment is, after all, only of instrumental value. We remain on the level of techniques. But what criterion shall we use to follow the lead of our personal priorities? We do have one that is underrated among conscientious, responsible people: joy.

## JOY ACCORDING TO "PESSIMISTIC" PHILOSOPHERS

Suppose someone openly adhered to the doctrine that there cannot be too much cheerfulness under any circumstances—even at a funeral. The sad truth is, I think, that he or she would be classified as shallow, cynical, disrespectful, irreligious, or mocking.

Søren Kierkegaard is an important figure here. He *seems* to take anguish, desperation, a sense of guilt, and suffering as the necessary, and sometimes even sufficient, condition of authentic living. But he also insists upon continuous joy as a condition of living. Whatever is done without joy is of no avail. "At seventy thousand fathoms depth" you should be glad. At seventy thousand fathoms, one should retain "a joyful mind." He sometimes calls himself Hilarius, the one permeated with *hilaritus* (the Latin word for cheerfulness).

*Dread* is the technical existentialist word for the kind of anxiety which opens the way to a deeper understanding of life. But according to Heidegger (another hero of modern pessimism), dread is not an isolated sensation of a negative kind. The mind is in a complex state in which dread cannot exist without joy; that is, one who thinks he has the dread experience but lacks joy, suffers from an illusion. Dread has an internal relation to joy.

Our problem is not that we lack high levels of integration (that is, that we are immature and therefore joyless) but rather that we glorify immaturity. Do the most influential philosophers of our time and culture represent high degrees of maturity and integration? I have in mind not only Heidegger, Sartre, Kierkegaard, Wittgenstein, but also Marx and Nietzsche. Tentatively, I must answer No. There are lesser known, but perhaps more mature philosophers, like Jaspers and Whitehead.

Should the world's misery and the approaching ecocatastrophe make one sad? . . . My point is that there is no good reason to feel sad about all this. According to the philosophies I am defending, such regret is a sign of immaturity: the immaturity of unconquered passiveness and lack of integration.

The remedy (or psychotherapy) against sadness caused by the world's misery is to do something about it. I shall refrain from mentioning Florence Nightingale, but let me note that Gandhi loved to care for, wash, and massage lepers; he simply enjoyed it. It is very common to find those who constantly deal with extreme misery to be more than usually cheerful. According to Spinoza, the power of an individual is infinitely small compared with that of the entire universe, so we must not expect to save the whole world. The main point—which is built into the basic conceptual framework of Spinoza's philosophy—is that of activeness. By interacting with extreme misery, one gains cheerfulness. And this interaction need not be direct. Most of us can do more in indirect ways by using our privileged positions in rich societies.

There are clear reasons for us not to concentrate all our efforts directly on extreme miseries, but rather to attack the causes, conditions, and factors indirectly contributing to this misery and, just as importantly, to encourage the factors which directly cause or facilitate the emergence of active (and therefore cheerful) work to alleviate misery.

Behind the prevailing widespread passivity found throughout the world, there is a lot of despair and pessimism concerning our capacity to have a good time. We tend to enjoy ourselves (except during vacations) in a private world of thoughtlessness, well insulated from the great issues of the day.

One of the strangest and next-to-paradoxical theses of Spinoza (and of Thomas Aquinas and others) is that knowledge of evil, or of misery, is inadequate knowledge. In short, there is no such object, whereas there is something good to know. Evil is always an absence of something, a lack of something positive. Their theory of knowledge holds that objects of knowledge are always something. When you say that you see that the glass is transparent, what you see, for instance, is a red rose behind the glass. You do not see the transparency which is not an object of perception.

In any event, while I do not think that the positive nonexistence of evil things can be shown without a great deal of redefinition of words, I nevertheless do not consider this view totally ridiculous. Like so many other strange points of view in major philosophies, it has an appeal and points in the right direction without perhaps stating anything clearly in the "scientific" sense.

## SPINOZA ON JOY

Spinoza operates with three main concepts of joy and three of sorrow. *Laetitia, hilaritas,* and *titillateo* are the three Latin terms for the positive emotions of joy. Translations of these terms are, to a surprising degree, arbitrary, because their function in Spinoza's system can be discovered only by studying the complex total structure of his system. Isolating one concept from the others is not possible. And the system is more than the sum of its parts. From a strict professional point of view, you must take it or leave it as a whole.

I translate *laetitia* as "joy"—a generic term comprising several important sub-kinds of joy. The main classification of joy is into *hilaritas* (cheerfulness) and *titillatio* (pleasurable excitement). *Hilaritas* is the serene thing, coloring the whole personality, or better, the whole world.

*Hilaritas* (cheerfulness) is defined by Spinoza as a joy to which every part of the body contributes. It does not affect only a subgroup of functions of the organism, but each and every one, and therefore the totality of the organism. Spinoza contends that there cannot be too much of *hilaritus.*

The other main kind of joy, *titillatio,* affects a sub-group of the parts of the body. If very narrowly based and strong, it dominates and thereby inhibits the other kinds of joy. Accordingly, there can be too much of it. Here Spinoza mentions love of money, sexual infatuation, and ambition. He also mentions other sources of joy which are all good in moderate degrees if they do not hamper and inhibit one another.

A second classification of joy is that derived from contemplation of our own achievement, creativity, or more broadly—activeness, and the joy derived from contemplation of causes of joy outside of us. The first he calls satisfaction, or repose in ourselves (*acquiescentia in se ipso*), the other he calls *amor*. There can be too much of them, however, because they sometimes refer to parts, not to the whole.

According to Spinoza, what refers to the whole of the body also refers to the whole of the conscious mind, and to the whole of the universe or, more generally, to the whole of Nature, insofar as we know it. This is understandable from Spinoza's so-called "philosophy of identity" which proclaims the ultimate identity of thought and matter, and from his theory of knowledge, which relates all our knowledge of the world to interaction with the body—just as biologists tend to do today.

Lack of self-acceptance (*acquiescentia in se ipso*) accounts for much of the passivity displayed by an important sector of the public in environmental conflicts. Many people are on the right side, but few stand up in public meetings and state how they, as private persons, feel about the pollution in their neighborhoods. They do not have sufficient self-respect, respect for their own feelings, and faith in their own importance. They do not have to fight themselves for the changes, it's only necessary that they state their feelings and positions in public. A small minority will then fight with joy—supported by that considerable sector of people.

The distinction between pervasive joy (covering all) and partial joy need not be considered an absolute dichotomy but rather exists in degrees. Joy may be more or less pervasive. Clearly, higher degrees of joy require high degrees of integration of the personality, and high degrees of such integration require intense cultivation of the personal aspect of interaction with the environment. It requires a firm grasp of what we call value priorities, but which Spinoza would call reality priorities, because of his resolute location of value among "objective" realities. Spinoza distinguishes degrees of realness and perfection. That which is perfect is complete. Integration of personality presupposes that we never act as mere functionaries or specialists, but always as whole personalities conscious of our value priorities, and of the need to manifest those priorities in social direct action.

The specific thing to be learned from Spinoza and certain modern psychologists is, however, to integrate the value priorities themselves in the world. We tend to say "the world of facts," but the separation of value from facts is, itself, mainly due to an overestimation of certain scientific traditions stemming from Galileo which confuses the *instrumental* excellence of the mechanistic worldview with its properties as a whole philosophy. Spinoza was heavily influenced by mechanical models of matter, but he did not extend them to cover "reality." His reality was neither mechanical, value-neutral, nor value-empty.

This cleavage into two worlds—the world of fact and the world of values—can theoretically be overcome by placing, as Spinoza does, joys and other so-called subjective phenomena into a unified total field of realities. But this is too much to go into here. I am more concerned with the place of joy among our total experiences. The objectivist conception of value is important, however, in any discussion in which technocrats tend to dismiss cheerfulness in the environment as something "merely subjective."

Spinoza makes use of the following short, crisp, and paradoxical definition of "joy" (*laetitia*): "Joy is man's transition from lesser to greater perfection." Somewhat less categorically he sometimes says that joy is the affect by which, or through which, we make the transition to greater perfection. Instead of "perfection" we may say "integrity" or "wholeness."

I consider to be of central importance the difference between these formulations and subjectivistic ones which proclaim that joy only *follows* or *accompanies* these transitions to greater perfection. The relation between joy and an increase in perfection is an *intrinsic* one, for Spinoza. That is, the two can be separated only conceptually, but not in practice. Such a realistic view of joy suggests that joyfulness, like color, attaches to, and forms, part of objects, but of course changes with the medium, and must be defined in terms of interaction with organisms. Joy is linked intrinsically to an increase in perfection, and an increase in perfection is linked to dozens of other increases, such as: an increase in power and virtue, an increase in freedom and rationality, an increase of activeness, an increase in the degree to which we are the cause of our own actions, and an increase in the degree to which our actions are understandable by reference to ourselves. Joy is thus a basic part of the conceptual structure of Spinoza's system.

An increase in power is an increase in the ability to carry out what we sincerely strive to do. Power does not presuppose that we coerce other people; a tyrant may be less powerful than some poor soul sitting in prison. This concept of power has a long tradition and should not be forgotten. What we strive to do is defined in relation to what actually happens; thus "to save the world from pollution" is not something anyone strives to do, but is rather a kind of limited effort to save the things around us.

Cheerfulness (*hilaritas*) requires action of the whole integrated personality and is linked to a great increase in power. With the absence of joy, there is no increase in power, freedom, or self-determination. Thus, lack of joy should be taken seriously, especially among so-called responsible people furthering a good cause. The joy of work, like any other partial joy, can dominate and subdue other sources of joy to such an extent that the overall result is stagnation or even a decrease in power. In Spinoza's terminology, this means a loss of perfection or integration, and increased difficulty in reaching a state of cheerfulness.

"To be happy" is often equated with enjoying oneself, laughing, or relaxing in the sense of being passive. Enjoying oneself by becoming intoxicated, which decreases the higher integrations of the nervous system, results in resignation. It means giving up the possibility of joyfulness of the whole person. Cheerfulness, in the Spinozistic sense, may not always be expressed in laughter or smiling, but in concentration, present-ness, activeness.

The example of Buddha may illustrate my point. Buddha was an active person, but had great repose in himself (*acquiescentia in se ipso*). Long before he died he is said to have reached Nirvana which, properly interpreted within Mahayana Buddhism, involves supreme integration and liberation of the personality, implying bliss or (in the terminology of Spinoza) *hilaritus*. Research by Stcherbatsky and others concerning the term *duhkha* (conventionally translated as "pain") shows that so-called pessimistic Buddhism also has a doctrine of joy as a central aspect of reaching freedom in Nirvana.

One may say, somewhat loosely, that what we now lack in our technological age is repose in oneself. The conditions of modern life prevent the full development of that self-respect and self-esteem which is required to reach a stable high degree of *acquiescentia in se ipso* (the term *alienation,* incidentally, is related to the opposite of *in se,* namely *in alio* wherein we repose in something else, something outside ourselves such as achievement in the eyes of others—we are "other directed").

*Humility,* as defined by Spinoza, is sorrow resulting from contemplation of one's own impotency, weakness, and helplessness. A feeling of sorrow always involves a decrease of perfection, virtue, and/or freedom. We can come to know adequately more potent things than ourselves. This gives us joy because of our activeness in the very process of knowing them. The realization of our own potency, and our active relation to the more potent, results in joy. Thus, instead of humility (which is a kind of sorrow) there are three kinds of joy: first, that resulting from the contemplation of our own power, however small, which gives us *acquiescentia in se ipso,* self-respect and contentedness; second, the joy resulting from increased personal, active knowledge of things greater than we are; and third, the joy resulting from active interaction which, strictly speaking, defines ourselves (as well as other objects or fragments) in the total field of reality (or in Nature, in Spinoza's terminology).

Adequate knowledge always has a joyful personal aspect because it reveals a power (never a weakness) in our personality. In Spinoza's words:

> Therefore, if man, when he contemplates himself, perceives some kind of impotency in himself, it does not come from his understanding himself, but

from his power of action being reduced. . . . To the extent that man knows himself with true rationality, to that extent it is assumed that he understands his essence, that is, his power.

We say with some haughtiness that Spinoza belongs to the age of rationalism, to the pre-Freudian, pre-Hitler era. But Spinoza in many ways anticipated Freud, and his term *ratio* must not be translated by our term *rational* or *rationality* without immediately adding that his *ratio* was more flexible, and was internally related to emotion. Rational action, for him, is action involving absolutely maximal perspective—that is, where things are seen as fragments of total Nature—which is, of course, not what we tend to call rational today. Spinoza was not an "intellectual" in the sense of modern Anglo-American social science.

Pity and commiseration (*misericordia* and *commiseratio*) are not virtues for Spinoza, and even less so for Gandhi, although they may have some positive instrumental value. Spinoza says that "commiseration, like shame, although it is not a virtue, is nevertheless good in so far as it shows that a desire for living honestly is present in the man who is possessed with shame, just as pain is called good in so far as it shows that the injured part has not yet putrified." A modest function, but nevertheless of instrumental value! Tersely, Spinoza adds, "a man who lives according to the dictates of reason strives as much as possible to prevent himself from being touched by commiseration." People who are crippled are among those who practically unanimously agree.

Commiseration is sorrow and therefore is, in itself, an evil. According to certain conventional morality, a duty should be carried out even if there is no joy. This might suggest that we had better disregard our duties if we are not permeated with joy. But this would seem to me to be rather fanatical, except when one adds a kind of norm concerning the high priority of developing the *capacity* for joy. "Alas! I cannot do my duty today because it does not fill me with joy. Better to escalate my efforts to experience joy!" Spinoza does not stress the remedy to the above situation—greater integration—but he presupposes it. The case of humility shows how *ratio* changes sorrows to joys: Spinozistic psychoanalysis tries to loosen up the mental cramps that cause unnecessary pain.

Freud worked with the tripartition: id, ego, and superego. The superego, through its main application in explaining neuroses, has a rather ugly reputation: it coerces the poor individual to try the impossible and then lets it experience shame and humility when there is no success. In Spinoza's analysis, the *ratio* also functions as a kind of overseer, but its main function is rather one of consolation. It directs our attention to what we can do rather than upon what we cannot, and eliminates feelings of necessary separation from others; it stresses the harmony of rational wills, and of well-understood self-interests.

A major virtue of a system like Spinoza's is the extreme consistency and tenacity with which consequences, even the most paradoxical, are drawn from intuitively reasonable principles. It meets the requirements of clarity and logic of modern natural science. The system says to us: "You do not like consequence No. 101? But you admit it follows from a premise you had admitted. Then give up the premise. You do not want to give up the premise? Then you must give up the logic, the rules of inference, you used to derive the consequence. You cannot give them up? But then you have to accept the consequence, the conclusion. You don't want to? Well, I suppose you don't want clarity and integration of your views and your personality." The rationality of a total view like Spinoza's is perhaps the only form of rationality capable of breaking down the pseudo-rational thinking of the conservative technocracy which presently obstructs efforts to think in terms of the total biosphere and its continued blossoming in the near and more remote future.

## THE PHILOSOPHICAL PREMISES OF ENVIRONMENTALISM

Personally, I favor the kind of powerful premises represented in Chinese, Indian, Islamic, Hebrew, as well as in Western philosophy—namely those which have the so-called ultimate unity of all life as a slogan. They do not hide the fact that big fish eat small ones, but stress the profound interdependence, the functional unity, of such a biospheric magnitude that non-violence, mutual respect, and feelings of identification are always potentially there, even between the predator and its so-called victim. In many cultures, identification is not limited merely to other living things, but also includes the mineral world, which helps us to conceive of ourselves as genuine surface fragments of our planet, fragments capable of somehow experiencing the existence of all other fragments: a microcosm of the macrocosm.

Another idea, right at the basis of a system from which environmental norms are derivable, is that of self-realization. The mature human individual, with a widened self, acknowledges a right to self-realization that is universal, and seeks a social order, or rather a biospherical order, which maximizes the potential for self-realization of all kinds of beings.

Level-headed and tough-minded environmentalists sometimes stress that it is sheer hypocrisy to pretend that we try to protect nature for its own sake. In reality, they say, we always have the needs of human beings in view. This is false, I think. Thousands of supporters of unpolluted so-called wastelands in Northern Labrador wish simply that those lands should continue to exist as they are, for their own sake. They are of intrinsic, and not only instrumental, value. To invoke *specifically* human needs to describe this situation is misleading, just as it is misleading to say that it is egotistical to share one's birthday cake with others because one *likes* to share with others.

Self-realization is not a maximal realization of the coercive powers of the ego. The "self" in the kinds of philosophy I am alluding to is something expansive, and the environmental crisis may turn out to be of immense value for the further expansion of human consciousness.

In modern education the difference between a world picture—or better, a world model—and a straightforward description of the world is slurred over. Atoms, particles, and wave functions are presented as parts of fragments of nature, even as *the* real, objective nature, as contrasted with human projections into nature—the "colorful" but subjective nature.

But so-called physical reality, in terms of modern science, is perhaps only a piece of abstract mathematical reality—a reality we emphatically do not live in. . . . [Our living environment] is made up of all the colorful, odor-filled, ugly or beautiful details, and it is sheer folly to look for an existing thing without color, odor, or any other homely qualities. . . . The significance of this subject is a broad cultural one: the rehabilitation of the status of the immediately experienced world, the colorful and joyful world. *Where* is joy in the world of fact? Right at the Center!

# 26 | DEEP ECOLOGY AND LIFESTYLE

## *Arne Naess*

THERE ARE A GREAT number of definite, more or less easily definable *tendencies* and *attitudes* which show themselves in the way people live. I am now focusing on the differences of lifestyles *within* an economic and social framework which the individual, alone, cannot be expected to change. Supporters of the Deep Ecology movement may be expected to at least try to live in harmony within what they accept as ecologically relevant guidelines, and to allow for more or less inevitable lapses. One should, of course, not look for "complete consistency," whatever that would mean. It would be practically impossible to formulate precise criteria for a consistent Deep Ecology lifestyle. Every formulation would have to be vague and highly dependent upon terminological idiosyncrasies.

It is agreed that it is important to clarify ecological consciousness and how it is revealed in action.

I have found it fruitful sometimes to simply list tendencies and attitudes characteristic of supporters of the Deep Ecology movement, focusing on Scandinavia, and freely enjoying my own terminological specialties. The order here adopted is not intended to reveal differences of importance, nor does it worry me that most items are overlapping. More worrisome is the methodology: I lean heavily on my personal observation.

1. Use of simple means. Avoidance of unnecessary complicated means to reach a goal or end.
2. Propensity to prefer activities most directly serving values in themselves and having intrinsic value. Avoidance of activities which are merely

Originally published in *The Paradox of Environmentalism,* edited by Neil Everndon (Ontario, Canada: Faculty of Environmental Studies, York University, 1984). Revised 1993. Reprinted with permission.

auxiliary, having no intrinsic value, or being many stages away from fundamental goals.

3. Anticonsumerism and minimization of personal property. This negative attitude follows from points 1 and 2.

4. Endeavor to maintain and increase the sensitivity and appreciation of goods of which there is enough for all to enjoy.

5. Absence or low degree of "novophilia"—the love of what is new merely because it is new. Cherishing old and well-worn things.

6. Efforts to dwell in situations of intrinsic value and to *act* rather than merely being busy.

7. Appreciation of ethnic and cultural differences among people, not feeling them as threats.

8. Concern about the situation of the Third and Fourth Worlds and the attempt to avoid a material standard of living too much different from and higher than the needy (global solidarity of lifestyle).

9. Appreciation of lifestyles which are universalizable, which are not blatantly impossible to sustain without injustice toward fellow humans or other species.

10. To go for depth and richness of experience rather than intensity.

11. To appreciate and choose, whenever possible, meaningful work rather than just making a living.

12. To lead a complex (not a complicated) life; trying to realize as many aspects of positive experiences as possible within each time-interval.

13. Cultivating life in community *(Gemeinschaft)* rather than in society *(Gesellschaft)*.

14. Appreciation of, or participation in, primary production—small-scale agriculture, forestry, fishing.

15. Efforts to satisfy vital needs rather than desires. Resisting the urge to "go shopping" as a diversion or therapy. Reducing the sheer number of possessions, favoring the old, much-worn, but essentially well-kept things.

16. Attempts to live in nature rather than just *visiting* beautiful places, and avoidance of tourism (but occasionally making use of tourist facilities).

17. When in vulnerable nature, living "light and traceless."

18. Tendency to appreciate all life-forms rather than merely those considered beautiful, remarkable, or narrowly useful.

19. Never use life-forms merely as means. Remain conscious of their intrinsic value and dignity even when using them as resources.

20. When there is a conflict between the interests of dogs and cats (and other pet animals) and wild species, a tendency to protect the latter.

21. Effort to protect local ecosystems, not only individual life-forms, feeling one's own community as a part of ecosystems.
22. Not only to deplore excessive interference in nature as unnecessary, unreasonable, and disrespectful, but to condemn it as insolent, atrocious, outrageous, and criminal—without condemning the people responsible for the interference.
23. Try to act resolutely and without cowardice in conflicts, but to remain non-violent in word and deeds.
24. Participate in or support of non-violent direct action when other ways of action fail.
25. Vegetarianism, total or partial.

There are many publically available sources for the study of Deep Ecology lifestyles, such as naturalists' and alternative lifestyle periodicals. In Norway, the periodical published by *The Future Is in Your Hands* deals extensively with the problems of young people, seeking to form new lifestyles and circles of friends. Perhaps more important is the direct contact with people achieved in direct actions.

In recent years, the practical possibilities of a highly developed Deep Ecological lifestyle have been reduced in Europe by economic policies that ruin small-scale enterprises. There is also a dominant tendency to standardize and regulate education and conditions of work. In short, the structuring of society is more detailed, leaving less room for subcultural independence. On the other hand, the reaction against this trend is strong. It would have greater impact if those who support the Deep Ecological movement were more politically active. There seems to be a 26th tendency, however: to find politics boring and distasteful.

In the seventies, when the movement was new and exciting, there was a tendency to be dogmatic: one *should* use bicycles; one *should not* go by air. Bears ought not to be shot under any circumstances. Hunting, even for ecological reasons, should be avoided. One should not visit non-industrial cultures because it would tend to weaken them. One should avoid every sport requiring mechanical means. Agriculture ought to be biodynamic; no poisons should be used. Et cetera, et cetera. Today there is more wisdom, less rigid rules. And the old Indian prayer is taken more seriously: "Great spirit, grant that I may not criticize my neighbor until I have walked a mile in his moccasins."

PART FOUR | # DEEP ECOLOGY AND ECOFEMINISM, SOCIAL ECOLOGY, THE GREENS, AND THE NEW AGE

# INTRODUCTION

AT TIMES, THE LONG-RANGE Deep Ecology movement has found itself at odds with other contemporary ecophilosophical analyses of the environmental crisis. Ecofeminism and Social Ecology both see themselves as alternative ecophilosophies that provide differing analyses of the root causes, and even the nature, of the ecological crisis, and propose different solutions to the ecocrisis in light of these analyses.

Ecology is, of course, a biological science concerned with studying the relations of organisms, species, and communities of species to each other, and to their environment. Thomas Berry has asserted that if we are to properly understand and deal effectively with the environment crisis, we must "reinvent the human at the species level." In other words, Berry is emphasizing that we must take seriously the radical biological message of Darwin, Thoreau, Muir, and the ecologists that we are "part and parcel" of the natural world within which our destiny is thoroughly intertwined with the destiny of other species and ecosystems.

It is the great anti-ecological illusion of the modernist Christian/Enlightenment paradigm to think that we humans have created, and live in, an urban technological "second nature" that, like a cocoon, is insulated from the natural world and natural constraints. (For further discussion of the "second nature" view, see the introduction to Part Two.)

From Thoreau and Muir to Leopold and Carson, the development of the contemporary ecological perspective has resulted from the efforts of ecologists and others who, philosophically and experientially, have "stepped back" from human society, usually by spending considerable time observing ecological processes in wild Nature. By so doing, they have attempted to overcome anthropocentrism and the "second nature" illusion by adopting an interspecies standpoint: what Leopold referred to as "thinking like a mountain."

Beginning in the mid-1980s, polemical attacks were directed at the Deep Ecology movement (and the statements of individual ecological activists) by Murray Bookchin and other Social Ecologists, and by various Ecofeminist theorists. Whereas the science of ecology has inspired the perspectives of Deep Ecology, Bookchin holds that the science of ecology is, for the most part, irrelevant to humans and human society (largely, it would seem, as a result of his advocacy of the "second nature" view). At the same time, however, he has appropriated the word "ecology" (and its positive connotations) in referring to his position as a Social Ecologist. Given their anthropocentric "second nature" perspective, it is understandable why Bookchin and other Social Ecologists reject the ecocentrism of the Deep Ecology platform, as well as analyses of the environmental crisis as stemming from anthropocentrism. Social Ecologists tend to be concerned primarily with issues of human social justice: they see ecological problems as essentially *political* and stemming from capitalism and problems of social hierarchy and social class domination (what has been referred to as the "left-Green" position).

There appear to be a number of Ecofeminist positions, but they all seem to reject the analyses of the roots of the environmental crisis in terms of anthropocentrism, pointing instead to long-standing Western cultural patriarchical attitudes of dominance over both women and Nature. Some Ecofeminist theorists write as if they believe in the "second nature" view, others do not. In any case, the root causes of the environmental crisis are seen by Social Ecologists and Ecofeminists to be essentially social justice and gender related, respectively. That is, they both find the environmental crisis to be the result of intraspecies, rather than interspecies, relationships.

In "The Deep Ecology–Ecofeminism Debate and Its Parallels," Warwick Fox examines the charges raised against Deep Ecology by Ecofeminists and Social Ecologists. Fox points out that Deep Ecology's ecocentrism logically and necessarily involves an egalitarian attitude toward all beings; thus it *subsumes* under its theoretical framework the egalitarian concerns of the various social movements, such as feminism and social justice.

Ecofeminists generally agree with Deep Ecology's ecocentrism; their criticism is directed at Deep Ecology's analysis of the environmental crisis as rooted in anthropocentrism. But why, Fox asks, should we focus on androcentrism (male-centeredness) as *the* root cause, rather than, for example, race, Westernization, or social hierarchy? For it is possible to imagine a society that has realized social, racial, and gender equality, but is still ecologically exploitive. This holds as well for Bookchin's social hierarchy analysis. Singling out either androcentrism or social hierarchy as *the* root cause of the environmental crisis, Fox argues, results in overly simplistic social and political analysis. Just as important is his claim that both Ecofeminists and Social Ecologists tend to remain anthropocentric in practice as well: they continue to focus on their respective human social and political agendas while practical strategies and the activism needed to ameliorate the ecological crisis, itself, receive from them a low priority or are ignored entirely.

Fox also discusses how Ecofeminists, Social Ecologists, and other critics misinterpret Deep Ecology's critique of anthropocentrism to mean that *humans* in general are the cause of the environmental crisis, often equating this view with misanthropy. Admittedly, confusion has arisen as the result of apparently misanthropic remarks made by individual ecological activists (for more discussion of this point, see the preface). As Fox points out, however, Deep Ecology's critique of anthropocentrism is directed at *human-centeredness* (a legitimating ideology), not at humans per se: a logical mistake made by critics that Fox refers to as "the fallacy of misplaced misanthropy." Fox further argues that anthropocentrism has been the main legitimating ideology used throughout history to justify the domination and destruction of Nature, hence Deep Ecology is justified in focusing upon anthropocentrism as a major cause of the environmental crisis.

On the other hand, Arne Naess has not been very impressed with the tenor of this "debate" from its very inception. He has said, "Away with all single-cause explanations of the ecological crisis!" Naess's approach to these issues is to point to the various movements that have recently converged to constitute the contemporary Green movement for social change: the peace movement, the social justice movement, and the ecology movement. His view is that it promotes only confusion to identify the various components of the Green movement with the ecology movement (see the Naess papers in Parts Five and Six and his paper "The Three Great Movements"). Naess points out that, despite philosophical differences, Ecofeminists, Social Ecologists, and Deep Ecologists tend to cooperate well in practice.

Deep Ecology has often been confused (by the media and by critics) with the New Age movement. In "Deep Ecology and the New Age Movement" I attempt to sort out these quite opposite perspectives. The New Age presents itself as a spiritual postmodern worldview, but for the most part, it is merely a continuation of the Baconian/Enlightenment technological "humans over Nature" vision. As such, New Age thinking easily translates into, and has now begun to permeate, the progress-oriented visions of modern industrial society and corporate megatechnology.

The intellectual component of the New Age movement has been inspired by the Jesuit priest Pierre Teilhard de Chardin and the technologist Buckminister Fuller. Both are radically anthropocentric and propose a total humanization and technological takeover of the Earth and its evolutionary processes. Morris Berman claims that New Age holistic cybernetic thinkers of the 1980s have produced what amounts to a "second nature" worldview which is totally disembodied and alienated from the Earth. Genetic engineers and nanotechnologists are prepared to dismantle and reassemble the Earth gene by gene, and molecule by molecule.

The Australian philosopher John Passmore has historically traced these

Western views of humans superiority and dominion over the Earth to the Platonic/Christian stewardship tradition, and of humans as perfecting Nature (i.e., converting "first nature" into "second nature") as beginning with Aristotle and continuing with the Baconian/Hegelian/Marxist and Teilhardian traditions.

New Age thinkers have recently allied themselves with James Lovelock's Gaia hypothesis while interpreting it anthropocentrically to justify large-scale global management of the biosphere. Bookchin's Social Ecology, despite his disclaimers, is very close to New Age thinking in proposing that humans should "take responsibility for" and direct the Earth's evolutionary processes. Bookchin's thinking is heir to the Hegelian/Marxist "humans perfecting Nature" tradition in holding that wild "first nature" must be made "free" by incorporating it into "second nature" thereby creating a new synthesis which he calls "free nature."

Thomas Berry, a Teilhard scholar, has rejected Teilhard's anthropocentrism and technological utopianism by reinterpreting Teilhard's cosmology along ecocentric lines. Similarly, the Deep Ecology movement, while admitting that humans are "very special beings," nevertheless promotes respect for, and protection of, the integrity of the biosphere, the wild, and the Earth's evolutionary processes. This necessarily involves a rejection of New Age anthropocentric "artificial world" megatechnology visions.

In "Leaving the Earth" (a selection from *In the Absence of the Sacred*) Jerry Mander further explores the theme of modern humanity's attempt to create an increasingly artificial "second nature." Disney World and the West Edmonton Mall are seen, by Mander, as highly controlled technocratic artificial environments that promote megatechnological utopias and fantasies, glorify consumption as a way of life, and prepare people psychologically for life in space colonies. As Mander and Jeremy Rifkin have both pointed out, however, contemporary urban people living in wholly artificial environments, their lives dominated by television and other electronic media, and alienated from wild Nature, are essentially already living in "space colonies" on Earth.

This is our contemporary version of Plato's cave: the "hyperreality" world that Umberto Eco calls "the absolutely fake." Mander points out that the "Disneyland syndrome" is now becoming universal—the world is becoming a sanitized facsimile of itself as it is commercially packaged into theme parks that cater to big-spending tourists. For example, Yosemite Valley has basically been a "Disneyland theme park" for years, a victim of "industrial tourism"; the fishing villages of Southeast Alaska are packaging themselves as theme parks, their streets lined with curio shops as larger and larger cruise boats line up in the harbors, waiting to disgorge thousands of tourists. Tom Birch further claims that designated wilderness areas are also hyperreal simulations of wildness (see his paper in Part Five).

# 27 | THE DEEP ECOLOGY-ECOFEMINISM DEBATE AND ITS PARALLELS

## *Warwick Fox*

## DEEP ECOLOGY'S ECOCENTRIC EGALITARIANISM

THE QUESTION OF THE relative merits of deep ecology and ecofeminism has recently received considerable attention, primarily from an ecofeminist perspective. This question has an obvious significance to anyone concerned with ecophilosophy and ecopolitics since it contrasts two of the most philosophically and socially influential approaches that have developed in response to ecological concerns. For deep ecologists in particular, the ecofeminist critique of deep ecology is of interest for at least two reasons in addition to the direct challenge that it presents to deep ecological theorizing. First, as I argue throughout this paper, the same criticism that can be made of simplistic forms of ecofeminism can be applied with equal force to critiques of deep ecology that proceed from simplistic versions of a broad range of social and political perspectives—the "parallels" of my title. Second, addressing the ecofeminist critique of deep ecology provides an opportunity to further elucidate the nature of deep ecology's concern with anthropocentrism.

Before examining the ecofeminist critique of deep ecology, which centers on deep ecology's negative or critical focus on anthropocentrism, it is important to outline deep ecology's positive or constructive focus. Deep ecology is concerned with encouraging an egalitarian attitude on the part of humans not only toward all *members* of the ecosphere, but even toward all identifiable *entities* or *forms* in the ecosphere. Thus, this attitude is intended to extend, for exam-

Originally published (in a somewhat longer version) in *Environmental Ethics* 11, no. 1 (Spring 1989). Reprinted with permission.

ple, to such entities (or forms) as rivers, landscapes, and even species and social systems considered in their own right. If deep ecologists sometimes write as if they consider these entities to be living entities, they do so on the basis of an extremely broad sense of the term *life*—a sense as broad as that implied in such expressions as "Let the river live!" It is ultimately of little consequence to deep ecologists, however, whether one wishes to consider the kind of egalitarianism they advocate as one that extends only toward living entities (in this extremely broad sense) or as one that extends toward both living and nonliving entities. Either way, the kind of egalitarian attitude they advocate is simply meant to indicate an attitude that, within obvious kinds of practical limits, allows all entities (including humans) *the freedom to unfold in their own way unhindered by the various forms of human domination.*

There are, of course, all sorts of problems involved in defining such things as how far these practical limits should extend or, in many cases, even where one entity ends and another begins. But, against this, it must be remembered that deep ecologists are not *intending* to advocate a specific set of guidelines for action; they are only intending to advocate a *general orientation.* Deep ecologists not only accept but welcome cultural diversity when it comes to effecting the specifics of this general orientation. After all, "the freedom to unfold in their own way unhindered by the various forms of human domination" applies to the unfolding of human cultures too. As Arne Naess puts it, where we draw the limit between justifiable and unjustifiable interference with respect to this general orientation "is a question that must be related to local, regional, and national particularities. Even then a certain area of disagreement must be taken as normal."[1] For deep ecologists, the only overriding consideration is that such limits should always be worked out *in the light of* the general orientation they advocate. Naess captures the sense of this general orientation while also conveying a sense of the cultural (and personal) diversity it allows for: "A rich variety of acceptable motives can be formulated for being *more reluctant* to injure or kill a living being of kind A than a being of kind B. The cultural setting is different for each being in each culture."[2] It is this general attitude of being reluctant, *prima facie,* to interfere with the unfolding of A *or* B— indeed, to desire that both should flourish—that characterizes the general orientation that is advocated by deep ecologists.

Deep ecologists have generally referred to this general orientation or attitude as one of "biospherical egalitarianism" or, more often (in order to suggest the intended comparison with an anthropo*centric* perspective more directly), "biocentric egalitarianism." However, because the prefix *bio-* refers, etymologically, to life or living organisms, it has sometimes been assumed that deep ecology's concerns *are* restricted to entities that are (in some sense) biologically alive. To correct this impression, Arne Naess and George Sessions have, in line with my preceding remarks, often pointed out that their sense of the term *life* is so broad, that it takes in "individuals, species, populations, habitat, as well as human and nonhuman cultures."[3] To avoid the possibility of confusion, however, I prefer to describe the kind of egalitarian attitude subscribed to by deep ecologists as *ecocentric* rather than *biocentric*. While there seems to be little reason for choosing between these terms on the basis of their ecological connotations, there are other grounds for preferring the term *ecocentric* to describe the kind of egalitarianism advocated by deep ecologists.[4] First, the term *ecocentric,* which etymologically means *oikos-,* home, or, by implication, Earth-centered, is more immediately informative than the term *biocentric,* which etymologically means life-centered and so requires an appended explanation of the broad sense in which the term *life* should be understood. Second, the term *ecocentric* seems closer to the spirit of deep ecology than the term *biocentric,* because, notwithstanding their broad usage of the term *life,* the motivation of deep ecologists depends more upon a profound sense that the Earth or ecosphere is *home* than it does upon a sense that the Earth or ecosphere is necessarily alive (you don't have to subscribe to some ecological form of *hylozoism* to be a supporter of deep ecology).

In accordance with this extremely broad, ecocentric egalitarianism, supporters of deep ecology hold that their concerns well and truly subsume the concerns of those movements that have restricted their focus to the attainment of a more egalitarian *human* society. Deep ecologists, in other words, consider their concerns to subsume the egalitarian concerns associated, for example, with feminism (as distinct from *eco*feminism), Marxism, antiracism, and anti-imperialism.[5] In the eyes of deep ecologists, the emergence of a distinct *eco*feminism, a distinct "green" socialism, and so on, are—at least in their best forms—attempts by feminists, Marxists-cum-socialists, and so on, to redress the human-centeredness of their respective perspectives.[6] Needless to say, deep ecologists welcome these developments and they recognize that ecofeminism, green socialism, and so on have their own distinctive theoretical flavors and emphases because of the different theoretical histories that inform them. Nevertheless, they see no *essential* disagreement between deep ecology and these perspectives, *providing* that the latter are genuinely able to overcome their anthropocentric legacies.

## THE ECOFEMINIST CRITIQUE
## OF DEEP ECOLOGY

With respect to ecofeminism and deep ecology in particular, many observers agree that the two perspectives have much in common—notwithstanding their different theoretical histories.[7] However, some ecofeminist writers have begun to perceive a significant tension between their perspective and that of deep ecology. In an evenhanded examination of ecofeminist criticisms of deep ecology, Michael Zimmerman has presented what is probably the clearest formulation of what I take to be the essential ecofeminist charge against deep ecology: "Feminist critics of deep ecology assert that [deep ecology] speaks of a gender-neutral 'anthropocentrism' [i.e., human-centeredness] as the root of the domination of nature, when in fact *androcentrism* [i.e., male-centeredness] is the real root."[8] There seems to be wide support for the view that this represents the essential ecofeminist criticism of deep ecology. For example, one of the main criticism made by Janet Biehl in her critique of deep ecology is that, "For ecofeminists the concept of anthropocentrism is profoundly, even "deeply" problematical. . . . By not excluding women from anthropocentrism, deep ecologists implicitly condemn women for being as anthropocentric as they condemn men for being—that is, for presuming to be above nature, for mastering it." Marti Kheel also notes at the outset of her critique of deep ecology that deep ecologists are concerned to "challenge the anthropocentric worldview" whereas for ecofeminists "it is the androcentric worldview that is the focal point of the needed shift." Likewise, the first difference in emphasis that Charlene Spretnak refers to in her comparison of deep ecology and ecofeminism is that of anthropocentrism versus androcentrism.[9]

Jim Cheney has claimed, nevertheless, in response to an earlier version of this paper, that it is wrong to regard Zimmerman's formulation as representing the essential ecofeminist charge against deep ecology. For Cheney, "The 'essential' [ecofeminist] charge is not that deep ecologists focus on *anthropo*centrism whereas the problem is really with *andro*centrism; rather, the central concern is . . . that deep ecology is *itself* in some sense androcentric."[10] In comparison to what I take to be the essential ecofeminist charge against deep ecology (as formulated concisely by Zimmerman), Cheney's formulation of the essential ecofeminist charge seems to represent a significant (if somewhat confusing) concession to deep ecology, since it suggests that ecofeminists are not overly concerned about deep ecologists' critical focus on anthropocentrism so long as deep ecologists do not formulate their critique of anthropocentrism in a way that is "itself in some sense androcentric." But whether Cheney's formulation represents a significant concession to deep ecology or not, my response to his charge is simple. The charge that I propose to address (as taken from Zimmerman's analysis) is clear-cut and serious—deep ecologists cannot deny that their *negative* focus is concerned, first and foremost, with anthropocentrism and ecofeminists cannot deny that their *negative* focus is concerned, first and foremost, with androcentrism. In contrast, the best that can be said about Cheney's claim that deep ecology is androcentric in its very formulation is that such a claim is entirely contentious.[11] Cheney's own recent attempt in *Environmental Ethics* to establish this claim is essentially based upon a misinterpretation of deep ecology as resting upon a "rights-based foundation."[12] Referring to a brief paper of my own, Cheney even acknowledges in his paper (albeit in a footnote) that if (as Fox claims) deep ecology does not rest upon "the language of intrinsic value and correlated concepts of rights, . . . then deep ecology is not subject to some of the criticisms I have offered."[13]

More recently, Cheney has abandoned his previous view of deep ecology and accepted that deep ecologists are primarily concerned with the development of a state of being of wider *identification* and, hence, with the realization of a more expansive (sense of) Self.[14] This understanding of deep ecology appears to have much in common with Cheney's characterization of ecofeminism as being concerned with an ethics of love, care, and friendship as opposed to a theory of rights, justice, and obligation.[15] However, Cheney argues instead that the deep ecological emphasis on the realization of a more expansive (sense of) Self is a "totalizing view" that represents "the desperate endgame of masculine alienation from nature."[16] What Cheney means by his highly abstract and potentially obfuscating reference to a "totalizing view" is that deep ecologists identify "with particulars only in the derivative sense that the logos of the cosmos threads its way through the cosmos, binds it together as a totality, a cosmos. Identification, for the deep ecologist, does not involve seeing or hearing the other or seeing oneself in the other, but rather involves seeing the other *sub specie aeternitas.*"[17]

What Cheney seems to object to in deep ecology, then, is not the emphasis on identification per se but rather the fact that deep ecologists emphasize identification within a cosmological context—that is, within the context of an awareness that all entities in the universe are part of a single, unfolding process. There is, however, a fundamental problem with arguing, as Cheney seems to want to, for a purely *personal* basis for identification (as opposed to a cosmological and, hence, *transpersonal* basis). Specifically, emphasizing a purely personal basis for identification—one that "leave[s] selves intact"[18]—necessarily implies an emphasis upon identification with entities with which one has considerable personal contact. In practice, this tends to mean that one identifies with *my* self first, *my* family next, *my* friends and more distant relations next, *my* ethnic grouping next, *my* species next, and so on—more or less what the sociobiologists say we are genetically predisposed to do. The problem with this is that, while extending love, care, and friendship to one's nearest and dearest is laudable in and of itself, the *other* side of the coin, emphasizing a purely personal basis for identification (*my*self first, *my* family next, and so on), looks more like the cause of possessiveness, war, and ecological destruction than the solution to these seemingly intractable problems. In contrast, to argue for a cosmological basis for identification is to attempt to convey a lived sense that all entities (including ourselves) are relatively autonomous modes of a single, unfolding process, that all entities are leaves on the tree of life. A lived sense of this understanding means that we strive, insofar as it is within our power to do so, not to identify ourselves exclusively with our leaf (our personal biographical self), our twig (our family), our minor subbranch (our community), our major subbranch (our race/gender), our branch (our species), and so on, but rather to identify ourselves with the tree. This necessarily leads, at the limit, to impartial identification with *all* particulars (all leaves on the tree).[19]

This distinction between personally based identification and cosmologically based identification certainly represents a difference in *theoretical* stance between Cheney's conception of ecofeminism on the one hand and deep ecology on the other. But whether this difference also reflects a basic difference between feminine and masculine modes of approaching the world (as Cheney wants to suggest) is a separate issue. On my reading of the literature, I do not see how anyone can—or why they would want to—deny that many women are *vitally* interested in cultivating a cosmological/transpersonal based sense of identification.[20] The cosmological/transpersonal voice *is* a "different voice" from the personal voice, but it does not seem to respect gender boundaries. Moreover, as the above discussion suggests, whatever one's view of the relationship or lack of relationship between these approaches and gender, a personally based approach to identification is vulnerable to criticism from an ecocentric perspective in a way in which a cosmological/transpersonal approach is not.

Because this brief examination of Cheney's critique of deep ecology suggests that there are major weaknesses with his claim that the essential ecofeminist charge against deep ecology is actually "that deep ecology is *itself*, in some sense androcentric," in what follows I, therefore, consider the essential ecofeminist charge against deep ecology to be the far more clear-cut and potentially far more serious charge (vis-à-vis Cheney's charge) that deep ecology "speaks of a gender-neutral 'anthropocentrism' as the root of the domination of nature, when in fact *androcentrism* is the real root."[21]

## PROBLEMS WITH THE ECOFEMINIST AND OTHER CRITIQUES

Having established the nature of the ecofeminist charge that I am concerned to address in what follows, it is important to note that this charge is *not* directed at deep ecology's positive or constructive task of encouraging an egalitarian attitude on the part of humans toward all entities in the ecosphere, but rather at deep ecology's negative or critical task of dismantling anthropocentrism. This distinction often seems to be overlooked by ecofeminist critics of deep ecology, who, presumably, are in general agreement with the constructive task of deep ecology.[22] But with respect to the critical task of these two perspectives, the fact remains that in the absence of a good answer to the ecofeminist charge, there is no reason—other than intellectual blindness or outright chauvinism in regard to issues concerning gender—why deep ecologists should not make androcentrism the focus of their critique rather than anthropocentrism. In addressing this challenge to the critical focus of deep ecology, I first make some general remarks about a certain style of social and political theorizing and then proceed to the essential deep ecological response to this ecofeminist charge.

To begin with, deep ecologists completely agree with ecofeminists that men have been far more implicated in the history of ecological destruction than women. However, deep ecologists also agree with similar charges derived from other social perspectives: for example, that capitalists, whites, and Westerners have been far more implicated in the history of ecological destruction than pre-capitalist peoples, blacks, and non-Westerners.[23] If ecofeminists also agree with these points, then the question arises as to why they do not also criticize deep ecology for being neutral with respect to issues concerning such significant social variables as socioeconomic class, race, and Westernization. There appears to be two reasons for this. First, to do so would detract from the priority that econfeminists wish to give to their own concern with androcentrism. Second, and more significantly, these charges could also be applied with equal force to the ecofeminist focus on androcentrism itself.[24] How does one defend the ecofeminist charge against deep ecology (i.e., that androcentrism is "the real root" of ecological destruction) in the face of these charges?[25] For deep ecologists, it is simplistic on both empirical and logical grounds to think that one particular perspective on human society identifies *the* real root of ecological destruction. Empirically, such thinking is simplistic (and thus descriptively poor) because it fails to give due consideration to the multitude of interacting factors at work in any given situation. (While on a *practical* level it can be perfectly reasonable to devote most of one's energy to one particular cause—if only for straightforward reasons to do with time and energy—that, of course, is no excuse for simplistic social *theorizing*.) Such thinking fails, in other words, to adopt an ecological perspective with respect to the workings of human society itself. Logically, such thinking is simplistic (and thus facile) because it implies that the solution to our ecological problems is close at hand—all we have to do is remove "the real root" of the problem—when it is actually perfectly possible to conceive of a society that is nonandrocentric, socioeconomically egalitarian, nonracist, and nonimperialistic with respect to other human societies, but whose members nevertheless remain aggressively anthropocentric in collectively agreeing to exploit their environment for their collective benefit in ways that nonanthropocentrists would find thoroughly objectionable. Indeed, the "green" critique of socialism proceeds from *precisely* this recognition that a socially egalitarian society does not necessarily imply an ecologically benign society.

An interesting example of the failure to recognize this point is provided by Murray Bookchin's anarcho-socialist inspired "social ecology" (I describe this approach as "anarcho-socialist" in inspiration because it advocates decentralism and cooperativeness and stands opposed to all forms of hierarchy). Bookchin is interesting in this context because, on the one hand, he correctly observes in the course of a highly polemical attack upon deep ecology that it is possible for a relatively ecologically benign human society also to be extremely oppressive internally (he offers the example of ancient Egyptian society), and yet, on the other hand, he fails to see that the reverse can also apply—that is, that it is possible for a relatively egalitarian human society to be extremely exploitative ecologically.[26] For Bookchin, to accept this latter point would be to argue against the basis of his own social ecology, since in his view a nonhierarchical, decentralist, and cooperative society is "a society that will live in harmony with nature *because* its members live in harmony with each other."[27] Bookchin's presentation of social ecology thus conveys no real appreciation of the fact that the relationships between the internal organization of human societies and their treatment of the nonhuman world can be as many and varied as the outcomes of any other evolutionary process. One may certainly speak in terms of certain forms of human social organization being more *conducive* to certain kinds of relationships with the nonhuman world than others. Bookchin, however, insists far too much that there is a straightforward, necessary relationship between the internal organization of human societies and their treatment of the nonhuman world. To this extent, his social ecology is constructed upon a logically facile basis. Moreover, it serves to reinforce anthropocentrism, since the assumption that the internal organization of human societies determines their treatment of the nonhuman world carries with it the implication that we need only concentrate on *interhuman* egalitarian concerns for all to become ecologically well with the world—a point I take up again later.[28]

In doing violence to the complexities of social interaction, simplistic social and political analyses of ecological destruction are not merely descriptively poor and logically facile, they are also morally objectionable on two grounds, scapegoating and inauthenticity. Scapegoating can be thought of in terms of overinclusiveness. Simplistic analyses target all men, all capitalists, all whites, and all Westerners, for example, to an equal degree when in fact certain sub-

classes of these identified classes are far more responsible for ecological destruction than others. Not only that but significant minorities of these classes
can be actively engaged in *opposing* the interests of both the dominant culture
of their class and those members of their class most responsible for ecological
destruction. Inauthenticity, on the other hand, can be thought of in terms of
underinclusiveness. Simplistic analyses are inauthentic in that they lead to a
complete denial of responsibility when at least partial responsibility for ecological destruction should be accepted. Such theorizing conveniently disguises the
extent to which (at least a subset of) the simplistically identified oppressed
group (e.g., women or the working class) also benefits from, and colludes with,
those most responsible for ecological destruction (e.g., consider the case of
animal destruction for furs and cosmetics consumed by Western and Western-
ized women, or the case of capitalists and unionists united in opposition to the
antidevelopment stance of "greenies"). It can, of course, be argued in response
that the hegemony of androcentrism or capitalism, for example, is such that
women or unionists effectively have *no* power to choose in our society and so
should not be burdened with *any* responsibility for ecological destruction. But
this surely overplays the role of social determination and to that extent only
serves to highlight the charge of inauthenticity. Moreover, attempting to escape
the charge of inauthenticity in this way directly contradicts the view of feminists or Marxists, to continue with the same examples, that women or the
working class *are* capable of self-conscious direction—of being a class *for*
themselves, a revolutionary class.

Yet another kind of objection to simplistic analyses of the kind to which I
have been referring is that while claiming to be "ecological" or "green," some
of these critics in fact remain anthropocentric—albeit in the passive sense of
serving to legitimize our continued preoccupation with interhuman affairs
rather than in the aggressive sense of overtly discriminating against the nonhuman world. Advocates of these approaches say in essence: "Since the real root
of our problems is androcentrism or capitalism, for example, we must *first* get
our interactions between humans right (with respect to gender issues, with
respect to the redistribution of wealth, and so on) and then everything else
(including our ecological problems) will fall into place." Any form of direct
concern with the question of the relationship between humans and the *nonhuman* world is thus trumped by concerns about the resolution of specific interhuman problems. The nonhuman world retains its traditional status as the
background against which the significant action—human action—takes place.

Not surprisingly, deep ecologists find it particularly frustrating to witness
representatives of simplistic social and political perspectives waving the banner
of ecology while in fact continuing to promote, whether wittingly or unwittingly, the interhuman and, hence, human-centered agenda of their respective

theoretical legacies. I have already commented on Bookchin's social ecology in regard to this point. Some ecofeminist writing is also relevant here. For example, the focus of Ariel Kay Salleh's critique of deep ecology is thoroughly interhuman. "To make a better world," she concludes, men have to be "brave enough to rediscover and to love the woman inside themselves," while women simply have to "be allowed to love what we are.[29] This conclusion follows from the fact that, in Salleh's version of feminism, women already "flow with the system of nature" by virtue of their essential nature."[30] Karen Warren and Michael Zimmerman have referred to this kind of approach to ecofeminism, according to which women are supposed to be "closer to nature" than men by virtue of their essential nature, as "radical feminism" (in contrast to liberal, traditional Marxist, and socialist feminism) and "essentialist feminism" respectively.[31] Warren correctly notes that "Radical feminists have had the most to say about eco-feminism," and both she and Zimmerman have made telling criticisms of this approach.[32] All I am drawing attention to here is the fact that this kind of "radical" approach simply serves to legitimize and, hence, to perpetuate our entirely *traditional* preoccupation with interhuman affairs. In accordance with the approach adopted by essentialist feminists, there is no need to give any serious consideration whatsoever to the possibility that women might, for example, discriminate against men, accumulate rather than distribute private wealth, be racist, support imperialism, or be ecologically destructive if the conditions of their historical subjugation were undone and the possibility of exercising genuine social and political power were available to them.[33] The upshot is that there is no need to worry about any form of human domination other than that of androcentrism. For deep ecologists, it's just another variation on the same old song—the song that reassures us that all will become ecologically well with the world if we just put this or that interhuman concern first.

I have objected to simplistic (and, hence, unecologically conceived) social and political analyses on the grounds that they are descriptively poor and logically facile, that they lend themselves to scapegoating on the one hand and are inauthentic on the other, and that even in their ecological guises, they are passively anthropocentric. Many who align themselves with the perspectives to which I have referred might well personally agree with the points I have made so far and consider that in virtue of this agreement, these objections do not really apply to their perspective. Thus, this kind of reaction can be quite common in the face of the sorts of objections I have made: "How could anyone be so stupid as to think that we ecofeminists (for example) are not also concerned about issues concerning socioeconomic class, race, and imperialism?" The problem is, however, that there is often a large gap between the alleged and often genuine personal concerns of members of a social and political movement and the theoretical articulation of the perspective that informs their movement. The fact that individual members of a social and political movement agree with the points I have made provides no guarantee whatsoever that the theoretical articulation of the perspective that informs their movement does not itself fall foul of these objections—and it is with this theoretical articulation that I have been concerned. By way of qualification, however, I do not in any way wish to assert that any of the objections I have made are necessarily fatal to the theoretical prospects of the social and political perspectives to which I have referred, since it is possible, at least in principle, for each of these perspectives to be revised or, at a minimum, suitably qualified so as not to fall foul of these objections.[34] But, that said, one must nevertheless be careful not to underestimate the significance of these objections, since presentations of the social and political perspectives to which I have referred continue to fall foul of them on an all too regular basis.

Variations on some (but not all) of the objections I have outlined would apply just as much to deep ecology if it were the case that deep ecologists were simply saying that humans as a whole have been far more implicated in the history of ecological destruction than nonhumans. (The ecofeminist charge against deep ecology implies that deep ecologists are saying precisely this: in turns on the contention that deep ecologists have been overinclusive in criticizing humanity *in general* for the destruction of the nonhuman world when the target of their critical attack should properly be the class of men and, of course, masculine culture in general.) However, this is *not* the essential point that deep ecologists are making, and it is here that we enter into the essential response by deep ecologists to the essential criticism made of their perspective by ecofeminists.

## THE ESSENTIAL DEEP ECOLOGICAL RESPONSE TO THE ECOFEMINIST CRITIQUE

The target of the deep ecologists' critique is not humans per se (i.e., a general class of social actors) but rather human-*centeredness* (i.e., a legitimating ideology).[35] It is not just ecofeminist critics who miss this point. Some other critics also miss it in an even bigger way by attacking deep ecologists not simply on the grounds that they *criticize* humanity in general for its ecological destructiveness, but rather on the grounds that deep ecologists are actually *opposed* to humanity in general—that is, that they are essentially misanthropic. According to Murray Bookchin, for example, in deep ecology " '*Humanity*' is essentially seen as an ugly 'anthropocentric' thing—presumably, a malignant product of natural evolution."[36] Henryk Skolimowski also suggests (albeit rather indirectly) that deep ecologists are misanthropic. "I find it rather morbid," he writes in *The Trumpeter,* "when some human beings (and the context suggests that he means deep ecologists) think that the human lot is the bottom of the pit. There is something pathological in the contention that humans are a cancer among the species. This kind of thinking is not sane and it does not promote the sense of wholeness which we need nowadays." In line with my remarks here, Alan Drengson, *The Trumpeter*'s editor and a prominent deep ecology philosopher, intervenes immediately at this point by adding parenthetically: "And it is certainly not the thinking of deep ecologists. Ed."[37]

The extent to which people in general are ready to equate opposition to human-centeredness with opposition to humans per se can be viewed as a function of the dominance of the anthropocentric frame of reference in our society. Just as those who criticize capitalism, for example, are often labeled as "Communists" and, by implication, "the enemy," when, in reality, they may be concerned with such things as a more equitable distribution of wealth in society, so those who criticize anthropocentrism are liable to be labeled as misanthropists when, in reality, they may be (and, in the context of environmentalism, generally are) concerned with encouraging a more egalitarian attitude on the part of humans toward all entities in the ecosphere. In failing to notice the fact that being opposed to humans-*centeredness* (deep ecology's critical task) is logically distinct from being opposed to humans per se (or, in other words, that being opposed to anthropo*centrism* is logically distinct from being misanthropic), and in equating the former with the latter, Bookchin and Skolimowski commit what I refer to as *the fallacy of misplaced misanthropy.*[38] Committing this fallacy in the context of criticizing deep ecology involves not just a crucial misreading of deep ecology's critical task, but also the oversight of two other considerations that contradict such a misreading. The first is that deep ecology's *constructive* task is to encourage an egalitarian attitude on the part of humans toward all entities in the ecosphere—including *humans.* The second is that deep ecologists are among the first to highlight and draw inspiration from the fact that not all humans have been human-centered either within the Western tradition or outside it. Far from being misanthropic, deep ecologists celebrate the existence of these human beings.

In making human-*centeredness* (rather than humans per se) the target of their critique, deep ecologists have contended that the assumption of human self-importance in the larger scheme of things has, to all intents and purposes, been the single deepest and most persistent assumption of (at least) all the *dominant* Western philosophical, social, and political traditions since the time of the classical Greeks—notwithstanding the fact that the dominant classes representing these traditions have typically adjudged themselves *more* human than others—and that, for a variety of reasons, this assumption is unwarranted and should be abandoned in favor of an ecocentric outlook.[39] Thus, what deep ecologists are drawing critical attention to is the fact that *whatever* class of social actors one identifies as having been most responsible for social domination and ecological destruction (e.g., men, capitalists, whites, Westerners), one tends at the most fundamental level to find a common kind of legitimation for the alleged superiority of these classes over others and, hence, for the assumed rightfulness of their domination of these others. Specifically, these classes of social actors have not sought to legitimate their position on the grounds that they are, for example, men, capitalists, white, or Western per se, but rather on the grounds that they have most exemplified whatever it is that has been taken to constitute the *essence of humanness* (e.g., being favored by God or possessing rationality). These classes of social actors have, in other words, habitually assumed themselves to be somehow *more fully human* than others, such as women ("the weaker vessel"), the "lower" classes, blacks, and non-Westerners ("savages," "primitives," "heathens"). The cultural spell of anthropocentrism has been considered sufficient to justify not only moral superiority (which, in itself, might be construed as carrying with it an obligation to help rather than dominate those who are less blessed), but also all kinds of domination within human society—let alone domination of the obviously nonhuman world.

That anthropocentrism has served as the most fundamental kind of legitimation employed by *whatever* powerful class of social actors one wishes to focus on can also be seen by considering the fundamental kind of legitimation that has habitually been employed with regard to large-scale or high-cost social enterprises such as war, scientific and technological development, or environmental exploitation. Such enterprises have habitually been undertaken not simply in the name of men, capitalists, whites, or Westerners, for example, but rather in the name of God (and thus our essential humanity—or our anthropocentric projection upon the cosmos, depending upon one's perspective) or simply in the name of humanity in general. (This applies notwithstanding the often sexist expression of these sentiments in terms of "man," "mankind," and so on, and notwithstanding the fact that certain classes of social actors benefit disproportionately from these enterprises.) Thus, to take some favorite examples, Francis Bacon and Descartes ushered in the development of modern science by promising, respectively, that it would lead to "enlarging the bounds of Human Empire" and that it would render humanity the "masters and possessors of nature."[40] Approximately three and a half centuries later, Neil Armstrong's moon walk—the culmination of a massive, politically directed, scientific and technological development effort—epitomized both the literal acting out of this vision of "enlarging the bounds of Human Empire" and the literal expression of its anthropocentric spirit: Armstrong's moon walk was, in his own words at the time, a "small step" for him, but a "giant leap for mankind." Here on Earth, not only do examples abound of environmental *exploitation* being undertaken in the name of humanity, but this also constitutes the fundamental kind of legitimation that is still most often employed for environmental *conservation* and *preservation*—it is implicit in every argument for the conservation or preservation of the nonhuman world on account of its use value to humans (.e.g, its scientific, recreational, or aesthetic value) rather than for its own sake or its use value to *nonhuman* beings.

The cultural pervasiveness of anthropocentrism in general and anthropocentric legitimations in particular are further illustrated when one turns to consider those social movements that have *opposed* the dominant classes of social actors to which I have been referring. With respect to the pervasiveness of anthropocentrism in general, it can be seen that those countermovements that have been most concerned with exposing discriminatory assumptions and undoing their effects have typically confined their interests to the human realm (i.e., to such issues as imperialism, race, socioeconomic class, and gender). With respect to the pervasiveness of anthropocentric legitimations in particular, it can equally be seen that these countermovements have not sought to legitimate their own claims on the basis that they are, for example, women, workers, black, or non-Western per se, but rather on the grounds that they too have exemplified—at least equally with those to whom they have been opposed—either whatever it is that *has* been taken to constitute the essence of humanness or else some redefined essence of humanness. While it would, in any case, be contrary to the (human-centered) egalitarian concerns of these countermovements to seek to legitimate their own claims by the former kind of approach (i.e., on the basis that they are, for example, women, workers, black, or non-Western per se), the pity is (from a deep ecological perspective) that these countermovements have not been egalitarian enough. Rather than attempting to replace the ideology of anthropocentrism with some broader, ecocentrically inclined perspective, these countermovements have only served to reinforce it.

It should be clear from this brief survey that the history of anthropocentrism takes in not only the assumption of the centrality and superiority of humans *in general,* but also the various claims and counterclaims that various classes of humans have made with regard to the exemplification of whatever attributes have been considered to be quintessentially human. Deep ecologists recognize that the actual historical reasons for the domination of one class by another (and here I also refer to the domination that humans as a class now exert over the nonhuman world) cannot be identified in any simplistic manner; they can be as complex as any ecological web or the evolutionary path of any organism. However, deep ecologists also recognize that claims to some form of human exclusiveness have tyically been employed to *legitimate* the bringing about and perpetuation of historical and evolutionary outcomes involving unwarranted domination. In consequence, deep ecologists have been attempting to get people to see that historical and evolutionary outcomes simply represent "the way things happen to have turned out"—nothing more—and that self-serving anthropocentric legitimations for these outcomes are just that.

What the ecofeminist criticism of deep ecology's focus on anthropocentrism overlooks, then, is the fact that deep ecologists are not primarily concerned with exposing the *classes of social actors* historically most responsible for social domination and ecological destruction, but rather with the task of sweeping the rug out from under the feet of these classes of social actors by exposing the most fundamental kind of *legitimation* that they have habitually employed in justifying their position. (This distinction between a concern with classes of social actors on the one hand and the most fundamental kind of legitimation they employ on the other hand should be apparent from the fact that deep ecology has been elaborated within a philosophical context rather than a sociological or political context—which is not to suggest that deep ecology does not have profound social and political implications.) Of course, ecofeminists, green socialists, and so on are also concerned with questions of legitimation, but they are generally concerned with these questions in a different sense than deep ecologists are concerned with them. The primary emphasis of ecofeminists, green socialists, and the other social and political analysts to whom I have referred is on the distribution of power in society and the ways in which that distribution is reinforced and reproduced. In this context, references to legitmation tend not to be to the "bottom line" rationale employed by these powerful classes (i.e., to legitimation in the fundamental or philosophical sense), but rather to the ways in which existing power structures utilize their sources of power to back up existing states of affairs (from overtly physical forms of power such as the police and the military to less tangible forms such as economic power and the manipulation of social status). To the extent that ecofeminists, green socialists, and so on *are* concerned to expose the fundamental, philosophical legitimation employed by the classes of social actors whose unwarranted degree of power is the focus of their critique, and to the extent that this concern extends out into a genuinely ecocentric perspective, it becomes difficult to see any significant difference between what they call ecofeminism, green socialism, and so on and what others call deep ecology (such differences as remain are simply differences of theoretical flavor and emphasis rather than differences of substance).

Deep ecologists want to unmask the ideology of anthropocentrism so that it can no longer be used as the "bottom line" legitimation for social domination and ecological destruction by *any* class of social actors (men, capitalists, whites, Westerners, humans generally—or even essentialist feminists!).[41] Thus, those who align themselves with certain perspectives on the distribution of power in human society (e.g., feminism, Marxism, antiracism, or anti-imperialism) misunderstand the essential nature of deep ecology if they see it in terms of their perspective *versus* deep ecology (e.g., in the case of ecofeminism and deep ecology, androcentrism *versus* anthropocentrism)—or if they criticize deep ecology on the basis that it has "no analysis of power." Rather, just as deep ecologists have learned and incorporated much from, and should be open to, a range of perspectives on the distribution of power in human society, so those who align themselves with these social and political perspectives can learn and incorporate much from, and should be open to, the deep ecologists' critique of the most fundamental kind of legitimation that has habitually been employed by those most responsible for social domination and ecological destruction.

# NOTES

1. Arne Naess, "Sustainable Development and the Deep Long-Range Ecological Movement," unpublished manuscript.

2. Arne Naess, "Intuition, Intrinsic Value, and Deep Ecology," *The Ecologist* 14 (1984): 202 (emphasis added). Naess fully accepts that "any realistic praxis necessitates some killing, exploitation, and suppression" ("The Shallow and the Deep, Long-Range Ecology Movement: A Summary," *Inquiry* 16 [1973]: 95). For more on the relevance of tradition and culture, see Naess's paper "Self-realization in Mixed Communities of Humans, Bears, Sheep, and Wolves," *Inquiry* 22 (1979): 231–41.

3. See the eight point list of "basic principles" of deep ecology proposed by Arne Naess and George Sessions and published in numerous places including Bill Devall and George Sessions, *Deep Ecology: Living as if Nature Mattered* (Layton, Utah: Gibbs M. Smith, 1985), chap. 5; and Arne Naess, "The Deep Ecological Movement: Some Philosophical Aspects," *Philosophical Inquiry* 8 (1986): 10–31.

4. *Biocentric* and *ecocentric* are equally useful in connoting the biosphere and the ecosphere respectively and these latter terms are themselves generally used interchangeably. However, where a distinction *is* made between the terms *biosphere* and *ecosphere,* it is the latter term that is taken as the more inclusive.

5. I am, of course, speaking here of the full realization of deep ecology's concerns, i.e., of the breadth of deep ecology's concerns *in principle.* In practice, however, deep ecologists, like everyone else, can fail to realize the full implications of their own principles.

6. In referring to *green socialism* and to *socialists,* I am aware that the term *socialism,* considered in its own right, is today popularly construed as referring to virtually the whole range of (human) social egalitarian concerns and that the concerns of socialism and green socialism might therefore be considered as subsuming the concerns of feminism and ecofeminism respectively. But there are nevertheless

significant differences between these approaches at the level of their theoretical flavors and emphases.

7. There is nothing to suggest that there is any incompatibility between deep ecology and an ecologically informed feminism in any of the works by the following authors, all of whom make explicit reference to both perspectives: Fritjof Capra, *The Turning Point: Science, Society, and the Rising Culture* (New York: Bantam Books, 1983), chap. 12; Don E. Marietta, Jr., "Environmentalism, Feminism, and the Future of American Society," *The Humanist,* May–June 1984, pp. 15–18, 30; Bill Devall and George Sessions, *Deep Ecology,* chap. 6; Charlene Spretnak, "The Spiritual Dimensions of Green Politics," appendix C in Charlene Spretnak and Fritjof Capra, *Green Politics: The Global Promise* (London: Paladin, Grafton Books, 1986); and Patsy Hallen, "Making Peace with Nature: Why Ecology Needs Feminism," *The Trumpeter* 4, no. 3 (1987): 3–14. Even those authors who do see a tension between these perspectives generally acknowledge that these perspectives at least bear a strong apparent similarity to each other. For example, Jim Cheney writes: "On the face of it, that *branch* of environmentalism called the 'deep ecology movement' seems to have answered the [ecofeminist] call for a nonhierarchical, nondomineering attitude toward nature ("Eco-Feminism and Deep Ecology," *Environmental Ethics* 9 [1987]: 115–45).

8. Zimmerman, "Feminism, Deep Ecology, and Environmental Ethics," *Environmental Ethics* 9 (1987): 21–44.

9. Janet Biehl, "It's Deep, But Is It Broad? An Eco-feminist Looks at Deep Ecology," *Kick It Over,* Winter 1987, p. 2A; Marti Kheel, "Ecofeminism and Deep Ecology," and Charlene Spretnak, "Ecofeminism: Our Roots and Flowering," *The Elmwood Newsletter,* Winter 1988, p. 7.

10. Personal communication, 21 April 1988.

11. Zimmerman ("Feminism, Deep Ecology, and Environmental Ethics," pp. 38–42) provides a thoughtful consideration of the various problems associated with the kind of claim that Cheney makes.

12. Cheney, "Eco-Feminism and Deep Ecology," p. 129.

13. Ibid., p. 133. The brief paper of mine that Cheney refers to is "A Postscript on Deep Ecology and Intrinsic Value," *The Trumpeter* 2, no. 4 (1985): 20–23. For a far more extensive critique of the view that deep ecology rests upon what Cheney refers to as "the language of intrinsic value and correlated concepts of rights," see my monograph *Approaching Deep Ecology: A Response to Richard Sylvan's Critique of Deep Ecology,* Environmental Studies Occasional Paper, no. 20 (Hobart: Centre for Environmental Studies, University of Tasmania, 1986).

14. Jim Cheney, "The Neo-Stoicism of Radical Environmentalism," unpublished early draft. This version of Cheney's critique of deep ecology follows his reading of my *Approaching Deep Ecology* and is, in large measure, a response to it.

15. See Cheney, "Eco-Feminism and Deep Ecology," p. 128.

16. Cheney, "Neo-Stoicism."

17. Ibid., p. 16.

18. Ibid., p. 15.

19. The fact that cosmologically based identification tends to be more *impartial* than personally based identification does not mean that it need be any less deeply felt. Consider Robinson Jeffers! For Jeffers, "This whole [the universe] is in *all its parts* so beautiful, and is felt by me to be so intensely in earnest, that I am *compelled* to love it" (quoted in Devall and Sessions, *Deep Ecology*, p. 101; emphasis added).

20. See, for example, Dolores LaChapelle, *Earth Wisdom* (Los Angeles: Guild of Tutors Press, 1978); Joanna Macy, "Deep Ecology and the Council of All Beings," and "Gaia Meditations (Adapted from John Seed)," *Awakening in the Nuclear Age,* Summer/Fall 1986, pp. 6–10 (both reprinted in *Revision,* Winter/Spring 1987, pp. 53–57); Freya Matthews, "Conservation and Self-Realization: A Deep Ecology Perspective," *Environmental Ethics* 10 (1988): 347–55; and Frances Vaughan, "Discovering Transpersonal Identity," *Journal of Humanistic Psychology* 25 (1985): 13–38.

21. Zimmerman, "Feminism, Deep Ecology, and Environmental Ethics," p. 37.

22. In a thoughtful analysis of the strengths and shortcomings of several varieties of feminism (liberal, traditional Marxist, radical, and socialist) for the development of a genuinely ecofeminist perspective, Karen J. Warren concurs that an ecologically informed feminism—"a transformative feminism"—would tie "the liberation of women to the elimination of all systems of oppression" ("Feminism and Ecology: Making Connections," *Environmental Ethics* 9 [1987]: 18). Unfortunately, however, many feminists who claim to be ecofeminists do not make their (presumed) commitment to an *ecocentric* egalitarianism particularly explicit, with the result that ecofeminist analyses can sometimes serve to reinforce anthropocentrism rather than overcome it. As for those ecofeminists, such as Warren, who are explicit about their commitment to an ecocentric egalitarianism, it becomes difficult to see any essential difference between their approach and that of deep ecology. As one ecofeminist-cum-deep ecologist said to me after reading Warren's article: "Why doesn't she just call it [i.e., Warren's vision of a transformative feminism] deep ecology? Why specifically attach the label *feminism* to it if she's advocating a genuinely nonprioritizing, biocentric egalitarianism?"

23. When I refer to any class of social actors, I expressly mean also to refer to the culture(s) associated with that class. However, I omit writing "men and their associated cultures," "non-Westerners and their associated cultures," and so on simply for ease of comprehension. In referring to capitalists and, hence, the culture of capitalism, I also mean to refer to "state capitalism" as found in the industrialized communist countries.

24. Indeed, even as I wrote this paper, a significant real-life example of such criticisms was being played out between the women of Greenham Common in the form of a "bitter dispute" over allegations of racism at the camp. Reports suggested that this dispute "threatens the world's most renowned peace camp after six years" (Deborah Smith, "Showdown at Greenham Common," *The Times on Sunday,* 25

October 1987, p. 27). Karen J. Warren similarly criticizes radical feminists—that group of feminists who "have had the most to say about ecofeminism"—for paying "little attention to the historical and material features of women's oppression (including the relevance of race, class, ethnic, and national background)" ("Feminism and Ecology," pp. 14–15).

25. Note that I am borrowing the phrase "the real root" from Michael Zimmerman's previously quoted formulation of what I consider to be the essential ecofeminist charge against deep ecology. I employ this phrase several times in the argument that follows.

26. Murray Bookchin, "Social Ecology Versus 'Deep Ecology,'" *Green Perspectives: Newsletter of the Green Program Project,* Summer 1987.

27. Ibid., p. 2 (emphasis added). This view is central to Bookchin's major statement of social ecology: *The Ecology of Freedom: The Emergence and Dissolution of Hierarchy* (Palo Alto: Cheshire Books, 1982).

28. This observation is in keeping with the anthropocentric flavor that many deep ecologists detect in Bookchin's work notwithstanding his avowed ecological orientation.

29. Salleh, "Deeper than Deep Ecology," p. 345. In another presentation of the ecofeminist sensibility, Don Davis also concludes by reiterating this conclusion of Salleh's ("Ecosophy: The Seduction of Sophia?" *Environmental Ethics* 8 [1986]: 151–62).

30. Salleh, "Deeper than Deep Ecology," p. 340.

31. Warren, "Feminism and Ecology," pp. 13–15, and Zimmerman, "Feminism, Deep Ecology," p. 40.

32. Warren, "Femimism and Ecology," p. 14. See also Alan E. Wittbecker, "Deep Anthropology: Ecology and Human Order," *Environmental Ethics* 8 (1986): 261–70, which provides a number of counterinstances to Salleh's essentialist feminist claim that the suppression of the feminine is "universal."

33. Stunningly obvious instances of these kinds of examples, such as the Prime Minister of England, Margaret Thatcher (the "Iron Lady"), sending warships to the Falklands, are typically explained in terms of the hegemony of androcentrism being such as to have overpowered the offending woman's essential nature. The implication is that if, as Salleh says, woman could just "be allowed to love what we are," then it would no longer be possible to find such examples.

34. Where revised, such perspectives would no doubt continue to differ from deep ecology in terms of their theoretical flavors and emphases, but they would not differ from deep ecology in terms of their essential concerns. Whether these revised perspectives would be recognizable or acceptable to their earlier supporters is of course an interesting question.

35. Ecofeminists, green socialists, and so on are also concerned with questions of legitimation, but generally in a different sense than deep ecologists are.

36. Bookchin, "Social Ecology," p. 3 (emphasis added).

37. Henryk Skolimowski, "To Continue the Dialogue with Deep Ecology," *The Trumpeter* 4, no. 4 (1987): 31. Skolimowski has previously been taken to task for the anthropocentrism inherent in his own approach: see George Sessions' review of Skolimowski's *Eco-Philosophy* in *Environmental Ethics* 6 (1984): 167–74. Since then Skolimowski has become a regular critic of deep ecology; see his articles "The Dogma of Anti-Anthropocentrism and Ecophilosophy," *Environmental Ethics* 8 (1984): 283–88 (Skolimowski's response to Sessions' review); "In Defence of Ecophilosophy and of Intrinsic Value: A Call for Conceptual Clarity," *The Trumpeter* 3, no. 4 (1988): 9–12 (this issue of *The Trumpeter* also carried replies from Bill Devall, Arne Naess, and myself); "To Continue the Dialogue with Deep Ecology"; and "Eco-Philosophy and Deep Ecology," *The Ecologist* 18 (1988): 124–27. I defend Sessions' reading of Skolimowski in my "Further Notes in Response to Skolimowski," *The Trumpeter* 4, no. 4 (1987): 32–34.

38. Much of Bookchin's case for his (mistaken) contention that deep ecology is essentially a misanthropic enterprise rests on certain statements by one or two significant figures in Earth First!—especially Dave Foreman and his personal, unhistorical, and abhorrently simplistic views on population control. However, Bookchin overlooks the surely obvious fact that Foreman says elsewhere in the same interview (p. 42), "I am speaking for myself, not for Earth First!," and both he and Foreman overlook the equally obvious fact that such a view runs contrary to the deep-ecological principle of encouraging an egalitarian attitude on the part of humans toward all entities in the ecosphere. In contrast to Foreman, Arne Naess says in a recent paper: "Sustainable development today means development along the lines of each culture, not development along a common, centralized line. But faced with hungry children humanitarian action is a priority, whatever its relation to developmental plans and cultural invasion" ("Sustainable Development and the Deep, Long-Range Ecological Movement").

39. There are two significant qualifications to be noted in this statement. First, I say "to all intents and purposes" because where these traditions have supposedly been primarily theocentric rather than anthropocentric, it has of course still been humans who have, by divine decree, had "dominion . . . over all the earth [which they are enjoined to 'fill and subdue'] . . . and over every living thing that moves upon the earth" (Genesis 1:26 and 1:28). From a deep ecological perspective, personalistic theocentrisms, in which humans are made in the image of a god to whom they have a privileged personal relationship, are simply anthropocentric projections upon the cosmos. Second, I say "since the time of the *classical* Greeks" (i.e., the Sophists, Socrates, Plato, and Aristotle) as distinct from the *early* Greeks, who initiated Western philosophy (i.e., the early and later Ionians, the Pythagoreans, the Eleatics, and the Atomists—often collectively referred to as the pre-Socratics), because, as Bertrand Russell has pointed out, "What is amiss, even in the best philosophy after Democritus [i.e., after the pre-Socratics], is an undue emphasis on man as compared with the universe" (Bertrand Russell, *History of Western Philosophy* [London: Unwin Paperbacks, 1979], p. 90). Russell's statement is meant to refer to humanity in general, although it also applies, of course, if its sexist

expression is read as representing its intended meaning (i.e., if "man" is read as "men"). It should be noted in this regard, however, that the reason why Russell's statement is true in the gender specific sense is, as I argue below, precisely because men have seen themselves as essentially *more* human than women—an observation that returns us to Russell's intended meaning in a dialectical manner. For excellent discussions of the anthropocentric nature of Western philosophy since the time of the pre-Socratics, see George Sessions, "Anthropocentrism and the Environmental Crisis," *Humboldt Journal of Social Relations* 2 (1974): 71–81 and George Sessions, "Spinoza and Jeffers on Man in Nature," *Inquiry* 20 (1977): 481–528.

40. Both quotes are from Brian Easlea's erudite and inspiring book *Liberation and the Aims of Science: An Essay on Obstacles to the Building of a Beautiful World* (London: Chatto and Windus, 1973), p. 253.

41. I include a reference to essentialist feminists here because, as Michael Zimmerman points out ("Feminism, Deep Ecology," p. 40), "In recent years, a number of feminists have favoured . . . an essentialist view [that women are essentially more attuned to nature than men] and have concluded that woman is *better* than man" (my emphasis). Karen Warren criticizes this point of view sharply ("Feminism and Ecology," p. 15): "The truth is that women, like men, are both connected to nature and separate from it, natural and cultural beings. . . . locating women either on the nature or on the culture side . . . mistakenly perpetuates the sort of oppositional, dualistic thinking for which patriarchal conceptual frameworks are criticized." But, even more fundamentally (since this is the end that such oppositional, dualistic thinking *serves*), essentialist feminism perpetuates the anthropocentric assumption that some humans are more equal than others by virtue of their essential nature.

# 28 | DEEP ECOLOGY AND THE NEW AGE MOVEMENT[1]

*George Sessions*

THE SO-CALLED NEW AGE is an amorphous movement that arose during the 1960s and '70s. The phrase "New Age" is used very loosely by journalists and others to refer to occult or other nonmainstream religious and spiritual practices, nontraditional psychotherapies, and new forms of consciousness. Gavin Miller, however, sees the "vague and poorly defined New Age Movement" as characterized by a belief in "evolutionary transformation and a new global consciousness." He cites New Age proponent David Spangler as claiming that the movement is based upon the belief that "the earth was entering a new cycle of evolution, which . . . would give birth to a new civilization." Jerry Mander sees the New Age as combining with the Gaia hypotheses (for instance, in the case of Timothy Leary's "star seeding" project) to provide a "techno-religious rationalization for . . . Space-Colonization-as-Evolution" where *"we* are [Gaia's] brain. We may even be the reason for evolution, its goal." Mander points out that

> a lot of New Age people *love* the idea of leaving the planet, being chosen by evolution to be its personal astronauts escaping into space. The prospect of personally fulfilling nature's evolutionary design is so thrilling an idea that its advocates don't see, or don't care, that it is only a modern-day continuation of Manifest Destiny, with the same outcome.[2]

The New Age movement presents itself as a postmodern spiritual world-view. Actually it provides a religious ideology for those (especially in the bio-technology, communications, and space technology industries) who see themselves as having a divine mandate for further technological progress, the

---

This essay is previously unpublished.

global electronics communication revolution, human colonization of outer space, and the human takeover of the Earth's evolutionary processes.

The goals (and jargon) of the New Age often overlap those of secular economic/megatechnology proponents who proclaim the dawning of a "new world order." For example, futurists such as Alvin Toffler write of a "Third Wave" of global planetization involving a "technosphere," "infosphere," and so forth. Toffler warns of "ecofascists" and an "eco-theocracy" who would impede this process. Futuristic thinkers such as George Gilder and Francis Fukuyama see the New Age goal of planetary consciousness as being achieved through the global unification of free markets with universal consumerism as a way of life. In many ways, the ideology of the New Age, whether in religious or secular form, has now permeated the megatechnology visions of contemporary industrial society, whether or not this is explicitly acknowledged.[3]

The New Age manifests itself in a couple of ways:

1. As a "pop culture" movement associated with California and Shirley MacLaine that promotes crystal and pyramid power, spiritual "channeling," astrology, and Eastern and Western versions of "pop psychology." Entrepreneurial New Age spiritual gurus provide workshops for corporations and command large fees. Several critics have taken "cheap shots" at Deep Ecology by attempting to associate it with the New Age. For instance, the environmental critic Alston Chase included both New Age and Deep Ecology proponents under the rubric of what he called the "California Cosmologists," claiming that these ideas were all spawned in California's "redwood think tanks." The Social Ecologist Murray Bookchin claimed, in an early tirade, that Deep Ecology had "parachuted into our midst from the Sunbelt's bizarre mix of Hollywood and Disneyland."[4]

2. As a more intellectual and social movement derived primarily from the writings of Buckminister Fuller and the Jesuit priest Pierre Teilhard de Chardin. As Gavin Miller points out, when Marilyn Ferguson (whose book *The Aquarian Conspiracy* was one of the first full-scale treatments of the New Age movement) "sent out a questionnaire in 1977 to people actively involved in mind-work and 'social transformation,' the person they most often named as influential in their ideas was Teilhard de Chardin." Ferguson's term *Aquarian Conspiracy* was inspired by Teilhard.[5]

The technologist Buckminister Fuller provides the main secular inspiration for the New Age movement. Fuller coined the phrase "spaceship earth" in 1951: an image of the Earth as a machine or vehicle with humans as the potential astronaut/pilots. In *An Operating Manual for Spaceship Earth* (1969) Fuller claimed that humans are now in a position to take control of the biological systems of the Earth. As a technological utopian, Fuller asserted that there is no human overpopulation problem; with modern technology there can be four billion billionaires on the planet! Engineers and computers, together with cybernetics and systems theory, will provide purely technological solutions to the world's problems. Like Teilhard, Fuller's megatechnology vision promotes the total humanization of the Earth. For example, in his book *Critical Path* Fuller proposed that "the power of the Amazon watershed be harnessed" and that we should

> take advantage of the hard-earned technique now provided by modern warfare that would approach this whole Brazilian jungleland from above, bombing it open, then parachuting [in equipment] . . . to carve out a complete polka-dot pattern of island airports over the whole country . . . [so that we can deploy] the Brazilian population over the whole of their land for the purpose of its development.

Humans, with their technology, have now achieved "the competence of God."[6]

Among New Age proponents, there is often a confusion between typically New Age themes and more ecological approaches. As Gavin Miller points out:

> New Age thinkers typically blend Teilhard de Chardin with popular psychology, meditation disciplines borrowed from Asia, and sometimes with thinkers who are opposed to global progress, such as Lewis Mumford and Ivan Illich. The New Age movement therefore hosts an often bizarre admixture of living close to nature and high-tech domination. Hence, for example, Stewart Brand's *CoEvolution Quarterly* in the 1970's became involved with space colony proposals."[7]

In this regard, one might also mention Michael Toms's influential New Directions radio program which is replete with New Age spiritual therapists and gurus of every hue. New Directions radio has simultaneously promoted the views of both Buckminister Fuller and John Muir.

## TEILHARD DE CHARDIN'S SPIRITUAL EVOLUTIONARY/MEGATECHNOLOGY VISION

Teilhard's cosmic story is told principally in his book *The Phenomenon of Man* (1959). It is characterized by a fusion of Christian anthropocentric spirituality with the ideas of evolution and inevitable human progress through technology. The end result, for Teilhard, is a "planetary culture" or "global civilization." Gavin Miller sees Teilhard's vision as infused with the idea of progress, which Miller characterizes in this context as the belief that the destiny of humans and human culture is to transcend the natural world and natural processes (the "second nature" theory); this transcendence will continue indefinitely as a way of liberating humans from Nature's constraints.

Teilhard deviates from scientific accounts of biological evolution by interpreting evolution as a goal-directed global progress leading necessarily to humans. As supposedly the highest form of consciousness on the planet, the spiritual destiny of humans is to technologically dominate the Earth and to replace the natural world and wild evolutionary processes with a human controlled artificial environment. As Teilhard comments upon this progress:

> In my opinion, the world of tomorrow will be born out of the "elected" group of those . . . who will decide that there is something big waiting for us ahead, and give their life to reach it. People *have* to decide for or against progress, *now*. And those who say no just have to be dropped behind.[8]

As Gavin Miller summarizes Teilhard's anthropocentric progress-oriented evolutionary cosmology:

> All matter is suffused with consciousness . . . and this consciousness provided a motive force for increasing complexity. Evolution is this forward movement from non-living matter to single-celled life, and then to more complex organisms. The most significant orthogenetic trend in evolution is towards increased brain power, towards reflection. Side branches of evolution such as those leading to plants or to insects have relatively little significance. With the arrival of human beings, consciousness rose to the power of reflection. . . .
>
> As the density of human enterprise and of thought increases, evolution converges around a center of attraction known as Omega. Scientific research leading to the harnessing of nature is the highest manifestation of humanity. . . . Human technological advance is the inevitable and manifest outcome of evolution; and we are poised to take over natural processes. This is a deterministic law of history.[9]

The Teilhardian scholar Conrad Bonifazi also provides a succinct statement of Teilhard's theology:

> In response to the question, What is the Earth? [Teilhard] would say, the earth is man! . . . In us, evolution may come to a halt, because we are evolution. . . . [Teilhard] envisages mankind, born on this planet and spread over its entire surface, coming gradually to form around its earthly matrix one single, hyper-complex and conscious arch-molecule, coextensive with the planet itself.[10]

This new layer of the Earth (Teilhard's "noosphere") results in global planetization: the Earth is totally enveloped by the "arch-molecule" of humanity and its consciousness living in a megatechnologically devised artificial environment ("second nature"). Miller points out that "firstly, the noosphere is a movement of convergence [toward the human species] which reverses the normal evolutionary flow [toward divergence, diversity] and speciation. Secondly, the noosphere is a vision based upon technology and communications . . . transportation and communications technology plays a particular role in the 'planetization' of civilization. . . . Thirdly, it is assumed that the processes of evolution become subject to human control; nature becomes subsumed into the noosphere." This is to be achieved through "the technological management of nature, usually under a global system, through 'holistic' 'post-industrial' means (i.e., electronics and genetic manipulation . . .)."[11]

As with Fuller and other technological utopians, human overpopulation is not a problem for Teilhard. The more quickly humans fill up the planet, the more quickly the noosphere is actualized. In anticipating the biotechnological takeover of the global evolutionary processes, Teilhard claimed

> Technology has a role that is biological in the strict sense of the word. . . . From this point of view, which agrees with that of Bergson, there ceases to be any distinction between the artificial and the natural, between technology and life, since all organisms are the result of invention; if there is any differ-ence, the advantage is on the side of the artificial . . . the artificial takes over from the natural. . . . [Human thought] suddenly bursts in, to dominate and transform everything on the earth.[12]

Teilhard's disdain for wild biological diversity parallels his dislike and sus-picion of human ethnic and cultural diversity which he sees as a source of global conflict: "the extremely varied groups into which mankind divides up [are] an unpleasing and unnecessary irregularity. . . ." This problem would also be solved with the attainment of the Omega Point and the global monocultural "planetary culture."[13]

Not only is the nonhuman world to be transformed by genetic manipula-tion, but, for Teilhard, humans themselves need to be improved by science and technology. Computers can be used to improve the human mind. Teil-hard's vision also includes a program of eugenics and psychological and biolog-ical engineering for humans to be applied at both the individual and social level. The historian and critic of megatechnology Lewis Mumford credits Teilhard with having "made explicit the underlying dogmatic premises of the metaphysics and theology of the megamachine."[14]

## TEILHARD TO THE EXTREME: NEW AGE DISEMBODIED CYBERNETICS

By elevating human consciousness to the supreme value, Teilhard perpetuates the Platonic/Christian/Cartesian tradition of mind/body dualism which deni-grates the value of the organic material world—the world of ecosystems, wild plants and animals, and even our own bodies. In a very perceptive essay, the historian Morris Berman faults New Age thinkers for precisely this problem: promoting an abstract, disembodied perception of reality, a form of pure mental process he calls "computer consciousness" and to which, he claims, modern technological society is becoming addicted.[15]

Berman claims that the holistic cybernetic thinkers of the 1980s—such as Ken Wilber, Rupert Sheldrake, Marilyn Ferguson, David Bohm, Douglas Hofstadter, and the late Gregory Bateson—have not fully overcome the mechanistic paradigm. Cybernetic holism actually dispenses with matter; it is "abstract and formal" and projects "a total vision of reality that circumscribes an entire world." Berman distinguishes between two types of holism: "the one, a sensuous situational, living approach to process" in which Nature is alive and sacred, the other an abstract manipulative cybernetic holism characteristic of many philosophical spokesmen for the New Age. The real issue, according to Berman, is not mechanism versus holism, but "whether the philosophical system is embodied or disembodied."[16]

When such New Age disembodied visions of reality are pushed to the extreme, we arrive at such projects as computer-simulated modeling of the natural world, electronic simulations of reality (such as "virtual reality"), "algeny" (the genetic manipulation of living tissue), the speculation of the nanotechnologists, and the "downloading" of human consciousness.[17]

Jeremy Rifkin argues that as our "outdoor" world of wild Nature and city streets becomes increasing polluted, ravished, and dangerous, "modern man and woman attempt to escape their last connection with the outside world by suppressing their own animal senses and freeing themselves from their own physical nature" by creating a "new indoor world" of electronic simulation. Dubbing the modern era the Age of Simulation, Rifkin claims that "with television, cinema, radio, stereos, CD players, and the like, modern man and woman can surround themselves with a second creation, an artifically conceived, electronic environment that is virtually sealed off from the world of living nature . . . proponents of virtual reality are eager to simulate every aspect of the human environment in hopes of creating a totally artificial living space."[18] Rifkin points to Jerry Mander's claim that "America has become the first culture to have substituted secondary, mediated versions of experience for direct experience of the world."[19]

Nanotechnology was conceived of by the physicist Richard Feynman and has been elaborated upon by Eric Drexler and Grant Fjermedal.[20] As explained by Mark Dowie, it goes even beyond genetic engineering in its attempt to

> zero down into the atomic structure of all materials and rearrange their molecules to get completely new forms, materials, and creatures. . . . Once they can move the atoms around and redesign the molecular chains . . . they will be able to redesign the whole world, molecule by molecule, and that's exactly

what they intend. It's the technological fix to end them all. . . . We won't need resources anymore since the resources are the molecules themselves from which they can make anything: trees, houses, animals, weapons, people. Eventually, they promise to eliminate death.[21]

The Carnegie Mellon scientist Hans Moravec proposes "downloading" the contents of human brains into robot computers. These machines will then evolve on their own, assuring human cultural evolution and allowing for a kind of human immortality. Moravec believes that the identity of a person is strictly tied up with consciousness, having nothing do with the body.[22]

Teilhard's obsession with human consciousness (mind, soul) and with totally altering and humanizing the Earth has its roots in Judeo-Christian "redemption" theology and the Christian story of the immaterial soul's singular importance and immortality. The pervasive influence (both explicit and implicit) of Christian metaphysics and mythos in our culture goes a long way toward explaining the appeal of Teilhard's vision (and similar visions) to scientists and others promoting New Age megatechnological utopian projects. For example, historian Lynn White, Jr., pointed out that despite the fact that many people in modern society "fondly regard themselves as post-Christians . . . no new set of basic values has been accepted in our society to displace those of Christianity. . . . we continue to live today very largely in a context of Christian axioms." White saw Marxism, like Islam (with their commitment to progress and the domination of Nature), as a Judeo-Christian heresy.[23]

Teilhard's metaphysics has its origins, like Francis Bacon's *New Atlantis,* in the story of the Fall. In the Genesis story, *both* humans and Nature fell from divine Grace; hence *both* humans and Nature are in a state of sin and in need of redemption. Conrad Bonifazi clearly brings out the redemption aspect of Teilhard's theology:

[For Teilhard] apocalyptic despair of this world is overarched by hope of transformation of the whole of creation . . . our implicit destiny in the myth of the fall, with its ramifications in the natural world, is spelled out in the myth of the restored paradise . . . there is undiminished hope of nature's inclusion with the processes of salvation.[24]

Teilhardian scholar Thomas Berry also points out that for Teilhard

the sense of progress was irresistible, the feeling that the great mission of the human was to exploit natural resources. . . . Teilhard became the heir to the imperial tradition in human-earth relations, the tradition of human control over the natural world. . . . Teilhard is the most faithful of all followers of Francis Bacon. . . . [He] is deeply involved in the total religious and humanist traditions in the West out of which this exploitive attitude developed.[25]

What better way to "redeem" the Earth (and to save one's soul) than to totally dismantle the Earth and rebuild it to human specifications, gene by gene, or molecule by molecule?

## HISTORICAL DEVELOPMENT OF THE STEWARDSHIP AND "MAN PERFECTING NATURE" IMAGES

Up to this point the emphasis has been on the Judeo-Christian religious influence of Teilhard on New Age ideology. But there are important Greek humanist and post-Renaissance philosophical influences as well, although the two major Western cultural strands of Judeo-Christian and Greek thought have not remained distinct throughout history. For example, Christianity was infused with Platonism in Saint Augustine's theology, Saint Thomas Aquinas incorporated Aristotle's thought into Christianity, and Greek humanist and Christian thought became intertwined and mutually reinforcing in post-Renaissance thought.

The Australian philosopher and historian of ideas John Passmore has provided an important analysis of the philosophical roots of the Western human/ Nature relationship in his early influential ecophilosophy book, *Man's Responsibility for Nature* (1974). Passmore divided the major Western views of the human/Nature relationship into three categories: (1) man as despot; (2) man as steward; and (3) man perfecting nature.

1. *Man as Despot.* In keeping with Lynn White's thesis, Passmore traced the view of humans as reckless exploiters and subduers of the Earth essentially to the historically dominant interpretation of Genesis in the Old Testament. Passmore felt this human/Nature position should be rejected.[26]

2. *Man as Steward.* Passmore traces the idea of human "stewardship" of the Earth to Plato and to the third-century A.D. post-Platonic philosopher Iamblichus. In trying to explain why man's immaterial and immortal soul would ever "immerse itself in matter," Iamblichus referred to a passage from Plato: "Man, they said, is sent to earth by God 'to administer earthly things,' to care for them in God's name."

A more recent version of the stewardship doctrine, according to Passmore, arose from seventeenth-century humanism and the statement by Sir Matthew Hale that "the end of man's creation was that he should be the viceroy of the great God of heaven and earth in this inferior world: his steward [sty-warden], *villicus* (farm manager), bailiff or farmer of this goodly farm of the lower world." As Passmore points out, "Man is still to think of himself, on Hale's view, as master over the world. . . ."[27]

A Christian version of stewardship was proposed in the 1960s by the prominent microbiologist René Dubos. Dubos based his stewardship position on the teachings of Saint Benedict, pointing out that the Benedictine order "actively intervened in nature" as farmers and builders. According to Dubos:

> Saint Benedict believed that it was the duty of the monks to work as partners of God in improving his creation or at least in giving it a more human expression. Implicit in his writings is the thought that labor is like a prayer which helps in recreating paradise out of chaotic wilderness.[28]

The Dubos/Benedictine view is that "chaotic wilderness" (wild ecosystems) serve no function or have no value in themselves. Humans are to be "masters over the world": to have "dominion" over the Earth, to manage and humanize it and to give the Earth, in the words of Dubos, "a more human expression." In a later book, *The Wooing of the Earth,* Dubos presents the image of the steward as a gardener weeding the Earth of "undesirable pests" and predators. He admits however that "the belief that we can manage the Earth and improve on Nature is probably the ultimate expression of human conceit, but it has deep roots in the past and is almost universal."[29]

The image of both the humanist and Christian versions of stewardship is of the Earth as a potential farm to be humanized and altered from its wild state. Paul Shepard underscores the essentially unecological aspect of this image:

> As agriculture replaced hunting and gathering it was accompanied by radical changes in the way men saw and responded to their natural surroundings. . . . [Agriculturalists] all shared the aim of completely humanizing the earth's surface, replacing wild with domestic, and creating landscapes from habitat.[30]

In the early 1970s, a theological debate broke out between Lynn White, Jr., and Dubos over the merits of Franciscan ecocentric equality versus Benedictine "man over Nature" stewardship.[31] In 1972, Dubos coauthored (with the economist Barbara Ward) *Only One Earth,* the commissioned report of the U.N. Stockholm Conference on the Human Environment. This helped enshrine the stewardship approach as the unofficial human/Nature philosophy of the United Nations environmental programs.

3. *Man Perfecting Nature.* The third major Western human/Nature position Passmore traced to Aristotle and the Stoic philosopher Posidonius. According to this view,

> man's responsibility is to perfect nature by cooperating with it [in the sense that] we speak, in this spirit, of an area still in something like its original condition as "not yet developed." To "develop" land, on this view, is to actualize its potentialities, to bring to light what it has in itself to become, and by this means to perfect it. . . . How is perfection to be judged: the presumption is still, in Aristotle's manner, that nature is at its best when it fulfills men's

needs—that this, indeed, is its reason for existing, what its potentialities are for. So to perfect nature is to humanize it, to make it more useful for man's purposes, more intelligible to their reason, more beautiful to their eyes. . . . Man does not complete the universe simply by being in it . . . he helps to create it.[32]

The Aristotelian/Stoic "man perfecting Nature" position came to full flowering, according to Passmore, within the German idealist metaphysical tradition of Fichte and Hegel. Martin Heidegger (who dissented in some important ways from this position, but is ultimately embedded in this tradition) claimed that Hegel's Christianized pantheism held that "man himself is the universe achieving consciousness."[33] Passmore claims that this position was later incorporated into the thinking of Karl Marx, Herbert Marcuse, Pierre Teilhard de Chardin, and Ian McHarg. Marcuse follows the thinking of Fichte, according to Passmore, in holding that there are

> two kinds of [human] mastery: a repressive and a liberating one. Man's relationship to nature, Marcuse is prepared to admit, must at first be repressive, but as he civilises nature, he at the same time liberates it, frees it, as Hegel also suggests, from its "negativity," its hostility to spirit. . . . So what is wrong with our treatment of nature is . . . that we have used it destructively, as distinct from seeking to humanize it, spiritualize it.[34]

Actually, both the stewardship and the "man perfecting Nature" positions have historically promoted the complete humanization of the Earth as a goal.

Passmore represents Teilhard's thinking as being part of the "man perfecting Nature" position: a position that he sees as a continuation of the Greek Aristotelian tradition into the more recent Christianized German idealism of Hegel. According to Passmore, Teilhard believed that humans "must work *with* the world. They are the first beings sufficiently rational to see what nature, through gradual evolution, is doing, and sufficiently powerful to help it on its path towards that final consummation for which 'the whole creation groaneth and travaileth until now.' "[35]

Passmore thought these two models of the human/Nature relationship were converging in the 1970s and he endorsed them as the West's unique contribution to a sound contemporary approach to Nature.

It is instructive to observe Passmore wrestle with the basic conflicts between his anthropocentric stewardship/man-perfecting-Nature position, and ecological principles such as Barry Commoner's so-called Laws of Ecology, in the closing chapter of his book. Commoner's Third Law, that "Nature Knows Best" (that "any major manmade change in a natural system is likely to be *detrimental* to that system"), was so troublesome to Passmore that he misquoted it to read, "detrimental to some member of [that system]."[36]

The year after his book appeared, Passmore withdrew his endorsement of the anthropocentrism of both the "stewardship" and the "man perfecting Nature" positions, claiming, "We do need a 'new metaphysics' which is genuinely not anthropocentric. . . . The working out of such a metaphysics is, in my judgment, the most important task which lies ahead of philosophy. . . . This is the only adequate foundation for effective ecological concern."[37]

## NEW AGE, GAIAN CONSCIOUSNESS, AND THE "BUSINESS MANAGERS" OF EVOLUTION

Almost all societies throughout history have held that the Earth is a living organism or animal. The eclipse of this belief in the West, at the beginning of the seventeenth century, was a result of the rise of the Cartesian/Newtonian scientific worldview, which characterized the world as a machine.[38] In the 1970s, James Lovelock, while under contract with NASA, revived the world-as-organism image, this time as a sophisticated cybernetic theory, which he referred to as the Gaia hypothesis.[39] Lovelock drew several controversial philosophical and environmental implications from his hypothesis.

First of all, Lovelock (like many other technologists) initially had little sympathy with environmentalists, calling them "misanthropes" and "Luddites." He held that Gaia has "vital organs" that need to be protected (such as the continental shelves and the rain forests) but otherwise claimed that the Earth is very resilient and can withstand considerable abuse. Even nuclear war, he held, might not seriously damage Gaia.[40] Lovelock seemed to suggest that the rest of Gaia (other than the "vital organs") is open to unlimited development. And so the Gaia hypotheses by itself, as Anthony Weston points out, seems to produce little in the way of an environmental ethic.[41]

Second, ancient animistic views of the world-as-organism held that intelligence (soul, consciousness) permeates the *entire* world animal.[42] For example, we find in Plato's *Timaeus* the doctrine that "a soul had been diffused throughout the body of the world." Teilhard's metaphysics held, to the contrary, that the consciousness of the world is located almost exclusively in humans. As Conrad Bonifazi expresses this idea: "The earth is a psycho-somatic entity. Its psyche, extending from the biosphere, is principally concentrated in human beings." In other words, *humans* are the Earth's consciousness.[43] Lovelock seemed to support this anthropocentric Teilhardian view when he claimed that "the evolution of *Homo sapiens,* with his technological inventiveness and his increasingly subtle communications network, has vastly increased Gaia's range of perception. She is now through us awake and aware of herself."[44]

The New Age movement was ecstatic about Lovelock's Gaia hypothesis and speculations: Gaia conferences were rapidly convened where the talk was of humans as the intelligence ("the eyes and the ears") of Gaia, of "perfecting Nature (Gaia)" through genetic engineering, a takeover of the Earth's revolutinary processes, and of global management and development schemes based on vast electronic satellite communications systems. For example, New Age writer Paul Vajk wrote that "should we find it desirable, we will be able to turn the Sahara Desert into farms and forests, or remake the landscape of New England. . . . We are the legitimate children of Gaia; we need not be ashamed that we are altering the landscapes and ecosystems of Earth."[45]

Lovelock also endorsed Norman Myers's *Gaia: An Atlas of Planetary Management* (1984), which called for an inventory of the Earth's "resources" as a basis for efficient global planning and exploitation. For Meyers, the rain forests constitute a "gene library" for humans; the oceans are a "remarkably rich 'resource realm.'" Genetic engineering will provide a major solution to the ecological crisis. Meyers concludes: "with the power of life in our hands, we could, for instance, make forests spring up on bare lands . . . [and] redeploy the genetic wealth of evolution to craft organisms to work in partnership with us. . . . It is time for humanity to use this power, and use it well." Gavin Miller comments that, for Meyers, "the ecological crisis thus moves us not to the preservation of nature, but to the replacement of nature."[46]

Miller sees the Gaia hypothesis, as developed and interpreted by Lovelock, as an example of what Morris Berman calls the "cybernetic dream." The social critic Ivan Illich has extended Berman's analysis to an overall critique of the New Age approach to the Gaia hypothesis, global management schemes, and planetary consciousness. Illich believes that only small-scale technologies can save us from Orwellian surveillance and management by technocratic elites.[47]

New Age historian William Irwin Thompson at one time expressed reservations about "all these General Systems theorists and computer scientists who would manage the planet," claiming that systems analysis is "simply the ideological camouflage for the emergence of an industrial managerial elite." His hope was that the sterilizing influence of industrialism could be neutralized by New Age mysticism.[48] But in *The American Replacement of Nature* (1991), Thompson looks more positively on the "cybernetic dream." He sees the United States as leading the way toward a planetary culture: "from a literary and European culture to a planetary and electronic one." America is preparing the world for a new global culture in which Nature will be replaced by a wholly artificial environment ("humanity's second nature"), which Thompson looks upon as evolutionary progress for humans. He also looks approvingly on the possibility of "downloading" the human mind into a computer.[49]

The political scientist Walter Truett Anderson doesn't count himself as part of the New Age movement, but he nevertheless writes in the "man perfecting nature" tradition when he says: "while most environmentalists are searching for ways to lessen human intervention in the natural world, I believe that intervention is, in a sense, human destiny, and that our task is to learn how we may sanely and reverently take responsibility for the global ecosystem and the course of evolution." Anderson proposes that humans become the "business managers" of the Earth's evolutionary processes.[50]

A religious/philosophical foundation for the New Age has been developed by the philosopher Henryk Skolimowski (who was inspired by Teilhard), which he calls Ecological Humanism. For Skolimowski, the world is sacred—a sanctuary—but humans are the priests of the sanctuary. He states:

> The coming age is to be seen as the age of stewardship: we are here . . . to maintain and creatively transform, and to carry on the torch of evolution. . . . The universe is to be conceived of as home for man . . . we are the custodians of evolution . . . its crowning glory. . . . Evolution is conceived of as a humanization and spiritualization of primordial matters.[51]

Like Teilhard, Skolimowski sees humans as the culmination of the Earth's evolutionary processes; correspondingly, he holds a graded hierarchy of intrinsic value with humans (by virtue of the quality of their consciousness) at the top of the pyramid:

> We cannot sustain all forms of life. Within the structure of evolution, the more highly developed the organism, the greater is its complexity and its sensitivity and the more reason to treat it as more valuable and precious than others. . . .[52]

This approach is not only unecological in suggesting that "lower" forms of life are expendable, it is also inconsistent with a scientific understanding of biological evolution. One is reminded of the note Darwin scribbled to himself in terms of thinking about evolution: "Never use the words *higher* and *lower*."[53]

An especially stark example of New Age fear of (and alienation from) wild Nature, together with a New Age program for domination and control, comes from the philosopher James Christian:

> Man has loved his earth; it nourished him. But he has also hated it for its relentless attempt to annihilate him. . . . Man is on the threshold of setting controls over ever-larger forces of nature—climate and earthquakes, for instance. The control of life and evolution is near . . . man may eventually establish control on a cosmological scale. . . . Man is now in process of taking control of his own evolutionary destiny, and, by default, the destiny of all other living creatures on his planet. . . . [This is] part of the grand transition man is now undergoing . . . from being a *passively produced organism* to being the *active controller* of life and destiny. . . . Controls have now spread to almost every area of human experience. Lagging behind, of course, is control of man

himself, but this appears to be the area wherein the next giant steps will be taken.[54]

Murray Bookchin has criticized the New Age as well as the Deep Ecology movements, but Bookchin's post-Marxist Social Ecology position actually comes close to promoting a secular version of the New Age. Bookchin characterizes Social Ecology as a postmodern *ecological* worldview, but, over the years, he has been staunchly opposed to such crucial ecological concerns as human overpopulation and the protection of wilderness and wild species while criticizing, in the process, key environmental thinkers such as George Perkins Marsh, William Vogt, and Paul Ehrlich. Thus, Bookchin essentially "missed" the Ecological Revolution of the 1960s: his main ecological concern during this period was urban pollution.

Like Skolimowski and Teilhard, Bookchin holds that there is a teleological direction to natural evolutionary processes that has led to greater and greater complexity and consciousness, finally culminating in humans.[55] As is typical of many social scientists who promote the anthropocentric concepts of the "social construction of reality" (and Nature as a "social category"), Bookchin holds that modern society has evolved from, but transcended, its origins in wild Nature (and natural laws and constraints). He describes this process in terms of the "two worlds" image: a "second nature" of civilized urban society that has evolved from "first nature" (the domain of wild ecosystems and tribal peoples). The ecological/social problem, for Bookchin, is to "free" and "perfect" both "first nature" and "second nature" in a new synthesis which he calls "free nature." (Incidentally, this is precisely the opposite of what Arne Naess means by "free nature.") Janet Biehl provides a clear account of Bookchin's utopian vision:

> There remains still another step . . . that must be made in natural and social evolution . . . that transforms second nature . . . into a "synthesis" of first and second nature in the form of a harmonious, conscious, and ecological "free nature." In free nature, both human and nonhuman nature come into their own as a rational, self-conscious, and purposeful unity. Humanity, as a product of natural evolution, brings its consciousness to the service of both first and second nature . . . by diminishing the impact of natural catastrophes, and promoting the thrust of natural evolution toward diversity and ending needless suffering, thereby fueling the creativity of natural evolution through its technics, science, and rationality.[56]

As Bookchin describes his vision of human intervention into the natural evolutionary processes:

> Natural evolution has not only provided humans with [the] *ability* but also the *necessity* to be purposive interveners into "first nature," to consciously

change "first nature" . . . *neither first nature nor second would lose its specificity and integrity.* Humanity, far from diminishing the integrity of nature, would add the dimension of freedom, reason, and ethics to first nature and raise evolution to the level of self-reflexivity that has always been latent in the very emergence of the natural world.[57]

Bookchin has suggested, for example, that humans could intervene to convert the "Canadian barrens" into an area "supporting a rich variety of biota."[58] This proposal unfortunately ignores the wild species, and the integrity of the ecosystems, now existing in the "Canadian barrens." What is at issue here is precisely the question of the *integrity* of nonhuman species and individuals in terms of their "otherness" and difference from humans, and a respect for the ongoing *integrity* of wild evolutionary processes.

Bookchin's Social Ecology position is an outgrowth of the Aristotelian/Hegelian/Marxist tradition and it remains essentially within German idealist "man perfecting nature" visions. As with Marcuse, the wild is "liberated" and made "free" for Bookchin when humans override natural spontaneous processes and "rationally" direct the Earth's evolutionary processes.[59]

## DEEP ECOLOGY AND THE NEW AGE

The leading environmental science textbook writer, G. Tyler Miller, saw the basic problem with Teilhardian New Age anthropocentrism in 1972 when he called for an end to Western unecological ideologies of human domination and control over the Earth:

> Our task is not to learn how to pilot spaceship earth [for Miller, the metaphor "spaceship earth" is itself an arrogant mechanistic misdescription of an organic Earth]. It is not to learn how—as Teilhard de Chardin would have it—to "seize the tiller of the world." Our task is to give up our fantasies of omnipotence. In other words, we must stop trying to steer. The solution to our present dilemma does not lie in attempting to extend our technical and managerial skills into every sphere of existence. Thus, *from a human standpoint our environmental crisis is the result of our arrogance toward nature.*[60]

A major breakthrough for Teilhard's anthropocentric orientation came, in a dramatic and forthright move, from the Catholic scholar (and president of the American Teilhard de Chardin Society) Thomas Berry. In 1982, Berry proposed a radical ecological revision of Teilhard's theology, claiming that "the opinion is correct that Teilhard does not in any direct manner support the ecological mode of consciousness." Berry pointed out that

> [Teilhard] fully accepted the technological and industrial exploitation of the planet as a desirable human activity. . . . Teilhard establishes the human as

his exclusive norm of values, a norm that requires the human to invade and to control rationally the spontaneities of nature . . . there is no question of accepting the natural world in its own spontaneous modes of being . . . this would be a treachery to the demands of the evolutionary process.[61]

Berry further states that Teilhard's position needs to be modified to reflect an ecocentric perspective:

the evolutionary process [Berry claims] finds its highest expression in the earth community seen in its comprehensive dimensions, not simply in a human community reigning in triumphal dominion over the other components of the earth community. The same evolutionary process has produced all the living and non-living components of the planet.[62]

The Christian scholar Jay McDaniel recently argues for the "stewardship as dominion" position. He characterizes this as "wise management undergirded by respect for life and environment." Instead of arguing for the merits of this position, he asserts that "our dominion is now irreversible" because there are now too many people on Earth. By holding the rather narrow view that a natural catastrophe is the only way the population can be reduced to a much smaller ecologically compatible level, he argues that our "best option" is

(1) to accept the ambiguity of such a high number of humans on the planet; (2) to stabilize that population as much as possible; and then (3) to find ways of allowing six to eleven billion people to live on the planet in ways that are ecologically wise. In the best of scenarios, we are doomed to dominion.[63]

For McDaniel, the image of humans as stewards (and "masters over the world") is a *fait accompli*. The Deep Ecology platform, by contrast, calls not only for population stabilization, but for the reduction of the size of the human population to allow for the full diversity and abundance of life forms on the Earth. In his desire to advocate the stewardship position, McDaniel overlooks the possibility of promoting vigorous but humane *long-range* programs of steady low birthrates throughout the world. Conservation biologists agree that 6 to 11 billion people on Earth is clearly ecologically unsustainable and will lead only to further human misery and a biologically impoverished Earth.

In contrast with the global consumerist "new world order" promised by corporate elites that is now merging with New Age megatechnology utopian visions, the Deep Ecology position advocates a vision of humans living creatively in harmonious ecological balance with the Earth and its nonhuman inhabitants.

Aldo Leopold viewed humans as just "plain members" of the ecological community, and as "only fellow-voyagers with other creatures in the odyssey of evolution." Thomas Berry holds, however, that humans are a unique species as a result of our self-reflexive consciousness. We are the only species that can appreciate the main features of the cosmological and biological evolutionary processes.

Arne Naess also believes that humans are "very special beings!" The problem, in Naess's view, is that we "underestimate our potentialities" both as individuals and as a species. Our ability to understand and identify with Life on Earth suggests a role primarily as "conscious joyful appreciator of this planet as an even greater whole of its immense richness."⁶⁴ We can become "ecological selves." As is typical throughout the history of our species, major religious/philosophical paradigm shifts often result in new/old perspectives on what it is to be human.

# NOTES

1. An earlier version of this paper was published as "Deep Ecology, New Age, and Gaian Consciousness," *Earth First! Journal* 7, 8 (1987): 27, 29–30. There is also a critique of New Age in B. Devall and G. Sessions, *Deep Ecology* (Utah: Peregrine Smith, 1985), pp. 5–6, 138–44. This revision (1993) has benefited enormously from Gavin C. Miller's excellent paper "Teilhard de Chardin and Environmental Thought," M.A. thesis, Faculty of Environmental Studies, York University, Ontario, Canada, 1993, submitted in revised form for publication to *Environmental Ethics*. I am most grateful to Gavin for giving me permission to draw from it.

2. Miller, ibid., p. 36; David Spangler, *Emergence: The Rebirth of the Sacred* (New York: Dell, 1984), p. 38; Jerry Mander, *In the Absence of the Sacred: The Failure of Technology and the Survival of the Indian Nations* (San Francisco: Sierra Club Books, 1991), pp. 146–48). Mander's book is a powerful critique of the corporate/consumer/megatechnology vision.

3. Alvin Toffler, *Powershift* (New York: Bantam Books, 1990), pp. 364–79; George Gilder, "The American 80's: Disaster or Triumph?" *Commentary* (Sept. 1990): 17–19; Francis Fukuyama, "The End of History," cited in Christopher Lasch, "The Fragility of Liberalism," *Salmagundi* 92 (Fall 1991): 5–18. See Miller, "Teilhard and Environmental Thought," pp. 38, 51.

4. Alston Chase, *Playing God in Yellowstone* (Boston: Atlantic Monthly Press, 1986), pp. 344–62; Murray Bookchin, *Remaking Society* (Boston: South End Press, 1990), pp. 11–12.

5. Miller, "Teilhard," pp. 35–36; Marilyn Ferguson, *The Aquarian Conspiracy: Personal and Social Transformation in the 1980's* (New York: St. Martin's, 1980), pp. 20, 434.

6. Buckminister Fuller, *Critical Path,* pp. 251, 297, 306. This reference was supplied to me by Bill McCormick.

7. Miller, "Teilhard," p. 112; Stewart Brand (ed.), *Space Colonies* (New York: Penguin, 1977).

8. Pierre Teilhard de Chardin, *Letters to Two Friends: 1926–1952* (New York: New American Library, 1968), pp. 153–55.

9. Miller, "Teilhard," p. 111.

10. Conrad Bonifazi, "Teilhard de Chardin and the Future," paper read at Rice University, Houston, Texas, October 1968.

11. Miller, "Teilhard," pp. 22–23, 35.

12. Teilhard de Chardin, *The Appearance of Man* (London: Collins, 1965), pp. 250–52; Teilhard de Chardin, *The Activation of Energy* (London: Collins, 1970), pp. 159, 304, 325; see also Julian Simon, *The Ultimate Resource* (Princeton: Princeton University Press, 1981).

13. Teilhard de Chardin, *The Phenomenon of Man* (New York: Harper and Row, 1959), p. 175. Miller, "Teilhard," p. 24.

14. Teilhard, ibid., pp. 282–83; Lewis Mumford, *The Pentagon of Power* (New York: Harcourt, Brace, Jovanovich, 1970), pp. 208–9, 314–17; Miller, "Teilhard," pp. 28, 95–96.

15. Morris Berman, "The Cybernetic Dream of the Twenty-first Century," *Journal of Humanistic Psychology* 26, 2 (1986): 24–51; for other critiques of "computer consciousness," see Theodore Roszak, *The Cult of Information* (London: Paladin, 1988); Jeremy Rifkin, *Time Wars* (New York: Henry Holt, 1987).

16. Berman, ibid., pp. 32, 41–42.

17. See Jeremy Rifkin, *Algeny: A New Word—a New World* (New York: Viking, 1983).

18. Jeremy Rifkin, *Biosphere Politics: A New Consciousness for a New Century* (New York: Crown Publishers, 1991), pp. 236–44.

19. Jerry Mander, *Four Arguments for the Elimination of Television* (New York: Morrow, 1978), p. 24.

20. Eric Drexler, *Engines of Creation: The Coming Era of Nanotechnology* (New York: Doubleday, 1987); Grant Fjermedal, *The Tomorrow Makers* (New York: Macmillan, 1986); see also Gregory Stock, *Metaman: The Merging of Humans and Machines into a Global Superorganism* (New York: Simon and Schuster, 1993).

21. Jerry Mander, *In the Absence of the Sacred*, pp. 181–82.

22. Hans Moravec, *Mind Children: The Future of Robot and Human Intelligence* (Cambridge: Harvard University Press, 1988); Moravec's views are discussed in Mander, ibid., pp. 183–86; Rifkin, *Biosphere Politics*, p. 245.

23. Lynn White, Jr., "Historical Roots of Our Ecologic Crisis," *Science* 155 (1967): 1203–7.

24. Conrad Bonifazi, *The Soul of the World: An Account of the Inwardness of Things* (Washington, D.C.: University Press of America, 1978): 218–21; for a critique of Bonifazi's Teilhardian theology, see George Sessions, "Review of Conrad Bonifazi, *The Soul of the World,*" *Environmental Ethics* 3, 3 (1981): 275–81; Judeo-Christian views of wilderness and primal peoples as evil and in need of "redemption" greatly influenced and rationalized the European invasion, settlement, and exploitation of the North American continent (as well as elsewhere throughout the world); this

is documented in the opening chapters of Roderick Nash, *Wilderness and the American Mind,* 3rd ed. (New Haven: Yale University Press, 1982).

25. Thomas Berry, *Teilhard in the Ecological Age* (Chambersberg, Penn.: Anima Books, 1982). One of the first Christian scholars to criticize Teilhard from an ecological perspective was Frederick Elder, who found Teilhard to be "fiercely anthropocentric." It is not without significance that Elder found two other leading American Christian theologians, Herbert Richardson and Harvey Cox, promoting on religious grounds a wholly artificial urban environment. As a basis for a new Christian ecotheology, Elder looked to the ecocentrism of Loren Eiseley (see Frederick Elder, *Crisis in Eden: A Religious Study of Man and the Environment* (Nashville, Tenn.: Abingdon Press, 1970).

26. John Passmore, *Man's Responsibility for Nature: Ecological Problems and Western Traditions* (New York: Scribner's, 1974), chaps. 1, 2.

27. Ibid., pp. 3–30.

28. René Dubos, *A God Within* (New York: Scribner's, 1972), pp. 135–74.

29. René Dubos, *The Wooing of the Earth* (New York: Scribner's, 1980), p. 79.

30. Paul Shepard, *The Tender Carnivore and the Sacred Game* (New York: Scribner's, 1973), p. 237.

31. See René Dubos, "A Theology of the Earth," and Lynn White, Jr., "Continuing the Conversation," in Ian G. Barbour (ed.), *Western Man and Environmental Ethics* (Reading, Mass.: Addison-Wesley, 1973); on April 6, 1980, a papal bull (issued by Pope John Paul II) was announced in Assisi proclaiming Saint Francis to be the patron saint of ecologists, but, as Lynn White pointed out, Benedictine views were attributed to Francis: specifically that Francis "considered nature as a marvellous gift from God to humanity." White quipped, "What *will* become of the dogma of papal infallibility if this sort of bungling continues?!" (personal correspondence, May 1, 1980). White had proposed Saint Francis as the "patron saint of ecology" in his 1966 "Historical Roots" paper.

32. Passmore, *Man's Responsibility for Nature:* 32–33.

33. Ibid., pp. 35, 34; for Heidegger's characterization of Hegel, see Michael Zimmerman, "Technological Culture and the End of Philosophy," in *Research in Philosophy and Technology,* vol. 2 (Greenwich, Conn.: Jai Press, 1979).

34. Passmore, p. 35.

35. Ibid., pp. 34–35.

36. Passmore, p. 185; for a statement of the "Laws of Ecology," see Barry Commoner, *The Closing Circle: Nature, Man, and Technology* (New York: Knopf, 1971), p. 41.

37. John Passmore, "Attitudes toward Nature," in R. S. Peters (ed.), *Nature and Conduct* (New York: Macmillan, 1975), p. 260.

38. See Conrad Bonifazi, *The Soul of the World,* p. ix.

39. James Lovelock, *Gaia: A New Look at Life on Earth* (New York: Oxford University Press, 1979).

40. Lovelock, *Gaia,* pp. 41, 116, 118ff.

41. Anthony Weston, "Forms of Gaian Ethics," *Environmental Ethics* 9, 3 (1987): 221. Weston's paper presents an excellent summary of Lovelock's hypothesis and an analysis of its ethical implications.

42. See David Abram, "The Perceptual Implications of Gaia," *The Ecologist* 15, 3 (1985): 96–103.

43. Bonifazi, *The Soul of the World*, p. 232.

44. Lovelock, *Gaia*, p. 148.

45. J. Peter Vajk, *Doomsday Has Been Cancelled* (Menlo Park, Calif.: Peace Publishers, 1978), p. 61.

46. Norman Meyers, *Gaia: An Atlas of Planet Management* (Garden City, N.Y.: Anchor Press, 1984), p. 257; Miller, "Teilhard," pp. 61–63.

47. Miller, "Teilhard," p. 89; Ivan Illich, *In the Mirror of the Past* (New York: Marion Boyers, 1992).

48. William Irwin Thompson, *Evil and World Order* (New York: Harper & Row, 1976), pp. 87, 89, 106; see also W. I. Thompson, *Passages about Earth* (New York: Harper & Row, 1974).

49. William Irwin Thompson, *The American Replacement of Nature* (New York: Doubleday, 1991), pp. 9, 113; see also W. I. Thompson (ed.), *Gaia 2: Emergence, The New Science of Becoming* (New York: Lindisfarne Press, 1991). For a discussion of Thompson's views, see Miller, "Teilhard," pp. 54–56.

50. Walter Truett Anderson, *To Govern Evolution: Further Adventures of the Political Animal* (New York: Harcourt Brace Jovanovich, 1987); for an ecological critique of biotechnology and the human takeover of Earth's evolutionary processes, see Rifkin, *Algeny.*

51. Henryk Skolimowski, *Eco-Philosophy: Designing New Tactics for Living* (London: Marion Boyers, 1981), pp. 54–55, 74–86; see also George Sessions, "Review of Skolimowski, *Eco-Philosophy,*" *Environmental Ethics* 6, 2 (1984): 167–74.

52. Skolimowski, ibid., pp. 83–84.

53. The Darwin quote appears in Roderick Nash, *The Rights of Nature: A History of Environmental Ethics* (Madison: University of Wisconsin, 1989), p. 42.

54. James Christian, *Philosophy: An Introduction to the Art of Wondering,* 3rd ed. (New York: Holt, Rinehart & Winston, 1981), pp. 357, 375, 381–82.

55. For a critique of Bookchin's evolutionary views and biotechnology proposals, see Robyn Eckersley, "Divining Evolution: The Ecological Ethics of Murray Bookchin," *Environmental Ethics* 11 (1989): 99–116; see also Kirkpatrick Sale, "Deep Ecology and Its Critics," *The Nation* 22 (May 14, 1988): 670–75.

56. Janet Biehl, "Dialectics in the Ethics of Social Ecology," in Michael Zimmerman, et al. (eds.), *Environmental Philosophy: From Animal Rights to Radical Ecology* (Englewood Cliffs, N.J.: Prentice-Hall, 1993), p. 387.

57. Murray Bookchin, "Social Ecology versus Deep Ecology," *Green Perspectives: A Newsletter of the Green Program* (Summer, 1987), p. 21; Bookchin, *The Philosophy of Social Ecology* (Montreal: Black Rose Books, 1990), pp. 182–83.

58. Murray Bookchin, "Recovering Evolution: A Reply to Eckersley and Fox," *Environmental Ethics* 12, no. 3 (1990): 272–73; for a discussion of Bookchin's proposals, see Andrew McLaughlin, *Regarding Nature: Industrialism and Deep Ecology* (Albany: State University of New York Press, 1993), pp. 215–17.

59. Murray Bookchin, *Remaking Society: Pathways to a Green Future* (Boston: South End Press, 1990), p. 204; for a comparison of the views of Bookchin and Marcuse, see Andrew Light, "Rereading Bookchin and Marcuse as Environmental Materialists," *Capitalism, Nature and Socialism* 4, no. 1 (1993): 69–98.

60. G. Tyler Miller, Jr., *Replenish the Earth: A Primer in Human Ecology* (Belmont, Calif.: Wadsworth, 1972), p. 53; see also G. Tyler Miller, Jr., *Living in the Environment: An Introduction to Environmental Science,* 6th ed. (Belmont, Calif.: Wadsworth, 1990).

61. Thomas Berry, *Teilhard in the Ecological Age* (Chambersburg, Pa.: Anima Books, 1982); quotes are from a selection from this book reprinted in Devall and Sessions, *Deep Ecology,* p. 143.

62. Ibid.

63. Jay McDaniel, "The Garden of Eden, the Fall, and Life in Christ: A Christian Approach to Ecology," in Mary Tucker and John Grim (eds.), *World Views and Ecology* (Lewisburg, Pa.: Bucknell University Press, 1993), pp. 74–75.

64. Arne Naess, "The Green Society and Deep Ecology" (The 1987 Schumacher Lecture), unpublished manuscript, p. 18; Arne Naess, "The Arrogance of Antihumanism?" *Ecophilosophy Newsletter* (1984): 8.

Michael Zimmerman has favorably compared Naess's views with the views of Murray Bookchin, but it is of course one thing to be primarily an "appreciator" of the biotic exuberance of the Earth, quite another to promote major intervention and control of the evolutionary processes; see Zimmerman, "Deep Ecology, Ecoactivism, and Human Evolution," *Revision* 13, 3 (1991): 127. Zimmerman continues to attempt to bring together the very different views of Deep Ecology and Social Ecology in his *Contesting Earth's Future* (Berkeley: University of California Press, 1994).

# 29 | LEAVING THE EARTH
## SPACE COLONIES, DISNEY, AND EPCOT

*Jerry Mander*

"You KNOW, JERRY, I feel like things are really closing in. There doesn't seem to be any escape now; nowhere that's not being made over."

Speaking to me was the artist Elizabeth Garsonnin. She continued:

"I can really identify with the young people today; how trapped they must feel. The natural world is almost gone, and it's being replaced by this awful hard-edged, commercial creation, with techno-humans running it. They're already in Antarctica. They're in all the jungles. They're tagging all the animals. Their satellites are photographing everything. They know what's in the ground and what's on the land. Soon they'll be on Venus and Mars. And they're inside human cells. Where is there left for the mind to flee? They've even invaded the subjective spaces, the fantasy world. As an artist I feel as if the sources of creation are being wiped out and paved over. It makes the only viable art protest art, but I hate that. It means they already have us confined; we can only react to *them*. I am so sad." . . .

## BANISHMENT FROM EDEN

Over the years, I have wondered about the apparently strong appeal of space travel and development to the public mind. I can understand why corporations, militaries, and governments want to promote departing from the planet, and I have mentioned its appeal to the New Age collective ego. But it hasn't been easy for me to grasp why the idea is so attractive to others. I finally

Originally published (in a longer version) in Jerry Mander, *In the Absence of the Sacred: The Failure of Technology and the Survival of the Indian Nations* (San Francisco: Sierra Club Books, 1991). Copyright © 1991 by Jerry Mander. Reprinted with permission of Sierra Club Books.

realized that space travel is not new; it is only the final stage of a departure process that actually began long ago. Our society really "left home" when we placed boundaries between ourselves and the earth, when we moved en masse inside totally artificial, reconstructed, "mediated" worlds—huge concrete cities and suburbs—and we aggressively ripped up and redesigned the natural world. By now, nature has literally receded from our view and diminished in size. We have lost contact with our roots. As a culture, we don't know where we came from; we're not aware we are part of something larger than ourselves. Nor can we easily find places that reveal natural processes still at work.

. . . As a corporate culture, we have begun to feel that one place is as good as the next; that it's okay to sacrifice this place for that one, even when the new place is not even on Earth. In the end, this leaves us all in a position similar to the millions of homeless people on our streets. In truth, we are all homeless, though we long to return.

My friend Gary Coates, an architecture professor at Kansas State University, . . . has argued provocatively that our quest for space is actually a distorted expression of a desire to return *home* to Eden, the place we abandoned. He sees our whole culture as caught in a replay of the Adam-and-Eve story.

In a recent conversation, Coates put it to me this way:

"Like all creation myths, the story of the Garden of Eden is not something that never happened or only happened long ago; it is something that is happening in every moment. . . . It was the murder of Abel, who represented a state of oneness with the earth, that set Cain off wandering in a never-satisfied quest for the return to, or re-creation of, paradise. Within the confines of our totally artificial environments on Earth, as they will soon also be in heaven, we also seek to re-enter Eden. In particular, the creation of the Leisureworlds, Disney Worlds, megamalls, Air Stream mobile home cities, lifestyle-segregated condominium communities, and especially genetic engineering, space coloni- zation, and terraforming of planets, are all updated forms of Cain's desire to return home by remaking the original creation. The tragedy is that in attempt- ing to recover paradise we accelerate the murder of nature. It's yet another repeat of the story of Cain and Abel, another acting out of the founding myth of Western history."

Coates is especially passionate about the role played today by theme-park environments; megamalls like Canada's West Edmonton Mall, and places like Disney World, Seaworld, and EPCOT Center. He argues that it is in these megamalls and theme parks that we are all being psychologically trained for our future in space. In those places, he adds, "we can see the emerging mind- scape and landscape . . . we can actually experience our existence as prepro- grammed participants in someone else's pre-engineered fantasies."

If not everyone can get to live in the utopian future world within plastic bubbles on Mars, everyone *can* experience more or less what it would be like right here on this planet in these self-contained bubbles of artificial life on Earth.

"Like the initiatory temples of Egypt and Greece," says Coates, "Disney World and the other worlds are the actual places where it is possible to understand fully the new mysteries. Space and time are collapsed and reality is re-created and fragmented just like on television. Things are only held together by the collage of stories that constitute the mythology of Progress. . . . When we are in Disney World or Seaworld or Leisureworld, as with television-world, we are inside someone else's story; we cannot tell what is reality and what is not. In the preplanned lifestyle communities, we construct our places of dwelling into stage sets for the re-creation of TV fantasies. We are finally figuring out how to live forever, disembodied inside our television sets, so that we shall never have to go outside again. This situation trains us well for the disconnected world of space colonies, robotics, genetic engineering, and Star Wars that are our "real" tomorrow-land. Combined, the theme parks reveal the logic and architecture of hyper-reality; the world Umberto Eco calls 'the absolutely fake.' "

Coates persuaded me that I should visit some of these places, and to view them as training grounds for a future disconnection from Earth. "They are every bit as powerful as the World's Fair of 1940," he said, "and with similar implications." So in 1988 I visited the West Edmonton Mall and EPCOT Center. Of the two, EPCOT is the more explicit in its goals. It *intends* to train people to live in and to like a certain kind of future. The West Edmonton Mall, on the other hand, is only a commercial shopping mall and amusement park, albeit the largest in the world. I doubt it was conceived as a preview of life in a Martian self-contained bubble environment. But it is such a preview nonetheless.

## THE WEST EDMONTON MALL, EDMONTON, CANADA

Edmonton is emphatically un-Martian. The city is the center of a spectacular natural landscape of sensuous grassy plains, wild rivers, great Rocky Mountains; it serves as the gateway to the untamed northern wilderness of Canada. But on the edge of the city is the West Edmonton Mall, and the point of that place is to re-create artificial versions of environments that are not in the vicinity. In that sense it is an otherworldly container of artificial reality planted into an alien landscape. In one visit you can get a fair sense of what would be considered crucial to a future life off the earth, where all human needs and pleasures are preplanned. Or, as the mall's brochure puts it, "The very best and most exciting natural wonders of the earth," within an environment of 889 stores. The brochure calls the mall "The Eighth Wonder of the World." And it is.

When I visited the mall, my favorite "natural environment" was the World Waterpark. Contained within a glass dome sixteen stories high, the Waterpark is the size of five football fields. It includes a giant concrete beach with a raging surf and real waves up to eight feet high, controlled by a computerized wave machine. Unfortunately, surfboarding was not permitted, although I saw dozens of people bodysurfing.

The air outside the mall was 20 degrees Fahrenheit on the day I visited, but inside the World Waterpark it was maintained at a constant 86 degrees. There were sunlamps for tanning and twenty-two water slides, including the Raging River, which simulates river rapids. You can rent rubber tubes and ride the "rapids" any day of the year.

If you prefer the open ocean to beaches, the West Edmonton Mall offers a "Deep Sea Adventure." You can take an underwater cruise in a thirty-three-foot submarine, which submerges and cruises in fifteen feet of water. Or you can pet the four Atlantic bottlenose dolphins swimming in the same miniocean in which the submarine cruises.

There are more than thirty aquariums throughout the mall, containing "more than 1,000 hand-picked specimens from the waters of Hawaii, Mexico, the Philippines, Australia, the Caribbean, South America, Japan, Canada, and the U.S.," according to the mall's brochure.

If your taste in natural wonders runs to birds and animals, the West Edmonton Mall has plenty. Glass-enclosed environments amidst the stores contain more than 250 exotic birds, including great flamingos from South America, several varieties of "intelligent and talented parrots," giant elands from South America, and many others. "All birds are housed in large aviaries," according to the developers, "which are representative of their natural habitats."

As for animals, there are mountain lions, tigers, spider monkeys, squirrel monkeys, black bears, French lopears, and jaguars, and your child can pet a "wide range of domestic animals throughout the complex." There are also 28,000 plants living nicely inside the mall, "many of which are rare and exotic species."

In addition to "natural wonders," the West Edmonton Mall offers some of the most romantic travel destinations on Earth. Want to be in Rome? The mall's Fantasyland Hotel features Roman rooms you can rent, with white marble, Roman statues and pillars, and an authentic Roman bath with mirrored walls. How about Arabia? Beds are surrounded with imitation sand dunes. The Polynesian rooms feature beds within a "warrior catamaran under full sail," as well as simulated volcanic eruptions. The West Edmonton Mall world traveler can also visit a re-creation of Bourbon Street, New Orleans, or a replica of a Parisian neighborhood on Europe Boulevard.

Elsewhere, the mall offers a full-sized ice-skating rink, an amusement park featuring a sixteen-story roller coaster, a 1.5-mile jogging track, a miniature golf course called Pebble Beach, a scaled replica of Christopher Columbus's ship *Santa Maria,* and, oh yes, 210 women's fashion stores, 35 menswear stores, 55 shoe stores, 35 jewelry stores, 11 major department stores, 19 movie theaters, 110 restaurants, 2 car dealerships, and 351 other miscellaneous shops, services, and natural wonders. Hey, if you can re-create such a complete world within a dome in Edmonton, Canada, why not do it on Mars?

## EPCOT CENTER, ORLANDO, FLORIDA

. . . Never having been to Disney World, I try to educate myself about the place. From the book *Walt Disney World,* published by the Disney Company, I learn the goal is "to make dreams come true." I also learn the place is ten times the size of Southern California's Disneyland, covering 27,000 acres—it is a self-contained total universe divided into four areas: the Vacation Kingdom, which contains all the hotels, golf courses, artificial lakes, water paradises, and artificial beaches; the Magic Kingdom, EPCOT Center, and within EPCOT, the World Showcase.

The largest and main attraction is the Magic Kingdom, itself divided into six "theme parks": Main Street, U.S.A.; Fantasyland; Adventureland; Frontierland; Liberty Square; and Tomorrowland. Each of these "theme parks" is an unabashed attempt to concretize our popular fantasies about American life and American adventure and travel. Each park reaches into our minds to pull out and re-create the movie and schoolroom images from our childhoods, and to put us in them as if they *were* real.

Main Street, U.S.A. is a prime example. According to the brochures, Main Street, U.S.A. "gives us a tantalizing look at the best of the 'good old days.' It is America between 1890 and 1910." It's a world of gingerbread houses, charming horse carts sharing the road with "old" cars, barbershop quartets, choo-choo trains, and penny arcades. No unions in this vision. No blacks-only and whites-only water fountains. No Indians. No poverty. It's a series of Hollywood images of America that might have emerged from the brain of Ronald Reagan.

Where Main Street, U.S.A. fictionalizes reality, Fantasyland makes "real" what has been imaginary: the Disney film characters. Cinderella is there with all the other cartoon people, including Peter Pan, Pinocchio, Snow White, the dwarfs, and all their cartoon environments of castles, drawbridges, forests, and fairylands.

As for Adventureland, the official Disney book says, "Disney Imagineers strove to make it 'a wonderland of nature's own design.' It is obvious to anyone who journeys through this exotic land that this direction was followed, leaf, stalk, and petal. A veritable United Nations of plants was assembled to represent the tropical regions of the world."

The word EPCOT is actually an acronym for Experimental Prototype Community of Tomorrow. "The dominions of Future World literally know no bounds," says the official Disney document, speaking the infinite-growth wisdom of corporate society. EPCOT Center was invented to make us comfortable with these nonboundaries of tomorrow. One exhibit puts EPCOT's goals very explicitly: to "help people who are unsure about these changes, or feel intimidated by futuristic [environments and] seemingly complex systems, the . . . exhibits are aimed at making us feel comfortable with computers and other implements of high technology."

. . . First, we dropped into Exxon Corporation's Universe of Energy. We entered a room that was set up as a huge theater. We were startled to realize that the rows of the theater were moving and rearranging themselves into a gigantic moving vehicle. A disembodied voice told us we were embarking on a "journey through time," to experience the history of the creation of energy. A diorama of the "world of dinosaurs" showed the creatures moving and threatening each other and us; strong scents were somehow emitted. The presentation effectively evoked a terrifying prehuman time. When our gigantic vehicle passed beyond the time travel, the loudspeaker said, "Welcome back, folks, to the twentieth century." Sighs of relief all around. Then the music suddenly alluded to *Star Wars* themes—with no credits to composers or performers—and we were launched into visions of tomorrow, a time "of unlimited electric energy" to fuel our dreams of a better world.

Next was the Horizons pavilion, created by General Electric Corporation. There, we were immediately put on a space shuttle to tomorrow, where they played almost exactly the same music as Exxon played (do these composers all know each other?), and where we could see dioramas of vast undersea cities and cities that float on top of the sea. We saw high-tech colonies in space. And in the section about the earth, we saw the most impressive display of all: a huge farm stretching to the horizon amidst what was once a desert. Now, we were told, the farm grows computer-controlled, worker-free, genetically engineered crops. The General Electric announcer kept repeating the slogan, "If we can dream it, we can do it."

Third, we visited "the land created by Kraft Foods Corporation." We were placed into little boats that floated downstream on a "journey to a place most of us have forgotten about: the place where food is grown." They showed the family farm—amidst appropriate odors of hay and dung—a wonderful relic from a bygone era. "Each year," came the voice over the loudspeaker, "the family farm is being replaced by business as farming becomes a science. With better seeds, better pesticides, and better techniques, we're moving into a new era." Soon after, our boat floated into a modern laboratory within a kind of greenhouse. Here was obviously where food is *now* grown. "This is what's called Controlled Environment Agriculture. . . . Nature by itself is not always productive," says the scientific voice of Kraft. We then floated past exhibits of totally mechanized farming. We saw new plant species now being developed that discard such wasteful elements as branches or trunks; we saw fruit growing directly out of plastic tubes. Many new species need no soil to grow in; they are hung in the lab and fed by an automatic, computer-controlled spray.

Throughout, we hear a chorus of children's voices singing a Woody Guthrie–type melody, "Let's listen to the land we all love . . ."

And so it went throughout EPCOT. The corporations and the new technologies are there to make our lives better. The future will be a lot better than the present. We don't need to maintain our charming but hindering bonds to such anomalies as land, family farms (or any farms), or community, or the natural world. All we need do now is relax, float in our little cars, and be awed with the skill, thoughtfulness, imagination, and devotion of these can-do visionary corporations and their astounding new tools. We can all look forward to a future of very little work, total comfort, and complete technological control of the environment, the weather, nature, and *us*. Our role? To trust their leadership and vision. To enjoy it, to live in it, and to watch it like a movie.

The technological visions of EPCOT Center didn't bother me much. I had seen such things before, all the way back to the 1940 World's Fair. What *really* got to me was walking around the grounds in the world of EPCOT. Like everywhere in Disney World, the grounds were perfectly groomed; so manicured that they seemed unreal, part of a stage set, which of course is what they were. The idea was to show the perfect control over the environment that technical experts can achieve. I never saw a loose piece of paper or a patch of brown grass. The rivers that meandered through the place were encased in concrete culverts, totally dead save for the movement of the waters—except for one little lake that had been stocked with minnows and other small fish. I was surprised at that until I realized these real life-forms were there on behalf of a small flock of pink flamingos, who ate them. Pink flamingos! Dreambirds.

Just as the "natural environment" at EPCOT had been perfected and packaged so as to eliminate any of nature's troubling variabilities, so had the people who worked there. Everyone wore green and white costumes, similar to the crew of "Star Trek." Everyone was clean and perfectly groomed. (The EPCOT representative who ushered around the Norwegian musicians told them that she had recently been criticized for allowing her fingernails to grow longer than one-sixteenth of an inch.)

Everyone at EPCOT smiled. Every question was answered in perfect sentences as if prerecorded. Everyone followed the rules to the letter. And it was clear that *we* had better follow the rules as well. . . .

The whole place is a visionary, futuristic projection of a utopian, computerized, technologized police state, where human behavior is as predefined as the perfect grass lawns. It is a logical extension of the corporate vision that has been steadily evolving for decades. We were shown a future where every blade of grass was in place, and the bird population is idealized to pink flamingos, all as part of an ideal future that includes every human being's emotions, genes, and experience. Brave New World. You either follow the lines or you are shipped out. The purpose? Efficiency, production, expansion, and a kind, measured, commodity-oriented, mesmerized, programmed, fictional, Disneyesque "happiness." . . .

## SAN FRANCISCO, THE THEME PARK

If places like the West Edmonton Mall and EPCOT Center are expressions of, and training grounds for, a culture preparing itself to depart from the planet, everyday life is becoming that way as well. The city of San Francisco, for example, where I live, has begun a process similar to many American cities, assessing its unique features and packaging them for a world of travel consumers hungry for a taste of unrooted, artificial-authentic experience. Whatever authenticity the city once had is quickly disappearing as its authentic features are converted into commodity form. This is the same logic as the West Edmonton Mall, which re-creates Bourbon Street and Polynesia in a domed environment in the freezing north of Canada. Uprooted as we all are, not attached to any place in particular, anyplace can now be anywhere, and authentic places can become "theme parks" of themselves.

When I first moved to San Francisco in 1960, the cable cars were transportation. My kids paid a quarter and rode them to school every day. Now, the cable cars have been reassessed. Most of the lines have been ripped out, save the ones that run from downtown hotels to Fisherman's Wharf. Now, a cable car costs $2.50 per ride, and you rarely see a San Franciscan on one. Similarly,

Fisherman's Wharf, which used to be for working fishermen, now has only a facade fishing fleet, to lure tourists. In fact, the entire city is rapidly becoming a replica of itself, and life within the city approaches what it would surely be like if lived inside Disney World. San Francisco is becoming "San Francisco, the theme park." Soon, we will find a way to re-create the 1989 earthquake.

Gary Coates put the trend this way: "I fully expect that before too long, some entire nation with a depressed economy, perhaps England, will change its name to Olde England, charge visitors a fee at the border, and hand them a book of tickets for the various attractions: Double-decker buses! Charming Shakespearean Stratford! Real soccer riots for your entertainment! The actual battlefield of the 300 Years' War between Olde England and Olde Ireland!"

Remaking authentic communities into packaged forms of themselves, re-creating environments in one place that actually belong somewhere else, creating theme parks and lifestyle-segregated communities, and space travel and colonization—all are symptomatic of the same modern malaise: a disconnection from a place on Earth that we can call Home. With the natural world—our true home—removed from our lives, we have built on top of the pavement a new world, a new Eden, perhaps; a mental world of creative dreams. We then live within these fantasies of our own creation; we live within our own minds. Though we are still on the planet Earth, we are disconnected from it, afloat on pavement, in the same way the astronauts float in space.

That our culture has taken this step into artificial worlds on and off the planet is a huge risk, for the logical result is disorientation and madness and, as Coates argues, the obsessive need to attempt to re-create nature and life.

PART FIVE | # WILDERNESS, THE WILD, AND CONSERVATION BIOLOGY

# INTRODUCTION

As a direct descendant of the Thoreau/Muir/Leopold tradition, and the Ecological Revolution of the 1960s, the long-range Deep Ecology movement is known for its emphasis upon, and advocacy of, the protection of wildness and wilderness areas. The 1984 Deep Ecology platform (the comment to point five) states:

> The fight to preserve and extend areas of wilderness, or near-wilderness, should continue and should focus on the general ecological functions of these areas (one such function: large wilderness areas are required in the biosphere to allow for continued evolutionary speciation of animals and plants). Most present designated wilderness areas and game preserves are not large enough to allow for such speciation.

However, the most important reasons for wilderness protection have been, and continue to be, widely misunderstood not only among the general public, but even by professional environmental ethics theorists. For example, the editors of a recent collection of readings, Donald VanDeVeer and Christine Pierce (*Environmental Ethics and Policy Book*, pp. 464–556), present the case for the importance of biodiversity protection but, in an entirely separate section, they discuss the importance of protecting wilderness. The reasons they give for wilderness protection are largely anthropocentric: aesthetics, recreational and "spiritual" values, its "positive influence on human character," and the development of American "frontier" virtues. The connections between wilderness protection, the protection of ancient forests, and the protection of biodiversity are not clearly made. Biodiversity protection, of course, requires wild habitat! The establishment of large protected wilderness areas and wildlife preserves is one of the most crucial ways to protect such habitat.

Further, VanDeVeer and Pierce quote the environmental ethicist Bryan Norton (*Toward Unity among Environmentalists,* p. 106), who claims that environmentalists and the Forest Service both agree that

> national forests will have a "productive" use (the Pinchot influence) and both accept the importance of aesthetic and amenity values (the Muir influence). Preservation organizations, [Norton] says, ". . . argue for wilderness whenever

possible as a counterforce against a perceived bias of foresters toward timber production over other aesthetic and moral goals."

In Norton's case, the ecological functions of wilderness areas are not even mentioned. Incidentally, the "unity" between environmentalists and the Forest Service that Norton alludes to is highly problematic: at present, the Sierra Club is voting to decide whether to adopt as policy a total ban on ancient forest cutting in the National Forests. But most significantly, Norton portrays Muir as being concerned with wilderness protection primarily for aesthetic reasons.

Even more strangely, Susan Armstrong and Richard Botzler, the editors of the anthology *Environmental Ethics* (1993), treat Thoreau's seminal essay on the wild ("Walking"), as well as Muir's writings, as a form of Nature (or wilderness) aesthetics.

While Muir's popular writings stressed the "religious/aesthetic" value of wilderness, Muir scholars since the 1980s (for example, Stephen Fox, Michael Cohen, Frederick Turner, Max Oelschlaeger) have solidly established Muir's basic ecocentric orientation. But even as early as 1967, Roderick Nash (*Wilderness and the American Mind*, pp. 128–29) claimed that Muir "valued wilderness as an environment in which the totality of creation existed in undisturbed harmony . . . [in wilderness humans] could feel themselves 'part of wild Nature, kin to everything.' From such knowledge came respect for 'the rights of all the rest of creation.'"

Muir did not have the vocabulary of modern ecologists at his disposal, but his thinking was essentially the same: what was left of wild Nature had to be protected, mainly in designated wilderness areas and National Parks, against the onslaught of commercial exploitation and the "progress" of human industrial expansion.

Muir's priorities were also essentially the same as modern ecologists. While many urban-oriented environmentalists see the protection of wilderness and wildness as peripheral and less important than industrial and urban pollution problems, Anne and Paul Ehrlich, in their book *Healing the Planet* (1991), express the judgment of most conservation biologists and professional ecologists when they claim that "the ravaging of biodiversity . . . is the most serious single environmental peril facing civilization" (p. 35).

Under the leadership of David Brower, the Sierra Club sponsored Wilderness Conferences throughout the 1950s and '60s that increasingly stressed the ecological importance of designated wilderness. Brower also promoted confrontational tactics designed to save the remaining wild areas. After he was ousted from office in 1969, the Sierra Club, along with other mainstream environmental organizations, reverted to their prior policies of anthropocentric, pragmatic, legalistic accommodation with the industrial establishment. In many cases, this involved major compromising on the preservation of some of the last wild places. In the 1980s, radical environmental groups, such as Earth First!, advocated an end to the compromising and a return to ecocentrism to get environmentalism back on the original Muir/Brower track.

In 1851, Henry David Thoreau made the radical and unprecedented statement "In wildness is the preservation of the world." Thoreau also remarked that "all good things are wild and free." These statements are increasingly being understood as the source of modern ecophilosophy and ecopsychology. They suggest that the modernist project of domesticating and destroying the wild, along with the corollary process of further domesticating human life and making it increasingly artificial and out of touch with the wild, is resulting in disaster. Not only must wild ecosystems, plants, and animals be protected; Thoreau and Muir were referring as well to the crucial importance of fostering *human wildness*.

Paul Shepard (in *Nature and Madness*, 1982) claims that humans are genetically programmed for wild environments and that there is a normal genetically based human ontogeny that involves bonding with wild nature. Industrial urban consumerist society "works," Shepard claims, only because modern urban humans who have not identified with wild Nature are "ontogenetically stuck," remaining in an adolescent stage of development. Psychologists, sociologists, and others point out that modern industrial/consumerist society, itself, inherently manifests destructive adolescent behavior. Gary Snyder also holds a similar view concerning the universality of a genetically based Paleolithic human nature (see Snyder, *The Practice of the Wild*, 1990). Influenced by Shepard and Snyder, the ecophilosopher Max Oelschlaeger (*The Idea of Wilderness*, 1991) has called for a return to "Paleolithic consciousness."

Thoreau and Muir also anticipated this reason for protecting wilderness. As Nash points out in the case of Muir (*Wilderness and the American Mind*, pp. 127–28):

> Muir believed that centuries of existence as primitive beings had implanted in modern men yearnings for adventure, freedom, and contact with nature that city life could not satisfy . . . "civilized man chokes his soul." . . . Recognizing in himself "a constant tendency to return to primitive wildness," Muir generalized for his race: "going to the woods is going home; for I suppose we came from the woods originally." Consequently, "there is a love of wild Nature in everybody" . . . "a little pure wildness is the one great present want, both of men and sheep."

If the genetically based "Paleolithic human nature" theory is true, the human need for the wild (and to *be* wild) goes far beyond such relatively superficial anthropocentric reasons for protecting wilderness as aesthetics, recreation, "positive influence on human character," and so on. This would place the *wild/domestic issue* (the intrinsic value of wild Nature and other species, the integrity of the Earth's ecological/evolutionary processes, and human genetically based psychological and physical well-being) as the *central* contemporary environmental, ecological, and ecophilosophical concern. (In this connection, see the papers by Glendinning, Turner, Snyder, and LaChapelle in Part One.)

In his paper "In Wildness Is the Preservation of the World," Jack Turner explores the meaning of Thoreau's famous statement. He points out that we have tamed our wilderness areas and trivialized our "wilderness experience." Those in the wilderness tourism and "Nature business," Turner claims, have contributed to this process by treating wilderness as a commodity. (In this connection, see the paper by Wayland Drew in Part Two.) Too often, the "Nature business" merely reflects and perpetuates the egoistic Disneyland consumerism and commercialization of industrial society. Turner claims that genuine experience of wildness requires that we live bioregionally as integral members of the wild community.

Theodore Roszak has criticized industrial tourism as a contemporary approach to the Earth's few remaining wild places. Luxury tourism to places like the Antarctic is merely an extension of cultural imperialism and urban-industrial domestication and dominance that turns all the world into a civilized artifact. Roszak adds that perhaps we have seen enough wildlife documentaries on TV. In his opinion, we should leave the wilderness and wildlife alone.

The historian Sherwood Anderson, in discussing the state of wilderness in Alaska, criticizes the impact of airplanes, helicopters, and other motorized vehicles on the Alaskan wilderness. The climbing of Mount McKinley has turned basically into a Disneyland spectacle. He also points to overly intrusive wildlife management practices by biologists, and by the National Park and Forest Services. Anderson recounts an incident in which the Forest Service tranquilized mountain goats and moved them by helicopter to the side of a highway in Kenai to provide "photo ops" for tourists. He suggests that perhaps enough wild animals have been radio-collared, tagged, and unnecessarily disturbed by biologists. It is time to respect the dignity, privacy, and "rights" of wild creatures in their natural habitats (see the bibliography for the Roszak and Anderson papers).

Thomas Birch, in "The Incarceration of Wildness," expands upon the themes of Turner and Roszak. He claims that the liberal tradition, and industrial society, attempt to domesticate, dominate, and incarcerate wildness (understood as the "other") by "extending" rights to the nonhuman, and by confining wildness in legally established wilderness areas. Drawing upon Jean Baudrillard's concepts of "hyperreality" and "simulacra," Birch claims that, like Disneyland, designated wilderness areas have become mere simulations of reality: in the case of wilderness areas, they are controlled, managed, and manipulated simulations of wildness. Designated wilderness areas, even in their current state, are nevertheless justified and crucial insofar as they preserve the nonhuman world for its own sake.

Developing themes raised by Zamiatin, Huxley, and Orwell (see the Drew paper, "Killing Wilderness," in Part Two), Birch claims that what is left of wildness in designated wilderness areas helps slow down the "bad faith" and total takeover of the world by the industrial "imperium." Wilderness areas also provide the potential for future "sacred space" and genuine wildness. Like Turner, Birch claims that we must move ultimately to bioregional ways of life. (For further discussions of the industrial/megatechnological society as being a Disneyland simulation of reality, see the selections by Mander and Sessions in Part Four.)

The next two papers focus on the new scientific discipline of conservation biology and its relation to wilderness and biodiversity protection. In "Ecocentrism, Wilderness, and Global Ecosystem Protection," I discuss some of the recent research by conservation biologists that demonstrates that existing designated wilderness areas and wildlife refuges are ecologically inadequate to protect wild species and allow for continued speciation. Ecologists and environmentalists have been proposing various forms of global ecosystem zoning since the late 1960s in order to protect biodiversity and wild ecosystems. It is claimed that the concepts of ecological restoration and mitigation are often misused to justify further wild ecosystem destruction.

Important recent refinements to ecosystem zoning proposals include Naess's concept of "free nature" and Paul Taylor's concept of the "bioculture." Naess claims that an acceptable ecological ideal for the Earth would consist of one-third wilderness, one-third free nature, and one-third bioculture. Dave Foreman discusses the Wildlands Project's North American Wilderness Recovery strategy for biodiversity protection (endorsed by E. O. Wilson, Paul Ehrlich, and other leading conservation biologists), which consists of greatly expanded wilderness areas and wildlife refuges, with interconnecting wildlife corridors.

Edward Grumbine, in "Wilderness, Wise Use, and Sustainable Development," examines recent challenges to the concept of designated wilderness areas, while drawing upon contemporary discussions of the problem of human/Nature dualism and the differences between wilderness, wildness, and the "other" (as explored, for instance, in the papers by Turner and Birch). A debate between two of the leading environmental ethics theorists, Holmes Rolston III and J. Baird Callicott, highlights some of these issues. As a Christian thinker, Rolston promotes wilderness protection but also subscribes to the "second nature" view (for a discussion of "second nature," see the introduction to Part Two). Rolston's "second nature" view is apparently a form of human/ nature dualism similar to the views of Murray Bookchin and Teilhard de Chardin wherein civilization is "postevolutionary" in having somehow evolved "out of nature." But whereas Rolston wants to protect wilderness, Bookchin wants to "free" the wild ("first nature") by incorporating it into civilization ("second nature") and by having humans "rationally" direct the evolutionary processes.

Contrary to Rolston, Callicott apparently overcomes human/Nature dualism by maintaining that modern civilization is still "embedded in nature." But proponents of designated wilderness areas, he claims, unrealistically try to preserve wilderness areas in a nonevolutionary "static" state. (Conservation biologists would deny this, as does Gary Snyder in his paper in Part Six. Thoreau and Muir also clearly saw that Nature and wilderness are not "static," but rather are in a continual state of process and evolution, and that these wild evolutionary processes themselves are to be protected.) Grumbine points out that Callicott, in basing his argument upon a problematic interpretation of Leopold, promotes the currently fashionable concept of "sustainable development" and apparently a continuation of the direction of megatechnological society and its utilitarian, managerial approach to "transforming" and "improving" Nature through further growth and development (for criticism of the concept of "sustainable development," see Part Six). Apparently, Callicott is uninterested in bioregional proposals and fails to see the need, as the Ehrlichs put it, to "reduce the scale of the human enterprise."

Grumbine also examines and criticizes the so-called Wise Use movement that proposes eliminating wilderness areas and most other forms of environmental protection in favor of total exploitation of the Earth.

As a biodiversity protection strategy, Grumbine favors an integrated "ecosystem management" approach that would "continue to focus on increasing the size and number of protected areas" such as designated wilderness. To accomplish this, conservation biologist Reed Noss has suggested that 50 percent of the contiguous United States be protected in wild nature reserves with interconnecting corridors. By comparison, Arne Naess thinks that at least 65 percent of the Earth should be protected with interconnecting wilderness areas, wild nature preserves, and "free nature"/bioregional living areas.

The issue of protecting biodiversity and wildness in the Third and Fourth Worlds is the subject of Arne Naess's paper "The Third World, Wilderness, and Deep Ecology." Naess is responding in part to a critique of Deep Ecology by a Social Ecologist from India, Ramachandra Guha (see bibliography). Guha claims that protection of wilderness, wildness, and biodiversity is not relevant to Third World concerns. The main concerns of the Deep Ecology movement are not relevant to what he sees as "the two fundamental ecological problems facing the globe: (i) overconsumption by the industrial world and urban elites in the Third World and (ii) growing militarization. . . ."

Guha's analysis strangely ignores what the vast majority of professional ecologists throughout the world consider to be the most serious global ecological problems: global human overpopulation, ozone layer depletion, the greenhouse effect, and current rates of wild habitat loss and species extinction. And so Guha sees the establishment of wildlife preserves in India for the protection of tigers and other endangered species as a form of elite ecological imperialism and "a direct transfer of resources from the poor to the rich."

Third World environmentalism, Guha claims, should place primary emphasis upon human issues of "equity and social justice." The Deep Ecology movement, he asserts, has little or no interest in the issues of restructuring society to achieve ecological sustainability and social justice, steady-state economics, and a "radical shift in consumption and production patterns." Guha further suggests that Deep Ecology is not relevant even to First World environmentalism: "A truly radical ecology movement in the American context," he claims, "ought to work toward a synthesis of the appropriate technology, alternate lifestyle, and peace movements."

In reply, Naess refers to Gary Snyder's point that, throughout history, humans have lived in wilderness in *moderate* numbers without appreciably reducing biological richness and diversity. But this is now not possible in First World countries where high-consumption lifestyles, and other highly destructive practices require the establishment of large designated wilderness areas to protect wildlife habitat and biodiversity.

Naess claims that Third World people must progress economically, while people in the rich countries must curtail their excessive consumption. But subsistence agriculture that destroys tropical forests cannot be considered long-term economic progress for the poor. The severe overpopulation in the Third World will require that most of the poor live in urban areas in the near future, and these urban areas will need massive improvements in living conditions.

Apart from the desperately poor, Naess believes that most people in the Third World are concerned about the protection of wildness and biodiversity, but such protection in the Third World will, to a large extent, take the form of living traditionally in ecologically benign ways in "free nature."

As a way of overcoming the apparent impasse between the central concerns of the Ecofeminists, the Social Ecologists, and supporters of the Deep Ecology movement, Naess suggests that the Green political movement is actually composed of four movements: (1) the antipoverty movement, (2) the social justice movement, (3) the alternative technology movement, and (4) the ecological movement. (In a more recent analysis, he revises this analysis to refer to the "three great movements": (1) the social justice movement, (2) the peace movement, and (3) the ecology movement.)

Naess suggests that Guha and others promote unnecessary confusion by identifying the Green movement (and all its component movements) with the ecology movement. The Deep Ecology movement strongly supports sustainability for all societies, but sustainability in the ecologically "wide" sense of protecting "the full richness and diversity of life forms on the planet." It is beneath human dignity, Naess claims, to aspire to less. (For another discussion of the Green movement and its various component movements, see Naess's paper in Part Six.)

# 30 | "IN WILDNESS IS THE PRESERVATION OF THE WORLD"

## *Jack Turner*

HANGING FROM THE CEILING of the visitor's center at Point Reyes National Seashore are plaques bearing famous quotations about the value of the natural world. The one from Thoreau reads: "In wilderness is the preservation of the world." This, of course, is a mistake. Henry didn't say "wilderness"; he said "wildness." But the mistake has become a cliché suitable for T-shirts and bumper stickers. So when a recent *Newsweek* article on wolf reintroduction says, " 'In wilderness,' Thoreau wrote, 'is the preservation of the world,' " I am not surprised. Confusing wilderness and wildness strikes me increasingly as a Freudian slip. It serves a repressive function, the avoidance of conflict, in this case the inherent tension between wilderness as property and wildness as quality.

Last year at a symposium on nature writing, William Kittredge was candid enough to admit that, "For decades I misread Thoreau. I assumed he was saying wilderness. . . . Maybe I didn't want Thoreau to have said wildness, I couldn't figure out what he meant."

I believe that mistaking wilderness for wildness is one cause of our increasing failure to preserve the earth, and that Kittredge's honesty pinpoints the key issue: we aren't sure what Thoreau meant by wildness, nor are we sure what we mean by wildness or why we should preserve it. I don't know either, so what follows is not an explication of Henry's famous saying but more of a prelude or a prolegomena to the issue.

This saying, perhaps Thoreau's most famous, is from his essay "Walking." Along with *Walden* and two other essays, "Resistance to Civil Government"

A slightly longer version of this essay was first published in *Northern Lights* 6, no. 4 (1991). Reprinted with permission.

(unfortunately called "Civil Disobedience" most of the time) and "Life Without Principle," it expresses the radical heart of Thoreau's life's work, and since he revised the essay just before his death, we may assume it accurately represents his thoughts on wildness.

The most notable thing about "Walking" is that it virtually ignores our current concerns with the preservation of habitats and species. His saying no doubt includes these things—he says "all good things are wild and free"—but Thoreau mainly talks about human beings, their literature, their myths, their history, their work and leisure, and of course their walking. He says, for instance,

> Give me for my friends and neighbors wild men, not tame ones. The wildness of the savage is but a faint symbol of the awful ferity with which good men and lovers meet.

And listen to the essay's opening lines:

> I wish to speak a word for Nature, for absolute freedom and wildness, as contrasted with a freedom and culture merely civil,—to regard man as an inhabitant, or a part and parcel of Nature, rather than a member of society.

Absolute freedom. Absolute wildness. Human beings as inhabitants of absolute freedom, absolute wildness. This is not the usual environmental rhetoric, and I agree with Kittredge: most of us simply don't know what Thoreau means.

Nor should we be surprised, for most people no longer have much experience with wild nature. But language and communication are social phenomena, and without common, shared experience, meaning is impossible. I would go so far as saying that in many inner cities, here and in the developing world, people no longer have the concept of nature. As a New York wit has it, Nature is something I pass through between my hotel and my taxi. As the population grows, the cause of preservation will become increasingly desperate.

What is equally unsettling is this: those people who have led a life of intimate contact with nature at its wildest—a buckaroo working the Owyhee country, a halibut fisherman plying the currents of the Gulf of Alaska, an Eskimo whale hunter, a rancher tending a small cow-calf operation, a logger with a chainsaw—are perceived as the enemies of preservation. The friends of preservation, on the other hand, are often city folk who depend on vacations in wilderness areas and national parks for their (necessarily) limited experience of wildness. The difference in degree of experience of wildness, the dichotomy of friends-enemies of preservation, and the notorious inability of these two groups to communicate shared values indicates the depth of our muddle about wilderness and wildness, and suggests again the increasingly desperate nature of our struggle.

We presume that the experience of wildness goes with wilderness (though the presumption ignores elements of our life that can also plausibly be thought of as wild: sex, dreams, rage). However, since wilderness is a place, and wildness a quality, we can always ask: How wild is our wilderness, and how wild is our experience there? My answer is, not very. There are many reasons, some of them widely acknowledged, and I will pass over them briefly. But there is one reason that is not widely accepted, a reason that is offensive to many minds, but that goes to the heart of Thoreau's opening lines: human beings are no longer residents of wild nature, hence we no longer consider ourselves part of a biological order.

"A little pure wildness is the one great present want," wrote John Muir. It is still true. Why isn't our wilderness wild and why is there so little experience of wildness there? Well, first of all the wilderness that most people visit (excluding Alaska and Canada) is too small—in space and time. Like all experience, the experience of the wild can be a taste or a feast, and feasts take time.

About one-third of our designated wilderness units are less than ten thousand acres, about four miles long on each side. An easy stroll. Some units, usually islands, are less than one hundred acres. I have been told that Point Reyes now has "wilderness zones" measuring several hundred yards, a point at which the word becomes meaningless. For comparison, recall that Disney World is twenty-seven thousand acres. *Disney World is nearly three times larger than a third of our wilderness areas.*

Even our largest wilderness units are small. Only 4 percent are larger than 500 thousand acres, an area twenty-seven miles on a side. And since many follow the ridges of mountain ranges, they are elongated to the point that they can be crossed in a single day by a strong hiker. True, some are adjacent to other wilderness areas and remote BLM lands and National Parks, but once you have visited the Amazon, Alaska, the Northwest Territories, or the Himalayas, our local wilderness seems very small indeed.

Without sufficient space and time, the experience of wildness is diminished or simply doesn't exist. Many people agree with Aldo Leopold: it should take a couple of weeks to pack across a true wilderness. It's a simple law: the farther you are from a road, and the longer you are out, the wilder your time. Two weeks is the minimum; a month is better. Until then the mind remains saturated with human concerns and blind to the concerns of the natural world. Until then the body remains bound to metronomic clocks and ignorant of natural biological rhythms, and the wilderness traveler remains ignorant of "forces more fundamental and more calming than the mechanical overlay they have so diligently clamped down on themselves" (Michael Young, *The Metronomic Society*).

Small wilderness units usually lack predators—sometimes simply a function of small size, sometimes a function of artificial borders created according to economic and political rather than ecological criteria. The result is the same: the wilderness is tamed. Predators are perhaps our most accessible experience of the wild. To come upon a grizzly track is to experience the wild in a most intimate, carnal way—an experience marked by gross alterations in attention, perception, body language, body chemistry, and emotion.

The tameness of wilderness is exacerbated by our current model for appropriate human use of the wild—the intensive and commercial recreation that requires trail systems, bridges, signs for direction and distance, back-country rangers, and rescue operations. These in turn create additional commercial activities that further diminish wildness—maps, guide books, guiding services, advertising, photography books, instructional films—all of which diminish discovery and surprise and independence and the unknown, the very qualities that make a place wild. Each of these reductions functions like the loss of a predator. It tames and domesticates the wilderness and eliminates wild experience.

The smallness, the artificial boundaries, the loss of predators, and the intensive recreational use all lead to replacing biological methods of growth and interaction with artificial methods of control—of plants, animals, humans, and events. Thus, animal populations are managed by controlled hunting, wild fires are suppressed, plants sprayed, and humans treated in a manner best described by the word "surveillance."

The wild then becomes a "problem" to be "solved" by further human intervention—scientific studies, state and federal laws, judicial decisions, political compromise, and administrative and bureaucratic procedures. Once this intervention begins, it never ends; it spirals into further and further human intrusion, rendering wilderness increasingly evaluated, managed, regulated, and controlled. That is, tamed.

Nibble by nibble, decision by decision, animal by animal, we have diminished the wildness of our wilderness. This hasn't just happened; *we have done it*. Thus diminished, wilderness becomes an area, a special unit of property treated like an historic relic or ruin—a valuable remnant. It becomes a place of "vacations" (a word related to *vacant,* empty). Humans are strangers there, foreigners to an experience that once grounded their most sacred beliefs and values. The wilderness as relic leads necessarily to tourism, and tourism in the wilderness becomes the primary mode of experiencing a diminished wild.

Wilderness as relic converts places into commodities. We should be concerned, for all tourism is a form of commerce and is to some degree destructive. Virtually everyone in the Nature Business feeds (literally) on wilderness as a commodity. We are enthralled with our ability to make a living in this exchange, but we tend to ignore the practical consequences to wilderness preservation and to ourselves. Preserving relics of tame wilderness and reducing experience there to tourism is not a free lunch. Compared with residency in a wild biological order, where the experience of wildness is part of everyday life, wilderness tourism is pathetic. It has some very bad consequences, and I want to mention several of them.

First, wilderness tourism ignores, perhaps even caricatures, the experience that decisively marked the founders of wilderness preservation and Deep Ecology—and I am thinking here of Thoreau, Muir, Leopold, and Murie. The kind of wildness they experienced has become very rare—an endangered experience. As a result, we no longer understand the roots of our own cause.

To read the works of these men and then to look at an issue of, say, *Sierra,* is to experience a severe disorientation. The founders had something we lack, something Thoreau called "Indian Wisdom." For much of their lives, these men lived in and studied nature before it became a "wilderness area."

Thoreau's knowledge of lands surrounding Concord was so vast some of the town's children believed that, like God, Henry had created it all. His knowledge of flora was so precise that a rare fern species not seen for a hundred years was recently rediscovered by examining his surveying notes. His essay on the succession of forest trees is one of the seminal essays of modern ecology. Muir made original contributions to the study of glaciers.

The works of Leopold and Murie are the classics in their field. To a considerable degree their lives were devotions to wild nature. Without such devotion there is no reason to believe there would be Thoreau's epiphanies on Katadin, Muir's mystical identification with trees, or Leopold's thinking like a mountain.

This is quite different from wilderness tourism, which is devoted to fun. We hunt for fun, fish for fun, climb for fun, ski for fun, and hike for fun. This is the grim harvest of the "fun hog" philosophy that drove the wilderness recreation boom for the past three decades. Despite the poetics and philosophical rhetoric of environmentalists, there is little evidence that either the spiritual or the scientific concerns of Muir, Thoreau, Leopold, and Murie (or the scientific concerns of conservation biology) have trickled down to most wilderness users.

Given the ignorance and arrogance of the fun hog, it is understandable that those who feel they will lose by increased wilderness designation—farmers, ranchers, loggers, commercial fishermen—are often enraged. Instead of a clash of needs, the preservation of the wild appears to be a clash of work versus recreation. Lacking a deeper experience of wildness and access to the lore, myth, metaphor, and ritual necessary to share that experience, there is no communication, no vision that might shatter the current dead-end of wilderness debate.

Both groups exploit the wild, the first by consumption, the second by alteration into a playpen. Either way, the quality of wildness is destroyed. Until we face that fact we will remain stuck. Meanwhile, the worship of wilderness designation becomes idolatry—the confusion of a symbol with its essence.

Second, with wilderness tourism we lose our most effective weapon for preserving wild nature: emotional identification. At the bedrock level, what drives both reform environmentalism and Deep Ecology is the practical problem of how to *compel* human beings to respect and care for wild nature. The tradition of Thoreau and Muir says that the best way to do it is raw, visceral contact with wild nature. True residency in the wild brings identification and a generalized NIMBY ("Not in my backyard!") response that extends sympathy to all the wild world. This is one of the most obvious lessons of primary cultures. Without such identification, solutions become abstract, impotent, and impractical. Right now impracticality and impotence dominate environmental thought.

For example, giving trees and animals moral rights analogous to the rights of humans has bogged down in a morass of value theory, and the aesthetic campaign to preserve the wild has done as much harm as good. It suggests (especially in a nation of relativists) that preservation is a matter of taste, a preference no more compelling than the choice between vanilla and chocolate. It leads to tedious arguments that begin with statements like "Who are you to say we shouldn't have snowmobiles in the Teton wilderness?", on the model of "Who are you to say I shouldn't eat chocolate?" This, in turn, leads inevitably to questions of egalitarianism and elitism, hence, directly into the dismal swamp of politics, which Henry said in "Walking" is the most alarming of man's affairs. Politicians are invariably people of the polis—city slickers. . . .

Philosophers have been no more helpful. Deep Ecologists are desperately trying to replace the philosophical foundations of the mechanical model of the world with philosophical foundations of an organic model. Unfortunately, these new foundations are not at all obvious to the lay public, and they are even less obvious to professional philosophers. . . . Worse yet, explications of these foundations rely on some of the most obscure ruminations of Spinoza, Whitehead, and Heidegger. This bodes ill for condors and rain forests. . . .

Third, wilderness tourism results in little art, literature, poetry, myth, or lore for most of our wild places. In "Walking," Thoreau says, "The West is preparing to add its fables to those of the East. The valleys of the Ganges, the Nile and the Rhine, have yielded their crop, it remains to be seen what the valleys of the Amazon, the Platte, the Orinoco, the St. Lawrence, and the Mississippi will produce." Well, nearly 150 years later it still remains to be seen.

If you ask for the art, literature, lore, myth, and fable of, say, the upper

Snake River, I would answer we are working on it, but it might be a while, because art that takes as its subject a place is created by people who live in that place. This is true of both wilderness and civilization. Joyce grew up in Dublin, Atget lived in Paris, Adams lived in Yosemite, Beston lived on Cape Cod. Many of our best writers on wilderness—Ed Abbey, Gary Snyder, Doug Peacock—worked as fire lookouts for the U.S. Forest Service. (There is probably a Ph.D. thesis here: "The Importance of Fire Lookouts in the Development of Western Nature Literature.") If our access to wilderness is limited to tourism, we have no reason to expect a literature and lore of the wild.

And yet, most of us, when we think about it, realize that after our own direct experience of wildness, art and literature, myth and lore have contributed most to our love of wild places, animals, plants, even, perhaps, our love of human wildness. For here is the language we so desperately lack, the medium so necessary to communicate a shared vision. Mere concepts and abstractions will not do because that which needs to be shared is beyond concepts and abstractions.

Fourth, without residency in the wild there will be no phenology of wild places, and this will be very unfortunate, for phenology, as Paul Shepard has reminded us, is the study of the mature naturalist—the gate through which nature becomes personal. Leopold published phenological studies of two counties in Wisconsin. Thoreau dedicated the last years of his life to studying the mysterious comings and goings of the natural world. Phenology requires a complete immersion in place over time, so the attention, the senses, and the mind can scrutinize and discern widely—the dates of arrivals and departures, the births, the flourishings, the decays and the deaths of wild things, their successions, synchronicities, dependencies, reciprocities, and cycles—the lived life of the earth.

To be absorbed in this life is to merge with larger patterns. Here ecology is not studied but felt. You know these truths the way you know hot from cold; they are immune from doubt and argument. Here is the intimate knowledge conservation biology often seeks to rediscover, the common wisdom of primary peoples. (And again, it is still the common wisdom of many people who actually work in nature.) This will not emerge from tourism in a relict wilderness.

So we are left with the vital importance of residency in wild nature, and a visceral knowledge of that wildness, as the most practical means of preserving the wild. What we need now is a new tradition of the wild that teaches us how human beings live best by living in and studying the wild without taming it or destroying it. Such a tradition of the wild existed; it is as old as the Pleistocene. Before the Neolithic, human beings were always living in, traveling through, and using lands we now call wilderness; they knew it intimately,

they respected it, they cared for it. It is the tradition of the people that populated all of the wilderness of North America, a tradition that influenced Taoism and informed major Chinese and Japanese poetic traditions. It is the
tradition that emerged again with Emerson and Thoreau (who once asked
"Why study the Greeks and the Romans? Why not study the American
Indian?"). . . .

In short, it is a tradition that could again compel respect, care, and love for
wild nature in a way that philosophical foundations, aesthetics, moral theory,
and politics cannot compel. It is a tradition we need to re-create for ourselves,
borrowing when necessary from native cultures, but making it new—a wild
tradition of our own.

A wild bunch is forming—an eclectic tribe returning to the wild to study,
learn, and express. From them shall come the lore, myth, literature, art, and
ritual we so require. Frank Craighead and John Haines are among the elders
of this tribe. And there is also Richard Nelson on his island, Doug Peacock
with his grizzlies, Terry Tempest Williams and her beloved birds, Hanna
Hinchman with her illuminated journals, Gary Nabhan with his seeds, Dolores LaChapelle and her rituals, Gary Snyder and his poems—all new teachers
of the wild.

The presence of these teachers is not sufficient, however. It will not help us
if this tradition is created for us, to be read about in yet another book. To
affect the self, the self must live the life of the wild, mold a particular form of
human character—a form of life. Relics will not do. Tourism will not do.

Out there is the great feeding mass we call the earth. We are, to go back to
Thoreau's opening lines, part and parcel of the earth, part and parcel of its
cycles, successions, and dependencies. We incorporate and are incorporated in
ways not requiring legal papers. We are creator and created, terrorist and
hostage, victim and executioner, a guest of honor and a part of the feast. We
inhabit a biological order that is terrifying in its identity and reciprocity. It is
expressed by Black Elk and his Wakan-Tanka, Lao Tzu and his Tao, the
Mahayana Net of Indra, the ecologist's food chain. It is a vision hidden from
the urban mind. This vision could inform everything from the most private
spiritual matters to the gross facts of nourishment and death. The only interesting question is how can we live it here and now, in this place, in these
times. . . .

# 31 THE INCARCERATION OF WILDNESS
## WILDERNESS AREAS AS PRISONS

*Thomas Birch*

## BAD FAITH IN WILDERNESS PRESERVATION?

AMERICAN PRESERVATIONISTS CHERISH THE belief that, as Roderick Nash
has stated it,

> Wilderness allocation and management is truly a cultural contribution of the
> United States to the world. Although other nations have established programs
> to preserve and protect tracts of land, it is only in the United States that a
> program of broad scope has been implemented, largely because of the fortu-
> itous combination of physical availability, environmental diversity, and cul-
> tural receptivity. Despite the continuing ambivalence of American society
> towards wilderness, the reserves should be regarded as one of the Nation's
> most significant contributions.[1]

While wilderness preservation is truly a significant contribution to world civilization, the question whether this contribution, as it is usually understood, is
entirely positive ethically is more problematic. As wilderness preservation is
generally understood and practiced by mainstream American tradition, and as
it often appears to others, particularly those Third and Fourth World peoples
who actually live on the most intimate terms with wild nature, it may well be
just another stanza in the same old imperialist song of Western civilization.[2]

Nash himself seems close to noticing this problem when he says that "Civilization created wilderness," and when he points out that "Appreciation of
wilderness began in the cities."[3] The urban centers of Western civilization are

A longer version of this essay was originally published in *Environmental Ethics* 12, 1 (1990).
Reprinted with permission.

the centers of imperial power and global domination and oppression. Whatever comes from them, including classic liberalism, is therefore likely to be tainted by the values, ideology, and practices of imperialism, as the mainstream white man (and his emulators) seeks to discharge (impose) his "white man's burden," the burden of his "enlightenment," on all the others, of all sorts, on this planet.

In his most recent book, *The Rights of Nature,* Nash suggests that

> ... liberty is the single most potent concept in the history of America. The product of both Europe's democratic revolutions and, following Frederick Jack Turner's hypothesis, the North American frontier, liberalism explains our national origins, delineates our ongoing mission, and anchors our ethics. Natural rights is a cultural given in America, essentially beyond debate as an idea. The liberal's characteristic belief in the goodness and intrinsic value of the individual leads to an endorsement of freedom, political equality, toleration, and self-determination.[4]

This is an accurate statement of what mainstream Western man has taken to be his beneficent burden, as he has sought to bring civilization and liberty (as he conceives it) first to the peoples and the land of North America and then to the entire planet.

Having established the liberal tradition as his starting point, Nash proceeds to subsume or appropriate (reduce) radical or "new" environmentalism into this story:

> Much of the new environmentalists' criticism of American tradition is warranted, but in adopting a subversive, counter-cultural stance, they overlooked one important intellectual foundation for protecting nature that is quintessentially American: natural-rights philosophy, the old American ideal of liberty that they themselves were applying to nature.[5]

Here Nash seems to be suggesting that the American ideals of liberty and natural rights have been overlooked in the new environmentalists' rhetoric but not in their action. Accordingly, Nash presents such diverse thinkers as Paul Shepard, Murray Bookchin, and the deep ecologists as best understood, not as subversive radicals who demand revolutionary changes in our environmental ethics and in our social structures, but as closet champions of the mainstream liberal tradition of natural rights, who would "extend" the benefits and protections of civilization to nature. Just as the once radical appearing abolitionist movement was an extension of our ethics to liberate blacks from exploitation by granting them rights, so the preservation of wilderness is essentially only a next step in the evolution of our liberal tradition, which now would allow even the freedom of self-determination for wild nature.

I suggest that belief in this liberal-tradition story involves self-deception—

that it is a cloaking story to cover and legitimate conquest and oppression that needs substantial correction if we are to understand wilderness and the ethics of our relationship with it. Still, if this liberal-tradition story were truly put into practice, if nature were allowed self-determination, then it would be transformed into a radically different story for us to inhabit. That is, this old story does contain some germs for its own transcendence. As things stand, however, self-determination is not permitted for nature, even in legally established wilderness reserves, in spite of much rhetoric to the contrary. Instead, wild nature is *confined* to official wilderness reserves. Why? Probably, I argue, because it would be self-contradictory for imperial power to allow genuine self-determination for the others it would dominate, since doing so would be an abrogation of its power.

John Rodman has exposed the dangers and limitations of our liberal tradition with regard to the animal liberation movement.[6] I am concerned here to do much the same thing with wilderness preservation and the liberation of nature movement. The nub of the problem with granting or extending rights to others, a problem which becomes pronounced when nature is the intended beneficiary, is that it presupposes the existence and the maintenance of a position of power from which to do the granting. Granting rights to nature requires bringing nature into our human system of legal and moral rights, and this is still a (homocentric) system of hierarchy and domination. The liberal mission is to open participation in the system to more and more others of more and more sorts. They are to be enabled and permitted to join the ranks and enjoy the benefits of power; they are to be absorbed. But obviously a system of domination cannot grant full equality to *all* the dominated without self-destructing. To believe that we can grant genuine self-determination to nature, and let its wildness be wild, without dis-inhabiting our story of power and domination, even in its most generous liberal form, is bad faith.

Bad faith is compounded if we believe that the Turner hypothesis, as cited by Nash, can be invoked to support the story of our culture's mission to bring freedom to the wilds of America. The explanatory power of Turner's frontier hypothesis, which proposes that the frontier produced "a culture of individualism, self-reliance, and diffused power—the culture of American democracy," has now been discredited as far as the history of American culture is concerned. Donald Worster writes that it is "a theory that has no water, no aridity, no technical dominance in it."[7] Patricia Limerick holds that it is "ethnocentric and nationalistic" and that "the history of the West is a study of a place undergoing conquest and never fully escaping its consequences."[8] Once we have demythologized American history, we see that Turner's frontier hypothesis is only an instance of a central myth of Western culture, the story that civilization brings light and order to the wild darkness of savagery—the legitimizing story that cloaks conquest, colonization, and domination. We deceive ourselves if we think that wilderness preservation can be adequately understood in terms of this suspect mythology. To overcome this self-deception we must attend to the less savory side of our tradition, to imperialism and domination (the sub-text of the liberal story as usually told).

It is therefore incumbent upon wilderness preservationists, especially those who are privileged to live in the centers of imperial power, to examine their position critically. Even though the establishment of wilderness reservations may well be the best gesture of respect toward nature that Western culture can offer at its present stage of ethical development, unless we Westerners see and acknowledge the shortcomings of this gesture we will languish in self-congratulatory bad faith. My aim here is to expose the bad faith that taints our mainstream justifications for wilderness preservation and to sting us out of it toward a more ethical relationship with wild nature, with wildness itself, and thereby with one another.

## BRINGING THE LAW TO THE LAND

At the center of Western culture's bad faith in wilderness preservation are faulty presuppositions about otherness, about others of all sorts, both human and nonhuman, and consequently about the "practical necessities" of our relationship with others. In speaking of "practical necessities" I am raising questions about how others *must* be related to in the deepest sense of *must*.[9]

Problems arise when the other is understood in the usual Western, and imperialistic, manner: as the enemy. In this sense, mainstream Western culture views the oppositional opportunities that otherness affords as adversarial. It presupposes that opposition is fundamentally conflictive, rather than complementary, or communal, or Taoist, or ecosystemic. At best, others are to be "tolerated," which is close to pitying them for their unfortunate inferiority. The central presupposition is thus Hobbist: that we exist fundamentally in a state of war with any and all others. This is perhaps the most central tenet of our guiding mythology, or legitimizing story, about the necessary manner of relationship with others. Thus, in practice, others are to be suppressed or, when need be, eradicated. This mythology is typical of, but not, of course, limited to mainstream Western culture. William Kittredge has given us a powerful summary of Western culture's leading story:

> It is important to realize that the primary mythology of the American West is also the primary mythology of our nation and part of a much older world mythology, that of law-bringing. Which means it is a mythology of conquest. . . . Most rudimentarily, our story of law-bringing is a story of takeover and dominance, ruling and controlling, especially by strength.[10]

In the case of wildland preservation, bad faith arises when we believe that the simple creation of legal entities such as wilderness areas (a land-use allocation or "disposition" category) can satisfy the practical necessities of relationship with wild land, and with wildness itself. To create legal entities such as wilderness areas is to attempt to *bring the law to wildness,* to bring the law to the essence of otherness, to impose civic law on nature. And this is *all* that it is as long as the customary story is still presupposed, even though it does reform the system of legal institutions. But this is precisely the same sort of reform as the incarceration of Native Americans (paradigm "others") on reservations, even with the putatively well-intended aim of making them over into "productive citizens," in place of the former practice of slaughtering them. Mere reform that is bound by the terms of the prevailing story not only fails to liberate us from the story, but also tends to consolidate its tyranny over us. The reform that appears to be a step in the right ethical direction backfires and turns out to increase the bad faith we have about the ethical quality of what is done. Finding the practical necessities of relationship with nature as other requires breaking the grip of our culture's imperialistic story. It further requires preserving wild land *in order* to help break the grip of this story. It is finally a matter of ethically resolving what Kittredge calls the struggle "to find a new story to inhabit."[11] Then, but only then, can bad faith be left behind.

As things stand for Western culture, committed as it is to the completion of an *imperium* over nature, wilderness reservations are "lockups."[12] The popular terminology of the opponents of wilderness areas about "locking up" wildland is accurate and insightful. The otherness of wildland is objectified into human resource, or value, categories and allocated by law to specific uses (thus bringing law to the land). Of course, as preservationists have often pointed out, allocations of land to specific hard uses such as intensive timber management, strip mining, motorized recreation, etc., are also "lockups," but the attempt to lock out exploiters by locking up wildland turns out, when properly understood, to be just another move in the imperial resource allocation game. This, in fact, is the language of the Wilderness Act of 1964, which states that its purpose is "to *secure* for the American people of present and future generations the *benefits* of an *enduring resource* of wilderness."[13] Wilderness areas in the United States are meant to serve four of the five main multiple uses for public lands: watershed, wildlife, grazing, and recreation. Only timber harvesting is excluded. Mining is often permitted.[14]

But what about the wildness itself? How could wildness be brought under the rule of law? By definition wildness is intractable to definition, is indefinite, and, although it is at the heart of finding utility values in the first place, wildness itself cannot plausibly be assigned any utility value because it spawns much, very much, that is *useless,* and much that is plain disutility. It is for this reason that it is so puzzling, to the point of unintelligibility, to try to construe wildness (or wilderness) as a resource, though we often hear wilderness called a resource. Since wildness is the source of resources, any attempt to construe it as a resource in terms of the rhetoric of resources reduces it to some set of resources.[15] Wildness itself, to the mind of the law-bringing imperium, is lawless; it is the paradigm of the unintelligible, unrepentant, incorrigible outlaw. How then is the imperium to deal with it?

All the usual attempts to subdue wildness by destroying its manifestations fail, although wildness may be driven into hiding for awhile, or, more accurately, may be lost sight of for awhile. Although the forest and the bison and the Indian may be exterminated, this does not affect wildness itself. In the case of wildness itself, there is nothing there to aim at and shoot. As what we might call the "soul" of otherness, wildness is no usual sort of other. To take the manifestations of wildness for the thing itself is to commit a category mistake. Wildness is still very much there and will not go away. How then is the imperium to deal with it, given that the usual strategies of conquest cannot work? Wildness cannot be ostracized, or exterminated, or chastened into discipline through punishment, reward, or even behavior modification techniques. Yet according to the dictates of the imperium, which claims total control, wildness must be, or at least must seem to be, brought into the system, brought under the rule of law. While the older ("conservative") factotums of the imperium still pursue the strategy of obliterating wildness by destroying its manifestations, the modern ("liberal") reformist factotums see the futility of the older strategy and therefore follow a more subtle strategy of "cooptation," or appropriation, through making a place for wildness within the imperial order and putting wildness in this place. The place that is made is the prison, or the asylum. When this place is made and wildness is incarcerated in it, the imperium is completed. Consider Foucault's observations:

> The carceral network does not cast the unassimilable into a confused hell; there is no outside. It takes back with one hand what it seems to exclude with the other. It saves everything, including what it punishes. It is unwilling to waste even what it has decided to disqualify.[16]

In this way, designated wilderness areas become prisons, in which the imperium incarcerates unassimilable wildness in order to complete itself, to finalize its reign. This is what is meant when it is said that there is no wilderness anymore in the contemporary world, in the technological imperium. There is, or will be soon, only a network of wilderness reservations in which wildness has been locked up.

To press the use of prison terminology, we may say that just as the "lockup" occurs at the end of the prison day, so wildness is locked up at the twilight time of modernism. To press prison terminology a bit more, we may say also that when wildness as prisoner "misbehaves" (by being its spontaneous self) the imperium "locks it down." A "lockdown" involves confining prisoners to their cells, revoking privileges, conducting searches, etc., to root out and correct the maleficence.[17]

Wilderness reservations are not intended or tolerated as places where nature is allowed to get out of control, even though a degree of aberrant behavior is permitted, just as a degree of it is permitted within the edifices of the penal system for humans. Wilderness reservations are not meant to be voids in the fabric of domination where "anarchy" is permitted, where nature is actually liberated. Not at all. The rule of law is presupposed as supreme. Just as wilderness reservations are created by law, so too can they be abolished by law. The threat of annihilation is always maintained. Just as a certain inmate, say a tree fungus, may be confined to the wilderness reservations by law, so too can it be exterminated by law, even within the reservation. The imperium does not, and cannot, abrogate these "rights," although it has arrogated them in the first place.


## OTHERNESS AS WILDNESS

At the center of the problem of Western culture's incarceration of wildness is its prevailing (mis)understanding of otherness as adversarial, as recalcitrant toward the law, as therefore irrational, criminal, outlaw, even criminally insane (like the grizzly bear). This understanding of the other is a part and product of Western culture's imperialistic mythology of law bringing. It is the meaning of otherness that the story of the imperium has created. It is an enforced misunderstanding, myth or story. Accordingly, texts such as Joseph Conrad's *Heart of Darkness* and E. M. Forster's *A Passage to India* have been incorporated into our literary canon and are taught in our educational institutions, as part of what is called the process of "the indoctrination of the young" by ruling elites,[18] or as what we may more politely call the inculcation and perpetuation of the mythology of Western culture.

If we are to understand what the creation of legally designated wilderness reservations amounts to ethically, then we must disentangle the threads of Western culture's mythology from the realities of otherness. Let us begin by emphasizing that the essence of otherness is wildness. If any other is to preserve its (his, her) identity as other, as other in relation to another person, society, species, or whatever, then it must at bottom resist accepting any *final* identity altogether. An other cannot *essentially* be what it is objectified, defined, analyzed, legislated, or understood to be if it is to be and remain an other. The maintenance of otherness requires the maintenance of a radical openness, or the maintenance of the sort of unconditioned freedom that permits sheer spontaneity and continuous participation in the emergence of novelty. . . .

## WILDERNESS AREAS AS "SIMULATIONS" OF WILDNESS, AND THE RISK OF THE REAL

Jean Baudrillard's brilliant and alarming analysis of modern Western culture starkly illuminates the uses to which imperial culture puts its wild others, both human and nonhuman. Baudrillard's analysis also explains the imperium's need to manufacture and maintain an adversarial sort of other to serve these uses. Briefly, these uses are to provide meaning and legitimation for the institution of imperial power and to enforce its reign with the threat of terror and chaos. For Baudrillard, modern Western culture is headed toward, and to a great extent has already reached, a condition of "hyperreality," and has taken up residence in a world of "simulation," a simulated world of "simulacra," with no remaining contact with reality, including ecological reality. In one of Baudrillard's more noted statements, "The very definition of the real has become: *that of which it is possible to give an equivalent reproduction.* . . . The real is not only what can be reproduced, *but that which is always already reproduced.* The hyperreal . . . which is entirely in simulation."[19]

In order to solidify its reign, to realize its goal of total control, power must create its own world, defined in its own terms, by means of models that are simulations of realities (of all sorts). Total control of such, and only such, simulacra is possible because they are reproducible and therefore fungible. Should any one of them stray from the grip of control, it can be eradicated and replaced with another. Appropriation into this throwaway world involves throwing away the former, and other, reality in favor of a simulation that is illusory: "We live everywhere already in an 'aesthetic' hallucination of reality."[20] Nevertheless, imperial power cannot afford to throw reality away entirely, because it needs some reality or semblance of reality to save its own meaningfulness and legitimacy.

Legally designated wilderness reserves thus become simulacra insofar as it is possible for the imperium to simulate wildness. The pressure on the imperium is to institute simulations of wildness in order to appropriate wildness into the imperium under the rubric of the model. Simulacra are produced according to the dictates of models, and we come to inhabit a modelling of reality that is purported to be all the reality there is. Otherness is incarcerated in simulacra, in models of otherness. But why must the imperium go to the trouble of preserving wild otherness, even if only as simulacra, rather than totally destroying this adversarial opposition and then forgetting about it altogether? Why does the imperium need to create and preserve its Genets and its wilderness preserves? At bottom, it is a matter of the imperium's need to preserve its own meaningfulness, to protect itself from "vanishing into the play of signs":

> Power . . . for some time now produces nothing but signs of its resemblance. And at the same time, another figure of power comes into play: that of a collective demand for *signs* of power—a holy union which forms around the disappearance of power. . . . When it has totally disappeared, logically we will be under the total spell of power—a haunting memory already foreshadowed everywhere, manifesting at one and the same time the compulsion to get rid of it (nobody wants it anymore, everybody unloads it on others) and the apprehensive pining over its loss.[21]

The whole point, purpose, and meaning of imperial power, and its most basic legitimation, is to give humans control over otherness. Once this is totally achieved, or perceived to be achieved, the game is over, and continuing to play it is meaningless. This holds true as much in the case of the manufactured hyperreality, which generates what is really an illusion or "hallucination" of total control, as it does for the real thing (which could be achieved only by some imperial eighteenth-century God the Father). The imperium must therefore attempt to keep its game, itself, alive by preserving its "reality principle," but preferably to the greatest extent possible by simulating this too. Thus, we are given Disneyland and the fantasy fare of television:

> Disneyland is there to conceal the fact that it is the "real" country, all of "real" America, which *is* Disneyland (just as prisons are there to conceal the fact that it is the social in its entirety, in its banal omnipresence, which is carceral). Disneyland is presented as imaginary in order to make us believe that the rest is real, when in fact all of Los Angeles and the America surrounding it are no longer real, but of the order of the hyperreal and of simulation. It is no longer a question of a false representation of reality (ideology), but of concealing the fact that the real is no longer real, and thus of saving the reality principle.[22]

## THE GROUND OF SUBVERSION

When Roderick Nash argues that "Civilization created wilderness," he quotes Luther Standing Bear:

> We did not think of the great open plains, the beautiful rolling hills and the winding streams with tangled growth as "wild." Only to the white man was nature a "wilderness" and . . . the land "infested" with "wild" animals and

"savage" people. . . . there was no wilderness; since nature was not dangerous but hospitable; not forbidding but friendly.[23]

The real point, which is not the point that Nash is trying to make out of what Luther Standing Bear has said, is that the wilderness, and now the wilderness reservations that the white imperium has created in obedience to its traditional story of law bringing, is an adversarial other to be subdued and controlled. In response I would argue that the other does not *have to be* an adversary or a simulation of an adversary. Certainly it is not an adversary for Luther Standing Bear. He sees the land in terms of a different story, a story which holds that the fundamental human relationship with nature, and with wildness itself, is participatory, cooperative, and complementary, rather than conflictive. At times, of course, and also in the terms of the other story, there is conflict, but normally wild nature sustains, sponsors, empowers, and makes human existence possible. Nature is wild, always wild, in the sense that it is not subject to human control. In this sense, humans are participants in a wildness that is far larger and more powerful than they can ever be, and to which human law bringing is so radically inappropriate as to be simply absurd. This is the sort of understanding of wilderness and its relationship with culture that we need to retrieve and reconstruct in postmodern society in response to the imperium's desire for total dominion.

It seems fair to take the RARE II (Roadless Area Review and Evaluation, second try) process in the United States as typical of and precedent setting for Western civilization's approach to wildland. The United States is, at the moment, the most powerful center of the imperium of Western culture, and the example of RARE II will be followed on the global level. Note that RARE II was implemented by the relatively liberal Carter administration and was intended as a reform of RARE I, to correct its mistakes. The purpose of the RARE process was to search out and evaluate the utilities of all remaining wildland in the national forests with the goal of determining its allocation or disposition, thereby giving it definition, bringing meaning into its nothingness, so that nothing remains unmanaged waste outside of the imperium. RARE II typifies the final step in the imperium's appropriation of wild nature, its most powerful enemy. The RARE process should be seen as a "search and destory" mission to discover and appropriate or exterminate the last vestiges of wild land in America, to complete the imperium. The acronym for the key instrument of wilderness evaluation in the field was WARS (Wilderness Attribute Rating System). As in the case of a racist joke, the subtext, or presupposition, of this cynical attempt at humor is near the surface and easily seen.[24]

The RARE II process thus marks the completion of the imperium's imposition of its network of control, bringing all wildland under management for some set of utilities. Whereas in the past there were wildland Guianas, which were ignored and to which wildness and wild nature were either let go or ostracized from civilization, places that were *outside* the system of management, but places where wildness could to some extent flower in its own integrities, with RARE II there are only legally designated wilderness areas or reservations in which wild nature, the ultimate other, has been locked into specific management schemata. Whereas, once upon a time, for example in the time of Homer, Western culture was a cluster of tenuously connected islands surrounded by a sea of wildness, civilization now surrounds (or so goes the deluded story) the last islands of wildness, and puts everything to use, wasting nothing. Even Genet is published—just as one of the recognized reasons for official wilderness is to benefit those "oddballs" who thrive on it, or even to permit the furtherance of their "self-realization." Wilderness and wildness are placed on the supermarket shelf of values along with everything else, and everything is enclosed *inside* the supermarket.

Yet there is a contradiction in the imperium's attempt to appropriate wildness, for, as we have seen above, it is not possible practically for the imperium to silence the subversive voice of the other completely or to stifle its glance. For the imperium, the problem with appropriating wildness by incarcerating it in the prisons of wilderness reservations is that the wildness is still there, and it is still wild, and it does "speak" to us. . . . When wildness speaks, it always says more than what the imperium would train it to say or train us to hear because wildness stays adamant in its own integrity, as other in its own unconditioned freedom. Thus, managing wildness is contradictory, even though managing official wilderness areas and prisons is not. There is an insurmountable tension in the notion of managing wildness, and of managing land *for* wildness. How much wildfire, how much insect evolution, for example, is to be permitted? We *cannot* know. Wildness is logically intractable to systemization. There can be no natural laws of wildness. . . .

## TOWARD RESIDENCE IN SACRED SPACE

Thinking of legally designated wilderness reserves as "sacred spaces" is not by itself enough to rescue official wilderness spaces from the totalizing grip of imperial power. Although there has always been a place for the sacred in the imperial order, in Western culture secular power has long ago triumphed over the church. As far as the imperium is concerned, the sacred, the mystical, and so forth are just the other side of the coin of criminal wild otherness.[25] Wilderness, like religion and morality, is fine for weekends and holidays, but during the working week it may in no way inform business as usual. Thus, the imperium incarcerates its sacred other in churches, convents, and ministries, but if its functionaries (like the Berrigans) take their sacred obligations out of the assigned area and, say, into the streets, they are imprisoned, or otherwise neutralized. It is perfectly fine with the imperium if, on weekends and holidays, some of its citizens wish to follow John Muir to the temples of the wilderness areas, rather than the usual churches—and this will probably hold for American Indian religions as well.[26] By making room for sacred space, the imperium confirms its tolerance, generosity, its rectitude, its beneficence, and it does so without having to abrogate *its* other (thus maintaining its bad faith). However, actually to inhabit, to live in, sacred space is an anathema, absolutely incompatible with the imperium:

> The idea that holiness inheres in the place where one lives is alien to the European tradition, for in that tradition sacred space is sundered, set aside, a place one goes only to worship. But to live in sacred space is the most forceful affirmation of the sacredness of the whole earth.[27]

For the imperium, only that which is other can be sacred, because all of the usual world, the mundane and the not-so-mundane, is taken to be profane, secular, objective. The imperium is committed to cordoning off sacred space, to separating it as other, effectively keeping it out of the center of our practical lives, and keeping us out of it and thus safe from its subversive effect. Wildness as wilderness land is incarcerated as sacred space. This is perhaps one of the main uses to which the imperial order puts wilderness. It consigns sacred space to the museum of holy relics, as one of the prime manifestations of the wildness it is compelled to incarcerate in order to demonstrate its total triumph.

The point, then, is that even the preservation of wilderness as sacred space must be conceived and practiced as part of a larger strategy that aims to make all land into, or back into, sacred space, and thereby to move humanity into a conscious reinhabitation of wildness. As Gary Snyder has pointed out:

> Inspiration, exaltation, insight do not end . . . when one steps outside the doors of the church. The wilderness as a temple is only a beginning. That is: one should not . . . leave the political world behind to be in a state of heightened insight . . . [but] be able to come back into the present world to see all the land about us, agricultural, suburban, urban, as part of the same giant realm of processes and beings—never totally ruined, never completely unnatural.[28]

Wilderness reserves should be understood as simply the largest and most pure entities in a continuum of sacred space that should also include, for example, wilderness restoration areas of all sizes, mini-wildernesses, pocket-wildernesses in every schoolyard, old roadbeds, wild plots in suburban yards, flower boxes in urban windows, cracks in the pavement, field, farm, home, and work-place, all the ubiquitous "margins." As Wendell Berry puts it:

> . . . lanes, streamsides, wooded fence rows . . . freeholds of wildness . . . enact, within the bounds of human domesticity itself, a human courtesy toward the wild that is one of the best safeguards of designated tracts of true wilderness. This is the landscape of harmony . . . democratic and free.[29]

Wilderness reserves make an indispensable contribution to establishing and inhabiting Berry's "landscape of harmony" writ large, which is how we should write it, a landscape that is thoroughly predicated upon and infused with wildness. The larger wilderness reserves, where the essence of otherness as wildness is most powerfully evident, continuously freshen, enliven, and em-power this infusion of wildness, on the analogy of water from mountain water-shed sources. The ideal goal, however, is a landscape that is self-sustaining and everywhere self-sufficient in wildness. Enough margins in some locales (per-haps including some Third World locales) could bring this about, or serve as the starting point toward reaching the goal of a larger harmony.

Because the landscape of harmony is an inhabited harmony with otherness and with others, respected in their own integrities, and thus a landscape, a "land" in Leopold's sense, and a form of human life that cooperates with others as complementary to us, it constitutes hope for an implacable counter-force to the momentum of totalizing imperial power. Furthermore, to a great extent, the margins, still exist, although we seldom notice them and neglect them. To achieve Berry's landscape of harmony we must, as it were, demar-ginalize the margins, including the legal wilderness reserves, and come to see and practice their continuing and sustaining primacy to all that we humans can value and construct. Then we can take up residence in wildness, where Luther Standing Bear lived, reinhabiting it now, of course, with different appropriate technologies and social forms. Then we can recover our endan-gered knowledge of reality and disempower the bad faith that the imperium puts upon us.

## THE JUSTIFICATION OF LEGAL WILDLAND ENTITIES

Wilderness reservations are best viewed as holes and cracks, as "free spaces" or "liberated zones," in the fabric of domination and self-deception that fuels and shapes our mainstream contemporary culture. Working to preserve wild nature, in wilderness reservations, or anywhere, is primarily, at this historical moment, an essential holding action, to stop the complete triumph of the bad faith of our culture, especially in regard to ecological reality, and to save us from ineluctably destructive self-deception. Although the culture may deceive itself and believe that wilderness reservations are successful appropriations of the wild and/or sacred and ethical opposition, in fact, their existence, properly understood, helps preserve and foster the possibility of liberation from our imperialist tradition. This subversive potential is what justifies their establishment.

From the ethical standpoint, the purpose and the only justification of laws is to help us fulfill our obligations, or to meet the practical necessities that are incumbent upon us. If legally created wilderness areas do, or can be made to, serve the subversive role I have pointed out, then the laws that create them are thereby ethically justified. Then wilderness reservations serve as a crucial counterfriction to the machine of total domination, slowing it down and creating a window through which a postmodern landscape of harmony may be found. But insofar as wilderness reservations, as they are so often (mis)understood, only serve the completion of the imperium, they are not justifiable. Wilderness must be preserved for the right reasons—to help save the possibility and foster the practice of conscious, active, continuing human participation in wildness, as well as to preserve others for their own sakes. The institution of legally designated wilderness reserves does make an essential contribution toward meeting this larger necessity. However, it is crucial to remember that, important as they are, legal wildland entities are not always and everywhere either the ethically sound or most effective means for meeting this larger necessity, especially if they are imperialistically understood and exported and colonially imposed, either domestically or internationally. I have suggested above what some of the other means may be. But on this question there is very much culturally and economically imaginative and sensitive work waiting to be done.

Of course, all of this looks to the possibility of a more ideal time, to a vision toward which we can struggle, when our practice of respect for nature has become so refined that preservationist laws would no longer be needed, a time when we have moved out of the imperium and taken up residence in wildness. The realization of this vision would mean recovering the sort of relation between humans and others, including human others, that Luther Standing Bear, for instance, sees as basic. It would mean realizing in contemporary practice what Leslie Marmon Silko has called "the requisite balance between human and *other*."[30] Others would then be seen and lived with as complementary to us, as we all live together in the wild and continuous composition of the world.

## NOTES

1. Roderick Nash, "International Concepts of Wilderness Preservation," in Hendee, Stankey, and Lucas, *Wilderness Management,* Misc. Publication No. 1365 (Washington, D.C.: U.S. Forest Service, 1978): 58.

2. For a forceful account of how First World wilderness preservation can appear to Third World peoples, see Ramachandra Guha, "Radical American Environmentalism and Wilderness Preservation: A Third World Critique," in *Environmental Ethics* 11 (1989): 71–83.

3. Roderick Nash, *Wilderness and the American Mind,* 3rd ed. (New Haven: Yale University Press, 1982), xiii, 44.

4. Roderick Nash, *The Rights of Nature* (Madison: University of Wisconsin Press, 1989), 10.

5. Ibid., 11.

6. See John Rodman, "The Liberation of Nature?" in *Inquiry* 20 (1977): 83–145, and "Four Forms of Ecological Consciousness Reconsidered," in Donald Scherer and Tom Attig (eds.), *Ethics and the Environment* (Englewood Cliffs, N.J.: Prentice-Hall, 1983), 82–92.

7. Donald Worster, *Rivers of Empire* (New York: Pantheon Books, 1985), 11.

8. Patricia Nelson Limerick, *The Legacy of Conquest* (New York: Norton, 1987), 21, 26.

9. I am using the term "practical necessities" in the sense offered by Bernard Williams: "When a deliberative conclusion embodies a consideration that has the highest deliberative priority and is also of the greatest importance (at least to the agent), it may take a special form and become a conclusion not merely that one should do a certain thing, but that one *must,* and that one cannot do anything else. We may call this a conclusion of practical necessity . . . a 'must' that is unconditional and *goes all the way down.*" Bernard Williams, *Ethics and the Limits of Philosophy* (Cambridge: Harvard University Press, 1985), 197–98.

10. William Kittredge, *Owning It All* (Saint Paul: Graywolf Press, 1987), 156–57.

11. Ibid., 64.

12. I am using the term *imperium* in the sense given by the *Oxford English Dictionary:* "command; absolute power; supreme or imperial power; Empire."

13. Section 2 (a) of the Wilderness Act of 1964; emphasis added.

14. See Section 4 (a)1 of the Wilderness Act of 1964, where consistency with the Multiple-Use Sustained-Yield Act is stipulated. The Wilderness Act permits the mining of claims established until 1984 for lands covered by the act. Roughly speaking, the legality of mining for other designated wilderness lands has been decided on a case by case basis. For an excellent account of wilderness values, see Holmes Rolston III, *Philosophy Gone Wild* (Buffalo: Prometheus Books, 1986), 180–205. Note further that the Wilderness Act, at Section 4 (d)4, explicitly reserves the right to further resource uses within designated wilderness areas: ". . . prospecting for water resources, water-conservation works, power projects, transmission lines, and other facilities needed in the public interest, including road construction and maintenance. . . ."

15. For a sound discussion of wilderness as the source of resources, and not a resource itself, see Holmes Rolston III, "Values Gone Wild," in *Philosophy Gone Wild,* 118–42.

16. Michel Foucault, *Discipline & Punish* (New York: Vintage Books, 1979), 301. Also see Foucault's *Madness and Civilization* (New York: Vintage Books, 1973).

17. See the Wilderness Act at Section 4 (d)1: "Such measures may be taken as may be necessary in the control of fire, insects, and disease, subject to such conditions as the Secretary deems desirable." For an interpretation of the Wilderness Act, see Hendee et al., *Wilderness Management,* 82. Note the current halt and reconsideration of the let-burn policy for wilderness fire management, as the result of the huge Yellowstone and Canyon Creek (Scapegoat Wilderness Area) fires in the summer of 1988.

18. See Noam Chomsky, *The Culture of Terrorism* (Boston: South End Press, 1988), 32. Chomsky quotes the first major publication of the Trilaterial Commission as saying that our educational institutions are responsible for "the indoctrination of the young."

19. Jean Baudrillard, *Simulations* (New York: Semiotext[e], 1983), 146–47.

20. Ibid., 147–48.

21. Ibid., 44–45.

22. Ibid., 25.

23. This is an opportune point to notice just how natural, appropriate, and even plausible it is for Roderick Nash, in his chapter on "The International Perspective" in *Wilderness and the American Mind,* to subsume wild nature and wilderness reservations into the rhetoric of international export-import commercialism. In this vein, he suggests that "national parks and wilderness systems might be thought of as institutional 'containers' that developed nations send to underdeveloped ones for the purpose of 'packaging' a fragile resource" (344). Such a packaging in containers, defined by *its* model of the wild other, and the experience of it (the "wilderness experience") is precisely what the imperium tries to achieve. Nash, *Wilderness and the American Mind,* xiii.

24. In the same vein, the acronym for the latest wilderness management practices is LAC (Limits of Acceptable Change).

25. See Guha, "Radical American Environmentalism and Wilderness Preservation" for development of this point.

26. Eventually either the recent negative Supreme Court decision on Indian religious rights to preserve sacred lands (*Lyng vs. Northwest Indian Cemetery Protective Association*) will be somehow softened by the courts or Congress will (slightly) strengthen the American Indian Religious Freedom Act. The logic of imperial power requires this sort of liberality. Of course, the imperium could never afford the liberality of classifying all land as sacred in any meaningful sense. But some designated and narrowly defined sacred areas will be allowed, or, to use the language of rights, "granted."

27. J. Donald Hughes and Jim Swan, "How Much of the Earth Is Sacred Space?" *Environmental Review* 10 (1986): 256.

28. Gary Snyder, "Good, Wild, Sacred," in Wes Jackson, et al. (eds.), *Meeting the Expectations of the Land* (San Francisco: North Point Press, 1984), 205.

29. Wendell Berry, "Preserving Wildness," in *Home Economics* (San Francisco: North Point Press, 1987), 151. The antithesis of the "landscape of harmony" is that of industrial monoculture—the landscape of the imperium.

30. Leslie Marmon Silko, "Landscape, History, and the Pueblo Imagination," *Antaeus* 57 (1986): 92. The "balance" we need to find is that which Silko says the Pueblo people had to find, and did, in order to become a culture. It is not the balance of cost-benefit analysis, but that of the dance, which requires loving, graceful integration of self and society within the wild whole of an otherness we revere.

# 32 | ECOCENTRISM, WILDERNESS, AND GLOBAL ECOSYSTEM PROTECTION

## *George Sessions*

## WILDERNESS: FROM MUIR TO PINCHOT TO MUIR

THE ECOPHILOSOPHER HOLMES ROLSTON III has quoted disapprovingly from a 1978 U.S. Forest Service document on "wilderness management" that asserts: "Wilderness is for people. . . . The preservation goals established for such areas are designed to provide values and benefits to society. . . . Wilderness is not set aside for the sake of its flora or fauna, but for people."[1]

It is disappointing to find Forest Service theorists in the late 1970s still promoting narrowly human-centered views of the function and values of wilderness. In so doing, they follow in the footsteps of the U.S. Forest Service founder, Gifford Pinchot, who once claimed "there are just people and resources." As the ideological archrival of John Muir at the beginning of the twentieth century, Pinchot promoted the anthropocentrism and utilitarian resource management mentality that has pervaded conservationist and land-use agency policy since the turn of the century.

It is somewhat ironic that Forest Service theorists continue with this unecological anthropocentric approach when we consider that Aldo Leopold (the *founder* of the Forest Service wilderness concept in the 1920s) published his justly famous ecocentric "land ethic" over forty years ago, and when profes-

Originally published (in a longer version) in *The Wilderness Condition,* edited by Max Oelschlaeger (San Francisco: Sierra Club Books, 1992). Copyright © 1992 by Max Oelschlaeger. Reprinted with permission of Sierra Club Books. Revised 1993.

sional ecologists have been promoting the ecological functions of wilderness at the Sierra Club Wilderness Conferences since the late 1950s.

Unlike the Forest Service, the National Park Service began to implement an ecological approach to its wilderness and wildlife policies in the spring of 1963, following the suggestions of its Advisory Board on Wildlife Management (the so-called Leopold Report, named for its chairman, Starker Leopold, the son of Aldo Leopold and a zoologist at the University of California at Berkeley). The Leopold Report proposed that the wilderness parks, using Yellowstone as a model, be treated as "biotic wholes." Leopold's committee, according to Alston Chase, was proposing "a philosophy of management that could be applied universally" (for instance, to the African wildlife reserves).[2]

Alston Chase blames the wilderness ecosystem approach for the decline of wildlife and ecological deterioration of Yellowstone, and has proposed instead a heavily manipulative scientific wildlife management approach—one that would turn Yellowstone into what some have described as a "natural zoo." Ecologists claim that, like most parks when established, Yellowstone does not comprise a complete ecosystem. For the ecosystem approach to work, a "Greater Yellowstone Ecosystem" must be established and legally protected. In addition, predator/prey balances must be reestablished, as through the reintroduction of the wolf.[3]

When Congress passed the Forest Reserve Act in 1891 enabling President Benjamin Harrison to set aside 13 million acres in "forest reserves," Muir had reason to believe they would be protected as wilderness. But the "forest reserves" later became National Forests, and Pinchot and the Forest Service had other plans for them. Following Pinchot's advocacy of the Resource Conservation and Development position, the Forest Service (as a branch of the Department of Agriculture) sees its primary function as serving as a handmaiden for industrial "resource" exploitation. Ecologically destructive activities such as mining, domestic animal grazing, and sport hunting, are allowed even within National Forest designated wilderness areas. And just as the Pioneers cleared wild forests to make way for agriculture, the Forest Service has facilitated and promoted the destruction of the last unprotected old growth (ancient) forest ecosystems in America to make way for agriculture in the form of biologically sterile monocultural "tree farms"—where the trees consist of one or two commercially valuable species, are even-aged, and grow in nice neat rows like a field of corn.

For the Forest Service, the forests are a *commodity* to be managed, "enhanced," and exploited: either as an agricultural crop to be "harvested" or as designated areas where "the wilderness experience" serves as a human recreational commodity. Forest economists decide these issues by assigning an economic value to the various human "uses" of the forests and computing a cost-benefit analysis.

Further, the forests are to be "enhanced"—and *domesticated*—by replacing ancient forest biodiversity with genetically manipulated "superior" (more economically valuable) trees which grow straighter and faster. One wonders about the wisdom of this now that the genetically "enhanced" domestic grains of the agricultural Green Revolution have turned sour. At present, geneticists are scouring the world for the genetic variability of whatever little pockets of wild grains still remain that have not been genetically tampered with. On the other hand, John Muir has already responded to this genetic tampering with the forests when he claimed that "all wildness is finer than tameness." Similiarly, for Thoreau: "In wildness is the preservation of the world."

As early as 1976, John Rodman pointed out:

> The charges frequently made in recent years by Preservationists and others—e.g., that the Forest Service is a captive (or willing) agent of corporate interests, that it allows ecologically-disruptive clear-cutting as well as cutting in excess of official quotas, while permitting grazing corporations to overgraze the land while paying fees far less than they would have to pay for the use of private land, etc.—represent less the latter-day capture of an agency by one or more of its constituents than a maturation of the basic principles of the founder [Pinchot]. The Forest Service is, in effect, a perennial government subsidy, in exchange for certain regulatory controls, to certain types of corporations.[4]

The massive clear-cutting of the last unprotected old-growth coniferous forests along the West Coast of North America (from California to Washington and into the Tongass National Forest in Southeast Alaska) is surpassed in unbridled destruction only by the unrestricted Canadian clear-cutting of British Columbia. At the present rate of clear-cutting along the British Columbia coast, this world's largest remaining temperate rain forest will be gone in fifteen years.[5] Surely, the loss of these last great ancient forest ecosystems in North America will go down as one of the great ecological crimes and blunders of this century, comparable to present rain forest destruction in the Amazon and the rest of Central and South America, Africa, Australia, and Southeast Asia. Japan's thirst for wood products for international markets has been primarily responsible for encouraging the destruction of 80 to 90 percent of the tropical forests in Sri Lanka and Southeast Asia over the last forty years. Japan is also a leading exploiter of the old-growth forests of Central and South America (including Brazil, Peru, and Chile) and the United States (including Southeast Alaska). Japanese corporations are now negotiating with Russia to clear cut the great pine forests of Siberia, the habitat of the Siberian tiger.

The destruction of the biodiversity of the last of the wild ancient forest ecosystems, and their replacement with unstable even-age tree plantations, is now occurring all over the world at an increasing rate.[6] Forestry critic Chris Maser points out that we are nowhere near attaining "sustainable forestry" even on those lands where tree cutting is appropriate, because we are training "plantation managers" instead of foresters. He writes: "We are liquidating our forests and replacing them with short-rotation plantations. Everything Nature does in designing forests adds to diversity, complexity, and stability through time. We decrease this by redesigning forests into plantations."[7] The destruction of ancient forests must cease, and a massive global effort should be made to try to *restore* diverse wild forest ecosystems. Fortunately, wide-scale public pressure is now being applied to modern forestry ideology to bring about major ecological reform. And even Pinchot-trained foresters are beginning to undergo a change of heart. As Canadian forester Bob Nixon recently remarked:

> As a forester, I learned to view forests as a source of industrial fibre. Now, I know that forests are much more than vertical assemblages of lumber, so very much more important than just a source of consumer products. . . . Natural forests, the new research tells us, are no longer something to move through, in the economic sense, in our quest for higher gains, but indeed a key element in the balanced functioning of planetary life.[8]

And how has wildness fared in Muir's National Parks under the anthropocentric orientation of twentieth-century America? The parks do not allow resource extraction within their boundaries, including their newly designated wilderness areas. But many of the parks have been damaged by NPS policies over the years that have catered to dominant American values and lifestyles, which see the parks as essentially natural "scenery" and recreational escapes for city-dwellers. This has encouraged a Disneyland atmosphere of excessive tourism and overdeveloped facilities, upgraded high-speed roads ("scenic drives"), mechanized recreation such as snowmobiling (which disturbs the tranquillity and the wildlife) and human overcrowding: what Edward Abbey called "industrial tourism."[9] In short, there has been a constant push from the commercially motivated to turn them into "theme parks" and international "roadside attractions."

## THE IMPLICATIONS OF CONSERVATION BIOLOGY FOR THE EARTH'S EVOLUTIONARY PROCESSES

The adequacy of currently designated wilderness areas and nature reserves throughout the world received a serious jolt in the 1980s from the findings of the new discipline of conservation biology.

In the 1960s, professional ecologists stepped outside their narrow areas of scientific expertise and began warning the public of the impending ecological disaster. They also proposed various public strategies to cope with these problems. The "intellectual activism" begun by these ecologists has been institutionalized into a new branch of ecology called "conservation biology." According to Mitch Friedman:

> Conservation biology considers the application of ecological theory and knowledge to conservation efforts. The development and utilization of this new discipline is a welcome advance in conservation, where ecological considerations tend to be overshadowed by political and economic forces, in part due to poor understanding of the effects of land-use decisions.[10]

Conservation biology has been spearheaded largely by Michael Soulé (an ecologist and a former student of Paul Ehrlich), who refers to conservation biology as a "crisis discipline" that has to apply its findings in the absence of certainty. This new field integrates ethical norms with the latest findings of ecological science.[11]

Soulé has provided scientific definitions for the terms "conservation" and "preservation." In his usage, "preservation" means "the maintenance of individuals or groups, but not for their evolutionary change." He proposes that "conservation" be taken to denote "policies and programs for the long-term retention of natural communities under conditions which provide for the potential for continuing evolution." Mitch Friedman carries this a step further by introducing the concept of "ecosystem conservation." This approach "involves the preservation of ecosystem wilderness: enough of the land area and functional components—the creatures *and* their habitat—to insure the continuation of processes which have co-evolved over immeasurable time."[12]

One can quibble over the choice of terms. "Conservation" has negative associations with Pinchot and the Resource Conservation and Development position. And "preservation" does not necessarily mean trying to maintain something in a static state, such as "preserving jam" or "deep-freezing" a wilderness. Perhaps "protection" would be a more neutral term. However, the term "ecosystem conservation" means protecting the ongoing dynamic continuum of evolutionary processes that constitutes the overall ecological health of the planet, in the sense described by Aldo Leopold.

It is thus clear that the *primary purpose* in setting aside and evaluating wilderness areas and wild nature preserves, from the standpoint of conservation biology and the ecological crisis, is the conservation and protection of wild plants, animals, and ecosystems (biotic diversity) and the continuation of wild evolutionary processes.

Based upon these objectives, we need to look at present global ecological realities. As Friedman points out:

An element of panic is present within the literature of conservation biology, as well as among the conservation community at large. This panic originates predominately from the present rate of species extinction, and the forecasts for impending mass extinction. We presently have scarcely a clue of even the total number of species on the planet, with estimates ranging between three and thirty-seven million. Yet, some researchers are predicting that anthropogenic extinctions, at current rates (which do not consider military disasters or other unpredictable events), may eliminate as many as a third of the planet's species over the next several decades (Meyers, 1987). This is shocking to anyone who treasures the intrinsic values of Earth's natural diversity and fecundity, or who fears for the fate of humanity and the planet as a whole. While most of these extinctions are occurring as a result of tropical rainforest deforestation, the same processes are occurring in temperate areas, including the United States (Wilcove et al., 1986).[13]

A further crisis that conservation biology has brought to public attention, as the result of ecological research in the 1980s, is that existing nature reserves (namely, national park and forest wilderness areas) do not meet realistic ecological criteria: they are too small and disconnected to protect biodiversity and ecological/evolutionary processes. Friedman claims:

> It is not enough to preserve some habitat for each species if we want to conserve ecosystems; the habitat must remain in the conditions under which the resident species evolved. For this reason, national forests, under present "multiple use" management, may not be effective nature reserves for many species.
>
> Historically, national parks and other reserves have been established according to political, or other nonbiological considerations. . . . To conserve species diversity, the legal boundaries of nature reserves should be congruent with natural criteria (Newmark, 1985). For instance, a reserve may be large [e.g., Everglades National Park] while still not protecting the ecological integrity of the area.
>
> Newmark (1985) suggests that reserves contain not only entire watersheds, but at least the minimum area necessary to maintain viable populations of those species which have the largest home ranges. Others have stated that complete, intact ecosystems should be preserved (Terborgh and Winter, 1980; Noss, 1985).[14]

In the 1970s Michael Soulé examined twenty wildlife reserves in East Africa, including the massive Tsavo and Serengeti national parks. He and his fellow researchers projected that

> all of the reserves will suffer extinctions in the near future. Their study predicts that a typical reserve, if it becomes a habitat island, will lose almost half of its large mammal species over the next 500 years . . . when a habitat island, for instance a national park surrounded by national forest, is reduced in size

(i.e., clearcutting along the park boundaries), the number of species in that island will decrease. The empirical evidence for the relaxation effect is alarming, and reflects the urgency with which we must re-evaluate our conservation strategies and remedy the situation.[15]

Edward Grumbine further points out that

Newmark (1985) investigated eight parks and park assemblages and found that even the largest reserve was six times too small to support minimum viable populations of species such as grizzly bear, mountain lion, black bear, wolverine, and gray wolf. A recent study by Salwasser et al. (1987) looked beyond park boundaries and included adjacent public lands as part of conservation networks. The results were the same. Only the largest area (81,000 square km) was sufficient to protect large vertebrate species over the long term. . . . Virtually every study of this type has reached similar conclusions: No park in the coterminus U.S. is capable of supporting minimum viable populations of large mammals over the long term. And the situation is worsening.[16]

Frankel and Soulé claim that "an area on the order of 600,000 square km (approximately equal to all of Washington and Oregon) is necessary for speciation of birds and large mammals."[17]

Christopher Manes quotes Soulé as saying that "for the first time in hundreds of millions of years significant evolutionary change in most higher organisms is coming to a screeching halt. . . . Vertebrate evolution may be at an end." Manes claims that Soulé's remarks may be as significant as the findings of Copernicus or Darwin in that "only a hundred or so years after Darwin 'discovered' our fundamental relationship to nature in terms of evolution, we are, according to Soulé, putting an end to it."[18]

The inescapable conclusion is this: there needs to be widespread public recognition that current global wilderness and nature preserve protection policies are failing miserably. Past policies and strategies have been based on inadequate ecological understanding. Humans have effectively clogged the evolutionary arteries of Mother Gaia.

Along with protecting the ozone layer, minimizing the severity of the greenhouse effect, and stabilizing (and then reducing) the growth and size of the human population, the most crucial ecological task facing humanity at this time is to devise and implement realistic nature reserve protection strategies.

## APPROACHES TO GLOBAL ECOSYSTEM PROTECTION ZONING

Even before conservation biologists were demonstrating the necessity for greatly expanded nature preserves throughout the world with interconnecting corridors, ecologists and environmentalists over twenty years ago had called for worldwide zoning to protect wild ecosystems and species. The first such proposal was made by David Brower in 1967. Declaring that less than 10 percent of the Earth had, at that time, escaped technological exploitation by humans, he proposed protecting the remaining wilderness and "granting other life forms the right to coexist" in what Jerry Mander called an Earth International Park.[19]

Another major zoning proposal was put forth in 1971 by the noted ecologist Eugene Odum. Odum proposed that:

> *The biosphere as a whole should be zoned,* in order to protect it from the human impact. We must strictly confine the Urban-Industrial Zone and the Production Zone (agriculture, grazing, fishing), enlarge the Compromise Zone, and drastically expand the Protection Zone, i.e., wilderness, wild rivers. Great expanses of seacoasts and estuaries must be included in the Protection Zone, along with forests, prairies and various habitat types. We must learn that the multiple-use Compromise Zone is no substitute, with its mining, lumbering, grazing, and recreation in the national forests, for the scientific, aesthetic, and genetic pool values of the Protection Zone. Such zoning, if carried out in time, may be the only way to limit the destructive impact of our technological–industrial–agri-business complex on earth.

In commenting upon Odum's proposal, John Phillips claimed that "to go so far as to zone the biosphere and set aside an adequate Protection Zone would be a supreme act of rationality by which the rational animal could protect the rest of life on earth, and himself, from his own irrational temptations."[20]

In 1973, Paul Shepard made a daring proposal for global ecosystem protection. In order to allow for the huge expanses of unmanaged wilderness needed "for ecological and evolutionary systems on a scale essential to their own requirements," he proposed that the interiors of continents and islands be allowed to return to the wild. Based on the now optimistic assumption that human population would stabilize by the year 2020 at 8 billion people, he proposed that humans live in cities strung in narrow ribbons along the edges of the continents. Hunting/gathering forays would range into the central wilderness, but there would be no permanent habitation.[21]

Based on his ecocentric orientation, Shepard foresaw the huge amounts of wilderness necessary for the healthy ecological and evolutionary functioning of the Earth. But his proposal has a number of practical and social/political problems, not the least of which would be (1) the physical problems involved in relocating humans to the edges of the continents, and (2) the pressures exerted by these concentrated human populations on the ocean shoreline ecosystems and estuaries. At this stage of history, it is probably more realistic to expand and interconnect ecosystem protection zones with the basically existing patterns of human settlement in mind.

Two other strategies that were developed to protect wild ecosystems are the Biosphere Reserve concept, as part of UNESCO's Man and the Biosphere Program, and the World Heritage Site system. According to Edward Grumbine:

> A model biosphere reserve consists of four integrated zones: a large protected core; a buffer zone; a restoration zone; and a stable cultural area where "indigenous people live in harmony with the environment." . . . the National Park Service has informally adopted the biosphere reserve model as a guide to regional land planning [and] after eighteen years, 41 biosphere reserves exist in the U.S. many of which occupy both national park and forest lands.[22]

Grumbine sees some possibilities with World Heritage Site designations, but he argues that there are serious problems with the Biosphere Reserve concept: the zones are not properly related and the "self-sustaining" core is not large enough to allow for speciation. He suggests that the biosphere reserve model be replaced by a national system of biological reserves.

## ECOLOGICAL RESTORATION, MITIGATION, AND STEWARDSHIP

Grumbine further argues that the establishment of biological reserves needs to be supplemented by a major program of *ecological restoration:*

> Restoration of damaged lands must be married to the goal of native diversity. This follows the *wilderness recovery* strategy of Noss (1986) and would include large scale restoration of natural fire cycles, recovery of threatened, endangered, and extirpated species, road closures and reforestation projects, stream rehabilitation to increase native anadromous fisheries, and much more (see Berger, 1985). Once an area was restored, nature would take its course with minimal interference from managers. The amount of work to be done would likely offset the loss of jobs in exploitive industries.[23]

The concept of ecological restoration is a crucial one for all of the zones, but serious problems emerge when developers try to use it as a justification for "mitigation" procedures: claiming that we can continue to develop (that is, *destroy*) wild ecosystems, displace wildlife, and then compensate these losses by "restoring" an equivalent area elsewhere. This is a shortsighted foolhardy approach, part of the overall "Disneyland syndrome" and the mentality that "human ingenuity and technological know-how can solve all our problems." This neglects the difficult and expensive process of restoration, together with the probability that restoration projects will be only partially successful. In all likelihood, they cannot reproduce the incredibly complex and diverse wild ecosystems that were destroyed. Further, mitigation procedures and environmental impact reports (EIR's), as they now exist in environmental law and as taught in environmental management programs in colleges and universities, function basically to "grease the skids" of continued growth and development as wildlife habitat is fragmented and destroyed, and wild flora and fauna relentlessly continue to disappear.

The anthropocentric/ecocentric debate has resurfaced in the context of trying to clarify the concept of "ecological restoration." Some restoration theorists argue for a stewardship approach in which restoration areas are to be treated as agricultural farms to be continuously manipulated and "enhanced" by humans (which is similar to the ideology of the Forest Service and their genetically "enhanced" forests). For instance, restoration theorist John Harper proposes the manipulative, interventionist, Baconian/Cartesian model of science as appropriate for ecology and restoration ecology:

> The *raison d'être* for a science of ecology is presumably the development of an understanding of the workings of nature that would enable us to predict its behavior and to manage and control it to our liking. . . . [Thus] the importance of a more manipulative, experimental approach to ecological research such as that represented by restoration ecology.

There is a play on words here, a bit of Orwellian Newspeak, with Harper's concept of ecological restoration. If one is going to continuously manipulate, there is no *ecological* restoration. By proposing the human-dominant managerial stewardship model for restoration ecology (the "participatory happy gardener" image of René Dubos) Harper seems totally unconcerned with the continual extension of human domesticity and the elimination of more wildness while, at the same time he assumes that humans are competent to manage Nature. Professional ecologists such as Frank Egler have countered that "Nature is not only more complex than we think, it is more complex than we *can* think!"[24]

Critics claim that proponents of nature preserves (which are largely free of human intervention and manipulation) view Nature as "static." But from Thoreau and Muir to modern conservation biologists, the protection of wildness in nature (or wilderness) preserves has been seen as the protection of wild evolutionary change: in Soulé's words, as the conservation of "natural communities under conditions which provide for the potential for continuing evolution." Ecological restoration should be followed, as Grumbine suggests, by allowing nature to take its course "with minimal interference from managers." Stewardship concepts of restoration should be confined to the bioculture.

# FREE NATURE, BIOCULTURE, AND BIOREGIONALISM

Arne Naess has added an important refinement to zoning proposals and eco-system protection strategies by distinguishing between *wilderness* protection zones (where people do not live and resource extraction is prohibited) and what he calls *free nature*. "Free nature" consists of areas of relatively sparse human habitation (for example, the foothills of the Sierra, parts of northern Europe, and much of the Third World) where wild natural processes are still essentially intact and dominant. These areas should be zoned to protect natural processes and wildlife while encouraging nonexploitive bioregional living. The remaining Fourth World tribal peoples who are still following traditional ways with minimal impact on wild ecosystems, can be thought of as living in free nature areas.[25]

One of the central features of thinking about ecological sustainable societies is the move toward decentralization and bioregional ways of life, which involves reinhabiting and restoring damaged ecosystems. But Roderick Nash, a major theorist and proponent of wilderness protection, has worried that a total movement toward bioregional reinhabitation of the Earth at this point (what he calls the "garden scenario") would be ecologically disastrous: "The problem, of course, is numbers. There are simply too many people on the planet to decentralize into garden environments and still have significant amounts of wilderness."[26] Elsewhere, Nash characterizes bioregionalism as "the contemporary attempt to 'reinhabit' wilderness areas."[27]

Nash is entirely justified in calling attention to the limitations of an overly ambitious bioregional program at this point in history. It is not clear, however, that the intent of contemporary bioregionalists is to reinhabit wilderness areas. Leading bioregional theorists such as Peter Berg, Gary Snyder, Raymond Dasmann, Thomas Berry, and Kirkpatrick Sale are fully aware of the importance of establishing greatly expanded wilderness/protection zones. Bioregional ways of life are appropriate for "free nature" and for ecologically restructured cities as suggested in such projects as Peter Berg's "green cities."[28] Redesigned ecological cities would contain wild and semiwild areas interspersed with human inhabited areas, either by protecting and expanding upon wild or near-wild areas that now exist near cities, or by restoring such areas.

Roderick Nash points out that "in 1982 [Edward] Abbey expressed his basic belief that humans had no right to use more than a portion of the planet and they had already passed that limit. Wild places must be left wild." In 1985, Stanford ecologist Paul Ehrlich claimed that "in a country like the United States, there is not the slightest excuse for developing one more square inch of undisturbed land." In their 1987 survey of world environmental problems,

Anne and Paul Ehrlich proposed that, as a general policy "the prime step [is] *to permit no development of any more virgin lands* . . . whatever remaining relatively undisturbed land exists that supports a biotic community of any significance should be set aside and fiercely defended against encroachment."[29] As the Ehrlichs point out, the 6 billion humans now on Earth have already destroyed or appropriated approximately 40 percent of biomass productivity on the land.[30]

Environmental ethicist Paul Taylor also promotes the idea of the protection of wilderness as species habitat. He claims that we must

> constantly place constraints on ourselves so as to cause the least possible inter- ference in natural ecosystems and their biota. . . . If [humans] have a sufficient concern for the natural world, they can control their own population growth, change their habits of consumption, and regulate their technology so as to save at least part of the Earth's surface as habitat for wild animals and plants.[31]

Taylor finds it necessary to distinguish between the basic needs of humans versus their nonbasic wants. To allow for sufficient amounts of species habitat, humans must reduce their nonbasic wants and consumption habits when these come into conflict with the basic needs of other species for survival and well-being. Taylor's analysis coincides with Naess's distinction between vital and nonvital needs and wants, which is incorporated into the Deep Ecology platform.[32]

Paul Taylor makes another important contribution to the discussion of eco-system protection zoning with his concept of the *bioculture.* He defines bioculture as "that aspect of any human culture in which humans create and regulate the environment of living things and systematically exploit them for human benefit."[33] Large-scale agriculture, pets, domestic animal and plant breeding, and "tree plantations" all belong to the human bioculture. Wilderness protection zoning, in effect, separates the world of the wild from the exploitive human activities of the bioculture. "Free nature" can be conceived of as a sort of hybrid buffer zone (where wild ecological processes predominate) situated between protection zones and biocultural zones.

Taylor's concept of the bioculture is a useful one. For instance, it helps us see that many movements are primarily involved with an ecological reform of the bioculture. The organic farm movement (inspired by Wendell Berry and Wes Jackson) is one example of this. The animal rights movement, in its concern with the "rights" of *all* animals, has, at least theoretically, failed to distinguish between the conditions of domestic animals in the bioculture and the very different situation of wild animals in wild ecosystems, sometimes with alarmingly anti-ecological results.

The present unecological goals and practices of the Forest Service (and similar practices worldwide) in clear-cutting wild forest ecosystems and replacing them with "tree plantations" can now be seen as an attempt to extend the bioculture at the expense of the wild. Taylor points out that the ethics of the bioculture differs fundamentally from the basically "noninterference" ethics appropriate to wilderness/protection zones. Perhaps some ecologically enlightened version of the "stewardship" model is appropriate for the bioculture, but not for wilderness/protection areas. Different kinds of problems arise when domestic animals gone ferral (and exotics) intrude in wild ecosystems, when wild animals stray from the protection zones into biocultural zones, and when there are mixed communities of wild and domestic as in "free nature."[34]

## WILDERNESS PROTECTION IN THE FIRST WORLD

The question still remains concerning how much of the Earth should be protected in wilderness and other ecosystem protection zones. The basic answer to this question has essentially been given by the recent research of the conservation biologists: enough habitat to protect the diversity and abundance of wild species, and the ongoing ecological health of the Earth, which involves, among other things, continued speciation and wild evolutionary change. Along these lines, Arne Naess has provided a future ecological vision toward which we can progress:

> I am not saying that we should have preserved the primordial forest as a whole, but looking back we can imagine a development such that, let us say, one third was preserved as wilderness, one third as free nature with mixed communities, which leaves one third for cities, paved roads, etc. [bioculture]. This would probably be enough, and I guess most people with influence in matters of the environment would agree. But of course, it is a wild fantasy, which is, incidentally, an important kind of wilderness![35]

To realize how ecologically out of balance we are in the United States, based upon Naess's suggestion, we have to consider Thomas Fleischner's point that "over 95% of the contiguous United States has been altered from its original state. Only 2% is legally protected from exploitive uses."[36] And even that 2 percent lacks adequate ecological protection. For example, Forest Service legally designated wilderness areas continue to allow mining, sport hunting, and domestic animal grazing within their boundaries. Legislative efforts are now being made to revise existing mining laws that have been the cause of much public land abuse. Some have claimed that, apart from ancient forest destruction, the greatest cause of ecological destruction on public lands (both wilderness and nonwilderness areas) is cattle and sheep grazing. Domestic animal grazing destroys the natural plant and grass communities, causes erosion, damages streams and other water supplies, competes with wildlife, results in federal programs to kill large numbers of large predators (including the poisoning and trapping of huge numbers of "nontarget" wildlife), and should be phased out.[37]

To begin to achieve an ecological land-use balance, once the ecologically destructive uses of now-existing Forest Service wilderness have been eliminated, the remaining 3 percent of *de facto* (nondesignated) wilderness should be placed in protection zones. This would bring the contiguous United States to a total to 5% protected habitat. That still leaves the contiguous United States approximately 30 percent short of a ratio of one-third wilderness, one-third free nature, and one-third bioculture (disregarding, for the present, the zoning of free nature).

Under the provisions of the Wilderness Act of 1964, the congressional battles over legal classification of wilderness in the National Parks and National Forests have already been fought, and mainline reform environmentalists have compromised severely in both cases, particularly the latter. Now the battle to zone land as wilderness is occurring over the 250 million acres administered by the Bureau of Land Management (BLM). The BLM is studying only 10 percent of its land (25 million acres) for possible wilderness designation (most BLM land is contracted out to private corporations and individuals for mining and domestic animal grazing). The projections are that, after the political wrangling and compromises are concluded, only 10 to 15 million acres will be legally protected. It must be remembered that the lands being discussed here (Park Service, Forest Service, and BLM) are *public* lands!

The Wildness Act of 1964, while framed and successfully lobbied by dedicated conservationists, is nevertheless a pre-ecological document and, accordingly, its stated purposes and provisions do not reflect the huge tracts of wilderness protection zones (and the degree of protection) required for species and wild ecosystem protection, especially for large mammal speciation. A recent news magazine article discussing the Wilderness Act and the upcoming BLM wilderness fight still couches the issues largely in terms of anthropocentric special-interest compromise politics: of wilderness recreation versus "motorized-recreation and commercial interests." The ecological issues are all but ignored.[38]

In order to boost the wilderness protection zone percentages toward the 30 percent figure, it would probably be necessary to place most Forest Service and BLM lands in protection zones and to restore them to wildlife habitat. A recent proposal by Deborah and Frank Popper of Rutgers University to return the Great Plains to buffalo habitat would also greatly increase ecosystem protection areas.

These strategies for protecting wildness and biodiversity have recently been refined and sophisticated. For instance, the Wildlands Project has been working closely with conservation biologists to develop a North American Wilderness Recovery Strategy. According to Dave Foreman:

> Going far beyond current National Park, Wildlife Refuge, and Wilderness Area systems, where individual reserves are discrete islands of wildness in a sea of human-modified landscapes, [conservation biologists] call for large Wilderness cores, buffer zones, and biological corridors. . . . Biological corridors would provide secure travelways between core reserves for the dispersal of wide-ranging species, for genetic exchange between populations, and for migration of organisms in response to climate change. Surrounding the core reserves would be buffer zones where increasing levels of compatible human activity would be allowed away from the cores. . . . Conservation biologists propose to begin with existing National Parks, Wilderness Areas, and other protected or unprotected natural areas [and enlarge and connect them]. . . . The key concept in this new Wilderness Area model is *connectivity*.[39]

Foreman has recently discussed the history of the bioregional/reinhabitation movement beginning with the writings of Gary Snyder, Peter Berg, and Raymond Dasmann. He claims that:

> The centerpiece of every bioregional group's platform should be a great core wilderness preserve where all the indigenous creatures are present and the natural flow is intact. Other wilderness preserves, both large and small, should be established and protected throughout the bioregion, and natural corridors established to allow for the free flow of genetic material between them and to such preserves in other bioregions. . . . These core wilderness preserves should be sacred shrines to us as reinhabitory people, but they transcend even their sacredness to us in simply being what they are—reserves of native diversity.[40]

## AN INTERNATIONAL PERSPECTIVE

Increasingly, our environmental problems are being recognized as global in scope and, as such, require effective international cooperation. Noel Brown, director of the United Nations Environmental Program, indicated that an Ecological Council (comparable to the Security Council) could soon be a reality.[41] With the human population predicted to soar to 10 to 15 billion people, if unchecked, by the middle of the next century (population biologists argue that 1 to 2 billion people worldwide, living comfortably at a basic-needs consumption level, would be maximum for what Naess calls "wide" ecological sustainability), the United Nations needs to reorganize its population control agencies and ecological protection programs to reflect a streamlined, effective, integrated biosphere approach to environmental problems. The United Nations General Assembly has already officially adopted an ecocentric orientation when it approved the World Charter for Nature in 1982. The charter asserts: "Every form of life is unique, warranting respect regardless of its worth to man, and, to accord other organisms such recognition, man must be guided by a moral code of action. . . . Nature shall be respected and its essential processes shall not be disrupted."[42] The severity of the ecological crisis must be fully appreciated, and the Charter for Nature needs to be reaffirmed and effectively implemented. Humanity has now entered an era of what some ecologists are calling *biological meltdown!*

The urgency of the ecological crisis suggests that the United Nations should give the highest priority to stabilizing the human population in the shortest time possible while ensuring that human dignity and the ideals of justice are protected. Birth control programs, including making contraceptives freely available to all who want them, have *quite recently* proven to be highly effective in dramatically reducing birthrates in certain Third World countries. It is just as important that population be stabilized, and then reduced, in First World countries. The massive funding and implementation of such programs is needed immediately throughout the world. The United Nations should continue to help feed the hungry and improve basic living conditions in Third World countries, and discourage consumerism and further industrialization throughout the world as part of an overall program of ecological and economic sustainability. Major educational programs should be instituted to "ecologize" the peoples of the world.

Unlike First World countries, which are now overdeveloped, overpopulated, and ecologically unsustainable, Third World countries need to improve their overall material standards of living, although along ecologically sustainable paths. It is unrealistic and unjust to expect Third World countries to turn to the protection of their wild ecosystems *as the expense* of the vital needs of their human populations. But the magnitude and severity of the global ecological crisis must be fully appreciated. Third World countries should be encouraged to adopt as high a priority as possible on the establishment of ecosystem protection zones, and the protection of large areas of free nature.

# NOTES

1. John Hendee, George Stankey, and Robert Lucas, *Wilderness Management* (Washington: USDA Forest Service Misc. Publication No. 1365, 1978), pp. 140–41; quoted in Holmes Rolston III, "Values Gone Wild," in Rolston, *Philosophy Gone Wild: Essays in Environmental Ethics* (Buffalo: Prometheus Books, 1986), p. 119.

2. Alston Chase, *Playing God in Yellowstone* (Boston: Atlantic Monthly Press, 1986), p. 33.

3. For a critique of Chase's views, see Dave Foreman, Doug Peacock, and George Sessions, "Who's 'Playing God in Yellowstone'?" *Earth First! Journal* 7, 11 (1986): 18–21.

4. John Rodman, "Resource Conservation—Economics and After," unpublished manuscript, Pitzer College, Claremont, Calif., 1976; see also Bill Devall and George Sessions, "The Development of Natural Resources and the Integrity of Nature," *Environmental Ethics* 6, 4 (1984): 293–322.

5. Joel Connelly, "British Columbia's Big Cut: Who Owns the Ancient Forests?" *Sierra* 76, no. 3 (1991): 42–53; see also Gary Snyder, *The Practice of the Wild* (San Francisco: North Point Press, 1990), pp. 116–43.

6. See Bill Devall (ed.), *Clearcut: The Tragedy of Industrial Forestry* (San Francisco: Sierra Club Books, 1994).

7. Chris Maser, *The Redesigned Forest* (San Pedro, Calif.: R&E Miles Publisher, 1988).

8. Bob Nixon, "Focus on Forests and Forestry," *The Trumpeter* 6, 2 (1989): 38.

9. Edward Abbey, *Desert Solitaire: A Season in the Wilderness* (New York: McGraw-Hill, 1968); see also Joseph Sax, *Mountains without Handrails* (Ann Arbor: University of Michigan Press, 1980).

10. Mitch Friedman, "How Much is Enough?: Lessons from Conservation Biology," in Mitch Friedman (ed.), *Forever Wild: Conserving the Greater North Cascades Ecosystem* (Mountain Hemlock Press [P.O. Box 2962, Bellingham, WA 98227], 1988), p. 34. I have drawn much of the following material on conservation biology from the excellent summaries in this book by Friedman and by Edward Grumbine, "Ecosystem Management for Native Diversity." For further discussions of the importance of conservation biology for environmentalism in the '90s, see James R. Udall, "Launching the Natural Ark," *Sierra* 76, 5 (1991): 80–89; Edward Grumbine, *Ghost Bears: Exploring the Biodiversity Crisis* (Washington, D.C.: Island Press, 1992).

11. Michael Soulé, "What Is Conservation Biology?" *Bioscience* 35 (1985): 727–34; quoted in Friedman, ibid.

12. Friedman, *Forever Wild,* pp. 1–2; see also O. H. Frankel and Michael Soulé, *Conservation and Evolution* (Cambridge: Cambridge University Press, 1981); Michael Soulé and D. Simberloff, "What Do Genetics and Ecology Tell Us about the Design of Nature Reserves?" *Biological Conservation* 35 (1986): 19–40.

13. Friedman, "How Much Is Enough?" p. 39; Norman Myers, "The Extinction Spasm Impending: Synergisms at Work," *Conservation Biology* 1 (1987): 14–21: A. P. Dobson, C. H. McLellan, and D. S. Wilcove, "Habitat Fragmentation in the Temperate Zone," in M. Soulé (ed.), *Conservation Biology: The Science of Scarcity and Diversity* (Sunderland, Mass.: Sinauer, 1986), pp. 237–56.

14. Friedman, ibid.; A. Runte, *National Parks: The American Experience* (Lincoln: University of Nebraska Press, 1987); W. D. Newmark, "Legal and Biotic Boundaries

of Western North American National Parks: A Problem of Congruence," *Biological Conservation* 33 (1985): 197–208; W. D. Newmark, "A Land-Bridge Island Perspective on Mammalian Extinctions in Western North American Parks," *Nature* 325 (1987): 430–32; R. M. May and D. S. Wilcove, "National Park Boundaries and Ecological Realities," *Nature* 324 (1986): 206–7; J. Terborgh and B. Winter, "Some Causes of Extinction," in B. A. Wilcox and Michael Soulé, *Conservation Biology: An Evolutionary-Ecological Perspective* (Sunderland, Mass.: Sinauer, 1980), pp. 19–133; R. F. Noss, "Wilderness Recovery and Ecological Restoration," *Earth First!* 5, no. 8 (1985): 18–19; R. F. Noss, "Recipe for Wilderness Recovery," *Earth First!* 6 (1986): 22, 25.

15. Friedman, "How Much Is Enough?" p. 37; C. Holtby, B. A. Wilcox, and Michael Soulé, "Benign Neglect: A Model of Faunal Collapse in the Game Reserves of East Africa," *Biological Conservation* 15 (1979): 259–70.

16. Grumbine, "Ecosystem Management," p. 46; W. D. Newmark, "Legal and Biotic Boundaries."

17. Friedman, "How Much Is Enough?" p. 43; Frankel and Soulé, *Conservation and Evolution*.

18. Michael Soulé, "Conservation Biology: Its Scope and Challenge," in M. Soulé and B. Wilcox (eds.), *Conservation Biology*, p. 166; quoted in Christopher Manes, *Green Rage: Radical Environmentalism and the Unmaking of Civilization* (Boston: Little, Brown, 1990), pp. 34–35.

19. David Brower, "Toward an Earth International Park," *Sierra Club Bulletin* 52, 9 (1967): 20.

20. Eugene P. Odum, *Fundamentals of Ecology* (Philadelphia: W. B. Saunders, 1971), p. 269; John Phillips, a philosopher/ecologist at St. Cloud State University in Minnesota, developed Odum's proposal in 1974 and presented it in "On Environmental Ethics," read at American Philosophical Association, San Francisco, 1978.

21. Paul Shepard, *The Tender Carnivore and the Sacred Game* (New York: Scribner's, 1973), pp. 260–73.

22. Edward Grumbine, "Ecosystem Management for Native Diversity," pp. 48, 52–53.

23. Grumbine, ibid.; R. F. Noss, "Recipe for Wilderness Recovery"; J. J. Berger, *Restoring the Earth: How Americans are Working to Renew Damaged Environments* (New York: Knopf, 1985).

24. John Harper, "The Heuristic Value of Ecological Restoration," in William Jordan (ed.), *Restoration Ecology* (Cambridge: Cambridge University Press, 1987), pp. 35–36; C. Mark Cowell, "Ecological Restoration and Environmental Ethics," *Environmental Ethics* 15, no. 1 (1993): 19–32; for critiques of stewardship models of ecological restoration, see Eric Katz, "The Big Lie: Human Restoration of Nature," *Technology and the Environment* (New York: JAI Press, 1992), pp. 231–41; Jamie Sayan, "Notes toward a Restoration Ethic," *Restoration and Management Notes* 7, 2 (1989): 57–59; see also Andrew McLaughlin, *Regarding Nature* (New York: State University of New York Press, 1993), pp. 214–17.

25. Arne Naess, "Ecosophy, Population, and Free Nature," *The Trumpeter* 5, 3 (1988).

26. Roderick Nash, *Wilderness and the American Mind,* 3rd ed. (New Haven: Yale University Press, 1982), pp. 380–84.

27. Roderick Nash, *The Rights of Nature,* pp. 270–71, n. 28.

28. See Peter Berg, Beryl Magilavy, Seth Zuckerman, *A Green City Program* (San Francisco: Planet Drum Books, 1989); Peter Berg (ed.), *Reinhabiting a Separate Country: A Bioregional Anthology of Northern California* (San Francisco: Planet Drum Foundation, 1978); Gary Snyder, "Re-inhabitation," in Snyder, *The Old Ways* (San Francisco: City Lights Books, 1977), pp. 57–66; Thomas Berry, "Bioregions: The Context for Reinhabiting the Earth," in Berry, *The Dream of the Earth,* pp. 163–70; Kirkpatrick Sale, *Dwellers in the Land: The Bioregional Vision* (San Francisco: Sierra Club Books, 1985).

29. Roderick Nash, *The Rights of Nature,* pp. 168–69; Paul Ehrlich, "Comments," *Defenders of Wildlife,* Nov./Dec. 1985; Anne and Paul Ehrlich, *Earth* (New York: Franklin Watts, 1987), p. 242.

30. Ehrlich and Ehrlich, ibid., p. 153.

31. Paul Taylor, *Respect for Nature: A Theory of Environmental Ethics* (Princeton: Princeton University Press, 1986), pp. 288, 310.

32. Ibid., pp. 269–77.

33. Ibid., pp. 53–58.

34. For a critique of the stewardship model as applied to agriculture, see Sara Ebenreck, "A Partnership Farmland Ethic," *Environmental Ethics* 5, 1 (1983): 33–45; Arne Naess, "Self-Realization in Mixed Communities of Humans, Bears, Sheep and Wolves," *Inquiry* 22 (1979): 231–42; Arne Naess and Ivar Mysterud, "Philosophy of Wolf Policies I," *Conservation Biology* 1, 1 (1987): 22–34.

35. Arne Naess, "Ecosophy, Population, and Free Nature," p. 118.

36. Thomas Fleischner, "Keeping It Wild: Toward a Deeper Wilderness Management," in Friedman, *Forever Wild,* p. 79.

37. For proposals to eliminate domestic grazing on public lands, see Denzel and Nancy Ferguson, *Sacred Cows at the Public Trough* (Bend, Ore.: Maverick Publications, 1983).

38. "The Battle for the Wilderness," *U.S. News and World Report* 107, 1 (July 1989): 16–21, 24–25.

39. See Dave Foreman and Howie Wolke, *The Big Outside* (New York: Harmony/Crown Books, 1992); John Davis (ed.), "The Wildlands Project: Plotting a Wilderness Recovery Strategy," *Wild Earth* (1993), special issue; Dave Foreman, "The Northern Rockies Ecosystem Protection Act and the Evolving Wilderness Area Model," *Wild Earth* 3, 4 (1993): 57–62.

40. Dave Foreman, "Who Speaks for Wolf?" in D. Foreman, *Confessions of an Ecowarrior* (New York: Harmony Books, 1991), pp. 37–50; for a bioregional ecologist's plan to save California's ecosystems and wildlife by limiting human population,

see Raymond F. Dasmann, *The Destruction of California* (New York: Macmillan, 1965).

41. See W. R. Prescott, "The Rights of Earth: An Interview with Dr. Noel J. Brown," *In Context* 22 (1989): 29–34.

42. *World Charter for Nature. United Nations General Assembly* (New York: United Nations, A/RES/37/7, Nov. 9, 1982); see also Harold W. Wood, Jr., "The United Nations World Charter for Nature," *Ecology Law Quarterly* 12 (1985): 977–96.

# 33 | WILDNESS, WISE USE, AND SUSTAINABLE DEVELOPMENT

## *Edward Grumbine*

## INTRODUCTION

As the third millennium c.e. approaches, ideas and images of wilderness in North America appear to be evolving toward some as yet unknown configuration. Evidence of these changes may be found in the number of recently published books and articles that critically reexamine various facets of the relationship between humans and wild nature. Philosopher Max Oelschlaeger has provided a developmental history of the idea of wilderness from the Paleolithic to the present.[1] There has been a lively exchange in *The Environmental Professional* over the role of wilderness as a cultural ideal and conservation strategy.[2] Biologists Reed Noss and Hal Salwasser have also debated similar issues in the conservation biology literature.[3] And botanists Arturo Gomez-Pompa and Andrea Kaus have weighed in with an attempt to "tame the wilderness myth" in the pages of *BioScience*.[4]

Dialogue over fundamental cultural matters does not take place in a vacuum. There are at least three reasons why wilderness is being reexamined today. The first reason derives from the pre-Darwinian roots of current Western conceptions of wilderness. In what Callicott labels "the received wilderness idea," people are seen as radically separated from nature, wilderness areas are considered to be pristine enclaves of nature untainted by human handiwork, and are believed to be operating in harmonious balance with the natural landscape they are embedded within.[5] This conventional image, familiar to both wilderness supporters and those who wish to develop wildlands, has been

Originally published (in a longer version) in *Environmental Ethics* 16, 3 (Fall 1994). Reprinted with permission.

legally codified in the 1964 Wilderness Act: "A wilderness, in contrast with those areas where man and his works dominate the landscape, is hereby recognized as an area where the earth and its community of life are untrammeled by man, where man himself is a visitor who does not remain."

This people/nature dualism informs both resource conservation, whose adherents believe that natural resources exist to be utilized for human benefit, and wilderness preservation, whose followers argue that a significant portion of landscapes should be protected in an undeveloped condition. The paradigmatic examples of these two camps have always been Gifford Pinchot and John Muir.[6] (Though many observers consider Muir to be the father of preservation, it must be noted that his thinking on the value of wild nature traveled well beyond that of most preservationists toward a unification of people with nature.)[7] The upshot of the radical Western split between people and nature is that *both* resource conservationists and wilderness preservationists, as long as they view nature as a collection of resources for humans, inhabit a world that categorically denies the full range of symbiotic relationships that may exist between people and wilderness. And, by focusing on nature as a fountain of inspiration or source of products, modern people have neglected the ecological theater and evolutionary play that drives the dynamic, ever-changing patterns and processes of Earth.

The second reason why the idea of wilderness is being critically reexamined is that science is finally beginning to offer theoretical and empirical insights into the ecological and managerial implications of the people/nature dualism. Conservation biology is providing compelling evidence as to why the image of conservation versus preservation has not served humans or nature well. Many species populations are losing their evolutionary viability, ecosystem functions (i.e., nutrient cycles, the water cycle, patterns of growth and decay) are being fundamentally altered by human activities, and at the biosphere level, the effects of greenhouse gases on Earth's atmosphere will likely affect nature reserves and managed landscapes in ways detrimental to both resource protection and extraction.[8]

Viewed in historical perspective, ecological dysfunction, once limited to particular species and specific locales, is now systemic from endangered gene pools to planetary climate change. Accordingly, conservation biology is attempting to understand the dynamics of these processes and advocate alternatives. Some environmentalists have seized upon the new field as providing irrefutable evidence that current efforts to preserve wilderness are grossly inadequate. The biodiversity crisis is challenging the fundamental logic of pristine wilderness set-asides surrounded by intensely managed multiple-use lands.[9]

The third reason why wilderness is undergoing reevaluation today is grounded in emerging political alternatives to the resource conservation/pres-

WILDERNESS & CONSERVATION BIOLOGY

ervation dichotomy. Two conflicting positions, either of which, if implemented, would alter current wilderness policies, are jostling for attention. One
alternative to the status quo, being explored by a broad spectrum of both
conservationists and preservationists, is "sustainable development." It is
claimed by many that sustainable development offers a long-term antidote to
the problem of humans destroying ecosystems more quickly than they can be
renewed by ecological processes.

A second position, represented by the Wise Use Movement (WUM), has
little broad-based political strength (as of yet). The WUM would like to expand the human hegemony over nature. WUM supporters "seek unrestricted
access to all natural resources for [private] economic use, benefit, and profit."[10]
This position, of course, is at odds with the sustainable development concept.
It is also completely against wilderness preservation in any form. But though
it may appear to be too radical to garner wide support, the potential political
influence of the WUM is not to be taken lightly.

The unresolved Western split between people and nature, the biodiversity
crisis, and nascent alternatives to long-standing land management policies provide insights into why the idea of wilderness is undergoing intense scrutiny in
the 1990s. Because these factors are interrelated and go down to cultural bedrock, they are difficult to untangle. As Oelschlaeger points out, any attempt to
review the assumptions of modernity, of which the relationship between humans and nature is clearly central, is difficult because "through the lens of
history human experience takes place entirely *outside* nature" (emphasis
added).[11] The idea of history in the West has subsumed wilderness to the
degree that we find ourselves living, as Aldo Leopold (1949) realized fifty years
ago, in an ecological "world of wounds."[12] For the 1990s, the upshot of this
cultural inheritance can be summarized succinctly: Ecologically, we have
erected a system of parks and wilderness areas that preserve scenic landscapes
but that lack ecological integrity; politically, we have assumed that such legal
designations would be sufficient to protect wild nature; philosophically, we
have spent much of our energy on debates over intrinsic versus instrumental
values in environmental ethics; and experientially, with more people having
less access to wildlands as populations grow and urbanization continues apace,
we have maintained, if not strengthened, the boundaries between wilderness
and civilization.

Given the current rate and scale of ecological deterioration and the depth
of our cultural predicament concerning our ongoing relationship with wild
nature, it is unfortunate that many of the papers reexamining wilderness are
shot through with arguments that tend to obfuscate rather than illuminate
many critical points. My aim in this paper is to reveal some of the conflicts
that persist over the idea of wilderness and clarify areas that need attention. I

also wish to provide notes toward the future of wilderness policy in North America as our ideas move away from viewing the world as a collection of resources toward an ecosystems view and beyond. I shall focus on two problems: the absence of a clear distinction between wilderness and wildness, and the role of wildness in any proposed revision of land management theory and practice.

## WILDNESS AND WILDERNESS

"I wish to speak a word for Nature," begins Henry David Thoreau in his essay "Walking," "for absolute freedom and wildness, . . . to regard man as an inhabitant, or part and parcel of Nature, rather than a member of society."[13] Thoreau uses the term *wildness* here, not *wilderness,* as is also the case later on in the essay where he states emphatically that "what I have been preparing to say is that in Wildness is the preservation of the world."[14] Callicott suggests that Aldo Leopold, a century later, was also "concerned primarily . . . with integrating an optimal mix of wildness with human habitation and economic utilization of the land."[15] Yet, if recent reexaminations of the wilderness idea provide any indication, we are still confused in our understanding of exactly what Thoreau and Leopold were driving at, the fact that *wildness* and *wilderness* are not equivalent in definition, meaning, or importance. Until we get clear on wildness and wilderness, we cannot be prepared to envision, let alone act upon, practical alternatives to the current ecological crisis.

In Oelschlaeger's view, humans have been erecting a boundary between themselves and nature since the advent of history.[16] This "fence" has become increasingly rigid over the centuries; the existence of the people/Nature dichotomy is one of the key assumptions of modernity. Civilization is both idealized and experienced as antithetical to wild nature. This assumption is not inconsequential—it allows most citizens of modern societies to inhabit a world that is, by any scientific reading of the facts, being destroyed by industrial imperialism. The people/nature split has led us to focus our efforts on preserving wilderness instead of protecting wildness. The idea of wilderness is culturally relative, of course, a fact pointed out by several observers.[17] Many nonindustrial cultures have no word or concept for wilderness. And, despite all the lofty pronouncements of preservationists, wilderness is still viewed by most citizens of industrial societies as a resource for humans.

Wildness, on the other hand, as "the process and essence of nature," is the *source* of resources and of human existence.[18] It is the generative framework within which all beings inhabit Earth. . . . Both Thoreau and Leopold saw wilderness as a cultural construct flowing from and dependent upon wildness.

In "Walking," Thoreau was careful to distinguish between people inhabiting nature and being members of society. Inhabiting for Thoreau, though he did not provide an explicit definition, was essential for both maintaining freedom *and* wildness in human culture. The two were inevitably linked for, if in wildness the world was to be preserved, then the loss of wildness would lead to certain ruin. Thoreau was probably the first person born of modernity to recognize the grave consequences of industrial civilization's project to dominate nature and contain wildness. Gary Snyder and Neil Evernden remind us again of the distinction between wildness and wilderness.[19] Snyder both clarifies and critiques Thoreau's bold assertion when he says that "wildness is not just the preservation of the world, it *is* the world."[20]

Wilderness areas, of course, may allow wild nature to live and breath to the degree that they are not subject to human control. And they are important (to humans) to the extent that they allow direct contact with wildness which may result in experiences that transcend the culturally relative categories of modern existence. Wilderness and wildness intersect where a river, mountain, bear, or beeplant spark an awareness in us that helps to break down the fence between people and nature, where value and valuer (or, to use the axiological categories of contemporary environmental ethics, instrumental and intrinsic values) appear as limited constructs.

Yet, the importance of protecting wildness goes deeper than the potential for healing the people/nature split. This dichotomy itself springs out of a fundamental paradox of human existence: the distinction between self and other.[21] Oelschlaeger argues that while "the Paleolithic mind did not distinguish the human enterprise from the natural world, . . . it did wonder at the miracle of existence and created an elaborate hunting mythology to account for reality."[22] If this is true, then consciousness of the other is not simply a phenomenon of history, but is part and parcel of human experience at least as far back as the formation of (proto-)culture. Wilderness bears on the distinction between self and other not in terms of erasing differences, but in the recognition of organic connections. The resolution of the paradox is found not in denying the distinctions between humans and other species, wolves and invertebrates, or any members of Earth's community of life, but in what we decide to make of the differences.

Philosopher Tom Birch is explicit concerning the usual Western position on the paradox of the other: "mainstream Western culture . . . presupposes that opposition is fundamentally conflictive, rather than complementary . . . or ecosystemic."[23] Taking conflict with otherness as our standard, we have narrowed our relationship with wildness to a combination of two approaches: (1) gaining power by dominating the world through objectifying the diversity of life and reducing it to resources for human consumption and (2) simply obliterating nature on a large scale and replacing it with developments (cities, factory farms, parking lots) of various kinds.

Both of these responses reinforce the Western concept of people being separated from nature and somehow outside the forces of evolution. But if evolutionary pathways may be modified by culture, but not ultimately overcome by these adaptations, then industrial societies have a problem. To paraphrase writer Barbara Allen, we haven't lost our relationship with wild nature, we have simply invented it in terms that do not allow us to erect a sustainable, cooperative relationship with it.[24]

. . . Evernden suggests that "perhaps even wildness is an inadequate term, for that essential core of otherness is inevitably nameless, and as such cannot be . . . made part of the domain of human willing."[25] To imply, however, as Callicott does that the concept of the other *reinforces* the people/nature split is to ignore this fundamental paradox that is, has been, and will continue to be part of the human condition.[26] And, to state, as Callicott has done recently, that "the ubiquity of man and his works has made the illusion of nature as Other all but impossible to maintain" is to confuse the eternal *presence* of otherness (shall I say wildness?) with the Western attempt to subdue it.[27]

The modern concepts of wilderness, wildness, and self/other may indeed be evolving. But old worldviews do not dissipate quickly and behaviors that put into practice new ways of being take even longer to become established as we feel our way from conflict toward complementarity. If a revised idea of wilderness does have a role in a sustainable future (and I believe emphatically that it does), then we must hook it to protecting wildness. And, if humans and their cultures are also fundamental expressions of wildness, then we must allow for wildness (and wilderness) to flourish in any conception of sustainable development.

## WHAT IS BEING SUSTAINED IN SUSTAINABLE DEVELOPMENT?

Many of Western culture's difficulties with allowing wildness to exist are revealed in the arguments of those writers who would substitute for the idea of wilderness the concept of sustainable development.[28] The debate between two of the principals in the discussion, philosophers J. Baird Callicott and Holmes Rolston, is grounded in contrasting views of the place of people in nature.

Holmes Rolston affirms a radical discontinuity between nature and culture, wilderness and civilization: "Humans now superimpose cultures on the wild nature out of which they *once emerged*" (emphasis added).[29] Rolston believes that human impositions upon nature, because they are the product of "deliberated human agency," are inevitably "artificial, unnatural." Elsewhere, Rolston has been careful to distinguish between degrees of naturalness, basing his definition on how closely human activities fit in with wild nature.[30] But in the wilderness debate, culture, for Rolston, "is a postevolutionary phase of our planetary history."[31] There could not be a more concise statement of separation between people and nature. Humans, according to Rolston, by virtue of their self-reflecting capacity and ability to intervene in the order of things, have today reached some kind of escape velocity and exited the evolutionary loop. Rolston recognizes an historical progression of culture evolving "out of nature" even while he champions respect for "our wild origins and our wild neighbors on this home planet."[32] But his support for wildness is problematic. In the context of modernity's attempt to dominate nature, otherness (to those who consider people to be "postevolutionary") likely remains an adversary, a competitor, a force against human projects. Given this, it is difficult to see how otherness can be accommodated, respected, or loved. If humans cannot recognize wildness in themselves or their cultures, it is doubtful that they will be able to respect wildness in either wild places or wild nonhuman beings.

At first glance, J. Baird Callicott appears to offer an alternative to Rolston that breaks down the people/nature fence and sets us firmly on a path toward revisioning wilderness. Callicott does not place people outside of nature. He "follow[s] Darwin in thinking that human culture is continuous with primate and mammalian proto-culture and that, no matter how hypertrophic it may lately have become, contemporary human civilization remains embedded in nature."[33] Reviewing the Western idea of wilderness, Callicott observes correctly that it perpetuates the human/nature dichtomy, that it is ethnocentric to the degree that it ignores the historical presence of people living in "pristine" ecosystems worldwide, and that it paints a static picture of nature as if, for example, the Yosemite Sierra in California would perpetually remain in the condition it was in when the area was designated a National Park in 1890. As an approach to conserving wildness, Callicott would scrap the outmoded Western concept of wilderness and replace it with a "postmodern, technologically-sophisticated, scientifically-informed" sustainable development that would reintegrate people with nature by limiting human enterprises to those that do not "compromise ecological integrity seriously."[34] As a paradigm for sustainable development, Callicott holds up Aldo Leopold's concept of land health, "Conservation is a state of harmony between man and land," and suggests that it presents an alternative to the use versus preserve status quo.[35]

Callicott's is a genuine attempt to move beyond the either/or nature of the wilderness debate. But he has not taken us far enough in the search for sustainable relationships between people and wildlands. First, Callicott does not consider the fundamental self/other paradox as part of the basic conditions of life on Earth for humans. Under the best of circumstances people will always be engaged in learning from and adjusting to the ecosystems they are in partnership with. To state this in terms of Leopold's ideal of conservation, harmony between people and nature is not so much a balanced state of grace as it is a dynamic complementarity that must be continuously renegotiated as individuals, cultures, and ecosystems evolve. From this perspective, the issue is not whether we can break down completely the wilderness/civilization dualism but whether we can reduce conflictive interactions and increase cooperative relations. With this distinction in mind, we can begin to comprehend some of the limits of Callicott's arguments for a sustainable development alternative to wilderness.

Much is being made today about new evidence that shows that humans have lived for thousands of years in what the Euro-American West has always considered untouched wilderness. Callicott uses this information to support his charge of ethnocentrism. A corollary of this is the degree to which primal peoples altered ecosystems before the arrival of Euro-Americans. From an ecological perspective, these issues are primarily questions of the rate and scale of human activities on the land. Before modern technology, the transformative power of humans was, by comparison, many times less than it is today. The fact that biologists and anthropologists are "discovering" that the Amazon Basin was "densely" populated and modified by humans says less about the state of wildness or land health of the region than it does about the persistence of modernity in denying the value (and even existence) of anything not part of the Euro-American image of wilderness and civilization.[36] Is Guatemala's Tikal National Park, part of the vast, sparsely settled Petén region of tropical forest, less healthy today even if we know that one thousand years ago much of the area was clearcut and cultivated by the Maya? Such information may prove Callicott's charge of ethnocentrism but the important point is not whether people lived (or live) in wild places but *how* they lived and continue to dwell in wildlands while accommodating wildness and what we might learn today about land health from considering their ways of life.

Callicott offers several suggestions that he believes would help integrate "a Third World approach to conservation" with efforts in the First World.[37] All his suggestions assume, however, that Third World peoples must be brought into the framework of the global, industrial economy. Extractive reserves and ecotourism, both currently in vogue with international conservation groups, will likely only continue Third World dependence on the industrial models of the First World. Such policies might teach forest peoples about the vagaries of global prices but will do little to educate the citizens of industrial societies with the wisdom derived from lives lived more closely following Leopold's conservation ideal. If there is to exist a sustainable development that enriches the wilderness idea, then there must be choices beyond either trying to integrate people into the global cash economy or continuing the destruction of wild ecosystems. Neither of these will genuinely further the quest for a working definition of land health a lá Leopold or help to reduce conflict between people and nature. A third path lies in stimulating nonindustrial local economies with local products for local use while simultaneously reducing both the rate and scale of the First World nation's consumption of resources. This is much easier said than done but we do not want to perpetuate past problems as we envision new sustainable approaches.

The main problem regarding wild places is how to increase their biological integrity while somehow constraining human development. If sustainable development is to succeed, there must be limits on how much habitat humans appropriate for themselves to the detriment of other living beings. This is problematic—the United States, a country that is very rich and relatively sparsely populated, has been able to protect formally only about 5 percent of its land from development. By most ecological accounts, this is nowhere near enough. For example, according to the best current information, to protect old-growth Douglas-fir ecosystems and their host of dependent species in the Pacific Northwest will likely require the region's timber cut to be decreased by over 80 percent from recent levels.[38] Columbia River salmon populations have plummeted since 1850 from 10–16 million fish to about 2.5 million today with 75 percent of current fish from hatchery stock.[39] At the national level, 59 percent of all species listed under the Endangered Species Act are either declining in population, extinct, or their status is unknown.[40] If one looks at the forest landscapes of North America and includes ecosystem processes such as wildfire in one's definition of land health (as Leopold surely would have), the disturbing conclusion is that, because the U.S. Forest Service has actively suppressed fire for almost a century, hundreds of millions of acres need a good clean burn today. Worldwide, three-quarters of all bird species are declining in population or threatened with extinction while the entire class of amphibians is losing ground.[41] And Soulé estimates that the following groups may "all but disappear" within the next century: nonhuman primates, large carnivores, and most of the hoofed animals.[42] Assuming that these data provide a rough estimate of how nonsustainable industrial culture has become, it may well be that conservation biologist Reed Noss's suggestion that 50% of the lower forty-eight states be protected in reserves "where humans do not dominate" does not go far enough.[43]

Given his knowledge of the biodiversity crisis, Callicott's disagreement with Noss's working proposal on the grounds that it is implicitly impractical, unreasonable, and misanthropic, borders on the disingenuous.[44] Callicott has neglected to make clear the *limits* of sustainable development. Defining these limits begins with asking three questions: What are we trying to sustain?, What are we attempting to develop?, and Who will benefit from these actions? If, following Callicott, we are trying to sustain biodiversity and ecosystem health, then we must explicitly recognize that a sustainable development alternative can succeed only if it is grounded upon an adequate system of ecological reserves. Callicott advocates "big wilderness," a national system of ecologically-defined reserves, cessation of old-growth logging, and elimination of livestock from western U.S. rangelands. All too often, however, Callicott's language betrays a tendency to portray humans as agents of control: "The past affords paradigms aplenty of an active, transformative, managerial relationship of people to nature";[45] a new generation of postindustrial technologies may make it possible for us to pursue many of our economic activities without compromising ecosystem health."[46] Callicott even offers Aldo Leopold as the head of an "ecological farm family [that] *actively manages its wild lands*" (emphasis added).[47] And, if both people and nature are to be the beneficiaries of the sustainable development alternative to wilderness, as Callicott would prefer, asking "Can we succeed as a global technological society in enriching the environment as we enrich ourselves?" poses problems for those who do not wish to be linked to such a new world order.[48] *Given the thrust of modernity, and the depth of the biodiversity crisis,* a "global technological society" is hardly compatible with "ecological exigencies."[49] I believe that such language, lacking humility and emphasizing management over restraint, is dangerous and as problematical as Rolston's denial of the fundamental wildness of human nature. There is a great deal of hubris here and very little of the sense of limits that will be required of humans in any transition toward sustainability.

## PERPETUATING CONFLICT: THE WISE USE MOVEMENT

Sustainable development is not the only general environmental policy option being discussed today. While environmentalists attempt to institute international debt-for-nature swaps, ecotourism, and extractive reserves, and scholars debate wilderness in academic journals, the WUM has grown quickly from a handful of individuals to a coalition of some 250 loose-knit groups with a common agenda.[50]

The WUM, as the name implies, does not focus exclusively on wilderness. But the movement's vision of working relations between people and nature is so narrowly construed as to be anathema for wildness in particular and sustainable development in general. The WUM has grown out of the Sagebrush Rebellion of the early 1980s. Its philosophical lineage in the U.S. can be traced back to what historian Craig Allin has called the "economics of superabundance" where resources are always unlimited and only labor is lacking.[51] The movement is a caricature of the "wise use" of Gifford Pinchot who first brought the concept to American conservation.

Most WUM supporters do not believe in either public lands or federal land management and seek to replace these with a no-holds-barred utilization of resources for private profit. The movement's manifesto, *The Wise Use Agenda,* includes the following among twenty-five goals: open access to mineral and oil resources in all wilderness areas, national parks, and wildlife refuges; logging and replanting of all U.S. old-growth forests; amendment of the Endangered Species Act to exclude nonadaptive species and those "species lacking the vigor to spread in range"; elimination of wetlands development restrictions; and so forth.[52]

Several charismatic leaders have worked together to create the organizational vision for the WUM. Ron Arnold, executive vice president of the Center for the Defense of Free Enterprise, a group which espouses an extreme form of the free-market economy, is the publisher of the *Agenda* and a key coordinator. Charles Cushman, president of the Multiple Use Land Alliance representing landowning inholders within national parks and national forests, is another important actor. People for the West!, the main lobbying group supporting the 1872 Mining Law, also figures prominently in the WUM. These three organizations are but representative of an extraordinary diversity of member groups, which include farmers, loggers, western water interests, cattlemen, off-road vehicle users, beach developers, miners, and more. . . .

The financial clout of the WUM is substantial. Extractive industries (mining corporations, timber companies), trade associations (the American Farm Bureau, National Cattlemen's Association), and off-road vehicle manufacturers (Honda, Kawasaki) have provided most of the funding up to the present. But contributions via direct mail from the growing membership are just beginning to be exploited. Alan Gottlieb, along with Arnold, one of the leaders of the Center for the Defense of Free Enterprise, has said "In the past five years we've raised $3 million for Wise Use issues, and $1 million of that came in the last year. The potential is way, way greater. We can reach five million households rather quickly."[53] . . .

The WUM, like the concept of sustainable development, appears to be a response to life in the 1990s where "environmental protection" is no longer at the margin of economic activity.[54] It might appear ironic that a movement bent on returning to the laissez-faire economics of the superabundance approach to nature of nineteenth century America would spring to life in an era of obvious limits. But, given the U.S. historical trend of increasing land use regulations (including wilderness designation and management) in response to declining amounts of roadless areas, productive grazing lands, uncut forests, economically recoverable oil, gas, and mineral deposits, etc., the rise of the WUM represents a last ditch attempt by the most radically utilitarian members of society to maintain their nonsustainable ways of life. While Callicott and others, however imperfectly, endeavor to conceive of a sustainable human partnership with nature nested within ecosystems, WUM supporters comprehend nature as embedded within a free-market economy based solely on the generation of private profits. Both sustainable development and the WUM do share common ground—each emphasizes the human *use* of nature. For Callicott sustainable development is proposed as a means for protecting biodiversity and ecosystem health. For the WUM, whose members see no value in wildness and little human relationship with nature beyond the pecuniary, use is the beginning and the end of the story. The movement is certain that success lies in perpetuating the old models of conflictive relationship that have strengthened the fence between people and nature. . . .

## TOWARD INTEGRATING WILDNESS WITH SUSTAINABLE LANDSCAPES

Aldo Leopold, according to philosopher Bryan Norton, envisioned conservation "as one culture's search for a workable, adaptive approach to living with the land," recognizing that "if a society's practices are not adaptive, . . . the culture with fail.[55] . . . Rolston, as we have seen, for all his support of wilderness, disregards the bonds connecting wild nature with culture. Callicott, for his part, places both people and nature in a wild nexus but, focusing on "active," "transformative," and "managerial" concepts of sustainability that might even "improve" nature as well as conserve it, fails to invoke meaningful limits on human projects.

If we are not careful in our attempts at redefining the people/nature boundary to bring human uses of nature into a role supportive of wildness, wilderness, once thought to be part of *the solution,* becomes *the problem.* For example, Gomez-Pompa and Kaus, after reviewing the Western concept of wilderness and finding the same ethnocentric problems that Callicott points out, state that "a belief in an untouched and untouchable wilderness has permeated global policies and politics in resource management . . . causing serious environmental problems."[56] . . .

Since the Western idea of wilderness is "mostly an urban perception, the view of people who are far removed from natural environments they depend upon for raw resources," Gomez-Pompa and Kaus propose that we tame the wilderness myth by paying attention to rural people's experience of being at home in nature, where conservation is part of a lifestyle and perception of working with ecosystems.[57] These authors have touched upon a key to resolving the dilemmas of accommodating human use while sustaining wildness. But they place too much weight on the distinction between urban and rural values—one need only to consider the WUM to acknowledge that there exists a wide range of rural attitudes toward conservation and wildness. Many rural people in the U.S. who derive their living directly from ecosystems are the same ranchers, loggers, and miners who form the grass roots constituency of the WUM.

A distinction more appropriate to the protection of wildness would be the one biologist Ray Dasmann has drawn between "biosphere people," those who draw support from planet-wide resources primarily through industrial fossil fuel economies, and "ecosystem people" who get their living primarily within the constraints of local ecosystems.[58] The driving engine behind biosphere values, of course, is the Western image of people fenced off from nature and the historical response of biosphere people to ecosystem people has been similar to that between biosphere people and wildness: domination. The value of Gomez-Pompa and Kaus's work is that they invite us to challenge this predominant view by reminding us that "Throughout the world, communally held resources have been managed and conserved by diverse human societies via cultural mechanisms that attach symbolic and social significance to land and resources beyond their immediate extractive values."[59] But what lies "beyond" extractive value? By what specific "cultural mechanisms" may people today experience what these values entail? Does wildness have a role to play here?

Answers to these questions may be found by attempting to discover what values, if any, limit ecosystem people's use of wild nature. Callicott characterized the relationship between humans and large carnivores in North America prior to Euro-American contact as one of "mutual tolerance."[60] Similarly, Rolston declares that "the Indians did not need or achieve" the idea that ecosystems might be so respected that people would only visit and not remain.[61] Yet, these statements do not capture the importance of what today we might call the sacred and how such beliefs might serve to set limits on human behavior in ecosystem cultures. A perusal of the anthropological literature on native people's relationship with grizzly bears, for example, suggests a far more meaningful relationship than mere "tolerance." Paul Shepard and Barry Sanders report that the Bear Mother Myth, which "may be the most persistent and widely-told tale" in the northern hemisphere, tells of both identity and distinction between the species and outlines appropriate ceremonies to honor bears.[62] Complex rites honoring bears are also described by Irving Hallowell, David Rockwell, and Richard Nelson.[63] Nelson considers a major tenet of

Koyukon ideology to be the fact that "humans and natural entities are involved in a constant spiritual interchange that profoundly affects [i.e. limits] human behavior."[64]

Contrary to Rolston's suggestion, indigenous peoples have often developed relations with wild places where only a limited human presence is allowed under certain circumstances. Snyder's account of a visit to a sacred place in the Australian outback in the company of aboriginal people of the Pintubi tribe proves that such practices still exist today, however tenuously.[65] My experience with the Mopan Maya of southern Belize has shown me that the Mopan do not travel to "wild" places indiscriminately and do not enter the forest without some modest ritual preparation.

The lesson here for biosphere people is that many ecosystem people are involved in relationships with their dwelling places that expand Dasmann's original concept of economically-based resource behavior to include a spiritually-based sense of enoughness that often limits their appropriation of what we would term "resources." Much evidence worldwide over the last several thousand years points toward ways of life based on respect and reciprocity that illuminate Leopold's original sense of conservation. This is not to deny that hunter-gatherers and neolithic agriculturalists caused extinctions at times. It is abundantly clear that people during the past 50,000 years, as they migrated into new areas of the planet, seem to have killed off numerous species.[66] There are few, if any, reasons to suspect that there existed an ongoing harmonious balance between people and nature throughout prehistory any more than we can find evidence of static, unchanging ecosystems today. Humans of the past were not exempt from the self/other paradox and it appears that *Homo sapiens* requires a period of adjustment as we settle in to new habitat before any possibility of sustainable ecosystem behavior may be achieved.[67] There are two distinctions, however, between human-caused extinctions of the past and those of the present. Past extinctions generally resulted from the overhunting of particularly vulnerable (large, flightless, etc.) species while those of today are due primarily to habitat destruction. Because of habitat loss, the current rate and scale of human-caused extinctions are unprecedented. The second distinction is that there exist today accessible models of "post-migration" human behavior (ecosystem peoples) that are available for biosphere people to learn from that seem to warrant the description "sustainable."[68]

Ecosystem behavior, whether supported in general terms by Leopold's land ethic or detailed specifically from anthropological accounts, depends upon a diminished fence between people and wildness. For, as Tom Birch points out, "a system of domination cannot grant full equality to *all* the dominated without self-destructing."[69] And, though profound cultural change is beyond the ken of most environmental policymaking, policies subscribed to today may set the stage for changes over the longer term.

## PROTECTING WILDNESS TODAY

How do we begin to move from preserving wilderness to protecting wildness? How do we start to embrace ecosystem ways of life and decrease our dependence on biosphere lifestyles? What follows are notes toward answers to these questions in North America.

For the present, the first step in any such strategy is to *continue to focus on increasing the size and number of protected areas, otherwise known as wilderness.* These lands are the last surviving remnants of wild diversity and they are faced with imminent development. But protection of biological diversity should be emphasized over preservation of scenic lands and recreational opportunities. Given the politics of wildlands protection in the U.S., the best hope for success will be to ground such an approach in the science of conservation biology. A conservation biology-based platform would include (1) habitat protection for viable populations of all native species; (2) areas large enough to encompass natural disturbance regimes; (3) a management timeline that allows for the continuing evolution of species and ecosystems; and (4) human use integrated into the system of protected areas that would provide for humans within the constraints of the above.[70]

Though the creation of such a system will be difficult, it is hard to justify anything less if full biodiversity sustainability is to be sought. Because most of the biodiversity and remaining roadless, undeveloped areas are found on U.S. federal lands, this strategy must focus on the public domain at the beginning. But given the lessons learned from the use vs. preservation approach to land management, it is obvious that this cannot remain the case for very long. State and private lands must soon be brought into biodiversity protection partnerships.[71]

A second step in the evolution toward an ecosystems partnership between culture and nature would be the implementation of ecosystem management within the landscape of use (multiple-use federal lands and private lands). The four conservation biology criteria (above) would apply to these lands as well. Many of Callicott's suggestions concerning the efficient use of nature with an emphasis upon appropriate, alternative technologies would be applicable on these lands. This is also where various Green alternatives to industrial society could provide direction. And it is here where the language and ideology of sustainable development might metamorphose into that of sustainable landscapes.

Landscape is a more appropriate image for sustainability than development for several reasons. It at once removes the focus from human projects which is implicit in "development" while, at the same time, describing a place that provides space for all species to live. It includes human use without excluding nonhuman beings and their needs. And it will be made more specific as diverse peoples in many different places begin to discover what it means to live within the constraints of local landscape conditions. To paraphrase Wendell Berry, our comprehension of sustainable landscapes will become more specific to the degree that we begin to live in them.[72]

The hope of protecting large wildlands with ecosystem management is that this strategy will begin to deal adequately with the biodiversity crisis while also providing a model that would serve the nature/culture system in two ways—sustaining wildness at the core of protected lands, as well as at the center of human communities. The promise of this strategy is that as people begin to gain direct experience with ecosystems by protecting biodiversity, wildness may become part of culture again. Surely, this was a major part of what Thoreau was proposing when he referred to wildness as "the preservation of the world."

## FUTURE WILD

Learning to live with nature in the near term will require much more than integrating landscape use with landscape protection. What Salwasser considers to be a "fact," that "more humans are going to demand more resources from remaining wildlands," must somehow be transformed into more humans demanding fewer resources through a combination of reduced consumption by biosphere people, greater technological efficiency, and an equitable redistribution of ecological goods and services.[73] Over time this must change into fewer humans demanding less. . . .

Much help during this difficult transition could be obtained from two sources. More citizens must demand action on environmental issues from their political representatives. A rise in grassroots organizing on both sides of the fence (witness the plethora of regional environmental groups and the WUM) is much in evidence, but the majority of citizens have not yet become involved. A second source of support must come from parents who would provide their children with direct contact with wild nature. With over 75 percent of the U.S. population now living in urban concentrations removed from wildlands, this is problematic. Given the long-term aspects of the transition to sustainability, however, it is imperative that young children be connected with wildness. Without direct experience with wild plants and animals, mountains, deserts, and rivers, it seems unlikely that children will value nature as they grow older. Paul Shepard believes that the crucial stages of childhood development must be partially "enacted within [wild] ecosystems" and that the destruction of ecological diversity in both places and cultures has had profound negative affects on human psychology.[74] Which brings us to the role of symbolic behaviors that might encourage humans to integrate wildness with culture.

After studying forest management policies and practices throughout southeast Asia, M. G. Chandrakanth and Jeff Romm conclude that secular prescriptions do not capture all the important interests and concerns of people.[75] Recognizing similar trends throughout the world, these authors suggest that debates over future policies "will not likely be resolved until [ policies] are explained and treated in religious as well as in legal, economic, and ecological terms."[76] This points us once again toward a critical distinction between biosphere and ecosystem peoples. What Gomez-Pompa and Kaus described as "cultural mechanisms that attach symbolic and social significance to land" are rooted in experience of the sacred that, mediated through a cooperative approach to self/other, may lead directly to limits on behavior.[77] Put in terms of the biodiversity crisis, legal reform (an Endangered Ecosystem Act), economic changes (inclusion of externalities in cost/benefit computations), scientific shifts (ecosystem management), as well as cultural revision of the Western idea of wilderness will not likely be sufficient to carry us very far beyond the threshold of sustainability. For the long term, what we need are cultural practices that resacralize the world. Philosopher Michael Zimmerman characterizes these as ceremonies that would allow Western people to incorporate wildness into the definition of "civilized" by way of social rituals that would enable one to "solidify . . . identification with the forest families—trees and squirrels, deer and birds—and that would . . . simultaneously initiate [one] into a human family which had appropriate respect for and relationship with the other families of the forest."[78] . . . Such approaches seek identification with nonhuman beings and a wonderfully expansive boundary between self and other, where, in Snyder's provocative descriptions, "the flora and fauna and landforms *are part of culture*" and culture itself is "a nourishing habitat."[79] . . .

The tasks required by the quest for sustaining wildness may in time bring humans to large-scale ecological restoration, returning wolves and grizzlies to California, Quebec, and Mexico while linking wildlands across the continent.[80] If so, we will have become a different people. . . .

## NOTES

1. Max Oelschlaeger, *The Idea of Wilderness* (New Haven: Yale University Press, 1991); see also Max Oelschlaeger, ed., *The Wilderness Condition* (San Francisco: Sierra Club Books, 1992).

2. Reed Noss, "Wilderness Recovery: Thinking Big in Restoration Ecology," *The Environmental Professional* 13 (1991): 225–34; J. Baird Callicott, "The Wilderness Idea Revisited: The Sustainable Development Alternative," *The Environmental Professional* 13 (1991): 225–47; J. Baird Callicott, "That Good Old-Time Wilderness Religion," *The Environmental Professional* 13 (1991): 378–99; Holmes Rolston, "The Wilderness Idea Reaffirmed," *The Environmental Professional* 13 (1991): 370–77.

3. Reed Noss, "Sustainability and Wilderness," *Conservation Biology* 5 (1991): 120–22; Hal Salwasser, "Sustainability As a Conservation Paradigm," *Conservation Biology* 4 (1990): 213–16.

4. Arturo Gomez-Pompa and Andrea Kaus, "Taming the Wilderness Myth," *BioScience* 42 (1992): 271–79.

5. Callicott, "The Wilderness Idea Revisited," 235.

6. See, in general, Roderick Nash, *Wilderness and the American Mind* (New Haven: Yale University Press, 1982); Stephen Fox, *The American Conservation Movement: John Muir and His Legacy* (Madison: University of Wisconsin Press, 1981).

7. Oelschlaeger, *The Idea of Wilderness,* 172–204.

8. For entrance into the rapidly expanding conservation biology literature, see Michael Soulé, ed., *Viable Populations for Conservation* (New York: Cambridge University Press, 1987); Michael Gilpin, "Population Viability Analysis," *Endangered Species Update* 6, 10 (1989): 15–18; David Wilcove, et al., "Habitat Fragmentation in the Temperate Zone," in *Conservation Biology: The Science of Scarcity and Diversity,* ed. Michael Soulé (Sunderland: Sinauer and Associates, 1986), 237–56; S. T. A. Pickett and John Thompson, "Patch Dynamics and the Design of Nature Reserves," in *Biological Conservation* 13 (1987): 27–37; A. J. Hansen, et al., "Conserving Biodiversity in Managed Forests," in *BioScience* 41 (1991): 382–92; S. T. A. Pickett, et al., "The New Paradigm in Ecology: Implications for Conservation Biology Above the Species Level," in *Conservation Biology: The Theory and Practice of Nature Conservation, Preservation, and Management,* eds. S. T. A. Pickett, et al., (New York: Chapman and Hall, 1992), 65–90; Robert Peters and Joan Darling, "The Greenhouse Effect and Nature Reserves," *BioScience* 35 (1985): 707–17; Robert Peters and Thomas Lovejoy, eds., *Biological Diversity and Global Climate Change* (New Haven: Yale University Press, 1992).

9. See, in general, R. Edward Grumbine, *Ghost Bears: Exploring the Biodiversity Crisis* (Washington, D.C.: Island Press, 1992).

10. Debra Callahan, "The Wise Use Movement," unpublished ms. from the W. Alton Jones Foundation, Washington, D.C., 1992, p. 2 (available from Cascade Holistic Economic Consultants, 3758 S.E. Milwaukee, Portland, OR 97202).

11. Oelschlaeger, *The Idea of Wilderness,* 7.

12. Aldo Leopold, "The Round River, " in *Round River,* Luna B. Leopold, ed., (Minocqua, Wisc.: Northword Press, 1991), 237.

13. Henry D. Thoreau, "Excursions and Poems," in vol. 5 of *The Writings of Henry David Thoreau* (Boston: Houghton Mifflin, 1906), 205.

14. Thoreau, "Excursions and Poems," 224.

15. Callicott, "The Wilderness Idea Revisited," 238.

16. Oelschlaeger, *The Idea of Wilderness,* 5.

17. Ibid.; see, in general, Callicott, "The Wilderness Idea Revisited"; Gomez-Pompa and Kaus, "Taming the Wilderness Myth."

18. Gary Snyder, *The Practice of the Wild* (San Francisco: North Point Press, 1990), 5.

19. See Snyder, *The Practice of the Wild,* and Neil Evernden, *The Social Creation of Nature* (Baltimore: Johns Hopkins University Press, 1992), 107–24.

20. Snyder, *The Practice of the Wild,* 6.

21. How one conceives of this distinction is, of course, fundamental. For a range of treatments of self/other dualism in Western experience see Morris Berman, *Coming to Our Senses* (New York: Simon and Schuster, 1989), 15–62; Evernden, *The Social Creation of Nature,* 88–103; Evelyn Fox Keller, *Reflections on Gender and Science* (New Haven: Yale University Press, 1985), 99; Theodore Roszak, *The Voice of the Earth* (New York: Simon and Schuster), 41–46; Robert Frodeman, "Radical Environmentalism and the Political Roots of Postmodernism: Differences that Make a Difference," *Environmental Ethics* 14 (1992): 319.

22. Oelschlaeger, *The Idea of Wilderness,* 12.

23. Tom Birch, "The Incarceration of Wildness: Wilderness Areas as Prisons," *Environmental Ethics* 12 (1990): 7.

24. Barbara Allen, "Letter to the editor," *Northern Lights* 8, 10 (1992): 29.

25. Evernden, *The Social Creation of Nature,* 121. Exploring these questions further is beyond the scope of this paper. For other treatments see Paul Shepard, "A Post-Historic Primitivism," in *The Wilderness Condition,* Max Oelschlaeger, ed. (San Francisco: Sierra Club Books, 1992), 40–89; Paul Shepard, *Nature and Madness* (San Francisco: Sierra Club Books, 1982), and Warwick Fox, *Toward a Transpersonal Ecology* (Boston: Shambhala Publications, 1990).

26. Callicott, "The Wilderness Idea Revisited," p. 240.

27. J. Baird Callicott, "La Nature Est Mort, Vive La Nature!" *Hastings Center Report:* 22, 5 (1992): 22.

28. For overviews of sustainable development, see Herman Daly and John Cobb, *For the Common Good* (Boston: Beacon Press, 1989); Daniel Korten, "Sustainable Development," in *World Policy Journal* 9, 1 (1991–92): 157–90; David Orr, *Ecological Literacy* (Albany: State University of New York Press, 1992).

29. Rolston, "The Wilderness Idea Reaffirmed," 370.

30. Holmes Rolston, "Biology and Philosophy in Yellowstone," in *Biology and Philosophy* 5 (1990): 244–245.

31. Rolston, "The Wilderness Idea Reaffirmed," 372.

32. Ibid., 377.

33. Callicott, "That Good Old-Time Wilderness Religion," 378.

34. Callicott, "The Wilderness Idea Revisited," 243.

35. Leopold, *A Sand County Almanac,* 207.

36. For discussion on humans in Amazonia see Gomez-Pompa and Kaus, "Taming the Wilderness Myth," 273–76.

37. Callicott, "The Wilderness Idea Revisited," 242–45.

38. K. Norman Johnson, et al., *Alternatives for Management of Late-successional Forests of the Pacific Northwest.* A report to the Agriculture Committee of the U.S. House of Representatives, October 8, 1991. 59pp.

39. John Williams, et al., "Declining Salmon and Steelhead Populations: New Endangered Species Concerns for the West," in *Endangered Species Update* 9, 4 (1992): 1–8.

40. USDI Fish and Wildlife Service, "Status of Endangered Species Recovery Program Is Detailed in Report to Congress," in *Endangered Species Technical Bulletin* 16 (9-12) (1991): 1, 9.

41. John Ryan, "Conserving Biological Diversity," in *State of the World—1992,* eds. Lester Brown, et al. (New York: W. W. Norton, 1992), 9–26.

42. Michael Soulé, et al., "The Millennium Ark: How Long a Voyage, How Many Staterooms, How Many Passengers?" *Zoo Biology* 5 (1986): 101–113.

43. Noss, "Wilderness Recovery," 226.

44. Callicott, "The Wilderness Idea Revisited," 244.

45. Ibid., 243.

46. Callicott, "That Good Old-Time Wilderness Religion," 379.

47. Callicott, "The Wilderness Idea Revisited," 239.

48. Ibid., 238.

49. Ibid., 243.

50. For a general description of the WUM, see Callahan, "The Wise-Use Movement."

51. Craig Allin, *The Politics of Wilderness Preservation* (Westport, Conn.: Greenwood Press, 1982), 12.

52. Ron Arnold, ed., *The Wise Use Agenda* (Bellevue, Wash.: Center for the Defense of Free Enterprise, 1988).

53. As quoted in Eric Brazil, " 'Wise-Use' Advocates Scorn the Rio Summit," in *San Francisco Examiner,* June 7, 1992, A1, A9.

54. Callahan, "The Wise-Use Movement," 2.

55. Bryan Norton, *Toward Unity Among Environmentalists* (New York: Oxford University Press, 1991), 58.

56. Gompez-Pompa and Kaus, "Taming the Wilderness Myth," 272.

57. Ibid.

58. Ray Dasmann, "Life-styles and Nature Conservation," *Oryx* 13, 3 (1976): 281–86.

59. Gompez-Pompa and Kaus, "Taming the Wilderness Myth," 273.

60. Callicott, "The Wilderness Idea Revisited," 242.

61. Rolston, "The Wilderness Idea Reaffirmed," 375.

62. Paul Shepard and Barry Sanders, *The Sacred Paw* (New York: Viking, 1985), 55–59.

63. Irving Hallowell, "Bear Ceremonialism in the Northern Hemisphere," *American Anthropologist* 28 (1926): 1–175; David Rockwell, *Giving Voice to Bear* (Niwot: Roberts Rinehart, 1991); Richard Nelson, *Make Prayers to the Raven* (Chicago: University of Chicago Press, 1983), 184–89.

64. Nelson, *Make Prayers to the Raven,* pp. 229–30. For a general discussion on this point written by tribal people, see Peggy Beck and Anna Walters, *The Sacred* (Tsaile, Ariz.: Navajo Community College Press, 1977), 11–22.

65. Snyder, *The Practice of the Wild,* 81–86.

66. Jared Diamond, "Man the Exterminator," in *Nature* 298 (1982): 787–89; Paul Martin and R. G. Klein, eds., *Quaternary Extinctions: A Prehistoric Revolution* (Tucson: University of Arizona Press, 1984).

67. William Burch, *Daydreams and Nightmares* (New York: Harper and Row, 1971), 49–50; Michael Soulé, "Conservation: Tactics for a Constant Crisis," in *Science* 153 (1991): 746.

68. For examples see Daniel Bromley, ed., *Making the Commons Work* (San Francisco: Institute for Contemporary Studies Press, 1992); David Feeny, et al. "The Tragedy of the Commons: Twenty-two Years Later," *Human Ecology* 18, 1 (1990): 1–17; Bonnie McCay and J. Atcheson, eds., *The Question of the Commons* (Tucson: University of Arizona Press, 1987); Edward Goldsmith, ed., *The Ecologist* 22, 4 (1992), special edition on the commons.

69. Birch, "The Incarceration of Wildness," 6.

70. For a full explication of this platform see Grumbine, *Ghost Bears,* 184–228.

71. See in general Michael O'Connell and Reed Noss, "Protecting Biodiversity on Private Lands," *Environmental Management* 6 (1992): 435–50.

72. Wendell Berry, "Conservation Is Good Work," *Wild Earth* 2, 1 (1992): 83.

73. Salwasser, "Sustainability As a Conservation Paradigm," 214.

74. Shepard, "Toward a Post-Historic Primitivism," 85.

75. M. G. Chandrakanth and Jeff Romm, "Sacred Forests, Secular Forest Policies and People's Actions," *National Resources Journal* 31 (1991): 141–57.

76. Ibid., 156.

77. Gomez-Pompa and Kaus, "Taming the Wilderness Myth," 273.

78. Michael Zimmerman, "The Blessing of Otherness," in *The Wilderness Condition,* ed. Max Oelschlaeger (San Francisco: Sierra Club Books, 1992), 245–70.

79. Snyder, *The Practice of the Wild,* 15, 37.

80. John Davis, ed. "The Wildlands Project," in *Wild Earth,* special issue no. 1, 1993.

# 34 | THE THIRD WORLD, WILDERNESS, AND DEEP ECOLOGY

*Arne Naess*

## I

THIS ARTICLE IS MOTIVATED by listening to some people from the Third World who express a suspicion that Deep Ecology is a new variant of Western domination and "neocolonialism": they fear that people of the Third World will be pushed out of their homes to make more room for spectacular animals. Some authors have expressed the opinion that Deep Ecology is for the rich nations that can afford the luxury of vast wilderness as habitat for wild species. In my opinion, however, it would indeed be tragic if such ideas were going to spoil the much-needed cooperation between supporters of the Deep Ecology movement throughout the various regions of the globe, including the Third World.

Throughout most of human history, all humans have lived in what we now call wilderness. As Gary Snyder points out:

> Just a few centuries ago, when virtually *all* was wild in North America, wilderness was not something exceptionally severe. Pronghorn and Bison trailed through the grasslands, creeks ran full of salmon, there were acres of clams, and grizzlies, cougar, and bighorn sheep were common in the lowlands. There were human beings, too: North America was *all populated.* There were people everywhere. . . . All of the hills and lakes of Alaska have been named in one or another of the dozen or so languages spoken by the native people.[1]

Prior to agriculture, our ancestors left few traces. Ecosystems were not appreciably changed for the most part, except by large fires, and probably

---

This essay (written in 1991) is previously unpublished. Published by permission.

through the extermination of some large animal species. But for the most part, landscapes and ecosystems were not irreversibly reduced in richness and diversity, and the basic ecological conditions of life were maintained. There is not today, nor was there ever, any essential conflict between humans in moderate numbers and a state of wilderness or wildness. There are reasons today, however, for some areas to be left entirely devoid of human settlement, and for limiting even short carefully arranged visits by scientists to a minimum, but this should be looked upon as an exceptional situation.

At present, there are old growth forests in Australia, for example, which are inhabited by ecologically conscious and careful people. This situation illustrates the essential compatibility of people living in wilderness with a presumably high quality of life—a "rich life with simple means." They use plants for food and other purposes, but they do not, of course, engage in subsistance agriculture.

What is considered a normal lifestyle in industrial countries is clearly incompatible with living in wilderness. Industrial people interfere so severely with natural processes that even a very small number of them can significantly alter the landscape. For example, it is widely recognized that people doing research in the Antarctic should use extreme care not to damage the ecosystems, but it is also clear that the rules are widely disobeyed.[2] Bad habits are difficult, but not impossible, to change!

It is unavoidable that some people concerned with the protection of wildlife and natural ecosystems tend to see a direct and global antagonism between human settlement and wilderness. But supporters of the Deep Ecology movement, like many others, know that wilderness, or wildness, need not be destroyed by people living in these areas (or nearby) and that they may enjoy a high quality of life.

It is not possible for people living in the United States to interfere as little with the wilderness as did the traditional American Indians, and Gary Snyder (and other articulate American supporters of the Deep Ecology movement) insist that there should be no further destruction of wilderness in America. Even what is now set aside in the United States as designated wilderness is interfered with too much. The traditional point of view of the U.S. Forest Service still has a lot of influence: "Wilderness is for people. . . . The preservation goals established . . . are designed to provide values and benefits to society. . . . Wilderness is not set aside for the sake of its flora or fauna, but for people."[3] It is not only the "*but* for people" that makes all the difference, from Gary Snyder's point of view, but also the term "society." People who live in wilderness, or who have their roots in wilderness, form communities rather than "societies." There is a vast difference between the slogan of the World

Wildlife Fund ("wilderness for people") and the meaning of the U.S. Forest Service phrase: "wilderness for American society."

Those people in the United States who are actively trying to stop the destruction of wilderness do not tend to publish *general proposals on how to treat apparently similar problems in the Third World*. At least this is true of theoreticians of the Deep Ecology movement. Nevertheless, there are writers who look upon "radical environmentalism," including Deep Ecology, as a threat to the poverty stricken people of the Third World. The opinion is not uncommon that people in the rich Western world tend to support wild animals and wilderness rather than poor people. However, the real question is: *How* can the poor be helped in a way that is sustainable in the long run?

Close cooperation between supporters of the Deep Ecology movement and ecologically concerned people in the poor countries requires that the latter trust the former's concern for the economic progress of the poor. But what is progress in this case? Is consumerism progress?

The principle formulated by Gary Snyder is applicable in Third World countries: that is, there is no inherent antagonism between human settlement and free nature, for it all depends on the *kind* of culture humans have. It should be a universal goal for mankind to avoid all kinds of consumerism and concentrate, instead, on raising the basic quality of life for humans, including the satisfaction of their economic needs.

The number of poor people in Third World countries is too large for all of them to dwell non-destructively in the tropical forests; more and more subsistence agriculture in these forests serves neither the best interests of the poor, nor does it protect the forests from destruction. Millions of people now live in the tropical forests in a broadly sustainable way; that is, without reducing the richness and diversity of life forms found there. But what is now happening is an *invasion* of these areas resulting in major disruption of the people and the communities who have been living there in harmony. The forests are clear-cut and burned, and subsistence agriculture is introduced. These practices cannot help the poor reach the goals of long-term economic progress. This is true as well of the large industrial operations in the forests and along the rivers.

The present ecological world situation requires a focusing of attention upon *urban* settlements; changing them in ways so that they will be appropriate and habitable places for the thousands of millions of people who now, and in the next century, will need a place to live. This gigantic effort will require mutual help between rich and poor countries. Significant economic progress for the poor is not possible through the extensive use of less fertile lands for agriculture. *There is no way out except through urbanization,* together with the willingness of the rich to buy products from the poor.

It has been pointed out that, from an ecological long-range perspective, the economies of some traditional North American native cultures were superbly sustainable in a broad sense. It has been noted that the philosophical, religious, and mythological basis for these economies, and for their social relations in general, was expressed through sayings which are eminently consistent with the fundamental attitudes found in the Deep Ecology movement. Similar sayings found in Eastern cultures have had an even greater impact. As the Indian social ecologist Ramachandra Guha (who has published what he sees as a Third World critique of Deep Ecology) claims, "The coupling of (ancient) Eastern and (modern) ecological wisdom seemingly helps consolidate the claim that deep ecology is a philosophy of universal significance."[4] The total views suggested among supporters of the Deep Ecology movement do, in a sense, couple "(ancient) Eastern and (modern) ecological wisdom." But there are reasons to be cautious here.

To cherish some of the ecosophic attitudes convincingly demonstrated by people from the East does not imply the doctrinal acceptance of any past definite philosophy or religion conventionally classified as Eastern. Heavy influence does not imply conformity with any beliefs: the history of ideas and contemporary philosophizing are different subjects. At any rate, there is ample reason for supporters of the Deep Ecology movement to refrain from questioning each other's ultimate beliefs. Deep cultural differences are more or less cognitively unbridgeable and will remain so, I hope.

Desperate people (including desperately poor, hungry people) will naturally have a narrow utilitarian attitude towards their environment. But overall, the people of the Third World, apart from the desperate minority, manifest a positive concern for the protection of free nature, and a respect for nonhuman living beings. At least this has been my experience while living among poor people in India, Pakistan and Nepal (and others in the Third World agree with me on this point). Without these experiences, I would not have talked about the international basis of a Deep Ecology movement.

Temporarily pressing problems of material need might monopolize their attention, but this is also true of people in similar circumstances in the West, despite their affluence. In short, there is a sound basis for *global* cooperation between supporters of the Deep Ecology movement and ecologically concerned people in the Third World, and also with people who try to understand and lessen the poverty in those regions. These people cooperate in movements against poverty which do not entail further large-scale deforestation. And there is no tendency to support animals at the expense of humans within the framework of this cooperation.

## II

To Social Ecologists in countries which are less affluent than the United States, it may look threatening when environmental activists in the United States declare "an unflinching opposition to human attacks on undisturbed wilderness."[5] Some activists even engage in un-Gandhian ecotage; for instance, destroying vehicles and other machinery while making sure that no one gets hurt in the process. So far, there have been very few authenticated cases of anyone being seriously hurt. Considering the vehemence of these struggles, and the passions involved, this should be considered a great victory.

Clearly, these intense personally involved activists are speaking about wilderness primarily in the United States, not necessarily about the situation on other continents. At least, this is true of supporters of the Deep Ecology movement, but this point can be easily overlooked by observers in the Third World. Unflinching opposition to the cutting down of *any* trees, or to the establishment of *any* new human settlements in any wilderness *what so ever* is a preposterous idea presumably held by no one. The real issue here for the Third World is: How much wilderness and wildlife habitat is it acceptable to continue to modify and destroy, and for what purposes?

In the richest nations of the world, the destruction of old growth forests still goes on. There is ample justification for activists in the United States to focus on these destructive, mindless, irreversible activities. The term "ecocriminality" is a suitable word to use for this forest destruction, and a question of great importance arises here: given their own unecological practices, do the rich nations deserve any *credibility* when preaching ecological responsibility to the poor countries?

One has to distinguish between three things: (1) the present dismal situation concerning the lack of protection of wilderness; (2) the estimates published by conservation biologists concerning the size of wilderness areas needed for continued speciation; and (3) the more-or-less realistic plans put forth by established environmental organizations (e.g. the World Wildlife Fund and the International Union for the Conservation of Nature) concerning how to improve the present state of affairs for protecting wildlife and wild ecosystems. (It should be pointed out that, given the estimates of Frankel and Soulé that an area on the order of six hundred square kilometers is necessary for the speciation of birds and mammals, of course nothing *specific* follows concerning how to achieve what is deemed necessary for this purpose.)

Is the idea that "the biosphere as a whole should be zoned" considered threatening to some in the Third World? Actually, it should be considered more of a threat directed against First World practices than toward any other nations. For, according to Odum and Phillips, establishment of protection zones "may be the only way to limit the destructive impact of our technological-industrial-agribusiness complex upon the earth."[6] This is clearly a warning directed more toward the destructive practices of the First World. Of course, if Third World elites try to copy First World excesses, then the situation would change.

## III

The movements supporting the establishment of "green" societies, and for a global Green movement, have their origin among people in the rich countries. It is understandable that they have not had much impact so far among people in the Third World, and that they are met with suspicion. The priorities among First and Third world countries are and, to some extent, must be, different. Furthermore, "green utopias," and even the everyday conceptions of what constitutes "greenness," tend to be rather uniform, as if green societies, in spite of the deeply different cultures and traditions of the world, would look very much alike.

It is to be hoped that there would be no standard green societies, no *Gleich-schaltung* of human institutions and behavioral patterns. Hopefully, economically sound societies of Africa, South America, and Southeast Asia would not resemble present rich countries except in certain rather superficial ways.

Some people think that "ecological sustainability" will be attained when policies have been adopted which will protect us from great ecological catastrophies. But it is beneath human dignity to have this as a supreme ecological goal! Ecological sustainability, in a more proper sense, will be achieved only when policies on a global scale protect the full richness and diversity of life forms on the planet. The former goal may be called "narrow"; the latter "wide" ecological sustainability. In short, it is my opinion that *a necessary, but not sufficient, criterion of the fully attained greenness of a society is that it is ecologically sustainable in the wide sense.* (The Bruntland Report admits of various interpretations, but it does envisage a sustainable "developed" country to be one that satisfies the wide sense of ecological sustainability.)

(A small digression: When I do not go into complex argumentation, but just announce that "it is beneath human dignity to aspire to less than *wide* ecological sustainability," I intend to express a personal view (and as with other assertions) thought to be *compatible* with supporters of the Deep Ecology movement. My assertions *that* supporters of the Deep Ecology movement have such and such attitudes or opinions are, of course, more or less certain, and should not be taken to assert that strictly everybody has those attitudes or opinions.)

## IV

It should be clear that the realization of wide ecological sustainability will require deep changes in the rich societies of the world having to do, in part, with policies of growth and overconsumptive lifestyles. If we accept that the realization of the goals of the Deep Ecology movement imply wide sustainability, two questions immediately arise: (1) does the realization of wide sustainability presuppose or require acceptance of the views of the Deep Ecology movement? and (2) does the realization of wide sustainability require significant changes in Third World societies?

If we answer "yes" to the first question, this might be interpreted as asserting that the realization of wide sustainability would require that most members of the relevant societies must accept the views of the Deep Ecology movement. As I see it, this is not necessary (and it would imply a change of heart of an extremely unlikely kind!). But a "yes" to the first question might be interpreted as the assertion that a sufficiently strong minority would be needed to bring about wide sustainability. This situation may well arise. (I don't mean to claim here that a definite answer to the first question is conceptually implied. A decisive "no" to this question is thinkable. It does seem clear, however, that the more people who explicitly or implicitly accept the views of the Deep Ecological movement, the better.)

As to question (2), a "yes" answer seems warranted as far as I can judge. In Third World countries at present there is a general tendency to attempt to follow an "economic growth and development" path which emulates the rich countries. This must be avoided, and to avoid it requires significant changes in the orientations of these societies.

What kinds of changes are necessary? A discussion of the nature of these changes has intentionally been left abstract and general in the Deep Ecology "platform." Point 6 of the "platform" states that "Policies must therefore be changed. These policies affect basic economic, technological, and ideological structures. The resulting state of affairs will be deeply different from the present."

It is obviously pertinent to ask: "Exactly which changes need to be made?" But times change. A short answer to this question seems much more difficult to provide in 1993 than it was in 1970. Practically every major concrete change envisaged in 1970 today seems either more difficult to realize, or not unreservedly desirable in the form it was proposed in 1970.

As a preliminary to serious practical discussion, one must specify which country, state, region, society, and community one has in mind. The distinction First World/Second World/Third World/Fourth World is still relevant. But practically all Deep Ecology literature has focused on rich countries even though there are many supporters in other kinds of countries. The "sustainability" literature is fortunately more diverse.

As an example of social and political change that was highly recommended in 1970, but not in the nineties, one may mention various forms of decentralization. Today the global nature of all the major ecological problems is widely recognized, along with the stubborn resistance of most local, regional, and national groups to give global concerns priority over the less-than-global, even when this is obviously necessary in order to attain wide global sustainability. To the slogan "Think globally, act locally" should be added a new one: "Think globally, act globally." Even if we take it for granted that your body is geographically at a definite place, nevertheless every action influences the Earth, and many of these may be roughly positive or negative. Actions are global in whatever locality you act. Many fierce local or regional conflicts have a global character, crossing every border and level of standard of living.

The moderately poor people in the Second and Third Worlds may seem more helpless, for example, than the coastal people of rich Arctic Norway, but the ecological conflicts are, to a remarkable degree, of the same kind. Communities who live largely by fishing within a day's distance from land in Arctic Norway are in extreme difficulties, because the resources of the Norway Sea, and even the vast uniquely rich Barent Sea, have been badly depleted. For the coastal people it is "a question of sheer survival" but, because Norway is a rich welfare state of sorts, there is no chance that they will go to bed hungry. If the policy makers had seen the intrinsic value, the inherent greatness of the ocean with its fullness of life (and not *only* its narrow usefulness as the source of big profits; e.g., trawling, ocean-factories), then the coastal people could have retained their way of life. They would not have lost their self-esteem by having to migrate to the cities. The supporters of the Deep Ecology movement in the rich countries are not in conflict with Deep Ecology supporters in the Third and Fourth worlds. Such behavior would be strange indeed, because the global perspective reveals the basic similarity of the situation among poor and rich.

The Sami people (wrongly referred to as Lapplanders), a Fourth World nomadic people living in the Arctic Soviet Union, Finland, Sweden, and Norway, have resisted being completely dominated by these four powerful states for the last four hundred years. When a big dam was proposed in their lands (as part of an unnecessary hydroelectric development), thousands of First World people joined them in protest. When a Sami was arrested for standing "unlawfully" on the shore of the river, the police asked him, "Why do you stay here?" He answered, "This place is part of myself." I know of no major ecological conflict anywhere which has not manifested the power and initiative of people who are not alienated from "free nature," but who protect it for its own sake as something which has meaning in itself, independently of its narrow human utility. This kind of motivation for protection of "free nature" adds substantially to the strong, but narrow, utilitarian motivation.

Sometimes the "environmental concern" of poor Third World communities seems to Westerners to relate to the "environment per se." As an example, the people of the Buddhist community of Beding (Peding) in the Rolwaling Himalaya live with the majestic holy mountain Gauri Shankar (Tseringma) straight above their heads. It has long been the object of religious respect. Some of us (mountaineers and Deep Ecology supporters) asked the people whether they wished to enjoy the profits they would get from expeditions by Westerners and Japanese trying to "conquer the mountain," or whether they preferred to *protect the mountain itself* from being trodden upon by humans with no respect for its cultural status. The families of the community came together and unanimously voted for protection. I had the honor of walking for a week with the chief of the community, Gonden, to deliver a document addressed to the King of Nepal in Kathmandu, asking him to prohibit the climbing of Gauri Shankar. There was no reply. The rich Hindu government of Nepal is economically interested in big expeditions, and the opinion of the faraway Buddhist communities of poor people carry little weight.

The work of Vandana Shiva and others shows how women in rural India continue to try to protect an economy that is largely ecologically sustainable. But do they have the power to resist Western inspired unecological development?

Consider an example from Africa. Large areas where the Masai live may be classified as areas of "free nature," if not wilderness. The Masai are not disturbed by the vast populations of spectacular animals on their lands, such as lions and leopards, together with hundreds of others, nor are these animals severely disturbed by the Masai. For a long time, there has been a remarkable compatibility between people and wild animals. As more or less nomadic herders, the Masai do not need land set apart for agricultural purposes.

What holds true for the Masai holds as well for a great number of other peoples and cultures in the Third World. Ecologically sustainable development may proceed in direct continuity with their traditional culture as long as population pressures remain moderate.

Lately, the Masai have been using more and more money for motor vehicles and other products they don't make themselves. This makes it tempting to sell parts of their territory to farmers looking for land for their many children. From the point of view of economic development, such sales are unfortunate because the relevant kind of subsistance agriculture does not lead to economic progress. The Masai can get sufficient cash through very carefully managed tourism and still have the traditional use of the land and preserve their cultural continuity. Some supporters of the Deep Ecology movement are working with the Masai to help them keep what is left of their land intact. An increase in subsistence farming, in this situation, is a blind alley. But the alternatives are all problematic and there are no easy answers to be found anywhere.

Individual arguments can be singled out and used and misused to defend a variety of mutually incompatible conclusions. In his paper, R. Guha warns that such is the case with arguments used by supporters of the Deep Ecology movement. And this does not happen only to Deep Ecology supporters in the United States.

After a speech I gave in Norway in favor of considering the Barent Sea seriously as a whole complex ecosystem (together with treating the living beings, including the tiny flagellates, as having intrinsic value) the politician considered to be the most powerful proponent of big fishing interests is said to have remarked, "Naess is of course more concerned about flagellates than about people." My point was that the present tragic situation for fishermen could have been avoided if policy makers had shown a little more respect for all life, not less respect for people. In every such case, one has reason to say that communication on the part of the supporters of Deep Ecology was imperfect. In this case, I certainly should have talked more about people than I did, but not to the exclusion of flagellates, radiolarians and all the other life forms which attract the interest of only a minority of people, and certainly not to the exclusion of ecosystems as a whole.

In 1985, at the international conservation biology conference in Michigan, a representative of a Third World country stood up and asked, "What about *our* problems?" Of course, it was strange for this person, and other representatives of the tropical countries, to hear discussions, day after day, on the future of biological processes in their countries without touching the main social and economic problems facing them. If the conference had been organized by the Green movement, the agenda would have been somewhat different. The discussions concerning how to deal with the ecological crisis would have taken up, let us say, only one third of the time. The other two-thirds would have concerned mainly social problems ("social justice," I would say) and peace. The representatives of the Third World could have introduced the latter two areas of concern and could have stressed that efforts to protect what is left of the richness and diversity of Life on Earth must not interfere with efforts to solve the main problems they have today.

Supporters of the Deep Ecology movement, however, might have raised the following question for discussion. "How can the increasing global interest in protecting all Life on Earth be used to further the cause of genuine economic progress and social justice in the Third World?"

Such questions will inevitably bring forth different and, in part, incompatible proposals. But as we explore these incompatible proposals, we must never lose sight of the importance of all humans everywhere of preserving the richness and diversity of Life on Earth.

# NOTES

1. Gary Snyder, *The Practice of the Wild* (San Francisco: North Point Press, 1990), 7.

2. See the Greenpeace report: *Greenpeace Antarctic Expedition 1989/90,* 53. Waste disposal procedures have improved but "many more changes are still needed if stations are to comply with the new waste disposal guidelines contained in ATCM Recommendation XV-3. Indeed, most stations have not even met the minimal guidelines agreed to by the treaty States in 1975."

3. Quoted from a valuable survey of the wilderness issues: George Sessions, "Ecocentrism, Wilderness, and Global Ecosystem Protection," in *The Wilderness Condition: Essays on Environmental and Civilization,* edited by Max Oelschlaeger (San Francisco: Sierra Club Books, 1992).

4. Ramachandra Guha, "Radical American Environmentalism and Wilderness Preservation: A Third World Critique," in *Environmental Ethics* 11, no. 1 (1989): 74.

5. Ibid., 74. "In contrast to the conventional lobbying efforts of environmental professionals based in Washington, [Earth First!] proposes a militant defense of "Mother Earth," and unflinching opposition to human attacks on undisturbed wilderness."

6. Sessions, "Ecocentrism. . . ."

PART SIX | # TOWARD THE TWENTY-FIRST CENTURY AND BEYOND
## *SOCIAL AND POLITICAL IMPLICATIONS*

# INTRODUCTION

SINCE THE 1980S, THE politics of ecology has centered around the concept
of "sustainable development." One year after adopting the World Charter for
Nature (which asserted that "Nature shall be respected and its essential processes shall not be disrupted"), the United Nations General Assembly, in 1983,
asked the Brundtland commission to formulate a "global agenda for change"
that would address the problems of the global environmental crisis. This even-
tuated in the 1987 Brundtland Report, which, for all practical purposes, has
nullified the Ecological Revolution of the 1960s and '70s—and the World
Charter for Nature—by officially sanctioning the era of materialism and heed-
less economic growth of the 1980s.

For example, Chris Lewis (see the introduction to Part Two) claims that the
Brundtland Report, *Our Common Future,* rejected the increasingly apocalyptic
warnings of scientists over the last forty years concerning the severity of the
ecological crisis, and ratified instead "the global post–World War II consensus
that economic growth and global development will create an abundant, peaceful, and just world." *Our Common Future* states:

> Our report . . . is not a prediction of ever increasing environmental decay,
> poverty, and hardship in an ever more polluted world among ever decreasing
> resources. We see instead the possibility for a new era of economic growth,
> one that must be based on policies that sustain and expand the environmental
> base. And we believe such growth to be absolutely essential to relieve the
> great poverty that is deepening in much of the developing world. (p. 1)

Lewis points out that "contradicting the optimistic conclusions of . . . the
Brundtland commission, [many of the world's leading] scientists assert that
progress and economic growth are, in fact, the causes of the global ecological
crisis. Indeed, progress has only intensified humanity's war against the natural
world." The unjustifiable optimism of the Brundtland Report, which flies in
the face of scientist's warnings about the environmental state of the world, is
also reflected in the sustainable development approach taken by the world's
leaders at the 1992 United Nations Conference on Environment and Development (UNCED) held in Rio de Janeiro.

In "The Shaky Ground of Sustainability," the leading environmental historian Donald Worster argues that the environmental goals of the 1960s and '70s Ecological Revolution have been compromised and obscured by the concept of sustainable development. To begin with, the word "sustainability" means different things to economists, political scientists, ecologists, and agrarian proponents such as Wendell Berry.

These problems, over the years, have been further compounded by shifting emphases and interpretations of the science of ecology. For example, the ecologist Daniel Botkin now argues that Nature is inherently chaotic, disorderly, and in continual flux. Botkin uses his interpretation of ecology in an attempt to support the anthropocentric view that humans must become the managers and controllers of Nature to provide Nature with order and "to make the Earth a comfortable home" for human civilization. Botkin criticizes the ecologists of the 1960s and '70s for being unnecessarily hostile to modern technology and progress.

Worster claims that the science of ecology has, by default, left the concept of sustainability with the economists. As a result of the recent interpretations of Botkin and others, the science of ecology now ironically appears to stand in the service of anthropocentric growth and development (although the new discipline of conservation biology seems to be returning ecology to its role as the "subversive science").

Worster criticizes the sustainable development ideal as resting on uncritical and unexamined anthropocentric assumptions. Further, the sustainable development approach travels the "easy road" of political compromise that fails to deal adequately with the ecological crisis. To remedy this situation, Worster proposes a return to the goals of the ecologists of the 1960s Ecological Revolution, and to the present environmental goals of the conservation biologists, by claiming that humanity's ultimate ecological priority should be the protection of biodiversity, wild ecosystems, and wild evolutionary processes.

Wolfgang Sachs provides a sophisticated political analysis and critique of the history and concept of development, "sustainable development," and the Rio UNCED Earth Summit. Sachs points out that it was President Harry Truman's 1949 inaugural speech that first defined nations of the Southern Hemisphere as "underdeveloped." It was essentially this definition that propelled the world into an economic production race, with Northern Hemisphere countries leading the pack. Contrary to the hopes and justification for continued development as expressed in the Brundtland Report, Sachs argues that the "social justice" rationale for development in the South has been a failure: the disparity between rich and poor is now greater than it was at the time of decolonization.

The Rio Earth Summit was a replay of older concerns, but now, according to Sachs, under the aegis of "sustainable development." The Rio conference managed to enshrine environmentalism as "the highest state of development-alism." The North demanded environmental accountability from the South while insisting upon continuing development and consumerism for itself. The South emphasized social justice while determined to follow the high-tech, high-consumption developmental path of the North. All of this development, however, works against both the environment and social justice.

Sachs claims that the concept of sustainable development is anthropocentric and concerned essentially with "the conservation of development, not for the conservation of nature." Nature becomes goods and services for human economic development; merely a "bargaining chip" in the ongoing political/economic struggles. Technocratic environmentalists (living in their illusory world of civilized "second nature") are concerned mainly with urban pollution, the scarcity of resources, and a technological "efficiency revolution." But, according to Sachs, technological efficiency without a radical change in society's goals is counterproductive.

The global ecological crisis has now resulted in the use of the concept of sustainability to support anthropocentric high-tech global resource and development management schemes for the Earth. (For critiques of global management schemes, which go hand in hand with the economic "new world order" being promoted by global corporate/economic elites, see Part Four; see also Jerry Mander's *In the Absence of the Sacred*.) By Westernizing the world, Sachs claims, the North has unwittingly destabilized its way of life. This is now seen by economic and political leaders as requiring worldwide management in order to protect Northern security.

In "Politics and the Ecological Crisis," Arne Naess points out that while ecological concern must lead to social/political activism, "everything, not just politics" needs to be changed. Nevertheless, in the 1960s, shallow anthropocentric environmentalists and "business as usual" economists and politicians proposed technological and legal solutions to the environmental crisis, while at the same time refusing to engage in philosophical discussions about the ecological crisis. By pointing out that crucial, unexamined anthropocentric assumptions underlie the politics of sustainable development, the analyses of Worster and Sachs further support Naess's claims.

Naess's answer to the "sustainability" quandary is to substitute the concept of "ecological sustainability" in place of the Brundtland/Rio advocacy of "sustainable development": more specifically, the concept of *"wide* ecological sustainability" (for a more complete account of "wide ecological sustainability" see the Naess paper in Part Five). As Naess uses the term, "narrow" ecological sustainability is anthropocentric in proposing politics that would try to protect mainly *humans* from ecological catastrophe. For Naess, *"wide* ecological sustainability" is ecocentric: it requires "the protection of the full richness and diversity of life forms on the planet." It is beneath human dignity, Naess claims, to aspire to less than *wide* ecological sustainability. Wide sustainability thus reflects the main concerns and goals of conservation biology and is consistent with Worster's conclusions concerning the ultimate ecological priority for humanity.

As Naess points out, ecological sustainability is only *one* of the goals of a Green society, the other two main goals being those of the peace movement and the social justice movement (what Naess calls "the three great movements"). These are separate goals and movements, however, and should not be confused with one another. Naess claims, however, that "considering the accelerating rate of irreversible ecological destruction worldwide, I find it acceptable to continue fighting ecological unsustainability whatever the state of affairs may be concerning the other two goals of Green societies." At times, the goals of these various movements will come into conflict: for example, when liberal immigration policies promoted by the social justice movement ignore ecological considerations.

Naess also points out that the Deep Ecology movement finds itself having to support trends toward both global institutions and decentralization. Global, national, and regional institutions may need to pressure the "smaller, less-polluted and [less-]damaged areas to adopt restrictions on ecologically damaging practices."

The next two papers, by Gary Snyder and Arne Naess, discuss some of the possible future directions for humanity in light of the worsening environmental crisis. Snyder is a leading theorist of the Deep Ecology bioregional/reinhabitory position. In "The Rediscovery of Turtle Island" (his most recent paper on the subject), Snyder attempts to come to grips with problems raised by the traditional Western dichotomies between mind and body, spirit and matter, and culture and nature.

As a result of the ecological perspective, we have been "thrown back" into the garden with the other animals, and the wall between nature and culture (between "first nature" and "second nature") has crumbled. Snyder discusses the instrumentalist orientations of anthropocentric proponents of wilderness preservation versus those who argue that since Nature is always changing, humans should feel free to transform it (furthering the discussion by Worster, and by Grumbine in Part Five). Both of these views treat Nature as a commodity. Nevertheless it is a "bum rap," Snyder claims, to attribute a "static" view of Nature to the wilderness preservationists.

There is a third way, inspired by the Native American traditions, ecosystem theory, and environmental philosophy, wherein future wilderness will be grounded in bioregional and watershed communities. Wilderness will exist primarily as wild species habitat. In some reinhabitory communities, wildlife corridors will be human-inhabited (what Naess refers to as "free nature").

Michael Zimmerman has also been concerned with the future of ecology (see the bibliography for Zimmerman's paper "The Future of Ecology"). One debate that particularly concerns him is whether national or global institutions will need to be called upon to help protect Nature (see Naess's views above), or whether environmental activism for social change should be strictly confined to the local and concrete grass roots level (views supposedly held by Snyder and Wendell Berry). Berry has explicitly criticized the possibility of acting on the global level to protect Nature: he claims it is impossible to "think globally." Further, the dangers of concentrating more power in regional, national, and global institutions have been emphasized by Birch (in Part Four) and others. Zimmerman's concerns are that we may be playing into the hands of those who will, in his words, force "everyone and everything to conform to a one-dimensional and totalitarian conceptual, political, or economic grid."

Snyder seems somewhat less worried about this than is Berry. In "The Rediscovery of Turtle Island," he mentions the California State Resources Agency, and some officials working at the federal level of the U.S. Forest Service and the Bureau of Land Management, who appear to be coming around to an ecosystem approach to land problems. In "Four Changes" (see Part Two) Snyder proposed a "cultural and individual pluralism, unified by a type of world tribal council." Zimmerman thinks that global organizations such as the United Nations, if they can be rechanneled to an ecocentric perspective from their "sustainable development" path, are needed to cope adequately with the environmental crisis.

In "Deep Ecology for the Twenty-second Century," Arne Naess provides us with an example of the *long-range* emphasis of the Deep Ecology movement by looking to the future to see what the prospects might be for both the human and the nonhuman inhabitants of the Earth. Naess claims that he is an *optimist* about the prospects for the twenty-second century! The extent of the irreversible environmental damage (species extinction, and so forth) that occurs during the twenty-first century—how far we will sink before heading back up—depends upon the environmental actions we take now. Therefore, we need ecological "activism on a high level immediately." Reemphasizing his concept of *wide* ecological sustainability, he examines some possible scenarios for the future. The need for future cooperation between "the three great movements" that comprise the Greens is discussed. Humans have special obligations toward their own kind, but it is also quite natural to extend and deepen our sense of caring for all creatures and the ecosystems of the Earth.

According to Naess, ecologically sustainable Green societies of the twenty-second century will look similar in some ways to presently existing societies.

While there will be big centers of commerce, learning, and the arts, in Naess's view, the *dominance* of greed, unecological production, and severe social injustice will have disappeared. Here Naess exhibits his deep philosophical commitment to *diversity* of all kinds. Substantial progress will also have been made toward a sustainable human population size.

There should also be many reinhabitory communities of the kind envisioned by Gary Snyder and others. Many supporters of the Deep Ecology movement believe that human habitation on Earth, including the cities, should ultimately be bioregional. It is also to be expected that the nature preserves with interconnecting corridors as proposed by the conservation biologists will have long since been securely in place.

# 35 | THE SHAKY GROUND OF SUSTAINABILITY

## *Donald Worster*

THE FIRST THING TO know when starting to climb a hill is where the summit is, and the second is that there are no completely painless ways to get there. Failing to know those things may lead one to take a deceptively easy path that never reaches the top but meanders off into a dead-end, frustrating the climber and wasting energy. The popular environmentalist slogan of "sustainable development" threatens to become such a path. Though attractive at first view, it appeals particularly to people who are dismayed by the long arduous hike they see ahead of them or who don't really have a clear notion of what the principal goal of environmentalism ought to be. After much milling about in a confused and contentious mood, they have discovered what looks like a broad, easy path where all kinds of folk can walk along together, and they hurry toward it, unaware that it may be going in the wrong direction.

Back in the 1960s and 1970s, when contemporary environmentalism first emerged, the goal was more obvious and the route more clear before they became obscured by political compromising. The goal was to save the living world around us, millions of species of plants and animals, including humans, from destruction by our technology, population, and appetites. The only way to do that, it was easy enough to see, was to think the radical thought that there must be limits to growth in three areas—limits to population, limits to technology, and limits to appetite and greed. Underlying this insight was a growing awareness that the progressive, secular materialist philosophy on which modern life rests, indeed on which Western civilization has rested for the past three hundred years, is deeply flawed and ultimately destructive to ourselves and the whole fabric of life on the planet. The only true, sure way to the environmentalist goal, therefore, was to challenge that philosophy fun-

A longer version of this essay was published in *Global Ecology*, edited by Wolfgang Sachs (London: Zed Books, 1993). Reprinted with permission.

damentally and find a new one based on material simplicity and spiritual richness.

I do not say that this conclusion was shared by everyone in those years who wore the label environmentalist, but it was obvious to the most thoughtful leaders that this was the path we had to take. Since it was so painfully difficult to make that turn, to go in a diametrically opposite direction from the way we had been going, however, many started looking for a less intimidating way. By the mid-1980s such an alternative, called "sustainable development," had emerged. First it appeared in the *World Conservation Strategy* of the International Union for the Conservation of Nature (1980), then in the book, *Building a Sustainable Society,* by Lester R. Brown of Worldwatch Institute (1981), then in another book, *Gaia: An Atlas of Planet Management,* edited by Norman Myers (1984), and then most influentially in the so-called Brundtland Report, *Our Common Future* (1987). The appeal of this alternative lay in its international political acceptability and in its potential for broad coalition among many contending parties. As Richard Sandbrook, executive vice-president of the International Institute for Environment and Development, explained: "It has not been too difficult to push the environment lobby of the North and the development lobby of the South together. And there is now in fact a blurring of the distinction between the two, so they are coming to have a common consensus around the theme of sustainable development."[1]

Lots of lobbyists coming together, lots of blurring going on—inevitably, lots of shallow thinking resulted. The North and South, we are told, could now make common cause without much difficulty. The capitalist and the socialist, the scientist and the economist, the impoverished masses and the urban elites could now all happily march together on a straight and easy path, if they did not ask too many potentially divisive questions about where they were going.

Like most popular slogans, sustainable development begins to wear thin after a while. Although it seems to have gained a wide acceptance, it has done so by sacrificing real substance. Worse yet, the slogan may turn out to be irredeemable for environmentalist use because it may inescapably compel us to adopt a narrow economic language, standard of judgment, and world view in approaching and utilizing the earth.

My own preference is for an environmentalism that talks about earth ethics and aesthetics rather than about resources and economics, that places priority on the survival of the living world of plants and animals on which our own survival depends, and that focuses on what nature's priceless beauty can add to our emotional well-being. I will return to that theme later, but first let us examine the shaky ground of sustainable development. So far we have not had a probing moral analysis of this slogan, despite all those books and reports mentioned above. Although I myself cannot offer any full analysis of it in so short a space, I do want to draw attention to the important subject of language and ask what is implied in that magic word of consensus, "sustainability."

## PROBING THE SLOGAN

The first and perhaps most difficult problem, one that seldom gets addressed, is the time frame that ought to be assumed. Is a sustainable society one that endures for a decade, a human lifetime, or a thousand years? . . .

Besides suggesting no clear time frame, the ideal of sustainability presents us with a bewildering multiplicity of criteria, and we have to sort out which ones we want to emphasize before we can develop any specific program of action. Among the dozens of possible sets of criteria, three or four have dominated public discussion of late, each based on a body of expertise, and they share little common ground.[2]

The field of economics, for example, has its own peculiar notion of what sustainability means. Economists focus on the point where societies achieve a critical take-off into long-term, continuous growth, investment, and profit in a market economy. The United States, for instance, reached that point around 1850, and has ever since been growing endlessly, despite a few recessions and depressions. By that standard any and all of the industrial societies are already sustainable, while the backward agrarian ones are not.[3] . . .

Still another group of experts, the political and social scientists, speak of "sustainable institutions" and "sustainable societies," which apparently refer to the ability of institutions or ruling groups to generate enough public support to renew themselves and hold on to power.[4] Sustainable societies are then simply those that are able to reproduce their political or social institutions; whether the institutions are benign or evil, compassionate or unjust, does not enter into the discussion. By this reasoning, the communist regimes of Eastern Europe and the Soviet Union have not proved to be sustainable and are being swept into the ashheaps of history.

These are all leading, important uses of the word found among various fields of expertise, and undoubtedly they all can be given very sophisticated (and far more precise than I have indicated) measurements. In contrast, we also have some simpler, more popular notions of the word. One of the clearest, most pithy, and least arcane definitions comes from Wendell Berry, the American writer and trenchant critic of all expertise. He called specifically for a more sustainable agriculture than we have today, by which he meant an agriculture that "does not deplete soils or people."[5] That phrase expresses, as so much of Berry's work does, an old-fashioned agrarian way of thinking, steeped in the folk history and local knowledge of his rural Kentucky neighbors. Like everything Berry writes, it has a concise, elemental ring, and the great virtue of recalling to our attention that people and the earth are interdependent, a fact that those specialized academic approaches by economists and the rest generally ignore.

In Berry's view the only truly sustainable societies have been small-scale agrarian ones; no modern industrial society could quality. His own model, which is based on the livelihood and culture of the Jeffersonian yeoman farmer, must be seen as part of the economic past; it has virtually disappeared from modern American life. One might ask, as Berry's critics regularly do, whether he is offering us more of a myth than a reality: did such non-depleting rural communities ever really exist in the United States, or are they only idealizations or indulgences in a false nostaligia? But even if we accept Berry's distinction between "sustainable agrarian" and "unsustainable industrial," it is still not clear what the preconditions for sustainability, or the measurement of its success, would be. What meaning can we give to the idea of "people depletion"? Is it a demographic or a cultural idea? And how much self-reliance or local community production does it require, and how much market exchange does it allow? For that matter, what is referred to in Berry's notion of soil depletion? Soil scientists point out that the United States has lost, on average, half of its topsoil since white, European settlement began; but then many of them go on to argue that such depletion is not a problem so long as we can substitute chemical fertilizers. Once more we are back in the muddle of whose expertise, language, and values are to define "sustainability." Berry would answer, I suppose, that we should leave the definition to local people, but national and international policy makers will want something more objective than that.

All those definitions and criteria are floating around in the air today, confusing our language and thinking, demanding far more of a consensus of meaning before we can achieve any concerted program of reform. To be sure, there is a widespread implication in the environmental literature I have cited that sustainability is at bottom an ecological concept: the goal of environmentalism should be to achieve "ecological sustainability." What that means is that the science of ecology is expected to cut through all the confusion and define sustainability for us; it should point out which practices are ecologically sustainable and which are not. Once again we are back in the business of looking for a set of expert, objective answers to guide policy. But how helpful really are those experts in ecology? Do they have a clear definition or set of criteria to offer? Do they even have a clear, coherent perception of nature to provide as a basis for international action?

## HOW HELPFUL ARE THE EXPERTS?

Ecologists traditionally have approached nature as a series of overlapping but integrated biological systems, or ecosystems. In contrast to most economists, for whom nature is not a relevant category of analysis, they have insisted that those systems are not disorganized or useless but self-organizing and productive of many material benefits that we need. The role of ecologists then, as we have generally come to understand it, is one of revealing to laymen how those ecosystems, or their modifications into agro-ecosystems, undergo stress from human demands and of helping us determine the critical point when that stress is so severe that they collapse.

If we accept that expert tutoring, the ecological idea of sustainability becomes, quite simply, another measure of production, rivaling that of the economists: a measure of productivity in the economy of nature where we find such commodities as soils, forests, and fisheries, and a measure of the capacity of that economy to rebound from stresses, avoid collapse, and maintain output. Unfortunately, compared to economists, the ecologists have recently become very uncertain about their own advice. Their indices of stress and collapse are in dispute, and their expertise is in disarray.

A few decades ago ecologists commonly believed that nature, when left free of human interference, eventually reaches a balance or equilibrium state where production is at a steady rate. The origins of this idea go back deep into the recesses of human memory, deep into the past of every civilization before the modern. For Westerners in particular the idea of nature as a balanced order has ancient Greek, medieval Christian, and eighteenth-century rationalist antecedents, and it survived even the profound intellectual revolution wrought by Charles Darwin and the theory of evolution through natural selection. From the time of its emergence in the late nineteenth century the science of ecology echoed that longstanding faith in the essential orderliness of nature, and until recently almost all ecologists would have agreed that sustainability is a matter of accommodating the human economy to that constancy and orderliness. Now, that is no longer the case.[6] . . .

When the idea of the super-organismic climax began to seem a little farfetched, ecologists replaced it with another concept of natural ecological order, the ecosystem. The ecosystem was a pattern of order in plant and animal assemblages that was based more on the study of physics than on analogies with the single living organism; in the ecosystem, energy and material flow in regular, orderly, efficient patterns. Human activity, warned ecologists like Eugene Odum much as Clements did before him, must conform to those patterns if we want to live in a harmonious, enduring relationship with nature.

Very recently, however, many ecologists have begun to question all those older ideas, theories, and metaphors, even to assert that nature is inherently *disorderly*. Some have tried to maintain that the ecosystem, like the climax stage, is a fiction that does not really describe the turbulence of the natural environment, or at least that such ideas are too vague or inflexible.[7] . . .

Many of these ideas appear in a recent book entitled *Discordant Harmonies*

(1990), which is self-described as "a new ecology for the twenty-first century." Here is how its author, Daniel Botkin, a leading California ecologist, sees the current situation in his science:

> Until the past few years, the predominant theories in ecology either presumed or had as a necessary consequence a very strict concept of a highly structured, ordered, and regulated, steady-state ecological system. Scientists know now that this view is wrong at local and regional levels . . . that is, at the levels of population and ecosystems. Change now appears to be intrinsic and natural at many scales of time and space in the biosphere.

"Wherever we seek to find constancy" in nature, Botkin writes, "we discover change."[8] . . . Here is Botkin again:

> Nature undisturbed by human influence seems more like a symphony whose harmonies arise from variation and change over every interval of time. We see a landscape that is always in flux, changing over many scales of time and space, changing with individual births and deaths, local disruptions and recoveries, larger scale responses to climate from one glacial age to another, and to the slower alterations of soils, and yet larger variations between glacial ages.[9]

But Botkin later makes a very telling amendment to that statement when he adds that "nature's symphony" is more like several compositions being played at once in the same hall, "each with its own pace and rhythm." And then he comes to what is really the practical upshot of his ecology for policy-makers, environmentalists, and developers: "We are forced to choose among these [compositions], which we have barely begun to hear and understand." Or one might say that after learning to hear all those discordances of nature, we humans must also assume the role of conducting the music. If there is to be any order in nature, it is our responsibility to achieve it. If there is to be any harmony, we must overcome the apparent discord. "Nature in the twenty-first century," this scientist concludes, "will be a nature that we make." Such a conclusion is where Botkin's science has been leading him all along: to a rejection of nature as a norm or standard for human civilization and to an assertion of a human right and need to give order and shape to nature. We are arriving, he proclaims, at a new view of Earth "in which we are a part of a living and changing system whose changes we can accept, use, and control, to make the Earth a comfortable home, for each of us individually and for all of us collectively in our civilizations." I believe that this new turn toward revisionism and relativism in ecological science is motivated, in part, by a desire to be less disapproving of economic development than environmentalists were in the 1960s and 1970s. Botkin criticizes that era for its radical, sometimes hostile, rejection of modern technology and progress. We need a science of ecology, he believes, that approaches development in a more "constructive and positive manner."[10]

## A PERMISSIVE ECOLOGY?

Those conclusions constitute what I would call a new permissiveness in ecology—far more permissive toward human desires than was the climax ecology of Frederick Clements and emphatically more permissive than the popular ecosystem ideas found among environmentalists of the 1960s and 1970s. This new ecology makes human wants and desires the primary test of what should be done with the earth. It denies that there is to be found in nature, past or present, any standard for, or even much of a limitation on, those desires. Botkin hints at this denial in the beginning of his book when he criticizes the environmentalism of the 1960s and 1970s as "essentially a disapproving, and in this sense, negative movement, exposing the bad aspects of our civilization for our environment. . . ." What we must do, he argues, is move away from that critical environmentalism toward a stance "that combine[s] technology with our concern about our environment in a constructive and positive manner."

This new turn in ecology presents several difficulties that I think the sustainable development advocates have not really acknowledged. In the first place, the whole idea of what is a normal "yield" or "output" from the natural economy becomes, if we follow Botkin's reasoning, far more ambiguous. Scientists once thought they could determine with relative ease the maximum sustained yield that a forest or fishery could achieve. They had only to determine the steady-state population in the ecosystem and then calculate how many fish could be caught each year without affecting the stock. They could take off the interest without touching the fixed capital. Botkin argues that it was just such assurance that led to over-fishing in the California sardine industry—and to the total collapse of that industry in the 1950s.[11]

But if the natural populations of fish and other organisms are in such continual flux that we cannot set maximum sustained yield targets, could we instead set up a more flexible standard of "optimum yield," one that would allow a more general margin for error and fluctuations? That is where most ecological sustainability thinking rests today. Harvest commodities from nature, but do so at a lightly reduced level to avoid overstressing a system in stochastic change. Call it the safe optimum notion. But that formula does not really address the more basic challenge implicit in recent ecological thinking. What can sustainable use, let alone sustainable development, mean in a natural world subject to so much disturbance and chaotic turbulence? Our powers of prediction, say ecologists, are far more limited than we imagined. To many, our understanding of what is normal in nature now seems to be arbitrary and partial.

The only real guidance Botkin gives us, and this is likewise true of most ecologists today, is that slow rates of change in ecosystems are "more natural," and therefore more desirable, than fast rates. "We must be wary," Botkin says, "when we engineer nature at an unnatural rate and in novel ways."[12] And that is all he really offers. But when we have to have more specific advice to manage this or that acre of land successfully, the ecologist is embarrassingly silent; he or she can hardly say any more what is "unnatural" or what is "novel" in light of the incredibly changeable record of the Earth's past.

In the much acclaimed partnership between advocates of ecological sustainability and of development, who is going to lead whom? This is the all-important question to ask about the new path that so many want us to take. I fear that in that partnership it will be "development" that makes most of the decisions, and "sustainable" will come trotting along, smiling and genial, unable to assert any firm leadership, complaining only about the pace of travel. "You must slow down, my friend, you are going too fast for me. This is a nice road to progress, but we must go along at a more 'natural' speed."

In the absence of any clear idea of what a healthy nature is, or how threats to that collective biological whole might impinge on us, we will end up relying on utilitarian, economic, and anthropocentric definitions of sustainability. That, it seems to me, is where the discussion is right now. Sustainability is, by and large, an economic concept on which economists are clear and ecologists are muddled. If you find that outcome unacceptable, as I do, then you must change the elementary terms of the discussion.

## FLAWS IN THE IDEAL

I find the following deep flaws in the sustainable development ideal:

First, it is based on the view that the natural world exists primarily to serve the material demands of the human species. Nature is nothing more than a pool of "resources" to be exploited; it has no intrinsic meaning or value apart from the goods and services it furnishes people, rich or poor. The Brundtland Report makes this point clear on every page: the "our" in its title refers to people exclusively, and the only moral issue it raises is the need to share what natural resources there are more equitably among our kind, among the present world population and among the generations to come. That is not by any means an unworthy goal, but it is not adequate to the challenge.

Second, sustainable development, though it acknowledges some kind of limit on those material demands, depends on the assumption that we can easily determine the carrying capacity of local regional ecosystems. Our knowledge is supposedly adequate to reveal the limits of nature and to exploit resources safely up to that level. In the face of new arguments suggesting how turbulent, complex, and unpredictable nature really is, that assumption seems highly optimistic. Furthermore, in light of the tendency of some leading ecologists to use such arguments to justify a more accommodating stance toward development, any heavy reliance on their ecological expertise seems doubly dangerous; they are experts who lack any agreement on what the limits are.

Third, the sustainability ideal rests on an uncritical, unexamined acceptance of the traditional worldview of progressive, secular materialism. It regards that worldview as completely benign so long as it can be made sustainable. The institutions associated with that worldview, including those of capitalism, socialism, and industrialism, also escape all criticism, or close scrutiny. We are led to believe that sustainability can be achieved with all those institutions and their values intact.

Perhaps my objections can be fully answered by the advocates of the sustainable development slogan. I suspect, however, that their response will, in the end, rest on the argument that the idea is the only politically acceptable kind of environmentalism we can expect at this point. It is desirable simply because it represents the politics of compromise.

Having been so critical toward this easy, sloganeering alternative, I feel obliged to conclude with a few ideas of my own about what a real solution for the global crisis will require. I grant that it will be more difficult to achieve, but would argue that it is more revolutionary in impact and more morally advanced.

We must make our first priority in dealing with the earth the careful and strict preservation of the billion-year-old heritage achieved by the evolution of plant and animal life. We must preserve all the species, sub-species, varieties, communities, and ecosystems that we possibly can. We must not, through our actions, cause any more species to become extinct. To be sure, we cannot stop every death or extinction, since the death of living things is part of the inevitable workings of nature. But we can avoid adding to that fateful outcome. We can stop reversing the processes of evolution, as we are doing today. We can work to preserve as much genetic variety as possible. We can save endangered habitats and restore those needed to support that evolutionary heritage. We can and must do all this primarily because the living heritage of evolution has an intrinsic value that we have not created but only inherited and enjoyed. That heritage demands our respect, our sympathy, and our love.

Unquestionably, we have a right to use that heritage to improve our material condition, but only after taking, in every community, every nation, and every family, the strictest measures to preserve it from extinction and diminution.

To conserve that evolutionary heritage is to focus our attention backward on the long history of the struggle of life on this planet. In recent centuries we have had our eyes fixed almost exclusively on the future and the potential affluence it can offer our aspiring species. Now it is time to learn to look backward more of the time and, from an appreciation of that past, learn humility in the presence of an achievement that overshadows all our technology, all our wealth, all our ingenuity, and all our human aspirations.

To conserve that heritage is to put other values than economic ones first in our priorities: the value of natural beauty, the value of respectfulness in the presence of what we have not created, and above all the value of life itself, a phenomenon that even now, with all our intelligence, we cannot really explain.

To learn truly to cherish and conserve that heritage is the hardest road the human species can take. I do not even know, though I have plenty of doubts, whether it is realistic at this point, given the state of global politics, to expect most nations to be ready or willing to take it. But I do know that it is the right path, while following the ambiguities, compromises, and smooth words of sustainable development may lead us into quicksand.

# NOTES

1. "World Commission on Environment and Development," in *Our Common Future* (New York: Oxford University Press, 1987), 64. See also R. Sandbrook, *The Conservation and Development Programme for the UK: A Response to the World Conservation Strategy* (1982), in *Our Common Future: A Canadian Response to the Challenge of Sustainable Development* (Ottawa: Harmony Foundation of Canada, 1989); and Raymond F. Dasmann, "Toward a Biosphere Consciousness," *The Ends of the Earth: Perspectives on Modern Environmental History,* edited by Donald Worster (New York: Cambridge University Press, 1988) 281–5.

2. I have found two books by Michael Redclift useful here: *Development and the Environment Crisis: Red or Green Alternatives?* (London: Methuen, 1984); and *Sustainable Development: Exploring the Contradictions* (London: Methuen, 1987). See also M. L'el'e Sharachchandram, "Sustainable Development: A Critical Review," *World Development,* vol. 19 (June, 1991), 607–21. Also, several of the essays in the symposium, *History of Sustained-Yield Forestry,* edited by Harold K. Steen (Durham, North Carolina: Forest History Society, 1984), especially the following: Robert G. Lee, "Sustained Yield and Social Order," pp. 90–100; Heinrich Rubner, "Sustained-Yield Forestry in Europe and Its Crisis During the Era of Nazi Dictatorship," pp. 170–75; and Claus Wiebecke and W. Peters, "Aspects of Sustained-Yield History: Forest Sustention as the Principle of Forestry—Idea and Reality," pp. 176–83.

3. Clem Tisdell, "Sustainable Development: Differing Perspectives of Ecologists and Economists and Relevance to LDCs," *World Development,* vol. 16, (March, 1988) 373–84.

4. Arthur A. Goldsmith and Derick W. Brinkerhoff define sustainability as a condition in which an institution's "outputs are valued highly enough that inputs continue." See their *Institutional Sustainability in Agriculture and Rural Development: A Global Perspective* (New York: Praeger, 1990) 13–14.

5. Wes Jackson, Wendell Berry, and Bruce Colman (eds.) *Meeting the Expectations of the Land: Essays in Sustainable Agriculture and Stewardship* (San Francisco: North Point Press, 1984) x.

6. For an example of how these older ecological theories still influence the advocates of sustainable development see P. Bartelmus, *Environment and Development* (London: Allen and Unwin, 1986) 44.

7. I have discussed some of these trends in my article "The Ecology of Order and Chaos," *Environmental History Review,* vol. 14 (Spring/Summer 1990) 1–18.

8. Daniel B. Botkin, *Discordant Harmonies: A New Ecology for the Twenty-first Century* (New York: Oxford University Press, 1990) 10, 62.

9. Ibid., 62.

10. Ibid., 6.

11. See also Arthur McEvoy, *The Fisherman's Problem: Ecology and Law in California Fisheries, 1850–1980* (New York: Cambridge University Press, 1986) 6–7, 10, 150–1.

12. Botkin (1990), 190.

# 36 | GLOBAL ECOLOGY AND THE SHADOW OF "DEVELOPMENT"

*Wolfgang Sachs*

THE WALLS IN THE Tokyo subway used to be plastered with advertising posters. The authorities, aware of Japan's shortage of wood-pulp, searched for ways to reduce this wastage of paper. They quickly found an "environmental solution": they mounted video screens on the walls and these now continuously bombard passengers with commercials—paper problem solved.

This anecdote exemplifies an approach to the environmental crisis which was also very much on the minds of the delegates who descended upon Rio de Janeiro for the "Earth Summit" (UNCED), to reconcile "environment" and "development." To put the outcome of UNCED in a nutshell: the governments at Rio came round to recognizing the declining state of the environment, but insisted on the relaunching of development. Indeed, most controversies arose from some party's heated defence of its "right to development"; in that respect, Malaysia's resistance to the forest declaration or Saudi Arabia's attempt to sabotage the climate convention trailed not far behind President Bush's cutting remark that the lifestyle of the United States would not be up for discussion at Rio. It is probably no exaggeration to say that the rain dance around "development" kept the conflicting parties together and offered a common ritual which comforted them for the one or other sacrifice made in favour of the environment. At the end, the Rio Declaration ceremoniously emphasized the sacredness of "development" and invoked its significance throughout the document wherever possible. Only after "the right to development" has been enshrined, does the document proceed to consider "the developmental and environmental needs of present and future generations"

A longer version of this essay was originally published in Wolfgang Sachs (ed.) *Global Ecology* (London: Zed Books, 1993). Reprinted with permission.

(Principle 3). In fact, the UN Conference in Rio inaugurated environmental-ism as the highest state of developmentalism.

Reaffirming the centrality of "development" in the international discussion on the environment surely helps to secure the collaboration of the dominating actors in government, economy and science, but it prevents the rupture re-quired to head off the multifaceted dangers for the future of mankind. It locks the perception of the ecological predicament into the very world-view which stimulates the pernicious dynamics, and hands the action over to those social forces—governments, agencies and corporations—which have largely been re-sponsible for the present state of affairs. This may turn out to be self-defeating. After all, the development discourse is deeply imbued with Western certainties like progress, growth, market integration, consumption, and universal needs, all notions that are part of the problem, not of the solution. They cannot but distract attention from the urgency of public debate on our relationship with nature, for they preclude the search for societies which live graciously within their means, and for social changes which take their inspiration from indige-nous ideas of the good and proper life. The incapacity to bid farewell to some of the certainties which have shaped the development era was the major short-coming of Rio. The great divide between development enthusiasts and devel-opment dissenters will be at the root of future conflicts about global ecology.

## TRUMAN AND WHAT FOLLOWED

Epochs rise slowly, but the development era opened at a certain date and hour. On January 20, 1949, it was President Harry Truman who, in his inauguration speech before Congress, drawing the attention of his audience to conditions in poorer countries, for the first time defined them as "underdeveloped areas."[1] Suddenly, a seemingly indelible concept was established, cramming the im-measurable diversity of the South into one single category—the underdevel-oped. That Truman coined a new term was not a matter of accident but the precise expression of a world-view; for him all the peoples of the world were moving along the same track, some faster, some slower, but all in the same direction. The Northern countries, in particular the United States, were run-ning ahead, while he saw the rest of the world—with its absurdly low per capita income—lagging far behind. An image that the economic societies of the North had increasingly acquired about themselves was thus projected upon the rest of the world: the degree of civilization in a country is to be indicated by the level of its production. Starting from that premise, Truman conceived of the world as an economic arena where nations compete for a better position on the GNP scale. No matter what ideals inspired Kikuyus,

Peruvians or Filipinos, Truman recognized them only as stragglers whose historical task was to participate in the development race and catch up with the lead runners. Consequently, it was the objective of development policy to bring all nations into the arena and enable them to run in the race.

Turning the South's societies into economic competitors not only required the injection of capital and transfer of technology, but a cultural transformation, for many "old ways" of living turned out to be "obstacles to development." The ideals and mental habits, patterns of work and modes of knowing, webs of loyalties and rules of governance in which the South's people were steeped, were usually at odds with the ethos of an economic society. In the attempt to overcome these barriers to growth, the traditional social fabric was often dissected and reassembled according to the textbook models of macroeconomics. To be sure, "development" had many effects, but one of its most insidious was the dissolution of cultures which were not built around a frenzy of accumulation. The South was thus precipitated into a transformation which had long been going on in the North: the gradual subordination of ever more aspects of social life under the rule of the economy. In fact, whenever development experts set their sights on a country, they fell victim to a particular myopia: they did not see a society which *has* an economy but a society which *is* an economy. As a result, they ended up revamping all kinds of institutions, such as work, schools or the law, in the service of productivity, degrading the indigenous style of doing things in the process. But the shift to a predominantly economic society involves a considerable cost: it undermines a society's capacity to secure well-being without joining unconditionally the economic race. The fact that the unfettered hegemony of Western productivism has made it more and more impossible to take exit roads from the global racetrack dangerously limits the space of maneuver for countries in times of uncertainty. Also in that respect, the countries of the North provide an ambiguous example: they have been so highly trained in productivism that they are incapable of doing anything but running the economic race.

After forty years of development, the state of affairs is dismal. The gap between front-runners and stragglers has not been bridged; on the contrary, it has widened to the extent that it has become inconceivable that it could ever be closed. The aspiration of catching-up has ended in a blunder of planetary proportions. The figures speak for themselves: during the 1980s, the contribution of developing countries (where two-thirds of humanity live) to the world's GNP shrank to 15 percent, while the share of the industrial countries, with 20 percent of the world population, rose to 80 percent. Admittedly, closer examination reveals that the picture is far from homogeneous, but neither the Southeast Asian showcases nor the oil-producing countries change the result that the development race has ended in disarray. The truth of this is more sharply highlighted if the destiny of large majorities of people within most Southern countries is considered; they live today in greater hardship and misery than at the time of decolonialization. The best one can say is that development has created a global middle class of individuals with cars, bank accounts, and career aspirations. It is made up of the majority in the North and small elites in the South and its size roughly equals that eight percent of the world population which owns a car. The internal rivalries of that class make a lot of noise in world politics, condemning to silence the overwhelming majority of the people. At the end of development, the question of justice looms larger than ever.

A second result of the development era has come dramatically to the fore in recent years: it has become evident that the race track leads in the wrong direction. While Truman could still take for granted that the North was at the head of social evolution, this premise of superiority has today been fully and finally shattered by the ecological predicament. . . . Economic expansion has already come up against its bio-physical limits; recognizing the earth's finiteness is a fatal blow to the idea of development as envisaged by Truman.

## AMBIGUOUS CLAIMS FOR JUSTICE

The UNCED process unfolded against this background of forty years of postwar history. As implied in the title of the Conference, any consideration of global ecology has to respond to both the crisis of justice and the crisis of nature. While the Northern countries' main concern was about nature, the South, in the run up to the Conference, managed to highlight the question of justice. In fact, during the debates leading up to UNCED, attentive spectators wondered if they had not seen it all before. Slogans, which had animated the 1970s discussions on the "New International Economic Order," kept creeping back to the forefront. Suddenly, calls for better terms of trade, debt relief, entry to Northern markets, technology transfer and aid, aid, and more aid, drowned the environmentalist discussion. Indeed, it was difficult to overlook the regressive tendencies in the controversy which opened up. The South, deeply hurt by the breakdown of development illusions, launched demands for further rounds of development. Already, in the June 1991 Beijing Declaration of the Group of 77, the point was made clearly and bluntly:

> Environmental problems cannot be dealt with separately; they must be linked to the development process, bringing the environmental concerns in line with the imperatives of economic growth and development. In this context, the right to development for the developing countries must be fully recognized.[2]

After the South's years of uneasiness in dealing with the environmental concerns raised by the North, the plot for Rio had finally thickened. Since the

North expects environmentally good behavior worldwide, the South, grasping this opportunity, discovered environmental concessions as diplomatic weapons. Consequently, the South reiterated the unfulfilled demands of the 1970s and opposed them to the North's ecological impositions. . . .

The Rio documents make clear that the South has no intention of abandoning the Northern model of living as its implicit utopia. In using the language of development, the South continues to subscribe to the notion that the North shows the way for the rest of the world. As a consequence, however, the South is incapable of escaping the North's cultural hegemony; for development without hegemony is like a race without a direction. Apart from all the economic pressures, adherence to "development" puts the South, culturally and politically, in a position of structural weakness, leading to the absurd situation in which the North can present itself as the benevolent provider of solutions to the ecological crisis.

Needless to say that this constellation plays into the hands of the Northern countries. With the blessing of "development," the growth fatalists in the North are implicitly justified in rushing ahead on the economic racetrack. The cultural helplessness of the industrial countries in responding adequately to the ecological predicament thus turns into a necessary virtue. After all, the main concern of the Northern elites is to get ahead in the competitive struggle between the United States, Europe, and Japan, achieving an ecological modernization of their economies along the way. They are light-years away from the insight that peace with nature eventually requires peace in economic warfare; consequently, a country such as Germany, for instance, manages to pose as a shining example of environmentalism, while pushing ahead with such ecologically disastrous free-trade policies as the European common market and the reform of GATT. The fact that "development," that race without a finishing line, remains uncontested, allows the North to continue the relentless pursuit of overdevelopment and economic power, since the idea of societies which settle for their accomplished stage of technical capacity becomes unthinkable. Indeed, such matters as limits to road-building, to high-speed transport, to economic concentration, to the production of chemicals, to large-scale cattle ranching, and so on, were not even pondered in Rio.

The unholy alliance between development enthusiasts in the South and growth fatalists in the North, however, works not only against the environment but also against greater justice in the world. For in most countries, while development has benefited rather small minorities, it has done so at the expense of large parts of the population. During the development era, growth was expected to abolish poverty. Instead, it led to social polarization. In many cases, communities which guaranteed sustenance have been torn apart in the attempt to build a modern economy. Southern elites, however, often justify their unmitigated pursuit of development by ritual reference to the persistence of poverty, cultivating the worn-out dogma that growth is the recipe against poverty. Locked in their interests of power and fixed on the lifestyle of the affluent, they fend off the insight that securing livelihoods requires a careful handling of growth. Yet the lesson to be drawn from forty years of development can be stated bluntly: the issue of justice must be delinked from the perspective of "development." In fact, both ecology and poverty call for limits to development. Without such a change in perspective, the struggle for redistribution of power and resources between North and South, which is inevitably renewed in facing environmental constraints, can be only what it was in the 1970s: a quarrel within the global middle class on how to divide the cake.

## EARTH'S FINITENESS AS A MANAGEMENT PROBLEM

"Development" is, above all, a way of thinking. It cannot, therefore, be easily identified with a particular strategy or program, but ties many different practices and aspirations to a common set of assumptions. . . .

Despite alarming signs of failure throughout its history, the development syndrome has survived until today, but at the price of increasing senility. When it became clear in the 1950s that investments were not enough, "man-power development" was added to the aid package; as it became obvious in the 1960s that hardship continued, "social development" was discovered; and in the 1990s, as the impoverishment of peasants could no longer be overlooked, "rural development" was included in the arsenal of development strategies. And so it went on, with further creations like "equitable development" and the "basic needs approach." Again and again, the same conceptual operation was repeated: degradation in the wake of development was redefined as a lack which called for yet another strategy of development. All along, the efficacy of "development" remained impervious to any counterevidence, but showed remarkable staying power; the concept was repeatedly stretched until it included both the strategy which inflicted the injury and the strategy designed for therapy. This strength of the concept, however, is also the reason for its galloping exhaustion; it no longer manifests any reactions to changing historical conditions. The tragic greatness of "development" consists in its monumental emptiness.

"Sustainable development," which UNCED enthroned as the reigning slogan of the 1990s, has inherited the fragility of "development." The concept emasculates the environmental challenge by absorbing it into the empty shell of "development," and insinuates the continuing validity of developmentalist assumptions even when confronted with a drastically different historical situation. In Rachel Carson's *Silent Spring,* the book which gave rise to the environmental movement in 1962, development was understood to inflict injuries on people and nature. Since the "World Conservation Strategy" in 1980 and later the Brundtland Report, development has come to be seen as the therapy for the injuries caused by development. What accounts for this shift?

Firstly, in the 1970s, under the impact of the oil crisis, governments began to realize that continued growth depended not only on capital formation or skilled manpower, but also on the long-term availability of natural resources. Foods for the insatiable growth machine, such as oil, timber, minerals, soils, genetic material, seemed on the decline; concern grew about the prospects of long-term growth. This was a decisive change in perspective: not the health of nature but the continuous health of development became the center of concern. In 1992, the World Bank summed up the new consensus in a laconic phrase: "What is sustainable? Sustainable development is development that lasts."[3] Of course, the task of development experts does not remain the same under this imperative, because the horizon of their decisions is now supposed to extend in time, taking into account also the welfare of future generations. But the frame stays the same: "sustainable development" calls for the conservation of development, not for the conservation of nature.

Even bearing in mind a very loose definition of development, the anthropocentric bias of the statement springs to mind; it is not the preservation of nature's dignity which is on the international agenda, but to extend human-centered utilitarianism to posterity. Needless to say, the naturalist and biocentric current of present-day environmentalism has been cut out by this conceptual operation. With "development" back in the saddle, the view on nature changes. The question now becomes: which of nature's "services" are to what extent indispensable for further development? Or the other way around: which "services" of nature are dispensable or can be substituted by, for example, new materials or genetic engineering? In other words, nature turns into a variable, albeit a critical one, in sustaining development. It comes as no surprise, therefore, that "nature capital" has already become a fashionable notion among ecological economists."[4]

Secondly, a new generation of post-industrial technologies suggested that growth was not invariably linked to the squandering of ever more resources, as in the time of smoke-stack economies, but could be pursued through less resource-intensive means. While in the past, innovations were largely aimed at increased productivity of labor, it now appeared possible that technical and organizational intelligence could concentrate on increasing the productivity of nature. In short, growth could be delinked from a rising consumption of energy and materials. In the eyes of developmentalists, the "limits to growth" did not call for abandoning the race, but for changing the running technique. After "no development without sustainability" had spread, "no sustainability without development" also gained recognition.

Thirdly, environmental degradation has been discovered to be a worldwide condition of poverty. While formerly the developmentalist image of the "poor" was characterized by lack of water, housing, health, and money, they are now seen to be suffering from lack of nature as well. Poverty is now exemplified by people who search desperately for firewood, find themselves trapped by encroaching deserts, are driven from their soils and forests, or are forced to endure dreadful sanitary conditions. Once the lack of nature is identified as a cause of poverty, it follows neatly that development agencies, since they are in the business of "eliminating poverty," have to diversify into programs for the environment. But people who are dependent on nature for their survival have no choice other than to pursue the last remaining fragments of its bounty. As the decline of nature is also a consequence of poverty, the poor of the world suddenly entered the stage as agents of environmental destruction. Whereas in the 1970s, the main threat to nature still appeared to be industrial man, in the 1980s environmentalists turned their eyes to the Third World and pointed to the vanishing forests, soils and animals there. With the shifting focus, environmentalism, in part, took on a different color; the crisis of the environment is no longer perceived as the result of building affluence for the global middle class in North and South, but as the result of human presence on the globe in general. No matter if nature is consumed for luxury or survival, no matter if the powerful or the marginalized tap nature, it all becomes one for the rising tribe of ecocrats. And so it could be that, among other things, an "Earth Summit" was called to reach decisions which should primarily have been the concern of the OECD—or even the G7.

The persistence of "development," the newly-found potentials for less resource-intensive growth paths, and the discovery of humanity in general as the enemy of nature—these notions were the conceptual ingredients for the type of thinking which received its diplomatic blessings at UNCED: the world is to be saved by more and better managerialism. The message, which is ritually repeated by many politicians, industrialists and scientists who have recently decided to slip on a green coat, goes as follows: nothing should be (the dogmatic version) or can be (the fatalist version) done to change the direction the world's economies are taking; problems along the way can be solved, if the challenge for better and more sophisticated management is taken up. As a result, ecology, once a call for new public virtues, has now become a call for new executive skills. In fact, Agenda 21, for example, overflows with such formulas as "integrated approach," "rational use," "sound management," "internalizing costs," "better information," "increased co-ordination," "long-term prediction," but by and large fails (except for some timid phrases in the hotly debated chapter "Changing Consumption Patterns") to consider any reduction of material standards of living and any attempts to slow down the accumulation dynamics. In short, alternatives to development are blackballed, alternatives within development are welcome.

Nevertheless, it was an achievement for UNCED to have delivered the call for environmental tools from a global rostrum, an opening which will give a boost to environmental engineering worldwide. But the price for this achievement is the reduction of environmentalism to managerialism. For the task of global ecology can be understood in two ways: it is either a technocratic effort to keep development afloat against the drift of plunder and pollution; or it is a cultural effort to shake off the hegemony of aging Western values and gradually retire from the development race. These two ways may not be exclusive in detail, but they differ deeply in perspective. In the first case, the paramount task becomes the management of the bio-physical limits to development. All powers of foresight have to be mustered in order to steer development along the edge of the abyss, continuously surveying, testing, and maneuvering the bio-physical limits. In the second case, the challenge consists in designing cultural/political limits to development. Each society is called upon to search for indigenous models of prosperity, which allow society's course to stay at a comfortable distance from the edge of the abyss, living graciously within a stable or shrinking volume of production. It is analogous to driving a vehicle at high speed towards a canyon, either you equip it with radar, monitors and highly trained personnel, correct its course and drive it as hard as possible along the rim; or you slow down, turn away from the edge, and drive leisurely here and there without too much attention to precise controls. Too many global ecologists—implicitly or explicitly—favor the first choice.

## BARGAINING FOR THE REST OF NATURE

Until some decades ago, quite a few tracts of the biosphere still remained untouched by the effects of economic growth. It is basically over the last thirty years that the tentacles of productivism have closed on the last virgin areas, leaving now no part of the biosphere untouched. More often than not, the human impact grows into a full-scale attack, tearing up the intricate webs of life. Since time immemorial humanity defended itself against nature, now nature must be defended against humanity. In particular danger are the "global commons," the Antarctic, ocean beds, tropical forests, with many species threatened by the voracious growth of demand for new inputs, while earth's atmosphere is overburdened with the residues growth leaves behind.

For that reason, the 1980s saw the rise of a global environmental consciousness, expressed by many voices, all deploring the threats to the earth's biosphere and the offense to the generations to come. The collective duty to preserve the "common heritage of mankind" was invoked, and "Caring for the Earth"[5] became an imperative which agitated spirits worldwide. Respect for the integrity of nature, independently of its value for humans, as well as a proper regard for the rights of humanity demanded that the global commons be protected.

International environmental diplomacy, however, is about something else. The rhetoric, which ornaments conferences and conventions, ritually calls for a new global ethic but the reality at the negotiating tables suggests a different logic. There, for the most part, one sees diplomats engaged in the familiar game of accumulating advantages for their countries, eager to outmaneuver their opponents, shrewdly tailoring environmental concerns to the interests dictated by their nation's economic position. Their parameters of action are bounded by the need to extend their nation's space for "development"; therefore in their hands environmental concerns turn into bargaining chips in the struggle of interests. In that respect, the thrust of UNCED's negotiations was no different from the thrust of previous negotiations about the Law of the Sea, the Antarctic, or the Montreal protocol on the reduction of CFCs; and upcoming negotiations on climate, animal protection or biodiversity are also hardly likely to be different.

The novelty of Rio, if there was one, lay not in commitments on the way to a collective stewardship of nature, but rather in international recognition of the scarcity of natural resources for development. The fragility of nature came into focus, because the services she offers as a "source" and a "sink" for economic growth have become inadequate; after centuries of availability, nature can no longer be counted upon as a silent collaborator in the process of "technical civilization." In other words, environmental diplomacy has recognized that nature is finite as a mine for resources and as a container for waste. Given that "development" is intrinsically open-ended, the logic underlying international negotiations is pretty straightforward. First, limits are to be identified at a level that permits the maximum use of nature as mine and container, right up to the critical threshold beyond which ecological decline would rapidly accelerate. This is where scientists gain supremacy, since such limits can only be identified on the basis of "scientific evidence"; endless quarrels about the state of knowledge are therefore part of the game. Once that hurdle has been overcome, the second step in the bargaining process is to define each country's proper share in the utilization of the "source" or the "sink" in question. Here diplomacy finds a new arena, and the old means of power, persuasion and bribery come in handy in order to maximize one's own country's share. And finally, mechanisms have to be designed to secure all parties' compliance with the norms stated by the treaty, an effort which calls for international monitoring and enforcement institutions. Far from "protecting the earth," environmental diplomacy which works within a developmentalist frame cannot but concentrate its efforts on rationing what is left of nature. To normalize, not eliminate, global overuse and pollution of nature will be its unintended effect.

Four major lines of conflict cut through the landscape of international environmental diplomacy, involving: rights to further exploitation of nature; rights to pollution; and rights to compensation; and overall, conflict over responsibility. In the UNCED discussions on the biodiversity convention, for example, the rights to further exploitation of nature held center stage. Who is entitled to have access to the world's dwindling genetic resources? Can nation states exert their sovereignty over them or are they to be regarded as "global commons"? Who is allowed to profit from the use of genetic diversity? Countries rich in biomass, but poor in industrial power were thus counterposed against countries rich in industrial power, but poor in biomass. Similar issues arise with respect to tropical timber, the mining of ocean beds, or to wild animals. Regarding the climate convention, on the other hand, diplomatic efforts were aimed at optimizing pollution rights over various periods of time. Oil-producing countries were not happy about any ceilings for $CO_2$ emissions, while small island states, understandably, hoped for the toughest limits possible. Moreover, the more economies are dependent on a cheap fuel base, the less the respective representatives were inclined to be strong on $CO_2$: the United States in the forefront, followed by the large newly industrialized countries, while Europe along with Japan could afford to urge stricter limits. . . . As the bio-physical limits to development become visible, the tide of the post-war era turns: multilateral negotiations no longer centre on the redistribution of riches but on the redistribution of risks.[6]

## EFFICIENCY AND SUFFICIENCY

Twenty years ago, "limits to growth" was the watchword of the environmental movement worldwide; today the buzzword of international ecology experts is "global change." The messages implied are clearly different.[7] "Limits to growth" calls on *homo industrialis* to reconsider his project and to abide by nature's laws. "Global change," however, puts mankind in the driver's seat and urges it to master nature's complexities with greater self-control. While the first formula sounds threatening, the second has an optimistic ring: it believes in a rebirth of *homo faber* and, on a more prosaic level, lends itself to the belief that the proven means of modern economy—product innovation, technological progress, market regulation, science-based planning—will show the way out of the ecological predicament.

The cure for all environmental ills is called "efficiency revolution." It focuses on reducing the throughput of energy and materials in the economic system by means of new technology and planning. Be it for the lightbulb or the car, for the design of power plants or transport systems, the aim is to come up with innovations that minimize the use of nature for each unit of output. Under this prescription, the economy will supposedly gain in fitness by keeping to a diet which eliminates the overweight in slag and dross. The efficiency scenario, however, seeks to make the circle square; it proposes a radical change through redirecting conventional means. . . . Optimizing input, not maximizing output, as in the post-war era, is the order of the day, and one already sees economists and engineers taking a renewed pleasure in their trade by puzzling out the minimum input for each unit of output. The hope which goes along with this strategic turnabout is again concisely stated by the World Bank: "Efficiency reforms help reduce pollution while raising a country's economic output."[8]

No doubt an efficiency revolution would have far-reaching effects. Since natural inputs were cheap and the deposition of waste mostly free of charge, economic development has for long been skewed towards squandering nature. Subsidies encouraged waste, technical progress was generally not designed to save on nature, and prices did not reflect environmental damages. There is a lot of space for correcting the course, and Agenda 21, for example, provides a number of signposts which indicate a new route. But the past course of economic history—in the East, West, and South—though with considerable variations—suggests that there is little room for efficiency strategies in earlier phases of growth, whereas they seem to work best—and are affordable—when applied after a certain level of growth has been attained. Since in the South the politics of selective growth would be a much more powerful way to limit the demand for resources, to transfer the "efficiency revolution" there wholesale makes sense only if the South is expected to follow the North's path of development. . . .

. . . But the efficiency strategy obviously plays into the North's hands: this way, they can again offer the South a new selection of tools for economic progress, at a price which will be scarcely different from that paid in the decades of technology transfer.

Environmentalists who refer exclusively to efficient resource management concentrate social imagination on the revision of means, rather than on the revision of goals. . . . An increase in resource efficiency alone leads to nothing, unless it goes hand-in-hand with an intelligent restraint of growth. Instead of asking how many supermarkets or how many bathrooms are enough, one focuses on how all these—and more—can be obtained with a lower input of resources. If, however, the dynamics of growth are not slowed down, the achievements of rationalization will soon be eaten up by the next round of growth. Consider the example of the fuel-efficient car. Today's vehicle engines are definitely more efficient than in the past; yet the relentless growth in number of cars and miles driven has canceled out that gain. And the same logic holds across the board, from energy saving to pollution abatement and recycling; not to mention the fact that continuously staving off the destructive effects of growth in turn requires new growth. In fact, what really matters is the overall physical scale of the economy with respect to nature, not only the efficient allocation of resources. Herman Daly has offered a telling comparison:[9] even if the cargo on a boat is distributed efficiently, the boat will inevitably sink under too much weight—even though it may sink optimally! Efficiency without sufficiency is counterproductive; the latter must define the boundaries of the former.

However, the rambling development creed impedes any serious public debate on the moderation of growth. Under its shadow, any society which decides, at least in some areas, not to go beyond certain levels of commodity-intensity, technical performance, or speed, appears to be backward. As a result, the consideration of zero-options, that is, choosing not to do something which is technically possible, is treated as a taboo in the official discussion on global ecology, even to the point of exposing some agreements to ridicule. . . .

## THE HEGEMONY OF GLOBALISM

"Sustainable development," though it can mean many things to many people, nevertheless contains a core message: keep the volume of human extraction/emission in balance with the regenerative capacities of nature. That sounds reasonable enough, but it conceals a conflict that has yet to win public attention, even though such fundamental issues as power, democracy and cultural autonomy are at stake. Sustainability, yes, but at what level? Where is the circle of use and regeneration to be closed? At the level of a village community, a country, or the entire planet? Until the 1980s, environmentalists were usually concerned with the local or the national space; ideas like "eco-development" and "self-reliance" had aimed to increase the economic and political independence of a place by reconnecting ecological resource flows.[10] But in subsequent years, they began to look at things from a much more elevated vantage point: they adopted the astronaut's view, taking in the entire globe at one glance. Today's ecology is in the business of saving nothing less than the planet. That suggestive globe, suspended in the dark universe, delicately furnished with clouds, oceans and continents, has become the object of science, planning and politics.

Modesty hardly seems to be the hallmark of such thinking. The 1989 special issue of the *Scientific American,* with the programmatic title "Managing Planet Earth," sets the tone:

> It is as a global species that we are transforming the planet. It is only as a global species—pooling our knowledge, coordinating our actions and sharing what the planet has to offer—that we may have any prospect for managing the planet's transformation along the pathways of sustainable development. Self-conscious, intelligent management of the earth is one of the great challenges facing humanity as it approaches the twenty-first century.[11]

Perceiving the earth as an object of environmental management is, on the cognitive level, certainly an outcome of space travel, which has turned the planet into a visible object, a revolution in the history of human perception.[12] But there is a political, a scientific and a technological reason as well. Politically, it was only in the 1980s that acid rain, the ozone hole and the greenhouse effect drove home the message that industrial pollution affects the entire globe across all borders. The planet revealed itself as the ultimate dumping ground. Scientifically, ecological research, after having for years mainly focused on single and isolated ecosystems like deserts, marshes and rain forests, recently shifted its attention to the study of the biosphere, that envelope of air, vegetation, water and rocks which sustains life globally. Technologically, as often in the history of science, it was a new generation of instruments and equipment which created the possibility of collecting and processing data on a global scale. With satellites, sensors and computers, the technology available in the 1990s permits the biosphere to be surveyed and modeled. As these factors have emerged simultaneously, human arrogance has discovered the ultimate dominion: planet Earth.

Only a few years ago, invoking the wholeness of the globe meant something else. Environmentalists waved around the picture of the earth taken from outer space, in order to remind the public of the majestic finiteness of the earth and to spread the insight that there is in the end no escape from the consequences of human action. While they appealed to the reality of the planet, inviting people to embrace humility, a new tribe of global ecocrats is ready to act upon the newly-emerged reality of the planet, imagining that they can preside over the world. Research on the biosphere is rapidly becoming big science; spurred by a number of international programs,[13] "planetary sciences," including satellite observation, deep-sea expeditions, worldwide data processing, are being institutionalized in many countries.

With this trend, sustainability is increasingly conceived as a challenge for global management. The new experts set out to identify the balance between human extractions/emissions on the one side, and the regenerative capacities of nature on the other, on a planetary scale, mapping and monitoring, measuring and calculating resource flows and biogeochemical cycles around the globe. According to Agenda 21:

> This is essential, if a more accurate estimate is to be provided of the carrying capacity of the planet Earth and of its resilience under the many stresses placed upon it by human activities.[14]

It is the implicit agenda of this endeavor to be eventually able to moderate the planetary system, supervising species diversity, fishing grounds, felling rates, energy flows, and material cycles. It remains a matter of speculation which of these expectations will ever be realized, but there is no doubt that the linkage of space travel, sensor technology and computer simulation has vastly increased the power to monitor nature, to recognize human impact, and to make predictions. The management of resource budgets thus becomes a matter of world politics.

Satellite pictures scanning the globe's vegetative cover, computer graphs running interacting curves through time, threshold levels held up as worldwide norms are the language of global ecology. It constructs a reality that contains mountains of data, but no people. The data do not explain why Tuaregs are driven to exhaust their waterholes, or what makes Germans so obsessed with high speed on freeways; they do not point out who owns the timber shipped from the Amazon or which industry flourishes because of a polluted Mediterranean sea; and they are mute about the significance of forest trees for Indian tribals or what water means in an Arab country. In short, they provide a knowledge which is faceless and placeless; an abstraction that carries a considerable cost: it consigns the realities of culture, power and virtue to oblivion. It offers data, but no context; it shows diagrams, but no actors; it gives calculations, but no notions of morality; it seeks stability, but disregards beauty. Indeed, the global vantage point requires ironing out all the differences and disregarding all circumstances; rarely has the gulf between observers and the observed been greater than between satellite-based forestry and the *seringueiro* in the Brazilian jungle. It is inevitable that the claims of global management are in conflict with the aspirations for cultural rights, democracy and self-determination. Indeed, it is easy for an ecocracy which acts in the name of "one earth" to become a threat to local communities and their lifestyles. After all, has there ever, in the history of colonialism, been a more powerful motive for streamlining the world than the call to save the planet?

Yet the North faces a problem. For the bid for global management has been triggered by a new historical constellation. Ever since Columbus arrived in Santo Domingo the North has by and large remained unaffected by the tragic consequences which followed his expansion overseas; others had borne the burden of sickness, exploitation and ecological destruction. Now, this historical tide seems about to turn; for the first time the Northern countries themselves are exposed to the bitter results of Westernizing the world. Immigration, population pressure, tribalism with mega-arms, and above all, the environmental consequences of worldwide industrialization threaten to destabilize the Northern way of life. It is as if the cycle which had been opened by Columbus is about to be closed at the end of this century. As a result, the North devises ways and means for protection and risk management worldwide. The rational planning of the planet becomes a matter of Northern security.

The celebrated control of (Western) man over nature leaves much to be desired. Science and technology successfully transform nature on a vast scale, but so far, with unpleasant as well as unpredictable consequences. In fact only if these consequences were under control would it be possible to speak of having accomplished domination over nature. It is here that technocratic environmentalism comes in. Seen from this angle, the purpose of global environmental management is nothing less than control of a second order; a higher level of observation and intervention has to be installed, in order to control the consequences of the control over nature. Such a step becomes the more imperative as the drive towards turning the world into a closely interrelated and expanding economic society continues unabated. Given that the continuing force of the development syndrome is an impediment to restraining the dynamics of worldwide industrialization, the obvious task is to prepare for regulating the transformation of nature globally in an optimal fashion. It is in that light that the *Scientific American* can elevate the following questions to key-issues for future decision-making:

> Two central questions must be addressed: What kind of planet do we want? What kind of planet can we get? . . . How much species diversity should be maintained in the world? Should the size or the growth rate of the human population be curtailed. . . ? How much climate change is acceptable?[15]

If there are no limits to growth, there surely seem to be no limits to hubris.

## NOTES

1. See the entry for "underdeveloped" in the *Oxford English Dictionary* (1989), vol. XVIII, 960. Extensive inquiries into the history of the development discourse can be found in Wolfgang Sachs (ed.) (1992) *The Development Dictionary: A Guide to Knowledge as Power,* London, Zed Books.

2. Beijing Ministerial Declaration on Environment and Development, June 19, 1991.
   I do not follow proposals to make a distinction between growth and development. It seems to me that "development" cannot be purified of its historical con-

text. For a distinction, see Herman E. Daly (1990) "Toward Some Operational Principles of Sustainable Development," in *Ecological Economics,* vol. 2, 1990, 1.

3. *World Development Report 1992* (1992), Oxford University Press (for the World Bank), New York, 34.

4. See for instance Salah El Serafy, "The Environment as Capital," in R. Costanza (ed.) (1991) *Ecological Economics: The Science and Management of Sustainability,* New York, Columbia University Press, 168–75.

5. The title of a major document, published jointly by IUCN, UNEP, and WWF in Gland, Switzerland, in 1991.

6. This change has been observed for the domestic scene by Ulrich Beck (1987) *Risikogesellschaft,* Frankfurt: Suhrkamp.

7. Frederick Buttels et al. (1990) "From Limits to Growth to Global Change: Constraints and Contradictions in the Evolution of Environmental Science and Ideology," in *Global Environmental Change,* vol. 1, no. 1, December, 57–66.

8. World Development Report 1992, op. cit., 114.

9. Herman E. Daly, "Elements of Environmental Macroeconomics," in R. Costanza (ed.), op. cit., 35.

10. For instance Ignacy Sachs (1980) *Stratégies de l'écodéveloppement,* Paris, Les Editions Ouvrières, 1980; or *What Now?* (1975), the report of the Dag Hammarskjöld Foundation.

11. William C. Clark, "Managing Planet Earth," *Scientific American,* vol. 261, September 1989, 47.

12. For an elaborate analysis of this aspect, see Wolfgang Sachs (1992) *Satellitenblick. Die Visualisierung der Erde im Zuge der Weltraumfahrt,* Berlin, Science Centre for Social Research.

13. For an overview see Thomas F. Malone (1986) "Mission to Planet Earth: Integrating Studies of Global Change," in *Environment,* vol. 28, no. 8, 6–11, 39–41.

14. Chapter 35.1 in the section "Science for Sustainable Development."

15. Clark, op. cit., 48.

# 37 | POLITICS AND THE ECOLOGICAL CRISIS
## AN INTRODUCTORY NOTE
### *Arne Naess*

"EVERYTHING IS POLITICS!" THIS was a powerful slogan in Western Europe during the 1960s, the years of student revolts. For the student, this slogan meant that the emerging environmental movement had to be similarly politicized; they felt that no real progress toward solving the ecological crisis would be made unless politicians were afraid of being kicked out of office if they attempted to block pollution and other ecological legislation. With no powerful pressure groups advocating strong environmental legislation, most politicians felt that they could not take the risk of moving from vague environmental promises to strong concrete proposals. Although the student radicals underestimated the strength of the traditional conservation movement, nevertheless they did have a beneficial influence on politically activating "nature lovers."

In Eastern Europe, the ecological movement was inevitably politicized, but with rather tragic results. Political leaders in these countries interpreted it, or pretended to interpret it, as an effort to politically undermine centralized industrial projects—thus a subversive activity. Consequently, even less was accomplished than in Western Europe.

It is important to note that Rachel Carson's *Silent Spring* (from which we can date the beginnings of the international deep ecological movement) insisted that *everything,* not just politics, would have to be changed. For example, without dwelling excessively on the pesticide controversy which Carson's book elicited, it nevertheless brought to light the issue of the covert cooperation of

Originally published in *ReVision* 13, 3 (1991). Reprinted with permission of the Helen Dwight Reid Educational Foundation. Published by Heldref Publications, 1319 18th Street, N.W., Washington, D.C. 20036-1802. Copyright 1991.

the U.S. Department of Agriculture with the pesticide industry. The controversy stemming from Carson's charges against the pesticide industry also made it clear that very powerful pressure groups would not only vote against necessary changes in the direction of responsible ecological policies, but that they also had the power and influence to monopolize the mass media with counterinformation. For instance, they claimed that there was no reason to ask for deep changes because the environmentalists were exaggerating. They claimed that new technologies, various natural science projects, and a few mild environmental laws were all that was needed to solve the environmental problems, and then they could get back to "business as usual." Thus, it was not necessary to hold discussions and engage in dialogues concerning fundamental philosophical issues surrounding the ecological crisis. It was not necessary to question the deepest premises of political behavior, nor to discuss the question of the behavior of humans on Earth. New technologies were soon invented, but they could not be introduced on the large scale required without strong political backing. As the tremendous social and political obstacles to the needed ecological changes were exposed, unhappily only a small minority of people in a minority of countries stood firmly behind the necessity of making these changes.

It is appropriate to talk of the "deep" and the "shallow" ecology movements as being characterized by marked differences in argumentation patterns. The deep argumentation pattern was generally rejected by industry and most of the public as leading to a blind alley, and as being pernicious because of its alarmist and even subversive character. I refer to this as an "argumentation pattern" because the differences between the "deep" and the "shallow" movements are not always discernible if we focus only on individual arguments. For example, the supporters of the Deep Ecology movement support many of the arguments made by shallow ecology proponents for certain changes, such as the move toward technologically "green" products.

Because of the multiplicity of political parties, and the relative ease with which political parties can be initiated in Western Europe, the politicization of the ecology movement has been easier to trace there than in the United States. It would be wrong to suppose however, that supporters of the Deep Ecology movement in the United States have been politically passive. Their politics have generally taken the form of infiltrating and influencing the two major political parties: the Democrats and the Republicans. There have also been occasional political victories, such as passing laws requiring major industries to choose less ecologically sensitive areas in which to locate their new factories.

## ECOLOGICAL SUSTAINABILITY

Moving now to the more philosophically fundamental issues of ecological politics, I wish to deal with the question: which are the *means* and which are the *ends* in the political fight for responsible ecological policies? With regard to ends, I propose the following axiom: *Long-range, local, district, regional, national, and global wide ecological sustainability is the criterion of ecologically responsible policies as a whole.*

Unsustainable policies can be viewed only as necessary ad hoc evils, and must only be temporary. When the norm of sustainability is used in what follows, it refers to the sense of wide sustainability as described in the above axiom.

It is now largely accepted among politicians that some sort of sustainability is a necessity. However, one should be prepared for usages of the term which are much narrower and weaker than the one suggested here. It actually might mean very little when a government or government-dominated agency declares a policy to be ecologically sustainable. The same holds as well for the term "biodiversity." "Maximize biodiversity!" is a very strong norm as promoted by conservation biologists, and it is derivable from our axiomatic norm of sustainability.

The goal of ecological sustainability is, however, only *one* of the goals of a Green society. A great deal of valuable literature has been devoted to outlining the characteristics of a Green society, and it is important to retain a vision of what we would consider a perfect Green society. Among the proponents of the ideals of a Green society, there is fairly substantial agreement that an established Green society is supposed to have reached three main goals, of which only one is ecologically sustainability. The two others are the goals of the peace movement and those of the social justice movement (if we allow the term "social justice" to have a wide meaning that includes the elimination of large scale human starvation and subjugation).

It is often asked, "What is the politics of the Deep Ecology movement? Don't Deep Ecology supporters have a political program?" These are badly posed questions. For there is no Green party political program derivable from the views which the supporters of the Deep Ecology movement have more or less in common.[1] Furthermore, the movement exists in many countries, and these countries have different traditions and different political systems.

Considering the accelerating rate of irreversible ecological destruction worldwide, I find it acceptable to continue fighting ecological unsustainability whatever the state of affairs may be concerning the other two goals of Green societies. I find this to be so even in spite of the completely obvious requirement that there needs to be significant progress toward the goals of the peace and the social justice movements in order fully to reach ecological sustainability. Because of the unique features of the ecological crisis, many political initiatives and goals relating to its solution must proceed with only minor reference to the ultimate goals of a Green society. The "greening" of policies must constantly be kept in mind, but not necessarily the ultimate steps towards a "perfect" Green society.

If there is any doubt concerning the need to act quickly on a number of ecological fronts, consider for example the proposed worldwide reforestation project. In 1988, The Worldwatch Institute outlined a plan to restore forests that involved the expenditure of between five and ten billion dollars from the year 2000 onwards. At present, we are clearer about the differences between a forest and a species-poor plantation of trees; thus, the costs of reforestation will be even higher than anticipated. The rich countries, of necessity, will have to bear the burden of most of these costs, if it is to be done at all.

In the early 1970s, there was substantial agreement over a number of features of Green societies; for instance, decentralization and the establishment of strong, fairly self-determining local communities. But it is now clear that, in areas of the world where pollution and other environmental problems are still minimal, the influential and powerful people in these areas tend to favor the kinds of development that people in more polluted areas increasingly resist. In order to save what can still be saved of areas contributing only moderately to the ecological crisis, political institutions in larger areas must pressure the smaller, less polluted and damaged areas to adopt restrictions on ecologically damaging practices. The anger, indignation, and fierce resistance to these restrictions by more local political institutions underscore the present deep-seated pressures to continue to "develop" along the lines of the most highly developed areas. I use the word "develop" with quotes because it is development inconsistent with the requirement of ecological sustainability. The unfortunate necessity of occasional coercion in these cases can be justified, in part, by an application of the norm of *universalizability* (i.e.—if ecological sustainability is a necessity for any area, then it is a necessity for all areas).

## CLASSES OF ECOLOGICAL UNSUSTAINABILITY

Let us suppose that we were to group areas into three classes: (1) those with a level of unsustainability considerably below the average, (2) those with roughly an average level of unsustainability, and (3) those considerably above the average level of unsustainability. Let us further suppose that a political party in the first class argues that certain unecological policies could justifiably be pursued because their implementation would only bring their area nearer the average level of unsustainability. This political party probably assumes that others in the first class would not do the same for, if they all did, it would significantly increase the average unsustainability—a situation contrary to what all classes now agree must be avoided. And so, people in the first class would have to be asked to follow a norm of forced status quo in terms of their degree of unsustainability, that is, a forced limitation on their self-determination in these matters. This course of action would protect these areas so that people would not later have to go through a severe period of transition toward sustainability. Thus, a thoughtless increase in unsustainability would be prevented, as well as the resulting necessary painful change of direction. This is not a question of arbitrary coercion, but rather of sanctions imposed within the limits of carefully considered legislation.

The above line of reasoning and proposed solution would, no doubt, be resisted within some "radical" environmental circles. The ghost of ecological dictatorship is liable to be raised, as well as that of undesirable hierarchical social/political structures. Therefore, it is important that as many people as possible clearly articulate the means and goals of policies that lead to a decrease of unsustainability.

One may justifiably object to the above classification scheme on the grounds that some areas now exist which have attained wide ecological sustainability (i.e., human and other activities do not result in a decrease in the full richness and diversity of life-forms in these areas). But such areas are certainly few and small. Not even Antarctica qualifies as fully sustainable.

The objection may also be raised that such a classification scheme should be applied mainly to states, countries, and other political and administrative units. But if we neglect geographical areas, the Earth's natural subdivisions would be ignored. For example, the eruption of Mount St. Helens decreased the richness and diversity of life-forms over a large area encompassing several political jurisdictions; this area went from class one or two to class three in a very short time. Thus, taking into consideration the Earth and its geographical subdivisions is of considerable importance in devising these classification schemes. Further, the biodiversity of the Mount St. Helens area should be restored—we wish to protect the richness and diversity of life whether decreases in richness and diversity are caused by humans or not. Another example is the Barents Sea, which is now a large class three area. In this case, the "criminal" policies of several countries, together with the irresponsibility shown by certain professions, have severely decreased the populations of various species of fish. It is open for discussion whether certain "natural" processes are also at fault, but the point of view taken is that, in the end, we wish the Barents Sea to recover.

On a national level, interesting conflicts along the above lines arise: for example, if Norwegian politicians agree to increased gas production from the North Sea area, it would also increase Norway's production of atmospheric carbon dioxide. If this happens, Norway will not be able to stay within the limits its government has promised the world it would not exceed. The government claims that the carbon dioxide production of an area larger than Norway (namely that of the European Common Market, and, of course, the world as a whole) will diminish as a result of their North Sea oil production. Since Norway would be exporting nearly all of the gas, the government points out that the importing countries would reduce their more ecologically unsound energy production of coal. If this were indeed the case, the increased development of the Norwegian gas industry would seem to be a step toward less unsustainability on a wider global scale.

But several relevant arguments can be offered against the government's decision. First, long-range sustainable global policy must be that of worldwide stabilization and reduction of the use of energy and, in particular, energy which is derived from nonrenewable resources. Secondly, the energy used to develop Norway's gas industry and to transport the gas to foreign countries would be considerable. If foreign countries were to indicate to Norway that they had a coal-reduction program, and were then to ask for gas to replace a certain percentage of their coal, the ecological situation would be quite different. Departments of foreign affairs around the world must become involved in these ecological considerations. At present, they are mainly preoccupied with commercial matters.[2]

From the point of view of the Deep Ecology movement, a trend toward both a centralization of political decisions and towards decentralization must be envisaged. The policies of local communities, in many areas of ecological conflict, must be controlled by regional and national political authorities. These authorities must be controlled, to a much greater extent, by institutions that are global (and not only international) in scope. But, of course, many ideals of strong local communities formulated in the sixties and seventies can be retained.

## GREEN POLITICS

Building a Green party at the national level is occurring only in the relatively few "democratic" countries. It is necessary for Green politics to spread to other parts of the world. But the content of the various Green party programs will have to adapt to differing political and ecological situations and will inevitably show great differences. Internal strife can be kept at a minimum by being clear about the differences between the fundamentalist and pragmatist positions in Green parties. Fundamentalists take a hard line on ecological issues; pragmatists are willing to consider compromises for the sake of social justice, for instance. Some compromises will have to be made. In Norway, fundamentalism has been strong, although there is a willingness to maintain the welfare profile of the political left. What follows is a short resumé of the Norwegian Green political program as one example of Green politics in a First World country.

The publication describing the Norwegian Green program consists of ten chapters, the first of which outlines the "basic values." The introductory statement in this chapter consists of six sentences, the first two of which are as follows: "We who are alive today have an obvious responsibility, in relation to future generations, for other life-forms and for the global community. The Greens wish to leave behind them an Earth at least as rich and diverse as the one we humans have inherited." The phrase "global community" does not mean the same as "human community," but refers rather to the coexistence of *all* living beings in the Earth's ecosphere. Richness and diversity is intended to include deep human cultural diversity, as well. Clearly, it is implied that we humans have many special obligations towards our fellow humans.

After the introductory note, there are twelve points outlining basic values, some of which are: current rates of social development can proceed only at the cost of the quality of life, which, after all, is a basic value; social and global solidarity implies reversing the trend toward the growing differences between rich and poor; the material standards in the rich countries must be reversed; and bureaucracy and the power of capital must also be reduced. These reductions are the inevitable consequences of emphasizing certain basic human values; they are not independent goals in and of themselves.

Other basic values in the Norwegian Green program include a technology adapted to nature and humans, cultural diversity, viable local communities, and a respect for nature and life. Other key issues include an increase in the minimum wage; the redistribution of wealth; decentralization and the support of small organizations; the participation of children and the young in productive work; ecological architecture that gives small children access to free nature, not just parks; transfer of military resources to environmental tasks; global cooperation and security; and the support of groups who work for alternative kinds of societies.

The above list of key issues provides an impression of the comprehensiveness of the Norwegian Green party program. Like most European Green parties, the Norwegian program tries to include the main concerns of the three great social movements of our time: the peace movement, the social justice movement, and the ecology movement. This is a formidable task and requires great discipline; but, in my opinion, the extreme positions within the three movements cannot all be accommodated. For example, antiracist feelings are strong in Norway, resulting in liberal immigration policies but, unfortunately, these policies often ignore ecological considerations. Because today's lifestyles in the richest countries of the world ensure gigantic waste per capita, com-

pared with lifestyles in poor countries, immigration from poor to rich countries creates more ecological stress. It is clear that the children of immigrants
will adopt the fatal consumption patterns of the rich countries, thereby adding
to the ecological crisis.

In my estimation, Green parties, including the Norwegian one, do not sufficiently see that solidarity and compassion for people in the Third World,
especially for the children, demand a tenfold increase in the contribution to
the daily fight against devastating hunger and degrading torture in many poor
countries as a more ecologically sound solution. The main driving force of the
Deep Ecology movement, as compared with the rest of the ecological movement, is that of *identification* and solidarity with all life. Humans are our
nearest, in terms of identification with all life: Green parties should include
political plans for participation in the fight against world hunger and for basic
human dignity. Green programs in the richest countries should include proposals to help poor countries which are invaded by immigrants from even
poorer countries. Immigration policies must be seen in a global context.

It is a widespread practice to accuse politicians, and the heads of political
parties, of being weak in their support of environmental matters, and of adopting Green slogans but never proposing strong actions towards solutions to the
ecological crisis. But party politicians must have voter support, and it is fairly
clear that powerful pressure groups will fight any decisive ecological program.
Politicians will not propose programs or projects that are unacceptable to the
leadership of major pressure groups whose well-organized effective action
supports special interests. Special-interest group democracy, as it functions
today, prevents major changes in ecological policies. People need help in recognizing their inconsistencies: for example, they may profess strong environmental concern but, through their actions, they support special interest groups
which prevent responsible ecological policies from being adopted, or even proposed, by the main political parties. What everybody can do in this situation is
to spend some time analyzing how they, directly or indirectly, support the
continuation of local, regional, or national policies which are ecologically irresponsible.

The special role of the Deep Ecology movement in political life has several
aspects. For one, it rejects the monopoly of narrowly human and short-term
argumentation patterns in favor of life-centered long-term arguments. It also
rejects the human-in-environment metaphor in favor of a more realistic
human-in-ecosystems and politics-in-ecosystems one. It generalizes most eco-
political issues: from "resources" to "resources for . . ."; from "life quality" to
"life quality for . . ."; from "consumption" to "consumption for . . ."; where
"for . . . " is, we insert "not only humans, but other living beings."

Supporters of the Deep Ecology movement have, as a main source of moti-, vation and perseverance, a philosophical/ecological total view (an ecosophy) that includes beliefs concerning fundamental goals and values in life, which it applies to political argumentation. That is, it uses *not only* arguments of the usual rather narrow kind, but also arguments from the level of a deep total view *and* with the ecological crisis in mind. But supporters of the Deep Ecology movement do not consider the ecological crisis to be the only global crisis; there are also crises of social justice, and of war and organized violence. And there are, of course, political problems which are only distantly related to ecology. Nevertheless, the supporters of the Deep Ecology movement have something important to contribute to the solution of these crises: they provide an example of the nonviolent activism needed in the years to come.

# NOTES

1. See the "Eight Points" as a suggestion for formulating a general, more or less, abstract platform for supporters of the Deep Ecology movement.
2. For a discussion of the principles of ecological diplomacy, see John E. Carroll (ed.), *International Environmental Diplomacy* (Cambridge: Cambridge University Press, 1988).

# 38 | THE REDISCOVERY OF TURTLE ISLAND

## Gary Snyder

*For John Wesley Powell, watershed visionary,*
*and for Wallace Stegner*

I

WE HUMAN BEINGS OF the developed societies have once more been expelled from a garden, the formal garden of Euro-American humanism and its assumptions of human superiority, priority, uniqueness, and dominance. We have been thrown back into that other garden with all the other animals and fungi and insects, where we can no longer be sure we are so privileged. The walls between "nature" and "culture" begin to crumble as we enter a posthuman era. Darwinian insights force occidental people, often unwillingly, to acknowledge their literal kinship with critters.

Ecological science investigates the interconnections of organisms and their constant transactions with energy and matter. Human societies come into being along with the rest of nature. There is no name yet for a humanistic scholarship that embraces the non-human. I suggest (in a spirit of pagan play) we call it "pan-humanism."

Environmental activists, ecological scientists, and pan-humanists are still in the process of re-evaluating how to think about, how to do policy, with Nature. The professional resource managers of the Forest Service and the Bureau of Land Management have been driven (partly from people of conscience within their own ranks) into re-thinking their old utilitarian view of the vast lands in their charge. This is a time of lively confluence, as non-governmental scientists, self-taught ecosystem experts from the communities, conservation-minded users, and land management agency leaders are finally getting together.

In the more rarefied world of ecological and social theory the confluence is rockier. Nature writing, environmental history, and ecological philosophy

---

Based on a talk given for "Reinventing Nature—Recovering the Wild," a conference held at the University of California at Davis, October 1993. Published by permission.

have become subjects of study in the humanities. Still there are many human-ists who think that knowledge of nature should be left entirely to the sciences. There are otherwise virtuous ("humane") historians and philosophers who unreflectively assume that the natural world is primarily a building-supply yard for human projects, with some pretty nursery plants available in one corner. As elegant and sophisticated as they might be at logic or aesthetics, when it comes to thinking about nature they are rather like absentee landlords.

Right now there are at least two sets of ideas circling about each other. One group, which we can call the "Savers," places great value on extensive preservation of wilderness areas and argues for the importance of the original condition of nature. This view has been tied to the idea that the mature condi-tion of an ecosystem is a stable and diverse condition technically called "cli-max." The other position holds that nature is constantly changing, that human agency has altered things to the point that there is no "natural condition" left, and that there is no reason to value climax (or "fitness") over any other suces-sion phase; and that human beings are not only part of nature but that they are also victors over nature and should keep on using and changing it. They can be called the "Users." The Savers view is attributed to the Sierra Club and other leading national organizations; to various "radical environmentalists" and to most environmental thinkers and writers. The Users view, which has supporters in the biological sciences, has already become a favorite of the World Bank and all those developers who are vexed by the problems that come with legislation that requires protection for creatures whose time and space is running out. It has been quickly seized on by the industry-sponsored populist-flavored "Wise Use" movement.

Different as they are in practice, they *both* reflect the instrumentalist view of nature that has long been a mainstay of Occidental thought. For Savers to wish to freeze some parts of nature into an icon of "pristine, uninhabited wilderness" is to treat it like a commodity, kept in a golden cage. They have also sometimes been insensitive to the plight of indigenous peoples whose home grounds were to be turned into a protected wildlife preserve or park; or the plight of local workers and farmers as logging and grazing policies change on public land.

The Users invocation of their concern for human welfare comes off as cyni-cal as their backers (mostly) lineup with the huge forces of governments and corporations, with NAFTA, GATT, and the sort of professionals who are "hired itinerant vandals" in Wendell Berry's phrase.

To say, as the Users do, that the natural world is subject to continual change and is shaped by history, is not a new insight. To say that human beings are fully part of nature is, for educated people, a truism, and totally fails to come to grips with the question of how to preserve natural variety. The need to protect world-wide biodiversity may be economically difficult and ethically controversial, but there are strong scientific *and* practical arguments in support of it. As for the Users' theoretical arguments against climax ecology theory, those earlier ecologists surely did reflect the progressive political tenor of the nineteen-thirties (and may have liked to see nature as a commune), but I have seen nothing in the writings of the older ecologists and preservationists to indicate that they doubted the ultimate rule of impermanence. By the same token there are ecological theorists today who are describing nature as though it were the trading floor of the stock market, chaos and all.

(And there are still some in the Users camp who, whether from a Judeo-Christian, Marxist-intellectual, or semi[idi]otic standpoint, would argue that human beings somehow amount to a qualitative leap away from biology, and have a new and unique fate.)

We would do well to leave these shaky and unproductive arguments behind. Hominids have *obviously* had some effect on the natural world going back for half a million or more years. So we should totally drop the use of the word "pristine" in regard to nature as meaning "untouched by human agency." "Pristine" should now be understood as meaning *virtually* pristine. An apparently untouched natural environment has in fact experienced some degree of human agency. Just as we could say of a west coast forest, "these woods have been impacted by deer, squirrels, and coyotes—but it's hard to see." Historically there were pre-agricultural environments where the human impact, rather like deer or cougar activities, was normally almost invisible to any but a tracker's eye. The greatest single pre-agricultural human effect on wild nature, yet to be fully grasped, was deliberate use of fire. In some cases human-caused fire seemed to mimic natural process, as with native burning in California. There were well-worn trails everywhere, as described by Alvar Nunez in his early-sixteenth-century walk across what is now Texas and the Southwest. But the fact still remains that in pre-industrial societies there were great numbers of species, vast grasslands, fertile wetlands, and extensive forests in mosaics of all different stages. Barry Commoner has said that the greatest destruction of the world environment—by far—has taken place since 1950.

Furthermore there is no "original condition" which once altered will never be redeemed. Original nature can be understood in terms of the myth of the "pool of Artemis"—the pool hidden in the forest that Artemis, Goddess of wild things, visits to renew her virginity. The wild has, nay *is,* a kind of hip, renewable virginity.

We are still laying the groundwork for a "culture of nature." The critique of the Judeo-Christian-Cartesian view of nature by which all developed nations excuse themselves for their drastically destructive treatment of the landscape, is well underway. Some of us would hope to resume, re-evaluate, re-create, and bring into line with complex science, that old view that holds the whole phenomenal world to be our being—multi-centered—"alive" in its own manner, and effortlessly self-organizing in its own chaotic way. Elements of this view are found in a wide range of ancient vernacular philosophies, and it turns up in a variety of more sophisticated but still tentative forms in recent thought. It would be a third way, not caught up in the dualisms of body and mind, spirit and matter, or culture and nature. It would be a non-instrumentalist view that extends intrinsic value to the non-human natural world.

There have been Euro-American scouting parties following a skein of old tracks that would cross the Occidental (and Postmodern) divide for several centuries. I am going to lay out the case history of one of these probes. It's a potentially new story for the North American identity. It has already been in the making for more than thirty years. I call it "The Rediscovery of Turtle Island."

## II

In January of 1969 I attended a gathering of Native American activists in Southern California. Hundreds of people had come from all over the west. After sundown we went out to a gravelly wash that came down from the desert mountains. Drums were set up, a fire started, and for most of the night we sang the pan-tribal songs called "49s". The night conversations circled around the idea of a native-inspired cultural and ecological renaissance for all of North America. I first heard this continent called "Turtle Island" there by a man who said his work was to be a messenger. He had his dark brown long hair tied in a Navajo men's knot, and he wore dusty khakis. He said that Turtle Island was the term that the people were coming to, a new name to help us build the future of North America. I asked him who or where it came from. He said "There are many creation myths with Turtle, east coast and west coast. But also you can just hear it."

I had recently returned to the west coast from a ten-year residence in Japan. It was instantly illuminating to hear this continent called "Turtle Island." The re-alignments those conversations suggested were rich and complex. I was reminded that the indigenous people here had a long history of subtle and effective ways of working with their home grounds. They had an exuberant variety of cultures and economies, and some distinctive social forms (such as communal households) that were found throughout the hemisphere. They sometimes fought with each other, but usually with a deep sense of mutual respect. Within each of their various forms of religious life lay a powerful spiritual teaching on the matter of human and natural relationships, and for some individuals a practice of self-realization that came with learning to see through non-human eyes. The landscape was intimately known, and the very idea of community and kinship embraced and included the huge populations of wild beings. Much of the truth of Native American history and culture has been obscured by the self-serving histories that were written on behalf of the present dominant society.

These points were already known to me from my youthful interest in environmental and Native Peoples' issues. Seeing them made fresh renewed my belief that a Native American cultural renaissance was coming, and put the emerging environmental movement into perspective. This gathering took place one year before the first Earth Day.

As I reentered American life during the spring of 1969, I saw the use of the term "Turtle Island" spread through the fugitive Native American newsletters and communications. I became aware that there was a notable groundswell of white people too who were seeing their life in the western hemisphere in a new way. Many whites figured that the best they could do on behalf of Turtle Island was to work for the environment, reinhabit the urban or rural margins, learn the landscape, and give support to Native Americans when asked. By late 1970 I had moved with my family to the Sierra Nevada and was developing a forest homestead north of the South Yuba River. Many others entered the mountains and hills of the Pacific Slope with virtually identical intentions, from the San Diego back-country north into British Columbia. They had begun the reinhabitory move.

Through the early seventies I worked with my local forest community, but made regular trips to the cities, and was out on long swings around the country reading poems or leading workshops—many in urban areas. Our new sense of the western hemisphere permeated everything we did. So I called the book of poems I wrote from that period *Turtle Island*.

The introduction says,

> Turtle Island—the old/new name for the continent, based on many creation myths of the people who have been living here for millennia, and reapplied by some of them to "North America" in recent years. Also, an idea found world-wide, of the earth, or cosmos even, sustained by a great turtle or serpent-of-eternity.
>
> A name: that we may see ourselves more accurately on this continent of watersheds and life-communities—plant zones, physiographic provinces, culture areas: following natural boundaries. The "USA" and its states and counties are arbitrary and inaccurate impositions on what is really here.
>
> The poems speak of place, and the energy-pathways that sustain life. Each living being is a swirl in the flow, a formal turbulence, a "song." The land, the planet itself, is also a living being—at another pace. Anglos, Black people, Chicanos, and others beached up on these shores all share such views at the

deepest levels of their old cultural traditions—African, Asian, or European. Hark again to those roots, to see our ancient solidarity, and then to the work of being together on Turtle Island.

Following on the publication of these poems I began to hear back from a lot of people—many in Canada—who were remaking a North American life. Many other writers got into this sort of work each on their own, a brilliant, and cranky bunch that included Jerry Rothenberg and his translation of Native American song and story into powerful little poem-events, Peter Blue Cloud's evocation of Coyote in a contemporary context, Dennis Tedlock's story-teller's representation of Zuni oral narrative in English. Ed Abbey's call for a passionate commitment to the wild, Leslie Silko's shivery novel *Ceremony,* Simon Ortiz' early poems and stories—and much more.

A lot of this followed on the heels of the back-to-the-land movement and the early seventies diaspora of longhairs and dropout graduate students to rural places. There are thousands of people from those days still making a culture: being teachers, plumbers, chair- and cabinet-makers, contractors and carpenters, poets-in-the-schools, auto mechanics, geographic information computer consultants, registered foresters, professional storytellers, forest service workers, river-guides, mountain-guides, architects or organic gardeners. Many simultaneously have mastered grassroots politics and the intricacies of public lands policies. Such people can be found tucked away in the cities, too.

The first wave of writers mentioned left some strong legacies—Rothenberg, Tedlock, and Dell Hymes gave us the field of Ethnopoetics (the basis for truly appreciating multicultural literature), Leslie Silko and Simon Ortiz opened the way for a distinguished and diverse body of new American Indian writing, Ed Abbey's eco-warrior spirit led toward the emergence of the radical environmental group Earth First! which (in splitting) generated the Wild Lands Project. Some of my own writings contributed to the inclusion of Buddhist ethics and lumber industry work-life in the mix, and writers as different as Wes Jackson, Wendell Berry and Gary Paul Nabhan opened the way for a serious discussion of place, nature in place, and community. The Native American movement has become a national presence, and the environmental movement has become (in some cases) big politics. Although the counter-culture has faded and blended in, its fundamental concerns are still a serious part of the dialog.

A key element in the debate is the question of our ethical obligations to the non-human world. The very mention of such a notion rattles the foundations of Occidental thought. Native American religious beliefs, although not identical coast to coast, are overwhelmingly in support of a full and sensitive acknowledgement of the subjecthood of nature. This in no way backs off from an unflinching awareness of the painful side of wild nature; seeing how everything is being eaten alive. The twentieth century syncretism of the "Turtle Island view" gathers ideas from Buddhism and Daoism and from the lively details of world-wide animism and paganism. Here too there is no imposition of ideas of progress or order on the natural world—Buddhism teaches impermanence, suffering, and no deity. "No self in self, no self in things." Buddhist teachings go on to say that the true source of compassion and ethical behavior is paradoxically none other than one's own realization of the insubstantial and ephemeral nature of everything. Much of animism and paganism celebrate the actual, in its inevitable pain and death, and offer no utopian hopes. Add to this contemporary ecosystem theory and environmental history, and you get a sense of what's at work. One recent philosophical outcome is "Deep Ecology" which informs the work of the Wild Lands Project, among others.

Conservation Biology, Deep Ecology, and such are given a community constituency and real grounding by the Bioregional movement. Bioregionalism applies commitment to this continent *place by place,* in terms of biogeographical regions and watersheds. It calls us to see our country in terms of its landforms, plant life, weather patterns, and seasonal changes—its whole natural history—before the net of political jurisdictions was cast over it. People are challenged to become "reinhabitory," that is to say, to become people who are learning to live and think "as if" they were totally engaged with their place for the long future. This doesn't mean some return to a primitive lifestyle or utopian provincialism, but simply implies an engagement with community and a search for the sustainable sophisticated mix of economic practices that would enable people to live regionally and yet learn from and contribute to a planetary society. (Some of the best bioregional work is being done in cities, as people try to restore neighborhoods.) Such people are, regardless of national or ethnic backgrounds, in the process of becoming something deeper than "American (or Mexican or Canadian) citizens"—they are becoming natives of Turtle Island.

Now in the nineties the term "Turtle Island" continues, modestly, to extend its sway. There is a Turtle Island Office, based in New York (with a newsletter) which is a national information center for the many bioregional groups which every other year hold a "Turtle Island Congress." Participants join in from Canada and Mexico. The use of the term is now standard in a number of Native American periodicals and circles. There is even a "Turtle Island String Quartet" based in San Francisco. In the winter of '92 I practically convinced the director of the Centro de Estudios Norteamericanos at the Universidad de Alcala in Madrid to change his department's name to "Estudios de la Isla de Tortuga." He much enjoyed the idea of the shift. We agreed: speak of the United States, and you are talking two centuries of basically English-speaking affairs; speak of "America" and you invoke five centuries of Euro-American schemes in the western hemisphere; speak of "Turtle Island" and a vast past, an open future, and all the life communities of plants, humans, and critters comes into focus.

## III

The Nisenan and Maidu, indigenous people who live on the east side of the Sacramento valley and into the northern Sierra foothills, tell a creation story that goes something like this:

> Coyote and Earthmaker were blowing around in the swirl of things. Coyote finally had enough of this aimlessness and said "Earthmaker, find us a world!" Earthmaker tried to get out of it, tried to excuse himself, because he knew that a world can only mean trouble. But Coyote nagged him into trying. So leaning over the surface of the vast waters, Earthmaker called up Turtle. After a long time Turtle surfaced, and Earthmaker said "Turtle, can you get me a bit of mud? Coyote wants a world." "A world" said Turtle, "Why bother. Oh well." And down she dived. She went down and down and down, to the bottom of the sea. She took a great gob of mud, and started swimming toward the surface. As she spiralled and paddled upward, the streaming water washed the mud from the sides of her mouth, from the back of her mouth— and by the time she reached the surface (the trip took six years) nothing was left but one grain of dirt between the tips of her beak. "That'll be enough!" said Earthmaker, taking it in his hands and giving it a pat like a tortilla. Suddenly Coyote and Earthmaker were standing on a piece of ground as big as a tarp. Then Earthmaker stamped his feet, and they were standing on a flat wide plain of mud. The ocean was gone. They stood on the land.

. . . and then Coyote began to want trees and plants, and scenery, and the story goes on with Coyote's imagining landscapes which then come forth, and he starts naming the animals and plants as they show themselves. "I'll call you skunk because you look like skunk." Those landscapes are there today.

My children grew up with this as their first creation story. When they later heard the Bible story they said "That's a lot like Coyote and Earthmaker." But the Nisenan story gave them their own immediate landscape, complete with details, and the characters were animals from their own world.

Mythopoetic play can be part of what jump-starts long-range social change. But what about the short-term? There are some immediate outcomes worth mentioning: A new era of community interaction with public lands has begun. In California a new set of ecosystem-based government/community joint management discussions are beginning to take place. Some of the most vital environmental politics is being done by watershed or ecosystem-based groups.

"Ecosystem management" by definition includes private landowners in the mix. In my corner of the northern Sierra we are practicing being a "human-inhabited wildlife corridor," an area that functions as a biological connector, and are coming to certain agreed-on practices that would enhance wildlife survival even as people continue to live there. Such a practice would be one key to preserving wildlife diversity in most Third World countries. We are all indigenous to this planet, this garden we are being called on by nature and history to reinhabit in good spirit. To restore the land one must live and work in a place. The place will welcome whomever approaches it with respect and attention. To work in a place is to bond to a place: people who work together in a place become a community, and a community, in time, grows a culture. To restore the wild is to restore culture.

My stepdaughter Kyungjin (KJ for short) was adopted at eighteen months from Korea. Her adoptive mother is of Japanese descent, her stepfather is a *haole,* her language is English. Her uncles and aunties are mostly Japanese-American people of the second and third generation who are farmers in the Great Central Valley. And now she lives in the Yuba river country, the mountain Nisenan territory of California. She sometimes has difficulty knowing how to see herself and will still announce "I am Korean" though she has little idea of what that might possibly mean. We play Korean music for her, she loves kimchee and gets a lot of it, and we promise to take her there for a visit someday. But then we tell her "Honey, you are a person of northern California. There are people from many different places here and lots of cultural styles and we respect them all. But who we are is what we are *here.*" And she walks a path to catch her ride to school through a forest where she stops and imitates the scolding of squirrels. She knows these critters are also neighbors in the 'hood. This also is learning culture.

She recently came home from school working at memorizing the Pledge of Allegiance. I taught her the poem that I had written for my (now grown) sons back in the mid-seventies, a pledge of allegiance that will be good on Turtle Island for centuries to come, regardless of changes in government:

### For All

> . . . I pledge allegiance
>
> I pledge allegiance to the soil
>     of Turtle Island
> and to the beings who thereon dwell
>     one ecosystem
>     in diversity
>     under the sun
> With joyful interpenetration for all.

# 39 | DEEP ECOLOGY FOR THE TWENTY-SECOND CENTURY

## Arne Naess

THIS IS NOT MY title! Why did my friends insist on this title? Because of many conversations of mine of the following kind:

NN: Are you an optimist or a pessimist?

NAESS: I'm an optimist!

NN: (Astonished) Really?

NAESS: Yes, a convinced optimist—when it comes to the twenty-second century.

NN: You mean, of course, the twenty-first century?

NAESS: No, the twenty-second! The lifetime of the grandchildren of our grandchildren. Aren't you interested in the world of those children?

NN: You mean we can relax because we have a lot of time available to overcome the ecological crisis?

NAESS: Not at all! Every week counts. How terrible and shamefully bad conditions will be in the twenty-first century, or how far down we fall before we start on the way back up, *depends upon what YOU* and others do today and tomorrow. There is not a single day to be lost. We need activism on a high level immediately.

The answer that I am an optimist is a reaction to the so-called doomsday prophets: people who talk *as if* they mean nothing can be done to straighten things out. They are few in number, but they are heavily exploited by people

Originally published in *The Trumpeter* 9, 2 (1992), and revised in 1993. Reprinted with permission.

in power who speak soothingly that the task ahead is not very formidable, and that government policies *can* turn the tide for the better. A telling example is the cover of the influential *Newsweek* magazine which, just before the Rio conference, used the headline "The End is Not Near." In the newsmagazine article, there was no pep talk, not even an admission that we are in for a great task that will require new thinking. This is just the opposite of slogans used when big corporations are "in the red" which proclaim "New Thinking! Greater Efforts Are Needed! New Leadership!" No slogans were offered like those of Churchill in 1940: "Of course we will win, but there will be many tears and much sweat to be shed."

In short, there is no time for overly pessimistic statements that can be exploited by passivists and those who promote complacency.

The realization of what we call *wide* ecological sustainability of the human enterprise on this unique planet may take a long time, but the more we *increase* unsustainability this year, and in the years to come, the longer it will take. How much is left of nature obviously depends upon what we do today and tomorrow. The appropriate message is of a simple, well-known kind: the recovery from our illness will take time, and for every day that we neglect to *seriously* try to stop the illness from getting worse, the more time it will take. Policies proposed today for attempting to heal the planet are not serious. The Deep Ecology movement is concerned with what can be done *today,* but I forsee no definite victories scarcely before the twenty-second century.

Roughly, I call ecological sustainability *wide* (or "broad") if and only if the change ("development") in life conditions on the planet is such that it ensures the full richness (abundance) and diversity of life-forms on the Earth (to the extent, of course, that humans can insure this). Every key word of this criterion, of course, needs clarification, but "wide" sustainability is obviously different from the "narrow" concept of ecological sustainability that is increasingly accepted politically: that is, the existence of short- and long-range policies that most researchers agree will make ecological *catastrophes* affecting narrow *human* interests unlikely. This kind of narrow sustainability is politically acceptable today as a *goal* for "global development." But broad ecological sustainability is concerned with overall ecological conditions on the Earth, not only with the interests of humanity, and the dangerous concept of development is avoided. By "development" is still meant something like an increase in Gross National Product, not an increase in the quality of life.

So the big open question is: How far down are we going to sink before we start heading back up in the twenty-second century? How far must we fall before there is a clear trend toward *decreasing* regional and global ecological unsustainability? It may be useful, in this connection, to consider some possible scenarios:

1. There is no major change in ecological policies and in the extent of worldwide poverty. Major ecological catastrophies occur as the result of the

steadily accumulating effects of a century of ecological folly. This dramatic situation forces new ecologically strict policies, perhaps through undemocratic, and even brutal, dictatorial military means used by the rich countries.

2. The same development continues except for a major change in the poor countries: there is considerable economic growth of the Western kind. Now there are five times as many people living unsustainably. A breakdown occurs very soon, and harsh measures are taken to fight chaos, and to begin a decrease in unsustainability.

3. and 4. Several similar developments ending in catastrophic and chaotic conditions, and subsequent harsh brutal policies implemented by the most powerful states. A turn towards sustainability, but only after enormous ecological devastation.

5. Ecological enlightenment, a realistic appreciation of the drastic reduction in the quality of life, increasing influence of the Deep Ecological attitude, and a slow decrease of the sum total of unsustainability. A trend toward decreasing unsustainability discernable by the year 2101.

Our hope: the realization of the rational scenario: one that guarantees the least strenuous path toward sustainability by the year 2101.

Now a few comments on the three great contemporary worldwide movements which call for grass roots activism:

First there is the *peace movement;* the oldest of the three which is, at present, remarkably dormant. But if military expenditures do not rapidly decrease from about 900 billion dollars per year, I expect it will revive. Then there are many movements which I include as part of the *social justice movement.* It includes the feminist movement and part of the social ecology movement. One might refer to the third movement by the use of the vague term *radical environmentalism,* because the use of the specific terminology of Deep Ecology will, sooner or later, elicit boredom and aggression. But a problem with the word "environmentalism" is that it smacks of the old metaphor suggesting humanity *surrounded* by something outside: the so-called environment of humans. But it will take a long time before radicalism ceases to be associated with the political *red-blue axis:*

## The Political Triangle

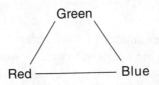

Broad ecological sustainability may be compatible with a variety of social and political structures, provided they all point towards the Green pole. Unfortunately, there is now (1993) a strong belief in Eastern Europe that policies must be Blue (for example, participation in world economic markets, etc.) *before* they point toward the Green pole.

It is not easy to be personally active in more than one of the three grass roots movements, but cooperation among the movements is essential. The ecological threat is not only one of war, but also of the immense military operations, and associated industrial activity, during peacetime. Cooperation between the ecological and the peace movements has been excellent for a long time. It is taking longer to establish close cooperation with all of the social justice movements. But because care, and the capacity to identify with all living beings, is so prominent in the Deep Ecology movement, injustice is taken seriously.

The small minority of supporters of the Deep Ecology movement who write in periodicals, talk in public, and organize conferences, meet people who are sometimes skeptical about their ethical concerns: is it true that they are much fonder of animals than humans? The answer is that, whatever the intensity of their fight for animals (or wilderness), they recognize the very special obligations we have for our fellow-humans. What we propose is not a shift of caring away from humans and towards non-humans, but rather an extension and deepening of overall caring. It is unwarranted to assume that the human potential for caring is constant and finite, and that an increase of caring for some creatures necessarily reduces caring for others. The next century will see a general increase in caring if the ecofeminists are at least partially right.

The societies developing in the twenty-second century, at the earliest I suspect, will not all look like the ideal Green societies envisioned since the sixties. Many will have traits more in common with what we have today. Will there be conspicuous consumption? Of course! But what is conspicuous, and what will secure prestige and wonder in that century, will require only moderate physical energy to achieve. Several tremendously important things will be different: there will be no political support of greed and unecological production. A tolerance of severe social injustice based on differences in levels of consumption will have disappeared.

To fight the *dominance* of something should be clearly distinguished from trying to *eliminate* something. We shall always need people who insist that their main goal in life has not been to amass money, but to create something useful in a world in which money is a measure of success and creative power. In sociology, we often talk about entrepreneurs in the wide important sense of socially highly energetic, creative, influential people. Their work is often controversial, sometimes clearly destructive, but they are required in any dynamic society.

I envision big, but not dominating, centers of commerce, learning and the arts, and big buildings and vast machinery for continued exploration in physics and cosmology. But in order to do something analogous to driving long distances in a conspicuous luxury car, a family would have to renounce many goods other people could afford. A good deal of the family's "Gaia-gift" would be spent on traveling in their prestigious car.

Rich people who work in the world of business, who are supporters of the Deep Ecology movement, ask in all seriousness whether Green utopian societies *must* look so dreary. Why portray a society which seemingly needs no big entrepreneurs, only organic farmers, modest artists, and mild naturalists? A capitalist society is, in a certain sense, a rather *wild* society! We need some degree of wildness, but not exactly of the capitalist sort. The usual utopian Green societies seem so sober and tame. We shall need enthusiasts of the extravagant, the luxurious, and the big. But they must not dominate.

In short, I do not envisage the *necessity* of any dramatic sudden turnaround in the social-political realm when I envisage things from the limited point of view of *overcoming the still-increasing ecological crisis.* But as mature human beings (I imagine that some of us are mature or on the way to becoming mature) we are also concerned about non-violence and social justice. It is not necessary for me to say anything more definite about these broad social and ethical issues at this point. But I see the value of expressing vague ideas concerning how one's own ideal Green societies might look. A Green society, in my terminology, is one that has, to some extent, solved not only the problem of reaching ecological sustainability, but has also ensured peace and a large measure of social justice. I don't see why so many people find reasons for despair. I am confident that humans have what is demanded to turn things around and achieve Green societies. This is how I, as a supporter of the Deep Ecology movement, feel today: impatient with the doomsday prophets and confident that we have a mission, however modest, in shaping a better future that is *not remote.*

# SELECTED BIBLIOGRAPHY

## PART ONE: WHAT IS DEEP ECOLOGY?

Abbey, Edward. *Desert Solitaire.* New York: McGraw-Hill, 1968.

——. *The Monkey Wrench Gang.* New York: Avon Books, 1976.

——. *Hayduke Lives.* Boston: Little, Brown, 1989.

Abram, David. "The Perceptual Implications of Gaia," *The Ecologist* 15 (1985): 96–103.

Berry, Thomas. *The Dream of the Earth.* San Francisco: Sierra Club Books, 1988.

Berry, Thomas, and Brian Swimme. *The Universe Story.* New York: HarperCollins, 1992.

Capra, Fritjof. *The Turning Point: Science, Society and the Rising Culture.* New York: Simon and Schuster, 1982.

Davis, John, ed., *The Earth First! Reader: Ten Years of Radical Environmentalism.* Salt Lake City, Utah: Peregrine Smith, 1991.

DeGroth, Teresa, and Edward Valauskas. *Deep Ecology and Environmental Ethics,* CPL Bibliography No. 185. Chicago: Council of Planning Librarians, 1987.

Devall, Bill. *Simple in Means, Rich in Ends: Practicing Deep Ecology.* Salt Lake City, Utah: Gibbs Smith, 1988.

——. *Living Richly in an Age of Limits.* Salt Lake City, Utah: Gibbs Smith, 1993.

——. "Deep Ecology and Radical Environmentalism." *Society and Natural Resources* 4 (1991): 247–58.

Devall, Bill, and George Sessions. *Deep Ecology: Living as if Nature Mattered.* Salt Lake City, Utah: Peregrine Smith, 1985.

Drengson, Alan. *Beyond Environmental Crisis: From Technocrat to Planetary Person.* New York: Peter Lang, 1989.

——. *Doc Forest and Blue Mountain Ecostery: A Narrative on Creating Ecological Harmony in Daily Life.* Victoria, B.C.: Ecostery House, 1993.

Ehrenfeld, David. *The Arrogance of Humanism.* Oxford: Oxford University Press, 1978.

Ehrlich, Paul, and Anne Ehrlich. *The Population Explosion.* New York: Simon and Schuster, 1990.

Elgin, Duane. *Voluntary Simplicity.* New York: William Morrow, 1981.

*Environmental Ethics.* Eugene Hargrove (ed.), Department of Philosophy, P.O. Box 13496, University of North Texas, Denton, TX 76203. Subscriptions $18/yr. The leading international academic journal dealing with Deep Ecology and environmental ethics.

Everndon, Neil. *The Natural Alien: Humankind and the Environment.* Toronto: University of Toronto Press, 1985.

———. *The Social Creation of Nature.* Baltimore: Johns Hopkins University Press, 1992.

Folsom, L. Edwin. "Gary Snyder's Descent to Turtle Island: Searching for Fossil Love." *Western American Literature* 15 (1980): 103–21.

Foreman, Dave. *Confessions of an Ecowarrior.* New York: Harmony Books, 1991.

———. *Books of the Big Outside.* P.O. Box 5141, Tucson, AZ 85703. Mail-order catalogue of many book titles on conservation biology, environmental history, and ecophilosophy.

Fox, Warwick. *Toward a Transpersonal Ecology: Developing New Foundations for Environmentalism.* Boston: Shambhala Publications, 1990. Important discussion of the development of the Deep Ecology movement, and exposition of Fox's ecopsychological "Transpersonal Ecology."

———. "Self and World: A Transpersonal, Ecological Approach." *ReVision* 13, 1 (1991): 116–21. Special *ReVision* issue on Deep Ecology, edited by Warwick Fox.

Glasser, Harold. "The Distinctiveness of the Deep Ecology Approach to Ecophilosophy." Unpublished manuscript, University of California, Davis, Dept. of Applied Science, 1991, pp. 1–28. Contains a critique of Fox's attempt to replace Deep Ecology with "Transpersonal Ecology."

Glendinning, Chellis. *My Names Is Chellis, and I'm in Recovery from Western Civilization.* Boston: Shambhala Publications, 1994.

Gordon, Anita, and David Suzuki. *It's a Matter of Survival.* Toronto: Stoddart Press, 1990.

Halper, Jon, ed. *Gary Snyder: Dimensions of a Life.* San Francisco: Sierra Club Books, 1991.

Hepworth, James, and Gregory McNamee, eds. *Resist Much, Obey Little: Some Notes on Edward Abbey.* Utah: Dream Garden Press, 1985.

LaChapelle, Dolores. *Earth Wisdom.* Silverton, Colo.: Way of the Mountain Center, 1978.

———. *Sacred Land Sacred Sex: Rapture of the Deep.* Durango, Colo.: Kivaki Press [585 E. 31st St.], 1988).

List, Peter C., ed. *Radical Environmentalism: Philosophy and Tactics.* Belmont, Calif.: Wadsworth, 1993.

Macy, Joanna. *World as Lover, World as Self.* Berkeley: Parallax, 1991.

Manes, Christopher. *Green Rage: Radical Environmentalism and the Unmaking of Civilization.* Boston: Little, Brown, 1990.

McKibben, Bill. *The End of Nature.* New York: Random House, 1989.

McLaughlin, Andrew. *Regarding Nature: Industrialism and Deep Ecology.* New York: State University of New York Press, 1993.

McLean, Wm. Scott, ed. *Gary Snyder: The Real Work.* New York: New Directions, 1980.

Metzner, Ralph. "The Emerging Ecological World View." In M. Tucker and J. Grim, eds., *Worldviews and Ecology.* Lewisburg, Pa.: Bucknell University Press, 1993, pp. 163–72.

Miller, G. Tyler. *Living in the Environment: An Introduction to Environmental Science.* 8th ed. Belmont, Calif.: Wadsworth, 1994.

Murphy, Patrick. *Understanding Gary Snyder.* Columbia, S.C.: University of South Carolina Press, 1992.

Naess, Arne. *Ecology, Community, and Lifestyle.* Cambridge, Cambridge University Press, 1989.

Oelschlaeger, Max. *The Idea of Wilderness: From Prehistory to the Age of Ecology.* New Haven: Yale University Press, 1991, pp. 260–80 (section on Gary Snyder).

———. *Caring for Creation: An Ecumenical Approach to the Environmental Crisis.* New Haven: Yale University Press, 1994.

———, ed. *After Earth Day: Continuing the Conservation Effort.* Denton: University of North Texas Press, 1992.

Rachaels, James. *Created from Animals: The Moral Implications of Darwinism.* Oxford: Oxford University Press, 1990.

Ronald, Ann. *The New West of Edward Abbey.* Reno: University of Nevada Press, 1988.

Roszak, Theodore. *Where the Wasteland Ends: Politics and Transcendence in Postindustrial Society.* Garden City, N.Y.: Anchor/Doubleday, 1972.

———. *The Voice of the Earth.* New York: Simon and Schuster, 1992. Lays out the foundations for the new field of ecopsychology.

Scarce, Rik. *Ecowarriors: Understanding the Radical Environmental Movement.* Chicago: Noble Press, 1990.

Seed, John; Joanna Macy; Pat Fleming; and Arne Naess. *Thinking Like a Mountain: Toward a Council of All Beings.* Philadelphia: New Society Publishers, 1988.

Sessions, George. "Gary Snyder: Post-Modern Man." In Halper, *Gary Snyder,* pp. 365–70.

———. "Radical Environmentalism in the 90s" and "Postscript: March 1992." *Wild Earth* 2, 3 (1992): 64–70.

———. "Deep Ecology as World View." In M. Tucker and John Grim, eds., *Worldviews and Ecology.* Lewisburg, Pa.: Bucknell University Press, 1993, pp. 207–27.

———. "Wilderness: Back to Basics." *Trumpeter* 11, 3 (1994).

———. "Paul Shepard: Ecological Elder." In Max Oelschlaeger, ed., *Nature's Odyssey: Essays on Paul Shepard.* Denton: University of North Texas Press, 1995.

Shepard, Paul. *Nature and Madness.* San Francisco: Sierra Club Books, 1982.

Snyder, Gary. *Turtle Island*. New York: New Directions, 1974.

———. *The Old Ways*. San Francisco: City Lights Books, 1977.

———. "Good Wild Sacred" (Schumacher Lecture). In Wes Jackson et al., eds., *Meeting the Expectations of the Land*. San Francisco: North Point Press, 1984.

———. *The Practice of the Wild*. San Francisco: North Point Press, 1990.

———. *No Nature: New and Selected Poems*. San Francisco: Pantheon Books, 1992.

———. *Coming into the Watershed*. New York: Pantheon Books, 1994.

Steuding, Bob. *Gary Snyder*. Boston: Twayne Publishers, 1976.

*Trumpeter: Canadian Journal of Ecosophy*. Alan Drengson, ed. P.O. Box 5853, Stn. B, Victoria, B.C., Canada V89 6S8. Subscriptions $20/yr. Semitechnical articles on Deep Ecology.

Zakin, Susan. *Coyotes and Town Dogs: Earth First! and the Environmental Movement*. New York: Viking Press, 1993.

Zimmerman, Michael, ed. *Environmental Philosophy: From Animal Rights to Radical Ecology*. Englewood Cliffs, N.J.: Prentice-Hall, 1993. Sections on Deep Ecology, Social Ecology, Ecofeminism, and environmental ethics.

## PART TWO: HISTORICAL ROOTS OF DEEP ECOLOGY

Bates, Marston. *The Forest and the Sea*. New York: Random House, 1960. Relevant selection reprinted in L. Forstner and J. Todd, eds., *The Everlasting Universe: Readings on the Ecological Revolution*. Lexington, Mass: D. C. Heath, 1971, pp. 46–56.

Booth, Annie, and Harvey Jacobs. "Ties That Bind: Native American Beliefs as a Foundation for Environmental Consciousness." *Environmental Ethics* 12, 1 (1990): 27–43.

Brower, David. *For Earth's Sake: The Life and Times of David Brower*. Salt Lake City, Utah: Peregrine Smith, 1990.

———. *Work in Progress*. Salt Lake City, Utah: Peregrine Smith, 1991.

Callicott, J. Baird. "Traditional American Indian and Western European Attitudes toward Nature." *Environmental Ethics* 4 (1982): 293–318. Reprinted in Robert Elliot and Arran Gare, eds., *Environmental Philosophy*. University Park: Pennsylvania State University Press, 1983, pp. 231–59.

———. *The World's Great Ecological Insights*. Berkeley: University of California Press, 1994.

———, ed. *Companion to a Sand County Almanac*. Madison: University of Wisconsin Press, 1987.

Cohen, Michael P. *The Pathless Way: John Muir and American Wilderness*. Madison: University of Wisconsin Press, 1984. Excellent account of the development of Muir's ecocentrism.

———. *The History of the Sierra Club: 1892–1970*. San Francisco: Sierra Club Books, 1988.

Cronen, William. *Nature's Metropolis.* New York: Norton, 1991.

———. "A Place for Stories: Nature, History, and Narrative." *Journal of American History* 78 (1992).

Dasmann, Raymond. *The Last Horizon.* New York: Macmillan, 1963.

Devall, Bill. "Reform Environmentalism." *Humboldt Journal of Social Relations* 6, 2 (1979).

———. "The Deep Ecology Movement." *Natural Resources Journal* 20 (1980): 299–322.

Drengson, Alan. "Shifting Paradigms: From the Technocratic to the Person-Planetary." *Environmental Ethics* 2, 3 (1980): 221–40.

Dunlap, Riley, and Angela Mertig, eds. *American Environmentalism: The U.S. Environmental Movement 1970–90.* Bristol, Pa.: Taylor and Francis, 1992.

Ferkiss, Victor. *Nature, Technology, and Society: Cultural Roots of the Current Environmental Crisis.* New York: New York University Press, 1993.

Fox, Stephen. *John Muir and His Legacy: The American Conservation Movement.* Boston: Little, Brown, 1981. Outstanding history of the Muir-inspired American conservation movement.

———. "Approaches to Environmental History." In Neil Everndon, ed. *The Paradox of Environmentalism.* Ontario: York University, Faculty of Environmental Studies, 1984, pp. 19–32. Critical discussion of the environmental history approaches of Donald Worster, Samuel Hays, and the Pinchot, gun club, and wildlife protection traditions.

French, Roderick. "Is Ecological Humanism a Contradiction in Terms?: The Philosophical Foundations of the Humanities Under Attack." In Hughes and Schultz, *Ecological Consciousness,* pp. 43–66. Perceptive discussion of the ecological views of Lynn White, Hans Jonas, Theodore Roszak, and Loren Eiseley.

Glacken, Clarence J. "Man Against Nature: An Outmoded Concept." In H. W. Helfrich, Jr., ed., *The Environmental Crisis.* New Haven: Yale University Press, 1970.

———. *Traces on the Rhodian Shore: Nature and Culture in Western Thought from Ancient Times to the End of the Eighteenth Century.* Berkeley: University of California Press, 1967.

Hargrove, Eugene C. *Foundations of Environmental Ethics.* Englewood Cliffs, N.J.: Prentice-Hall, 1989, pp. 14–47. Critique of the history of anthropocentrism in Western philosophy.

Harney, T. R., and Robert Disch, eds. *The Dying Generations: Perspectives on the Environmental Crisis.* New York: Dell, 1971.

Hughes, J. Donald. *Ecology in Ancient Civilizations.* Albuquerque: University of New Mexico Press, 1975.

———. *American Indian Ecology.* El Paso: Texas Western Press, 1983.

Hughes, J. Donald, and Robert Schultz (eds.), *Ecological Consciousness: Essays from the Earthday X Colloquium, University of Denver, April 21–24, 1980* (Washington D.C.: University Press of America, 1981).

Kvaloy, Sigmond. "Ecophilosophy and Ecopolitics." *North American Review* 259, 2 (1974): 16–28.

Lawrence, D. H. "Pan in America." In E. McDonald, ed., *Phoenix.* New York: Macmillan, 1936. Reprinted in L. J. Forstner and J. Todd, eds., *The Everlasting Universe: Readings on the Ecological Revolution.* Lexington, Mass: Health & Co., 1971. Outstanding discussion of the animistic perception of Native Americans.

Leopold, Aldo. *A Sand County Almanac.* New York: Oxford University Press, 1949.

Lewis, Chris. "Telling Stories About the Future: Environmental History and Apocalyptic Science." *Environmental History Review* 17, 3 (1993): 43–60. Excellent history of scientist's warnings about ecological crisis, and critique of William Cronon and other environmental historian's cultural relativism and views of progress.

Mander, Jerry. *In the Absence of the Sacred: The Failure of Technology and the Survival of the Indian Nations.* San Francisco: Sierra Club Books, 1991.

Martin, Calvin. "The American Indian as Miscast Ecologist." In J. Donald Hughes and R. C. Schultz, eds., *Ecological Consciousness,* pp. 137–48.

———. *In The Spirit of the Earth.* Baltimore: Johns Hopkins University Press, 1992.

Marx, Leo. "American Institutions and Ecological Ideals." *Science* 170 (1970): 945–52. Marx, a literary critic, challenged the scientific establishment to evaluate the severity of the environmental crisis in 1970. The "establishment" did not begin to issue official environmental warnings until the 1990s.

Meeker, Joseph. *The Comedy of Survival.* New York: Scribner's, 1974.

Meine, Curt. *Aldo Leopold: His Life and Work.* Madison: University of Wisconsin Press, 1988.

Merchant, Carolyn. *The Death of Nature: Women, Ecology, and the Scientific Revolution.* New York: Harper and Row, 1983.

Nash, Roderick. *Wilderness and the American Mind.* 3rd ed. New Haven: Yale University Press, 1982.

———. *The Rights of Nature: A History of Environmental Ethics.* Madison: University of Wisconsin Press, 1989.

———, ed. *American Environmentalism: Readings in Conservation History.* 3rd ed. New York: McGraw-Hill, 1990.

Nelson, Richard. *Make Prayers to the Raven.* Chicago: University of Chicago Press, 1983.

Oelschlaeger, Max. *The Idea of Wilderness: From Prehistory to the Age of Ecology.* New Haven: Yale University Press, 1991.

———, ed. *Nature's Odyssey: Essays on Paul Shepard.* Denton: University of North Texas Press, 1995.

Passmore, John. *Man's Responsibility for Nature: Ecological Problems and Western Traditions.* New York: Scribner's, 1974.

Ponting, Clive. *A Green History of the World: The Environment and the Collapse of Great Civilizations.* New York: St. Martin's Press, 1992.

Pursell, Carroll, ed. *From Conservation to Ecology.* New York: T. Y. Crowell, 1973.

Rodman, John. "The Dolphin Papers." *North American Review* 259 (1974): 3–26. Reprinted in Daniel Halpern, ed., *On Nature.* Berkeley: North Point Press, 1989.

Sale, Kirkpatrick. *The Green Revolution: The American Environmental Movement 1962–1992.* New York: Hill and Wang, 1993.

Sessions, George. "Anthropocentrism and the Environmental Crisis." *Humboldt Journal of Social Relations* 2, 1 (1974): 81–91.

———. "Spinoza and Jeffers on Man in Nature." *Inquiry* (Oslo) 20, 4 (1977): 481–528.

———. "Shallow and Deep Ecology: A Review of the Philosophical Literature." In Hughes and Schultz, *Ecological Consciousness* (1981), pp. 391–462.

———. "The Deep Ecology Movement: A Review." *Environmental Review* 11, 2 (1987): 105–25.

Shepard, Paul. *Man in the Landscape.* New York: Knopf, 1967.

———. *The Tender Carnivore and the Sacred Game.* New York: Scribner's, 1973.

———. *Nature and Madness.* San Francisco: Sierra Club Books, 1982.

Taylor, Bob. *Our Limits Transgressed: Environmental Political Thought in America.* Lawrence: University Press of Kansas, 1992.

Toulmin, Stephen. *The Return to Cosmology: Postmodern Science and the Theology of Nature.* Berkeley: University of California Press, 1982.

Turner, Frederick. *Rediscovering America: John Muir in His Time and Ours.* San Francisco: Sierra Club Books, 1985.

Vecsey, C., and R. W. Venables, eds. *American Indian Environments: Ecological Issues in Native American History.* Syracuse: Syracuse University Press, 1980.

Wall, Derek. *Green History: An Anthology of Environmental Literature, Philosophy, and Politics.* New York: Routledge, 1994.

White, Lynn, Jr. "The Historical Roots of Our Ecologic Crisis." *Science* 155 (March 10, 1967): 1203–7. Reprinted in Lynn White, *Machina Ex Deo* (Cambridge: MIT Press, 1968); D. VanDeVeer and C. Pierce, eds., *Environmental Ethics and Policy Book* (Belmont, Calif.: Wadsworth, 1994); and innumerable ecological anthologies of the early 1970s.

———. "Continuing the Conversation." In Ian G. Barbour, ed., *Western Man and Environmental Ethics.* Reading, Mass.: Addison-Wesley, 1973, pp. 55–64.

Worster, Donald. *Nature's Economy: The Roots of Ecology.* San Francisco: Sierra Club Books, 1977.

———. "Seeing Beyond Culture." *Journal of American History* 76 (1990). A critique of William Cronen's relativism and views of "second nature."

## PART THREE: ARNE NAESS ON DEEP ECOLOGY AND ECOSOPHY

Cheney, Jim. "Review of Naess, *Ecology, Community, and Lifestyle.*" *Environmental Ethics* 13, 3 (1991): 263–73.

Curley, E. M. "Man and Nature in Spinoza." In Jon Wetlesen, *Spinoza's Philosophy of Man*. Oslo: Universitetsforlaget, 1978, pp. 19–26.

Drengson, Alan, ed. *The Trumpeter* 9, 2 (1992). Special issue: "The Long-Range Deep Ecology Movement and Arne Naess."

Fox, Warwick. *Toward a Transpersonal Ecology: Developing New Foundations for Environmentalism*. Boston: Shambhala Publications, 1990. Chap. 4 on Arne Naess.

———. "Intellectual Origins of the 'Depth' Theme in the Philosophy of Arne Naess." *The Trumpeter* 9, 2 (1992): 68–73. Special issue on Arne Naess.

Glasser, Harold. "The Distinctiveness of the Deep Ecology Approach to Ecophilosophy." Unpublished manuscript, University of California, Davis, Dept. of Applied Science, 1991, pp. 1–28.

Gullvag, Ingemund, and Jon Wetlesen, eds. *In Sceptical Wonder: Inquiries into the Philosophies of Arne Naess on the Occasion of His Seventieth Birthday*. Oslo: Universitetsforlaget, 1982.

Hampshire, Stuart. *Two Theories of Morality*. New York: Oxford University Press, 1977. Comparison of Aristotle and Spinoza.

Lloyd, Genevieve. "Spinoza's Environmental Ethics." *Inquiry* 23, 3 (1980): 293–312.

Matthews, Freya. *The Ecological Self*. London, Routledge, 1990.

Naess, Arne. *Interpretation and Preciseness: A Contribution to the Theory of Communicative Action*. Oslo: Norwegian Academy of Sciences, 1953.

———"Reflections about Total Views." *Philosophy and Phenomenological Research* 25 (1964): 16–29.

———. *Gandhi and the Nuclear Age*. New Jersey: Bedminister Press, 1965.

———. *Elements of Applied Semantics*. London: Allen and Unwin, 1966.

———. *Scepticism*. New York: Humanities Press, 1968.

———. *Four Modern Philosophers: Carnap, Wittgenstein, Heidegger, Sartre*. Chicago: University of Chicago Press, 1968.

———. *The Pluralist and Possibilist Aspects of the Scientific Enterprise*. Oslo: Universitetsforlaget, 1972.

———. *Gandhi and Group Conflict: An Exploration of Satyagraha*. Oslo: Universitetsforlaget, 1974.

———. *Freedom, Emotion, and Self-Subsistence: The Structure of a Central Part of Spinoza's Ethics*. Oslo: Universitetsforlaget, 1975.

———. "Spinoza and Ecology." *Philosophia* 7, 1 (1977): 45–54.

———. "Notes on the Methodology of Normative Systems." *Methodology and Science* 10 (1977): 64–79.

———. "Through Spinoza to Mahayana Buddhism, or Through Mahayana Buddhism to Spinoza?" In Jon Wetlesen, *Spinoza's Philosophy of Man*. Oslo: Universitetsforlaget, 1978, pp. 136–58. Reply to Wetlesen's interpretation of Spinoza.

———. "Self-Realization in Mixed Communities of Humans, Bears, Sheep and Wolves." *Inquiry* 22 (1979): 231–41.

————. "Modesty and the Conquest of Mountains." In Michael Tobias and H. Drasdo, eds., *The Mountain Spirit*. New York: Overlook Press, 1979, pp. 13–16.

————. "Environmental Ethics and Spinoza's Ethics: Comments on Genevieve Lloyd's Article." *Inquiry* (Oslo) 23, 3 (1980): 312–25.

————. *Communication and Argument: Elements of Applied Semantics*. Oslo: Universitetsforlaget, 1981.

————. "How My Philosophy Seemed to Develop." In Andre Mercier and Maja Svilar, eds., *Philosophers on Their Own Work*, vol. 10. Bern: Peter Lang, 1983, pp. 209–26.

————. "A Defense of the Deep Ecology Movement." *Environmental Ethics* 6, 3 (1984): 265–70. A reply to Richard Watson.

————. "The World of Concrete Contents." *Inquiry* 28 (1985): 417–28. A sophisticated account of Naess's position on skepticism, Gestalt perception, and ontology.

————. "Identification as a Source for Deep Ecological Attitudes." In Michael Tobias, ed., *Deep Ecology*. San Diego: Avant Books, 1985. Reprinted in Peter List, ed., *Radical Environmentalism*. Belmont, Calif.: Wadsworth, 1993, pp. 24–38.

————. "Deep Ecology and Ultimate Premises." *The Ecologist* 18 (1988): 4–7.

————. "Tvergastein: An Example of Place." Unpublished manuscript, 1988.

————. *Ecology, Community, and Lifestyle*. Cambridge: Cambridge University Press, 1989.

————. " 'Man Apart' and Deep Ecology: A Reply to Reed." *Environmental Ethics* 12, 2 (1990): 185–92.

————. "The Encouraging Richness and Diversity of Ultimate Premises in Environmental Philosophy." *The Trumpeter* 9, 2 (1992): 53–60.

————. "Beautiful Action: Its Function in the Ecological Crisis." *Environmental Values* 2, 1 (1993): 67–71.

Reed, Peter. "Man Apart: An Alternative to the Self-Realization Approach." *Environmental Ethics* 11 (1989): 53–69.

Reed, Peter, and David Rothenberg. *Wisdom in the Open Air: The Norwegian Roots of Deep Ecology*. Minneapolis: University of Minnesota Press, 1993.

Rothenberg, David. *Is It Painful to Think?: Conversations with Arne Naess*. Minneapolis: University of Minnesota Press, 1993.

Sessions, George. "Western Process Metaphysics: Heraclitus, Whitehead, and Spinoza." In Bill Devall and George Sessions, *Deep Ecology*. Salt Lake City, Utah: Peregrine Smith Books, 1985, pp. 236–42. Points out that Spinoza's rational metaphysical system is like Zen Buddhism in leading to direct intuitive knowledge and experience of the world.

————. "Arne Naess and the Union of Theory and Practice." *Trumpeter* 9, 2 (1992): 73–76.

Watson, Richard. "A Critique of Anti-Anthropocentric Biocentrism." *Environmental Ethics* 5, 3 (1983): 245–56.

Wetlesen, Jon. *The Sage and the Way: Spinoza's Ethics of Freedom.* Oslo: Universitetsforlaget, 1978.

Wienpahl, Paul. "Spinoza and Mysticism." In Jon Wetlesen, ed., *Spinoza's Philosophy of Man.* Oslo: Universitetsforlaget, 1978, pp. 211–24.

———. *The Radical Spinoza.* New York: New York University Press, 1979.

Zimmerman, Michael. "Arne Naess: Celebrant of Diversity." *The Trumpeter* 9, 2 (1992): 61–62.

## PART FOUR: DEEP ECOLOGY AND ECOFEMINISM, SOCIAL ECOLOGY, THE NEW AGE, AND THE GREENS

Berman, Morris. *The Reenchantment of the World.* Ithaca, N.Y.: Cornell University Press, 1981.

———. "The Cybernetic Dream of the Twenty-First Century." *Journal of Humanistic Psychology* 26, 2 (1986): 24–51. Reprinted in John Clark, ed., *Renewing the Earth: The Promise of Social Ecology.* London: Green Print, 1990. Outstanding critique of New Age cybernetic disembodied thinking.

———. *Coming to Our Senses.* New York: Bantam, 1989.

Borgman, Albert. *Technology and the Character of Contemporary Life.* Chicago: University of Chicago Press, 1984.

Burnham, David. *The Rise of the Computer State.* New York: Vintage, 1980.

Cheney, Jim. "Ecofeminism and Deep Ecology." *Environmental Ethics* 9 (1987): 115–45.

Cuomo, Christine. "Unraveling the Problems in Ecofeminism." *Environmental Ethics* 14, 4 (1992): 351–63. A critique of ecofeminist theory.

Davion, Victoria. "How Feminist Is Ecofeminism?" In Karen Warren, ed., *Ecofeminist Philosophy.* New York: Routledge, 1994. A critique of ecofeminist theory.

Devall, Bill. "Deep Ecology and Its Critics." *The Trumpeter* 5, 2 (1988): 55–60.

Eckersley, Robyn. "Divining Evolution: The Ecological Ethics of Murray Bookchin." *Environmental Ethics* 11 (1989): 99–116. A critique of Bookchin's evolutionary views.

Gaard, Greta, ed. *Ecofeminism: Women, Animals and Nature.* Philadelphia: Temple University Press, 1993.

Hallen, Patsy. "Making Peace with Nature: Why Ecology Needs Ecofeminism." *The Trumpeter* 4, 3 (1987): 3–14.

Harrington, Michael. "To the Disney Station." *Harpers* (Jan. 1979): 35–44.

Hay, Peter, and Marcus Haward. "Comparative Green Politics: Beyond the European Context." *Political Studies* 36 (1988): 433–38.

Krieger, Martin H. "What's Wrong with Plastic Trees?" *Science* 179 (1973): 450–71.

Mander, Jerry. *In the Absence of the Sacred: The Failure of Technology and the Survival of the Indian Nations.* San Francisco: Sierra Club Books, 1991. The first half of this book is a devastating critique of the corporate/consumer/megatechnology vision.

McKibben, Bill. *The Age of Misinformation.* New York: Random House, 1992.

Milton, J. P., and M. T. Favor. *The Careless Technology.* New York: Natural History Press, 1971.

Naess, Arne. "A European Looks at North American Branches of the Deep Ecology Movement." *The Trumpeter* 5, 2 (1988): 75–6.

———. "The Three Great Movements." *The Trumpeter* 9, 2 (1992).

Rifkin, Jeremy. *Algeny.* New York: Penguin Books, 1984.

———. *Time Wars: The Primary Conflict in Human History.* New York: Henry Holt, 1987. How "computer consciousness" speeds up time in society.

———. *Declaration of a Heretic.* New York: Routledge, 1987.

———. *Biosphere Politics.* New York: Crown Publishers, 1991.

———. "The Clinton Dilemma." *Tikkun* 8, 3 (1993): 14–18, 75–79. Rifkin points to the incompatibilities in the Clinton administration's advocacy of high-tech and continued economic growth versus the social/ecological necessity of attaining a sustainable society.

Ritzer, George. *The McDonaldization of Society.* London: Pine Forge Press, 1993.

Roszak, Theodore. *The Cult of Information.* London, Paladin, 1988. A powerful critique of "computer consciousness."

Sale, Kirkpatrick. "Deep Ecology and Its Critics." *The Nation* 22 (May 14, 1988): 670–75.

Schickel, R. *The Disney Version.* New York: Simon and Schuster, 1968.

Sessions, George. "Radical Environmentalism in the 90's." In M. Oelschlaeger, ed., *After Earth Day.* Denton: Univ. of North Texas Press, 1992, pp. 17–27. Discussion of Deep Ecology, Murray Bookchin, Green Politics, and Earth First! (See also next title.)

———. "Postscript: March 1992." *Wild Earth* 2, 3 (1992): 64–70.

Shiva, Vandana. *Staying Alive: Women, Ecology, and Development.* London: Zed Books, 1992.

Sorkin, Michael. "See You in Disneyland." In M. Sorkin, ed., *Variations on a Theme Park.* New York: Hill and Wang, 1992.

Spretnak, Charlene. "The Spiritual Dimensions of Green Politics." In Charlene Spretnak and Fritjof Capra, *Green Politics: The Global Promise.* New York: Dutton, 1984.

———. "Ecofeminism: Our Roots and Flowering." In Irene Diamond and Gloria Orenstein, eds., *Reweaving the World: The Emergence of Ecofeminism.* San Francisco: Sierra Club Books, 1990.

Winner, Langdon. *Autonomous Technology: Technics Out of Control as a Theme in Political Thought.* Cambridge: MIT Press, 1977.

———. *The Whale and the Reactor.* Chicago: University of Chicago Press, 1986.

Zimmerman, Michael. "Feminism, Deep Ecology, and Environmental Ethics." *Environmental Ethics* 9 (1987): 21–44.

———. "Deep Ecology and Ecofeminism: The Emerging Dialogue." In Diamond and Orenstein, eds., *Reweaving the World*.

———. "Rethinking the Heidegger-Deep Ecology Relationship." *Environmental Ethics* 15, 3 (1993): 195–224.

———. *Contesting Earth's Future: Radical Ecology and Postmodernity*. Berkeley: University of California Press, 1994. Discussion of Deep Ecology, Ecofeminism, Capra, Roszak, and Bookchin.

Zimmerman, Michael, J. Baird Callicott et al., eds., *Environmental Philosophy: From Animal Rights to Radical Ecology*. Englewood Cliffs, N.J.: Prentice-Hall, 1993. Sections on Environmental Ethics, Deep Ecology, Ecofeminism, and Social Ecology.

## PART FIVE: WILDERNESS, THE WILD, AND CONSERVATION BIOLOGY

Anderson, Lorraine, ed. *Sisters of the Earth*. New York, Vintage, 1991.

Anderson, Sherwood. "The End of American Wilderness." *Environmental Review* 9 (1985): 197–209. Provocative discussion of the negative impact of machines, biologists, and National Park management policies on Alaska's plants, animals, and wildness.

Armstrong, Susan, and Richard Botzler, eds. *Environmental Ethics*. New York: McGraw-Hill, 1993. Section 3 on the Aesthetic Value of Nature.

Bergon, Frank, ed. *The Wilderness Reader*. New York: New American Library, 1980.

Burks, David, ed. *Place of the Wild: A Wildlands Anthology*. Washington, D.C.: Island Press, 1994. Important "cutting edge" collection of papers on Wildlands Project, wilderness, and the wild.

Davis, John, ed. "The Wildlands Project: Plotting a North American Wilderness Recovery Strategy." *Wild Earth,* Special Issue, 1993.

DeBlieu, Jan. *Meant to Be Wild: The Struggle to Save Endangered Species through Captive Breeding*. Golden, Colo.: Fulcrum, 1993. An even-handed discussion of the pros and cons of captive breeding of endangered species.

Devall, Bill, ed. *Clearcut: The Tragedy of Industrial Forestry*. San Francisco: Sierra Club Books, 1994.

Devall, Bill, and George Sessions. "The Development of Natural Resources and the Integrity of Nature." *Environmental Ethics* 6, 4 (1984): 293–322.

DiSilvestro, Roger. *Reclaiming the Last Wild Places: A New Agenda for Biodiversity*. New York: Wiley and Sons, 1993.

Drengson, Alan. "Beyond Empire Resourcism to Ecoforestry." *The International Journal of Ecoforestry* 1, 1 (1994).

Ehrenfeld, David. *The Arrogance of Humanism*. New York: Oxford University Press, 1978. Critique of anthropocentric "resource" approach to wild plants, animals, and ecosystems.

Ehrlich, Paul. *The Machinery of Nature: The Living World around Us—and How It Works.* New York: Simon and Schuster, 1986.

Ehrlich, Paul, and Anne Ehrlich. *Extinction: The Causes and Consequences of the Disappearance of Species.* New York: Random House, 1981.

———. *The Population Explosion.* New York: Simon and Schuster, 1990.

———. *Healing the Planet: Strategies for Resolving the Environmental Crisis.* Reading, Mass.: Addison-Wesley, 1991. See chapter 1 on ecosystem and biodiversity protection.

Foreman, Dave, and Howie Wolke. *The Big Outside: A Descriptive Inventory of the Big Wilderness Areas of the United States.* New York: Harmony Books, 1992.

Fromme, Michael. *Regreening the National Parks.* Tucson: University of Arizona Press, 1991.

Grumbine, Edward. *Ghost Bears: Exploring the Biodiversity Crisis.* Washington D.C.: Island Press, 1992.

Guha, Ramachandra. "Radical American Environmentalism and Wilderness Preservation: A Third World Critique." *Environmental Ethics* 11, 1 (1989): 71–83. Reprinted in VanDeVeer and Pierce, *Environmental Ethics and Policy Book,* pp. 548–56.

*International Journal of Ecoforestry.* United States Ecoforestry Institute, P.O. Box 12543, Portland, OR 97212. Subscriptions $25/yr.

Johns, David. "The Relevance of Deep Ecology to the Third World." *Environmental Ethics* 12, 3 (1990): 233–52. Reply to Guha's critique of Deep Ecology.

Livingston, John. *The Fallacy of Wildlife Conservation.* Toronto: McClelland and Stewart, 1981.

McNeely, Jeffrey, K. Miller et al., eds. *Conserving the World's Biological Diversity.* Washington, D.C.: World Resources Institute, 1990.

Mowat, Farley. *Sea of Slaughter.* Boston: Atlantic Monthly Press, 1984.

Naess, Arne. "Intrinsic Value: Will the Defenders of Nature Please Rise?" *Conservation Biology* (1986): 22–34. Keynote Address to the Second International Conference on Conservation Biology held at University of Michigan, May 1985.

———. "Should We Try to Relieve Extreme Cases of Extreme Suffering in Nature?" *PanEcology* 6 (1991): 1–5.

Nash, Roderick. *Wilderness and the American Mind.* 3rd ed. New Haven: Yale University Press, 1981.

———. *American Environmentalism: Readings in Conservation History.* 3rd ed. New York: McGraw-Hill, 1990.

Norton, Bryan. *Why Preserve Natural Variety?* Princeton: Princeton University Press, 1990.

———. *Toward Unity among Environmentalists.* New York: Oxford University Press, 1991.

Noss, Reed F. "Wilderness Recovery: Thinking Big in Restoration Ecology." *The Environmental Professional* 13 (1991): 225–34.

Noss, Reed F., and Allen Cooperrider. *Saving Nature's Legacy: Protecting and Restoring Biodiversity.* Washington, D.C.: Island Press, 1994.

Oelschlaeger, Max. *The Idea of Wilderness: From Prehistory to the Age of Ecology.* New Haven: Yale University Press, 1991.

———. ed. *The Wilderness Condition: Essays in Environment and Civilization.* San Francisco: Sierra Club Books, 1992.

Peacock, Doug. *Grizzly Years: In Search of the American Wilderness.* New York: Holt, 1990.

Primack, Richard B. *Essentials of Conservation Biology.* Sunderland, Mass.: Sinauer, 1993. Excellent new textbook on conservation biology.

Rodman, John. "The Liberation of Nature?" *Inquiry* (Oslo) 20 (1977): 83–145. Superb critique of animal liberation, legalistic approaches to Nature, and a sensitive discussion of the wild.

Rolston, Holmes III. *Philosophy Gone Wild: Essays in Environmental Ethics.* Buffalo, N.Y.: Prometheus Books, 1986.

Roszak, Theodore. "Leave the Wilderness Alone!" *New Scientist,* no. 1613 (1988): 63–64.

Schaller, George. *The Last Panda.* Chicago: University of Chicago Press, 1993. Schaller documents the recent scandalous wildlife protection policies that have endangered the panda in China.

Seidman, Mike. "Zoos and the Psychology of Extinction." *Wild Earth* 2, 4 (1992): 64–69. Excellent critique of the human motives for keeping wild animals in zoos.

Sessions, George. "Ecocentrism, Wilderness, and Global Ecosystem Protection." In Max Oelschlaeger, ed., *The Wilderness Condition,* pp. 90–130. Part II of the longer version of this paper has an evaluation of the arguments for the protection of wilderness.

———. "Paul Shepard: Ecological Elder." In Max Oelschlaeger, ed., *Nature's Odyssey: Essays on Paul Shepard.* Denton: University of North Texas Press, 1995.

Shepard, Paul. *The Tender Carnivore and the Sacred Game.* New York: Scribner's, 1973.

———. *Thinking Animals: Animals and the Development of Human Intelligence.* New York: Viking Press, 1978.

———. *Nature and Madness.* San Francisco: Sierra Club Books, 1982.

———. "A Post-Historic Primitivism," in Max Oelschlaeger, ed., *The Wilderness Condition,* pp. 40–89.

———. *The Others.* New York: Farrar, Straus and Giroux, 1994.

Snyder, Gary. *The Practice of the Wild.* San Francisco: North Point Press, 1990.

Soulé, Michael, ed. *Conservation Biology: The Science of Scarcity and Diversity.* Sunderland, Mass.: Sinauer, 1986.

———, ed. *Viable Populations for Conservation.* Cambridge: Cambridge University Press, 1987.

Soulé, Michael, and Bruce Wilcox, eds. *Conservation Biology: An Evolutionary-Ecological Perspective.* Sunderland, Mass.: Sinauer, 1980.

Turner, Frederick. *Beyond Geography: The Western Spirit against the Wilderness.* New York: Viking Press, 1980.

VanDeVeer, Donald, and Christine Pierce, eds. *Environmental Ethics and Policy Book.* Belmont, Calif.: Wadsworth, 1994.

Western, David, and Mary Pearl, eds. *Conservation for the Twenty-first Century.* Oxford: Oxford University Press, 1989.

Westra, Laura. *An Environmental Proposal for Ethics: The Principle of Integrity.* Lanham, Md.: Rowman & Littlefield, 1994. Philosophical defense of the ecosystems approach to environmental ethics.

*Wild Earth.* John Davis and Dave Foreman, eds. P.O. Box 455, Richmond, VT 05477. Subscriptions $25/yr. Focuses on Deep Ecology, conservation biology, and strategies for protection of wildness and biodiversity.

Wilson, E. O. *Biophilia.* Cambridge: Harvard University Press, 1984.

———. *The Diversity of Life.* Cambridge: Harvard University Press, 1992. Outstanding discussion by a leading conservation biologist of the complexity of wild ecosystems and the need to protect biodiversity.

———., ed. *Biodiversity.* Washington, D.C.: National Academy Press, 1988.

Wilson, E. O., and Stephen Kellert, eds. *The Biophilia Hypothesis.* Washington, D.C.: Island Press, 1993.

Wolke, Howie. *Wilderness on the Rocks.* Tucson, Ariz.: Ned Ludd Books, 1991.

## PART SIX: TOWARD THE TWENTY-FIRST CENTURY AND BEYOND

Andruss, Van, ed. *Home: A Bioregional Reader.* New York: New Society Publishers, 1990.

Barnet, Richard, and John Cavanaugh. *Global Dreams: Imperial Corporations and the New World Order.* New York: Simon and Schuster, 1994.

Berg, Peter, et al. *A Green City Program.* 2nd ed. San Francisco: Wingbow Press, 1990.

Berry, Wendell, *Sex, Economy, Freedom and Community.* New York: Pantheon, 1993.

Bowers, C. A. "The Conservative Misinterpretation of the Educational Ecological Crisis." *Environmental Ethics* 14, 2 (1992): 101–27.

———. *Education, Cultural Myths, and the Ecological Crisis.* Albany: State University of New York Press, 1992.

Caldicott, Helen. *If You Love This Planet: A Plan to Heal the Earth.* New York: Norton, 1992.

Chomsky, Noam. *The Prosperous Few and the Restless Many.* Berkeley: Odonian Press, 1993. Articles on the New Global Economy (NAFTA and GATT).

Cobb, John Jr. *Sustainability: Economics, Ecology, and Justice.* Maryknoll, N.Y.: Orbis

Books, 1992. Good ecological critique of NAFTA, GATT, and other "free trade" agreements.

Colchester, Marcus, and Larry Lohmann, eds. *The Struggle for Land and the Fate of the Forests*. London: Zed Books, 1993. The fight for the forests in the Third World.

Craig, Paul; Harold Glasser; and Willett Kempton. "Ethics and Values in Environmental Policy." *Environmental Values* 2, 2 (1993): 137–57.

Daily, Gretchen, and Paul Ehrlich. "Population, Sustainability, and Earth's Carrying Capacity." *Bioscience* 42, 10 (1992): 761–71.

Daly, Herman. *Steady State Economics*. 2nd ed. Washington, D.C.: Island Press, 1991.

Daly, Herman, and John Cobb. *For the Common Good: Redirecting the Economy toward Community, the Environment, and a Sustainable Future*. Boston: Beacon Press, 1989.

Dobson, Andrew, ed. *The Green Reader: Essays toward a Sustainable Society*. San Francisco: Mercury House, 1991.

Douthwaite, Richard. *The Growth Illusion*. Tulsa, Okla.: Council Oaks Books, 1992.

Durning, Alan. *How Much Is Enough?: The Consumer Society and the Future of the Earth*. New York: Norton, 1992. Worldwatch Institute researcher argues for an end to consumerism and excessive advertising in industrialized countries.

Earth Island Books. *The Case against Free Trade: GATT, NAFTA, and the Globalization of Corporate Power*. Berkeley: North Atlantic Books, 1993.

Eckersley, Robyn. *Environmentalism and Political Theory: Toward an Ecocentric Approach*. Albany: State University of New York Press, 1992.

Ehrenfeld, David. *Beginning Again: People and Nature in the New Millennium*. Oxford: Oxford University Press, 1993.

Ehrlich, Anne, and Paul Ehrlich. *Earth*. New York: Franklin Watts, 1987.

Ehrlich, Paul, and Anne Ehrlich. *Healing the Planet: Strategies for Resolving the Environmental Crisis*. Reading, Mass.: Addison-Wesley, 1991.

Frodeman, Robert. "Radical Environmentalism and the Political Roots of Postmodernism." *Environmental Ethics* 14, 4 (1992): 307–19.

Garreau, Joel. *The Nine Nations of North America*. Boston: Houghton Mifflin, 1981, chap. 8, "Ecotopia," pp. 245–86.

Gowdy, John. "Progress and Environmental Sustainability." *Environmental Ethics* 16, 1 (1994): 41–55. An economist critiques progress and economic growth from an ecological perspective.

Guha, Ramachandra. "Radical American Environmentalism and Wilderness Preservation: A Third World Critique." *Environmental Ethics* 11, 1 (1989): 71–81. Guha argues that wild ecosystem and biodiversity protection should not be a central ecological concern for the Third World, or even the First World.

Gunn, Alastair. "Environmental Ethics and Tropical Rain Forests." *Environmental Ethics* 16, 1 (1994): 21–40. A New Zealand ecophilosopher examines environmental problems from a Third World perspective.

Harrison, Paul. *The Third Revolution: Environment, Population and a Sustainable World*.

London: I. B. Tauris, 1992. Excellent treatment of Third World environmental and population problems.

Hawkin, Paul. *The Ecology of Commerce.* San Francisco: HarperCollins, 1993.

Johns, David M. "The Relevance of Deep Ecology to the Third World." *Environmental Ethics* 12, 3 (1990): 233–52. A reply to Guha.

Katz, Eric, and Lauren Oechsli. "Moving Beyond Anthropocentrism: Environmental Ethics, Development, and the Amazon." *Environmental Ethics* 15, 1 (1993): 49–59. Argues against Guha that any Third World development policy must be viewed from the ecocentric context of humanity's moral obligations to wild ecosystems, animals and plants.

Kemmis, Daniel. *Community and the Politics of Place.* Norman: University of Oklahoma Press, 1990.

Krall, Florence. *Ecotone: Wayfaring on the Margins.* Albany: State University of New York Press, 1994.

McLaughlin, Andrew. "Ecology, Capitalism, and Socialism." *Socialism and Democracy* (1990): 69–102.

———. *Regarding Nature: Industrialism and Deep Ecology.* Albany: State University of New York Press, 1993.

Naess, Arne. "Ecosophy, Population, and Free Nature." *The Trumpeter* 5, 3 (1988): 113–19.

———. *Ecology, Community, and Lifestyle.* Cambridge: Cambridge University Press, 1989), chaps. 5 and 6. Extensive discussions of ecological economics and politics.

———. "Sustainable Development and Deep Ecology." In Ron and J. Engel, eds., *Ethics of Environment and Development.* Tucson: University of Arizona Press, 1990, pp. 87–96.

———. " 'Man Apart' and Deep Ecology: A Reply to Reed." *Environmental Ethics* 12, 2 (1990): 185–92. Naess addresses the issue of the compatibility of Self-Realization as wide identification with the idea of nonhuman Nature as "wholly other."

———. "Sustainability! The Integral Approach." In O. Sandlund, K. Hindar, and A. Brown, eds., *Conservation of Biodiversity for Sustainable Development.* Oslo: Scandinavian University Press, 1992, pp. 303–10.

———. "The Politics of the Deep Ecology Movement." In Peter Reed and David Rothenberg, eds., *Wisdom in the Open Air.* Minneapolis: University of Minnesota Press, 1993, pp. 82–99.

Norberg-Hodge, Helena. *Ancient Futures: Learning from Ladakh.* San Francisco: Sierra Club Books, 1991.

Orr, David. *Ecological Literacy.* Albany: State University of New York Press, 1992.

Paulke, Robert. *Environmentalism and the Future of Progressive Politics.* New Haven: Yale University Press, 1989.

Redclift, M. *Sustainable Development: Exploring the Contradictions.* London: Methuen, 1987.

Routley, Val, and Richard Routley. "Social Theories, Self Management, and Environmental Problems." In D. Mannison, M. McRobbie, and R. Routley, eds., *Environmental Philosophy*. Canberra: Philosophy Dept., RSSS, Australian National University, 1980, pp. 217–332.

Sachs, Wolfgang, ed., *Global Ecology*. London: Zed Books, 1993. Important critiques of the Rio conference, the concept of "sustainable development," and ecology and the Third World.

Sagoff, Mark. *The Economy of the Earth*. New York: Cambridge University Press, 1988.

Sale, Kirkpatrick. *Dwellers in the Land: The Bioregional Vision*. San Francisco: Sierra Club Books, 1985.

Sessions, George. "Ecophilosophy, Utopias and Education." *Journal of Environmental Education* 15, 1 (Fall 1983).

Shepard, Paul. "Place in American Culture." *North American Review* (Fall 1977): 22–32.

Shiva, Vandana. *Monocultures of the Mind: Biodiversity, Biotechnology and the Third World*. Malaysia: Third World Network, 1993.

Sklar, Holly, ed. *Trilaterialism: The Trilaterial Commission and Elite Planning for World Management*. Boston: South End Press, 1980.

Snyder, Gary. *The Practice of the Wild*. San Francisco: North Point Press, 1990.

———. *Coming into the Watershed*. New York: Pantheon, 1994.

*Third World Resurgence*. Third World Network, 87 Cantonment Road, 10250 Penang, Malaysia. Subscriptions $20/yr. Third World development looked at from ecological and social justice perspectives.

Weston, Anthony. *Is There Life on Earth?* Philadelphia: Temple University Press, 1994. Discussion of how to make our cities more ecologically compatible.

Zimmerman, Michael. "The Future of Ecology," in Max Oelschlaeger, ed., *After Earth Day: Continuing the Conservation Effort*. Denton: University of North Texas Press, 1992, pp. 170–83.

# ABOUT THE CONTRIBUTORS

Thomas Berry is director of the Riverdale Center for Religious Research in New York. He is the author of *The Dream of the Earth* (1988) and coauthor of *The Universe Story* (1992).

Thomas Birch is a professor of philosophy at the University of Montana. He is the book review editor of *Environmental Ethics* and has written a number of papers in ecophilosophy.

Fritjof Capra is a research physicist and the author of *The Tao of Physics* (1975) and *The Turning Point* (1982). He is also the founder of the Elmwood Institute in Berkeley, California.

Wayland Drew teaches English at Bracebridge High School in Ontario, Canada. He is author of *A Sea Within* (1984), *The Wabeno Feast* (1973), and other books.

Dave Foreman was a cofounder of Earth First! and is now executive editor of *Wild Earth*. He is the coauthor of *The Big Outside* (1992) and the author of *Confessions of an Ecowarrior* (1991).

Warwick Fox is a National Research Fellow at the Center for Environmental Studies at the University of Tasmania, Australia, and the author of *Toward a Transpersonal Ecology* (1990).

Chellis Glendinning is a psychologist who lives in Tesuque, New Mexico. She is the author of *When Technology Wounds* (1990) and *My Name Is Chellis, and I'm in Recovery from Western Civilization* (1994).

Edward Grumbine is director of the Sierra Institute, University of California, Santa Cruz Extension, and the author of *Ghost Bears: Exploring the Biodiversity Crisis* (1992).

Del Ivan Janik is professor of English at the State University of New York at Cortland.

Dolores LaChapelle is director of Way of the Mountain Center in Silverton, Colorado. She is the author of *Earth Festivals* (1973), *Earth Wisdom* (1978), *Sacred Land Sacred Sex* (1988), and *Deep Powder Snow* (1993).

Richard Langlais is a doctoral candidate in human ecology at Göteborgs University in Sweden and the author of *Road News from Tibet* (1992).

Jerry Mander is Senior Fellow at the Public Media Center in San Francisco,

California. He is the author of *Four Arguments for the Elimination of Television* (1977) and *In The Absence of the Sacred* (1991).

Andrew McLaughlin is associate professor of philosophy at Lehman College, City University of New York, and the author of *Regarding Nature: Industrialism and Deep Ecology* (1993).

Arne Naess is professor emeritus of philosophy, and was for many years the chairman of the philosophy department at the University of Oslo, Norway. He is the author of *Ecology, Community and Lifestyle* (1989) and many books and papers on empirical linguistics, philosophy of science, Spinoza, Gandhi, and ecosophy.

John Rodman is a professor of political science at Pitzer College, Claremont, California, and the author of many important papers in ecophilosophy.

Wolfgang Sachs is a fellow at the Institute for Cultural Studies in Essen, Germany. He is author of *For Love of the Automobile* (1992) and editor of *The Development Dictionary* (1992) and *Global Ecology* (1993).

George Sessions is chairman of the philosophy department at Sierra College in Rocklin, California. He is the coauthor of *Deep Ecology* (1985) and the coeditor of *Environmental Philosophy* (1993).

Paul Shepard is professor emeritus of human ecology at Pitzer College, Claremont, California. He is the author of *Man in the Landscape* (1967), *The Tender Carnivore and the Sacred Game* (1973), *Thinking Animals* (1978), and *Nature and Madness* (1982), and the coauthor of *The Sacred Paw* (1985).

Gary Snyder is professor of English at the University of California, Davis. He is the author of *Turtle Island* (1975), *The Practice of the Wild* (1990), *Coming into the Watershed* (1994), and many other books of poetry and essays.

Jack Turner holds an advanced degree in philosophy from Cornell University and has taught philosophy at the University of Illinois. He has climbed extensively in the Himalayas and is now chief guide for the Exum Guide Service and School of Mountaineering in Grand Teton National Park. He lives in Moose, Wyoming.

Donald Worster is professor of environmental history at the University of Kansas. He is the author of *Nature's Economy* (1977), *Dust Bowl* (1979), and *Rivers of Empire* (1985) and the editor of *Ends of the Earth* (1988).